THE WORKS OF JONATHAN EDWARDS

VOLUME 18

Harry S. Stout, General Editor

Oh that my wayes were directed
to keepe thy Statutes. Ps. 119. 5.

W. Simpson Sculp:

Plate from Francis Quarles, *Emblemes* (London, 1635). Courtesy Beinecke Rare
Book and Manuscript Library, Yale University.

JONATHAN EDWARDS

The "Miscellanies"

(Entry Nos. 501 – 832)

EDITED BY
AVA CHAMBERLAIN

WRIGHT STATE UNIVERSITY

New Haven and London

YALE UNIVERSITY PRESS, 2000

Funds for editing The Works of Jonathan Edwards
*have been provided by The Pew Charitable Trusts, Lilly
Endowment, Inc., and The Henry Luce Foundation, Inc.*

*Published with assistance from The Exxon Education
Foundation.*

*Set in New Baskerville type by The Composing Room
of Michigan, Inc., Grand Rapids, Michigan.*

*Printed in the United States of America by Vail-Ballou
Press, Binghamton, New York.*

Library of Congress Cataloging-in-Publication Data

*Edwards, Jonathan, 1703–1758
    The "miscellanies" (Entry nos. 501–832) / edited by
Ava Chamberlain.
       p.   cm. — (The works of Jonathan Edwards ; v. 18)
    ISBN 0-300-08330-0 (alk. paper)
       1. Theology, Doctrinal.   I. Chamberlain, Ava.
II. Title.
BT75.2.E39   2000
230'.58—dc21   99-058552*

*A catalogue record for this book is available from the
British Library.*

*The paper in this book meets the guidelines for permanence
and durability of the Committee on Production Guidelines
for Book Longevity of the Council on Library Resources*

10   9   8   7   6   5   4   3   2   1

EDITORIAL COMMITTEE FOR
THE WORKS OF JONATHAN EDWARDS

PREVIOUSLY PUBLISHED

PAUL RAMSEY, ed., *Freedom of the Will*
JOHN E. SMITH, ed., *Religious Affections*
CLYDE A. HOLBROOK, ed., *Original Sin*
C. C. GOEN, ed., *The Great Awakening*
STEPHEN J. STEIN, ed., *Apocalyptic Writings*
WALLACE E. ANDERSON, ed., *Scientific and Philosophical Writings*
NORMAN PETTIT, ed., *The Life of David Brainerd*
PAUL RAMSEY, ed., *Ethical Writings*
JOHN F. WILSON, ed., *A History of the Work of Redemption*
WILSON H. KIMNACH, ed., *Sermons and Discourses, 1720–1723*
WALLACE E. ANDERSON AND MASON I. LOWANCE, eds., *Typological Writings*
DAVID D. HALL, ed., *Ecclesiastical Writings*
THOMAS A. SCHAFER, ed., *The "Miscellanies," a–500*
KENNETH P. MINKEMA, ed., *Sermons and Discourses, 1723–1729*
STEPHEN J. STEIN, ed., *Notes on Scripture*
GEORGE S. CLAGHORN, ed., *Letters and Personal Writings*
MARK VALERI, ed., *Sermons and Discourses, 1730–1733*

CONTENTS

ILLUSTRATIONS

Preparation of the Text

The text of Jonathan Edwards is reproduced in this Edition as he wrote it in manuscript, or, if he published it himself, as it was printed in the first edition. In order to present this text to modern readers as practically readable, several technical adjustments have been made. Those which can be addressed categorically are as follows:

1. All spelling is regularized and conformed to that of *Webster's Third New International Dictionary*, a step that does not involve much more than removing the "u" from "colour" or "k" from "publick" since Edwards was a good speller, used relatively modern spelling, and generally avoided "y" contractions. His orthographic contractions and abbreviations, such as ampersands, "call'd," and "thems." are spelled out, though pronounced contractions, such as "han't" and "ben't," are retained.

2. There is no regular punctuation in most of Edwards' manuscripts and where it does exist, as in the earliest sermons, it tends to be highly erratic. Editors take into account Edwards' example in punctuation and related matters, but all punctuation is necessarily that of the editor, including paragraph divisions (especially in some notebooks such as the "Miscellanies") and the emphasizing devices of italics and capitalization. In reference to capitalization, it should be noted that pronouns referring to the deity are lower case except in passages where Edwards confusingly mixes "he's" referring to God and man: here capitalization of pronouns referring to the deity sorts out the references for the reader.

3. Numbered heads designate important structures of argument in Edwards' sermons, notebooks, and treatises. Numbering, including spelled-out numbers, has been regularized and corrected where necessary. Particularly in the manuscript sermon texts, numbering has been clarified by the use of systematic schemes of heads and subheads in accordance with eighteenth-century homiletical form, a practice similar to modern analytical outline form. Thus the series of subordinated head number forms, 1, (1), *1*, a, (a), in the textual exegesis, and the series, I, *First*, 1, (1),

1, a, (a), in Doctrine and Application divisions, make it possible to determine sermon head relationships at a glance.

4. Textual intervention to regularize Edwards' citation of Scripture includes the correction of erroneous citation, the regularizing of citation form (including the standardization of book abbreviations), and the completion of quotations which Edwards' textual markings indicate should be completed (as in preaching).

5. Omissions and lacunae in the manuscript text are filled by insertions in square brackets ([ ]); repeated phrases sometimes represented by Edwards with a long dash are inserted in curly brackets ({ }). In all cases of uncertain readings, annotation gives notice of the problem. Markings in the text designate whole word units even when only a few letters are at issue.

6. Minor slips of the pen or obvious typographical errors are corrected without annotation. Likewise, Edwards' corrections, deletions, and internal shifts of material are observed but not noted unless of substantive interest.

7. Quotations made by the editor from the Bible (AV) and other secondary sources are printed *verbatim ac literatim*. Edwards' quotations from such sources are often rather free but are not corrected and are not annotated as such unless significant omissions or distortions are involved.

Acknowledgments

During my tenure as a research editor for *The Works of Jonathan Edwards*, I had the good fortune to assist Thomas A. Schafer as he prepared *The "Miscellanies," Nos. a–500* for publication. Tom introduced me to the "Miscellanies" manuscripts. He also shared with me over the course of many lunchtime conversations his understanding of this difficult collection of writings, and this insight has informed my work on this volume at every stage in its preparation. In addition, beginning in the late 1940s, Prof. Schafer made the manuscript transcriptions that served as the foundation for this volume. He also did the initial editing of Nos. 501–600 and provided me with his research on the dating of several key entries.

General Editor Harry S. Stout not only is responsible for the ongoing success of the Edition, he made possible my participation in this project and has generously encouraged and supported my work. Executive Editor Kenneth P. Minkema assisted me in countless ways as both a colleague and friend. He researched numerous footnotes, carefully read my edited text, answered endless questions and was always available for conversation. Douglas A. Sweeney, Kyle P. Farley, and Peter J. Thuesen, past and present members of the Edition staff, also provided valuable research assistance. James Stout keyed in much of the original transcript of the entries. George Levesque checked the Latin and Greek portions of the text, and Eric Friedland supplied the Hebrew. M. X. Lesser furnished me with his edition of *Justification by Faith Alone*, and Mark Valeri kindly shared with me his transcription of Joseph Bellamy's student notebook. Susan Laity, manuscript editor at Yale University Press, as she has done with so many other volumes in the Edition, carefully read the entire manuscript. I also want to thank Michael McGiffert and an anonymous reader for their thorough and perceptive reviews of this volume.

A number of individuals are responsible for nurturing my interest in Edwards over the years. Wayne Proudfoot introduced me to Jonathan Edwards when I was a graduate student at Columbia University and has consistently encouraged my work on this volume. The friendly conversation and professional support of Wilson H. Kimnach, Stephen J. Stein, and John F. Wilson has helped to sustain my interest in Edwards. Several consultations with Amy Plantinga Pauw and Douglas Sweeney, the editors of the two remaining "Miscellanies" volumes, were also quite helpful. Finally, the sincere faith of my parents, Hiram and Evelyn Chamberlain, instilled in me a lasting interest in the religious life; it is to them that I dedicate this volume.

I received financial assistance from *The Works of Jonathan Edwards* for the preparation of this volume and for several research trips to New Haven. The Beinecke Rare Book and Manuscript Library, which houses the manuscripts published in this volume, has supplied invaluable staff support. William E. Rickert, associate provost of Wright State University, arranged my release from some of my teaching responsibilities to facilitate preparation of this volume. Funding for this volume and for the Edition as a whole has been provided by the Pew Charitable Trusts, Lilly Endowment, Inc., and the Henry Luce Foundation, Inc.

EDITOR'S INTRODUCTION

T̲HIS volume of *The Works of Jonathan Edwards* is the second in a projected series of four containing Jonathan Edwards' theological notebooks, called the "Miscellanies."[1] Edwards regularly made entries in this series throughout his ministerial career, writing the first in 1722, while a young supply preacher in New York City, and the last in 1758, the year of his death. The entries are sequentially numbered; the nine manuscript volumes that compose the "Miscellanies" contain more than 1,400 entries.[2] They vary widely in length. The shortest are one-line cross-references to other texts, while the longest are the equivalent of small treatises. Unlike others of Edwards' notebooks, this series was not limited to a single subject; hence the name "Miscellanies." Edwards ranged widely throughout the theological loci of Reformed Christianity, giving each entry a brief title that specified the principal topic of the composition. To control this large and diverse collection of materials, Edwards also maintained an elaborate index, which he called the "Table," that organized the entries by subject headings that generally corresponded to their various titles.[3]

The initial volume of the "Miscellanies," edited by Thomas A. Schafer, contains entry Nos. a–500 and covers the time period from November 1722 to July–August 1731.[4] This volume contains Nos. 501–832, which carries the series to approximately January 1740, several months after Ed-

1. Thomas A. Schafer edited the first volume, *The Works of Jonathan Edwards, 13, The "Miscellanies," a–500* (New Haven, Yale Univ. Press, 1994). The editors of the two forthcoming volumes are Amy Plantinga Pauw and Douglas A. Sweeney. No. 1069, "Types of the Messiah," is published in *The Works of Jonathan Edwards, 11, Typological Writings*, ed. Wallace E. Anderson and Mason Lowance, Jr., with David Watters (New Haven, Yale Univ. Press, 1993), 191–324. (After the initial citation, individual volumes in the Yale Edition are referred to as *Works*, followed by the volume number.)

2. All MSS volumes but one are in the Beinecke Rare Book and Manuscript Library, Yale University, New Haven, Conn. Book 6 is in the Trask Library, Andover-Newton Theological School, Newton Centre, Mass. Throughout the present volume it is assumed that all JE's MSS are at the Beinecke Library unless otherwise specified.

3. The "Table" to the "Miscellanies" is published in *Works, 13*, 113–50.

4. A capitalized "No." with numerals always refers to "Miscellanies" entries; lower case is used for all citations of other MSS of JE.

wards' delivery of the sermon series known as *A History of the Work of Redemption* and shortly before the outbreak of the Great Awakening in New England later that year.[5] The "Miscellanies," notes Schafer, "trace the intellectual development and maturation of one of America's foremost theologians, providing valuable insights into his mind and spirit."[6] If entry Nos. a–500 "reveal the genesis and incubation of Edwards' most characteristic ideas prior to their first exposition before a larger public," then Nos. 501–832 record the development of those ideas as Edwards first emerges in the public sphere as a spokesperson for orthodox Calvinism.[7] In the 1730s Edwards not only assumed a prominent role in colonial New England church politics but also acquired an international reputation as an evangelist for his leadership of the revivals in the Connecticut River Valley.

Edwards' Religious and Pastoral Experience during the 1730s

In 1729, after several years as Solomon Stoddard's assistant, Edwards became pastor of the church in Northampton, the largest parish in western Massachusetts. From this advantageous position, he began to build his reputation among the ministerial elite in colonial New England. In July 1731 he delivered a public lecture in Boston, and the sermon was so well received that the local clergy recommended its immediate printing. The lecture, *God Glorified in Man's Dependence,* was Edwards' first publication. His second, a sermon entitled *A Divine and Supernatural Light,* was preached first in Northampton in 1733 and then printed in Boston early the following year.[8] These two sermons publicly positioned Edwards as a defender of evangelical Calvinism, unsympathetic to the liberal viewpoint becoming increasingly popular in the Anglo-American evangelical community. In *God Glorified* he maintains that God has absolute sovereignty in the redemption of humankind, while in *Divine and Supernatural Light* he emphasizes the natural incapacity of the human faculties truly to know and love God. Together the sermons not only display the keen intellect and eloquent voice of an ambitious young minister but openly declare his allegiance in a conflict soon to rupture the unity of colonial New England.

Two events related to this conflict accelerated Edwards' rise to prominence. Both spanned the years 1734–36. In May 1734 the First Church

5. For the dating of Nos. 501–832, see below, pp. 43–48.
6. *Works, 13,* 1.
7. *Works, 13,* 2.
8. Both of these sermons are published in *The Works of Jonathan Edwards, 17, Sermons and Discourses, 1730–1733,* ed. Mark R. Valeri (New Haven, Yale Univ. Press, 1999), 196–216, 405–26.

in Springfield, seeking to replace its recently deceased minister, invited Robert Breck, a young graduate of Harvard College, to preach with a view to settlement.[9] Breck's reputation for questionable behavior and liberal theology, however, preceded him. He had been suspected of theft while an undergraduate at Harvard, and while a candidate for the ministry in Windham, Connecticut, he reportedly voiced unorthodox views from the pulpit. Learning of his candidacy in Springfield, various members of the ministerial association of Hampshire County began to mobilize in opposition to his ordination. Edwards had attended the meeting in 1731 that formally organized the Hampshire Association, and he regularly participated in its twice-yearly sessions. As the Breck affair escalated, Edwards emerged as one of the most vocal opponents of his ordination. In November 1734 he was one of the six members of the Association to caution Springfield not to proceed with ordination, and throughout 1735 he was a frequent signatory of letters addressed to Springfield from the association, which attempted to influence the parish's conduct of the affair.[1]

Ignoring the demands of the Hampshire Association, the Springfield church, with the support of several Boston ministers, ordained Robert Breck in January 1736. This act ended only one phase of the controversy, for it precipitated a pamphlet war that extended for more than a year. In response to a letter printed in the *Boston Gazette*, the association published a narrative account of the controversy, which in turn elicited an anonymous defense of the Springfield church's proceedings.[2] The Hampshire Association ended the debate with its publication of *A Letter to the Author of the Pamphlet* in 1737.[3] It is testimony both to Edwards' involvement in the Breck affair and to his increasing stature as a minister in the county that he was asked to write this final defense of the association's conduct.[4]

The Breck affair was largely responsible for "the great noise" that Edwards notes "was in this part of the country about Arminianism" in 1734.[5]

9. For an account of the Breck affair, see *The Works of Jonathan Edwards, 12, Ecclesiastical Writings*, ed. David D. Hall (New Haven, Yale Univ. Press, 1994), 4–17.

1. See *The Works of Jonathan Edwards, 16, Letters and Personal Writings*, ed. George S. Claghorn (New Haven, Yale Univ. Press, 1998), 58–64.

2. *A Narrative of the Proceedings of Those Ministers of the County of Hampshire, Etc. that have Disapproved of the Late Measures Taken in Order to the Settlement of Mr. Robert Breck* . . . . (Boston, 1736); *An Examination of and Some Answer to a Pamphlet, Entitled, A Narrative and Defense* . . . (Boston, 1736).

3. *A Letter to the Author of the Pamphlet called An Answer to the Hampshire Narrative* (Boston 1737); see *Works, 12*, 91–163.

4. For evidence of JE's authorship of this unsigned pamphlet, see *Works, 12*, 5, n. 2.

5. *The Works of Jonathan Edwards, 4, The Great Awakening*, ed. C. C. Goen (New Haven, Yale Univ. Press, 1972), 148.

Edwards responded to this noise on several levels. He not only opposed Breck's settlement, but to counter the spread of liberal Christianity in his local Northampton congregation he preached a two-part lecture on justification by faith, which was "most evidently attended with a very remarkable blessing of heaven to the souls of the people in this town."[6] This lecture was a response to the Breck affair, and as a consequence Edwards was accused of "meddling with the controversy in the pulpit."[7] It also helped to spark a religious revival in Northampton and other neighboring parishes.

The details of the awakening along the Connecticut River Valley in 1734–35 are well known.[8] According to Edwards' published account, the revival began in Northampton when, in response to the sudden death of two young people in the spring of 1734, "there began evidently to appear more of a religious concern on people's minds." By December, he relates, "the Spirit of God began extraordinarily to set in, and wonderfully to work among us." In the following months "a great and earnest concern about the great things of religion and the eternal world became universal in all parts of the town."[9] The excitement was sustained until the summer of 1735, when Joseph Hawley, Edwards' uncle by marriage, slit his throat in despair of his eternal salvation. During this time the revival spread to thirty-two other towns in the Connecticut Valley, making it the largest awakening experienced in New England up to that time.

This awakening was widely perceived to be divine vindication of evangelical Calvinism. Edwards himself considered "the late work of God in this place" to be "a remarkable testimony of God's approbation of the doctrine of justification by faith alone," a principal target of the liberal critique.[1] Although the Hampshire County ministers had been unable to keep Breck out of the Springfield pulpit, they appeared to be winning their campaign against Arminianism by other means. Edwards, however, ensured that his work on behalf of the association did not alienate Breck's influential Boston supporters. At the height of both the Breck affair and the awakening, in May 1735, Edwards sent to Benjamin Colman, pastor of Boston's Brattle Street Church, a narrative account of the course of the revival in the Connecticut Valley. Colman had signed the certificate of or-

---

    6. *Works, 4,* 149.

    7. *Works, 4,* 148.

    8. For an account of the Connecticut Valley awakening, see *Works, 4,* 19–25.

    9. *Works, 4,* 148–49.

    1. *Discourses on Various Important Subjects . . . Delivered at Northampton, Chiefly at the Time of the Late Wonderful Pouring Out of the Spirit of God There,* (Boston, 1738), p. ii.

thodoxy that Breck had presented to the Springfield church and apparently supported his ordination.[2] But he was sufficiently impressed by Edwards' account that he sent an extract of it to his London correspondent, John Guyse. It was primarily through Colman's efforts that *A Faithful Narrative* was published, first in London in 1737, and then in Boston the following year.[3] This book would rapidly propel Edwards to a position of international prominence in the Anglo-American evangelical world.

In 1734–35 Edwards laid the foundation for his reputation both as a defender of Calvinism and as an evangelist. In the remaining years of the decade, as the successive editions of *A Faithful Narrative* issued from the press, this reputation spread widely both in the colonies and abroad. Building on this popular acclaim, Edwards published in 1738 a revised version of *Justification by Faith Alone* and four other revival-related sermons under the title *Discourses on Various Important Subjects*.

As his celebrity grew, Edwards became increasingly frustrated with his congregation's failing spiritual condition. Exacerbating this frustration was Northampton's recently acquired reputation for extraordinary piety. Learning that *A Faithful Narrative* had been well received in London, Edwards wrote to Colman that "it is a great damp to that joy to consider how we decline, and what decays that lively spirit in religion suffers amongst us, while others are rejoicing and praising God for us." However, he was "ashamed, and ready to blush," not only on account of the backsliding but also at the return of contentiousness and party spirit.[4] Edwards had reported in *A Faithful Narrative* that his congregation "remarkably appeared united in dear affection to one another," but this fruit of the awakening apparently did not endure.[5]

The building of a new meetinghouse was one source of renewed contention among the people of Northampton.[6] In November 1735 the church approved the construction, but because of disagreement about its cost and location work did not begin until the following summer. The order of seating in the new meetinghouse also proved divisive: for the first time wealth was given precedence over age as a determinant of social sta-

2. *Works, 12*, 103, n. 7.

3. For a full account of the publication history of *A Faithful Narrative*, see *Works, 4*, 32–46.

4. JE to the Reverend Benjamin Colman, Northampton, May 19, 1737, in *Works, 16*, 67.

5. *Works, 4*, 184.

6. For an account of the building of the new meetinghouse, see Patricia J. Tracy, *Jonathan Edwards, Pastor: Religion and Society in Eighteenth-Century Northampton* (New York, Hill & Wang, 1979), 125–29, and Ola Elizabeth Winslow, *Jonathan Edwards, 1703–1758* (New York, Collier Books, 1961), 160–63.

tus, and men and women were permitted to sit together in family pew boxes. What Edwards called "one of the most amazing instances of divine preservation, that perhaps was ever known in the land" underscored the urgent need for the construction. On March 13, 1737, just as Edwards began to open the text of his morning sermon, the gallery of the old meetinghouse "sunk, and fell down, with the most amazing noise, upon the heads of those that sat under."[7] If the revival was the first "surprising work of God" to occur in Northampton during Edwards' ministry, then the collapse of the gallery was the second, because "so mysteriously and wonderfully did it come to pass, that every life was preserved."[8] Edwards also interpreted the incident as a warning from God, but even this portentous sign failed to spark another revival. He reported to Colman that "it has had in no wise the effect that ten times less things were wont to have two or three years ago."[9] It did not even quicken the pace of construction, for the spire of the new meetinghouse was not raised until the following July and the building was not formally dedicated until December.

Twice as large as the old building, the new meetinghouse reflected Edwards' rapidly expanding reputation. With the change in venue also came a change in Edwards' preaching style. The internationally famous author of *A Faithful Narrative* began to preach treatises from the pulpit. The sermon series was a traditional Puritan vehicle for the exposition of doctrine, and in 1738–39 Edwards mastered and transformed this homiletical style by delivering three extended series from his new pulpit. The month before the dedication of the building, in November 1737, Edwards began to preach a nineteen-preaching-unit series on Matthew 25:1–12, the parable of the wise and foolish virgins. The series extended at least until February and must have been completed by the end of March, because between April and October 1738 Edwards delivered the twenty-one-unit series on I Corinthians 13, known as *Charity and Its Fruits*.[1] In March 1739, only five months after finishing the *Charity* series, he began the thirty-unit series on Isaiah 51:8, known as *A History of the Work of Redemption*.[2] In the series on the wise and foolish virgins, Edwards delineates a list of the un-

7. JE to the Reverend Benjamin Colman, Northampton, March 19, 1736/37, in *Works, 16*, 65.

8. Ibid., 66.

9. JE to Colman, May 19, 1737, in *Works, 16*, 68.

1. See *The Works of Jonathan Edwards, 8, Ethical Writings*, ed. Paul Ramsey (New Haven, Yale Univ. Press, 1989), 123–397.

2. See *The Works of Jonathan Edwards, 9, A History of the Work of Redemption*, ed. John F. Wilson (New Haven, Yale Univ. Press, 1989).

certain and certain signs of grace that anticipates *Religious Affections* (1746) at almost every point. In the *Charity* series he continues this theme, although he concentrates on the nature of true Christian practice, the chief sign of grace. In the *Redemption* series, however, he shifts his focus from the internal application of redemption in the heart of the saint to its external application in history. By means of these three sermon series Edwards displayed to his congregation in their new meetinghouse the full extent of his rhetorical power. Undoubtedly he was also trying to spark another revival. In 1740 George Whitefield would arrive in New England and accomplish that task for him.

The Nature, Purpose, and Use of "Miscellanies" Nos. 501–832

"Miscellanies" Nos. 501–832 trace Edwards' intellectual development during this crucial period in his career as a Puritan minister and theologian. The internal narrative they provide is, however, indirect, for the entries themselves include few references to external events. Nos. 501–832 contain only one date, a cross-reference in No. 625 to a "sermon on Cant. 1:3, preached June 1733."[3] In fact, citations of sermons are the strongest links to external events found in this group of entries, for after January 1733 each of Edwards' sermon manuscripts contains a notation of the date of its composition. Apart from these oblique references to specific preaching occasions, Edwards makes no mention of his public activities in these miscellanies. Nevertheless, thematic connections can be discerned between specific entries and the social context in which they were presumably composed. Many entries written in the 1730s, for example, consider various stages of the morphology of conversion, a topic that occupied Edwards during the awakening and that he considered at length in *A Faithful Narrative*. Similarly, many address some aspect of the liberal critique of Calvinist Christianity, a topic related to Edwards' involvement in the Breck affair. But Edwards discusses neither of these events explicitly.

Also absent from the "Miscellanies" are references to Edwards' private affairs and his spiritual life. Edwards regularly kept a diary of his religious experiences for only a few years in his youth.[4] The journal in which he con-

3. The MS of this sermon on Cant. 1:3 provides the additional information that it was preached "at Boston," probably as a public lecture. We can speculate that JE included this date in the "Miscellanies" entry to mark the occasion of his delivery of a lecture in Boston. But it is equally likely that he did so to distinguish it from one on the same text that he had preached in 1728.

4. For JE's "Diary," see *Works, 16,* 759–89.

tinuously made entries throughout his career was the "Miscellanies." The content of this theological journal appears impersonal; it contains no record of such events in Edwards' family life as the birth of a child or the death of a relative, nor does it include reflections on his spiritual condition.[5] Very few entries are even written in the first person. It is at times possible to discern personal referents in the subtext of Edwards' abstract theological analysis. For example, in No. 810 he comments that "the deliverance of the Christian church will be preceded by God's raising up a number of eminent ministers that shall more plainly and fervently and effectually preach the gospel than it had been before." But we can only speculate that Edwards saw himself as one of these eminent and powerful preachers.

The personal dimension of these writings will come more clearly into focus if we abandon the assumptions that the affective inner life of an author must dwell first and foremost on the self. The "Miscellanies" are a record of Edwards' affective inner life, but it is a life centered on God and not the self. In his "Personal Narrative," Edwards exclaims that he "love[s] the doctrines of the gospel: they have been to my soul like green pastures." His ardor is so strong that "only mentioning a single word, causes my heart to burn within me: or only seeing the name of Christ, or the name of some attribute of God."[6] The "Miscellanies" trace Edwards' communion with this most excellent love object. Self-scrutiny was a distraction, if not a temptation, leading him away from "this sweetness." "The sweetest joys and delights I have experienced," he reveals, have been "in a direct view of the glorious things of the gospel." It is "a loss that I cannot bear, to take off my eye from the glorious pleasant object I behold without me, to turn my eye in upon myself, and my own good estate."[7] Edwards composed the "Miscellanies" not simply as an intellectual exercise but as a devotional discipline, which transcended in its aim the self-centered diary. Refusing "to turn his eye in upon himself," he recorded his heart's delight in the "glorious things of the gospel." This was his lifelong pursuit, to draw near to God through an understanding of doctrine.

Because it is a journal focused on God and not the self, the "Miscellanies" do not conform to the standards of any common literary genre. They are therefore frequently interpreted as private writings containing rough drafts or notes for sermons and treatises that Edwards was planning to write. This characterization is only partially accurate. The "Miscella-

5. JE kept a record of domestic events, such as births and deaths, in the "Blank Bible."
6. *Works, 16*, 799–800.
7. *Works, 16*, 800.

nies" are private writings insofar as Edwards apparently did not intend the text as it stands for publication. Unlike other of his notebooks, however, various features of the "Miscellanies" manuscripts lend them a public character. Edwards composed the "Miscellanies" in complete sentences, first writing rough drafts that he would later carefully edit and transcribe—using his "public" hand—into the notebooks. As a result, each of the entries is a complete composition on a discrete topic, with the exception of those that are cross-references or additions to earlier entries. At times, Edwards linked a series of entries together by cross-references to form a more extended composition. He even elaborately structured the longer entries, dividing them into sections and subparts and appending multiple corollaries. Furthermore, he does not present his ideas in a tentative fashion. Only once in Nos. 501–832 does he indicate any hesitation about an argument or conclusion when he added to No. 595, an entry about infant baptism, the comment, "These things about baptism doubtful." Apart from this one retraction, Edwards articulates his ideas with a certainty uncharacteristic of mere notes or rough drafts.

The fact that Edwards apparently allowed his colleagues and students to read and study his compositions in the "Miscellanies" also gives them a public character. In 1758, when Edwards moved to Princeton to assume the presidency of the College of New Jersey, he left "some of his long papers"—undoubtedly a reference to the folio-sized "Miscellanies" notebooks—and "manuscript sermons" in the care of Samuel Hopkins and gave him permission to use them freely.[8] In 1765–66, Jonathan Edwards, Jr., wintered with Hopkins as he prepared for ordination. Hopkins, who still had possession of Edwards' manuscripts, used them as a precis of Reformed theology to correct some of Edwards, Jr.'s unorthodox views.[9] Hopkins may have acquired this teaching technique when he was training as a ministerial candidate with Edwards, Sr.[1] What is certain is that both Hopkins and Edwards, Jr., considered the "Miscellanies" to be of publishable quality, and both issued advertisements to solicit support for such a venture.[2] The "Miscellanies," therefore, are better described not as private

8. Samuel Hopkins to Joseph Bellamy, Jan. 19, 1758 (Presbyterian Historical Society, Philadelphia, Pennsylvania).

9. See Robert L. Ferm, *Jonathan Edwards the Younger: 1745–1801* (Grand Rapids, Eerdmans Publishing Co., 1976), 22.

1. That JE used the "Miscellanies" as a teaching tool is suggested by the fact that Joseph Bellamy, while training with JE for the ministry, kept a notebook that looks suspiciously like an imitation of the "Miscellanies." Bellamy's notebook is housed in the library of Yale Divinity Scool, New Haven, Conn.

2. *Works, 13*, 545–46.

but as quasi-public writings, having a status analogous to the letter, which in the eighteenth century was often composed for a broad audience.

If the "Miscellanies" are not strictly private writings, neither are they simply notes or drafts for planned compositions. Edwards did use the "Miscellanies" as a repository for ideas that he intended to develop in future, fully public compositions, such as sermons and treatises. But precisely because of their quasi-public status the entries have a complexity and finality that surpasses their relation to Edwards' published writings. To assess which themes dominate Nos. 501–832 and to trace their course of development, we must therefore view the "Miscellanies" not only as a sourcebook but also as a composition in its own right. Each of these perspectives reveals a different facet of this rich, multidimensional text. And insofar as entries that appear important in relation to Edwards' published texts may be less significant when viewed in the context of the "Miscellanies" as a whole, the latter perspective also functions as an important corrective to the former.

Reading the miscellanies that Edwards wrote in the 1730s retrospectively from the perspective of his mature writings, we perceive in embryo the ideas that form the core of some of his most famous published treatises. For example, several entries express concepts that Edwards later developed at length in *Freedom of the Will*. No. 830, which has a line running along the entirety of its left margin indicating its use elsewhere, contains in outline form the substance of Edwards' argument in *Freedom of the Will*. Not only does its first sentence echo the title of the treatise by its use of the phrase "present prevailing notion of liberty," but it addresses the concept of liberty of indifference, which is the principal focus of Edwards' argument in the treatise. In both the entry and the treatise he calls this concept of liberty "absurd" because it leads to conclusions obviously contrary to common sense, and he uses similar examples in both texts to demonstrate this point.[3] In No. 573 he defines volitional ability in the same terms he would use some twenty years later in the treatise. "[I]n the vulgar and more ordinary use of the expression," Edwards writes, "if we say a man has it in his own power to do or not, we ordinarily mean no other than that he can do it if he has a mind to do it, or chooses to do it."[4] And in No. 657

3. For JE's discussion of liberty of indifference, see *The Works of Jonathan Edwards, 1, Freedom of the Will*, ed. Paul Ramsey (New Haven, Yale Univ. Press, 1957), 203–16, and *passim*. His exclamation in the entry, "But how absurd are these things!" is echoed in the treatise by the statement, "This is grossly absurd" (p. 205).

4. Cf., "In the strictest propriety of speech, a man has a thing in his power, if he has it in his choice, or at his election: and a man can't be truly said to be unable to do a thing, when he can do it if he will" (*Works, 1*, 162).

Edwards develops the distinction only implied in No. 573 between the commonsense meaning of free will and the "metaphysical" meaning constructed by philosophers. Anticipating the infinite regress argument he will later use with such force in *Freedom of the Will*, Edwards reasons that this metaphysical notion of liberty is not only artificial but also inconsistent, "for it supposes that there [is] a volition or act of the will before the first act."[5]

A similar relation can be discerned between various entries from the 1730s and *The Nature of True Virtue*, which Edwards wrote in 1755. The most important of these is No. 530. In this entry Edwards identifies two different types of self-love and argues that only "a man's love to his own proper, single, and separate good" is contrary to love of God. He also makes the distinction, central to the argument in the treatise, between love of benevolence and love of complacence.[6] However, in two other entries, which have "use lines" down their left margins, Edwards also introduces ideas that he will later develop in the treatise. In No. 623 he explains how at the Day of Judgment natural conscience will "be in its most perfect exercise" making the damned "convinced in conscience that their punishment is just."[7] And in No. 821, which continues the discussion of self-love, he argues that the affections of gratitude and pity only appear to be virtues natural to humankind; because they "arise from self-love," they actually are devoid of moral virtue.[8] Some of these concepts Edwards first expressed publicly in *Charity and Its Fruits*, but not until his composition of *True Virtue* were they presented in a format that Edwards himself intended for formal publication.

Because of the significance later scholars have attributed to Edwards' Stockbridge treatises, entries such as these, which he wrote while in Northampton, attract attention. These entries are important insofar as they display the genesis of what are now considered Edwards' most characteristic ideas and help locate the historical context in which those ideas

5. Cf. "Arminians improve these terms, as terms of art, and in their metaphysical meaning, to advance and establish those things which are contrary to common sense, in a high degree. . . . [T]hey have introduced a new strange liberty, consisting in indifference, contingence, and self-determination; by which they involve themselves . . . in great obscurity, and manifold gross inconsistence" (*Works, 1,* 429; see also pp. 343–49). For the infinite regress argument, see pp. 171–74.

6. JE also discusses self-love in No. 534. For the distinction between types of self-love and between benevolence and complacence, see *Works, 8,* 575–88, 542–49.

7. See the discussion of natural conscience in *Works, 8,* 589–99.

8. JE develops the concept of natural conscience in *Works 8,* 588–99. For his discussion of gratitude and pity as expressions of self-love, see pp. 575–88, 605–08.

were first expressed. But to read Nos. 501–832 solely from the perspective of Edwards' Stockbridge treatises gives a distorted view of the "Miscellanies" text itself. In retrospect, ideas appear important that during the 1730s were not Edwards' dominant preoccupation. If we view this portion of the "Miscellanies" as a composition in its own right, neither free will nor true virtue qualifies as a major theme. And if we view it as a source-book, the connections that most clearly manifest themselves are to texts written contemporaneously with this set of entries, such as *Justification by Faith Alone* or *A History of the Work of Redemption*. In the remainder of this introduction, I will therefore consider the major themes in Nos. 501–832 both as they develop in the "Miscellanies" text itself and as they relate to Edwards' published writings.

Major Themes in "Miscellanies" Nos. 501–832

Five themes dominate "Miscellanies" Nos. 501–832: justification by faith alone; spiritual knowledge, which includes both the "new spiritual sense" and Christian practice; the rationality of the Christian religion; the history of the work of redemption; and conversion and the religious life. True, these five themes do not account for all the subjects Edwards considers in this set of entries. Furthermore, to organize the entries according to these five themes imposes an external structure on the text. Because these themes do not uniformly correspond to rubrics used by Edwards to index entries in the "Table" to the "Miscellanies," it is unlikely that Edwards himself would have grouped the entries in precisely the fashion they are considered below. But judging either by the frequency of entries on a given topic or by the length and complexity of individual entries, these are the subjects that preoccupied Edwards in the 1730s. That he publicly issued, or planned to issue, a major statement on each of these topics from either the pulpit or the press confirms their importance.

JUSTIFICATION BY FAITH ALONE

In 1734 Edwards preached a two-unit lecture on justification (Rom. 4:5) that, in a revised and expanded form, was published in 1738 as *Justification by Faith Alone*, the first and most prominent piece in *Discourses on Various Important Subjects*. As Edwards prepared first to write this lecture and then to revise it for publication, justification emerges in the "Miscellanies" as a dominant theme. There is consequently a close relation between the "Miscellanies" and *Justification by Faith Alone*. In fact, this text, perhaps more than any other, supports the interpretation of the "Miscellanies" as a collection of notes and drafts that Edwards intended for use in future publications. The original 1734 lecture relies only minimally on the "Miscellanies." But as Edwards revised his lecture for publication, he incorporated into it many ideas first articulated in miscellanies entries. Edwards probably wrote the concentration of justification-related entries extending from Nos. 668 to No. 729 as he revised the lecture for publication; however, the earliest entry having a direct relation to the published discourse is No. 315, which dates from 1727. From this entry to No. 729, the last written before the publication of the discourse, there are thirty-one entries listed in the "Table" under the heading of "Justification." Excerpts, revisions, and paraphrases of the majority of these entries can be found throughout *Justification by Faith Alone*. Although Edwards used the original lecture as the framework for the discourse, in significant measure he pieced together the discourse from compositions made first within the "Miscellanies."

The correspondence between the "Miscellanies" and *Justification by Faith Alone* is not exact. Issues that Edwards addresses at length in the original lecture—such as the claim "that when it is said, we are not justified by the works of the law it means only the works of the ceremonial law, not the moral law"—are neglected in the "Miscellanies."[9] Other issues that are integral to the discourse but absent from the lecture—such as the distinction between moral and natural fitness—are the subject of numerous entries. Moreover, both the lecture and the discourse are overtly polemical texts.[1] At the outset of the lecture Edwards establishes its polemical context by giving his "congregation a brief account of the opinion that is by some maintained that I would oppose in this discourse."[2] Similarly, in the preface to *Discourses on Various Important Subjects*, Edwards explicitly identifies the viewpoint that he opposes as "the Arminian scheme of justification by our own virtue."[3] In neither the lecture nor the discourse does Edwards name a specific minister or theologian as his opponent;

9. Lecture on Rom. 4:5 (Nov. 1734). The doctrine of this lecture is the same as that of the published discourse: "We are justified only by faith in Christ, and not by any manner of goodness of our own." JE delivered it probably as a mid-week lecture over two separate preaching occasions. Its fifty-four leaves contain numerous marks and annotations made while JE was revising the text for publication.

1. The Breck controversy was not the only occasion for JE's delivery of the original sermon. As C. C. Goen points out, in Nov. 1734, the month of the sermon's delivery, William Rand, minister at Sunderland, was reported to have "'advanced some new notions as to the doctrines of justification'" (*Works*, *4*, 17).

2. Lecture on Rom. 4:5 (Nov. 1734), L. 1r.

3. *Discourses on Various Important Subjects*, p. iv.

however, he gives a clear indication of the complex of views he associates with "Arminianism."[4] According to Conrad Cherry, Edwards maintains in *Justification by Faith* that "the essence of Arminianism is its neonomianism," which "conceives faith as a new kind of obedience and the gospel as a new kind of law."[5] Anri Morimoto identifies Edwards' interpretation of the Arminian doctrine of justification with three claims: that "to justify means to pardon"; that "there is no imputation of Christ's righteousness"; and that "sincere obedience is sufficient in order to receive justification," for God "regards our imperfect human effort as perfect."[6] In the discourse Edwards structures his argument to address each of these points; in the "Miscellanies," however, he focuses on a more limited range of issues.

Unlike his practice in the lecture and the discourse, Edwards rarely refers in the "Miscellanies" to the polemical context in which he wrote entries on justification by faith. No. 829, which explicitly mentions "Arminians" whose "scheme" implies "that we are justified by our own merit," is exceptional. In keeping with the general lack of contextualization in the "Miscellanies," Edwards' opponent must be inferred from the course of argumentation he pursues. The principal issue that runs throughout these entries is the role of faith in the act of justification. Edwards considers several methods of clarifying this issue that were either absent from or undeveloped in the lecture. He distinguishes between different meanings of the word "condition" in order to specify the sense in which faith is a condition of justification (Nos. 315, 412, 659). In No. 669 he addresses the question "whether faith and repentance are two distinct things that in like manner are the conditions of justification." This entry forms the substance of the fifth objection appended to the discourse, but more important, Edwards begins to explore in this entry the two-part definition of jus-

---

4. Thomas A. Schafer notes, "There was probably not, in 1734, an avowed Arminian in the Puritan pulpits of New England; but the works of English divines like Samuel Clarke, John Tillotson, Isaac Barrow, and Daniel Whitby were beginning to be read" ("Jonathan Edwards on Justification by Faith," *Church History*, 20 [Dec. 1951], 55). On Arminianism in New England, see also Conrad Cherry, *The Theology of Jonathan Edwards: A Reappraisal* (1966; rep. Bloomington, Indiana Univ. Press, 1990), 188–215; Francis Albert Christie, "The Beginnings of Arminianism in New England," *Papers of the American Society of Church History*, Second Series, III (1912), 153–72; Gerald J. Goodwin, "The Myth of Arminian-Calvinism in Eighteenth-Century New England," *New England Quarterly*, XLI (June 1968), 213–237; C.C. Goen's introduction to *Works*, 4, 1–18; Perry Miller, *Jonathan Edwards* (1949; rep. Amherst, Univ. of Massachusetts Press, 1981), 101–30; and Conrad Wright, *The Beginnings of Unitarianism in America* (Boston, Beacon Press, 1955).

5. Cherry, *The Theology of Jonathan Edwards*, 187.

6. Anri Morimoto, *Jonathan Edwards and the Catholic Vision of Salvation* (University Park, Pennsylvania State Univ. Press, 1995), 76.

A page from "Miscellanies," Book 1, featuring entry No. 669, "Justification." Courtesy Beinecke Rare Book and Manuscript Library, Yale University.

tification that dominates the discourse. "Justifying faith," he writes, "is conversant about two things. It is conversant about sin to be rejected and to be delivered from, and about positive good to be accepted and obtained." Building upon this distinction, Edwards argues in the discourse that justification does not simply consist in pardon, or the remission of sins, as his Arminian opponents maintain, but also includes the imputation of Christ's active righteousness.

Because "condition" is an ambiguous term that can describe the relation between justification and not only faith but various other graces (Nos. 315, 412), Edwards prefers in the discourse the aesthetic language of "fitness" or "suitableness." Although this approach is present in the lecture, Edwards develops it much more thoroughly in the "Miscellanies." Faith, he argues in No. 507, is "the active suitableness, or rather suiting, of the receiver with Christ and his redemption. 'Tis the active, direct suiting and according of the soul to the Redeemer, and to his salvation" (see also Nos. 416, 659). Fitness language avoids the causal connotation of the term "condition," but to ensure that his doctrine of justification does not make faith into a work, Edwards also distinguishes between "moral" and "natural" fitness (Nos. 647, 670, 682, 712). By this distinction Edwards attempts to eliminate from his doctrine of justification the implication that human acts have by nature a virtue or merit respected by God. "A person is morally fit for a state," he writes in No. 647, "when by his excellency or odiousness his excellency or odiousness commends him to it." To call the relation between faith and justification one of moral fitness is, therefore, equivalent to Arminianism, for it assumes that the human act of faith has in itself an excellency or loveliness that merits eternal salvation. A relation of natural fitness, however, has no implication of merit because it depends only upon "the beauty of that order there [is] in uniting those things that have a natural agreement and congruity, the one with the other" (No. 712).

Edwards also distinguishes between natural and moral fitness in order to defend the doctrine of imputation. Arminians considered this doctrine to be irrational and unjust, for it appears to assert that at the moment of justification the righteousness earned by Christ is transferred to one who is by nature unworthy to receive it. To describe the relation between faith and justification as one of natural fitness answers this charge more effectively than the traditional forensic explanation. Characterizing justification as meaning simply that believers are "looked on [as] suitable that Christ's satisfaction and merits should be theirs" obscures its ontological foundation, without which imputation appears to be the unjust transference of an alien righteousness.[7] The concept of natural fitness emphasizes that imputation is preceded by a preexisting union with Christ. As Edwards states in No. 712, "God will neither impute Christ's righteousness to us, nor adjudge his benefits to us, *unless we be in him;* nor will he look upon us as being in him without an actual unition to him." Because the union with Christ, which occurs by faith, creates the ontological foundation necessary for imputation, it is fitting that the faithful are justified. "God sees it fit," Edwards writes in No. 568, "that they only that are one with Christ by their own act, should be looked upon as one in law." It is fitting that Christ's righteousness is transferred to the elect, for "[w]hat is real in the union between Christ and his people, is the foundation of what is legal."[8] By grounding justification in the reality of union with Christ, therefore, the concept of natural fitness rebuts the Arminian objection to imputation without making justification into a reward for meritorious works.

Although Edwards insists that justification is not conferred as a reward for faith, he also claims that God "does in some respect give [believers] happiness as a testimony of his respect to the loveliness of their holiness and good works" (No. 627). In both the "Miscellanies" and the discourse he attempts to resolve this apparent contradiction by differentiating between the quality of works before and following the union with Christ that occurs by faith. Before union there is nothing in human nature morally fit for a reward; following union, however, it is appropriate to speak of both moral fitness and reward. The "good works" of the saints "are not lovely to God in themselves," Edwards writes in No. 627; "they are lovely to him in Christ and beholding them not separately and by themselves, but as in Christ" (see also No. 712). Because of the imputation of Christ's righteousness, works acquire a virtue or merit that renders them subject to reward. The reward that saints receive for the perceived holiness of their works is not justification, however, but glorification. To identify justification as the reward would contradict Edwards' assertion that the relation between faith and justification is one of natural, not moral, fitness. It is "heaven itself with all its glory and happiness" that is conferred upon the saints as a reward for the holiness of their works (No. 671; see also No. 793). Edwards can therefore maintain that the communion of saints in heaven is hierarchical. Although all who are justified will ultimately be

---

7. *Justification by Faith Alone,* in *Discourses on Various Important Subjects,* p. 17.

8. JE repeats this assertion in *Justification by Faith Alone,* p. 16. See Schafer's discussion of this passage ("Jonathan Edwards and Justification By Faith," 58–60) and Morimoto's response (pp. 84–90).

glorified, "the degree of their happiness will be according to the degree of their holiness and good works" (No. 671).

The distinction between natural and moral fitness is integral to *Justification by Faith Alone*. Absent from the 1734 lecture, it is developed by Edwards in the "Miscellanies" for use in the published discourse. However, Edwards' analysis of the relation between faith and works did not end with publication of *Justification by Faith Alone*. No. 729, which he incorporated into the discourse's discussion of evangelical obedience, was probably the last justification-related entry written before publication. But it was the first entry listed under the new "Table" headings of "Justification, Obedience" and "Justification, Perseverance." A series of issues concerning obedience to the law, perseverance in the faith, and Christian practice generally, emerge as a dominant theme in the miscellanies of the latter 1730s. These issues arise from Edwards' extended analysis of the doctrine of justification by faith, and they ultimately transform every aspect of his soteriology, including his concept of spiritual knowledge.

SPIRITUAL KNOWLEDGE

In 1948 the *Harvard Theological Review* published an essay by Perry Miller called "Jonathan Edwards on the Sense of the Heart."[9] This essay contained the text of "Miscellanies" No. 782, which has the multiple title "Ideas. Sense of the Heart. Spiritual Knowledge or Conviction. Faith," along with Miller's commentary on the entry. With this publication Miller laid the foundation for the image of Edwards he would so persuasively portray in his intellectual biography *Jonathan Edwards*, which was published the following year.[1] In No. 782 Edwards uses Lockean empiricism to articulate the distinctive element in the religious experience of the regenerate, which he called the "new spiritual sense." Considered in isolation, the entry allowed Miller to depict Edwards as an heir not of Calvin but of the Enlightenment, who "rejected the metaphysics and psychology of original Puritanism, and substituted Newton and Locke."[2] Insofar as Miller's biography shaped the discourse about Edwards for at least a gen-

---

9. Perry Miller, "Jonathan Edwards on the Sense of the Heart," *Harvard Theological Review* 41 (1948), 123–45. Miller's edition of No. 782 is fairly accurate; more problematic is his assertion that the entry "probably dates from Edwards' later years in Northampton and may roughly be ascribed to about 1745" (p. 124). JE wrote the entry in the winter of 1738–39; see "Note on the Text," pp. 45–46 below.

1. Miller, *Jonathan Edwards*. Miller also drew extensively on this entry in "The Rhetoric of Sensation," in *Errand into the Wilderness* (Cambridge, Harvard Univ. Press, 1956), 167–83.

2. Miller, *Jonathan Edwards*, 194.

eration, entry No. 782, and other writings that supported his perspective, became the foundational texts for Edwards' scholarship. Although Miller's portrait of Edwards has been widely criticized, these texts continue to define the discipline and to generate scholarly debate.[3]

No. 782 is the culmination of a series of entries on the new sense and such related topics as faith and the witness of the Spirit. Edwards wrote the first number in this series while a supply preacher in New York (No. aa), and he regularly returned to this subject throughout the 1720s and 1730s. Following his composition of the long, synthetic essay that comprises No. 782, he made only one additional entry in this series of any substance (No. 1090). Edwards' development in the "Miscellanies" of the concept of the new spiritual sense appears, therefore, to reach a climax with this entry. However, a different course of development will emerge if we read No. 782 in the context of the "Miscellanies" manuscripts as a whole. At approximately the same time that he composed No. 782 Edwards wrote another entry, No. 790, entitled "Signs of Godliness," in which he maintains "that good fruits, or good works and keeping Christ's commandments" are the "best signs of godliness." No. 782 should be read in conjunction with No. 790. These two entries describe two distinct means available to the regenerate for obtaining spiritual knowledge. The new spiritual sense affords the saint a sure conviction of the truth of the Christian faith, while Christian practice is the most reliable means of acquiring personal assurance of salvation. But because No. 782 was published as an independent essay and because the new spiritual sense played a leading role in Miller's program to make Edwards accessible to a modern audience, this concept has been considered in isolation from the totality of Edwards' thought.[4] As a result, the new spiritual sense has frequently been identified as the means of assurance, a power that Edwards in his mature thought attributes primarily to Christian practice.

3. See Terrence Erdt, *Jonathan Edwards: Art and the Sense of the Heart* (Amherst, Univ. of Massachusetts Press, 1980); Paul Helm, "John Locke and Jonathan Edwards: A Reconsideration," *Journal of the History of Ideas* 7 (1969), 51–61; David Lyttle, "The Sixth Sense of Jonathan Edwards," *The Church Quarterly Review* 167 (1966), 50–59; Michael J. McClymond, "Spiritual Perception in Jonathan Edwards," *The Journal of Religion* 77 (April 1977), 195–216; Claude A. Smith, "Jonathan Edwards and 'the Way of Ideas,'" *Harvard Theological Review* 59 (1966), 153–73. The most sustained critique of Miller's interpretation of JE is Cherry, *The Theology of Jonathan Edwards.*

4. A recent example of this tendency is Leon Chai, *Jonathan Edwards and the Limits of Enlightenment Philosophy* (New York, Oxford Univ. Press, 1998), 22–35. Notable exceptions are Wayne Proudfoot, "Perception and Love in *Religious Affections*," in *Jonathan Edwards's Writings: Text, Context, Interpretation,* ed. Stephen J. Stein (Bloomington, Indiana Univ. Press, 1996), 122–36; and John E. Smith, "Jonathan Edwards: Piety and Practice in the American Character," *Journal of Religion* 54 (1974), 166–80.

In one of his best-known sermons, Edwards explains the function of the new sense with little reference to the concept of Christian practice. In August 1733 he delivered to his Northampton congregation a lecture that was published in revised form the following year under the title *A Divine and Supernatural Light*.[5] Written around the time he composed Nos. 628 and 630, which both have the title "Spiritual Knowledge. Faith," it reflects the content of these and several other miscellanies entries (e.g. Nos. 397, 471, 489, 540).[6] In this sermon Edwards maintains that the regenerate receive at the moment of conversion "a new, supernatural principle of life and action." Because this new principle includes the capacity to perceive "the divine excellency of the things revealed in the Word of God," saints thereby obtain a "spiritual and saving conviction of the truth and reality of these things." Edwards emphasizes that this new sense of divine excellency "is given immediately by God, and not obtained by natural means"; it is therefore "attainable by persons of mean capacities, and advantages, as well as those that are of the greatest parts and learning." But he mentions Christian practice only as an afterthought, when he remarks in his final exhortation that spiritual light "has its fruit in an universal holiness of life."[7]

The miscellanies from the 1730s reveal how Edwards arrived only gradually at a recognition of the importance of Christian practice. This topic clearly displays how the "Miscellanies" provide a record of Edwards' intellectual development more precise than that available in his published sermons and discourses. In the early 1730s, when *Divine and Supernatural Light* was written, there is little discussion in the "Miscellanies" of persevering obedience through trials of faith—which is the essence of Christian practice—as the best evidence of a godly disposition. Only after the Connecticut Valley revivals does this subject emerge in the "Miscellanies" as a dominant theme. No. 695, written in 1736, is his first entry with the title "Perseverance" since No. 467, which dates from 1730. As it became evident that many of the presumed converts in Northampton had failed to persevere, Edwards begins to argue that not only faith but also perseverance is a condition of justification. And perhaps because the backsliders alerted him to the error of identifying as the means of assurance "the inward witness of the Spirit, the feeling of soul-assuring inward experi-

---

5. See *Works*, *17*, 405–26. For a discussion of the relation between the original sermon and the published discourse, see *Works*, *10*, 111–13.

6. Valeri notes the importance of Nos. 489, 540, 628, and 630 (*Works*, *17*, 40). See *Works*, *13*, 462–63, 512–14, 533.

7. *Works*, *17*, 411, 413, 410, 423–24.

ence," he shifts the locus of assurance from immediate experience to persevering Christian practice (No. 800).

Edwards initially considers perseverance as a necessary precondition for the confirmation of the angels. In No. 515 he postpones the confirmation of the angels until the moment "when Jesus Christ ascended into heaven" (see also Nos. 570, 591, 593, 744). God kept the angels "in a state of trial, from the beginning of the world till the ascension of Christ." This long period of probation ensured that the angels had "a thorough trial of their obedience" before their confirmation. In particular, they were not confirmed until "after they had seen Christ in the flesh, for this was the greatest trial of the angels' obedience that ever was." In No. 664b Edwards expands the concept of perseverance to include not only angels but also saints. In this entry Edwards argues that "every creature, before he receives the eternal reward of his obedience, should have some considerable trial of his obedience." Obedience to God's law is insufficient to display "the creature's respect to God and his authority" unless he "meets with some trial, i.e. some opposition to obedience." Therefore, both angels and saints must persevere through such trials, as did Christ, who "had immensely the greatest trial of obedience that ever was."

Edwards began to write entries entitled "Perseverance" only after establishing in No. 664b that perseverance through trials of faith is a universal requirement for salvation. In No. 695 he considers perseverance as a feature distinguishing the covenant with Adam from the covenant of grace (see also Nos. 755, 774). As he revised *Justification by Faith Alone* for publication, however, he attempts to delineate the relation between justification and perseverance. Reflecting his increasing recognition of the importance of this doctrine, he comments in No. 729 that "Calvinian divines" have not "sufficiently set forth" the manner in which perseverance is "necessary to salvation." In earlier entries Edwards had maintained that the union with Christ obtained by faith was the sole condition of justification, but here, and in several subsequent entries, he modifies this viewpoint (Nos. 795, 808). He continues to insist that "a sinner is justified on his first act of faith," but he gives to perseverance a status almost equivalent to faith by arguing that perseverance is contained "virtually in that first act." To explain the relation between justification and perseverance Edwards again uses the aesthetic language of "fitness." Although faith "renders it congruous that we should be accepted to a title to salvation," faith has this congruity only because God looks upon perseverance "as if it were a property of the faith, by which the sinner is then justified." If perseverance were not virtually contained in the act of faith, "it would be

The first two pages of entry No. 729, "Perseverance," from "Miscellanies," Book 2. Courtesy Beinecke Rare Book and Manuscript Library, Yale University.

needful," as the Arminians claim, "that the act of justification should be suspended, till the sinner had persevered in faith" (see also No. 695).

As Edwards worked through the relation between justification and perseverance, his understanding of the new spiritual sense also began to shift. In No. 686 Edwards equates the new spiritual sense with the means of assurance by reasoning that the regenerate acquire assurance of their union with Christ through "a kind of immediate and intuitive evidence of the soul's relation to God." A saint "knows there is an union, for he sees it, or feels it, so strong that he can't question it, or doubt of it." By No. 729, however, he is associating the means of assurance not with an immediate "witness of the Spirit" but with perseverance. In this entry Edwards asserts "that not only the first act of faith, but after-acts of faith, and perseverance in faith, do justify the sinner." After-acts of faith, such as perseverance, enter into justification because they "have as great and greater hand in the manifestation of the futurition of salvation to us . . . as the first act; for our knowledge of this may be mainly from after-acts, and from a course of acts." It is this insight that Edwards develops at length in No. 790.

No. 790 is the first entry in the "Miscellanies" entitled "Signs of Godliness," but it continues the course of inquiry Edwards began in the numbers on spiritual knowledge and perseverance. In this entry Edwards adopts the view traditionally maintained by orthodox divines, that good works or sanctification is the best evidence of justification. The "best signs of godliness," he asserts, are "doing good works, and bringing forth good fruit perseveringly, through trials" of faith. He recommends that we judge not only others but also ourselves by this sign, and even insists that it is "principally by men's works, practice, or fruits that they are to be judged at the last day." Sensing an inconsistency with the concept of the witness of the Spirit, he redefines this more intuitive means of assurance to coincide with his developing doctrine of Christian practice. In No. 790 Edwards no longer equates the Spirit's witness with the "immediate testimony of the Spirit of God himself to our souls that we are the children of God"; instead, he argues that it signifies the internal perception of "those exercises of grace and exertions of soul whence good external practice in speech or behavior immediately result."

Edwards himself clearly suggests that the new spiritual sense should be understood in conjunction with Christian practice in a sermon series he delivered from his Northampton pulpit in the winter of 1737–38. Written approximately a year before Nos. 782 and 790, this nineteen-unit series on the parable of the wise and foolish virgins (Matt. 25:1–12) delineates an extensive list of the signs of grace that incorporates both the new sense and Christian practice. Bringing together the insights he would further articulate in Nos. 782 and 790, Edwards maintains, first, that the only truly distinguishing mark of the saint is the knowledge of divine excellency that is acquired by means of the new spiritual sense in the conversion moment; and second, that the most reliable means of achieving subjective certainty of the presence of this new sense is persevering Christian practice.[8] That Edwards reiterates this two-fold division in *Religious Affections* is an indication that it represents his mature view of the means of spiritual knowledge. In this treatise Edwards emphasizes Christian practice to distance his understanding of evangelical Calvinism from the antinomianism and enthusiasm of the radical New Lights. The "Miscellanies" suggest that Edwards first confronted his own latent antinomianism in the aftermath of the Connecticut Valley awakening, as his backsliding congregants painfully displayed to him that immediate experience was an unreliable means of assurance: it produced hypocrites more often than saints.

THE RATIONALITY OF THE CHRISTIAN RELIGION

Edwards first considered writing a treatise entitled "A Rational Account of the Principles and Main Doctrines of the Christian Religion" as early as 1724, for he included it in a list of projects that he made on a letter leaf while a tutor at Yale.[9] In the 1730s he sporadically made notes to himself about the content and organization of the treatise on a sheet of paper, which has as its heading a proposed title nearly identical to the one stated above.[1] From Edwards' projected outline it appears that he intended to write a systematic theology or, to use the eighteenth-century term, "body of divinity," which would have considered such standard "heads" of Reformed theology as the being and attributes of God, the relations of the persons in the Trinity, the ends of creation, the fall of humankind, and the means of salvation through Christ.[2] "Miscellanies" No. 832, written in the winter of 1739–40, supplies further information about the "Rational Account." In this entry, entitled "Preface to Rational Account," Edwards identifies the treatise as an effort to prove "that the present fashionable

---

8. For a consideration of this course of inquiry, see Ava Chamberlain, "Brides of Christ and Signs of Grace: Edwards's Sermon Series on the Parable of the Wise and Foolish Virgins," in *Jonathan Edwards's Writings*, 3–18.

9. *Works, 13*, 4–5, 7, 15. JE subsequently incorporated this leaf into his "Catalogue of Reading"; it is therefore usually called the "Catalogue letter" leaf.

1. The heading of the outline reads, "A Rational Account of the Main Doctrines of the Christian Religion Attempted." This outline is published in *Works, 6*, 396–97.

2. See *Works, 6*, 396.

divinity is wrong." He also refers to the debate, which dominated the Anglo-American world in the late seventeenth and early eighteenth centuries, concerning the "reformation of manners," and aligns himself with the evangelical view that the only means to achieve lasting moral reform is through a revival of piety.[3] There is no direct evidence extant that Edwards pursued this project after 1740. Around this time he appears to have abandoned it for a more historical approach to the exposition of Christian doctrine. Before this date, however, Edwards was actively planning to write the "Rational Account."

Edwards used the "Miscellanies" to explore themes he was planning to pursue in the "Rational Account." The fact that "Rational Account" was, according to Thomas Schafer, one of the names by which Edwards initially referred to the "Miscellanies" indicates the close relation between the notebooks and this proposed treatise.[4] He may have abandoned this designation for the "Miscellanies" as the content of the notebooks ranged beyond the apparent subject matter of the treatise; however, many miscellanies entries written in the 1720s and 1730s are related to it. One link between the "Miscellanies" and the "Rational Account" is suggested by Edwards' proposed title for the treatise. A portion of the title—the words "Christian Religion"—appears in the "Miscellanies" as the topic of a new subject heading in 1725, around the time he listed the "Rational Account" on the "Catalogue letter" leaf. And "Christian Religion" emerges as a dominant theme in the miscellanies of the 1730s as he prepared to write the "Rational Account."

The relation between the "Christian Religion" entries and the "Rational Account" is further specified by another of Edwards' proposed titles for the treatise, "A Rational Account of Christianity, or, The Perfect Harmony between the Doctrines of the Christian Religion and Human Reason Manifested."[5] This formulation of the title describes more precisely the aim of the "Rational Account." Edwards intended this treatise to be not simply a systematic theology but a demonstration of the rationality or reasonableness of Christian doctrine. Correspondingly, the rationality of Christian doctrine is also the subject of most of the miscellanies entries entitled "Christian Religion." For example, in No. 514 Edwards asserts

---

3. For a discussion of this debate, see Richard P. Gildrie, *The Profane, the Civil, and the Godly: The Reformation of Manners in Orthodox New England, 1679–1749* (University Park, Univ. of Pennsylvania Press, 1994), and Michael J. Crawford, *Seasons of Grace: Colonial New England's Revival Tradition in Its British Context* (New York, Oxford Univ. Press, 1991), 19–51.

4. *Works, 13*, 6–7; for an example of such a reference, see *Works, 6*, 306.

5. This title is also listed on the "Catalogue letter" leaf.

that "what the Scripture reveals of the future happiness of the righteous, is exceeding rational, and excellently fit and congruous." And in No. 752 he argues that "[i]f there be a revelation that God makes to the world, 'tis most reasonable to suppose, and natural to expect, that he should therein make known . . . what manner of being he is." Making the link even more explicit, he states in No. 547 that the "Christian revelation gives us a most rational account of the design of God in his providential disposition of things," and in No. 596 that "the gospel gives us a most rational account of a full recovery from our fallen state."

The demand that religion must conform to the principles of reason was integral to English Enlightenment thought, and it was within this context that Edwards prepared to write the "Rational Account." In *An Essay Concerning Human Understanding* (1690), John Locke established the principle that "Nothing that is contrary to, and inconsistent with the clear and self-evident Dictates of Reason, has a Right to be urged, or assented to, as a Matter of Faith."[6] Although Locke accepted the possible validity of revealed truths, he insisted that revelation must be subjected to the judgment of reason. God may reveal truths that are beyond the scope of reason, but they cannot be contrary to reason, because reason "can never require or enable me to believe that, which is contrary to it self."[7] In *The Reasonableness of Christianity* (1695), he further maintained that the validity of revealed truths may be confirmed by signs or evidences, chief among which were the performance of miracles and the fulfillment of prophecy.[8] Using these principles, Locke rejected such easy targets as transubstantiation and papal infallibility, while he retained many of the fundamental doctrines of traditional Christianity.

The deists accepted Locke's claim that religion must contain nothing contrary to reason but drew from it much more radical conclusions.[9] In *Christianity Not Mysterious* (1696) John Toland criticized the view that mir-

---

6. John Locke, *An Essay Concerning Human Understanding*, ed. Peter H. Nidditch (Oxford, Claredon Press, 1975), bk. IV, ch. 18, § 10, p. 696.

7. Locke, *Essay*, bk. IV, ch. 18, § 6, p. 693.

8. Locke also discusses the evidentary value of miracles in the *Essay*, bk. IV, ch. 19, § 15, pp. 704–05.

9. For the deist controversy, see James M. Byrne, *Religion and the Enlightenment: From Descartes to Kant* (Louisville, Westminster John Knox Press, 1996); Gerald R. Cragg, *Reason and Authority in the Eighteenth Century* (Cambridge, Cambridge Univ. Press, 1964); Peter Gay, *The Enlightenment: An Interpretation*, Vol. I, *The Rise of Modern Paganism* (New York, Alfred A. Knopf, 1966); Peter Gay, ed., *Deism: An Anthology* (Princeton, D. Van Nostrand Co., 1968); Henry F. May, *The Enlightenment in America* (New York, Oxford Univ. Press, 1976); and John Redwood, *Reason, Ridicule and Religion: The Age of Enlightenment in England, 1660–1750* (London, Thames and Hudson, 1976).

acles testify to the truth of revelation, maintaining that both miracle and mystery are affronts to reason. In *A Discourse of the Grounds and Reasons of the Christian Religion* (1724), Anthony Collins undermined the evidential value of prophecy by arguing that none of the Old Testament prophecies had been literally fulfilled. And Matthew Tindal forcefully expressed in *Christianity As Old As Creation* (1730) the fundamental principle of all deist thought, that a purely rational religion has no place for supernatural revelation, for the content of revelation is either irrational or superfluous. The assault by free-thinkers and deists such as these elicited from more orthodox divines an attempt to defend Christianity on rational grounds. This response was, according to Henry F. May, a "tactical mistake," because the orthodox formulations of several key doctrines—such as the Trinity, the incarnation of Christ, and the eternal damnation of the wicked—appeared self-evidently irrational.[1] In the face of these difficulties many retreated into such compromise positions as Arianism, Socinianism, and latitudinarianism.

Edwards intended the "Rational Account" to be transatlantic assault upon deism, which had as yet no vocal exponents in New England.[2] Without retreating from Reformed orthodoxy, he systematically addresses in the "Christian Religion" entries each of the elements of the deist critique. Those having the single title "Christian Religion" generally consider the deists' principal claim, that supernatural revelation is superfluous to a purely rational religion. In No. 544 Edwards maintains that if God exists it is "unreasonable" to suppose "that he should never speak." Because it "is a property of all intelligent beings, that God has made in his own image, to speak," it is "strange that any should imagine that the supreme intelligence should never speak." His most common argument, however, is that revelation is necessary, for by means of it God has disclosed truths unavailable to human reason. Revelation is not superfluous because without it humankind would never, for example, have "come to any tolerable knowledge of future rewards and punishments" (No. 514). The New Testament revelation, in particular, is needed to obtain a "distinct knowledge of the future invisible world that we are to be in after death" (No. 582). Similarly, "if the Scriptures are not a revelation of God, then mankind . . . are left wholly and entirely in the dark both about God's works of creation and providence" (No. 752).

1. May, *Enlightenment in America*, 23.
2. See A. Owen Aldridge, "Natural Religion and Deism in America before Ethan Allen and Thomas Paine," *The William and Mary Quarterly*, 3rd Series, *LIV* (October 1997), 835–48.

Most "Christian Religion" entries have subtitles that specify the particular aspect of the deist critique they address. In those having the subtitle "Christ's Miracles," Edwards argues that miracles are testimony both of Christ's divinity and the truth of the gospel revelation. "What more could we desire of a man that pretends to come from God," he writes in No. 584, "than to give us such evidences of his power as these?" (see also, Nos. 512, 518[b]). In those having the subtitle "Mysteries," Edwards directly responds to the deists' objection to revelation, that it contains many things beyond the scope of human reason. He maintains in No. 583 that, given the disparity between the capacities of divine and human reason, it would be "unreasonable to expect any other, than that there should be many things in such a revelation that should be utterly beyond our understanding, and seem impossible." Such things are not inherently beyond reason; the redeemed will one day acquire an understanding of Christian mysteries, as the thirteen-year-old boy whom Edwards describes in No. 652 is capable of understanding the apparently mysterious fact "that a piece of any matter of two inches square[3] was eight times so big as one of but one inch square." Other "Christian Religion" entries examine such issues as divine providence (Nos. 525, 547), immortality of the soul (No. 547) and resurrection of the dead (Nos. 552, 608). There are also many entries, not specifically entitled "Christian Religion," that have a similar aim or subject matter. Those that consider the eternity of hell torments, for example, are probably related to the "Rational Account," for this doctrine was considered not only by deists but also by liberal divines to be one of the least defensible aspects of reformed Christianity (see Nos. 557–559, 572, 574, 575).

In the miscellanies of the 1730s, especially in the entries on "Christian Religion," Edwards constructs a defense of the rationality of Christian faith against the deist critique. Unlike the latitudinarian opponents of the deists, however, Edwards' rational defense did not weaken his adherence to the fundamental doctrines of Reformed orthodoxy. He remains convinced of the rationality of these doctrines at least in part because he uses a standard of rationality not shared by his opponents. He accepted the position first articulated by Locke that religious belief must conform to the principles of reason, but tempered it with the belief that divine, not human, reason was the ultimate standard of judgment. Consequently, he frequently presupposes not only the existence of God but the truth of the very doctrine that is the object of demonstration. There are miscellanies

---

3. I. e. cubed.

entries that treat what are now considered the classical proofs for the existence of God. Nos. 587 and 650 contain variants of the ontological argument, and in Nos. 651 and 749 Edwards articulates what was the foundation for all eighteenth-century natural theology, the design or teleological argument. Equally common, however, is the sort of circular reasoning found in No. 519. "If there must be a revelation," Edwards asserts in this entry, "this is convincing that the Christian revelation is the true [one], that it has been by means of this revelation, and this only, that the world has come to the knowledge of the one only true God." For Edwards, a conviction of the truth of Christianity was finally grounded not in human reason but in the perception of divine excellency conveyed by the new spiritual sense. This higher form of conviction was ultimately unavailable for public discussion, for to the unredeemed, who lack the perception of excellency, talk about it is "foolishness" and "words without a meaning" (No. 683). A purely rational defense of Christian doctrine would have required Edwards to use, as did the latitudinarians in their anti-deist polemic, the standard of rationality advocated by his opponents. To avoid this "tactical mistake" Edwards may have abandoned the "Rational Account" and adopted a more historical approach to the defense of Christian doctrine.

THE HISTORY OF THE WORK OF REDEMPTION

In a letter written near the end of his life Edwards described several of the theological projects on which he was currently working. In addition to continuing his polemic against the Arminians, which he had begun in *Freedom of the Will,* he indicates that he is preparing to write two "great work[s]."[4] The first he entitles "A History of the Work of Redemption," suggesting that it was to be a revision of the sermon series he had preached on the history of redemption in 1739.[5] The second, entitled "The Harmony of the Old and New Testament," was apparently a wholly new project. His failure to mention the "Rational Account" supports the contention that he abandoned this project sometime after 1740. Other evidence indicates that, although Edwards discontinued work on the "Rational Account," he did not reject his plans to write a response to the deist critique of revealed religion. Both "A History of Redemption" and "The

4. JE to the Trustees of the College of New Jersey, Stockbridge, Oct. 19, 1757, in *Works, 16,* 727–29.

5. This sermon series was published posthumously in 1774, under the title *A History of the Work of Redemption* (see *Works, 9*).

Harmony of the Old and New Testament" may have occupied the vacuum created by the absence of the "Rational Account."

Edwards intended to employ in both of these proposed treatises the same approach to confute deist claims.[6] Many orthodox and latitudinarian opponents of the deists maintained that, in addition to miracles, prophecy was evidence of the truth of the Christian revelation. The fulfillment of Old Testament prophecies of the messiah demonstrated the divinity of Christ, the unity of the Testaments, and the supernatural origin of the Scriptures. In neither the outline of the "Rational Account" nor the "Christian Religion" entries written in the 1730s did Edwards emphasize this aspect of the deist debate; by the end of his life, however, it had become the core of two major theological projects. Like the "Rational Account," "A History of the Work of Redemption" was to be "a body of divinity," in which "every divine doctrine, will appear to greatest advantage in the brightest light." But in this treatise Edwards intended to use "an entire new method" for the exposition of doctrine, which he describes as "being thrown into the form of a history, considering the affair of Christian theology, as the whole of it, in each part, stands in reference to the great work of redemption by Jesus Christ." Similarly, in "The Harmony of the Old and New Testament" he planned to show how prophecies and types of the Messiah in the Old Testament were fulfilled by Jesus Christ and to demonstrate "the harmony of the Old and New Testament, as to doctrine and precept."[7]

Edwards' movement away from a systematic defense based upon rationality to a historical defense based upon prophecy began to occur in the 1730s. That Edwards drafted a preface to the "Rational Account" in "Miscellanies" No. 832 indicates that in the winter of 1739–40 he was still actively planning to write this treatise. However, the previous year he delivered to his Northampton congregation a thirty-sermon series tracing God's redemptive work "from the fall of man to the end of the world."[8] This series suggests that by 1739 Edwards viewed God's action in history as an alternative means of defending the truth of the Christian revelation against deism. The anti-deist orientation of *A History of the Work of Redemption* is displayed most clearly in the Application sections of the series.

6. For an analysis of the polemical context in which Edwards conceived *The Harmony of the Old and New Testament*, see Kenneth P. Minkema, "The Other Unfinished 'Great Work': Jonathan Edwards, Messianic Prophecy, and 'The Harmony of the Old and New Testament,'" in *Jonathan Edwards's Writings*, 52–65.

7. *Works, 16*, 727–28.

8. *Works, 9*, 116.

In these sections Edwards frequently draws conclusions or inferences that address a specific aspect of the deist critique of revealed religion.

For example, having considered the succession of divine dispensations from the fall of humankind to the establishment of the Roman Empire, Edwards concludes in Sermon 13 that this history demonstrates "that Jesus of Nazareth is indeed the Son of God" and "that the Christian religion is the true religion." The deists may argue that "some subtile, cunning persons contrived this history and these prophecies, so as all to point to Jesus Christ on purpose to confirm it that he was the messiah," but the composition of the Hebrew scriptures "long before Christ was born" proves this explanation fallacious.[9] Similarly, having considered the succession of divine dispensations from the incarnation of Christ to the present day, Edwards concludes in Sermon 25 that this history is "great evidence of the truth of the Christian religion, and that the Scriptures are the word of God." Not only must Christianity be true because God has preserved it from "the violent and perpetual opposition that has ever been by the corruption and wickedness of mankind against this church." But the fulfillment of those prophecies concerning the establishment and growth both of the Christian church and of the Antichrist demonstrates "the divine authority of the Scriptures."[1]

The "Miscellanies" provide further evidence that in the 1730s Edwards became increasingly confident that the argument from history was more persuasive than the argument from reason. Edwards did not begin to write "Christian Religion" entries with the specific subtitle "Prophecies of the Messiah" until the 1740s (i.e. Nos. 891, 922). However, within the "Christian Religion" entries of the 1730s two topics suggest the future direction of his course of inquiry. In those entries having the subtitle "Christians the True Israel" Edwards demonstrates the validity of the claim fundamental to all Christian interpretation of prophecy, that the "promises that were made by the prophets to the people of Israel concerning their future prosperity and glory, are fulfilled in the Christian church according to their proper intent" (No. 597; see also Nos. 601, 649, 658). And in those entries having the subtitle "Love of Enemies, Praying Against Them," he harmonizes an apparent contradiction between the testaments, that in the gospels Jesus enjoins his followers to love their enemies, while "old testament saints" seem "to hate personal enemies" and "to pray for their hurt" (No. 600; see also No. 640).

9. *Works, 9,* 281–82.
1. *Works, 9,* 442, 444, 449.

To chart more precisely the development of the work of redemption theme we must look beyond the "Christian Religion" entries and consider the entire array of miscellanies written in the 1730s. The "Redemption" series did mark a sudden shift in Edwards' response to the deist challenge, but it did not reflect a new area of inquiry. Two entries written before the series particularly indicate Edwards' increasing interest in salvation history.[2] No. 702, the longest entry Edwards wrote during the 1730s, is entitled "Work of Creation. Providence. Redemption." This entry outlines the central thesis of *A History of the Work of Redemption*, which is set out in the first sermon of the series, "that all God's works, both of creation and providence, are subordinate to the work of redemption." Although the different components of this work may appear unrelated, they are, Edwards argues, "all one scheme, one contrivance." And No. 664b is a long, synthetic entry having multiple subtitles indicating its consideration of the entire range of salvation history, from "Fall of Angels" and "Fall of Man" to "Day of Judgment" and "Consummation of All Things." In this entry Edwards begins to develop what James Davidson has called the "afflictive model of progress," which functions as one of the most important unifying motifs of *History of Redemption*.[3] According to this model, every stage of the work of redemption is marked by the suffering of the elect and the persecution of the church in the world. Christ most clearly displays this universal feature of redemption history, because the "sufferings that he underwent in obedience to the Father were by far the greatest that ever any elect creature endured." But "every creature, before he receives the eternal reward of his obedience," also must "have some considerable trial" (No. 664b; see also No. 791).

Within the miscellanies of the 1730s there are numerous other redemption-related entries, including those designated "Satan Defeated," "Millennium," "Consummation of All Things," and "New Heavens and New Earth." So many entries refer either directly or indirectly to the work of redemption that John Wilson has concluded that "this was *a*, if not *the*, central focal point" of Edwards' "theological reflection."[4] Even the "Lord's Day" entries may bear upon this theme. Edwards suggests in No. 751 that his defense of the Christian sabbath was intended to

2. See also John Wilson's discussion of the relation between the "Miscellanies" and the Redemption series in *Works*, 9, 13–17.

3. James West Davidson, *The Logic of Millennial Thought: Eighteenth-Century New England* (New Haven, Yale Univ. Press, 1977), 129.

4. *Works*, 9, 15. For a comprehensive list of redemption-related entries, see Stephen Stein's list of apocalyptic themes in the "Miscellanies" in *Works*, 5, 461–62.

counter the arguments of the "anti-sabbatarians," who maintained, contrary to the belief that "certain appointed days should be wholly dedicated to God's service," that "we ought to dedicate all our time to God."[5] But if we view Edwards' "Lord's Day" entries in relation to the themes that dominate the miscellanies of the 1730s, anti-sabbatarianism is clearly a secondary concern. Scripture supports sabbatarianism insofar as it designates the Lord's Day as "that day of the week that is to be kept holy to God" (No. 536). More important, however, Christianity's transference of the sabbath from the seventh day of the week to the first is a sign of the progress of God's work of redemption, for it marks the abolition of the Old Testament dispensation and the introduction of the New.

Throughout this period Edwards also frequently wrote entries entitled "Wisdom of God in the Work of Redemption," a rubric he had first introduced in the "Miscellanies" in 1728 (No. 337). Although this set of entries appears to relate to Edwards' developing interest in the history of redemption, it may be more closely connected to the "Rational Account." In the "Wisdom of God" entries Edwards emphasizes the logic and rationality of the Christian scheme of salvation. As their title indicates, these entries focus on God's wise contrivance of the plan of redemption. For example, many consider Christ's role as the agent of salvation: why the incarnation was necessary (Nos. 510, 571, 604, 615, 633); that Christ came at the most appropriate time (No. 569); and why the Mediator must be the "middle person" between the Father and the Holy Spirit (Nos. 614, 733, 781). Edwards proposed in the "Rational Account" to defend the doctrines of the Christian faith by demonstrating their rationality. Integral to this project would have been a demonstration of the rationality of redemption itself; accordingly, in the outline to the "Rational Account" Edwards reminds himself "[t]o explain the doctrine of the Trinity before I begin to treat of the work of redemption."[6] Given their emphasis upon divine contrivance, the "Wisdom of God" entries may therefore reflect his efforts to develop this theme.[7]

The relation between the "Wisdom of God" entries and the "Rational

---

5. For a comprehensive treatment of the anti-sabbatarian debate, see Winton U. Solberg, *Redeem the Time: The Puritan Sabbath in Early America* (Cambridge, Harvard Univ. Press, 1977).

6. *Works, 6,* 396.

7. In *The Reasonableness of Christianity,* Locke also considers "the admirable contrivance of the divine wisdom of the whole work of our redemption, as far as we are able to trace it by the footsteps which God hath made visible to human reason" (*The Reasonableness of Christianity,* ed. George W. Ewing [Washington, D.C., Regnery Publishing, 1965], 101–102).

Account" may also explain why Edwards virtually discontinued this rubric following his composition of the "Redemption" series. After No. 781, which was written several months before the "Redemption" series, this set of entries tapers off; according to the "Table," Edwards wrote only four more "Wisdom of God" entries at much later dates (Nos. 904, 944, 1005, 1133). He also made his last entry with the title "Satan Defeated" (No. 815) soon after his delivery of the "Redemption" series. Edwards' discontinuance of the "Wisdom of God" entries parallels both his movement away from the "Rational Account" and his growing conviction that salvation history—grounded in the fulfillment of both prophetic and apocalyptic projections of the future of the church—represented Christianity's best line of defense against the deists. One indication of Edwards' new approach is his introduction in the "Miscellanies" of a new redemption-related rubric not long after his composition of the last "Wisdom of God" entry. Edwards wrote No. 802, entitled "Progress of Redemption," during or shortly after the "Redemption" series. This rubric, which grows in prominence in the 1740s, absorbed earlier themes, like "Satan Defeated," and eclipsed the "Wisdom of God" entries. In contrast to the "Wisdom of God" entries, those entitled "Progress of Redemption" emphasize how God's action in history gradually moves forward in time toward the salvation of the elect and the ultimate display of God's glory. These entries do not neglect God's wise contrivance of the work of redemption, because by definition that which moves forward in time toward a specific end must be designed to achieve that end. But they focus more on how the design manifests itself in time than on its abstract logic.

The "Miscellanies" confirm what Edwards' failure to write the "Rational Account" and his plan to revise "A History of the Work of Redemption" only suggest, that over time he concluded that the argument from history was more persuasive than the argument from reason. The "Miscellanies" also help to identify when this shift in methodology began to occur. In the 1730s these notebooks were the principal locus of Edwards' preparations to write the "Rational Account." In the latter part of this decade, however, entries addressing historical themes grow in prominence. And by the end of the decade, Edwards had produced not the "Rational Account" but a sermon series describing the history of the work of redemption. That this shift occurred after the Connecticut Valley awakening may give some indication of its cause. Having witnessed a decisive moment in salvation history, Edwards turned to history to pursue his debate with the deists.

CONVERSION AND THE RELIGIOUS LIFE

In *A History of the Work of Redemption* Edwards identifies religious revival as the engine driving salvation history. From the "days of Enos," when there "was the first remarkable pouring out of the Spirit through Christ," to the premillennial period, when the "work of conversion shall break forth and go on in such a manner as never has been like to," the history of redemption is marked by periodic revivals in piety.[8] The Connecticut Valley awakening was itself one such moment of the extraordinary dispensation of God's grace. Although Edwards himself drew no millennial conclusions about the 1734–35 revival in *A Faithful Narrative*, his promoters did not hesitate to remark that "this wonderful work may be considered as an earnest of what God will do towards the close of the Gospel day."[9] This dramatic display of God's action in history reinforced, if it did not create, Edwards' conviction of the truth of the narrative traced in *History of Redemption*.

As revival is the manifestation of the work of redemption on a local or regional level, so conversion is its manifestation on an individual level. What Edwards, like other Puritan divines, calls "the application of redemption" in the soul is but the smallest unit in the scheme of salvation.[1] It reflects in microcosm what God enacts in macrocosm in the course of world history. Edwards conjectured that during the Connecticut Valley awakening "more than 300 souls were savingly brought home to Christ" in Northampton "in the space of half a year."[2] So many conversions in so short a time gave Edwards ample opportunity to observe a multiplicity of dramatic religious experiences, which he described at length in *A Faithful Narrative*. Although he insists that there is "an endless variety in the particular manner and circumstances in which persons are wrought upon," his account was rapidly accepted in the Anglo-American evangelical community as the normative expression of the morphology of conversion.[3]

---

8. *Works, 9,* 141, 460.

9. This statement was made in the preface to the 3rd edition (Boston 1738) of *A Faithful Narrative* (*Works, 4,* 141).

1. *Works, 9,* 120.

2. *Works, 4,* 158.

3. *Works, 4,* 185, 25–29. For discussion of the Puritan "morphology of conversion," see Edmund S. Morgan, who coined the phrase in *Visible Saints: The History of a Puritan Idea* (1963; rep. Ithaca, Cornell Univ. Press, 1982), Charles Lloyd Cohen, *God's Caress: The Psychology of Puritan Religious Experience* (New York, Oxford Univ. Press, 1986), Charles E. Hambrick-Stowe, *The Practice of Piety: Puritan Devotional Disciplines in Seventeenth-Century New England* (Chapel Hill, Univ. of North Carolina Press, 1982), Perry Miller, "'Preparation for Salvation' in Seventeenth-Century New England," in *Nature's Nation* (Cambridge, Harvard Univ. Press, 1967), pp. 50–77, and Norman Pettit, *The Heart Prepared: Grace and Conversion in Puritan Spiritual Life* (New Haven, Yale Univ. Press, 1966).

The miscellanies of the 1730s reflect Edwards' preoccupation with the phenomenology of the religious life. No single entry offers an extended analysis of the succession of stages before and after conversion. But the internal application of redemption in the heart of the saint is as dominant a motif in Nos. 501–832 as its external application in history. Puritan divines commonly claimed that before conversion the sinner experiences both conviction and humiliation, and Edwards inherited from his grandfather Stoddard an evangelical emphasis upon these two preparatory stages. In the "Miscellanies" he consistently insists that before conversion the unredeemed must experience "a sense of guilt, of the evil nature of sin," and "of the agreeableness and connection between that and the punishment" (No. 528). Accompanying this conviction of sin is a corresponding "humiliation, or sense of their own unworthiness" and "of the vanity of all their other confidences" (No. 645).

Edwards' interest in the stages of conviction and humiliation appears in such entries as these to be primarily pastoral and homiletical. The majority are one-paragraph notations containing a brief comment on preparation, an apt typological representation of the need for conviction and humiliation, or a cross-reference to an imprecatory sermon. The relation to sermon composition is even more evident in the longer entries, for they generally are compilations of Scripture passages indicating, for example, "that trusting in our own righteousness is fatal to the soul" (No. 637; see also Nos. 645, 674). Sermons, not miscellanies, were evidently Edwards' principal locus for developing the morphology of conversion.[4]

The series of entries on the sin against the Holy Ghost also relates to the preparatory stages of conviction and humiliation. In 1730 Edwards had composed a four-part analysis of the conditions necessary to commit the unpardonable sin (No. 475). During the Connecticut Valley revival his pastoral interest in the subject acquired new urgency. In *A Faithful Narrative* he observes that people under conviction may "have great fears that they have committed the unpardonable sin, or that God will surely never show mercy to them that are such vipers; and are often tempted to leave off in despair."[5] The possible consequences of such a melancholy condition were forcefully impressed upon Edwards by the suicide of his uncle Joseph Hawley in the latter days of the revival. Following the awakening, therefore, he returned to the topic of the sin against the Holy Ghost, care-

---

4. For the relation between the "Miscellanies" and JE's sermon composition, see *Works, 10,* 74–90.

5. *Works, 4,* 165.

fully delineating in three lengthy entries (Nos. 703, 706, 707) the rare combination of factors necessary to place oneself beyond the scope of God's redemption. He indicates by cross-references that these entries are additions to No. 475. Together, the four comprise a short essay on a subject that Edwards recognized he must master in order to effectively counsel parishioners suffering extreme spiritual distress.

The polemical context in which Edwards developed his views concerning the morphology of conversion begins to emerge in entries on the means of grace. Rejecting the antinomian claim that reliance upon the means compromises the freeness of God's grace, Edwards maintains "that God's manner is to bestow his grace on men by outward means," such as preaching and the sacraments (No. 538). But he carefully articulates the role of the means of grace to avoid the Arminian claim that sincere striving for salvation merits regeneration as a reward. Although there is a "greater probability" that those who diligently seek salvation will be converted, the means of grace "have no influence to produce grace, either as causes or instruments" (Nos. 538, 539). Before conversion, the means do no more than supply the mind with the "matter for grace to act upon." By conveying speculative ideas to the mind and engaging the natural affections of the heart, they create the "opportunity for grace to act, when God shall infuse it" (No. 539). Common grace enhances the operation of the means, for it "assists the faculties of the soul to do that more fully, which they do by nature," but regeneration occurs only when the Spirit of God infuses a "new and supernatural principle," which "causes the faculties to do that that they do not by nature" (No. 626).

During the 1730s Edwards employed two different theological models to describe the transformation that occurs in the sinner at the conversion moment. The first and more traditional approach focused on the doctrine of justification by faith. Edwards began this course of inquiry in his Master's thesis[6] and pursued it throughout the 1730s, not only by regular composition of miscellanies on justification but by preaching the two-unit lecture that in a revised form was published in 1738 as *Justification by Faith Alone*. After the publication, however, Edwards never again gave extended consideration to this doctrine in his published writings, although he continued to write entries on justification in the "Miscellanies" and other notebooks. His own analysis of the doctrine of justification, espe-

---

6. *Quaestio: Peccator Non Iustificatur Coram Deo Nisi Per Iustitiam Christi Fide Apprehensam* (1723). See *The Works of Jonathan Edwards, 14, Sermons and Discourses, 1723–1729*, ed. Kenneth P. Minkema (New Haven, Yale Univ. Press, 1997), 47–66.

cially his consideration of the relation between justification and perseverance, led him away from justification as the central organizing concept of his soteriology.

After the Connecticut Valley revival, the backsliding of Edwards' Northampton congregation made him increasingly aware of the importance of persevering Christian practice in the religious life. As a result, in both the "Miscellanies" and *Justification by Faith Alone* he attempts to construct an analysis of justification that gives to perseverance a status almost equivalent to faith. The orthodox doctrine of justification could, however, accommodate this innovation only with difficulty. The strain is most evident in his explanation of how not only faith but also perseverance is a condition of justification. By insisting that the "sinner is justified on his first act of faith," Edwards avoids the Arminian view "that the act of justification should be suspended, till the sinner had persevered in faith." But he elevates the status of perseverance by asserting that faith "virtually contains" perseverance, which "God has respect to" and looks "upon as if it were a property of the faith, by which the sinner is then justified" (No. 729). This concept of "virtual perseverance" clearly exposes the limits of the orthodox doctrine of justification. For example, in No. 795 Edwards attempts to defend the apparently contradictory position that, although it is "impossible that we should fail of salvation" after the first act of faith, there are some "conditions of salvation," such as perseverance, "on which salvation may be so suspended," that we may "perish for want of them." In this passage, Edwards' orthodoxy prevents him from identifying *actual* perseverance as a condition of justification, but to express the meaning of *virtual* perseverance he is forced to use language suggesting the Arminian view.[7]

Although Edwards' analysis of justification could not easily accommodate his understanding of perseverance, it did point toward a more adequate conceptual vehicle. To explain how the first act of faith virtually contains perseverance, Edwards appeals to the "actual union of the soul with Christ," which occurs in the conversion moment (No. 729). Because Christ "has actually persevered through the greatest imaginable trials," Edwards reasons in No. 695, "we shall stand and persevere in him." Hav-

---

7. No. 847 contains an even more striking passage: "And even justification itself does in a sense attend and depend upon these after-works of the Spirit of God upon the soul. The condition of justification in a sense remains still to be performed, even after the first conversion, and the sentence of justification in a sense remains still to be passed, and the man remains still in a state of probation for heaven, which could not be, if his justification did not still depend on what remained to be done."

ing "persevered not only for himself, but for us," we "are sealed in him to persevering life." Moreover, Edwards appeals to the union between the believer and Christ to explain more than the concept of perseverance. It is the foundation for the fitness that naturally obtains between faith and justification and the fitness that morally obtains between good works and the degree of the saint's reward in heaven. Edwards also uses the reality of this union to counter Arminian objections to the concept of imputation.[8] In fact, the primary focus of Edwards' analysis of the doctrine of justification is not the forensic transaction that occurs by means of justification but the ontological transformation that occurs by means of union with Christ. "What is real in the union between Christ and his people," he writes in No. 568, "is the foundation of what is legal." As the limitations of the doctrine of justification became increasingly evident, a second model of conversion, which operates exclusively on this "real" or ontological level, displaced justification as the central organizing concept of Edwards' soteriology.

The doctrine of the new spiritual sense developed alongside justification by faith in both the sermons and the "Miscellanies." Although rooted in the Calvinist tradition, Edwards articulated this model of conversion in terms drawn from the empiricist philosophy of John Locke.[9] Edwards began to construct the doctrine of the new spiritual sense early in his ministerial career; *A Divine and Supernatural Light* (1734) is the best-known example of a theme that he had frequently addressed in sermons of the 1720s.[1] This course of inquiry reached its first climax in 1738, the year *Justification by Faith Alone* issued from the press. In the winter of 1737–38 Edwards preached a sermon series on the parable of the wise and foolish virgins, which contained the most complete expression of the doctrine of the new spiritual sense to date. In the winter of 1738–39 he composed No. 782, the most extended analysis of the new sense found in the "Miscellanies." And after 1738 Edwards continued his investigation of the doctrine of the new spiritual sense for many years in both his notebooks and his sermons. Unlike the doctrine of justification, this course of inquiry reached a second climax in 1746 with the publication of *Religious Affections*.

The concept of the new spiritual sense reflects the polemical context

---

8. See above, pp. 12–18, for a discussion of these issues.

9. For a discussion of the Calvinist roots of JE's concept of the new spiritual sense, see Terrence Erdt, *Jonathan Edwards: Art and the Sense of the Heart* (Amherst, Univ. of Massachusetts Press, 1980), 1–20.

1. For two early treatments of this theme, see *Works, 14*, 67–98, 246–77.

in which Edwards' views on the morphology of conversion developed. Contrary to the Arminian view that conversion occurs through a quantitative improvement of the faculties, Edwards uses this concept to portray conversion as "a work that is done at once, and not gradually." Infusion of the new spiritual sense effects a qualitative change that "differs not only in degree, but in nature and kind from . . . anything that is ever found in natural men" (No. 673). By restoring the capacity lost at the fall to perceive "the excellency and glory of divine things," it produces an ontological transformation of the human faculties. It transforms the cognitive faculty insofar as the perception of excellency "directly evidences the truth of religion to the mind" (No. 628). And it transforms the volitional faculty insofar as excellency has "a loveliness immensely above all, worthy to be chosen and pursued and cleaved to and delighted [in] far above all" (No. 739). There is therefore no immediate causal relation between striving for salvation and obtaining it, for the "exercises" of the new spiritual sense "are something diverse in nature and kind from, and above all that belongs to, or proceeds from, human nature as such" (No. 818).

The new spiritual sense also afforded Edwards a means to maintain what the doctrine of justification by faith could depict only with difficulty, that true conversion necessarily results in persevering Christian practice. After infusion of the new sense, Edwards asserts, "grace is the principle that reigns and predominates in the heart of a godly man." Because "God predominates in the stated established choice and election of his heart" the saint has the capacity of acting in accordance with the will of God (No. 739). And this is a capacity that the saint cannot lose, for the covenant of grace promises that once "infused into the hearts of men" grace "shall remain there and put forth acts there after the manner of an abiding, natural, vital principle of action, a seed remaining in us" (No. 629). It acts "in the soul habitually, and according to such a stated constitution or law," that it establishes "a foundation for a continued course of exercises, as is called a principle of nature" (No. 626). Unlike justification, therefore, the new sense ensures that conversion is looked upon not as the end of the religious life but as the beginning of a new stage, in which the saint by persevering through repeated trials of faith obtains both sanctification and assurance, and is thereby prepared for the full revelation of divine glory that will occur after death.

To explore this second model of conversion Edwards adopted a new homiletical form, the sermon series, commonly used by Puritan divines for the exposition of doctrine. As the text of his first series he chose the parable of the wise and foolish virgins, which several of his predecessors, such as Thomas Shepard and Thomas Manton, had used to depict the relation between conversion and persevering Christian practice. And he follows the traditional interpretation of the parable insofar as he equates the oil in the wise virgins' lamps with the new spiritual sense and the flame with Christian practice. For the text of his second series, which he preached immediately upon completion of the virgins series, Edwards chose another passage (I Cor. 13) that afforded him the opportunity to construct a detailed description of the nature of Christian practice. Although *Charity and Its Fruits* identifies "Christian love" as the distinguishing mark of the saint, this principle is structurally identical to the new spiritual sense insofar as it "will dispose" the saint "to all proper acts of respect both to God and men."[2] *Justification by Faith Alone* displayed the limitations of the orthodox doctrine of justification. But in these two series Edwards demonstrates that the new spiritual sense is an expansive concept, capable of comprehending the Christian life in all its stages. Together with *History of Redemption*, these series articulate the conceptual framework that will guide Edwards through the theological upheaval soon to rupture the unity of the New England Congregational establishment.

* * *

"Miscellanies" Nos. 501–832 are a record of Edwards' intellectual development during a formative period in his career as a Puritan minister and theologian. In the early 1730s his orthodox Calvinism positioned him as an opponent of the Arminianism and deism that were acquiring increasing support within the Anglo-American evangelical community, and he was developing in his sermons and notebooks a variety of theological strategies designed to counter these views. In addition to his ongoing preparation to write a systematic defense of Christian doctrine, he published sermons on divine sovereignty (1731) and spiritual light (1734) and preached a two-part lecture on justification by faith that was published in a revised form in 1738. However, between the initial delivery of *Justification by Faith Alone* and its publication an event occurred that dramatically altered the course of Edwards' intellectual development. The Connecticut Valley awakening was the defining moment of Edwards' early ministerial career. Not only did his narrative account of the revival establish his international reputation as an evangelist, but his reflection

2. *Works, 8,* 132, 134.

on the revival and its aftermath in Northampton permanently transformed his work as a theologian.

The "Miscellanies" trace the effects of the Connecticut Valley awakening on the direction of Edwards' theological inquiry. Each of the major themes in Nos. 501–832 was affected by it. The revival was one factor in Edwards' ultimate decision to abandon his plans to write a rational defense of the Christian faith. This unprecedented example of God's redemptive power encouraged him to adopt a more historical approach to counter the deist critique of revealed religion. Equally significant was the backsliding of Edwards' Northampton congregation in the years following the revival. This frustrating circumstance forced him to pay greater attention to the role of persevering Christian practice in the religious life, which in turn created difficulties for his developing doctrine of justification by faith. It also suggests why after the revival Edwards gave greater prominence to the doctrine of the new spiritual sense and shifted the means of assurance from immediate experience to persevering Christian practice. Having failed to reverse the declining piety of his own congregation Edwards emphasized the model of conversion that most effectively articulated his increased appreciation of the role of perseverance in the religious life.

Note on the Text

The "Miscellanies" (Nos. a–1360) consists of nine consecutively numbered manuscript notebooks.[3] Entry Nos. 501–832 comprise parts of two of these notebooks, and all of a third.[4] Nos. 501–688 take up roughly the latter half of Book 1, which was constructed by Edwards from a gathering of separately folded folio sheets. This volume has no cover, although it most likely had one at one time. Its pages, now disbound, are brittle and the margins are ragged.

Book 2 contains entry Nos. 689–760. It is a quarto volume in good condition. The cover is half a piece of oil cloth (presumably a ream wrapper) with a multicolored stamp; the other half forms the cover of Book 2 of "Notes on Scripture."[5] The volume, inscribed "Vol. II" by Edwards on the

---

3. For a description of the "Miscellanies" notebooks, see *Works, 13,* 153–55.

4. Some miscellanies entries have appeared in earlier collections of JE's writings, as well as in monographs, articles, and other publications. A complete list of "Previous Publication of the 'Miscellanies'" can be found in *Works, 13,* 545–57. See especially pp. 554–55 for earlier appearances of entries that are included in this volume.

5. See the illustration in *Works, 15,* 37.

first manuscript page, is an infolded quire, which he stitched and paginated himself, pages 1–188. The final leaf in this volume, which Edwards used to write the conclusion of an addendum to No. 717, is unnumbered. With the first entry in Book 2, No. 689, entitled "Visible Church," Edwards began the practice of writing runningheads over long entries. In some cases the runninghead initially described the subject of the entry, and then consisted merely of the entry number (as in No. 710, "The Occasion for the Fall of the Angels").

Entry Nos. 761–832 are in Book 3. This folio volume is in generally good condition, although the edges of its pages are a bit more tattered than those in Book 2. Its cover is made from a coarse brown ream wrapper with a red seal on the back reading "Super Fine." As with Book 2, the entire volume is an infolded quire, which Edwards constructed himself, with two separately folded sheets at the end. He also inscribed the volume "III" on the front and back covers. A small piece of paper is tipped in between leaves 4 and 5, on which Edwards wrote additions to No. 772. A later owner of the manuscript numbered the pages (except the tipped-in fragment), pages 1–134. No. 832, ending on page 74, falls a little more than halfway through the volume.

In this set of entries Edwards uses an ink that ranges from medium to dark brown in color. His handwriting is generally neat and legible, although over time it becomes somewhat larger and looser than in the earliest entries, which are written in a small, tight hand. There are relatively few deletions and emendations. Edwards does at times strike through and interlineate words and phrases, but the entries do not have the appearance of rough drafts. As he prepared the manuscripts for transcription, Jonathan Edwards, Jr., lightly edited scattered entries, generally using a noticeably darker, black ink.[6]

Thomas A. Schafer, the editor of entry Nos. a–500, developed an elaborate methodology for dating Edwards' early manuscript corpus.[7] Using the watermarks in the paper on which Edwards wrote and an analysis of his ink, handwriting, and orthography, Schafer was able to establish a chronology not only for the early miscellanies entries but also for the sermons composed before 1733 and a variety of other manuscripts.[8] This method cannot be employed with equal precision much further than "Miscellanies" No. 500. Around the time of the composition of this entry

6. See *Works, 13*, 158–60, for a more detailed description of JE's handwriting and style of composition.
7. For a description of this method, see *Works, 13*, 59–89.
8. Schafer summarizes the results of this research in a chronological chart, *Works, 13*, 89–109.

Edwards, according to Schafer, "purchased a relatively large quantity of foolscap in two batches, one bearing English/GR and the other London/GR watermarks." He constructed sermon booklets from the first batch for at least two years.[9] This uniformity of watermark makes it impossible to establish parallels between the paper used for sermons in this period and others of Edwards' manuscripts, including the "Miscellanies." Furthermore, unlike Book 1 of the "Miscellanies," which is made from a gathering of sheets containing a variety of different watermarks, Books 2–8 are infolded quires.[1] This method of construction greatly reduces the number of different watermarks in the notebooks. Book 2, made from ninety-five pieces of quarto-sized paper, contains only one watermark, and all sixty-three sheets of Book 3 have the same watermark, with the exception of the two separately folded sheets at the end. And because Edwards presumably stitched together these notebooks in advance, the paper from which they are made reflects Edwards' paper stock at the time of his construction of the notebooks and not at the time of his composition of any given entry.

Despite these limitations, it is possible to determine approximate dates for the composition of Nos. 501–832. Schafer concludes that Edwards wrote Nos. 501–510 between July and August 1731.[2] Using this date as a starting point, a chronology for the composition of the remaining entries can be projected by drawing on resources both internal and external to the "Miscellanies" manuscripts themselves.

The most significant resource for constructing this chronology are Edwards' frequent cross-references within the miscellanies entries themselves to his sermon manuscripts. Beginning in January 1733 Edwards noted in the upper-right-hand corner of each sermon booklet the date of its composition. A cross-reference in a specific miscellanies entry to a sermon written after this date, which is integral to the "Miscellanies" text and not a later addition to the manuscript, establishes the earliest possible date for the composition of the entry (its *terminus a quo*). For example, entry No. 612 consists of a direction to "see sermon on I Cor. 11:29, the doctrine and the reason." The manuscript of this sermon indicates that Edwards composed it in January 1733. No. 612, therefore, could not have been written earlier than this date, although it may have been written later. Table 1 lists the integral references to dated sermons in Nos. 501–

9. *Works, 13,* 88.
1. For an explanation of paper terminology, see *Works, 13,* 10, n. 2.
2. See *Works, 13,* 89, 109.

832 and the date of the composition of each sermon.[3] This date in turn is the earliest possible date for the composition of the entry.

**Table 1.   Integral References to Dated Sermons in "Miscellanies,"
Nos. 501–832**

Entry Number	Sermon Text	Date
612	I Cor. 11:29	Jan. 1733
614	Eph. 3:10	Mar. 1733
625	Cant. 1:3	June 1733
678	Rom. 2:10	Dec. 17[35][4]
696	Cant. 1:3	June 1733
	Rev. 5:5	Aug. 1736
698	Is. 53:3	Aug. 1736
753	Matt. 9:2	M.S. not extant
756	I Cor. 13:8 (#14)	Oct. 1738
788	Gen. 3:11	Feb. 1739
801	Rom. 12:4–8	Aug. 19, 1739
802	Is. 51:8 (#18)	June–July 1739[5]
803	Is. 51:8 (#28)	Aug. 1739
807	Is. 51:8 (#29)	Aug. 1739
819	Matt. 25:1–12	Winter 1737–38[6]

This sequence of sermon references forms an approximate chronology for the composition of Nos. 501–832, which can be refined by drawing on several other sources of evidence. Integral references to published texts at times supply additional dates. In No. 666 Edwards lists the scripture texts used by Isaac Watts in *An Essay toward the Proof of a Separate State of Souls*, published in 1732. And in No. 820 he cites his own discourse on *Justification by Faith Alone*, which was issued in 1738. There are also nu-

3. Within Nos. 501–610 there are a number of integral cross-references to sermons written prior to Jan. 1733. According to Schafer, these sermons were all written during 1731–32, but because their MSS do not contain dates of composition the cross-references to them in the "Miscellanies" do not supply specific *termini a quo* for any entries.

4. This date is Schafer's approximation. Due to MS damage, the last two digits of the date are no longer legible.

5. JE delivered his sermon series on Is. 51:8 between March and August 1739. The MS does not contain a date for Sermon 18, but given that Sermon 16 is dated June 17, JE must have preached the 18th unit in late June or early July. See *Works, 9*, 5–7.

6. JE delivered his sermon series on Matt. 25:1–12 between Nov. 1737 and March 1738.

merous references within this set of entries to manuscripts other than Edwards' sermons. Many of these references are later additions, and many cite manuscripts without precise dates of composition. However, a few of the references to "Notes on Scripture" do provide evidence for the dating of several miscellanies entries. Nos. 721, 756, and 784 contain integral citations to discrete "Scripture" notes that Stephen J. Stein has dated with some precision.[7] The most significant of these are the reference in No. 721 to "Notes on Scripture" no. 265 (dated between August and November 1737) and that in No. 784 to no. 319 (dated January 1739).[8]

There are also cross-references to the "Miscellanies" in Edwards' other manuscript writings, which at times help date an entry or confirm the dating of an entry. For example, there are datable references in "Notes on Scripture" to miscellanies entries, such as that in "Scripture" no. 381 (written after August 1739) to No. 811. And the series on Is. 51:8 cites "Miscellanies" No. 802 in Sermon 18 (June–July 1739) and No. 803 in Sermon 28 (August 1739).[9] Most significant, there is an integral reference in the manuscript of the lecture on justification by faith (Rom. 4:5), which Edwards delivered in November 1734, to "Miscellanies" No. 668. This reference indicates that No. 668 was composed no later than November 1734 (its *terminus ad quem*). Ink comparisons made by Thomas Schafer further suggest a composition date approximately the same as that of the lecture. The thin, grainy, but rimming ink in which Edwards wrote the lecture generally matches that used in Nos. 667, 668, and the beginning of No. 669.[1] Therefore, insofar as the lecture on justification marked the beginning of the revival in Northampton, entry No. 668 locates the approximate point in the "Miscellanies" manuscripts at which this crucial event occurred.

In the absence of cross-references, content parallels between miscellanies entries and Edwards' other writings can at times supply approximate dates. For example, Edwards' discussion of the parable of the wise and foolish virgins (Matt. 25:1–12) in the last paragraph of No. 710 is insuf-

---

7. For the dating of "Notes on Scripture," see *Works, 15*, 41–46.

8. In addition, No. 756 refers to "Notes on Scripture" no. 305 (April–Oct. 1738). There are several other integral references in Nos. 501–832 to "Scripture" notes, but their composition dates have not been precisely determined.

9. See *Works, 9*, 353, n. 3; 491, n. 4. These cross-references are later (but not much later) additions; they were probably made at the time of the composition of the entry cited.

1. In the middle of No. 669 the ink changes to a stiff, gray-brown color, and by the end of the entry it becomes tan and mangy in appearance. The sermon on Luke 16:6 contains this same sequence of ink variations. It therefore appears that JE wrote No. 669 at the same time as this sermon, in Feb. 1735.

ficient to establish a date alone, but it confirms what other evidence suggests, that this entry was composed in 1737–38, around the time Edwards preached his sermon series on this text. The content of several entries on justification by faith and related issues is sufficiently similar to that of *Justification by Faith Alone* to provide evidence for dates. Edwards incorporated into his 1734 lecture excerpts, revisions and paraphrases of numerous miscellanies entries written both before the lecture and while he was preparing it for publication.[2] The content parallels occur with the greatest frequency between entry Nos. 568 and 729. There are entries before No. 568 that informed Edwards' revision of the lecture, and there are entries following No. 729 that reflect issues discussed in the discourse. But the fact that the discourse contains many verbatim excerpts from Nos. 568–729 and none from entries after No. 729 suggests that Edwards submitted his manuscript to the publisher soon after the composition of this entry. Edwards, therefore, could not have written No. 729 later than 1738, the date of the publication of the discourse, and he apparently composed the concentration of justification-related entries from No. 668— written in November 1734, the date of the delivery of the lecture (see above)—to No. 729 as he revised the lecture for publication.

The approximate date for the composition of No. 832, the final entry in the set of "Miscellanies" included in this volume, is winter 1739–40. The reference in No. 807 to Sermon 29 of the series on Isaiah 51:8 indicates that this entry was written no earlier than August 1739. The cross-references in Nos. 819 and 820, being to texts written earlier than 1739, do not carry the chronology forward. However, the integral reference in No. 841 to a sermon on Luke 15:22, dating from January 1740, establishes that this entry was written no earlier than this date. We can therefore conclude that No. 832 was written in the winter of 1739–40, several months after the completion of the "Redemption" series but not many months into the new year.

The following chronological table has been constructed from the evidence summarized above. It does not include every datable entry, many of which are listed in Table 1, above, but focuses on particular landmark dates. Because the chronology depends heavily upon cross-references, the dates are generally approximations based on estimations of the earliest or latest possible date of composition.

This tentative chronology suggests that the rate at which Edwards wrote

---

2. See the discussion of the relation between the "Miscellanies" and *Justification by Faith Alone*, above, pp. 12–18.

Table 2.   Selected Dates for the Composition
of "Miscellanies," Nos. 501–832

Entry	Date
501–510	July–Aug. 1731
612	No earlier than Jan. 1733
625	No earlier than June 1733[3]
668	Nov. 1734
698	No earlier than Aug. 1736
729	No later than 1738
756	No earlier than Oct. 1738
788	No earlier than Feb. 1739
807	No earlier than Aug. 1739
832	Winter 1739–40

miscellanies entries slowed over time. For example, it appears that he spent less time with his notebooks during the Connecticut Valley revival, presumably as his pastoral responsibilities made increasing demands upon his time. Although he made 167 entries between July 1731 and November 1734, from November 1734 to August 1736 he made only thirty-one. However, rate of composition must be factored together with length of entry. As entries decrease in number they tend to increase in length. Taken together, the total length of the thirty-one entries composed during and immediately following the revival is approximately half that of the 167 entries composed in the preceding three and a half years. And although Edwards wrote almost exactly the same number of entries during these three and a half years as he wrote during the next five years, in total length the second half of this set of entries is more than twice that of the first. Following the revival, as Edwards began to experiment with more extensive literary forms, such as the discourse and the sermon series, he also began to devote to individual miscellanies entries the sustained attention necessary to compose what are in effect complete theological essays.

---

3. Ink comparisons made by Schafer show that the sermon on Cant. 1:3 was written in an ink identical to that found in Nos. 621–22. Nos. 626–28 are written in the same ink as *A Divine and Supernatural Light* (Matt. 16:17), dated Aug. 1733. It is therefore likely that JE wrote No. 625 between June and August 1733.

THE "MISCELLANIES,"
ENTRY NOS. 501 – 832

501. FALL OF MAN. Adam had a sufficient assistance of God always present with him, to have enabled him to have obeyed, if he had used his natural abilities in endeavoring it; though the assistance was not such as it would have been after his confirmation, to render it impossible for him to sin. Man might be deceived, so that he should not be disposed to use his endeavors to persevere; but if he did use his endeavors, there was a sufficient assistance always with him to enable him to persevere. See No. 436.

502. CHRIST'S RIGHTEOUSNESS. 'Tis most agreeable to the tenor of the Scripture that believers shall partake with Christ in that exaltation and glory which the Father gives him in reward for his obedience, his doing the work which he did in the world by the Father's appointment. The whole mystical Christ shall be rewarded for this, which is the same thing as the having Christ's righteousness imputed to them.

503. CEREMONY. See sermon on Luke 10:38–44, under the second doctrine.[1]

504. CONDITION OF JUSTIFICATION. REPENTANCE. FAITH. The freedom of grace appears in the forgiving of sin upon repentance, or only for our being willing to part with it; just after the same manner as the bestowment of eternal life, only for accepting of it. For to make us an offer of freedom from a thing only for quitting of it, is equivalent to the offering the possession of a thing for the receiving of it. God makes us this offer, that if we will in our hearts quit sin, we shall be [free] from it, and all the evil that belongs to it and flows from it; which is the same thing as the offering us

1. The second doctrine of the sermon on Luke 10:38–42 (n.d., [summer 1731]) states, "The most acceptable way of showing respect to Christ is to give hearty entertainment to his Word." Under this doctrine JE lists several "ways that men take to show respect" to Jesus Christ, "while they neglect this way." As the fourth of these false means of respect, he discusses how "papists" and members of the Church of England "make a show of respect to Christ by a great deal of pomp and ceremony in his worship."

freedom only for accepting it. Accepting in this case is quitting and parting with, in our wills and inclinations. So that repentance is implied in faith; 'tis a part of our willing reception of the salvation of Jesus Christ, though faith with respect to sin implies something more in it, viz. a respect to Christ as him by whom we have deliverance. Thus by faith we destroy sin. See Gal. 2:18, with my note.[2]

505. HELL TORMENTS. When the law was given at Sinai, it was in a very different manner from that in which the word of God was delivered by Christ. At Sinai, the terrors of the law—God's justice and wrath ready to revenge the breaches of it—chiefly were represented by the appearances there; and doubtless God's wrath upon sinners that suffer the curse of the law is answerable to those appearances. The appearances [there] were very awful thunders and lightnings and earthquakes, so that they could not endure. God spake out of the fire; the fire that God spake out of was a dreadful fire. Deut. 4:11, "And the mountain burnt with fire unto the midst [of heaven], with darkness, clouds, and thick darkness. And the Lord spake unto you out of the midst of the fire"; and v. 36, "Out of heaven he made thee to hear his voice, that he might instruct thee: and upon earth he showed thee his great fire; and thou heardest his words out of the midst of the fire." God's vengeance on the breakers of that law, will be answerable to those significations of it, for Moses himself testifies, that according to God's fear, so is his wrath (Ps. 90:11).

506. CHRIST'S SATISFACTION. FIRST COVENANT, ETC. It may be objected, that although [eternal] death fulfills the threatening, "Thou shalt surely die" [Gen. 2:17], as it may very fairly be understood; yet Adam did not understand it so, but took it that he personally must surely die. I answer, that perhaps Adam did not probably distinctly know, that the suffering the eternal wrath of God was meant by that threatening; he understood it only in the general, that it was [to] be a destruction of him, not particularly conceiving of all that misery that was naturally implied in that expression. He therefore understood that he personally, and perhaps his posterity if he had any, were certainly to be destroyed: and it was fulfilled in his and his posterity's temporal death, so as to be consistent with

2. In 1731 JE acquired from Benjamin Pierpont an interleaved Bible, in which he recorded notes on particular Bible verses throughout the course of his career. In this "Blank Bible" note JE states that "by believing in Christ as a savior from eternal death we destroy sin, and that because there is repentance necessarily implied in the nature of this faith." It ends with a cross-reference to the current "Miscellanies" entry, No. 504.

the words as he understood them; though it might be mitigated, so as to be more gentle than he feared, in not being with that wrath, and being followed by a resurrection. And so far as they were not understood by Adam, God is obliged by them only according to their proper and fair construction. Adam had a distinct notion of this, that the frame of his body was to be destroyed; but had no distinct notion about the doleful state of the soul the dissolution of the body was to usher in. See Nos. 1083, 357.

Corol. Hence we see why it was needful, that temporal death should be inflicted on Adam and all his posterity, except in some extraordinary instances, though eternal death may be wholly escaped.

507. JUSTIFICATION. See Nos. 416, 632. 'Tis upon the account of faith that God looks upon it as meet, that such and such should be looked upon as having an interest in Christ and his redemption; because faith, or the mind's receiving or closing with Christ as Mediator, is (if I may so express it) the active suitableness, or rather suiting, of the receiver with Christ and his redemption. 'Tis the active, direct suiting and according of the soul to the Redeemer, and to his salvation and the nature of it—to salvation as salvation—and under the notion and quality of a free gift, a suiting with the way wherein it is procured and made ours. 'Tis the immediate suiting of the faculties of the soul, a suiting of judgment and sense and disposition of the soul. The mind don't receive as the body receives, by taking with [the] hand or by opening the door; mental or spiritual reception can be nothing else but the suiting or according of the mind to a thing declared and proposed.

You may say, other graces are a suiting of the soul to salvation, as for instance love to God. I answer, not directly, in that sense that we speak of; in that sense, love to God is rather a suiting or according of the soul to the nature of God.

This suiting or agreeing of the faculties of the soul to salvation, renders it meet for an interest in salvation in a quite different manner from what righteousness, or moral excellency, renders anyone meet for happiness, as being a suitable testimony of God's respect to that excellency. This suiting that we speak of, is only that of compliance, agreeing, or closing of the faculties [with Christ]. Christ having purchased salvation, God waits for nothing else but this. Righteousness being already fulfilled, if there be only this, it renders it suitable to receive it, as 'tis a next capacity and disposition in the subject for it. The soul by it is suited as the socket for the jewel that is set in it; by this the soul admits it, as things transparent admit light when opaque bodies refuse it. Why should there be a declared belonging of Christ's salvation to that soul that disagrees and refuses and wars against it?

508. WISDOM OF GOD IN THE WORK OF REDEMPTION. As 'tis so ordered in redemption, that thereby man's dependence should become greater on God, and man should be brought nearer to God; so God hereby acquires a greater right to the creature. The creature was God's before, as he created it, and as it was absolutely dependent on God for its being; now besides that, 'tis God's as he has created it again. 'Tis God's as he hath redeemed [it] from a state infinitely worse than nothing, and brought it to a state vastly better than its former being before the fall; and then, when it could not be done without infinite expense. So that hereby God acquires an infinitely great and strong right to the redeemed: for the right is equal to the expense that obtained it, since that expense was necessary, and the benefit of the redeemed equal to the expense; which is not only to the glory of God, but will be matter of rejoicing to the redeemed, to think that God hath so great a right to them, and will make [them], with so much the more earnestness of consent and desire, yield up themselves to God, and devote themselves to serve and glorify him.

509. HELL TORMENTS. That God should so lay out himself, and do things so astonishingly great to redeem man, argues the exceeding greatness of his misery; and so doth the work of redemption's being made so much of, that all the great works of God that were wrought in the world before, and all laws and divine constitutions, must be so contrived as to be only introductory to it. Everything must be so ordered as to be a shadow; it must be so much prophesied of, spoken of so often in such an exalted manner, in songs and psalms, that all the events in the world must be only so many preparations for it. Doubtless 'tis a redemption from a very great misery, as well as to a great happiness, or it would not be made so much of.

510. WISDOM OF GOD IN THE WORK OF REDEMPTION. One design of God in the gospel, is to bring us to make God the object of our undivided respect, that he may engross our regard every way, that whatever natural inclination there is in us, he may be the center of it, and that God may be all in all. Thus there is a natural inclination in the creature, not only to the adoration of a glorious being infinitely superior, but to friendship, to love and delight in a fellow creature, one that may be familiarly conversed with and enjoyed; and virtue and holiness don't destroy or weaken this inclination.

That God therefore might also be the object of the exercise of this natural inclination of ours, of our love and friendship to a companion, God is come down to us, has taken our nature, and is become one of us, that he might be our companion; so that there is now provision made, that we may have sufficient vent for all our inclination and love, in God and towards him. (Christ conversed in the most mild, sweet, familiar, and humane manner with his disciples.) If this inclination in us be sanctified and governed and directed by a holy principle, as it ought to be, we shall need no other kind of person to exercise it upon than Jesus Christ; but in him it can be immensely better satisfied, than in any other object. There is everything in him, in the highest perfection, that tends to answer this inclination of ours. He stands in a relation to us the most advantageous for this possible. He has those qualifications that are the most endearing and qualifying for a friend possible; and he hath done that for us which, above all things conceivable, tends to attract our hearts and unite them to him, in entire love and confidence.

If God had not thus descended to us, this inclination to friendship and love to a companion might have been subordinate to a supreme regard to God; as holiness and the image of God might have been the main qualification that moved the choice of a companion and attracted love, and as this friendship might be improved to holy purposes, jointly to adore and assist each other in serving and glorifying God. But yet the heart doth not so universally and undividedly center in God, as when this love to a companion is subordinate to the adoration of God, and improved to the purposes of serving and glorifying of God; but also when the person who is the immediate object of it, is God.

511. CONVICTION. This is one great design and end of God in suffering man to fall, that by a sense of evil he might have the greater sense of good. How congruous therefore is it, that God should prepare man by a sense of evil, which consists in sin and misery, for a sense of good; especially that good which consists in a salvation from those evils.

512. CHRISTIAN RELIGION. CHRIST'S MIRACLES were such as were properly divine works, and are often spoken of as such in the Old Testament, particularly his walking on the water, when in a storm and the waves were raised. Job 9:8, "Which alone spreadeth out the heavens, and treadeth on the waves of the sea."

His stilling the tempest and raging of the sea. Ps. 65:7, "Which stilleth the noise of the seas, the noise of their waves." Ps. 107:29, "He maketh the

storm a calm, so that the waves thereof are still." Ps. 89:8–9, "O Lord God
of hosts, who is a strong Lord like unto thee, or to thy faithfulness round
about thee? Thou rulest the raging of the sea: when the waves thereof
arise, thou stillest them." Ps. 93:4, "The Lord on high is mightier than the
noise of many waters, yea, than the mighty waves of the sea." Job 38:8–11,
"Or who shut up the sea with doors . . . and said, Hitherto shalt thou come,
and no further: and here shall thy proud waves be stayed?"

Casting out devils. Job 41, with Ps. 74: 13–14 and Is. 51:9.

Feeding a multitude in the wilderness. Deut. 8:15–16, "Who brought
thee forth water out of the rock of flint, who fed thee in the wilderness."
Christ did that which the children of Israel questioned whether God
could do, Ps. 78:19, 20, 23–25, "Can God furnish a table in the wilderness?" And Ps. 146:7, "Which giveth food to the hungry."

Telling men's thoughts. Amos 4:13, "That declareth unto man what is
his thought."

Raising the dead. Ezek. 37. Is. 26:19, "Thy dead men shall live, together
with my dead body shall they arise. Awake and sing, ye that dwell in the
dust: for thy dew is as the dew of herbs, and the earth shall cast out the
dead." Ps. 68:20, "He that is our God is the God of salvation; and unto God
the Lord belong the issues from death." I Sam. 2:6, "The Lord kills, and
he makes alive; he bringeth down to the grave, and bringeth up." So Deut.
32:39, "See now that I, even I, am he, and there is no God with me: I kill
and I make alive." See II Kgs. 5:7.

Opening the eyes of the blind. Ps. 146:8, "The Lord openeth the eyes
of the blind." Is. 29:18; 35:5; 42:7.

Healing the leprosy. II Kgs. 5:6–7, compared with Deut. 32:39.

Unstopping the ears of the deaf. Is. 29:18; 35:5.

Healing grievous sores, or wounds, or issues. Job 5:17–18.

Christ healed such diseases, as of old were appointed to by types of our
souls' diseases, or the corruption of our nature, such as the plague of leprosy, and issues of blood.

Loosing the tongue of the dumb. Is. 35:6.

Causing him that hath an impediment in his speech to speak plain. Is.
32:4.

Lifting up her that was bound and bowed together by a spirit of infirmity. Ps. 146:7–8, "The Lord looseth the prisoners: the Lord raiseth them
that are bowed down."

Restoring the lame. Is. 35:6.

Healing the sick. Ps. 103:3, "Who forgiveth all thine iniquities, and who
healeth all thy diseases." Remarkable is that place, Ex. 15:26.

Christ joined pardoning sins with his healing the sick. When one came to be healed, he several times first told him that his sins were forgiven; and when the Jews were stumbled at it, and found fault that he should pretend to forgive sins, then immediately upon it he heals the person's disease, that they might believe that he had power to forgive sins, and tells 'em that he does it for this end (Matt. 9:2–8; Mark 2:3–12; Luke 5:18–26). Now if Christ were an impostor, can it be believed that [God] would so countenance such horrid blasphemy as this would be, as to enable him to cure the disease by a word's speaking—a work which God appropriates to himself as his own work, and joins it to forgiving iniquities, and mentions them as both alike his peculiar works? Would God give an impostor this attestation to his blasphemous lie, when he pretended to do [it] as an attestation? Christ urges this argument with the Jews, when they found fault with his calling himself the Son of God. John 10:37, "If I do not the works of my Father, believe me not."

There are three other things that are[3] to [be] remarked of Christ's miracles, viz. (1) that they were such as it was prophesied he would work; (2) they were works of mercy and love, no needless miracles; and (3) they were lively types of the great spiritual works of God and the Redeemer.

513. INCARNATION. See Nos. 487, 624. It seems to me reasonable to suppose, that that which the man Christ Jesus had his divine knowledge by, that he had his union with the divine Logos by. For doubtless, this union was some union of the faculties of his soul; but Christ had his divine knowledge by the Holy Ghost. Acts 1:2, "After that he through the Holy Ghost had given commandments unto the apostles."

514. CHRISTIAN RELIGION. Without divine revelation, 'tis impossible the world should ever [have] come to any tolerable knowledge of future rewards and punishments. I believe the world, without revelation, never would have come to any determination that there was any future rewards and punishments, but would have remained in midnight darkness about it. But if they could have found out that there was to be any such thing, they would have been forever ignorant, whether they were eternal or temporal, and of what kind they were; the nature, kind, and degree, and circumstances of the happiness of heaven; what it was they were to enjoy, and with what qualifications. These things would forever have been as much unknown, as how that part of the universe is formed that is beyond the

---

3. MS: "is."

starry heavens. Indeed, what the Scripture reveals of the future happiness of the righteous, is exceeding rational, and excellently fit and congruous: that those that are holy shall hereafter be made perfectly holy, that they shall enjoy a happiness that is holy and spiritual, that they shall see God, and be in his presence, and everlastingly enjoy his love. But the world never would have found out this.

515. CONFIRMATION OF THE ANGELS. See Nos. 442; and 702, corol. 4. The fall of the angels that fell, was a great establishment and confirmation to the angels that stood. They resisted a great temptation by which the rest fell, whatever that temptation was, and they resisted the enticement of the ringleaders which drew away multitudes; and the resisting and overcoming great temptation, naturally tends greatly to confirm in righteousness. And probably they had been engaged on God's side, in resisting those that fell, when there was war, rebellion raised in heaven against God. All the hosts of heaven soon divided, some on one side and some [on the other]; and standing for God, in opposition and war against those that were his enemies, naturally tended to confirm their friendship to God. And then they saw the dreadful issue of the fallen angels' rebellion, how much it was to their loss. They saw how dreadful the wrath of God was, which tended to make them dread rebellion, and sufficiently careful to avoid it. They now learnt more highly to prize God's favor, by seeing the dreadfulness of his displeasure; they now saw more of the beauty of holiness, now they had the deformity of sin to compare it with.

But when their time of probation was at [an] end, and they had the reward of certain confirmation by having eternal life absolutely made certain to them, is uncertain. However, there are many things that make it look exceeding probable to me, that whenever this was done, it was through the Son of God; that he was the immediate dispenser of this reward, and that they received it of the Father through him.

1. We have shown before (No. 320) that it was in contempt of the Son of God, that those of them that fell rebelled; it was because they would not have one in the human nature to rule over them. How congruous therefore is it, that those that stood should be dependent on him for their reward of confirmation, in contempt of whom the others had rebelled, that God should thus honor his Son in the sight of the angels, that had been thus contemned by the angels that fell, in their sight. It was congruous that Christ, who was despised and rejected by a great number of the angels, should become the foundation upon which the rest should be built for eternal life. Ps. 118:22, "The stone which the builders refused, the

same is become the head of the corner." This makes it seem probable to me, that the time of their confirmation was when Jesus Christ ascended into heaven; for,

(1) It was Jesus Christ in the human nature that was despised and rejected by the rebelling angels; it was congruous therefore, that it should be Jesus Christ in the human nature that should confirm them that stood.

(2) It was also congruous that their confirmation should be deferred till that time; that before they were confirmed, they might have a thorough trial of their obedience in that particular wherein the rebelling angels were guilty, viz. in their submission to Jesus Christ in the human nature. It was congruous therefore, that their confirmation should be deferred, till they had actually submitted to Christ in man's nature as their King; as they had opportunity to do when Christ in man's nature ascended into heaven. And,

(3) It seems very congruous that this should be reserved to be part of Christ's exaltation. We often read of Christ's being set over the angels, when he ascended and sat at the right hand [of God]; and that then he was made head of all principality and power, that then all things were put under his feet, that then God the Father said, "Let all the angels of God worship him" [Heb. 1:6]. It was very congruous that Christ should have this honor immediately, after such great humiliation and sufferings. And,

(4) It was fit that the angels should be confirmed after they had seen Christ in the flesh, for this was the greatest trial of the angels' obedience that ever was. If the other angels rebelled only at its being foretold that such an one in man's nature should rule over them, if that was so great a trial that so many angels fell in it; how great a trial was [it] when they saw a poor, obscure, despised, afflicted man, and when they had just seen [him] so mocked and spit upon, and crucified and put to death, like a vile malefactor! This was a great trial to those thrones, dominions, principalities, and powers, those mighty glorious and exalted spirits, whether or no they would submit to such an one for their sovereign Lord and King.

(5) It was very fit that God should honor the day of the ascension and glorious exaltation of his Son, which was a day of such joy to Christ, with joining with it such an occasion of joy to the angels, as the reception of their reward of eternal life; that when Christ rejoices, who had lately endured so much sorrow, the heavenly hosts might rejoice with him.

Obj. 1. It may be objected that it was a long time for the angels to be kept in a state of trial, from the beginning of the world till the ascension of Christ. But [I answer] there might very fitly be a longer time of trial for those mighty spirits, than for others.

Obj. 2. That the angels could not enjoy that quiet and undisturbed happiness for all that while, if they were all the time unconfirmed, and did not certainly know that they should not fall. I answer, there was no occasion for any disresting fears. For they never could be guilty of rebellion without knowing, when they were going to commit it, that it was rebellion, and that thereby they should forfeit eternal life and expose themselves to wrath, by the tenor of God's covenant. And they could not fall, but it must be their voluntary act; and they had perfect freedom of mind from any lust, and had been sufficiently warned and greatly confirmed when the angels fell: so that there was a great probability that they should not fall, though God had not yet declared and promised absolutely that they should not. They were not absolutely certain of it; this was an occasion of joy reserved for that joyful and glorious day of Christ's ascension.

(6) The angels are now confirmed, and hence have been since Christ's ascension; for Christ, since he appeared in the flesh, gathered together and united into one society, one family, one body, all the angels and saints in heaven and the church on earth. Now 'tis not to be supposed that part of this body are in a confirmed state, and part still in a state of probation. But,

2. The second argument that the angels are confirmed by Christ, we learn by Scripture: that Christ is the head of the angels, and that the angels are united to him as part of his body. Which holds forth, that he is not only their head of government, but their head of communication; he is the head from whence they derive their good. And 'tis manifest that he that is their head of government, should be their head of communication too; Christ is therefore the head from whence the angels receive communication of good. But how well doth this agree with their receiving their reward of obedience from him! God, in making Christ head of angels and men, hath made him his dispenser of his benefits to all universally. 'Tis therefore most probable, [that he] who now dispenses the blessings of the angels' reward to them, is he from whom they first received that reward; that God bestowed it upon them at first through his hands. And this also confirms that the time of the angels' confirmation was at Christ's ascension; for then was he made the head of the angels, then were all things put under his feet.

3. It [is] most congruous that that person that is to judge the angels, and that shall publicly declare the unalterable condemnation of those that fell, and also shall publicly declare the unalterable confirmation of those that stood, should be the same person that acted the part of a judge before, when they were first confirmed. He that is the judge of the angels

at the last day, publicly before heaven, earth, and hell to confirm them, is probably the same person that was their judge, when they were first confirmed in heaven. The Father hath committed all judgment to the Son, and this he did to Christ God-man; for the committing all judgment to him was done at Christ's first exaltation, and the first fruits of it was probably his confirming the angels as their judge. See table concerning the order in which things in this "Miscellanies" [entry] are to be placed, col. 1.[4]

4. Christ being called the "tree of life, that grows in the midst of the paradise of God" (Rev. 2:7). If we consider the use of the tree of life that grew in the midst of the earthly paradise, it was to confirm man in life, in case of obedience; if he had stood, he was to have received the reward in that way, by eating the fruit of that tree. Christ, being the tree of life in the heavenly paradise, is so to all the inhabitants of that paradise. See Nos. 570, 591, 664[b], §§ 6–9.

Corol. 1. Here we may observe the wonderful analogy there is in God's dispensations towards angels and men.

Corol. 2. Here we may take notice of the manifold wisdom of God. What glorious and wonderful ends are accomplished by the same events in heaven, earth, and hell; as particularly by those dispensations of providence in Christ's incarnation, death, and exaltation. How manifold are the wise designs that are carried on in different worlds, by the turning of one wheel!

Corol. 3. Here we may observe how the affairs of the church on earth and of the blessed assembly of heaven are linked together. When the joyful times of the gospel begin on earth, which begin with Christ's exaltation, then joyful times begin also in heaven amongst the angels there, and by the same means. When we have such a glorious occasion given us to rejoice, they have an occasion given them. So long as the church continued under a legal dispensation, so long the angels continued under law; for since their confirmation, the angels are not under law, as is evident by what I have said in my note on Gal. 5:18.[5] So doubtless at the same time, there was a great addition to the happiness of the separate spirits of the saints, as the resurrection of many of them with Christ's resurrection is an

---

4. JE's "Table" to the "Miscellanies" contains a similar citation, under the entry entitled "Confirmation of the angels"; the table to which these citations refer, however, has been lost. See *Works, 13*, 128.

5. The "Blank Bible" note on Gal. 5:18 is a cross-reference to "Notes on Scripture," no. 196. All references to "Notes on Scripture" designate the four-volume series of "Scripture" notebooks compiled by JE over the course of his ministry. For the text of no. 196, see *The Works of Jonathan Edwards, 15, Notes on Scripture*, ed. Stephen J. Stein (New Haven, Yale Univ. Press, 1998), 108–15.

argument. And in the general, when God gradually carries on the designs of grace in this world, by accomplishing glorious things in the church below, there is a new accession of joy and glory to the church in heaven. Thus the matter is represented in John's Revelations;[6] and 'tis fit that it should be thus, seeing they are one family.

516. SATISFACTION OF CHRIST.[7] The sufferings of Christ herein differed from the sufferings of the damned in hell, that Christ had immensely a greater sense of the worth of the good that he lost, viz. the manifestation and enjoyment of the love of God; and therefore, when God forsook him and hid his face from him, it was so much more grievous.

There were these things gave him a sense of the worth of the enjoyment of the Father's love: (1) He infinitely loved the Father; and the love of the man Christ Jesus was in some sort infinite, and proportionable was his desire of the love of the Father. (2) He had actually been infinitely happy in the enjoyment of the Father's love, so that he knew more by experience of the worth of it, than any angel or saint in heaven. And (3) the Father's love was infinite to him. It was a greater thing to have the expressions and manifestations of great love interrupted, than lesser love; the loss by the interruption was greater. As a sense of evil increases a sense of good, so a sense of good doth as much increase a sense of evil. See Nos. 265, 664, 1005.

517. HUMILIATION. It appears by that text, "If we would judge ourselves, we should not be judged of the Lord" (I Cor. 11:31–32), that men are not brought thoroughly to judge themselves, as justly liable to the punishment which the law threatens, but by saving repentance.

518[a]. FAITH, JUSTIFICATION.[8] Faith, when spoken of as compared with works, or an universal and persevering obedience, it may be said alone to be the condition of salvation, if by "condition" we mean that which of itself, without the actual performance of the other, will, according to the tenor of the divine promise, give a man a certainty of life.

6. For a discussion of texts illustrating this point, see the last paragraph of No. 777, pp. 432–34.

7. JE made two previous starts at No. 516, but cancelled both:

"516. CONVERSION. One foundation of Mr. Stoddard's being so positive of persons always knowing the time of their conversion, extraordinary cases excepted, was

"516. HELL TORMENTS. The greatness of hell torments was signified by the excessive heat of Nebuchadnezzar's furnace, which was a type of hell."

8. This entry is cancelled by a single vertical line two inches to the right of its left margin.

518[b]. CHRIST'S MIRACLES. CHRISTIAN RELIGION. Christ, by the works which he wrought, showed "that he had an absolute and sovereign power over the course of nature," and over the spiritual and invisible world, and "over the bodies and souls of men," as Dr. Sharp observes.[9] It was not so with other prophets that were wont to work miracles. They could not work what miracles they pleased, or when they pleased. They could not work miracles, but only when they were excited and directed to it by a special command or impulse from heaven. But Christ wrought miracles in a constant course, from the time of the beginning of his public ministry. They sought to him for it, and he did them as of his own power at all times. It was under that notion that they came to him for it, that he was able; and this Christ required, that they should believe, in order to it, which never any prophet pretended to. Moses was shut out of Canaan, partly for working a miracle in his own name, and not sanctifying the Lord God: "Must we fetch water out of this rock?" said he [Num. 20:10]. The prophets never pretended that they themselves had properly any power to work miracles, but disclaimed it. God never subjected the course of nature to them, to work miracles by their own word and command upon all occasions. Care was taken that in all the miracles that God wrought, wherein he made any use of the prophets, that it should be visible that what was done, was done only by God; and that what they said or did, upon which the miracle was wrought, was by particular revelation from heaven.

They that came to Christ that he might work miracles for them, did [it] in the faith of that by his own power and holiness he was able to do it for them. The leper said, "Lord, if thou wilt thou canst make me clean" (Matt. 8:2). He believed that Christ could work miracles when he would. This Christ approved of. Matt. 8:8, "But speak the word only, and my servant shall be healed." Matt. 9:18, "My daughter is even now dead: but come and lay thine hand on her, and she shall live." Matt. 9:28, "Believe ye that I am able to do this? They said unto him, Yea, Lord." Matt. 9:21, "If I may but touch his garment, I shall be whole." See Matt. 16:9. Christ there reproves the disciples, because they were afraid of wanting bread, not remembering how he had fed multitudes in the wilderness; which implies that he was able to do the like again, when he was pleased. He cast out devils as of his own power and authority. Mark 1:27, "With authority commandeth he even the unclean spirits, and they do obey him." And Christ

9. John Sharp, *Fifteen Sermons Preached on Several Occasions* (London, 1700; vol. 1, 6th ed. London, 1729; vol. 2, 2nd ed. 1729). Vol. 1, Sermon VI, "Preached at White-Hall on the Twentieth of March, 1684–5," p. 178.

as having power of his own to work miracles, gave power to his disciples, as Matt. 10, Mark 3:14–15 and 6:7–13, and Luke 9 and 10. And so miracles were wrought in Christ's name by the apostles and multitudes of other disciples. Moses did not work those miracles that were wrought in his time, nor did he in the least pretend to any such thing. But Christ did pretend to work his miracles; they are often spoken of, and he himself speaks of them, as works that he did, yea, and declares himself fellow with God in working. John 5:17, "My Father worketh hitherto, and I work."

519. CHRISTIAN RELIGION. If there must be a revelation, this is convincing that the Christian revelation is the true [one], that it has been by means of this revelation, and this only, that the world has come to the knowledge of the one only true God. Till this came, all the world lay in ignorance of him; but when this came, it was successful to bring the world to the acknowledgment of him. And 'tis from hence that all that part of the world that owns the one only true God, whether Christians, Jews, Mahometans, or deists, have received. If there be a true revelation in the world, 'tis not to be supposed that God would so order things, that it should not be by that true revelation, but by a false one, an imposture, that the world should come to the knowledge of the true God.

And this is evidential, that the Christian revelation is that which God designed as the proper means to bring the world to the knowledge of himself, rather than other revelation and rather than human reason. For 'tis unreasonable to suppose that God would so order that another means, which God did not design as proper means for the obtaining this effect, should actually obtain it, and that only. If the Christian revelation ben't the proper means to bring the world to the knowledge of the true God, 'tis strange that the world, who were before ignorant of him, should be brought to knowledge of him by it, and no part of it ever brought to the knowledge of him by any other means; which may be supposed to be the means which God designed.

520. FEW SAVED. See Shepard's *Sincere Convert,* paragraph at the bottom of the 83rd page and the top of the 84th.[1] The following seem to be some of the reasons why there are but few of fallen men chosen to eternal life:

1. The edition of Thomas Shepard's *The Sincere Convert* that JE used cannot be identified. The paragraph to which he refers is probably located in the first sermon of ch. V, which takes as its doctrine, "That the number of them that shall be saved is very small." This section can be found in the 1st ed. (London, 1640) on pp. 120–44.

1. Hereby it becomes more sensible and remarkable that they are dependent on the sovereign power and grace of God for salvation, and that it is his work, that their redemption is owing only to him. Because 'tis a remarkable and strange thing, that a few should be so different from all the rest of mankind, that they should become so different in themselves, and be in so different state. When [there is] such a distinction of a small part from the common mass, it the more commands notice; and it is natural to inquire what should be the cause of it. It is natural to inquire why these few, in these respects, are so different from all the rest, that are of the same kind of beings, of the same original, and otherwise in the same circumstances. 'Tis natural to conclude that there is some extrinsic cause of the distinction; it don't look as if it were from anything in their nature: for then, why are none of the rest so? Why so few of all mankind, when all have the same nature? When a few are exceptions from all the world, 'tis more apparent that divine power and sovereign will makes the difference. If the generality were so, we should be ready to think there was something in man's nature that tended to it, or that there are some efficacious causes of it in man himself, or in what belongs to him, or in the common state or circumstances of mankind. But the smallness of the number leads us to seek a cause out of that nature which is common to mankind. The redeemed themselves are put in mind by it, that the cause that distinguishes them is not in themselves.

That the difference is owing to divine election, is more apparent. If the generality were saved and but few perished, a designing of those many to salvation could hardly be called an election. "Election" seems to denote a choosing out one or a few out of many, a choosing a portion out of the common mass; but if the multitude or mass itself was taken, and only a few distinguished ones left, this could hardly be called an election. The divine sovereign will is more obviously the cause of the distinction in such an election, when a few are distinguished from the generality and are chosen to a supernatural state, than if the generality were designed to this state, and only a few left in their natural state. If the generality were in a state of grace, we should be more ready to look upon that state as natural.

That which is rare is more taken notice of, and looked upon as more wonderful. Those works that are ordinary, though they are very great, ben't so much admired as those that are more rare. Thus the power of God in the works of nature is as great as in miracles; yet the power of God is more notable and remarkable in miracles: miracles are therefore spoken of in Scripture as works of the great power of God.

2. This teaches that the saints don't belong to this world, that this world is not their country, because they are only some few that are chosen out

of the world (John 15:19). "These are they that are redeemed from amongst men, being the firstfruits unto God and to the Lamb" (Rev. 14:4). The world is fallen and lost; 'tis only a number that God hath set his love upon, that are redeemed. The world is in a perishing state; 'tis sinking down into eternal perdition; 'tis set on fire of hell, and is burning up in the dreadful flames. Those are only a few chosen ones, that are plucked from the common ruin (see Num. 23:9).

3. By reason of there being so few saved, the grace and love of God towards those that are saved, will be the more valued and admired; and that upon two accounts.

(1) There is the same kind of cause why it should be so, as why a man that escapes some great evil will rejoice the more, the narrower his escape is. If the generality of an army was condemned to die, and only a certain small number was to be saved by lot, those upon whom this happy lot fell, would rejoice so much the more for the smallness of the number; every time they think how narrow their escape was, they will prize the blessing of life the more. And when men are saved by the free and sovereign will of a benefactor, and not by chance, that don't alter the case as to the joy of him that is saved: for he considers his being involved with others in the same state of misery and danger, as prior to the will of the benefactor to deliver him from that misery and danger; and his danger before his deliverance was so much the greater, by how much the fewer there were to be saved.

(2) Any good that is enjoyed is valued and admired according as it appears great or small in comparison, both according to the degree by which it excels something else that it is compared with, and also according to the number excelled. The same riches, the same esteem, the same pleasures, the same advantages every way that a king has, would not be so valued, were not the person hereby so distinguished and exalted above such a multitude. So, he that outrun in the Olympic games. So the creature admires the love of God, for his being thereby so distinguished and exalted above so many.

Upon these accounts, if God should by some miracle or wonder of providence wherein the divine hand was visible, and from a peculiar favor and love, snatch a man out of a sinking ship, he would be more affected with God's favor and love to him in particular, than if God had, by a miracle, stopped the leak and saved the ship and whole crew. This world is like a sinking ship.

521. WISDOM OF GOD IN THE WORK OF REDEMPTION. DEATH OF THE SAINTS. There is this good comes by the saints' dying: they thereby are

able to have something of an idea of what Christ suffered for them; they themselves taste of death, and so are the better able to judge how wonderful Christ's love to them was in dying for them.

522. NO PROMISES TO UNCONVERTED MEN'S SEEKING SALVATION. It was not meet that God should make any promises of success to unregenerated seekers of salvation. For it is not meet that any should have absolute promises of success, unless they do what they can, or if they are slack and partial and ben't thorough in seeking. Nor is it meet that absolute promises should be made to such as are thorough in seeking, unless they are persevering in it. It is not meet that God should promise men success, if they would be engaged in seeking during any limited time, as for a day or month or year. Therefore, it was not meet that God should make any absolute promises of success to any unconverted seekers; for no unconverted man will be thorough in striving for eternal life, and be fixed and persevering in it.

The Arminians say that God has promised that if men will make a good improvement of common grace, he will give special. Then I would ask, how long must a man make a good improvement of common grace, in order to be entitled to that promise? Will it be a performance of the condition of the promise, if a man doth it for a day or a week? If it be said, that a man must go on in making a good improvement of it, waiting for the fulfilling of the promise in God's time; I answer, that I believe that God has promised special grace to those that are faithful in the improvement of common grace, and continue so to be: but there are none but those that have special grace, that do thus. There is no promise of grace but what is implied in that, "To him that hath shall be given" [Luke 8:18]. God makes promises of grace only to grace.

523. ANTICHRIST. The two empires of Antichrist and of the Mahometans seem to have been raised up on purpose, that the glory of the power and dominion of Jesus might appear in overcoming and overthrowing the mightiest empires of the world, and in establishing his own empire upon their ruins. It was foretold that the kingdom of Christ should break in pieces and consume all the four mighty monarchies that have been in the world; which was represented by the stone's smiting the image, and breaking in pieces the iron, the clay, the brass, the silver, and the gold, and making of them like the chaff of the summer threshing floor, and the wind's carrying them away, so that no place was found for them [Dan. 2:35]. Now the Antichristian and the Mahometan empires, they

comprehend all those parts of the earth that have been subject to those four monarchies.

That Christ's victory therefore might be the more visible, and his triumph the more glorious, God hath so ordered it that the empire of these parts of the world should be set on such a foot, that the very being of it must be overthrown and utterly abolished, by the setting up the kingdom of Christ in those parts of the world. Thus the being of Antichrist's kingdom must be abolished, if Christ sets up his own kingdom. The Antichristian empire being fundamentally opposite to Christ's, the dominion of Christ and the dominion of Antichrist over the same parts of the world, are inconsistent one with another. Now when Christ overcame the Roman empire in Constantine's time, it was not to the abolition of the empire itself, but only the heathenism of it. The victory over the earthly power and empire therefore, was not so visible and remarkable, because the strife was not about the being of that power and empire, as it was when the Greeks strove with the Persians, and afterwards the Romans with the Greeks, [when] the prevailing of the empire of the one overthrew the empire of the other.

When Christ overcomes the powers of earth so as to abolish their very being, his superiority is the more visible, because it is to be supposed that that earthly power will exert itself to its utmost to preserve its own being. God therefore saw meet, that the power and dominion of the Roman empire should come to stand on such a foot, as that the being of it should be incompatible with Christ's dominion, that Christ might be glorified in overthrowing [it] and setting up his own kingdom upon its ruins. And it seems to me also very probable that the case will be so ordered, that the prevailing of Christianity will also abolish the being of the Mahometan empire.

524. WISDOM OF GOD IN THE WORK OF REDEMPTION. See sermon on Job 11:12, Inf. I.[2]

525. PROVIDENCE. CHRISTIAN RELIGION. That God takes care of and governs the world is evident, because "the same ends, designs, and motives (whatever they were) that induced God to create the world, will oblige him forever to take care of it and look after it," as Abp. Sharp ob-

2. The doctrine of the sermon on Job 11:12 (n.d., [1731–32]) states "that man is naturally a proud creature." In this entry JE probably intended to refer to the 1st reason under the use of instruction, in which he considers how from the nature of pride we "learn one reason why Christ appeared in such mean low circumstances in the world."

serves.[3] For whatever end it was that [God] gave the world a being, to be continued in being it must be supposed that the continuance of the being of the world, so long as God does continue [it] in being, or so long as he made it to be continued in being, is that which as much concerns the obtaining of God's end, as the first giving of it being. It is not to be supposed that God answered his end merely in making a world, and that if [it] had dropped into nothing the next moment, his design would have been fully obtained.

And further, if so, we must necessarily suppose that the manner of the world's continuance in being, or its manner of existing from time through the several parts of its continuance, is as much to be looked at, in order to the obtaining God's end, as the manner of its existing at first; i.e. it must concern God as much, to see and take care of the manner of [the] world's existence from time to time, as it did to see and take care after what manner it should be first made. And it is evident that God *did* take care how the world was first made, by the visible and remarkable contrivance of every part of it.

Again, 'tis evident that it must of necessity be more agreeable to the divine will, that the world should exist in one manner, than another. It can't be that God should be indifferent to all possible manners of existence of the world; and therefore he must of necessity take care how it exists from time. 'Tis evident that he is not indifferent to all manners of the world's existence; for if so, he would have taken no care how it existed at first, which it is evident he did.

Again, 'tis evident that God, in the first creation of the world, in his creating it in such a manner, had respect to the manner of its future existence, for the contrivance of it in innumerable instances, and indeed in every instance, was with an eye to its future existence. So that 'tis evident, that [he] is not indifferent to the manner of the world's being in continuance. He that takes care of the manner of the world's being in its continuance, in the first making of [it], shows that he is concerned how the affairs of the world proceed.

God concerned himself in the manner of the existence of the world in its creation, in minute circumstances, such as the particular form and shape and position of every minutest part; he chose one position and one manner rather than another, in every minutest particular. And there is no reason can be given, why God should not choose one manner of existence

3. Sharp, *Fifteen Sermons* (see above, No. 518[b], p. 63, n. 9), Vol. 1, Sermon XIII, "Preached Before the King and Queen at White-Hall, the 12th of November, 1693," p. 374.

rather than another in all circumstances, at any other time, as well as that of the world's first existence.

As to God's moral government of intelligent creatures, how unreasonable is it to suppose, that God intended that those creatures that he made in his own image, in the image of his own intelligent nature, should have no concern with that being who is their author and pattern, when God has made them capable of understanding of him, and knowing their[4] own dependence on him, and seeing the manifestations which he makes of himself, and capable of knowing their obligations to him?

526. WISDOM OF GOD IN THE WORK OF REDEMPTION. God made the world for his own glory. And Jesus Christ has this honor, to be the greatest instrument of glorifying God that ever was, and more than all other beings put together. Yea, he is so the great means or author of the glory of God, that what others do towards it is in a dependence upon what he does; the actions of others are to God's glory through him, and 'tis as his servants, and under his direction, and by his influence.

Agreeable to this, it was so ordered that Christ should be the great means of bringing the world from heathenism, to the knowledge of the true God and the true religion. Therefore, it was reserved for him to be the revealer of glorious divine truths, which were in a great measure kept hid till he came. Therefore, he probably was appointed to cast out Satan and his angels out of heaven when they sinned; therefore, I suppose, it was by him that the elect angels were confirmed. Therefore, he is appointed judge of the world, and is to glorify God at the day of judgment, by declaring his righteousness, by destroying all his enemies, and glorifying his elect. Therefore is Christ the grand medium of all communications of grace and happiness from God, by which especially God glorifies himself. Christ has this honor, that the pleasure of the Lord should prosper in his hands.

527. HELL TORMENTS, their greatness. When I read some instances of the monstrous and amazing cruelty of some popish persecutors, I have such a sense of the horridness of what they did, that the extremity of hell torments don't seem too much for them. So if we were sensible of the evil and horrid nature of all sin, the misery of hell would not seem at all more than a just and equal punishment. 'Tis no argument that sin is not of such a horrid nature, that we that are guilty of it are not sensible of the hor-

---

4. MS: "his."

ridness of it, for the actions of those persecutors did not seem horrid to them, as they do to us; the devilish spirit of pride and cruelty made it not seem so. Nor is it any argument why sin should not be punished with such an extreme misery, that although sin be of so dreadfully evil a nature, yet we that commit it are not sensible of it, and so are to be in a great measure excused. For 'tis the wickedness of our temper and nature that makes us insensible of it; as we don't think those persecutors don't deserve to be extremely punished, because they had no sense of the horridness of what they did, because it was their devilish disposition that made it not seem horrid to them.

528. CONVICTION. HUMILIATION. It is very plain, in order to a sense of the sufficiency of Christ's satisfaction for our sins, and the propriety and fitness of our guilt's being looked upon as removed by Christ's redemption, or our sense of its suitableness to God's nature and glory that it should be pleasing to him to look upon our guilt as satisfied for by Christ's redemption; it is absolutely necessary that we should have a view of both, viz. both of our guilt, and also of Christ's redemption. There must be a sense of guilt, of the evil nature of sin, and of the demerit of it, of the agreeableness and connection between that and the punishment; and there must also be a sense of Christ's redemption, that is, a belief of the truth and reality of it, and a sense of the nature of it. And here 'tis necessary that the sense of guilt should be first, which is first in fact, and is first in order of nature: and thus undoubtedly it ordinarily is first, in legal conviction; then [follows] gracious repentance, and then succeeds the explicit acting of faith on Jesus Christ. A sense of sin and guilt, being first in the order of nature, must of necessity be either before the other, or with it; it can't be after it.

529. HEAVEN. There can be no doubt, but that the saints in heaven shall see the flourishing and prosperity of the church on earth: for how can they avoid it, when they shall be with the King himself, whose kingdom this church is, and that as King manages all those affairs. Shall the royal family be kept in ignorance of the success of the affairs of the kingdom? They shall also be with the angels, those ministers by which the King manages those affairs. In the flourishing of Christ's kingdom here on earth, consists much of Christ's mediatorial glory, and of the reward that the Father promised him for his performing what he did on earth in the work of redemption. The happiness of the saints in heaven consists much in that, that they are with Christ and are partakers with him in that glory and

reward. The saints are not only with the King that reigns over this kingdom, but they reign with him in the same kingdom; they sit with him in his throne. And therefore it is said that they shall reign on earth [Rev. 5:10]; that is, when the time of the flourishing and prosperity of Christ's kingdom comes on earth, when he shall reign here in such a glorious manner in his kingdom of grace, they shall reign with him. So they are said to reign with him a thousand years [Rev. 20:4, 6]. Therefore, doubtless, they are not ignorant of the flourishing of the church here on earth.

Can it be supposed that the saints in heaven had not notice of Christ's incarnation, and did not know what he did here upon earth, and that they had no notice when he was crucified and buried and rose again? And if so, why should they be ignorant of what succeeded, as of the pouring out of the Holy Ghost at Pentecost, and how the kingdom which Christ had thus laid the foundation of, flourished? Why should their knowledge of the affairs of Christ's kingdom on earth cease, as soon as Christ was ascended?

The saints in heaven are under infinitely greater advantages to take the pleasure of beholding how Christ's kingdom flourishes, than if they were here upon earth: for they can better see and understand the marvelous steps that divine wisdom takes in all that is done, and the glorious ends he accomplishes, and what opposition Satan makes, and how he is baffled and overthrown. They can see the wise connection of one event with another, and the beautiful order of all things that come to pass in the church in different ages, that to us appear like confusion. They will behold the glory of the divine attributes in his works of providence, infinitely more clearly than we can.

The greatest objection that I think of against this, is that of Simeon, who had it revealed to him that he should not see death before he had seen the Lord's Christ; and when he saw him said, "Now lettest thou thy servant depart in peace, for mine eyes have seen thy salvation" [Luke 2:29–30], as though he should [have] missed of the pleasure and satisfaction of seeing this salvation, if he had died before. But shall we conclude from hence, that if Simeon had died before, he would not have known of Christ's birth? He surely at least would have seen this salvation, when Christ ascended into heaven. But the case was thus: Simeon was now more willing to die, more willing to venture his soul into another world, and he should die in much stronger hope, because his faith in God's salvation was abundantly strengthened by this sight. He had the greater assurance that when he did depart, he should depart in peace, for his eyes had actually seen the salvation which God had provided for souls; and was therefore more fully persuaded, that his soul should be safe and happy in a future state. Or if otherwise, it was because the state of separate souls in that particular was not known to him.

Indeed, 'tis desirable to live to see the flourishing of God's church upon this account, that those saints that live to see it, will probably be partakers in that spiritual prosperity. Their souls will receive a portion of the Spirit that is then plentifully poured out, and so will be increased in grace and holiness; their own souls will prosper, and will be partakers of the prosperity of the church. And besides, they will have a more glorious opportunity to do good, in having a hand in promoting that public prosperity.

An objection may be raised from Eccles. 9:5–6, "The dead . . . have no more a portion forever in anything done under the sun." But see an answer in my note on the verse.[5]

530. LOVE TO GOD. SELF-LOVE. Whether or no a man ought to love God more than himself. Self-love, taken in the most extensive sense, and love to God, are not things properly capable of being compared one with another: for they are not opposites, or things entirely distinct; but one enters into the nature of the other. Self-love is a man's love of his own pleasure and happiness, and hatred of his own misery; or rather, 'tis only a capacity of enjoyment or suffering. For to say a man loves his own happiness and pleasure, is only to say that he delights in what he delights [in]; and to say that he hates his own misery, is only to say that he is grieved or afflicted in his own affliction. So that self-love is only a capacity of enjoying or taking delight in anything.

Now surely 'tis improper to say that our love to God is superior to our general capacity of delighting in anything. Proportionable to our love to God is our disposition to delight in his good. Now our delight in God's good can't be superior to our general capacity of delighting in anything; or which is the same thing, our delight in God's good can't be superior to our love to delight in general: for proportionably as we delight in God's good, so shall we love that delight. A desire of and delight in God's good, is love to God; and love to delight is self-love. Now the degree of delight in a particular thing, and the degree of love to pleasure or delight in general, ben't properly comparable one with another; for they are not entirely distinct, but one enters into the nature of the other. Delight in a

5. In the "Blank Bible" note on Eccles. 9:5–6, JE explains that although the dead "have no more a reward of the labor they have taken under the sun for a worldly possession . . . they may have a portion in the affairs of the church that respect another world."

particular thing includes a love to delight in general. A particular delight in anything can't be said to be superior to love to delight in general: for always in proportion to the degree of delight is the love a man hath to that delight. For he loves greater delight more than less, in proportion as it is greater; if he did not love it more, it would not be a greater delight to him.

Love of benevolence to any person is an inclination to their good. But evermore equal to the inclination or desire anyone has of another's good, is the delight he has in that other's good if it be obtained, and the uneasiness if it be not obtained. But equal to that delight, is a person's love to that delight; and equal to that uneasiness, is his hatred of that uneasiness. But love to our own delight or hatred of our own uneasiness, is self-love; so that no love to another can be superior to self-love, as most extensively taken.

Self-love is a man's love to his own good; but self-love may be taken in two senses, as any good may be said to be a man's own good in two senses. (1) Any good whatsoever that a man any way enjoys, or anything that he takes delight in, it is thereby his own good. Whether it be a man's own proper and separate pleasure or honor, or the pleasure or honor of another, our delight in it renders it our own good, in proportion as we delight in it. 'Tis impossible that a man should delight in any good that is not his own; for to say that, would be to say that he delights in that in which he does not delight. Now take self-love for a man's love to his own good in this more general sense, and love to God can't be superior to it.

But (2) a person's good may be said to be his own good, as 'tis his proper and separate good, which is his and what he has delight in directly and immediately. And love to good that is a man's own in this sense, is what is ordinarily called self-love; and superior to this, love to God can and ought to be.

Self-love is either [(1)] simple mere self-love; which is a man's love to his own proper, single, and separate good, and is what arises simply and necessarily from the nature of a perceiving willing being. It necessarily arises from that, without the supposition of any other principle. I therefore call it simple self-love, because it arises simply from that principle, viz. the nature of a perceiving willing being. Self-love taken in this sense, and love to God are entirely distinct, and don't enter one into the nature of the other at all.

There is (2) a compounded self-love, which is exercised in the delight that a man has in the good of another; it is the value that he sets upon that delight. This I call compounded self-love, because it arises from a compounded principle. It arises from the necessary nature of a perceiving and willing being, whereby he loves his own pleasure or delight; but not from this alone. But it supposes also another principle that determines the exercise of this principle, and makes that to become its object which otherwise cannot: a certain principle uniting this person with another, that causes the good of another to be its good. The first arises simply from his own being, whereby that which agrees immediately and directly with his own being, is his good; the second arises also from a principle uniting him to another being, whereby the good of that other being does in a sort become his own. This second sort of self-love is not entirely distinct from love to God, but enters into its nature.

Corol. Hence 'tis impossible for any person to be willing to be perfectly and finally miserable for God's sake, for this supposes love to God to be superior to self-love in the most general and extensive sense of self-love, which enters into the nature of love to God. It may be possible, that a man may be willing to be deprived of all his own proper separate good for God's sake; but then he is not perfectly miserable but happy, in the delight that he hath in God's good: for he takes greater delight in God's good, for the sake of which he parts with his own, than he did in his own. So that the man is not perfectly miserable, he is not deprived of all delight, but he is happy. He has greater delight in what is obtained for God, than he had in what he has of his own; so that he has only exchanged a lesser joy for a greater.

But if a man is willing to be perfectly miserable for God's sake, then he is willing to part with all his own separate good. But he must be willing also to be deprived of that which is indirectly his own, viz. God's good; which supposition is inconsistent with itself. For to be willing to be deprived of this latter sort of good, is opposite to that principle of love to God itself, from whence such a willingness is supposed to arise. Love to God, if it be superior to any other principle, will make a man forever unwilling, utterly and finally to be deprived of this part of his happiness, which he has in God's being blessed and glorified; and the more he loves him the more unwilling he will be. So that this supposition, that a man can be willing to be perfectly and utterly miserable out of love to God, is inconsistent with itself.

Note. That love of God which we have hitherto spoken of, is a love of benevolence only. But this is to be observed, that there necessarily accompanies a love of benevolence, a love of appetite, or complacence; which is a disposition to desire or delight in beholding the beauty of another, and a relation to or union with him. Self-love in its most general extent, is very much concerned in this, and is not entirely distinct from it. The difference is only this, that self-love is a man's desire of or delight in his own happiness, and this love of complacence is a placing of his happiness, which he thus desires and delights in, in a particular object.

This sort of love, which is always in proportion to a love of benevolence, is also inconsistent with a willingness to be utterly miserable for God's sake: for if the man is utterly miserable, he is utterly excluded [from] the enjoyment of God; but how can man's love of complacence towards God be gratified in this? The more a man loves God, the more unwilling will he be, to be deprived of this happiness.

531. LORD'S DAY. It is to be observed to have been God's manner, gradually to abolish old constitutions and gradually to introduce new ones. John was the forerunner of Christ, and his baptism was only to prepare the way for his appearing; but his baptism did not wholly cease as soon as he appeared, but gradually decreased, and Christ gradually increased (as John 3:30 and context, and ch. 4 at the beginning), as the day star don't immediately disappear at the sun's rising, but gradually goes out. So the worship of the Jewish [religion] was not abolished at once, but gradually. God for some time continued a degree of his blessing upon the rites of the Jewish worship (till the destruction of Jerusalem) to Christianized Jews, that had not yet had the cessation of them and the grounds of it fully revealed to 'em; and the apostles themselves were wont to attend them, many of them for a considerable time. Thus the moon and stars gradually disappear, and daylight gradually comes on. So it was with respect to the sabbath. The seventh-day sabbath was for some time kept as a holy day by the Christian church, at least amongst the Jews; and as the observation of the Christian sabbath more and more prevailed, the Christian sabbath and Jewish sabbath both were kept for a while, till the Jewish sabbath gradually ceased, and the Christian sabbath only prevailed.

532. RIGHTEOUSNESS OF CHRIST. It seems strange to me, that those that hold that Christ's merits are imputed to us, or, which is the same thing, that he merited for us, or that we have the benefit of his merit, should deny that his active righteousness is imputed to us. For what was it that Christ merited by, if it was not by his righteousness; or what should there be that ever anyone should merit or deserve anything by, besides their righteousness or goodness? If anything that Christ did or suffered, merited or deserved any [reward], it was by virtue of the goodness or

righteousness or holiness of it. If there was any merit in Christ's suffering and death, it must be because there was an excellent righteousness or holiness in that act of laying down his life, as there was shown in it a transcendent love to the Father; and it was a glorious act of obedience to him.

533. LAW OF NATURE. The Apostle says, Rom. 2:14–15, that "the Gentiles, which have not the law, do by nature the things contained in the law; these, having not the law, are a law unto themselves: which show the work of the law written in their hearts, their conscience also bearing witness." In order to men's having the law of God made known to them by the light of nature, two things are necessary. The light of nature must not [only] discover to them that these and those things are their duty, i.e. that they are right, that there is a justice and equality in them, and the contrary unjust; but it must discover to 'em also, that 'tis the will of God that they should be done, and that they shall incur his displeasure by the contrary. For a law is a signification of the will of a lawgiver, with the danger of the effects of his displeasure, in case of the breach of that law.

The Gentiles had both these. Their natural consciences testified to the latter after this manner: natural conscience suggests to every man the relation and agreement there is, between that which is wrong or unjust, and punishment; this naturally disposes men to expect it. To think of wrong and injustice, especially such as often is seen without any punishment to balance it, is shocking to men's minds. Men therefore are naturally averse to thinking that there will be no punishment, especially when they themselves are great sufferers by injustice, and have it not in their power to avenge themselves; and the same sense made guilty persons jealous lest they should meet with their deserved punishment. And this kept up in the world, among all nations, the doctrine of a superior power that would revenge iniquity; this sense of men's consciences kept alive that tradition, and made it easily and naturally received. The light of nature discovered the being of a deity otherwise; but this sense of conscience upheld this notion of him, that he was the revenger of evil, and it also made them the more easily believe the being of a deity itself. God also gave many evidences of it in his providence amongst the heathen, that he was the revenger of iniquity. When the light of nature discovered to 'em that there was a God that governed the world, they the more easily believed him to be a just being, and so that he hated injustice, because it appeared horrid to think of a supreme Judge of the universe, that was unjust. Gen. 18:25, "Shall not the Judge of all the earth do right?"

534. RESTRAINING GRACE AND CORRUPTION OF MAN'S NATURE. See sermon on Matt. 10:17.[6] Mere self-love, if it be the sole governing principle in the heart and without restraint, will dispose one to delight in another's misery, because self-love seeks its own comparative happiness, or to diminish its comparative misery, which is obtained in the depression of others. This seems to be the cause that the devils do delight in others' misery; for they are governed wholly and solely by mere simple self-love, and 'tis without any restraint.

Self-love will delight in cruelty and putting others to pain, because it appears to it as an exercise of power and dominion. One's power over another appears in being able to afflict another; that shows them to be in their power. For all regard their own comfort and happiness, and would not part with it if they were free; and the more one is afflicted by another, the more it shows him to be in his power, because there is the greater incitement to the sufferer to show his liberty, if he had it, in delivering himself. When anyone is affronted or crossed, self-love will excite [him] to be cruel in revenge, because self-love makes men seek prodigiously to advance themselves; and this is one thing wherein the greatness and power of anyone appears, that his wrath shall be terrible, that it shall appear a terrible thing to offend him.

There is no degree of self-advancement, but what self-love, if it be the sole governing principle, will make men to seek, for there is no other principle to be a balance to it, or to limit its desires. If there be only self-love that bears rule, it will be contented with nothing short of the throne of God; and so there will be no limits to a man's revenge, and other manifestations of pride.

535. FATHERS. There can be no doubt of it, but that we may do well to make use of arguments from what is said by the fathers, and from the accounts that history gives us of the church in times near the apostles, for the confirmation of [the] truth of a doctrine or goodness of a practice: for arguments may in many cases be very rationally drawn from thence, to that purpose. They may in themselves be very rational, probable arguments; and surely every argument may have influence on our minds, according to the degree of force it really and indeed has in[7] itself.

---

6. The sermon on Matt. 10:17 (n.d., [1731–32]) states as its doctrine "that the nature of man is so corrupted that he is become a very evil and hurtful creature." One reason for this corrupt disposition, JE maintains in the 3rd point under the doctrine, is that "man naturally has no other principle to direct and govern him in his actions, but only self-love."

7. MS: "is in."

But this I am satisfied of, that God never designed that the dependence of his church should be at all upon them. That is, that it was God's design, when he gave the church the Scriptures, so to make and dispose them, and to put so much into them, and in such a manner, that they should be completely sufficient of themselves, that they should hold forth to us things sufficient for us to know, and that they should be sufficiently there exhibited,[8] and that in all important matters, whether in doctrine or practice, the Scriptures should sufficiently explain themselves; so that we should have no need of joining unto them the writings of the fathers or church historians, and being acquainted with them, in order to our being directed and determined in any important matter: for this reason, because the church never was, is not, nor ever will be capable of being so well acquainted with them, as to be capable of judging by them, but only those of the church that are learned men. It is not sufficient that the teachers of the church can, and can tell others, unless they could lead their hearers to see and understand the evidence that arises from thence, that they may judge for themselves. 'Tis not sufficient ground for them to believe that there is such evidence from the fathers and church history, because that learned man that happens to [be] their teacher tells them so; because other learned men say otherwise. The Scriptures are not so large, but that all may be well acquainted with them; and ministers may so lead men's understandings, that they may see the evidence that may be fetched from thence, themselves.

This being not the design of providence, that any of our dependence should be upon any other ancient ecclesiastical writings besides the holy Scripture, there is not that safety in trusting to 'em. We han't that ground to expect that care of divine providence to order it, so that we should not be led into unavoidable mistakes, either about the affairs of those times, or in the conclusions we draw from them. We can't be so sure of the care of providence, that things should not come to us so, as that we should unavoidably be led into error about them; that the authors should not be corrupted, and yet we have no means to discover that they are so, or to determine wherein. Though the arguments we go upon may seem very probable, yet seeing that we han't the care of divine providence here to depend upon, we can't be so assured that [we] are not deceived in judging of the state, doctrines and practice of the primitive church, and the arguments we draw from thence concerning the doctrines and institutions of the apostles.

8. MS: "exhibited or with sufficient."

It seems to me that God would have our whole dependence be upon the Scriptures, because the greater our dependence is on the Word of God, the more direct and immediate is our dependence on God himself. The more absolute and entire our dependence on the Word of God is, the greater respect shall we have to that Word, the more shall we esteem and honor and prize it; and this respect to the Word of God will lead us to have the greater respect to God himself. If we were forced to join the fathers with the Scriptures, as though they were not sufficient of themselves, or not so sufficient as that we can well judge of some important things by them alone without the fathers, this will take off something of our respect to the Scriptures. And here will be a temptation, to exalt other writings to be sharers with God's Word in the respect we pay them.

God did not intend to cumber us with a rule of greater bulk than the Bible. 'Tis a mercy of God, an instance of his care of his church, that their rule is so fully and completely contained within so small a compass, that it is so compendious, that 'tis not beyond the capacity of ordinary Christians to manage it, and become well acquainted with it; though here is also room enough, for the most learned forever to exercise their study and scrutiny. They that introduce the fathers, and tack them to our Scripture rules—as not being enough, sufficiently to direct us in some important things without them—do us no kindness. They frustrate God's forementioned merciful care of his church; they make our rule so prodigiously bulky that [it] is to most of the church unmanageable, and what they can never be well acquainted with; and instead of making our way to the knowledge of truth more plain and direct, they make it more obscure and exceedingly roundabout. Our rule, instead of becoming the more easy and clear for it, becomes exceedingly the more difficult and perplexed.

Therefore, if the writings of the fathers and accounts of the primitive church seem to make it probable that the apostles taught such a doctrine or instituted such a practice, if the same also seems probable from Scripture, this is a confirmation that we understand the Scripture right. And if we have not seen it before in the Scripture, or have understood the Scriptures in time past otherwise, if we are anything doubtful about the mind of the Scripture in the matter, this may well put us upon searching the Scripture more diligently. But it must be the Scripture at last that must determine us. That way that the scale is turned by the Scriptures alone, that way must we be determined; and we ought to look upon the matter as undetermined, till it is determined by Scripture alone.

536. LORD'S DAY. The first day of the week being called in Scripture the Lord's day,[9] sufficiently marks it out to be that day of the week that is to be kept holy to God. God has been pleased to call it by his name. God's putting his name upon anything, or anything's being called by God's name, denoted the holiness of it and its appropriatedness to God. Thus God put his name upon the people of Israel of old (Num. 6:27); they were called by God's name, as 'tis said, II Chron. 7:14. They were called God's people, or the Lord's people; this denoted that they were a holy and peculiar people above all others. So the city Jerusalem was a city that was called by God's name (Jer. 25:29; Dan. 9:18–19); this denoted that [it] was a holy city, a place chosen of God for holy uses, above all other cities. So the temple is said to be an house that was called by God's name (I Kgs. 8:43, and often elsewhere); that is, it was called God's house, or the Lord's house. This denoted that it was a house appropriated to holy uses above all other houses, that it was a holy place. So the first day of the week's being called by God's name, being called God's day, or the Lord's day, denotes that 'tis a holy day, a day appropriated to holy uses above all other days in the week. The appellation of "Lord's day" denotes a day consecrated to an holy use and to the remembrance of Christ, as the appellation of "the Lord's Supper" denotes a supper so consecrated.[1]

That by which the sabbath day was distinguished from other days, consisted in two things, viz. God's hallowing of it, and his blessing it. But when God put his name upon anything, or appointed that it should be called after his name, it betokened both these things:

1. It betokened that God hallowed or sanctified it, and that it was holy. Thus the temple of old was called by God's name, and he had put his name there, so as by God's appointment, to be called the house of the Lord (I Kgs. 8:43); by this it was hallowed or sanctified, as appears by I Kgs 9:7, "And this house, which I have *hallowed* for my name." So of old the people of Israel were called by God's name (Jer. 14:9), and God had put his name on them (Num. 6:27), so that by God's appointment they were called *his people;* and hence they are said to be an holy nation or people (Ex. 19:6; Deut. 7:6, 14:2, 26:19). So Jerusalem was the city that was called by God's name; it was the place that God had chosen to put his name there (II Chron. 6:6; Jer. 25:29; Dan. 9:18), so that it was called the city of the

9. There is no Scripture passage that directly calls the first day of the week "the Lord's day." The statement "I was in the Spirit on the Lord's day" (Rev. 1:10) is understood to be a reference to "the first day of the week, when the disciples came together to break bread" (Acts 20:7).

1. The rest of the entry was written later, in space left below No. 462, and was designated as an addition to No. 536.

Lord, the city of the great King (Ps. 48:2; Matt. 5:35); hence 'tis so often called the holy city.

[2.] So also when God put his name upon anything, or appointed it should be called by his name, it betokened that God had blessed it, or had annexed his blessing to it. Ex. 20:24, "In all places where I record my name I will come unto thee, and I will bless thee." This was denoted by the people Israel's having God's name put upon them; as Num. 6 at the latter end, "On this wise shall ye bless the people: The Lord bless thee, and keep thee: the Lord make his face to shine upon thee, and be gracious unto thee: the Lord lift up his countenance upon thee, and give thee peace. And *they shall put my name upon the children of Israel, and I will bless them.*" Therefore the prophet makes use of this as an argument with God, that he would be with his people and bless them. Jer. 14:9, "Yet thou, O Lord, art in the midst of us, and we are *called by thy name;* leave us not." And so also the prophet Daniel, in the 9th chapter of his prophecy, 18th and 19th verses, uses this argument concerning both the people and city. So God's calling the temple by his name, denoted that God had annexed his blessing[2] to that house, so that there was especial encouragement that his blessing might be found there; which was to bless an *holy place,* in the same sense as God has blessed the sabbath, or *holy time.* See I Kgs. 8:43, "Hear thou in heaven thy dwelling place, and do according to all that the stranger calleth to thee for: that all the people of the earth may know thy name, to fear thee, as do thy people Israel; and that they may know that this house, which I have builded, is *called by thy name.*" And as God has promised that in *all places* where he puts his name that he will come to us and will [bless us], so by a parity of reason we may expect that in *all times* on which he puts his name (as he has on the Christian sabbath), in them he will come to us and will bless us.

And the following places do show that God's putting his name on anything did betoken that God had both hallowed and blessed it. So concerning the people of Israel, Deut. 28:9–11, "The Lord shall establish thee an *holy* people unto himself, as he hath sworn unto thee, if thou shalt keep the commandments of the Lord thy God, and walk in his ways. And all the people of the earth shall see that thou art *called by the name of the Lord; and they shall be afraid of thee. And the Lord shall make thee plenteous* in goods, in the fruit of thy body, and in the fruit of thy cattle, and in the fruit of thy ground which the Lord sware unto thy fathers to give thee." So concerning the temple, II Chron. 7:16, "For now have I chosen and *sanctified*

---

2. MS: "blessed."

this house, that *my name* may be there forever: *and mine eyes and my heart shall be there perpetually.*" So that since the Lord has been pleased to call the first day of the week by his name (Rev. 1:10), we may conclude that this is the day that the Lord hath blessed and hallowed; and therefore that he has appointed this day to be kept as a sabbath holy unto himself (Gen. 2:3).

537. GRACE. SPIRIT'S OPERATION. There is no gift or benefit that is so much in God, that is so much of himself, of his nature, that is so much a communication of the Deity, as grace is; 'tis as much a communication of the Deity, as light [is] a communication of the sun. 'Tis therefore fit that when it is bestowed, it should be so much the more immediately given, from himself and by himself. There is no good that we want or are capable of, so nextly in God; and therefore 'tis fit that there should be none so nextly from him.

As this may show us, why God will bestow this good more immediately and directly; so also, why he will especially exercise and manifest his sovereignty and free pleasure in bestowing of this gift. God's grace is eminently his own. God's creatures, the sun, moon and stars, etc., are his own to dispose of as he pleases; but with more eminent reason, that which is so nearly pertaining to the very nature of God, as his grace, the actings and influences of his own Spirit, the communications of his own beauty and his own happiness. God will therefore make his sovereign right here more eminently to appear, in the bestowment of this.

538. PROMISES. ENCOURAGEMENTS. Though there be no promise to any seekers of grace but gracious ones, yet there must be a greater probability of their conversion who seek—though not after a gracious manner, though they are not thorough and sufficiently resolved in seeking—than of others who wholly neglect their salvation; or not so great an unlikelihood of it, upon these accounts. The more persons seek their salvation, the less sin they commit; for there is[3] no other way of seeking, but only avoiding sins of omission and commission: and surely, the more persons sin and provoke God, the more are they exposed to his wrath, and so to be denied his mercy.

And again, we know that God's manner is to bestow his grace on men by outward means; otherwise, to what purpose is the Bible, and sabbath, and preaching, and sacraments, or doctrinal knowledge of religion? And

3. MS: "for this."

therefore, if persons are out of the way of those means, there is no likelihood of their receiving grace, because God bestows his grace by means. And so the more they are in the way of means, the more they attain of means, the more they are concerned with them, and the more they attend them, the more are they in the way of being met with by God, and receiving his grace, by those means.

539. MEANS OF GRACE. Grace is from God as immediately and directly as light is from the sun; and that notwithstanding the means that are improved, such as word, ordinances, etc. For though these are made use of, yet they have no influence to produce grace, either as causes or instruments, or any other way; and yet they are concerned in the affair of the production of grace, and are necessary in order to it.

They are concerned in this affair either immediately or remotely. As they are immediately concerned, it is not either as adjuvant causes or instruments, but only as by them the Spirit of God has an opportunity to cause acts of grace in the soul; and that grace, as immediately from him, may have an opportunity to act more fully and freely and suitably to the nature of things, i.e. to the nature and works of God, and our own state and nature, and the relation there is between God and us and others. The means of grace have to do in this affair of the production of grace, or any act of it, in our souls, no otherwise than as those means cause those effects in our souls; whereby there is an opportunity for grace to act, and to act suitably to the nature of things, as it proceeds and flows from the Holy Ghost. God don't see meet to infuse grace, where there is no opportunity for it to act, or to act in some measure suitably.

If it be inquired, what I mean by grace's acting suitably to the nature of things, and whether or no grace can act at all, and not act suitably to the nature of things: I answer, it acts suitably so far as it does act, as to the matter of the act; but it may be so, that it may act very partially and lamely, like a man that has but one leg or arm or a hand, [or is] without any feet, etc., and mayn't have any opportunity to act otherwise. Thus for instance, I don't know but it is possible for God to infuse a principle of grace into the heart of a man, that never has been informed that Christ is any more than a man; or believes that there are some things God can't do, and that he is sometimes mistaken; or has a notion of Father, Son and Holy Ghost as three distinct gods, friends one to another. But the actings of grace will be very unsuitable to the nature of things; it must act very lamely or monstrously, and so unsuitably, that I believe God ordinarily don't see meet that it should be, where there is no opportunity for it to act no better.

But that it may appear, how that outward means are no otherwise concerned in this affair of the production of grace, any otherwise than as by the effects these means cause in our souls, give opportunity for grace to act as infused or excited, we will consider what effects they do produce in our souls. And they are of three kinds: (1) They supply the mind with notions, or speculative ideas, of the things of religion. (2) They may have an effect upon mere natural reason, in a measure to gain the assent of the judgment. (3) They may have an effect upon the natural principles of heart, to give, in a degree, a sense of the natural good or evil of those things that they have a notion of, and so may accordingly move the heart with fear, etc. Now none of these effects are any way concerned in the existing or acting of grace in the heart, any otherwise than as they afford an opportunity for it to act, or to act more freely and suitably; as we shall show concerning each of them.

1. The means of grace, such as the Word and sacraments, supply the mind with notions, or speculative ideas, of the things of religion, and thus give an opportunity for grace to act in the soul; for hereby the soul is supplied with matter for grace to act upon, when God shall be pleased to infuse it. And this matter is by those means there upheld and so disposed, as that it may be more capable of, and fitted for, the acting of grace upon it in a suitable manner, or in a manner most agreeable to the nature of things. The matter which the principle of grace acts upon, is those notions or ideas that the mind is furnished with, of the things of religion; or of God, Christ, the future world, the saints, the attributes of God, the works of God, those things that Christ has done and suffered, etc. If there could be a principle of grace in the heart without these notions or ideas there, yet it could not act, because it could have no matter to act upon.

Now they are the means of grace, such as the Scriptures, instructions of parents and ministers, sacraments, etc., that supply our minds with those ideas and notions: and the end of these means is to supply our minds with them, and to supply us with them more fully, and to revive and maintain those ideas in our minds; and that the attention of our mind to them may be more strong, that they may be, as much as may be, not only habitually, but actually existing in our minds, and that [those] ideas, as to their actual existence, may be clear and lively, and that they may be disposed in the most advantageous order. And thus the means of grace have no influence to work grace, but only give such notions to our minds, and so disposed, as to give opportunity for grace to act, when God shall infuse it; as Elijah, by laying fuel upon the altar, and laying it in order, gave opportunity for the fire to burn, when God should send it down from heaven. Here,

(1) It is needful, in order to give this opportunity, that these notions should be true; for those that are false ben't proper fuel for the fire. A false notion gives no opportunity for grace to act, but on the contrary, will hinder its acting. Thus if a man has been taught that God is a foolish and unjust being, these notions of folly or injustice in God, give no opportunity for a principle of grace to act towards God; but on the contrary, tend to prevent. Therefore, those outward means that do most exhibit the truth to our minds, give us the greatest advantage for the obtaining grace.

(2) The more fully we are supplied with these notions, the greater opportunity has grace to act, and to act more suitably to the nature of things when God infuses it, because it has more objects to act upon, and one object illustrates another; so that we han't only more notions, but all our notions are the more clear, and more according to truth. So that this is another thing that means do: they more and more fully and purely supply our minds with matter for grace to act upon. Here therefore, is the benefit of frequent and abundant instructions; here is the benefit of study and meditation, and comparing spiritual things with spiritual.

(3) The more lively these notions are, the more strong the ideas, the greater opportunity for grace to act if infused. Surely, if the existence of these ideas gives an opportunity, then the more perfect the actual existence of them is, the greater opportunity. The stronger and more lively the impression with which the ideas actually exists, the more perfect is its existence; as when we look on the sun, our idea of it has a more perfect existence, than when we only think of it by imagination, because the impression is much stronger. Therefore here is the advantage of clear, convincing instructions, of setting forth divine things in a clear light; here is the advantage of divine eloquence, in instructing, warning, counseling, etc.: they serve as they give more strong and lively impressions of the truth. The stronger reasons and arguments are offered to confirm any truth, or to show the eligibleness of any practice, it serves as it gives those ideas that are the matter that grace acts upon, and disposes them in such order, sets them in such light, that grace, if in the heart, shall have the greater opportunity to act more fully and more according to its tendency, upon them. Reasonings and pathetical counsels and warnings do give an opportunity for grace another way also, by the effect they have upon natural principles; of which I shall speak by and by.

(4) The oftener these notions or ideas are revived, and the more they are upheld in the soul, the greater opportunity for the Spirit of God to infuse grace, because he hath more opportunity, hath opportunity more constantly. The more constantly the matter for grace to work upon is upheld,

the more likely are persons to receive grace of the Spirit. 'Tis the wisest way to maintain the opportunity, for we know not when the Spirit's time is.

2. Means may have an effect upon our reason, in a degree, to gain the assent of that. (Note: By mere reason, I mean that wherein there is merely the exercise of the speculative faculty, wholly distinct from and independent of a sense of heart, wherein is not only the exercise of the speculative understanding, but also of the disposition, inclination, or will of the soul. Spiritual understanding includes this, as we have shown elsewhere. See No. 540.)[4] But that effect which means have upon mere reason, is no otherwise concerned in the affair of the production of grace in the soul, [than] only as hereby the soul is so prepared for it, that grace, when communicated from the Spirit of God, will have a better opportunity to act. For the judgment of mere reason, concurring with that conviction which arises from the heart's sense of the divine excellency of spiritual things, strengthens the assurance; and the mind's having the stronger and more confirmed belief of the truth of spiritual things, love and other graces flow out the more freely and fully towards those objects that are thus believed to be real. The more fully realized the being of the objects of grace's actings, the greater[5] opportunity will there be for the new nature to exert itself towards them.

The knowledge of the rational arguments that are brought to prove the truth of religion, whether they have any effect upon mere natural reason or no, prepares the mind for grace another way: viz. as hereby the mind has ideas and notions set in that order, has those arguments present, that when grace has removed prejudices and given eyes to see, they will see the connection and relation of the ideas, and the force of the arguments. But this belongs to the foregoing way, wherein means give opportunity for grace to act.

3. The third effect of means is upon the natural principles of heart, to give in a degree a sense of the natural good or evil of those things that the mind has a notion, or speculative idea, of, and so may accordingly move the heart with fear, and desire, etc.; and by this means also, the soul may be the better prepared for grace. For these effects upon the natural prin-

---

4. Although the reference to No. 540 is a later addition, the preceding note is integral to the text of the entry. That spiritual understanding includes the exercise of both reason and will is a frequent theme in JE's writings; see, for example, Nos. 397 and 489 (*Works, 13*, 462–63, 533). Prior to the composition of No. 539, JE had also explored the difference between speculative and spiritual understanding in two sermons, *A Spiritual Understanding of Divine Things Denied to the Unregenerate* (I Cor. 2:14) and *Profitable Hearers of the Word* (Matt. 13:23). See *Works, 14*, 67–96, 243–77.

5. MS: "the are the greater."

ciples of heart remaining and existing with the supernatural principle of heart when infused, the actings of the soul may be greater and more suitable, and the effects that follow greater, than otherwise would be. Thus if a person has been deeply possessed with a sense of the dreadfulness of divine wrath and with great fear of it, when afterwards the soul comes to have a sense of the grace and love of God, this appears the more glorious, because the mind is already possessed with a deep sense of the dreadfulness of that evil, which this grace and love delivers from; and the preciousness of love is illustrated by the dreadfulness of the opposite, wrath. God is more loved for his grace and goodness to him. And then grace more naturally exercises itself in awful and humble reverence, which is most suitable to our nature and state, and the relation we stand in to God: for being in a mind that was before prepared by so deep a sense of the dreadfulness of God's anger, these effects upon natural principles direct the stream of grace into that channel.

Thus we have shown how that means are concerned in the affair of the production of grace. They are also concerned in another way, more remotely: (1) as they restrain from sin, whereby God might be provoked to withhold grace; (2) as means excite to attend and use means. Thus men are persuaded by the Word to hear and read the Word, and to meditate upon it, to keep sabbaths, to attend sacraments, etc.; counsels of parents may persuade to a diligent use of means. See No. 542.[6]

Corol. 1. Hence it follows, that attending and using means of grace is no more than a waiting upon God for his grace, in the way wherein he is wont to bestow [it]; 'tis watching at wisdom's gates, and waiting at the posts of her doors.

Corol. 2. By what has been said, we see the necessity of means of grace in order to the obtaining grace; for without means there could be no opportunity for grace to act, there could be no matter for grace to act upon. God gives grace immediately; but he don't give immediately and by inspiration, those ideas and speculative notions, that are the matter that grace acts upon. Neither will God give grace, where there is no opportunity for it to act.

540. SPIRITUAL UNDERSTANDING. Remember, when speaking of the creation of man, and the state and nature with which he was created, to distinguish between mere speculative and notional understanding, and

6. No. 542 lists a third way "that means are more remotely concerned in the affair of the production of grace" (see below, p. 89).

that which implies a sense of heart, or arises from it, wherein is exercised not merely the faculty of understanding, but the other faculty of will, or inclination, or the heart; and to make a distinction between the speculative faculty and the heart; and then to show how many principles of heart God created man with, viz. natural and supernatural principles.

541. SPIRIT'S OPERATION. In the order of beings in the natural world, the more excellent and noble any being is, the more visible and immediate hand of God is there in bringing them into being; and the most noble of all, and that which is most akin to the nature of God, viz. the soul of man, is most immediately and directly from him: so that here, second causes have no causal influence at all. Second causes have something to do in bringing the body into being; but they have no influence here, but the soul is directly breathed from God (Heb. 12:9, Eccles. 12:7, Zech. 12:1). And so it is in the moral and spiritual world; the most noble and excellent gift and qualification, wherein [lies] the glory and happiness of that most noble creature, the soul of man, is immediately from God. This is the excellency and dignity of this excellent and noble being, the soul, of which God is the immediate Father. All notional knowledge and outward virtue without this, is but the body without the spirit; 'tis the soul of all virtue and religious knowledge.

542. MEANS OF GRACE. See No. 539. (3) Another way[7] that means are more remotely concerned in the affair of the production of grace, is that in the use of them persons do seek and strive for grace; and this prepares the heart for it. Earnestly seeking and taking pains for grace, prepares the heart highly to prize it, and make much of it when obtained; and their natural powers and principles are hereby already awakened, and got into such a way of acting, that they are the more prepared to concur with grace.

543. LORD'S DAY. It is evident by Matt. 24:20, "Pray that your flight be not on the sabbath day," that it was the design of Christ, that a day should be kept in the Christian church as a sabbath; and also that the Lord's day is well called by the name of the sabbath, as well as the Jewish sabbath.

544. CHRISTIAN RELIGION. It seems to me a kind of unreasonable thing, to suppose that there should be a God without any word of his; that there

7. In the third to last paragraph of No. 539, JE lists two ways in which means are remotely concerned in the production of grace. The present entry constitutes a third (see above, p. 88).

should be a God, an intelligent voluntary being, that has so much concern with [us], and with whom we have infinitely more concern than with any other being, and yet that he should never speak. It is a property of all intelligent beings, that God has made in his own image, to speak; they are hereby distinguished from inferior creatures. It is therefore strange that any should imagine that the supreme intelligence should never speak, that there should be no word of his.

545. HELL TORMENTS. See No. 491. We are taught by the Scripture that God will punish wicked men, to show the dreadfulness of his wrath and the greatness of his power, that they shall be punished with everlasting destruction from the glory of God's power. And it seems by the Scripture that God will show his power upon wicked men, as being enraged, and as [an] enraged man lays out his strength—it so seems by Nahum at the beginning; Deut. 29:20, 32:22, 40–42; Rev. 19:15, and many other places. As Mr. Halyburton observes, "the power of man produces greater effects, when anger and fury make him strain as it were every sinew and nerve, than when he is cool and in a sedate composed frame: as Samson in such a case pulled down the pillars of the house."[8]

And when the wicked at the day of judgment see the immense and terrible greatness and awful majesty of God, and also see how exceedingly he abhors sin, and how he is provoked with them, as it will then appear; they will expect it, their own hearts will forebode it, that now their sufferings must be answerable to that great power, excited by fierceness of wrath. When they shall see the awful majesty of God, they will doubtless fear the more; but Moses tells us, that according to his fear, so is his wrath [Ps. 90:11]. God's wrath, which they shall experience, will doubtless be at least in the compounded proportion of that manifestation of majesty and of abhorrence of their sins, which they shall then see.

One thing that is implied in that fear or terribleness of God that Moses speaks of, according to which his wrath will be, consists in that appearance of power and might that there is in God. God's wrath will be according to the manifestation or glory of God's power, at the day of judgment. Now the punishment of wicked men don't answer this part of God's fear or terribleness by its eternity; the terribleness of God's might don't so much appear in making their punishment eternal,[9] as in the degree of suffering.

8. Thomas Halyburton, *The Great Concern for Salvation* (London, 1722), p. 158.
9. MS: "eternity."

I know it will be ready to [be] objected, that such an extreme degree of suffering is incredible, that 'tis incredible that [God] should ever make any creature so miserable. But there is no arguing from hence; for God will have no respect or consideration at all of the welfare of those that are damned, nor any concern lest they should suffer too much—they are the godly only, that God afflicts in measure (Is. 27:8, Jer. 30:11)—but only that justice should take place. God will cast upon them and not spare; he will have no pity upon them; he will stir up all his wrath; he will utterly forsake them; they shall be "given over unto death" (Ps. 118:18). The creature will be utterly lost and thrown away of God. As to any concern God will have for it, God will have a concern for justice, but no sort of concern for the creature. This is evident, because he makes their sufferings eternal. We can therefore make no guess to what degree they will suffer, by that; nor can we say to what degree they will not suffer. I can't say, from any concern that God will have for them lest they should [be] too much tormented, any otherwise than merely, that they ben't punished beyond strict justice, that their torment won't rise more beyond any torment in this world than any man can rise by multiplication of numbers. No degree of misery whatever is incredible, merely because 'tis so great, or that God can't find it in his heart to inflict so great misery. But if it be incredible upon any account, it must be because 'tis beyond what severe justice will allow of. The truth is, those that die in sin, there is no mortal can tell to what degree they shall or shall not be tormented.

The exceedingness of the misery of the damned, may be argued from the fears and amazing expectations of wicked men at the end of the world, from those things that they then shall see and hear. If we now do but see a flash of lightning and hear a clap of thunder, or feel the shock of an earthquake, what awful things do they seem to suggest to us, of the anger and displeasure of God. If we hear a severe clap of thunder, and imagine any person aimed at by it, and it directed upon him in divine wrath, what a terrible apprehension does that suggest to our minds of that wrath, and of the inexpressible misery of the person that is subject to it, if he be in the meantime sensible. And if we do but behold and hear a hurricane, or great whirlwind, or a mighty storm of hail or rain, or behold and hear the falls of a great river, or the raging of a sea in a storm, or of the flames when only a house is on fire, and do but imagine in our own minds, that this is from divine wrath, or that they are significations and emblems of that wrath: what an apprehension will it give us of the misery [of] him against whom this wrath rages.

What amazing fears, then, will the wicked have begotten in their minds, of their approaching misery—when the earth shall be shaken out of its place; when God shall arise and terribly shake the earth even from its foundation, and the mountains shall totter and sink and be overturned in God's anger, and the rocks shall be thrown down; yea, when the mountains shall skip like rams, and little hills like lambs, and shall be cast into the midst of the sea, and the waves shall roar, and heaven and earth shall be all rent in pieces with amazing thunders; when the heavens shall be passing away with a great noise, and they shall see not only a house or city, but the world in a conflagration immensely greater and fiercer than any fire that now we see: and all this they shall know to be significations of the anger of God against them, whose majesty and terrible greatness they shall see at the same time, as he appears in the clouds of heaven. What expectations will these things give them of misery; what fears will they beget in them! Christ tells us that the extraordinary things that will be seen, will cause men's hearts to fail them for fear; but according to God's fear, so is his wrath. They shall find it as dreadful as these things foreboded.

They shall always to eternity continue to see such amazing significations of God's wrath; for the heavens and earth which now are, that are reserved and kept in store on purpose against the day of their perdition, will eternally be wracked and rent and in flames. What an apprehension would the sight of such strong, mighty and raging flames of such a great furnace, suggest to the mind of a beholder of wrath; but the wrath felt will be answerable thereto.

The heat of so great a fire must needs be immensely great. When a house is on fire, the heat in the midst of it is exceedingly beyond what is in a small fire; but how fierce will be the flames when heaven and earth shall be in a conflagration! The apostle Peter says, "the elements shall melt with fervent heat" (II Pet. 3:10).

Corol. Neither doth God care how much blessedness the saints enjoy; he is not careful lest they should enjoy too much, or lest their enjoyments should be too exquisitely delighting.

546. SEPARATE STATE. HELL TORMENTS. HEAVEN. It may possibly seem strange that the torments of the wicked should be so great, while they are only in prison in order to their judgment and punishment. But there is no other difference in God's dealing with sinners in this respect, from the treatment of malefactors by human judges and rulers, but what naturally arises from the difference of the nature and qualifications of the judges, and the difference of the ends of judgment. Men commit supposed malefactors to prison in order to a determination whether they are guilty or no,

the matter not being yet sufficiently determined. But God, who imprisons wicked men, certainly and infallibly understands whether they are guilty or not; they are not imprisoned that it may be determined whether they are guilty, but because it is determined and known that they are. The end of human judgment is to find out whether a man be guilty or no; but the end of divine judgment is only to declare their guilt, and God's righteousness in their punishment. The guilt of wicked men is infallibly determined when they die: it is fit therefore, that they should be bound in chains of darkness and misery; it is fit that[1] God's enemies, and rebels against him, and the objects of his eternal wrath should be imprisoned in dark and dismal recesses, while they are reserved for execution; 'tis fit that the prison of the objects of divine wrath, should be a doleful, horrid abode.

So it is fit that those who are his elect, that he hath chosen to make the objects of his love, should be reserved in a paradise in order to that. 'Tis fit that she that God hath chosen for his spouse, and his choice of whom he has declared, should be reserved in a blissful abode, while she is kept against the time of marriage. 'Tis fit that in the meantime she should have blessed communion and conversation with God. The glorification of the souls of the saints at their death is a marriage, in comparison of their conversion, and their state of grace here; but 'tis but an espousal, a state of conversation with Christ in order to marriage, compared with the glory that shall be after the resurrection. So the state of the damned separate spirits, though it be inexpressibly doleful, yet 'tis but as a confinement in chains and a dark dungeon in order to execution, in comparison of their misery after the day of judgment. See note on Matt. 18:34.[2]

547. CHRISTIAN RELIGION. GOD'S END IN CREATION AND PROVIDENCE. IMMORTALITY OF THE SOUL. There is doubtless some design that God is pursuing, and scheme that he is carrying on, in the various changes and revolutions that from age to age happen in the world; there is some certain great design to which providence subordinates all the successive changes that come to pass in the state of affairs of mankind. All revolutions from the beginning of the world to the end, are doubtless but various parts of one scheme, all conspiring for the bringing to pass the great

---

1. MS: "that the prison where."

2. In this "Blank Bible" note JE quotes Phillip Doddridge's *Family Expositor: or, a Paraphrase and Version of the New Testament: with Critical Notes* (6 vols. London, 1739–56) on the text to the effect that "'imprisonment is a much greater punishment in the eastern parts of the world than here'" (Vol. 2, § 95, p. 33, n. *h*). JE apparently thinks this contrast in punishments comparable to that of the damned before and after the day of judgment.

event which is ultimately in view. And the scheme will not be finished, nor the design fully accomplished, the great event fully brought to pass, till the end of the world and the last revolution is brought about. The world, it is most evident, is not an everlasting thing; it will have an end, and God's end in making and governing the world will not be fully obtained, nor his scheme be finished, till the end of the world comes. If it were, he would put an end to it sooner; for God won't continue the world, won't continue to uphold it, and dispose and govern it, and cause changes and revolutions in it, after he has nothing further that he aims at by it.

God don't fully obtain his design in any one particular state that the world has been in at one time, but in the various successive states that the world is in, in different ages, connected in a scheme. 'Tis evident that he don't fully obtain his end, his design, in any one particular state that the world has ever been in; for if so, we should have no change. But God is continually causing revolutions. Providence makes a continual progress, and continually is bringing forth things new in the state of the world, and very different from what ever were before; he removes one that he may establish another. And perfection will not be obtained till the last revolution, when God's design will be fully reached.

Nor yet are the past states of the world abolished by revolutions because they are in vain, or don't do anything towards promoting his design in creating the world; if so, providence would never have ordered them, the world never would have been in such a state. There remains therefore no other way, but that the various successive states of the world do in conjunction, or as connected in a scheme, together attain God's great design.

Corol. 1. Hence it may be argued, that the intelligent beings of the world are everlasting, and will remain after the world comes to an end. If the perception and intelligence of the world don't remain after the world comes to an end, then as soon as ever the world comes to an end, the world and all that pertains to it, and its various successive states and revolutions, the whole absolutely ceases and come to nothing; nothing remains of it all. It is at once all as if nothing had been; so that when the world and all its revolutions are finished, nothing is obtained. As soon as ever the last revolution, or the last part of the scheme is finished—when we have but now supposed God first perfectly reaches his great design, and accomplishes what he had in view in making the world—he reaches nothing, he accomplishes nothing; but only is just where he was before he made the world, or so much as entered upon his scheme. There is nothing remains that can be supposed to be the thing reached or brought forth, as the great thing aimed at in all that God had for so many ages been doing: the great event that is struck out at last, in the consummation of all things, is the same nothing from which things began! There is no benefit, nor glory, nor honor to God himself, nor to any other, remains. God has no benefit that he enjoys, remaining; he has gained no knowledge, no new idea, by all that has happened; there remains no declarative glory of God, nor any benefit to any other being, but all is just as it was before God set out in his work. So that at the end of the world, at the close of all things, when the great design of the whole scheme is to be fully attained, nothing at all is attained. See Nos. 867, 1006.

Corol. 2. It is an argument of the truth of the Christian revelation; for there is nothing else that informs what God's design [is in] that series of revolutions and events that are brought to pass in the [world], what end he seeks, and what scheme he has laid out. (Agreeable to the challenge God makes to the gods and prophets and teachers of the heathen world, Is. 41:22–23.) 'Tis most fit that the intelligent beings of the world should be made acquainted with it; they are the beings that are principally concerned in it. The thing that is God's great design, is something concerning them; and the revolutions by which it is to be brought to pass, are revolutions among them and in their state. The state of [the] inanimate, unperceiving part of the world, is nothing regarded any otherwise, than in a subserviency to the perceiving or intelligent [part]. And then 'tis most rational to suppose, that God should reveal the design he has [been] carrying on to his rational creatures: that as God has made them capable of it, they may [be] actively falling in with it and promoting it, and acting herein as the subjects and friends of God.

The Christian revelation gives us a most rational account of the design of God in his providential disposition of things, a design most worthy of an infinitely wise, holy, and perfect being; and of the way and means of God's accomplishment of it. It gives us an account of the principal parts of the scheme, in the principal providences from the beginning of the world to the end of it, and particularly of the manner how all shall be perfected in the consummation of all things.

548. CONVICTION. See sermon on Matt. 25:8, first particular under the second doctrine. HUMILIATION. See second particular under second doctrine.[3]

---

3. The second doctrine of the sermon on Matt. 25:8 (n.d., [1731–32]) states that "when Christ comes, wicked men's hopes of salvation and seeming evidence of conversion will at once totally vanish and disappear." At this time sinners will be "thoroughly convinced of their sin and guilt," and because of this new state of conviction they will, JE states as the first particular, "know they never saw the sufficiencies of Christ"; and as the second, "see the insufficiency of their own righteousness to remove that guilt."

549. CHURCH DISCIPLINE. RULING ELDERS. See my note on I Cor. 12:28. POWER OF THE BRETHREN. See note on II Cor. 2:6.[4]

550. HELL TORMENTS. The devils, their tormenting wicked men in another world, seems to be represented by the unclean fowls of the air and beasts of the earth preying upon men's dead bodies; which was a punishment often threatened to ungodly, accursed men.

551. LORD'S DAY. The ancient sabbath was to be in imitation and commemoration of God's resting from the work of creation, and his being refreshed, and his being pleased and refreshed at the beholding of his work when finished, when he saw it all very good (Ex. 31:17). But the ground of that refreshment was soon at an end when man fell, and the world that he had created very good was so totally ruined, and God was so burdened and wearied with the sin and corruption of the world, that instead of continuing to rejoice and be refreshed in the view of it, he repented that he had created it, and it grieved him at the heart (Gen. 6:6).

It was fit therefore, that that day, that was kept in remembrance of that rest and refreshment of the Creator which so soon ceased, should cease and give place to another day of rest and joy, kept in remembrance of God's glorious and never failing rest and refreshment, which he had when he had completed the restoration of the fallen, corrupted world. Therefore 'tis said, "Be ye glad and rejoice *forever* in that which I create: for, behold, I create Jerusalem a rejoicing, and her people a joy" [Is. 65:18].

552. RESURRECTION. CHRISTIAN RELIGION. The doctrine of the general resurrection at the end of the world, upon many accounts seems to me a most credible doctrine. There are a multitude of resemblances of it in nature and providences, which I doubt not were designed on purpose to be types of it. It seems credible upon this account, that the work of the Redeemer is [a] wholly restoring work from beginning to end; and it seems rational to think, that he would therefore go through with it, and would make a *thorough* restoration, and repair all the ruins that were

---

4. In the "Blank Bible" note on I Cor. 12:28, JE argues against the office of ruling elder. Although in the early church Christ "marked out" persons for "work in the church" by giving them "miraculous gifts," this does not mean that "there are so many distinct standing offices in the church as there were extraordinary gifts." The "Blank Bible" note on II Cor. 2:6, which contains a cross-reference to the previous note, similarly argues for a limitation of lay power. The text may "be rightly translated 'of many' rather than 'before many,'" JE maintains, "yet it might be 'of many,' and not by the whole congregation by virtue of any power vested in the brethren."

brought upon the world by sin. 'Tis the glory of the Restorer, that he appears as an all-sufficient and complete Restorer.

553. END OF THE CREATION. There are many of the divine attributes that, if God had not created the world, never would have had any exercise: the power of God, the wisdom and prudence and contrivance of God, and the goodness and mercy and grace of God, and the justice of God. It is fit that the divine attributes should have exercise. Indeed God knew as perfectly, that there were these attributes fundamentally in himself before they were in exercise, as since; but God, as he delights in his own excellency and glorious perfections, so he delights in the exercise of those perfections.

'Tis true that there was from eternity that act in God within himself and towards himself, that was the exercise of the same perfection of his nature. But it was not the same kind of exercise: it virtually contained it, but there was not explicitly the same exercise of his perfection. God, who delights in the exercise of his own perfection, delights in all the kinds of its exercise. That eternal act or energy of the divine nature within him, whereby he infinitely loves and delights in himself, I suppose does imply fundamentally goodness and grace towards creatures, if there be that occasion which infinite wisdom sees fit. But God, who delights in his own perfection, delights in seeing those exercises of his perfection explicitly in being, that are fundamentally implied.

554. WISDOM OF GOD IN THE WORK OF REDEMPTION. ANGELS. 'Tis probable that the angels in heaven had notice of the election of men before the fall; and that God, when he created this lower world in their view, and created man the inhabitant of it, he might give to those spectators some intimations of his design with them; and that they then knew that God's delights were with the sons of men, and that they were to be a peculiarly favored race. It seems probable (as I have elsewhere said),[5] that it was some intimations of the peculiar favor that God had to them, and the dignity to which he designed to advance the human nature above theirs, that was the occasion of the rebellion of some of them.

They therefore, knowing God's love to them, and election of them, before they fell, were doubtless greatly surprised when men fell and had sinned against God: for they could no way conceive how it was possible now, consistent with the rule which God had fixed with men and with the

5. No. 320. For a similar cross-reference, see above, No. 515, p. 58.

glory of God, for God now to fulfill his own decree, and accomplish upon men those eternal designs of love, that he had given them a general intimation of. They were all astonished. Such a thought, as that God should be frustrated and overreached by his enemy the devil, was what they could not entertain; but yet they could not conceive of any way for God honorably to fulfill his declared design in creating men. They had seen that the angels that sinned, perished without remedy; and it never entered into their thoughts, that there was any other way for a sinning creature. They concluded and took it for certain, that if any creature sinned, they must necessarily perish eternally. They could no way conceive how the wisdom of God could help out in this case. They were all, the wisest angel in heaven was perfectly, nonplused. They could not [but] have their thoughts excited and set to work to the utmost, to think it could be. Man must be happy, and the object of that high favor of God, notwithstanding this fall; for it was the decree of God, and that they knew. This must necessarily put every angel upon a trial of the utmost of his own thought and wisdom. And everyone soon found that they could devise nothing; it was a thing sealed with seven seals. God did as it were give them the trial first, as is said of opening the sealed book in the Revelation [Rev. 5:1–9].

Thus were they prepared for the greater admiration of the wisdom of God, when God should come to reveal his own counsels respecting this matter. They were prepared by this astonishment, for a greater astonishment, when God should come to reveal the immense depths of his own wisdom in this affair.

Probably it was kept secret from 'em for ages, that they might have the more thorough trial of their wisdom. And they saw that God still after the fall was not disappointed—he had not let fall his design—but that he still did intend men, though fallen, for that peculiar favor and honor that he had spoken of. They perceived, by what God said to our first parents, that he had a design of redeeming of them; and how earnestly did they wait, to see how God would accomplish it! And as God gradually gave further and further intimations of his design and the manner of it, how engaged their attention, and how deep and fixed their contemplation! These things the angels desired to look into (I Pet. 1:12), as was typified by the posture of the cherubim over the ark, fixedly and as in deep attention looking down into it.

It seems to me, that they never had the mystery fully unfolded to 'em till Christ's incarnation; and then was this contrivance, and the accomplishment of it, seen of angels (I Tim. 3:16); and then was made known "to principalities and powers in heavenly places the manifold wisdom of

God, according to the eternal purpose which he purposed in Christ Jesus our Lord" (Eph. 3:10–11). They were the more filled with admiration when they had this contrivance revealed to them, that they not only had it unfolded to 'em, but see it accomplished.

And how great was their admiration, when they not only see men restored, but that such was the divine contrivance that it brought forth good out of evil, made it only an occasion of their far greater glory. How great was their admiration, when they saw Satan in everything so totally baffled, and become a means of his own confusion in that wherein he thought he had disappointed God and ruined mankind.

555. HEAVEN. SEPARATE STATE. ANGELS. The saints are spectators of God's providences relating to his church here below. See note on Heb. 6:15.[6] One end of the creation of the angels, and giving them such great understanding, was that they might be fit witnesses and spectators of God's works here below, and might behold all parts of the divine scheme, and see how it was accomplished in the divine works and revolutions from age to age. Mortal men, they see but a very little; they have a very imperfect view of God's providences in the world while they live, and they don't live long enough to see more than a very small part of the scheme. God saw fit that there should be creatures of very great discerning and comprehensive understandings, that [should] be spectators of the whole series of the works of God; and therefore they were created in the beginning of the creation, that they might behold the whole series, from the beginning to the consummation of all things. And therefore we read that they sang together and shouted for joy, when they beheld God forming this lower world (Job 38:7). So we are taught that they were spectators of the work of redemption and the progress of it (I Tim. 3:16, Eph. 3:10). And as God has made them to be spectators of the great works of divine wisdom and power, so that their minds may be the more engaged and entertained, God allows them to have a subordinate hand in them, and he improves them as his messengers and servants in bringing them to pass.

Hence I argue that undoubtedly the souls of departed saints are also spectators of the same things, for they go to be in heaven with the angels. The angels carry 'em to paradise; and we can't suppose that they leave 'em there, and that the only opportunity they have to converse with an-

6. In this "Blank Bible" note JE states that Heb. 6:15 "is an evidence that the saints in heaven are acquainted with the affairs of the church here on earth, and also that a considerable part of their happiness consists in seeing the dispensations and works of God's grace towards the church on earth, and the discovering of his glory therein."

gels, from their death till the end of the world, is while they are in their way from earth to Abraham's bosom. The saints, even on earth, have from time to time been admitted to converse with angels; and shall they not, much more familiarly, when they go to be with Christ in paradise?

The spirits of just men made perfect are reckoned as of the same society with the angels, and as dwelling with them in Mount Zion, the city of the living God, the heavenly Jerusalem [Heb. 12:22–23]; which the Apostle elsewhere calls "Jerusalem which is above" [Gal. 4:26], by which he doubtless means, in heaven. Why should not the saints go to be with the angels, when they go from their bodies? Seeing they are of the same family, the angels are their brethren; why should they [be] kept separate from the angels, who are their brethren in the same family? As the angel in the Revelation tells John, he is of his brethren (Rev. 22:9). And if any would understand that not of a proper angel, but the departed soul of one of the saints, then will it make much to our present purpose. If one of them was sent to reveal to John the providences of God relating to the church on earth, then doubtless departed saints are acquainted with them. But that the departed saints do dwell in heaven with the angels, is more evident because we learn by Eph. 3:15 that the whole family is in heaven and in earth. Departed saints are doubtless of the family; the angels, they also are of the family; saints and angels are all gathered together in one in Christ (Eph. 1:10; and Col. 1:16, 20). But none can doubt, but that heaven is the dwelling place of the angels.

It is no privilege to be continued in this world, to have opportunity to see here the success of the gospel and glorious things accomplished in the church. If this had been any privilege, the man Christ Jesus should have been allowed it. He saw very little success while he was here, of all that he did and suffered; the success was chiefly after he went to heaven, and there he can see it better than if he were here. And this is part of his promised glory, that he there sees the success of his redemption, and his own kingdom carried on and flourishing in this world (Is. 53:10–12). And 'tis the will of Christ, that departed saints should be with him where he is, that they may behold this glory of Christ which the Father gives him, and be partakers of him in it (John 17:24).

556. HADES. If the souls of departed saints are in any state of existence at all, between their death and resurrection, 'tis unreasonable to suppose that they should be all that while kept away from Christ; especially considering what Christ has said (John 12:26, and 14:3, and 17:24), and also considering what the Apostle said, when speaking of dying, that he had

"a desire to depart, and to be with Christ" [Philip. 1:23]. If it be said, that the Apostle did not mean that he should be with Christ's human nature, but if it was his divine nature he meant, yet he was doubtless to be with the divine nature of Christ in a manner very different [from] what the saints are here: he was to be where were the glorious manifestations of the presence of Christ in his divine nature. And then, if the departed saints are where they behold and enjoy the glorious presence of Christ in his divine nature, why should they[7] not be admitted to be where is his human nature? When they enjoy the glorious and immediate manifestations of his presence in one nature, and that in his original and highest nature, why should they not behold [him] in the other inferior nature?

557. ETERNITY OF HELL TORMENTS. It is to be considered that the wicked in hell will forever continue sinning, exercising malice, and blaspheming, etc.; and 'tis surely therefore no wonder, that God should forever continue punishing. And if any think that 'tis incredible, that God should leave any to continue forever sinning as a punishment of their sins here, as a judicial consequence of their sins, let it be considered what have been the judicial consequences of that one sin of our first parents, their eating of the forbidden fruit: the corruption of the nature of all mankind, and all the actual sins that ever have been committed in the world of mankind, and all the temporal calamities that the world has suffered, the corruption and ruin the world has suffered, and all the punishments of sin in another world, whether they be eternal or no. If it be credible, that all these things should be the judicial consequences of that one sin, I don't see why it should seem incredible, that God should eternally give a man up to sin for his own sin. See No. 559.

558. DEGREE OF HELL TORMENTS. When we think of the extreme degree of hell torments, we are ready to be shocked by it, and are ready to say within ourselves, "How can such an infliction consist with the merciful nature of God?" But the saints in heaven, though they'll have a more adequate and lively idea of the greatness of their misery, yet will not be at all shocked by it; and very much because they'll also, at the same time, have a truer and more lively apprehension of the evil of sin, two ways, viz. 1. as they'll see the odiousness of sin in general, and 2. as they'll see how great the corruption of nature is, and principle of enmity against God that is in the hearts of the sufferers, and how great acts of sin it extends to, or

7. MS: "why they should."

how great sins that is the principle or seed of in their hearts. For their circumstances will try them, and cause corruption most violently to rage and to show itself, what it is; and it will seem no way cruel in God to inflict such extreme sufferings on such extremely wicked creatures.

559. ETERNITY OF HELL TORMENTS. See No. 557. If it be just in God, in judgment for one sin to lead[8] to another, and yet just for him to punish both, then is it just with him to leave men to continue in sin to all eternity? For as long as they continue sinning, they continue deserving to be punished; and therefore, by the hypothesis, it still continues to be just to leave 'em to commit other sins, and so *in infinitum.*

560. WISDOM OF GOD IN THE WORK OF REDEMPTION. SATAN DEFEATED. Says one, "The old serpent thought, by means of the woman he had undone all forever, to all intents and purposes; whereas behold, the woman by her seed is to bruise his head, and restore all according to the eternal scheme."—Blackwell's *Schema Sacrum.*[9]

561. GOSPEL, NO ENCOURAGEMENT TO SIN. See sermon on Gal. 2:17.[1]

562. ETERNITY OF HELL TORMENTS. See sermon on Rev. 19:2–3.[2]

563. HUMILIATION. 'Tis God's manner, upon extraordinary humiliations, to give extraordinary comforts. Hence persons have thought, that there is a humiliation goes always before conversion: for the first extraordinary comforts that have been observed, they call their conversion; and it is generally observed, that extraordinary humiliation goes before it.

564. CHRISTIAN RELIGION. Reasonableness of the Christian doctrine of the end of the world, and day of judgment, and the state of man that will succeed it—because this is a state of confusion, the wicked dwelling here among the righteous. See sermon on Luke 13:7, especially the rea-

---

8. MS: "leave."

9. Thomas Blackwell, *Schema Sacrum, or a sacred scheme of natural and revealed religion* (Edinburgh, 1710; 3rd ed. Edinburgh, 1725), p. 192. This sentence occurs in ch. X, entitled "Adam's Breach of the foresaid Covenant; as the Fourth remarkable Event in Time, for bringing about the Eternal Scheme . . ."

1. The doctrine of the sermon on Gal. 2:17 (n.d., [1731–32]) is the same as the title of the entry, "The gospel is no encouragement to sin."

2. In his sermon on Rev. 19:2–3 (n.d., [1731–32]), JE maintains that "'tis not inconsistent with the attributes of God to punish ungodly men with a misery that is eternal."

sons given why hell is the fittest place for wicked men, under the use of exhortation.[3]

565. HEAVEN. SEPARATE SPIRITS. The happiness which the departed souls of the saints enjoy with Christ before the resurrection, is proleptical, or by way of anticipation. This is not the proper time of their reward; the proper time of the reward and glory of saints is after the end of the world, when an end shall be put to the world's state of probation. Then succeeds the state of retribution, when all the present dispensation of the covenant of grace shall be ended, and Christ shall have brought all enemies under his feet, and shall have fully accomplished the ends and designs of his mediatorial kingdom, and his own glory shall be fully obtained, and he shall have fully finished God's scheme in the series of revolutions in divine providence. Then will be the time of Christ's joy and triumph; and then will be the proper time of judgment and retribution, and then will be the proper time of the reward and glory of Christ's followers.

The state that spirits of just men are in now, is not the proper state of their reward; 'tis only a state wherein they are reserved against the time of their reward. 'Tis the time wherein the pure, chosen, espoused virgin is reserved in the King's house against the day of marriage; and the joy and blessedness that they now enjoy with Christ, in their conversation with him, though it be to us unspeakably great, is only by way of prelibation of what is future, and therefore vastly short of it. Such is God's overflowing love to them, that while they are only reserved for their designed glory, they shall be reserved in blessed abodes; as a king would entertain the virgin that he reserves for marriage, and whom he loves with a strong and ardent love, in no mean manner, but a way suitable to his love to her, and his design concerning her. The state of the blessed souls in heaven is not merely a state of repose, but of a glorious degree of anticipation of their reward, as is evident by Heb. 6:12; see my note on it.[4]

Thus 'tis God's way, from his overflowing goodness to his people, to grant a prelibation of blessings before the proper season. So the church of the old testament had an anticipation of gospel benefits, before Christ came and the gospel days commenced. So the saints here are allowed in a measure to anticipate the blessedness that is to succeed the fall of Antichrist. Rev. 6:9–11, "I saw under the altar the souls of them that were slain for the word of God, and for the testimony which they held: and they

3. The MS of the sermon on Luke 13:7 is not extant.

4. This "Blank Bible" note states that Heb. 6:12 is "an evidence that those saints that are dead are in a state of reward, and not in a state of inactivity and insensibility."

cried with a loud voice, saying, How long, O Lord, holy and true, dost thou not judge and avenge our blood on them that dwell on earth? And white robes were given to every one of them; and it was said unto them, that they should rest yet for a little season, until their fellow servants also and their brethren, that should be killed as they were, should be fulfilled." Those white robes were the glory and reward which God gave them beforehand, the earnest of what was to be after Antichrist's fall. So the saints here in this world have that light, holiness and joy, that is an anticipation and earnest of what they are to have in heaven. And what they have now in heaven, is but an earnest of what they are to have afterwards, at the consummation of all things, when all things come to be settled in their fixed and eternal state. Therefore the apostles so often speak of the reward and glory of saints at Christ's second coming, and encourage Christians with that, without any mention of the glory which they shall receive before. See Exposition on Revelation, no. 59.[5]

566. LAW. SIN. DUTY. It hardly seems to me true to say, that the command of God is the prime ground of all the duty we owe to God. Obedience is but one part of the duty we owe to God. 'Tis our duty to love God, to honor him, and have a supreme regard to him, and submit to him, and praise him, and obey him. These are distinct duties. To obey God is not a general [duty], that under which the rest are properly included as particulars; that don't comprise the general nature and reason of all the rest. It is not the prime reason or ground of our obligation to love and honor God, that [it] is our duty to obey him.

I acknowledge that we are commanded to love and honor God, and therefore ought to love and honor him in obedience to that command, seeing God has commanded it. But our obligation to obedience is not the prime ground of our duty to love him and honor him; but on the contrary, our obligation to love and honor God, and to exercise a supreme regard to God, is the very proper ground of our obligation to obey. That is the very reason, that 'tis our duty to do as God bids us, because we owe such a supreme regard, love and honor to him, as disobedience is quite contrary to.

A command of any being can't be the prime foundation of obligation, because there must be something prior, as reason why a command is obligatory, and why obedience is due to it; as, if anyone should ask me, why I

5. See *The Works of Jonathan Edwards, 5, Apocalyptic Writings*, ed. Stephen J. Stein (New Haven, Yale Univ. Press, 1977), 149–58.

am obliged to obey God more than the king of France, it would not be proper for me to answer, "Because God commands me to obey Him." There is something prior to God's command, that is the ground and reason why his command obliges.

567. LOVE TO GOD. If a man has any true love to God, he must have a spirit to love God above all, because, without seeing something of the divine glory, there can be no true love to God; but if a man sees anything of divine glory, he'll see that he is more glorious than any other: for whereinsoever God is divine, therein he is above all others. If men are sensible only of some excellency in God that is common with him to others, they are[6] not sensible of anything of his divine glory. But so far as any man is sensible of excellency in God above others, so far must he love him above others. See No. 739.

568. FAITH. JUSTIFICATION. 'Tis fit that in order to an union between two living, acting beings, so as that they should be looked upon one, there should be the mutual act of each, the consent of both, that each should receive [the] other, and actively join themselves to each other. 'Tis not for the goodness or loveliness of the grace of faith that makes God to look upon it fitter that they that believe should have an interest in Christ, than others; but only because 'tis that act on their part which makes 'em one. God sees it fit that they only that are one with Christ by their own act, should be looked upon as one in law. What is real in the union between Christ and his people, is the foundation of what is legal; that is, it is something that is really in them and between them, uniting [them], that is the ground of the suitableness of their being accounted as one by the Judge. There is a wide difference between its being looked on it suitable, that Christ's satisfaction and righteousness should be theirs, that believing because an interest in Christ's satisfaction and righteousness is but a suitable reward of faith, or a suitable testimony of God's respect to the amiableness and excellency of their faith; I say, there is a wide difference between this, and its being looked on suitable, that Christ's satisfaction and righteousness should be theirs, because Christ and they are so united that they may be well looked upon one. See No. 632.

569. WISDOM OF GOD IN THE WORK OF REDEMPTION. Christ came in the fullness of time. It would not have been so well for Christ to have come

6. MS: "he is."

presently after the fall; for it was needful, that men should be first seen in a fallen [state] after the world was peopled, that it might be seen and thoroughly proved and remembered, what calamity and misery mankind were under before the redemption, what a doleful state the world was in while left under the dominion of Satan. It must not be before the flood, because then it would not be within memory, as it is now. It must not be soon after the flood; for then it would be before the world is well peopled, and before the apostasy from the true God to heathenism is so great universal, which was needful in order to the redemption's being conspicuous.

570. CONFIRMATION OF ANGELS. See No. 515. We learn by Col. 1:16–20 that it was the design of the Father that his Son should have the preeminence in all things, not only with respect to men, but with respect to angels, thrones, dominions, principalities and powers; and there are some things there mentioned, wherein he has the preeminence, viz. that they were created by him and for him, and that they consist by him, and that every creature has all fullness in him. Why then hath not Christ the preeminence with respect to the angels, as he is the dispenser of God's benefits to them, so that they should have all fullness in him, and particularly that the gift of eternal life should be from his hands?

One thing mentioned, wherein God's will that his Son in all things should have preeminence, and that all fullness should dwell in him, is that by him he reconciles all things to him[self], whether they be things in heaven or things on earth. If this be understood only to extend to man, yet if it be one thing wherein God's will that his Son should in all things have the preeminence, and that all fullness should dwell in him, that 'tis by him that men are brought to an union with God, why would it not be another, that by him the angels also are brought to their confirmed union with him; when it is plainly implied in what the Apostle says, that 'tis the Father's design that Christ should in all things have the preeminence, with respect to the angels as well as with respect to men, and that both angels and men should have all their fullness in him? If they have their fullness in him, I don't see how it can be otherwise, than they should have their reward and eternal life and blessedness in him.

Again, it is said (I Cor. 8:6) that all things are of God the Father, and all things by Jesus Christ. God gave the angels their being by Jesus Christ; and I don't see why this would not be another instance of all things being by him, that he gives them their eternal life by Jesus Christ. This is one instance of men's being by him, and is intended in those words that follow, "and we by him."

571. HEAVEN. WISDOM AND GLORIOUSNESS OF THE WORK OF REDEMP-
TION. When the saints get to heaven, they shall not merely see Christ, and
have to do with him as subjects and servants with a glorious and gracious
Lord and Sovereign, but Christ will most freely and intimately converse
with them as friends and brethren. This we may learn from the manner
of Christ's conversing with his disciples here on earth. Though he was the
supreme Lord of the disciples, and did not refuse, yea, required their
supreme respect and adoration, yet he did not treat them as earthly sov-
ereigns are wont to do their subjects; he did not keep them at an awful distance, but all along conversed with them with the most friendly familiarity, as with brethren, or a father amongst a company of children. So he did
with the twelve, and so he did with Mary and Martha and Lazarus; he told
his disciples that he did not call 'em servants, but he called them friends
[John 15:15].

So neither will he call his disciples servants, but friends, in heaven.
Though Christ be in a state of exaltation at the right hand of God, and appears in an immense height of glory, yet this won't hinder his conversing
with his saints in a most familiar and intimate manner. He won't treat his
disciples with greater distance for his being in a state of exaltation, but he
will rather take them into a state of exaltation with him. This will be the
improvement Christ will make of his own glory, to make his beloved
friends partakers with him, to glorify them in his glory; as Christ says to
his Father, John 17:22–23, "And the glory which thou hast given me have
I given them; that they may be one, even as we are one: I in them, and thou
in me, that they may be made perfect in one." For we are to consider that
though Christ be greatly exalted, yet he is exalted not as a private person
for himself only, but he is exalted as his people's head; he is exalted in
their name and upon their account, and as one of them, as their representative, as the firstfruits. He is not exalted that he may be more above
them, and be at a greater distance from them, but that they may be exalted with him. The exaltation and honor of the head is not to make a
greater distance between the head and the members, but the members
and head have the same relation and union as they had before, and are
honored with the head.

Christ, when he was going to heaven, comforted his disciples with that,
that after a while he would come and take them to himself, that they might
be with him again; and we ben't to suppose, that when the disciples got to
heaven, that though they found their Lord in a state of infinite exaltation,
yet that they found him any more shy or keeping a greater distance from
them than he used to do. No, he embraced 'em as friends; he welcomed

'em home to their common Father's house; he welcomed them to their common glory who had been his friends here in this world, that had been together here, and had here together partook of sorrows and troubles. Now he welcomed 'em to their rest, to partake of glory with him. He took 'em and led them into his chambers, and showed them all his glory; as Christ prayed, John 17:24, "Father, I will that they also, whom thou hast given me, be with me where I am; that they may behold my glory, which thou has given me." And there ensued without doubt a most pleasant and free conversation between Christ and his disciples, when they met together in their common rest and glory.

Christ did not behave [differently] towards his disciples after they had seen his transfiguration than before, no, nor after his resurrection; nor will he in his highest exaltation in heaven.

Christ took on him man's nature for this end, that he might be under advantage for a more familiar conversation than the infinite distance of the divine nature would allow of; and such a communion and familiar conversation is suitable to the relation that Christ stands in to believers, as their representative, their brother, and the husband of the church. The church's being so often called the spouse of Christ, intimates an admittance to the greatest nearness, intimacy and communion of good. Christ will conform his people to himself: he'll give them his glory, the glory of his person; their souls shall be made like his soul, their bodies like to his glorious body; they shall partake with him in his riches, as co-heirs in his pleasures. He will bring them into his banqueting house, and they shall drink new wine with him. They shall partake with [him] in the honor of judging the world at the last day, when Christ shall descend from heaven in the glory of his Father, in such awful and dreadful majesty, with all his holy angels with [him], and all nations shall be gathered before [him]. The saints at the same time shall be as familiar with Christ as his disciples were when he was upon earth; they shall sit with him to judge with him.

As Christ died as the head of believers and in their name, and was exalted in their name, so shall he judge the world as their head and representative. It was God's design in this way to confound and triumph over Satan, viz. by making man, that he so despised and envied, and thought to have had slaves to god it over, and thought to have glutted his pride and malice and envy with his blood, and in his everlasting misery—I say, by making him his judge. It was God's design that the elect of mankind should be Satan's judge; and therefore, the head of 'em, the elder brother of them, is appointed to this work in the name of the rest, and the rest are to be with him in it. God gave Christ "authority to execute judgment because he is the Son of man" (John 5:27), partly upon this account we have mentioned.

The conversation of Christ's disciples in heaven shall in[7] many respects be vastly more intimate than it was when Christ was on earth, for in heaven the union shall be perfected (see note on John 20:17).[8] The union is but begun in this world, and there is a great deal remains in this world to separate and disunite them; but then all those obstacles of a close union and most intimate communion shall be removed. When the church is received to glory, that is her marriage with Christ; and therefore doubtless the conversation and enjoyment will be more intimate. This is not a time for that full acquaintance and those manifestations of love, which Christ designs towards his people.

When saints shall see Christ's divine glory and exaltation in heaven, this will indeed possess their hearts with the greater admiration and adoring respect; but this will not keep 'em at a distance, but will only serve the more to heighten their surprise and pleasure, when they find Christ condescending to treat them in such a familiar manner.

The saints being united to Christ, shall have a more glorious union with and enjoyment of the Father, than otherwise could be, for hereby their relation becomes much nearer. They are the children of God in a higher manner than otherwise they could be; for being members of God's own natural Son, they are partakers of his relation to the Father, or of his sonship. Being members of the Son, they are partakers of the Father's love to the Son and his complacence in him. John 17:23, "I in them, and thou in me; thou hast loved them as thou hast loved me"; and [v.] 26, "That the love wherewith thou hast loved me may be in them"; and 16:27, "The Father himself loveth you, because ye have loved me, and have believed that I came out from God." So they are in their measure partakers of the Son's enjoyment of his Father: they have his joy fulfilled in themselves, and by this means they come to a more familiar and intimate conversing with God the Father, than otherwise ever would have been. For there is doubtless an infinite intimacy between the Father and the Son; and the saints being in him shall partake with him in it, and of the blessedness of it.

Such is the contrivance of our redemption, that thereby we are brought

---

7. MS: "be."

8. According to this "Blank Bible" note, Jesus' "repelling" of Mary Magdalene when she went to embrace him signifies "that familiarity and full enjoyment of Christ is not allowed before his ascension." Although "Christ might not see it upon all accounts meet to suffer a woman to embrace him," Mary Magdalene—and by implication all believers—will in heaven "have a more intimate and full enjoyment of him than now."

to an immensely more glorious and exalted kind of union with God and enjoyment of him, both the Father and the Son, than otherwise could have been. For Christ being united to the human nature, we have advantage for a far more intimate union and conversation with him, than we could possibly have had if he had remained only in the divine nature. So we, being united to a divine person, can in him have more intimate union and conversation with God the Father, who is only in the divine nature, than otherwise possibly could be. Christ, who is a divine person, by taking on him our nature, descends from the infinite distance between God and us, and is brought nigh to us, to give us advantage to converse with him. So on the other hand, we, by being in Christ, a divine person, ascend nearer to God the Father, and have advantage to converse with him. This was the design of Christ to bring it to pass, that he and his Father and his people might be brought to a most intimate union and communion. John 17:21–23, "That they all may be one; as thou, Father, art in me, and I in thee, that they also may be one in us: that the world may believe that thou hast sent me. And the glory which thou hast given me have I given them; that they may be one, even as we are one: I in them, and thou in me, that they may be made perfect in one." Christ has brought it to pass, that those that the Father has given him should be brought into the household of God, that he and his Father and they should be as it were one society, one family; that his people should be in a sort admitted into that society of the three persons in the Godhead. In this family or household, God [is] the Father, Jesus Christ is his own natural and eternally begotten Son. The saints, they also are children in the family; the church is the daughter of God, being the spouse of his Son. They all have communion in the same spirit, the Holy Ghost.

Corol. 1. Seeing that God hath designed man for such exceeding exaltation, it was but agreeable to his wisdom to bestow [it] in such a way as should abase man and exalt his own free grace, and wherein man's entire and absolute and universal dependence on God should be most evident and conspicuous.

Corol. 2. 'Tis easy to observe that wisdom of God, that seeing he designed him for[9] such a height of glory, that it should be so ordered that he should be brought to it from the lowest depths of wretchedness and vileness.

Corol. 3. Hence we may learn something how vastly greater glory and happiness the elect are brought to by Christ than that which was lost by

9. MS: "from."

the fall, or even than that which man would [have] attained to if he had not fallen. For then, man would never have had such an advantage for an intimate union and converse with the Father or Son, Christ remaining at an infinite distance from man in the divine nature, and man remaining at an infinite distance from the Father, without being brought nigh by an union to a divine person.

Corol. 4. Hence we may see how God hath confounded Satan, in actually fulfilling that which was a lie in him, wherewith he deluded poor man and procured his fall, viz. that they should be as gods. When Satan said so, he did not think that this would really be the fruit of it; he aimed at that which was infinitely contrary, his lowest depression, debasement and ruin. But God has greatly frustrated him in fulfilling of it, in making the issue of that eating that fruit to be the advancement of the elect to such an union with the persons of the Trinity, and communion with them in divine honor and blessedness; and particularly, has united one of them, the head and representative of the rest, in a personal union with the Godhead, and so to the honor, dominion and work of God, in ruling the world and judging it, and particularly judging them (the devils), in which all the rest of the elect in their measure partake with him.

572. EXTREMITY OF HELL TORMENTS. This confirms it with me, that the misery is exceeding great, that God hath so every way contrived to glorify his Son as Savior, or hath so ordered in all respects that his salvation should be exceeding. Now a part of the gloriousness of his salvation consists in this, that 'tis salvation from so great misery; and the greater the misery, still the more glorious the salvation. Therefore I believe that God would so order it, that that misery should be very exceeding great.

573. FREE WILL. I don't scruple to say that God has promised salvation to such things as are properly in man's own power. Those things in man unto which salvation is promised as the conditions of, are of two sorts. They are either,

1. Those acts which consist and are complete in the mere immanent exercise of the will or inclination itself; such are the internal breathings of love to God, and exercises of faith in Christ. These are absolutely necessary to salvation, and salvation is promised to them. These, in the most ordinary way of using the expression, can't be said to be in a man's own power or not in his power: because when we speak of things being in man's power or not in his power, in our common discourse, we have respect only to things that are consequential to his will, that are considered as the ef-

fects of his will; and not of the mere simple and first motions of the will itself. If we say a thing is in a man's power, we mean that he can do it if he
will; and so a prior act of the will determining is supposed. Neither can
these things, in the vulgar and ordinary use of the expression, be said not
to be in a man's power: because when we say a thing is not in anyone's
power, we mean that he can't do it if he will; but this is absurd, to say of
the very simple and mere acts of the will itself, that we can't do them if we
will, for the willing is the doing, and the doing of 'em consists in the willing of 'em. Or,

2. The other kind of conditions to which salvation is promised, are
those actions, or a way and course of those actions, that are the effects of
the will, and depend upon it, which flow from it; which are properly called
voluntary actions. These also are conditions of salvation, and have salvation promised to them. Thus salvation is very often promised to an universal obedience, and a steadfast and faithful perseverance in it through
the changes, difficulties and trials of life. Now this sort of condition a man
may be said properly to have in his own power, in the vulgar and more ordinary use of such an expression. For if we say a man has it in his own
power to do or not, we ordinarily mean no other than that he can do it if
he has a mind to do it, or chooses to do it, or all things considered had
rather do it than not. If we can't be properly said to have everything in
our power that we can do if we choose to do it, then we can't be said properly to have it in our own power to [do] anything but only what we actually do.

And so a man may be said properly to have it in his power to do that
which he surely will not, as the case may be, or the case being as it is. Thus
a man may have it in his own power to sell his estate and give the money
to his poor neighbor; and yet the case may be so at the same time—he
may have so little love to his neighbor and so great a love to his possessions, and the like—that he certainly will not do it. There may be as much
of a connection between those things in the qualities and circumstances
of the man, and his refusing to give his estate to his neighbor, as between
any two theorems in the mathematics. He has it in his power as much as
he has other things, because there wants nothing but his having a mind
to do it, or his being willing to do [it]; and that is required in all other
things, and in this no more than in everything else. So a man has it in his
power, in the voluntary actions of his life, universally and steadfastly and
faithfully to obey God's commands, and cleave to and follow Christ
through all difficulties and trials; though it be certain that without love to
God and faith in Jesus Christ, no man will do it. And there is a sure con-

nection between our being without these (as we all naturally are) and a not thus universally and perseveringly obeying God, and cleaving to Christ.

A man can avoid drunkenness if he will, and he can avoid fornication if he will; and so he can all other ways of wickedness if he chooses to avoid 'em, every one. And he can persevere in it if he holds of that mind, if he continues to choose to avoid them all; and God has promised salvation to men if they will thus do. If one should promise another a certain reward, if he would approve himself his faithful friend by a persevering adherence to his interest, the case might be so, that there might be such remarkable trials, and such a succession of 'em, that the man certainly would not fulfill this condition unless he be a sincere friend; but yet the fulfilling is in his own power and at his own choice.

574. ETERNITY OF HELL TORMENTS. The wicked, when they are cast into hell, will continue sinning still. Yea, they will sin more than ever; their wickedness will be unrestrained. Such torments must needs be, to an unsanctified [mind], an occasion of a fearful exercise of enmity and rage against God. Therefore if it ben't incredible that God should cast men into hell at all for the sins they have been guilty of in this life, then, seeing they continue sinning, 'tis not incredible that their misery there should be continued. For if we should suppose that the punishment that the sins of this life deserve is but finite, that it deserves only a temporary misery, yet while they are suffering that, they continue sinning still, and so contract a new debt; and again, while they are paying that, they contract another, and so on *in infinitum*.

575. ETERNITY OF HELL TORMENTS. ETERNAL DEATH. The eternal death and destruction and misery which the ungodly are to suffer, is not an eternal annihilation; for they are to suffer the same kind of punishment with the devils, as is most evident, Matt. 25:41, "Depart, ye cursed, into everlasting fire, prepared for the devil and his angels." But the devil's punishment is not to be eternally annihilated, but to be forever tormented, for this is what he trembles in expectation of. Therefore he besought Christ not to torment him before the time [Matt. 8:29]. And we have an account how this shall be executed, Rev. 20:10, "And the devil that deceived them was cast into the lake of fire and brimstone, where the beast and false prophet are, and shall be tormented day and night for ever and ever"; plainly intimating that he shall be tormented with them. It might have better been rendered, "And *they* shall be tormented day and

night for ever and ever" (for the word "tormented" is in the plural number), i.e. they three, the devil, the beast, and the false prophet, for this is evidently the meaning. And this is said to be "the second death" in the 14th verse. And no doubt but the wicked shall die the second death: for if men don't suffer it, it can't be called the second death, for the devils suffer no other death. 'Tis called the second only with respect to wicked men, for they die a death before this, which is the first death. In Rev. 2:11 it is promised that he that overcomes "shall not be hurt of the second death," implying that others shall; and it is said, that they that have part in the first resurrection, "on such the second death hath no power" (20:6), implying that it hath power on others. We know that wicked men will suffer another death after they rise from the first, and surely that is the second. And it is expressly said of the worshippers of the beast, that they "shall be tormented with fire and brimstone in the presence of the holy angels, and in the presence of the Lamb, and the smoke of their torment shall ascend up for ever and ever, and they have no rest day nor night" (14:10–11); and doubtless it will be so with other wicked men.

576. HEAVEN'S HAPPINESS. When I think how great this happiness is, sometimes it is ready to seem almost incredible. But the death and sufferings of Christ make everything credible that belongs to this blessedness; for if God would so contrive to show his love in the manner and means of procuring our happiness, nothing can be incredible in the degree of the happiness itself. If all that God doth about it be of a piece, he will also set infinite wisdom on work to make their happiness and glory great in the degree of it. If God "spared not his own Son, but delivered him up for us all, how shall he not with him also freely give us all things?" [Rom. 8:32]. Nothing could have been such a confirmation of their blessedness as this. If nothing be too much to be given to man, and to be done for man in the means of procuring his happiness, nothing will be too much to be given to him as the end, no degree of happiness too great for him to enjoy.[1]

577. BAPTISM. *Ques.* How far, and in what manner, are regeneration of the heart and the grace of the Spirit, connected with baptism in infants? This may be resolved in answer to several more particular questions.

1. Whether or no all that are regularly admitted to baptism are spiritually regenerated? *Ans.* No. The Apostle and other inspired persons bap-

---

1. The last sentence is a later addition, written at the end of No. 575. Except for a line showing that it belongs with No. 576, the location of its placement is not indicated.

tized many adult persons that were hypocrites, but they were regularly admitted to baptism. Philip baptized Simon Magus, but yet he indeed had no part nor lot in the spiritual benefits of the gospel, and was yet in the gall of bitterness and bond of iniquity. He was regularly admitted to baptism, because in what was visible he was a Christian. But if an adult person may be regularly admitted to baptism, and regeneration not be connected with it, I don't see why an infant mayn't; especially when the parents of the infant in whose right the child is baptized are, as Simon Magus was, a Christian only visibly and not really.

2. Whether or no all the children of godly or believing parents, that are baptized, are regenerated? *Ans.* No. Because experience shows, that multitudes of such show no signs of grace at all, as they come to be capable of acting in the world; and prove wicked when they grow up.

3. Whether or no we may conclude that all baptized children of godly parents that die in infancy are regenerated, and in a state of grace?

[*Ans.* No. But we can't conclude that the baptized children of godly parents that die in infancy are not more likely to be regenerated],[2] for then the parents in such a case would have no greater ground of encouragement concerning their children's salvation, nor any more reason to hope for it, for their earnestly and believingly praying for its salvation. And when they saw their child like to die, it would be their duty to pray earnestly for the salvation of their child's soul, and yet might know that they have no more reason to hope for their child's salvation for that; so that they have no motive of this nature to earnestness [in] prayer. And if they have been enabled believingly and with their whole hearts to dedicate their child to God in baptism, they have no more reason to hope that God accepts it as one of his children for that. Which things seem to me unreasonable.

But saving grace seems to me by the promises of God's Word to be thus far connected with baptism in infants. If the parents do sincerely, believingly and entirely, with a thorough disposition, will and desire, dedicate their child to God that they bring to baptism, if that child dies in infancy, the parents have good grounds to hope for its salvation; and have[3] also good grounds to hope, that if the child don't die in infancy, that the blessing of God will attend their thorough care and pains to bring up their child in the nurture and admonition of the Lord. So that by that means

---

2. The lack of a direct answer to the third question and the awkwardness of the phrasing suggest that several words were omitted due to scribal error.

3. MS: "has."

they may be brought to salvation, they that do thoroughly dedicate their children to God, will be willing to take thorough care to bring 'em up for God. See No. 595.

578. HUMILIATION. 'Tis true that humiliation is necessary in order to a true receiving of Christ. A becoming as a little child is necessary in order to a right receiving the kingdom of heaven, because Christ tells us that unless we receive it as a little child, we cannot enter into it. But however, it don't hence follow, that a man becomes as a little child before his conversion. That is a thing wrought in conversion, as is evident by Matt. 18:3, "Except ye be converted, and become as little children, ye shall not enter into the kingdom of heaven"; which is spoken with respect to humility, as Christ explains himself in the verse following: "Whosoever therefore shall humble himself as this little child."

579. DEGREE OF HELL TORMENTS. See sermon on I Cor. 10:8–11, in that part where it is showed how the deluge was a type of the destruction and misery of hell.[4]

580. FREE GRACE. SPIRIT'S OPERATION. It is often observed that attainments of great excellency or value are not had without great difficulty. God hath made the road to such attainments hard and difficult, and it is wisely ordered that it should be so upon many accounts. If those things that are the most excellent and of distinguishing worth, were as easy to be come at as other things, this would destroy their distinction from other things, or would destroy our sense of their distinction. Silver and gold, if they were as easy to be come at as brass and iron, the distinction of silver and gold in value would thereby be destroyed. And if learning and the noblest arts and sciences were as easily come at as inferior attainments, this would tend to destroy the sense of their distinction among mankind; they would be despised and neglected. And then 'tis fit that it should be required, in order to our obtaining those things that are indeed very excellent, by a labor and endeavor after them in some measure answerable; that none may attain to them but those that are sensible of the worth of them, and are prepared to prize them suitably when attained, by giving the price of a diligent and laborious and constant pursuit for them.

---

4. In the sermon on I Cor. 10:8–11 (n.d., [1731–32]) JE uses the flood as one example of the doctrine, which states that "those awful temporal destructions that we have an account of God's bringing on wicked men of old, are types and shadows of God's eternal judgments."

This is the way whereby providence upholds the dignity of the more excellent temporal attainments. But 'tis not [an] adequate or sufficient way with respect to the highest and most excellent attainment, of spiritual wisdom and true sanctification. If the way of obtaining this should be only as difficult, or but a little more difficult, than the way of obtaining the most excellent of temporal blessings, it would be no way answerable or proportionate to its worth and excellency, which is infinitely superior; but if it should be vastly more difficult, the terms would be disproportionate to man's faculties and abilities. The way therefore of man's coming at this greatest of blessings, that is most suitable to the nature and infinite excellency and value of it, is that it should be required of man that he should seek it above all things, with the greatest earnestness, diligence and constancy; and that God should insist upon it, that men that desire and would hope to obtain, should thus seek it, because 'tis absurd not earnestly to desire and seek that which is so excellent and is attainable: but that the obtaining it should not properly depend upon any human labors or endeavors at all, but upon his own free and sovereign grace to bestow it on whom he will. 'Tis fit that God should reserve this infinitely most precious blessing to be bestowed according to his own free and sovereign pleasure, as being too great and excellent to be dependent on anything else.

581. END OF THE CREATION. GLORY OF GOD. When God is said (Prov. 16:4) to make "all things for himself," no more is necessarily understood by it, than that he made all things for his own designs and purposes, and to put them to his own use. 'Tis as much as to say that everything that is, that comes to pass, is altogether of God's ordering, and God has some design in it; 'tis for something that God aims at and will have obtained, that this or the other thing is or happens, whatever it be. Even sin and wickedness itself, it comes to pass because God has a use for it, a design and purpose to accomplish by it. Things don't happen merely to fulfill the desires or designs of some other being, some adversary of God. But all that is or comes to pass, 'tis of God's will and for his pleasure that it happens, and for his ends; and 'tis not primarily of the will of some other, and for their purposes.

Obj. But then we are taught nothing by that addition, "for himself." If it had been said, "God hath made all things," that would have implied as much as that God made them for his own ends; for if God made things designedly, it must be for some end. See No. 586.[5]

---

5. No. 586 contains an answer to the objection. See below, p. 121.

582. CHRISTIAN RELIGION. See note on Luke 7:13.[6]

If the New Testament ben't a true revelation of God, then God never has yet given the world any clear revelation of a future state. But if a revelation be needful upon any account, [it] is upon this, viz. that we may have some certain and distinct knowledge of the future invisible world that we are to be in after death, and after this world comes to an end. We must therefore suppose that God did design a further revelation than the Old Testament, because a future state was not clearly revealed by that. And 'tis not credible that God should defer it to this time, partly by reason of its being so long since the finishing of that revelation, which is above two thousand years. If that revelation was only introductory to another, 'tis hardly credible that there should be so long a space between the introduction, and that other revelation which it was an introduction to. And besides, this clearer revelation of a future state would now be out of season, because all the world have already received the doctrine of a future world for many ages. If God designed a true revelation, 'tis not probable that[7] any false revelation should anticipate it, and do its work beforehand. And upon many other accounts that might be mentioned, is it incredible that revelation should still be deferred.

583. CHRISTIAN RELIGION. MYSTERIES. 'Tis very unreasonable to make it an objection against the Christian revelation, that it contains some things that are very mysterious and difficult to our understandings, and that seem to us impossible. If God will give us a revelation from heaven of the very truth concerning his own nature and acts, counsels and ways, and of the spiritual and invisible world, 'tis unreasonable to expect any other, than that there should be many things in such a revelation that should be utterly beyond our understanding, and seem impossible.

For when was there ever a time when, if there had been a revelation from heaven of the very truth in philosophical matters, and concerning the nature of created things—which are of a vastly lower nature, and must be supposed to be more proportioned to our understandings—and there would not have been many things which would have appeared, not only to the vulgar but to the learned of that age, absurd and impossible? If

6. This reference originally constituted the whole number. When JE began the next paragraph, he wrote a new "Christian Religion" heading, then deleted it and included the new entry under No. 582. The new material, however, is on a different topic from that of the "Blank Bible" note on Luke 7:13, which seeks to show that we can infer the divinity of Christ's miracles from the fact that he performed them with compassion.

7. MS: "that he ~~would defer it~~ that."

many of those positions in philosophy which are now received by the learned world as indubitable truths, had been revealed from heaven to be truths in past ages, they would be looked upon as mysterious and difficult, and would have seemed as impossible as the most mysterious Christian doctrines do now. And I believe that even now, if there should come a revelation from heaven of what is the very truth in these matters, without deviating at all to accommodate it to our received notions and principles, there would be many things in it that would seem to be absurd and contradictious. I do now receive principles as certain, which once if they had been told me, I should have looked upon 'em as difficult as any mystery in the Bible. Without doubt, much of the difficulty that we have about the doctrines of Christianity, arises from wrong principles that we receive. We find that those things that are received as principles in one age, and are never once questioned, it comes into nobody's thought that they possibly may not be true; and yet are exploded in another age, as light increases. If God makes a revelation to us, he must reveal to us the truth as it is, without accommodating himself to our notions and principles; which would indeed be impossible, for those things which are our received notions in one age are contrary to what are so in another. The Word of God was not given for any particular age, but for all ages. It surely becomes us to receive what God reveals to be truth, and to look upon his Word as proof sufficient, whether what he reveals squares with our notions or not.

I rather wonder that the Word of God contains no more mysteries in it; and I believe 'tis because God is tender of us, and considers the weakness of our sight, and reveals only such things as he sees that man, though so weak a creature, if of an humble and an honest mind, can well enough bear. Such a kind of tenderness we see in Christ towards his disciples, who had many things to say, but forbore, because they could not bear 'em yet. And though God don't depart from truth to accommodate his revelation to our manner of thinking; yet I believe he accommodates himself to our way of understanding in his manner of expressing and representing things, as we are wont to do when we are teaching little children.

584. CHRISTIAN RELIGION. CHRIST'S MIRACLES. What can be more reasonable than to believe a man, when he comes and tells us that he is sent from God, and will heal the diseases of our souls; and tells us, that we may believe him, [that] he'll heal the diseases of our bodies; and accordingly heals all sorts at all times, of all manner of diseases, by a touch or word's speaking; and plainly shows that he can do it when he will, and let the dis-

ease be what it will? He tells us that he will dispossess Satan of our souls, and free us from his power and dominion; and to prove that he has power to do as he says, he before our eyes dispossesses him of the bodies of men that he possessed, does it very often, and for a long time together: so as plainly to show that he has power over those unclean spirits, and can conquer 'em and eject 'em and restrain 'em as he will, and do what he will with them. He tells us that he will deliver us from spiritual and eternal death, and also from temporal death; that he will raise us from [the] dead, and give us eternal life, so that we shall live forever and not die. And to prove this, he gives us sensible evidence that he has power over men's lives, not only by prolonging men's lives, but even by restoring of them after they are dead; and besides, rises from the dead himself. He tells us that he will bestow heavenly glory upon us, will translate us to heaven; and to confirm us in that he will so do, tells us that we shall see himself after his death ascend into heaven.

What more could we desire of a man that pretends to come from God, and to have power to do these things for us, than to give us such evidences of his power as these? He tells us that he will undertake for us, and appear for us before [God], and that he will ask mercy for us of him; and tells us that we need no doubt but that, if he appears for us and pleads for us, he shall procure acceptance for us: for God so loves him, that he always hears him, and grants what he asks of him. And that we may see that it is true, he does in our hearing ask of God strange things, such as particularly ask of God, concerning a dead man that had been dead four days, that he may come to life again; and tells God that he asks it for this end, that we may see how that he always hears him, and grants what he requests: and accordingly at his request the dead man comes to life. See No. 716.

585. HEAVEN'S HAPPINESS. It has sometimes looked strange to me, that man should be ever brought to such exceeding happiness as that of heaven seems to be, because we find that here providence won't suffer any great degree of happiness. When men have something in which they hope to find very great joy, there will be something to spoil it; providence seems watchfully to take care that [men] should have no exceeding joy and satisfaction here in this world. But indeed this, instead of being an argument against the greatness of heaven's happiness, seems to argue for it; for we can't suppose that the reason why providence won't suffer men to enjoy great happiness here, is that he is averse to the creature's happiness, but because this is not a time for it. To everything there is an appointed season and time, and 'tis agreeable to God's method of dispen-

sation that a thing should be sought in vain out of its appointed time. God reserves happiness to be bestowed hereafter; that is the appointed time for it, and that is the reason he don't give it now. No man, let him be never so strong or wise, shall alter this divine establishment by anticipating happiness before his appointed time.

'Tis so in all things. Sometimes there is an appointed time for a man's prosperity upon earth, and then nothing can hinder his[8] prosperity. And then when that time is past, then comes an appointed time for his adversity; and then all things conspire for his ruin, and all his strength and skill shall not help him. History verifies this with respect to many kings, generals and great men. One while they conquer all, and nothing can stand before 'em; all things conspire for their advancement, and all that oppose it are confounded. And after a while it is right the reverse. So has it been with respect to the kingdoms and monarchies of the world. One while is their time to flourish, and then God will give all into their hands, and will destroy those that oppose their flourishing. And then after that comes the time of their decay and ruin, and then everything runs backward and all helpers are vain. See Jeremiah, ch. 27.

586. END OF CREATION. See No. 581.[9]

Ans. This seems to be added, because some things seem to come to pass thwarting God's designs and purposes, as particularly the sin and wickedness there is in the world. This is added to obviate such a thought, as though God were frustrated, or his aims thwarted and frustrated by wicked men; and therefore it follows, "and even the wicked" [Prov. 16:4]. God makes all things for himself, i.e. that he may be the owner and user of it; which is true of everything, for he never ceases to be the owner of anything that he hath made. And when he gives things to others, 'tis not as when we give; he don't cease still to be the owner and user of it. He continues to dispose of it for his own ends as much as ever. When Solomon says that God made all things for himself, it seems to be an expression of much the same import as that in Rev. 4:11, "Thou hast made all things, and for thy pleasure they are and were created"; i.e. all things came into being at thy will and pleasure, and for thy will [and] pleasure, or for the accomplishment of what thou wilt, or of thine own designs and purposes. So we are to understand that that is said of Christ, Col. 1:16, "All things

8. MS: "their."

9. In this entry JE answers the question that he posed in the final paragraph of No. 581. See above, p. 117.

are made by him, and for him"; i.e. all things are made by him, and for his ends and purposes.

587. BEING OF GOD. NECESSARY EXISTENCE. God is a necessary being, as it is impossible but that God should exist, because there is no other way. There is no second to make a disjunction; there is nothing else supposable. To illustrate this by one of God's attributes, viz. eternity: it is absolutely necessary that eternity should be, and it is, because there is no other way. To say "eternity or not eternity" is no disjunction, because there is no such thing to make a supposition about as "no eternity." Nor can we in our minds make any such supposition as "not any eternity"; we may seem to make such a supposition in words, but it is no supposition, because the words have no sense in thought to answer them. They are words as much without any sense in thought that they should signify, as these, a crooked straight line, or a square circle, or a six-angled triangle. If we go to suppose that there is no eternity, it is the same as if we should say or suppose that there never was any such thing as duration; which is a contradiction, for the word "never" implies eternity, and 'tis the same as to say there never was any such [thing] as duration from all eternity. So that in the very denying the thing, we affirm it.

588. ETERNITY OF HELL PUNISHMENT, the justice and suitableness of it. See sermon on Ezek. 7:10, second particular under the doctrine.[1]

589. CHRIST'S MEDIATION. DEGREES OF GLORY. CHRIST'S RIGHTEOUSNESS. See Nos. 403 and 367. Christ and believers all have a right in that righteousness that Christ wrought out; it is a good common among them. And it being imputed to all, they all are entitled to benefit by it, by virtue of that original and eternal rule of righteousness which we call the law, or covenant of works; and the benefit of it that they are all entitled to by virtue of that rule, is eternal life, or a full and perfect and eternal happiness; and one to whom that righteousness belongs is entitled to no more benefit by that rule simply, than another. The case may be so, that one can challenge more than another can, because his capacity may be larger, and he may need more; but what each one's capacity shall be is a thing that the law determines not. And therefore I say, no one can challenge more benefit by the law simply, than another.

That matter of each one's capacity remains to be determined by God,

---

1. The MS of the sermon on Ezek. 7:10 is not extant.

either arbitrarily, or in what way, or agreeably to what other additional constitution, he himself shall be pleased to establish. And God has been pleased to establish this further constitution, that everyone's capacity shall be determined according to his holiness and his good works here in the world. This constitution being subjoined to the law, one believer by the law, or covenant of works, may challenge a greater benefit by Christ's righteousness than another; and Christ can challenge immensely greater benefit than any believer. For as I said before, if it were once determined what each one's capacity should be, one could challenge more benefit by the law than another: for everyone can challenge that by the law, to have happiness according to his capacity. Indeed it is requisite that the capacity of the head should be immensely larger than of the rest of the parts of the body; and so it was requisite that he should be more holy and do better works than others, that he might have a greater capacity, according to that forementioned constitution. God sees meet that the same rule should hold throughout the body, to the head and all other parts; as Christ is become one of us, so he has his reward in common with us, and in some respect by the same rules.

590. CHRIST'S RESURRECTION. CHRISTIAN RELIGION. *Ques.* Why was not Christ, after he rose from the dead, during his stay upon earth, with his disciples as he was before? Why was he not with them constantly, dwelling with them and going in and out with them? *Ans.* The very different states that Christ and his disciples were now in, would not allow of it. Christ before his death, and while in a state of humiliation, was in like state with them. He was subject to hunger and thirst as they were; he needed sleep as they did; he needed the like defense from the weather that they did, and the like: and then he was in a state suitable for a cohabitation with them. But when he was risen from the dead, the case was exceedingly altered. He no longer continued in a state of humiliation, but then began his exaltation; he put off mortality; he put off all the infirmities of his body; the nature of his body was exceedingly different from theirs, as things celestial differ from terrestrial. Mortal beings ben't apt for a cohabitation with immortal, nor terrestrial with celestial, nor corruption with incorruption.

And then, if Christ had constantly been with his disciples, and dwelt with them, and gone in and out with them amongst men as before, then he must have appeared either in his former mean state or in his glorified state. If he had appeared in his former mean state, that would have been to have continued his state of humiliation after his resurrection, and finishing the work of redemption, and his triumph over the powers of darkness. He must have remained still in the form of a servant; he must still [have] remained empty of his glory, or with his glory veiled. And[2] the circumstances of the disciples, yet in their corrupt and mortal state, and the state of this world, would no way admit of his appearing as an inhabitant of this world, and dwelling here with them, in his glorified state. The disciples were not meet to dwell with a glorified Savior: that would have been to have exalted them to a glorified state as to their objective glory and happiness, while they the subjects remained still in their corrupt, infirm and mortal state; which would have been no way suitable. God will not thus mix and confound heaven and earth.

591. CONFIRMATION OF THE ANGELS. See Nos. 515 and 570. It is an argument that it was Christ that confirmed the angels and adjudged [it] to them for their reward, because this was an act of judgment, was the proper act of a judge, whereby judgment was passed whether they had fulfilled the law or no, and were worthy of the reward of it, by the tenor of it. But Christ is constituted universal Judge of all, both angels and men. John 5:22, "For the Father judgeth none, οὐδένα, but hath committed all judgment to the Son." And Christ is not only constituted the Judge of men but of angels; I Cor. 6:3, "Know ye not that we shall judge angels?" If this be meant only of the evil angels, yet that shows that Christ's power of judging is extended beyond mankind to the angelic nature; and if [he] be constituted the Judge of the evil angels, that will confirm me that he is of the good too, as he is the Judge of both good and bad of mankind. And Christ tells us that all power is given him in heaven and in earth (Matt. 28:18); and we are often particularly told as to the good angels, that he is made their Lord and Sovereign, and that they are put under him. The Apostle, in Rom. 14:10–12, speaking of Christ's being universal Judge, before whose judgment seat all must stand and to whom all must give an account, speaks of it as meant by those words in the Old Testament:[3] "As I live, saith the Lord, every knee shall bow to me, and every tongue shall confess to God"; which place of the Old Testament the Apostle refers to in Philip. 2:9–11, "Wherefore God also hath highly exalted him, and given him a name above every name: that at the name of Jesus every knee should bow, of things in heaven, and things in earth, and things under the earth; and that every tongue should confess that Jesus is Lord, to the glory of God the Father."

2. MS: "And on the other hand."
3. JE's quotation is from Rom. 14:11, in which Paul paraphrases Is. 45:23.

And these things are spoken of Christ God-man. For in this last-mentioned place, 'tis mentioned as the reward of his being found in fashion as a man and humbling himself; and in that other place, and in that place in Romans, his being universal Judge, and every knee's bowing to him, and every tongue's confessing to him, is spoken of him as God-man: for it is said that he died, rose, and revived that he might have this honor and authority [Rom. 14:9]. So in John 5:27, 'tis said that the Father "hath given him authority to execute judgment also, because he is the Son of man." So that if he has acted the part of a judge towards the elect angels, it must be since his incarnation; and we know that he is to judge angels at the last day as God-man.

Corol. Hence Christ is the tree of life in the heavenly paradise, to all the inhabitants of it. If our first parents had stood in their obedience, and were meet for their reward of eternal life, then they were to be brought to the tree of life, and were to receive it from that tree by eating the fruit of it, as though eternal life was the fruit of that tree. Thus it [was] in the earthly paradise, the dwelling place of man; and there was also a tree of life in the heavenly paradise, the dwelling place of angels. When they had stood in their obedience, and were looked upon of God meet for the reward of eternal life, they were brought to Jesus to receive the reward at his hands; which they in God's account especially became worthy of by their being willing to be subject to him as God-man, and being willing to depend on him as their absolute Lord and supreme Judge.

592. HELL TORMENTS. The spiritual misery of [the] damned will very much consist in the sense of the immense hatred and displeasure of God. I speak not of feeling or fearing the effects of God's displeasure, but of the apprehension of that displeasure simply considered. Such is the nature of the soul, that simple apprehension of the hatred of another is unpleasant to it. It begets an uneasiness in a man to have his neighbors at odds with him; and how great a trouble would it be to a man to have all around him, all that he sees and has to do with, ill-affected to him, hating and despising him! A man in such a case could have but little comfort of his life; and that not only because he feels or is afraid of the effects of their ill will, the mischief that they do or will do him, but because he looks upon the dislike, hatred and contempt of his fellow creatures itself a calamity. Some would regard it less than others, as some men would regard less than others any other particular calamity that is not his total and perfect ruin; which yet don't argue that it is not in itself a calamity. Some may less regard such a calamity because they have more of other enjoyments to fly

to, to support them; or because they have their minds habitually more engaged, and their attention more fixed on other enjoyments; and from other causes that might be mentioned, that by no means infer that it is not in itself a calamity.

The hatred or contempt of another is more regarded, and the apprehension of it more afflictive,

1. According to the apprehension we have of a man's being. Therefore the sense of another's contempt and hatred causes greater uneasiness when a man is present than when absent; for when he is[4] present, we have a more lively apprehension of his being. Hence enemies love to keep apart.

2. According as the person hating or contemning appears great or considerable, i.e. according to the degree of greatness that appears, and according to the degree of the appearance of that greatness, the liveliness of the idea or apprehension we have of it. There are a great many things that contribute to the appearance or apprehension that we have of a man's greatness or considerableness: the evidences and manifestations we see of his wisdom and capacity, the outward show in the countenance and gesture, a splendid and pompous way of living, the reputation he has among others, the respect they show him. These and other such like things tend to strike the imagination, and greatly enliven the apprehension we have of his[5] considerableness. If we see a man to be in general reputation and honor, this renders the apprehension of his hatred or contempt [more afflictive] on two accounts, viz. as this gives more of an impression of his greatness; and secondly, as by this means he is like to influence others to the like temper towards us—but 'tis the former reason only that belongs here.

3. According as his contempt or hatred appears great, i.e. according to the degree of the dislike that appears, and according to the degree of the appearance, or liveliness of our sense of it. Thus there will be a greater affliction while the person hating or contemning is showing his hatred or contempt by reproachful words, or by his actions and behavior, than when he is absent, and we see not the expressions of his dislike, because we have then a more lively idea of it upon this account. The more we are concerned with persons, the more afflictive is their hatred, for our concern with them keeps us in the way of their expressions of their hatred, and gives frequent occasion for the reviving our apprehension of them and

4. MS: "they are."
5. MS: "their."

their enmity. Partly for this reason, a man would not very much mind the hatred of a man dwelling in the East Indies, because he did not come in his way to express his dislike and enmity, and to revive and enliven the uneasy idea. In such a case we han't that lively apprehension of the being of a man and his considerableness; we don't see those evidences and manifestations of his considerableness.

4. A man will suffer from the apprehension of the dislike of another, in some proportion as the quantity of remaining good is greater or smaller. If a man is hated and contemned by one, but is loved and esteemed as much by another that appears as considerable as he, or if by many who together appear as considerable, the one will balance the other.

From these things we may in some measure gather how greatly wicked men in another world will suffer from the apprehension of God's displeasure. Now indeed, in this world, they commonly very little regard it, for they have very little sense of the being of God; they see nothing of him, they are very insensible of the greatness of God, and have no lively apprehension of his displeasure. Their minds are exceedingly stupefied as to the apprehension of these things, and are exceedingly diverted, being wholly taken up about worldly enjoyments and the objects that are around them, and affect their senses.

But in another world the soul shall be stripped of stupefying flesh and sense, and taken from all those worldly objects and enjoyments that now engage and take up the mind; and then they will be sufficiently sensible of the being of God. They shall then see that he is, doubtless in a more full and clear manner, and with vastly more perfect apprehension, than we now see one another to be, or than we see the sun to be; and also shall see how great a being God is, and shall have the most quick and strong apprehensions of his greatness; shall perpetually have the greatest and clearest apprehensions of his infinite greatness and considerableness; shall see that he is immensely more considerable than all other beings put together; shall see that he is the great all, and all without him are nothing; shall be sensible of God's presence continually with them, and of a most near concern with them; shall see then that their being and all things appertaining to them, are every moment from God; shall see the infinitely near concern God hath in all things, how all things are made by him, and that by him all things consist, and that by him all things are disposed and done, and that all things are absolutely and entirely and in all respects dependent upon him; and shall know that God perfectly and implacably hates them, and infinitely loathes and contemns them; and shall perpetually have the most strong and vivid apprehension of that divine hatred and contempt, [stronger and more vivid] than one man has of the hatred of another when he is in his presence, and hears and sees him manifest his enmity, as much as words and behavior can do.

There will be more perfect ways without doubt for conveying things to the minds of those that are in another world, than the signs that men use here. 'Tis suitable that wicked men should know and be sensible how God hates their sins, and them for them; and no doubt but God will make them to know it sufficiently, and that he will convey it to their apprehensions in far more perfect ways. And then they shall [have] nothing to fly to for a support; they shall have the esteem and good will of no other being, nor shall they have any enjoyment wherewith to comfort themselves. The horror, therefore, that they will sustain in a sense of God's displeasure, will, by what has been already said, be great in proportion to the degree of the sense they will have of the being of God, and the degree of his greatness apprehended, and the degree of apprehension or sense of it, and the degree of the displeasure, hatred and contempt apprehended, and the impression or liveliness of the apprehension, and destituteness of other enjoyments to take refuge in.

Corol. 1. Hence we may see how that disgrace and contempt will be a very great part of the misery of the damned. Nothing will make men more uneasy here, than to be despised and contemned by their fellow creatures; they look upon nothing as a greater injury from them than contempt. By what has been said, we may learn how [much] more sinners will suffer in another world, in apprehension of God's contempt of them.

Corol. 2. Hence reason tells us that the misery of the damned will certainly be inexpressibly and inconceivably great, for merely their being perfectly hated of God, and their being sensible of it, will unavoidably render it so. And doubtless they are perfectly hated of God; or else no account can be given of God's making them eternally and desperately miserable,[6] without hope or possibility of help. And doubtless they are made sensible of it; for surely 'tis meet that the delinquent should be made sensible of the just displeasure of his Lord and Judge.

593. CONFIRMATION OF THE ANGELS. See Nos. 591, 570, 515. The angels, we know, were especially then given to Christ God-man, when he ascended. Then it was that he was made the head of all principality and power; and the great congruity of it confirms me, that when they once were given to Christ God-man, then they were in [a] confirmed state and

---

6. MS: "misery."

incapable of perishing. For 'tis most congruous that there should be no possibility of any such thing as perishing or death in his hands who is the prince of life, and the end of whose very being in such a constitution of his person, was life and salvation. 'Tis congruous that in such an one there should be only life and no death, which is so disagreeable to his character and work, and the nature of his kingdom.

594. CHRIST'S MEDIATION, RIGHTEOUSNESS, SACRIFICE. DEGREES OF GLORY. See sermon on Rev. 5:12, throughout.[7] See also note on I Cor. 15:41.[8]

595. BAPTISM. See No. 577. The parent don't give his child to God with a thorough disposition, will and desire, that is not willing and disposed to be thorough in taking pains in the child's education, that he may bring it up for God. It is in the baptism of infants as it is in the baptism of adult persons; only in the one the person acts for himself, in the other the parent acts for him. In baptism of an adult person, if it be regularly administered, the person baptized does make a visible dedication of himself to God. But notwithstanding, if he ben't sincere in it, he is not entitled to the blessings signified and sealed in baptism. So in baptism of an infant, if it be regular, the parent or parents make a visible dedication of the child to God; but if he don't do it sincerely, the child is not saved upon that account. If the adult person does sincerely and believingly give up himself to God, baptism seals salvation to him: so if the parent sincerely and believingly dedicates the infant to God, baptism seals salvation to it. If the adult person did sincerely and with his whole heart dedicate himself to God, he will afterwards live a holy life. He will be so thorough in his care and pains to avoid sin, and serve and glorify God, that he will be universally holy, and in that way will come to eternal life; the promise of it is sealed in his baptism. So if a parent did sincerely and with his whole heart dedicate his child to God, he will afterward take thorough and effectual care in bringing up his children in the nurture and admonition of the Lord, continuing in prayer and dependence on God for them; and in that way it is sealed to them, that ordinarily they shall obtain success.

7. The doctrine of the sermon on Rev. 5:12 (n.d., [1731–32]) states that "Christ was worthy of his exaltation upon the account of his being slain." In explication of this doctrine JE considers (1) "what is meant by exaltation and to what degree [Christ] is exalted"; (2) "in what respects he is worthy" of exaltation; and (3) "why he is worthy."

8. Reference uncertain. There is no note on this text in either the "Blank Bible" or the "Notes on Scripture."

A parent that has believingly and entirely given up his child to God, yet mayn't be absolutely certain of the salvation of his child if it dies in infancy; as an adult person that has truly given up himself to God, mayn't be certain of his own salvation, because he is not absolutely certain whether he was sincere in it. Though the promise of the salvation of a baptized child that dies in infancy, to a parent that thoroughly dedicates it to God, be absolute, yet there is reason why the parent should earnestly pray for its salvation; as an adult believer may have reason earnestly to pray for his salvation, and when dying to commend his spirit into Christ's hands, as Stephen did.

Note. A parent may himself be a true believer, and yet not entirely give up his child to God. A person may be a true believer, that yet has not acted that faith for his child, that he has for himself. (These things about baptism doubtful.) [9]

596. CHRISTIAN RELIGION. We can't reasonably suppose that mankind in their primitive state, or when God first created them, were in the same corrupt state wherein they are now; mankind are doubtless fallen from a better and more excellent state, that they were once in. Now if God has not wholly forsaken and given over mankind in their fallen state, but still has a kindness and favor for them, 'tis most reasonable to suppose that God has a design to restore them to the state from whence they are fallen. For if the almighty and all-sufficient God be yet man's friend, still continues his love to him, he'll forgive him his ill deserts, and will doubtless repair his losses, and change him from his loathsomeness and hatefulness, and help him out of his misery. For if he still is so gracious as to continue still to make him the object of his divine love, and to receive him into favor, why should he suffer him to remain hateful and miserable without changing or helping him? This don't become an all-sufficient friend; it rather becomes such a friend not only perfectly to restore man, but to do it with advantage, to exalt him to a more excellent state than he was in before.

But we have [no] notice given us of any restoration, any other way than by the gospel; and the gospel gives us a most rational account of a full recovery from our fallen state, and obtaining our primitive happiness, and advancement to a much greater happiness by Jesus Christ. But if the gospel ben't true, and we have no benefit by any merits of a mediator,

9. This comment is a later (though probably not much later) addition. It is not clear whether it refers to the whole number or only to the note at the end.

there is no reason why we should expect ever to be fully restored, much less to be more than restored. For if we suppose God will of his absolute mercy forgive upon our repentance and sincere endeavors to conform to his laws, yet we can't expect that our reward will be any greater than in proportion to our goodness: which doubtless in the best [of men], in the present state of mankind, is vastly short of what man had before he fell; and so the happiness that the best of men are brought to now falls vastly short of what man lost or missed of.

597. CHRISTIAN RELIGION. CHRISTIANS ARE TO BE LOOKED UPON AS GOD'S PEOPLE, ISRAEL. See No. 49. The seed of Abraham and of Israel are continued in the Christian church. Christians, though according to the flesh descended of the Gentiles, yet are looked upon as being of that same people that came up out of Egypt, and dwelt in Canaan under judges and kings; they are Israel, and the seed of Abraham, according to the true intent and meaning of the words as used by the prophets, and as taken and understood by the Jews themselves. So that promises that were made by the prophets to the people of Israel concerning their future prosperity and glory, are fulfilled in the Christian church according to their proper intent, and as the Jews themselves might well understand them. For,

1. They that were proselyted to the true worship of the God of Israel, and to an observance of the rules that Israel were under, were by the law and custom of the nation always from the beginning looked upon as being of the same people, of the congregation or church of Israel. Ex. 12:48, "Let all his males be circumcised, and he shall be as one that is born in the land." There were many strangers in the congregation of Israel that came up out of Egypt, that God covenanted with together with the natural seed of Israel, made the same covenant with them, as appears by Ex. 12:38, "And a mixed multitude went up with them," [and] Deut. 29:10–13. And the stranger is there mentioned as being of that people that God had established, to be a people for himself, and that he might be unto them a God; and Abraham and Isaac and Jacob are there mentioned as being their common father. And it was after appointed that the stranger should be as one born in the land, and that there should be one law for them and the stranger; and strangers that worshipped the true God according to his institutions, were to be of the congregation or church of Israel. Only there was an exception made of the Moabites and Ammonites, that they should [not] enter into the congregation of the Lord till the tenth generation, and an Edomite till the third generation.

When strangers served the same God, they were of the same people; as

Ruth who was a Moabitess says, "Thy people shall be my people, and thy God shall be my God" [Ruth 1:16]. So that by the Law of Moses itself, those that joined themselves to the God of Israel, and worshipped him according to the ordinances of Israel, were of Israel. And 'tis no objection, that the Christians don't worship God according to the ordinances given to Israel by Moses, those ordinances having now ceased; for this alters not the case, whether they be the same ordinances that God gave Israel then, or those that he gave Israel afterwards. He that joins to the God of Israel, and the ordinances that Israel are under at that time, he is an Israelite according to the Law. There is no reason why God's altering the ordinances of his worship in Israel should make any alteration in this matter, or why he that is a proselyte to the God of Israel and ordinances of Israel now, since the alteration of those ordinances, should not be an Israelite, as well as before that alteration.

The ordinances of the Christian worship are ordinances as much given to God's people of Israel as the ordinances of the Law of Moses were. Christ was sent to the lost sheep of the house of Israel; he came to his own. When he sent forth the apostles, he first sent them to the Jews and bid 'em not go by the way of the Gentiles, nor enter into the cities of the Samaritans. And after his resurrection the apostles at first for some time preached only to the Jews; and the Christian church at first was only of the Jews.

The proselytes, as well as those that were the descendants of Israel according to the flesh, were to keep the Passover in commemoration of the deliverance of the children of Israel out of Egypt, as being concerned in that affair, and as being of the people that were then delivered, as well as others, as appears by Ex. 12:48–49. And so they were to keep those other feasts that were in commemoration of other remarkable events pertaining to Israel. So they were circumcised, as a sign of their being the children of Abraham.

And as it was the law, so it was the custom of the Jews from the beginning, to look upon proselytes as belonging to the congregation and people of Israel. As we have observed already that there were strangers with the congregation of Israel in the wilderness when they entered into covenant with God; and afterwards we find mention of persons as of the people of Israel that were descended of other nations: as Uriah the Hittite, Obil the Ishmaelite (I Chron. 27:30), Araunah or Ornan the Jebusite, and Zelek the Ammonite (II Sam. 23:37; I Chron. 11:39), Ithmah the Moabite (I Chron. 11:46), Obed-edom the Gittite (II Sam. 6:10–11). So it was with Ittai the Gittite, and the six hundred men that came up with him with David from Gath (II Sam. 15:18–22). So it was with many of the Jebusites, Zech. 9:7, where 'tis prophesied that in gospel times other Gentiles shall be as they. So it was with the Kenites, according to Moses' promise to Hobab, "We are journeying to the place of which the Lord said, I will give it you: come thou with us, and we will do thee good: for the Lord hath spoken good concerning Israel. And it shall be, if thou go with us, yea, it shall be, that what goodness the Lord shall do unto us, the same will we do unto thee" (Num. 10:29, 32). Which promise is doubtless made to everyone that will go with them, and join with them as Jethro did, as it is prophesied of the Gentiles in gospel times that they should (Zech. 8:23). And so it was with the Gibeonites: a whole nation, by joining to Israel in their worship of Jehovah, became of Israel; and that according to the Law, Deut. 29:10–13, where is particular mention of the hewer of the wood and drawer of the water as God's covenant people, and children of Abraham, Isaac and Jacob. So it was with those spoken of, Esther 8:17 (compare Esther 9:27 and Zech. 8:23). 'Tis prophesied that in gospel times the Gentiles should be given to the Jews as their children, Ezek. 16:61 (see note).[1]

Besides the accounts which the holy Scriptures give us, that the Jews looked upon a proselyte as a proper Israelite is confirmed by other accounts. The Talmud gives this account (see Wall, *Of Infant Baptism*, intro., p. lxxi, a quotation out of the Talmud), "When a proselyte is received, he must be circumcised: and then when he is cured, they baptize him in the presence of two wise men, saying; Behold, he is an Israelite in all things." And as Mr. Wall says in the same page, "the same continues to this day to be the practice of the present Jews. For so Leo Modena,[2] in his history of them, speaking of a proselyte's admission, [says], 'They take and circumcise him: and as soon as he is well of his sore, he is to wash himself all over in water: and this is to be done in the presence of three rabbins. And so thenceforth he becomes as a natural Jew.'" [On] p. lxxii he quotes out of Gemara Babylon[3] (*ad tit.* Cherithoth) this passage, "And, if he be not baptized; he remains a Gentile." Persons are still made

1. The "Blank Bible" note on Ezek. 16:61 states, "Here the Gentiles, that are represented by Sodom, are spoken of as those that should thereafter become children of God's Israel . . . and in this chapter, those that were the posterity of those patriarchs according to the flesh are not reckoned in the sight of God as their posterity, but rather the posterity of the heathen."

2. Leone Modena (1571–1648) was an Italian rabbi and scholar whose writings were highly regarded by Christian Hebraists. Wall is perhaps quoting from Modena's *Historia de' riti Ebraici* (Paris, 1637).

3. I.e. the Babylonian Talmud. Cherithoth (Keritot) is a tractate in the Babylonian Talmud.

Israelites by baptism according to Christ's institution, though circumcision ceases.[4]

Dion Cassius[5] the historian gives the same account; his words as quoted by Prideaux (*Connection,* Pt. II, p. 434), are, "The country is called Judea, and the people Jews. And this name is also given to as many others as embrace their religion, though of other nations." There is a remarkable instance of this, in a whole nation that by this means became Jews or Israelites before Christ came. Hircanus, conquering the Edomites, or Idumeans, "forced them to become proselytes to the Jewish religion, and hereon being incorporated into the Jewish nation, as well as into the Jewish church, they thenceforth became reputed as one and the same people, and at length the name of Edomites or Idumeans being swallowed up in that of Jews, it became lost, and no more heard of" (Prideaux, *Connection,* Pt. II, p. 433).[6] And so the Jews that we read of in Christ's time, were a people mixed of the posterity of those that before were Jews and of those Edomites. Herod the Great, the king of the Jews, was of the offspring of those Edomites. There can be no reason why people now that join themselves to the God of Israel, and embrace the religion that he has instituted for Israel, should not be accounted true Israelites, as well as those Edomites.

Obj. 1. But then the proselytes among the Jews were accounted Jews and Israelites because they came and joined themselves to that people; none were Israelites but one of these two ways, either by being the natural offspring of Jacob, or by joining to them that were so. The people or company began with Jacob's children according to the flesh; though persons of other nations soon began to be added, and so continued to be added to from other nations from age to age, down to Christ's time, as a snowball gathers by rolling, yet the original company were the natural offspring of Jacob.

Ans. So it was in the Christian church. The Christian church first began with Jews, and was for some time made up only of Jews; and they proselyted or converted the Gentiles, and brought 'em to join with them. It was

---

4. William Wall, *The History of Infant Baptism. In Two Parts. The First, Being an Impartial Collection of all such passages in the writers of the four first Centuries do make for, or Against it. The Second, Containing several Things that do help to illustrate the said History* (London, 1705; 3rd ed., London, 1720), pp. lxxi–lxxii.

5. Dio Cassius (c. 150–235 C.E.), a Roman historian, makes frequent reference to Jewish religious practices and political activities in his multivolume *History of Rome.*

6. Humphrey Prideaux, *The Old and New Testaments Connected in the History of the Jews and Neighbouring Nations, from the Declensions of the Kingdoms of Israel and Judah to the Time of Christ* (2 vols. London, 1716–18; 9th ed., 4 vols. London, 1725), vol. 3, pt. II, bk. V, pp. 434, n. *w,* and 433.

they that laid the foundation for all the proselytism of the Gentiles that ever has been since. And the Gentile proselytes or converts were added to the Jewish-Christian church; and so, in process of time, the Christian Jews and Gentiles were mixed and blended together, and all distinction was lost, as it was with the Jews and Edomites before Christ's time.

Obj. 2. But the proselytes were the more properly reckoned as of the nation of the Jews, because they submitted themselves to their government, to their kings and priests or rulers: so the whole kingdom were denomi-, nated Israel, because the seed of Israel were the governing part.

Ans. 1. The supreme and absolute Lord, King and Judge, and great high priest and captain, and common head of government and influence that Christians are under, that rules and disposes all things in the Christian church, and that is all in all among them, was a Jew, was the natural seed of Abraham and Israel. And the apostles, who under Christ have the principal rule in the Christian church in all ages, and sit as it were on twelve thrones judging the twelve tribes of Israel, were Jews.

Ans. 2. Whether the civil government of Israel was in the hands of one of the natural offspring of Jacob, or one that was according to the flesh descended of other nations, if he were now of the people of Israel, that altered not the case. Thus Herod was king of the Jews though descended of the Idumeans.

Ans. 3. The Law nor custom did not make it essential that they should be under the temporal government of those that were Israelites, but only that they should embrace the Jewish religion. Thus proselytes were Israelites when the Jews were subject to the government of the Chaldeans and Romans.

Obj. 3. All that were of that company or society were called Israel, because the natural posterity of Israel were the prevailing part; the greater number were of them and so their name prevailed. They were so much the greater part, that the name of Israel swallowed up the names of other nations that were mixed with them.

Ans. 1. The Law don't make it necessary that the natural Israelites should be the major or prevailing part as to number. Proselytes by the Law should have kept the Passover in commemoration of Israel's coming out of Egypt, though they had been more in number than the natural posterity of those that did come out of Egypt; the language of which would have been, that they were of the same people, and as such were concerned in that transaction as well as their natural posterity.

Ans. 2. If the greater part of the people had happened to have been the posterity of the Idumeans, that would not have deprived the society of the name of Israel, nor that part of them that were descended of another nation. It was not their prevailing in number that denominated the whole company Israel, but their prevailing in religion; their being prevalent in that respect, that they brought the rest to submit to their God, and to embrace their laws and institutions, and to be subject to the spiritual government of Israel.

Ans. 3. It was particularly prophesied of Israel in the times of the gospel, that those [who] were the natural offspring of the Gentiles should prevail in number, should be the greater part of God's people; as will be shown by and by.[7]

Obj. 4. The proselytes dwelt in the land of Israel, but Christians dwell in all parts of the world.

Ans. It was not necessary that they should dwell in the same land in order to their being looked upon as of Israel. For the Jews after the captivity into Babylon never generally dwelt in the land of Canaan; and before Christ's time they were scattered all over the world (as the Christians are), and proselytes [were] among them as we learn by Acts 2:9–10.

Obj. 5. Those of the Jewish nation that the Christian Gentile converts joined to, were not the body of the people but only a small part of it, for the greater part of the Jewish nation never embraced Christianity; and so the Christian converts never joined themselves to the nation, but only to a party of them.

Ans. 1. This is no more of an objection why proselytes joining themselves to them should not upon that account be looked upon Israelites, than why proselytes joining themselves to the Jews after the captivity of the ten tribes, should not be accounted Israelites: for the ten tribes were the major part of the nation.

Ans. 2. Those Jews of which the Christian church at first was made up, were the whole body of the people that were truly Israelites; they were the whole of God's Israel. The rest were rejected from being God's people, as much as the ten tribes were when they were removed out of God's sight. They forsook and went off from Israel; they were broken off from that stock by unbelief that the Gentiles might be grafted on. They forsook the God of Israel, the King of Israel, the priesthood, temple worship and ordinances of Israel; and God withdrew the tokens of his presence from among them, and removed 'em out of his sight by sending them into captivity, as he did the ten tribes. According to the Apostle's observation, "They are not all Israel, that are of Israel" [Rom. 9:6]. So that

---

7. I.e. in the second part of this entry.

those that the Christian proselytes joined themselves to were the remnant of Israel, or that part of the nation of Israel that yet remained and had not departed, and were not rejected from being any more of Israel, or God's people. God threatened (Num. 14:12) that he would disinherit the whole congregation of Israel, and make of Moses a great nation. If he had so done, proselytes joining themselves to his posterity would have been Israelites nevertheless for his being but one of so many hundred thousands.

Obj. 6. Converts or proselytes might well be looked upon as of the same society or "congregation" (as the Scripture phrase is), but how could they justly be looked upon as standing in such a relation to Abraham or Israel as to be properly accounted their children, and be called by the name of Israel?

Ans. 1. 'Tis evident that the natural relation that any bare to Abraham or Israel, was not the main foundation of their being denominated children of Abraham or of Israel, in divine style, but some relation that is more spiritual; as appears by Gen. 21:12, "In Isaac shall thy seed be called." That is, he and his posterity shall be accounted thy seed, and not any other of thy posterity; and accordingly Ishmael, the son of his handmaid, and the children that he had by his lawful wife Keturah, were excluded. Thus the Apostle argues from hence, Rom 9:7, "Neither, because they are the seed of Abraham, are they children: but, In Isaac shall thy seed be called." And so in Esau and Jacob, that were both the sons of Isaac by the same woman and at the same birth, and though Esau was the first-born.

That which is sufficient to cause that those that are the natural posterity shall not be children, is also sufficient to cause that those that are not his natural posterity may be children. A certain spiritual relation may make those children that are not his natural offspring; as far, or in the same sense degree and manner, as the want of it makes those not his children, that are his natural offspring. If divine constitution may retrench the measure of the denomination of Abraham's seed, so as that it shall fall short of the limits of his natural progeny, doubtless it may also extend it beyond them.

Ans. 2. They were well looked upon as standing in so near a relation to Abraham and Israel, by reason of the relation they stand in to Jesus Christ, who was the seed of Abraham and Israel: they are "Christ's, and therefore Abraham's seed, and heirs according to the promise" (Gal. 3:29). Christians are a great deal more *of* Christ, and are derived from him in greater and more noble and important respects, and more truly and really, than persons are of, and derived from a progenitor of whom they are the natural offspring. The natural derivation of children from progenitors is but a type and shadow of our derivation from Christ. Christians are the seed of Christ, who was the natural seed of Abraham and Israel, who was the principal part of their natural seed; and indeed not properly a part, but *instar totius.*[8] for he is the end and sum of all the promises made to Abraham, Isaac and Jacob respecting their seed. And the reason and ground of that constitution of God, whereby some of their posterity were reckoned their seed and not others, was the relation that they bare to this promised seed, Jesus Christ.

Ans. 3. Gentile Christians are spiritually the descendants of Jews; the Gentile converts are spiritually begotten of the Jews. For as we have observed already, the Christian church originally was only of Jews, and those Christian Jews begat the Gentile converts: as the apostle Paul to the Corinthians professes himself to be their father, and tells 'em that he had begotten them through the gospel [I Cor. 4:15]. The Jewish church was the mother of the Gentile converts and brought them forth, according to the language of the prophets.

2. It appears that Gentile Christians are of God's Israel, according to the true intent and meaning of the prophets, when they foretold to Israel their future prosperity and glory. For those prophecies do explain themselves. They, at the same time that they are foretelling the future glory and prosperity of Israel, do foretell that the Gentiles shall be added to them, as an accession to the congregation of Israel. "And the Gentiles shall come to thy light, and kings to the brightness of thy rising. Lift up thine eyes round about, and see: all they gather themselves together, they come to thee: thy sons shall come from far, and thy daughters shall be nursed at thy side" (Is. 60:3–4). "All the flocks of Kedar shall be gathered together unto thee, the rams of Nebaioth shall minister unto thee: they shall come with acceptance on mine altar" (v. 7). "Surely the isles shall wait for me, and the ships of Tarshish first, to bring thy sons from far, their silver and their gold with them, unto the name of the Lord thy God, and unto the Holy One of Israel, because he hath glorified thee" (v. 9). "Lift up thine eyes round about thee, and behold: all these gather themselves together, and come to thee. As I live, saith the Lord, thou shalt surely clothe thee with them, as with an ornament, and bind them on thee, as a bride doth" (Is. 49:18); 'tis evident that the Gentiles are here meant, by the 6th and

8. The model for the whole.

by the 21st and 22nd verses. See Is. 2:2–3, 44:3–5, 55:5, 56:3, 5–7, and especially v. 8; Hos. 2:23.

Yea it was prophesied, that those that should join themselves to them, of the Gentiles, should be many more than the Jews, and that the greater part of God's people should be of them. Zech. 8:22–23, "Yea, many people and strong nations shall come to seek the Lord of hosts in Jerusalem, and to pray before the Lord. Thus saith the Lord of hosts; In those days it shall come to pass, that ten men shall take hold out of all languages of the nations, even shall take hold of the skirt of him that is a Jew, saying, We will go with you: for we have heard that God is with you." Is. 54:1–3, "Sing, O barren, and thou that didst not bear; break forth into singing, and cry aloud, thou that didst not travail with child: for more are the children of the desolate than the children of the married wife, saith the Lord. Enlarge the place of thy tent, and let them stretch forth the curtains of thine habitations: spare not, lengthen thy cords, and strengthen thy stakes; for thou shalt break forth on the right hand and on the left; and thy seed shall inherit the Gentiles"; with v. 5, "The God of the whole earth shall he be called." See Is. 49:5–6, 66:7–8; Ps. 87, throughout.

And not only so, but it was prophesied also that the body of the people of the Jews should be rejected, and should no longer be God's people, and that the Gentiles should be taken in their room. Is. 65 at the beginning, "I am sought of them that asked not for me; I am found of them that sought me not: I said, Behold me, behold me, to a nation that was not called by my name. I have spread out my hands all the day to a rebellious people, which walketh in a way that was not good, after their own thoughts." Mal. 1:10–11, Is. 49:20–22. In Ps. 125:5 the righteous are called God's Israel, in a plain distinction from all the wicked. See note on Deut. 33:5.[9]

And 'tis also prophesied that God's people should not be confined to the land of Canaan, but should dwell in other countries. "Enlarge the place of thy tent, stretch forth the curtains of thine habitations: spare not, lengthen thy cords, and strengthen thy stakes; for thou shalt break forth on the right hand and on the left; for thy seed shall inherit the Gentiles" (Is. 54:2–3). And in Mal. 1:10–11 it is prophesied that they shall neither be confined to the land of Canaan in their dwelling, nor to the temple

9. The "Blank Bible" note on Deut. 33:5 states, "The name by which Israel is here called is 'the Upright One,' signifying that they only are truly of God's Israel, or Israelites indeed, but those that are upright or without guilt."

there in their worship; but that they shall dwell from the rising of the sun to the going down of the same, and that in all parts of the world incense should be offered, and a pure offering.

In Is. 65:1–7 is foretold the calling the Gentiles and rejecting the Jews; but yet in vv. 8–10 it is foretold that not all the Jews shall be rejected, but that a certain number of them shall be brought forth from among the rest, and be owned and blessed as God's people; and then in vv. 11–15 is showed the great difference God will make between his people and the body of the people of the Jews that were wicked. And when the prophets are foretelling great future prosperity to God's people, to Israel and Zion, we generally find they at the same time denounce terrible judgments to the wicked, making a distinction between the people of Israel or Zion, and the wicked. See No. 601 and Nos. 649, 658; see also "Fulfillment of the Prophecies of the Messiah," § 142.[1]

598. CHRISTIAN RELIGION. SCRIPTURE. Much of the Scripture is apt to seem insipid to us now, and as though there were no great matter of instruction in it, because those points of instruction that are most plainly contained in it, is old to us. 'Tis what we and everybody has been taught from our infancy, and has been most plainly taught this many hundred years in the world, so that the doctrines seem self-evident; so plain to us now, that there seems to have been no need of a particular revelation of such things, especially of insisting upon 'em so much. But it seems exceeding different to us now from what it would have done, if we had lived in those times when the revelation was given, when the things were in great measure new, at least as to that distinctness and expressness of their revelation. 'Tis so now with some of those that seem to us very plain points of what is now called natural religion. If we had an idea of the state the world was in then, when God gave the revelation, they would appear glorious instructions, bringing great light into the world, and most worthy of God. We are ready to despise that that we are so used to, and that is so common and old to us and to the world, as the children of Israel despised manna.

1. "Miscellanies," No. 1068, in itself a small treatise of 144 manuscript pages, is entitled "Fulfillment of the Prophecies of the Messiah." Section 142 begins, "Though it be foretold that the bigger part of the Jews should be rejected and destroyed, and the Gentiles called in their room, in the days of the Messiah's kingdom, yet it is foretold that the Jews should not all be rejected, but that a small part of that nation should be reserved and saved, and should receive the blessings of the Messiah's kingdom."

599. CHRISTIAN RELIGION. CONCERNING THE ABROGATION OF THE CEREMONIAL LAW. TESTAMENTS. DISPENSATIONS. See notes on Jer. 3:16 [–17] and I Chron. 23:26.[2]

600. CHRISTIAN RELIGION. LOVE OF ENEMIES, PRAYING AGAINST THEM. It was not a thing allowed of under the old testament, nor approved of by the old testament saints, to hate personal enemies, to wish ill to them, to wish for revenge, or to pray for their hurt; except it was as prophets, and as speaking in the name of the Lord. So that there is no inconsistence between the religion of the old testament and new in this respect. The apostle Paul himself doth thus imprecate vengeance on his enemies. II Tim. 4:14, "Alexander the coppersmith did me much evil: the Lord reward him according to his works." Revenge or a desire of it was forbidden by the Law of Moses, Lev. 19:18. Yea, there love of our enemy is implicitly commanded: for he that we are to love as ourselves, is the same that we are there forbidden to avenge ourselves upon, which is doubtless our enemy, or he that injures us. And doing good to enemies is required by the Law of Moses. Ex. 23:4–5, "If thou meet this enemy's ox or his ass going astray, thou shalt surely bring it back to him again. If thou seest the ass of him that hateth thee lying under his burden, and wouldest forbear to help him, thou shalt surely help with him."

And this was agreeable to the sense of the saints of those times; as appears by Job 31:29, "If I rejoiced at the destruction of him that hated me, or lifted up myself when evil found him." Prov. 24:17, "Rejoice not when thine enemy falleth, nor let thine heart be glad when he stumbleth"; and 17:5, "He that is glad at calamities shall not be unpunished." We can't think that those imprecations we find in the Psalms and prophets were out of their own hearts, for cursing is spoken of as a very dreadful sin in the Old Testament. And David, whom we have oftener than any others praying for vengeance on enemies, by the history of his life was a man of a spirit very remote from a spiteful, revengeful spirit; yea, we have no such instance in all the Old Testament, as appears by his behavior when persecuted by Saul, when he heard of his death, and upon occasion of the death of Ishbosheth and Abner, and Shimei's cursing him, etc. And he

2. According to Jer. 3:16–17, the throne of God, which used to be identified with the ark, will in the future be located in Jerusalem. This change, JE concludes in his "Blank Bible" note on these verses, "could not be done without a change of the law. So that here is an explicit prophecy that the law shall be changed in gospel times." Similarly, the "Blank Bible" note on I Chron. 23:26 states that "the ceremonial law was in part altered before Christ's time."

himself in the Psalms gives us an account of his wishing well to his enemies and doing good to them (Ps. 7:4), praying for them and grieving at
their calamities (Ps. 35:13–14); and when he prayed for those dreadful
curses upon Achitophel, he was especially far from a revengeful frame, as
appears by his behavior when Shimei cursed him. And some of the most
terrible imprecations that we find in all the Old Testament, are in the New
spoken of as prophetical, even those in the 109th Psalm; as in Acts 1:20.
See notes on Jer. 12:3 and Matt. 1:19.[3]

601. CHRISTIANS, THE TRUE ISRAEL. See No. 597.[4]

Corol. Hence, that was a true title that was written on Christ's cross in
Hebrew and Greek and Latin, "JESUS OF NAZARETH THE KING OF THE JEWS"
[John 19:19]: he is King of the Jews, and only of the Jews, in his kingdom
of grace. There was a special providence in ordering that the inscription
should be so written, and not that "he said, 'I am the King of the Jews,'"
which was the accusation intended by it. I believe this is what St. John
would intimate to us, John 19:21–22. See Nos. 649, 658.

602. CHRISTIAN RELIGION. See note on Ps. 74:13–14.[5]

603. CORRUPTION OF NATURE. REMAINS OF SIN IN THE GODLY, how that
all they do is polluted with sin. See note on Col. 3:17.[6]

604. WISDOM OF GOD IN THE WORK OF REDEMPTION. CHRIST'S RIGHT-
EOUSNESS. It was a thing infinitely honorable to God, that a person of infinite dignity was not ashamed to call him his God, and to adore and obey
him as such. This was more to his honor than if any mere creature of any
possible degree of excellency and dignity had so done.

3. The "Blank Bible" note on Jer. 12:3 is simply a reference to "Notes on Scripture," no. 108,
which comments on Is. 52:7 (*Works, 15,* 81). The "Blank Bible" note on Matt. 1:19 states, "This
is a remarkable and eminent instance of a Christian spirit; and this verse is an evidence that that
meekness, gentleness, forgiveness, and kindness to enemies that the gospel prescribes were duties under the law, and before Christ came."

4. This entry is a corollary to No. 597. See above, p. 140.

5. The "Blank Bible" note on Ps. 74:13–14 observes, "Christ then obtained a signal victory
over Satan . . . when he overthrew Pharaoh and his host in the Red Sea. Then was in a measure
fulfilled that curse on the old serpent, Gen. 3:15. . . . Pharaoh was typically that dragon and
leviathan."

6. JE asks in this "Blank Bible" note, "why can't what we do be accepted, but by Christ?" He answers that humans are infinitely ill-deserving and condemned creatures; even the holy actions
of the godly are corrupt.

605. ORIGINAL SIN. SPIRIT'S OPERATION. FLESH AND SPIRIT. See note on Gal. 5:17.[7]

606. REGENERATION NOT BAPTISM. See a paper laid up in one of the shelves of the scrutore.[8]

607. CHRISTIAN RELIGION. See note on I Cor. 15:11.[9]

608. CHRISTIAN RELIGION. The RESURRECTION of the dead is a doctrine exceeding consonant to the tenor of the gospel of Christ. There is a great congruity between this and other doctrines about the redemption of Christ. For if God appointed his Son to redeem mankind from the calamities and miseries that are come upon them by the fall, 'tis most meet that this redemption should be complete, and that all the evils of the fall should be abolished and delivered from, of which one is death. 'Tis rational to suppose that the eternal Son of God, if he did undertake the work and [was] to be at so great expense and difficulty in it, that he would make thorough work on't. And 'tis congruous that this enemy, death, should first actually take possession, that redemption of Christ from death should be the more visible, remarkable and glorious; that he should not deliver men by preventing the evil, but that the evil should first actually be, that the power and sufficiency of the Redeemer in redeeming may be the more conspicuous and glorious, and his grace therein the more taken notice of.

609. CONSUMMATION OF ALL THINGS. THE DELIVERING UP OF THE KINGDOM. [See] No. 664, § 9; see No. 736. Christ God-man shall reign after he has delivered up the kingdom to the Father, but not as he doth now. Now he reigns by a delegated authority, as a king's son may reign in some part of his dominions as his viceroy or over the whole, by having the whole government and management committed to him and left with him for a

---

7. The "Blank Bible" note on Gal. 5:17 begins, "By this [text] with the context it seems that grace in the heart is no other than the spirit of God dwelling in the heart and becoming a principle of life and action there."

8. This paper cannot now be identified. The "scrutore" (cf. *escritoire*) was JE's desk; a photograph of it appears as the frontispiece of *Works, 13*.

9. In the "Blank Bible" note on I Cor. 15:11, JE maintains, "There was no such thing as any difference among the apostles in the doctrines that they preached, or as one's finding fault with another's thought; but all acknowledged each other's doctrine." Paul exemplifies this unanimity of doctrine.

time. But then Christ will reign as a king's son may reign in copartnership with his father. Now he reigns by virtue of a delegation or commission; then he will reign by virtue of his union with the Father. Now things are managed in Christ's name; they are left to his ordering and government, and the Father reigns by the Son. Then the Father will take the government upon himself, and things will be managed in his name, and the Son shall reign in and with the Father. As it can't be said that the Father does not reign now, [when] the kingdom is in the hands of his Son; so neither can it be said that the Son will not reign then, when the kingdom shall be delivered up into the hands of the Father. The government of the world takes its rise now from the Son as the head and spring of it; and the Father reigns now by virtue of the relation of the Son and his government to him, as his Son [is] infinitely near and dear to him, the same with him in nature and will, as being in the Son and the Son from him, commissionated and instructed by him, acting and influencing by the same Spirit. And so the Father now governs all, by the Son. Then the government of the universe will be from the Father, will take its rise from him. And then the Son will reign by virtue of the Father's relation to him and his to the Father, as being [in] his Father the same in nature and will, the Son being his perfect image; and being in the Father, being his fellow admitted to fellowship and communion with him in government; and the Spirit of the Father by which he actuates and influences, being also his Spirit. Thus the Son then will reign in and with the Father. God the Father is now king of the world; he is he that sits upon the throne, as he is often represented in the Revelation, though the kingdom be in the hands of the Son. So Christ will be king of the church and of the world after the Father has taken the kingdom into his own hands.

Christ will forever continue to reign over all things, for two reasons: first, because 'tis his natural right. As he is a divine person, the natural Son of God, he has a right to reign forever, as he is the Father's proper heir. Second, he will reign forever in reward for what he did in the work of redemption; upon this account he will [be] admitted by the Father to reign with him. As the saints shall be set on thrones and shall reign forever and ever as a fruit of Christ's righteousness, so much more shall Christ reign forever in reward for his own righteousness. It is said of the saints after the resurrection, that "they shall reign forever and ever" (Rev. 22:5); and we have it explained how they shall reign, viz. by sitting with Christ on his throne (3:21), whence 'tis evident that Christ shall reign forever on that throne, as it is said in Rev. 22:3, that the throne of God and the Lamb shall be in the new Jerusalem, or church in her state of consummate glory, after the resurrection. Heb. 10:12, "For ever sat down on the right hand of God." See Mastricht, pp. 1096b and 482a.[1]

610. SELF-RIGHTEOUSNESS, the manner of its working in persons while under CONVICTIONS, see sermon on Rom. 3:13–18, the first seven pages of the application; and whence it arises and the manner of its working, see sermon on Luke 18:14.[2]

611. COVENANT OF WORKS, why the moral law was not expressly given to our first parents, as well as the precept of not eating the forbidden fruit, see note on I Tim. 1:9.[3]

612. SACRAMENT of the Lord's Supper is an ordinance eminently and peculiarly sacred, see sermon on I Cor. 11:29, the doctrine and reason.[4]

613. MILLENNIUM. That there will be a vastly more glorious propagation of the true religion before the end of the world, is what I am con-

1. "Quintus ergo passus hujus dispensationis, erit in consummatione seculorum, quam textus dicit, quando cap. X. 1. Angelus fortis, narratur, pedem dextrum habuisse super mare, & sinistrum super terram, h.e. sibi subjagasse universum orbem, hinc jurasse non fore ab hoc tempus amplius vs. 6. Quod confirmatur etiam Psal. CII. 27. Heb. I. 10. 11. 12. Jes. LXVI. 17. 2 Pet. III. 7. 10. 11. 12. 13. Qui nunc sunt coeli & terra——repositi servantur igni——veniet——dies ille Domini, quo coeli cum stridore praeteribunt, elementa vero aestuantia solventur, terraque & quae in ea sunt opera exurentur" (p. 1096, col. 1). "Resp. Argumentum duplici nititur falsa hypothesi: A. quod functio Christi regia, eadem sit cum sacerdotali, quam supra cap. V. §. VI. ex professo rejecimus. B. quod in terris Mediator non fuerit Sacerdos, quam refutavimus cap. vii. §. xvi. (2) Quod potestas illa omnis, in coelo & in terra, quae cum regia coincidit, de qua Matth. xxviii. 19. post ascensionem demum ei collata fuerit, cum Apostoli emitterentur per universum orbem terrarum, id quod factum demum post ascensionem" (Peter van Mastricht, *Theoretico-Practico Theologia* [Rhenum, 1699], p. [5]82, col. 1). See below, p. 310, n. 1.

2. The sermon on Rom. 3:13–18 (n.d., [1731–32]) has only one use, which is "of conviction to natural men of the vanity and unreasonableness of trusting in their own righteousness." In the first seven pages of this use, which in its entirety comprises two complete sermon units, JE considers how "persons generally will be ready to condemn self-righteousness in words" while entertaining "a high opinion of their own righteousness." The sermon on Luke 18:14 (Nov. 1736) takes as its doctrine, "A self-righteous spirit, or a disposition to trust in a man's own righteousness, is abominable unto God."

3. The "Blank Bible" note on I Tim. 1:9 states, "This may be given as a reason why the precepts of the moral law were not expressed by God to our first parents, as well as that positive precept of not eating the forbidden fruit. There is not that need of God's expressly and particularly forbidding these and those immoralities to one that is perfectly righteous."

4. The doctrine of the sermon on I Cor. 11:29 (Jan. 1733) states, "The sacrament of the Lord's Supper is a very sacred ordinance." Under this doctrine JE lists 5 reasons why the Lord's Supper is "more eminently sacred and holy" than "all the ordinances of divine worship that God has instituted."

firmed in by this, that there has been no propagation of Christianity yet, but what Satan hath emulated as to the extent of it. He in the extent of Mahometanism has vied with the extent of the Christian church, as the magicians in Egypt for a while vied with Moses in the wonders they wrought. It seems [to] me highly probable that Christ will go on in propagating his church till he has vastly outdone Satan, as Moses went on till the magicians could vie with him no longer. And particularly I believe that the Christian church will be so propagated as to swallow up Mahometanism and root it out of the world, as Moses' rod swallowed up the Egyptians' rods. The propagation of the Christian church is often spoken of in Scripture as a glorious instance of the conquering power of God and Christ; and therefore, without doubt, it shall be carried far as to be vastly beyond what Satan has done to vie with Christ.

614. WISDOM OF GOD IN THE WORK OF REDEMPTION. That our Mediator should be neither the Father nor the Spirit[5] but the middle person between them, was fit and necessary, upon a like account as it was necessary that he should be neither God the Father nor one of fallen men but a middle person between them. It was not meet that the Mediator should be the Father, because he sustained the rights of Godhead and was the person offended and to be appeased by a mediator. It was not fit that he should be one of fallen men, because they were those whose mediator he was to be or that he was to mediate for. It was not fit that he should be either God the Father nor a fallen man, because he was to be mediator between the Father and fallen man. Upon the same account, 'tis not fit that he should be either the Father or the Spirit, for he is to be mediator between the Father and the Spirit. In being mediator between the Father and the saints, he is mediator between the Father and the Spirit. The saints as saints act only by the Spirit in all their transactings wherein they act by a mediator; i.e. in all their transactings with God, they act by the Spirit, or rather it is the Spirit of God that acts in them. They are the temples of the Holy Ghost. The Holy Spirit dwelling in them is their principle of life and action. There is need of a mediator between God and the Spirit, as the Spirit is a principle of action in a fallen creature. For even those holy exercises that are the actings of the Spirit in the fallen creature, can't be acceptable nor avail anything with God as from the fallen creature, unless it be by a mediator. The Spirit in the saints is it that seeks blessings of God through a mediator, that looks to him by faith and depends on him for it.

5. MS: "the Son."

'Tis not suitable that the same person that seeks should be mediator for itself for the obtaining the things that it seeks. See this better expressed in sermon on Eph. 3:10, in the eighth and ninth pages of the sermon.[6]

615. WISDOM OF GOD IN THE WORK OF REDEMPTION. It was requisite that Christ in order to redeem man should take on him the very nature of man and not any other created nature. If he had took on him the nature of an angel and had obeyed and suffered in that, it would not have been sufficient, for obeying the commands of God in an angelical nature would [not] have answered the law that was given to man. Man's law required the obedience of that nature, an obedience performed with the strength and under the circumstances [and] imperfections of that nature, and the temptations that it is liable to. It was therefore essential that Christ should be in the same nature, because the law could not be properly answered unless the ends for which God gave the law are answered; which was, that his authority might be submitted to and honored, by his commands being perfectly obeyed and authority perfectly yielded to in such a nature, in a nature of that strength and those circumstances. This is one end of God's creating another sort of intelligent beings besides the angels, that his authority might be submitted to and glorified in [such] a nature, under circumstances so differing from the circumstances of their nature. It was therefore essential in order to Christ answering the design of man's law, without which the law can't be satisfied, that he should obey in man's nature; and indeed, without this he don't obey the same law. 'Tis not the difference of positive commands that makes a different law; it is the difference of natures only that doth that. It may well enough be said that there is no other law but the moral law, for all positive precepts that are or can be are included in the moral law; because this is one of God's moral laws, that we should yield obedience to all God's precepts, whatever they are. The moral law is the same in the same natures, and can be different only in different natures.

616. WISDOM OF GOD IN THE WORK OF REDEMPTION. SATAN DEFEATED. What the fallen angels have done for the ruin of mankind, has only proved an occasion of mankind's being exalted into their stead and to fill up that room that was left vacant in heaven by their fall.[7] The beholding this must

6. On these two pages of the sermon on Eph. 3:10 (March 1733) JE discusses why "it was meet that the Mediator should not be either the Father or the Spirit but a middle person between them." See Worcester ed., *4*, 135–36.

7. MS: "fallen."

needs be exceeding cross and mortifying to Satan, to think that he must be cast down from such a height of glory to so low and abject a state, to such disgrace and misery; and that men, creatures so inferior to him, whom he so envied and thought to have made his vassals, should be advanced into his place in glory; and that what he has done should be the means or occasion of bringing of it about, for under the first covenant there was no promise of heavenly glory.

617. COVENANT OF GRACE. See Nos. 1091, 825, 919, 1091. It seems to me there arises considerable confusion from not rightly distinguishing between the covenant that God makes with Christ and with his church or believers in him, and the covenant between Christ and his church or between Christ and men. There is doubtless a difference between the covenant that God makes with Christ and his people, considered as one, and the covenant of Christ and his people between themselves. The covenant that a father makes between a son and his wife, under one or considered as one, must be looked upon different from the marriage covenant or the covenant of the son and his wife between themselves. The father is concerned in this covenant only—as a parent in a child's marriage—directing, consenting and ratifying. These covenants are often confounded, and the promises of each called the promises of the covenant of grace without due distinction; which has perhaps been the occasion of many difficulties and considerable confusion in discourses and controversies about the covenant of grace.

All the promises of each of these covenants are conditional. To suppose that there are any promises of the covenant of grace, or any covenant promises, that are not conditional promises, seems an absurdity and contradiction. These covenants differ in their conditions. The condition of the covenant that God has made with Jesus Christ as a public person, is all that Christ has done and suffered to procure redemption. The condition of Christ's covenant with his people or of the marriage covenant between him and men, is that they should close with him and adhere to him.

They also differ in their promises. The sum of what is promised by the Father in the former of these covenants, is Christ's reward for what he has done in the work of redemption and success therein. And the sum of what is promised in Christ's marriage covenant with his people, is the enjoyment of himself and communion with him in the benefits he himself has obtained of the Father by what he has done and suffered; as in marriage the persons covenanting give themselves and all that they have to each other. And indeed we may say that the sum of all that Christ promises in his covenant with his people, is that he will give himself to them. In marriage the persons covenanting, giving themselves to each other, do give what they have to each; the union which they mutually consent to infers [and] confers communion. This promise of the covenant of Christ with his people, implies eternal life of both soul and body. The happiness of eternal life, it consists in the enjoyment of Christ and in communion with him or partaking with him in the happiness and glory of his reward, who is rewarded with the eternal life and glory of both soul and body. It includes sanctification and perseverance; these are included in the enjoyment of Christ and communion with Christ. It includes justification; this also is a part of believers' communion with Christ, for they in their justification are but partakers of Christ's justification. They are pardoned and justified in Christ's acquittance and justification as Mediator. The promises of the incarnation of Christ and of his obedience and sacrifice, were included in the covenant between Christ and believers before these things were actually accomplished. These were included in Christ's promise of giving himself to believers. If he gives himself to believers, as is promised in this marriage covenant, then he must represent them. If Christ gives himself to sinners, of course, justice due to the sinners takes hold on him, and all the sinners' obligations lie upon Christ. These things necessarily follow from Christ's making himself one with them, as he doth in his marriage covenant.

In the promise of the Father's covenant with the Son are included eternal life, perseverance, justification; and not only so, but regeneration or conversion; the giving faith, and all things necessary in order to faith, [such] as the means of grace, God's Word and ordinances: for all these things are included in the success of what [Christ] has done and suffered and are parts of his reward. Hence it appears that many of the things promised in both these covenants are the same, but in some things different. So that those things that are promises in one of these covenants, are conditions in another. Thus regeneration and closing with Christ, is one of the promises of the covenant of the Father with Christ, but is the condition in the covenant of Christ with his people. So, on the other hand, the incarnation, death and sufferings of Christ, are promises in Christ's covenant with his people, but they are the conditions of the covenant of the Father with his Son. The things concerned in both covenants being some of them the same and to the same persons, don't cause but that the covenants are not entirely different: as if a father gives an estate to his son and his future wife, the son in his marriage covenant gives himself and his estate to her that he takes to wife; yet the covenants are entirely different and not at all to be confounded.

Both these covenants are revealed to us, and we are concerned in both; both are our consolation. We are concerned in the covenant between the Father and Son, because in that covenant God transacted with him as a public person or as our head, and therefore transacts with believers as in Christ or as being parts of Christ. We are concerned in the covenant between Christ and us as being one of the parties contracting. In the former, we are concerned as being of one of the parties contracting or belonging to it; but in the latter, we are concerned as being distinctly and by ourselves one of the parties contracting. That that is together but one of the parties contracting in the former, is in the latter distinguished into two parties contracting one with another.

The promises of the former of these covenants being revealed, do become the promises of the Father to believers. These are the promises that are given us in Christ; that is, they are promises made to us by the Father as being in Christ, being parts of Christ and so having a right to the same blessing that are promised to Christ himself, our head.

God often speaks in his Word of the covenant he has made with his people, comparing it to the covenant between husband and wife. By this covenant is intended the covenant between Christ and his people.

The promises of a new heart, and a right spirit, and of writing God's law on our heart, etc., that we have in the Word of God, are in different respects promises of both these covenants. These promises, as they respect the first regeneration, belong to God's covenant with his Son. As they respect what is done in the work of sanctification after conversion, they belong also to Christ's covenant with his people. As they denote the public prosperity and glory of the church, they likewise belong[8] to both covenants. For the conversion of sinners to Christ is one thing wherein the church's glory consists, and what every saint looks upon as part of his prosperity, and so is part of that prosperity that Christ has promised to his people for their comfort.

Corol. 1. The revelation and offer of the gospel is not properly called a covenant till it is consented to. As when a man courts a woman [and] offers himself to her, his offer is not called a covenant, though he be obliged by it on his part. Neither do I think that the gospel is called a covenant in Scripture, but only when the engagements are mutual.

Corol. 2. What has been said may something illustrate to us the different respects in which the first closing with Christ and a perseverance in faith and holiness may be said to be conditions of the covenant of grace. There is the

---

8. MS: "it likewise belongs."

like difference between them, as there is between a woman's consenting to be the wife and accepting for her husband him that offers himself to her and courts her, and the duty that she in her covenant promises toward her husband, viz. cleaving to him and being faithful to him as a wife till death.

Both these are in some respects the condition of the covenant—both her accepting him for an husband, and her being faithful to him as a wife till death—but not in the same respects. For the former is so much the condition alone, that as soon as she has performed it, she is at once entitled to him as an husband and so to his love and kindness as such, and to communion in his possessions, before the actual performance of the duty she has promised. She may also be entitled to his instruction and care of her, his wisdom and endeavors to cultivate love, and best assistance to enable her to behave towards him as she ought in her place. But yet her being actually faithful to him till death, may also be so much the condition; as that his accepting [her] as a wife, was as looking upon her faithfulness to him as already virtually performed in her accepting him to be her husband and promising faithfulness, and her supposed disposition to be faithful to her promises. See sermons on Ps. 111:5 and Gal. 3:16.[9]

618. SATAN DEFEATED. Christ poured the greater contempt upon Satan in his victory over him, by reason of the manner of his preparing himself to fight with him, and the contemptible means and weapons he made use of to overthrow him. When he was preparing to encounter that proud and potent enemy, the method he took was not to put on his strength and to deck himself with glory and beauty, but to lay aside his strength and glory and to become weak, to take upon him the nature of a poor, feeble, mortal man, a worm of the dust, that in this nature and state he might overcome Satan; like David who, when he went to fight with Goliath, put off the princely armor that Saul armed him with. The weapons that Christ made use of in fighting with the hellish giant were his poverty, afflictions, reproaches and death. His principal weapon was his own cross, the ignominious instrument of his own death. These were seemingly weak and despicable weapons, and doubtless Satan disdained 'em, as much as Goliath did David's stones that he came out against him with. But with such weapons as these, Christ in a human, weak, mortal nature overthrew all the power and baffled all the craft of hell.

9. The doctrine of the sermon on Ps. 111:5 (Aug. 1745) states, "God never fails in any instance of faithfulness to the covenant engagements he has entered into in behalf of mankind"; that of the sermon on Gal. 3:16 (Feb. 1746) states, "In the divine transactions and dispensations relating to man's salvation, Christ and believers are considered, as it were, as one mystical person."

619. SATAN DEFEATED. Nothing can more clearly manifest to the heavenly hosts that God is the supreme and absolute disposer of all things, than to see God carry on his designs from age to age, so as at last to bring forth those great events and fulfill his great ends by a most powerful and subtle enemy; as he doth by Satan, who, in all that he doth, to his utmost, endeavors to frustrate and counterwork him. Neither can anything more show the wisdom of God in his government of the world.

620. JUSTIFICATION. Faith is the condition of salvation because it trusts in Christ and ascribes salvation to him. Repentance is the condition because it renounces confidence in self and disclaims the glory of salvation. So that neither of them justifies as a work, for the nature of the one is to renounce works, and the nature of the other is to depend on the works of another.

621. CHRIST'S AGONY IN THE GARDEN. It may be asked why Christ should suffer so much beforehand; why was it necessary that he should have two turns of suffering the wrath of God, one upon the cross and another before he was apprehended in the garden?

Ans. The reason might be this: Christ might have a specimen of his sufferings beforehand, that he might know what it was that he was going to suffer, that he might have an idea what those sufferings were that must be undergone to make atonement for sin, that his undertaking them might be more his own act and choice. The undergoing those sufferings and his abiding their approach, could not be fully and perfectly his own actual choice as man, unless he knew what they were. But he could not fully know what they were, he could not have a clear and full idea of [them], without in a considerable measure feeling them. For a clear idea of sorrow, or joy, or any act, exercise or passion of the mind, is the very same thing in a degree existing in the mind that it is an idea of, as I have shown in my discourse about the Trinity.[1] The sufferings that Christ felt in the garden seem to be from an idea he had of his approaching sufferings on the cross, as appears by Christ's expressing himself.[2] God saw fit to give Christ a very full understanding what his approaching sufferings were, just before they came, before he was apprehended, when he had yet opportunity to flee;

[1]. See *An Unpublished Essay of Edwards on the Trinity*, ed. George P. Fischer (New York, Charles Scribner's Sons, 1903), pp. 81–84. JE wrote the first eight pages of this essay, which include the passage on "reflex ideas" to which he refers in this entry, in the first few months of 1730.

[2]. JE perhaps has in mind Jesus' prayer in the garden to "let this cup pass from me: nevertheless, not as I will, but as thou wilt" (Matt. 26:39).

that his choosing them and abiding them might be his own act as man, that it might not be said that he undertook to suffer he knew not what. It was the will of God that that should be the act of Christ, both of the divine and human nature, that it might be a glorious manifestation of the love of both natures towards man, and it might be a more meritorious act of obedience. See No. 653.

See this more fully spoken to in sermon on Luke 22:44, under the fourth thing proposed under the first proposition.[3]

622. CHRIST'S MEDIATION. Mr. Watts' 3rd vol. of sermons, p. 185.[4] "'Twas this very blood in the virtue of which Jesus himself was raised from the dead. Heb. 13:20, 'The God of peace brought again from the dead our Lord Jesus, that great Shepherd of the sheep, through the blood of the everlasting covenant.' 'Twas in the virtue of this blood that he ascended and appeared before God in heaven: Heb. 9:12, 'Christ by his own blood entered into the holy place, having obtained eternal redemption for us.'

"Did the cursed guilt of our sins bring the Son of God down from heaven to earth, did it smite him to death, and lay him low in the grave? But the power of his complete atonement has broken the bonds of death, and the grave, this has brought him back to life again, and raised him from earth to heaven; and by the same blood of his cross he has opened an effectual way for our rising from the dead, and our final admission into the place of blessedness. As Aaron the Jewish high priest might not dare to venture into the Holy of Holies without the blood of expiation, so Christ, our great high priest, when he had once taken our sins upon him, might not ascend into heaven into the presence of God, till in the language of Scripture he could carry his own blood with him,[5] till he could show a full atonement."

623. CONSCIENCE. Let this be added to No. 472. This appears, because natural conscience may be in its most perfect exercise in those in whom

---

3. The first proposition of the sermon on Luke 22:44 (Oct. 1739) states, "The soul of Christ in his agony in the garden had a sore conflict with those terrible views and amazing apprehensions that he then had." Under the fourth particular JE discusses "what may be supposed to be the special ends of God's giving Christ those terrible views of his last sufferings." By showing Christ his future suffering, God ensured that he would "take up the cup" willingly and with human foreknowledge of what lay ahead.

4. Isaac Watts, *Sermons on Various Subjects* (3 vols. London, 1723), p. 185. JE quotes from Sermon VI of Vol. III, which is entitled "The Atonement of Christ."

5. Perhaps a reference to Heb. 9:12.

sin and corruption have its most perfect dominion and exercise. As, for instance, in the devils and damned: their consciences are not stupid, but thoroughly awakened, and fully do their office; they have the most perfect sense of good and evil of that kind. But yet they can't be said properly to see more of the hatefulness or deformity of sin in general, or their own sins, than some wicked men on earth, who yet have not their consciences in any measure so fully enlightened and awakened. They will be sensible and convinced in conscience that their punishment is just. They'll be so far convinced of their own wickedness, that they'll see fully and clearly that it has deserved so dreadful a punishment, even at the same time that they feel it; which argues an illumination of conscience far beyond what any have in this world. And yet this will be without seeing anything of the hatefulness of their sins. It can, therefore, be nothing else but a sense of the equality and answerableness of such a displeasure of God to their sins, from the sight they will have of the awful greatness and majesty of God.[6]

624. INCARNATION OF THE SON OF GOD. See Nos. 487 and 513. Another thing that confirms that Christ's union with the Godhead is by the communication of the Holy Ghost not by measure to him, is what Christ says in vindication of himself, when the Jews accused him of blasphemy for making himself God and saying that he and his Father are one, in John 10:36. "Say ye of him, whom the Father hath sanctified, and sent into the world, thou blasphemest; because I said, I am the Son of God?" He mentions that as sufficient warrant for his saying that he was the Son of God, and that he and the Father were one, and making himself equal with God, viz. that the Father had sanctified [him]. 'Tis by that that he becomes the Son of God. But 'tis the Holy Ghost that is the sanctifier; God sanctified Christ no otherwise than by communicating his Holy Spirit to him. His being sanctified made him God as it made him a divine person. His being sent into the world, i.e. upon the work and office that he came upon, made [him] God by office. See No. 709.

625. EXCELLENCY OF CHRIST. See sermon on Cant. 1:3, preached June 1733.[7]

6. There is a vertical line down the left margin of this entry, indicating that JE used it in another composition. Cf. the chapter on "Natural Conscience" in *The Nature of True Virtue* (*Works, 8,* 589–99).

7. The doctrine of the sermon on Cant. 1:3 states "that Jesus Christ is a person transcendently excellent and desirable." The sermon MS includes the notation "at Boston, June 1733," which indicates that JE probably first delivered it as a public lecture in Boston.

626. SPIRIT'S OPERATION. NATURE. GRACE. COMMON GRACE. SPECIAL REGENERATION. See No. 471. Natural men may have convictions from the Spirit of God, but 'tis from the Spirit of God only as assisting natural principles, and not infusing any new and supernatural principle. That conviction of guilt which a natural man may have from the Spirit of God, is only by the Spirit's assisting natural conscience the better and more fully to do its office. Therein common grace differs from special, that common grace is only the assistance of natural principles; special is the infusing and exciting supernatural principles. Or (if any of these words are too abstruse) common grace only assists the faculties of the soul to do that more fully, which they do by nature; as man's natural conscience will by mere nature render him in a degree sensible of guilt. It will accuse a man and condemn him when he has done amiss. The Spirit of God, in those convictions which natural men sometimes have, assists conscience to do this in a further degree, and helps this natural principle against those things that tend to stupefy it and to hinder its free exercise. But special grace causes the faculties to do that that they do not by nature; causes those things to be in the soul that are above nature, and of which there is nothing of the like kind in the soul by nature; and causes them to be in the soul habitually, and according to such a stated constitution or law that lays such a foundation for a continued course of exercises, as is called a principle of nature—such as a principle of life in a plant or animal, or a principle of sensation or natural appetite, etc.

627. JUSTIFICATION. FREE GRACE. REWARDS. See Nos. 671 and 688. God, in rewarding the holiness and good works of believers, does in some respect give them happiness as a testimony of his respect to the loveliness of their holiness and good works, for this is the very notion of a reward, but in a very different sense from what would have been if man had not fallen. For a man to have eternal life for his works, in the sense that would have been if we had performed perfect obedience, is to have eternal life as a testimony of God's respect to our loveliness; as we are beheld separately by ourselves and to the loveliness of what we do considered in itself, and as it is in us as separately by ourselves. But when God rewards the good works of believers, 'tis in testimony of his respect to the loveliness of their good works in Christ: for their good works are not lovely to God in themselves, but they are lovely to him in Christ and beholding them not separately and by themselves, but as in Christ. See how in note on Col. 3:17.[8]

8. See above, No. 603, p. 142, n. 6.

If we had never committed but one sin and at all other times had exercised perfect holiness and performed perfect obedience, yet looking upon us as we are by ourselves, with all that belongs to us, we should be in no degree lovely persons but hateful, though we had performed many lovely acts; and no one act of holiness is a lovely act in itself and without consideration of any relation to Christ, unless it be a perfect act.

Two things come to pass, relating to the saints' reward for their inherent righteousness, by virtue of their relation to Christ: (1) that any of their inherent righteousness or good works, are acceptable and lovely to God and looked upon meet to be rewarded at all; and (2) that they [are] looked upon worthy of so great a reward, or that God looks upon it suitable that they should be so exceedingly rewarded as they shall [be]. If we suppose that all the deformity of the saints' works is hid by Christ, so that God beholds and has respect to them simply with regard to their holiness, yet that holiness, when thus simple and by itself, is but small; yet God doth exceedingly reward it with a much greater reward probably than he would have done Adam's perfect obedience. This is again because God beholds them as in Christ. Their holiness and good works, what little of it there is, receive vastly greater value than otherwise they would have, by virtue of their relation to Christ; and that because God looks upon them as persons of greater dignity. Is. 43:4, "Since thou wast precious in my sight, thou hast been honorable." The same love and obedience in a person of greater dignity, is more valuable than in one of lesser dignity. Believers are become immensely more honorable persons in God's esteem, by virtue of their relation to Christ, than man would have been considered as by himself; as a mean person becomes more honorable when married to a king. "According to the tenor of the first covenant, the person was to be accepted only for the work's sake; but in the covenant of grace, the works are accepted for the person's sake." Mr. Vinke in *Morning Exercises*.[9]

628. SPIRITUAL KNOWLEDGE. FAITH. That spiritual light that is let into the soul by the Spirit of God, discovering the excellency and glory of divine things, it not only directly evidences the truth of religion to the mind, as this divine glory is an evident stamp of divinity and truth; but it sanctifies the reasoning faculty, and assists it to see the clear evidence there is

9. Peter Vinke's sermon, "How Gospel-grace the Best Motive to Holiness?" was published in Samuel Annesley's *Casuistical Morning-Exercises. The Fourth Volume. By Several Ministers In and About London* (London, 1689), pp. 69v–76v. JE quotes from a passage that appears on p. 72v of this volume.

of the truth of religion in rational arguments. And that two ways, viz. first, as it removes prejudices and so lays the mind more open to the force of argument; and also secondly, as it positively enlightens and assists it to see the force of rational arguments, not only by removing prejudices but by adding greater light, clearness and strength to the judgment in this matter. See how one way, No. 408.[1]

629. MEANS OF GRACE. The Word and ordinances and works of God are means of grace, as they give opportunity for the proper and fit exercise of grace, and are in a sort means of that exercise; though not in the same manner as things are the means of the exercise of natural principles, because not only the principle of grace, but every exercise of it, is the immediate effect of the sovereign acting of the Spirit of God. Indeed, in natural things, means of effects, in metaphysical strictness, are not proper causes of the effects, but only occasions. God produces all effects; but yet he ties natural events to the operation of such means, or causes them to be consequent on such means according to fixed, determinate and unchangeable rules, which are called the laws of nature. And thus it is that natural means are the causes of the exercises of natural principles. But means of grace are not means of the exercises of grace in such a manner. For the actings of the Spirit of God in the heart are more arbitrary and are not tied to such and such means by such laws or rules, as shall particularly and precisely determine in a stated method every particular exercise and the degree of it; but the Holy Spirit is given and infused into the hearts of men only under this general law, viz. that it shall remain there and put forth acts there after the manner of an abiding, natural, vital principle of action, a seed remaining in us.[2]

---

1. See *Works, 13,* 469–70.
2. At this point JE crossed out the remainder of this paragraph and a following paragraph with large X marks. He directed, by means of cue marks, that a paragraph written at the end of No. 631 be substituted for the deleted material. This new composition is included in the text as the final paragraph of the current entry. The deleted material reads as follows: "that it should be putting forth itself, from time to time, as opportunity and advantage from those means presents; that its exercises should ordinarily be, from time to time, consequent on those antecedents in a measure, as the exertions of natural vital principles in plants and animals are consequent on those antecedents that are called natural causes, such as the influence of the sun, and rain, and due cultivation, food, physic, etc.; that when there are the antecedents (those that give suitable opportunity) answerable exercises of grace should follow in some measure in an ordinary and stated way, not precisely determinate and certain as in natural effects, but so far that the obtaining those antecedents should be a very likely way to have those exercises; and the having the most of these antecedents and so thereby the most opportunity for the exercise of grace, should be the likeliest way to have the most of the exercises of grace. But innumerable

Means of grace are so much less properly means either of the habit or exercises of grace, as the dependence or connection between them and the effect is less. The dependence or connection is so much less, as the law by which the effect is consequent is more general and less certain and determinate as to particulars.

630. SPIRITUAL KNOWLEDGE. FAITH. That belief of the truth may be saving that doth most directly depend on rational arguments. See the two foregoing.[3] Believing the truth of divine doctrines, is one of those suitable exercises of grace that God insists that there should be opportunity for, in order to his bestowing grace. Rational arguments give opportunity for it; they give opportunity for such a belief with a less degree of grace. They give opportunity for a fuller and more established belief, less liable to be shocked by temptation with the same degree of grace.

631. FREE WILL. It don't at all excuse persons for not doing such duties, as loving God, accepting of Christ, etc., that they can't do it of themselves; unless they would if they could, and, if they would if they could, unless they would do it from good principles. For that woulding[4] is as good as no woulding at all, that is in no wise from any good principle. But unless men would love God from some real respect to God or sense of duty, that is, of the goodness of their duty, or disposition to their duty, as in itself good and lovely, and not merely from an aversion to pain and desire

---

things are concerned as means, that are concurring in the degree of opportunity given for the exercise of grace; as innumerable things are to be considered, if every thing should be brought into consideration, that is concerned as a natural cause in the degree of the flourishing of a plant.

"So that means of grace, are means of the exercises of grace when once the principle is infused; and the degree of the principle given differing from natural causes only in this, that the effect in natural things in all its circumstances, is connected with the antecedent by a precise and unalterable rule. And here the effect is connected with the antecedent only by a general law, not so particular and precise as to all times and circumstances, but leaving room for variation according to God's arbitrary determination in particulars."

3. This appears to be a reference to Nos. 628 and 629. But, unlike No. 628, No. 629 does not directly discuss the issue of rational demonstrations of religious truths. The other "foregoing" entry to which JE refers is probably No. 408, which is cited at the end of No. 628 (See *Works, 13,* 469–70).

4. As explained by John E. Smith, JE used this word "to refer to very weak inclinations which do not represent genuine convictions and do not issue in action." See *The Works of Jonathan Edwards, 2, Religious Affections,* ed. John E. Smith (New Haven, Yale Univ. Press, 1959), 99, n. 2.

of pleasure, it is in no wise from any good principle. See sermon on Rev. 3:20, answer to second objection under the first use.[5]

632. FREE GRACE. FAITH. JUSTIFICATION is that qualification that renders it suitable in God's esteem that persons should have a declared interest in Christ and his redemption, upon three accounts, viz.:

1. That 'tis an active uniting of the person to Christ, and therefore God looks upon it suitable, that such as believe should be looked upon one with Christ. See No. 568.

2. 'Tis a receiving and accepting the gift. God don't look upon it suitable that the gift, or a right to the gift, should be conferred on an intelligent acting being, that at the same time disapproves of, rejects and opposes the gift. It would be very unsuitable to unite such blessings to an acting willing being, where there is no accord or union of the act or will with the blessing bestowed, but the contrary. See No. 507.

3. It receives and accepts the gift, or is the person's active uniting with the gift, with its qualities and relations, viz. as a free gift, the gift of God, the fruit of his power, etc. It acknowledges the author of the gift, and that glory and perfection of God, that is exercised in giving—his power, holiness, justice, faithfulness and grace that the gift depends upon—and gives the glory to the proper author. When we say that faith is the condition of justification, 'tis no more than to say, 'tis the condition of God's making known his decree, that they shall have the benefit of Christ's righteousness. For without those things forementioned, what good could be obtained by his declaring such a decree? Abundance of evil would be the consequence. But God, in the rule of his making known his decree in this matter, doubtless aims at some good. See No. 6.

633. WISDOM OF GOD IN THE WORK OF REDEMPTION. DIVINITY OF THE SON OF GOD. God would not give us any person to be our redeemer, but one that was of divine and absolutely supreme dignity and excellency, or that was the supreme God, lest we should be under temptation to pay him too great respect: lest if he were not the supreme God, we should be under temptation to pay him that respect, which is due only to the supreme

5. In the first use of the sermon on Rev. 3:20 (March 1734) JE endeavors "to convince sinners how justly they may be left [to] perish forever in that they ben't willing that Christ should be theirs and they his." In response to the second objection under this use JE argues (1) that "'tis no excuse that persons can't receive Christ of themselves, unless they would do it if they could"; and (2) that "there is no excuse to 'em unless they would do it from a good principle."

[God]; and which God, who is a jealous God, will by no means allow to be paid to an inferior being. Men are very liable to be tempted to set those too high from whom they have received great benefits. They are prone to give them that respect and honor that belongs to God only. Thus the gentile world deified and adored their kings that did great things for them, and others from whom they received great benefits. So Cornelius was tempted to give too great respect to Peter, he being the person that God had marked out to be his teacher and guide in things pertaining to eternal salvation. So the apostle John could scarce avoid adoring the angel that showed him those visions; he fell down to worship him once and again. Though the first time he had been strictly warned against it, yet the temptation was so great that he did it again (Rev. 19:10 and 22:8). This that they were under temptation to, was greatly disallowed of by God. When Cornelius fell down before [him], "Peter took him up, saying, Stand up; I myself also am a man" [Acts 10:26]. So when the people at Lystra were about to offer divine worship to Paul and Barnabas, when they heard of it, "they rent their clothes, and ran in among the people, crying out, Sirs, and saying, Sirs, why do ye these things? We also are men of like passions with you, and preach unto you that ye should turn from these vanities, unto the living God, which made heaven, and the earth, and the sea, and all things that are therein" (Acts 14). And when John was about to adore the angel, how strictly was he warned against it. "See thou do it not," says he, "for I am thy fellow servant, and of the brethren, the prophets, that have the testimony of Jesus Christ: worship God" [Rev. 19:10]. And God has been careful to guard against it; so he hid the body of Moses that it might be no temptation to idolatry. But if anything can be a temptation to give supreme respect and honor to one that is not the supreme being, this would be a temptation, viz. to have a person that is not the supreme being to be our redeemer, to have such an one endure such great sufferings out of love to us, and thereby to deliver us from such extreme and eternal misery, and to purchase for us so great and eternal happiness. God therefore, in wisdom, has appointed such a person to be our redeemer that is of absolutely supreme glory and excellency, that we may be in no danger of loving and adoring him too much; that we may prize him, exalt him, for the great things that he has done for us as much as we will, and as his love to us, and his sufferings for us, and the benefits we receive by him, can tempt us to without danger of exceeding.

Christ has done as great things for us, as ever the Father did. His mercy and love have been as great and wonderful, and we receive as much benefit by it, as we do by the love and mercy of the Father. The Father never did greater things for us, than to redeem us from hell and bring us to eternal life. But if Christ had not been a person equal with the Father, and worthy of our equal respect, God would not have ordered it so that the temptation to love and respect to the Son, that we have by kindness received, should be equal with what we have to love and respect to the Father.

634. RESURRECTION. NEW HEAVEN AND NEW EARTH. That the settled and everlasting abode of the righteous after the resurrection, shall not be here upon this earth, but in heaven, in that world of glory where the man Christ Jesus now is, seems rational upon this account, viz. that it seems most rational to suppose that the saints, when they receive their consummate glory, should be removed to be brought to Christ, to be gathered home to him, of whom are all things, and to whom are all things, than that they should remain unmoved, and Christ should remove and change his place, to take up his everlasting abode in that which is their native place. 'Tis fit that in the consummation of all things, that all things should be gathered together to God, that the less should remove and be brought home to the greater, and not the greater change place to come to the less. Christ, when he ascended into heaven, he ascended to his fixed and everlasting abode of glory; and the promise is that Christ will take believers home to him, that though he will come again, yet it will be to take them to himself. See Notes on Revelation, nos. 62 and 73.[6] See No. 743.

635. CONVICTION. HUMILIATION. Bad wounds must be searched to the bottom; and oftentimes when they are very deep they must be lanced, and the core laid open, though it be very painful to endure, before they can have a good cure. The surgeon may skin them over, so that it may look like a cure without this, without much hurting the patient, but it will not do the patient much good. He does but deceive him for the present, but it will be no lasting benefit to him; the sore will break out again. This figures forth to us the case of our spiritual wound. The plague of our hearts, which is great and deep and must be searched, must be lanced by painful conviction. The core must be laid open. We must be made to see that fountain of sin and corruption there is, and what a dreadful state we are in by nature, in order to a thorough and saving cure. Jer. 8:11, speaking of the teachers of Israel, their prophets and priests, "They have healed the hurt of the daughter of my people slightly, saying, peace, peace, when there is no peace."

6. See *Works*, 5, 158 and 166–67.

A child is not brought forth by the mother without grievous pain. This is a type of the pains and inward distress that there is in the soul before it becomes the spiritual mother of Christ.

636. FAITH, SAVING, may be built upon rational arguments, or rational arguments may savingly convince the soul of the truth of the things of religion. Nicodemus, when he "came to Jesus by night, said unto him, Rabbi, we know that thou art a teacher come from God: for no man can do these miracles that thou dost, except God be with him" [John 3:2]. He was a true believer; and though now he was cowardly and came by night, yet afterwards he appeared openly as one of his disciples in a time of greater trial, viz. when he, with Joseph of Arimathea, came to anoint the body of Jesus (John 19:39, compared with Mark 15:43). The woman of Samaria believed, because Jesus told her all that ever she did (John 4:29), though that might not be the only thing that convinced her. John 6:26, "Verily, verily, I say unto you, ye seek me, not because ye saw the miracles, but because ye did eat of the loaves, and were filled." Christ reproves the Jews for not believing, though he had done such miracles. John 5:36, "But I have greater witness than that of John: for the works which the Father hath given me to finish, the same works that I do, bear witness of me, that the Father hath sent me." And 10:24–26, "Then came the Jews round about him, and said unto him, How long dost thou make us to doubt? If thou be the Christ, tell us plainly. Jesus answered them, I told ye, and ye believed not: the works that I do in my Father's name, they bear witness of me. But ye believe not, because ye are not of my sheep." And vv. 37–38, "If I do not the works of my Father, believe me not. But if I do, though ye believe not me, believe the works; that ye may know, and believe, that the Father is in me, and I in him." John 11:15, "But I am glad for your sakes that I was not there, to the intent that ye might believe." John 11:42, "And I know that thou hearest me always: but because of the people that stand by I said it, that they may believe that thou hast sent me." John 12:37, "Though he had done so many miracles before them, yet they believed not on him." John 13:18–19, "He that eateth bread with me hath lift up his heel against me. Now I tell you before it come to pass, that, when it come to pass, ye may believe that I am he."[7] John 14:28–29, "I go away, and come again unto you. And now I have told you before it come to pass, that, when it

7. The MS at this point reads, "John 11:15, speaking of Lazarus's death, 'And I am glad for your sakes that I was not there, to the intent ye may believe.'" JE must have forgotten to delete this passage after interlineating a reference to John 11:15 a few lines above it.

come to pass, ye may believe." John 14:11, "Believe me that I am in the Father, and the Father in me: or else believe me for the very works' sake." John testifies that he saw the soldier pierce Christ's side, and says that he bears record that we might believe (John 19:34–35). He means either as it proved that he was really dead, and so that when he rose, he rose from the dead; or that the Scripture was fulfilled in him that says, "a bone of him shall not be broken," as in the next verse. John 20:30–31, "And many other signs truly did Jesus in the presence of his disciples, which are not written in this book: but these are written, that ye might believe that Jesus is the Christ, the Son of God; and that believing ye might have life through his name." Thomas was convinced by thrusting his hand into his side. Christ bids him do it, and "not be faithless but believing"; and when he had done it, he cries out, "My Lord and my God." He believed by reasoning from what he had perceived with his external senses; Christ says to him, "Thomas, because thou hast seen, thou hast believed" (John 20:24–29).

How often have we an account in the Acts of the Apostles, reasoning and disputing with men to bring them to believing, and of many being brought to believe through that means. How often did they use that argument, especially of the resurrection of Christ.

637. TRUSTING IN OUR OWN RIGHTEOUSNESS for justification or acceptance with God, or the having the ground of our expectation of God's favor in a high and false apprehension of our own excellency, as related to God's favor, is a thing fatal to the soul, and what will prevent salvation.[8] This is evident,

I. By Rom. 9:31–32. "But Israel, which followed after the law of righteousness, hath not attained to the law of righteousness. Wherefore? because they sought it not by faith, but as it were by the works of the law." Here 'tis evident,

1. That this that Israel did that is here spoken of is fatal, because 'tis said they attained not to the law of righteousness for this reason; this is given as the main reason of their missing of it. And then it's evident by the context, for that is what the Apostle is speaking of, viz. how the greater part of that nation miss of salvation and shall be vessels of wrath; and indeed, this is what he is upon throughout the whole chapter.

2. That by seeking or following after the law of righteousness by the works of the law, is meant seeking justification by the works of the law. For

---

8. MS: "salvation appears."

what is here expressed by following after the law of righteousness, is in the preceding verse, where the Apostle is evidently speaking of the same thing, called following after righteousness, by which is doubtless intended a becoming righteous in the sight of God, or to his acceptance. When it is said, Israel sought or followed after the law of righteousness by the works of the law, 'tis as much as to say, Israel sought and expected to be found in God's appointed way of justification by performing the works of the law.

3. 'Tis evident that by the works of the law here is meant not only a conformity to Jewish ordinances of worship, but our own moral righteousness or excellency, consisting in our obedience to the laws of God in general, whether moral, ceremonial or whatever; because what is called here the works of the law, is called in the third verse of the next chapter their own righteousness, where the same thing is evidently intended by the reference the Apostle has there to what is said here. And doubtless by the works of the law is meant the same as the Apostle means by the righteousness of the law in the fifth verse of the next chapter, where that expression is evidently used as synonymous with our own righteousness (v. 3), and so they are used as synonymous (Philip. 3:6, 9). But doubtless by their own righteousness is meant the same as their own goodness or moral excellency, and not only that part of it that consisted in their obedience to the ceremonial law. And again, we often find the works of the law set by this Apostle in opposition to the free grace of God, and therefore thereby must be intended our own excellency. For wherein does grace appear, but in being bestowed on them that are no more excellent, that are so unworthy, so far from deserving anything? Rom 3:20, 24, 27, 28; and Titus 3:5, where, instead of works of law, the Apostle says works of righteousness; Rom. 11:6 and 4:4; Gal. 5:4; Eph. 2:8, 9.

And then where the Apostle speaks of the works of the law, when speaking of this matter of justification, he evidently means not only works of the ceremonial, but also moral law, as Rom 3:20 with the context; and in other places where this matter is treated of, which it is needless to mention.

4. Seeking or following after justification by the works of the law or by our own righteousness, is fatal, as it is a self-exaltation, and upon the account of that high opinion there is of, and dependence upon, our own excellency in it. For doubtless 'tis fatal to our salvation upon the account of that in it, wherein it is especially opposite to God's design in the way of our salvation. This way of man's seeking his own salvation is fatal to man, doubtless because of that in it by which it is contrary to God's way, or to his aim in the way that he has contrived; which is that salvation should be

wholly for Christ's sake, and that free grace alone should be exalted, and boasting be excluded, and all glory should belong to God and none to us (Rom. 3:27, Eph. 2:19, Rom. 4:2, I Cor. 1:29–31). Doubtless, therefore, seeking justification by the works of the law is fatal upon the account of the boasting that is included in it. The end of the law is that men may be sensible they have nothing of their own to plead. Rom. 3:19, "That every mouth may be stopped."

And then 'tis evident that this was the error of the Jews, that are those that are here spoken of, by the accounts we have of them, viz. that they had a high conceit of their own righteousness, and looked upon themselves as very acceptable, and highly valued in the sight of God upon that account. This kind of pride and self-dependence, is what the Pharisees are so often found fault with for, who were the leading sect among the Jews, and were heads and leaders in the Jews' opposition to the gospel (Math. 6:2, 5, 16; Math. 7:3–5; Luke 16:15; Luke 18:9–12). And this is mentioned as the fault of the Jews in general (Rom. 2:17–23). And this is prophesied of as that for which the Jews should be rejected, when the gentiles should be called (Is. 65:6, with the context).

II. Again, it is evident that trusting in our own righteousness is fatal to the soul by Rom. 10:3, "For they, being ignorant of God's righteousness, and going about to establish their own righteousness, have not submitted themselves unto the righteousness of God." This is evidently spoken as a thing fatal to them, by the manner of the Apostle's introducing it, having said that it was his heart's desire and prayer for them that they might be saved, then shows how they fail of it. 'Tis evident also by the last verses of the preceding chapter, where the Apostle is speaking of the same thing in those forementioned words, which occasion these. 'Tis evident also by the 16th and following verses. And here, by their going about to establish their own righteousness, is not merely intended going about to establish a way of justification of their own devising, but going about to establish something as the matter of their justification that was their own or that was of themselves. And so by their being ignorant of and not submitting themselves to God's righteousness, is meant that they were ignorant how they were entirely dependent on God, and on his imputation, in this affair of justification; did not understand nor believe this doctrine of imputed righteousness, or righteousness from God; did not yield to be justified by righteousness merely from God, as imputed by him. I look upon it that 'tis here called God's righteousness, not chiefly because 'tis the righteousness of Christ, a divine person, but rather as 'tis wholly and immediately received from God, or as 'tis righteousness of, or from, God

(Philip. 3:9); what is not at all from ourselves, but merely by God's imputation. See Rom. 4:3–6 ff. But that by going about to establish their own righteousness, is meant going about to establish something of their own as the matter of their justification, is evident by the connection with the 32nd verse of the foregoing chapter, compared with the fifth verse of this. 'Tis evident that here, by their own righteousness, is meant the same as works of the law there. Again, 'tis evident by the meaning of this phrase, of [their] own righteousness, when used elsewhere by this Apostle, as Philip. 3:9.

III. Again, it is evident by Gal. 5:2–4, "Behold, I Paul say unto you, that if ye be circumcised, Christ shall profit you nothing. For I testify again to every man that is circumcised, that he is a debtor to do the whole law. Christ is become of no effect unto you, whosoever is justified by the law, is fallen from grace"; together [with] 4:10–11, "Ye observe days, and months, and times, and years. I am afraid of you, lest I have bestowed upon you labor in vain." Now the Apostle could not mean that merely the being circumcised would render Christ of no profit or effect to a person, for we read that Paul himself took Timothy and circumcised him because of the Jews (Acts 16:3). Therefore, 'tis a being circumcised under some particular apprehension, or notion, or with some certain view, that must be the thing that is fatal; and the Apostle must mean that Christ shall profit them nothing if they are circumcised under that notion or with that view that those Jews were, that were zealous for it and urged the necessity of it to them. But they were zealous of it as a thing that gave them great dignity, and on the account of which they were highly esteemed of God as something to be boasted of or gloried in, as Gal. 6:12–14 and 5:26 and 6:3; that which they sought praise by (Rom. 2:29). They looked upon themselves as holier and more acceptable to God upon that account than other men. They trusted in it. They held it absolutely necessary to salvation, "And certain men which came down from Judea taught the brethren, and said, Except ye be circumcised after the manner of Moses, ye cannot be saved" (Acts 15:1). They looked upon it necessary, not merely as obedience to any plain command of God is necessary to salvation, but in the same manner as it was necessary to any person's admission into the Jewish nation, or his being of Israel according to the flesh. It was the very qualification that admitted them; the principal thing by which they were made Israelites, and by which they challenged a right to the privileges of an Israelite. Circumcision was a type of regeneration and admitted men into the outward Israel, in the same manner as regeneration does to the kingdom of heaven. Therefore the Apostle says in the sixth chapter of this epistle, "Neither circumcision availeth any thing, nor uncircumcision, but a new creature." The Jews put circumcision instead of regeneration, instead of that faith that is wrought in regeneration, or instead of that righteousness of Christ that faith has or that is virtually in faith, supposing that they were justified by works and not by faith. And therefore it is said in the sixth verse of the context of the place we are upon [Gal. 5:6], "For in Jesus Christ neither circumcision availeth any thing, nor uncircumcision; but faith which worketh by love." It was a greater manifestation of self-ignorance and a self-exalting disposition, to make so much of so little a matter, such a trifle in themselves, than if it were some considerable matter.

Again, 'tis evident that this is spoken of as fatal, not merely as a piece of superstition, as it was a part of the ceremonial law which was abolished, but as they trusted in it as a part of righteousness or moral excellency; which is evident by the whole epistle and by the words immediately following, where the Apostle explains himself, "Christ is become of no effect to you, whosoever of you are justified by the law, are fallen from grace" [Gal. 5:4]; where 'tis evident that the thing that the Apostle testifies is seeking justification by the works of the law, as opposite to justification by mere grace, which can be no other than seeking justification by the righteousness of the law, as containing some excellency or dignity in it.

And when the Apostle says in the third verse, "For I testify to every man that is circumcised, he is debtor to do the whole law," the argument is this: if ye seek to be justified by this or any other work of the law, you are obliged to perfect obedience to the law of God in order to your having your aim, i.e. justification, because the law appoints that as the condition of justification. For that is the language of the law, "he that doth them shall live in them" (Gal. 3:12). The Apostle don't mean only that he is a debtor to do the whole ceremonial law: and this is evident by the same argument used by this Apostle to the same persons against the same error in this very epistle, as 3:10, "For as many as are of the works of the law are under the curse: for it is written, Cursed is every one that continueth not in all things which are written in the book of the law to do them"; and vv. 11–12, "But that no man is justified by the law in the sight of God, it is evident: for, the just shall live by faith. But the law is not of faith: but the man that doth them shall live in them." 'Tis against seeking justification by the works of the law in this sense that the Apostle writes in this epistle, as is evident by 2:16–19. It appears by the objection the Apostle there proposes and answers, viz. that seeking to be justified without the works of the law, would be an encouragement to sin. Now what is the opposite of sin but a moral righteousness or goodness? Seeking justification by the works of the law in this sense, was the error that the Galatians ran into; that was the occasion of the Apostle's writing this epistle, as is evident there by the context, especially the beginning of the next chapter. That it was the whole law of God that the Apostle meant when speaking of justification by the works of the law, is evident also by 3:10, 12–13, 19, 21–22.

So it was upon the same account that the Apostle was afraid of the Galatians, lest he had bestowed upon them labor in vain, because they observed "days, and months, and times, and years" (as 4:10–11), viz. because he feared they did it, as trusting in those performances as a righteousness, or in the moral excellency of them to commend them to God. This is evident by the context and by the forementioned passages of the epistle. The observing these things in itself was no sign that they trusted in them as a righteousness, because God once required them; but they were a sign of it under their circumstances. For it was now revealed with sufficient evidence that they were abolished; and those that were not overfond of them, and did not make much of them as placing the essence of religion much in them, and did not think them to be acceptable to God upon their own account, generally were easily persuaded that they were abolished. It was only those who were very zealous of them, or chiefly they that yet observed them. And observation will show that those that set much by ceremonies and outward forms and trifles in religion, and spend their zeal much about them, do ordinarily make a righteousness of them, are proud of them and depend upon them to commend them to God. The looking on such outward rites and forms as highly acceptable to God in themselves, they betray a mean thought of God and a high thought of man. They that are truly convinced of sin, they see so much of the evil of those things that are in themselves sinful and do more immediately flow from the wickedness of the heart, and of their obligation to moral and spiritual duties, that they see these to be of immensely greater importance, than mere external ceremonies. The beggarly elements of the world, they see that the flesh is not worthy to be gloried in. Thus David, when convinced of sin, was sensible of the worthlessness of ceremonies in comparison of heart holiness. Ps. 51:16–17, "Thou desirest not sacrifice; else would I give it: thou delightest not in burnt offering. The sacrifices of God are a broken spirit; a broken and a contrite heart, O God, thou wilt not despise."

And then probably the Apostle feared that the Galatians made a righteousness of these observances, because he knew the character of those false teachers that endeavored to lead them into it, that they were a proud, pharisaical, self-righteous sort of persons. There were some that observed days and times that the Apostle had charity for. Rom. 14:5–6, "One man esteemeth one day above another: another esteemeth every day alike. Let every man be fully persuaded in his own mind. He that regardeth the day, regardeth it to the Lord; and he that regardeth not the day, to the Lord he doth not regard it."

IV. It appears to be fatal because 'tis the direct contrary of that humiliation and self-abasement for sin that we are so often taught to be necessary in the word of God. See many texts enumerated in the papers of Scripture Signs of Godliness.[9]

V. 'Tis opposite to and inconsistent with that in faith, which is one ground of its being made the condition of our justification, viz. that it gives the glory of our acceptance with God to Christ. See No. 632.

VI. It is a confirmation of this, that God took so much care that the children of Israel should not entertain any such conceit, that it was for their righteousness that God bestowed such and such favors upon them (Deut. 9:4–6, Ezek. 36:22–32).

VII. It appears also by the parable of the Pharisee and publican. Luke 18:9–14, "And he spake this parable unto certain that trusted in themselves that they were righteous, and despised others: Two men went up into the temple to pray," etc. "I tell you, this man went down to his house justified rather than the other," i.e. this and not the other. Here 'tis evident, first, that the trusting in themselves that they were righteous, is intended the same as trusting in their own righteousness or moral goodness for justification and acceptance with God. For 'tis his moral goodness is what the Pharisee rehearses over before God in his prayer. And he depended upon it for justification, as is evident by the expression, trusted in themselves that they were righteous, or had matter for justification; and 'tis evident that this is the thing that was sought by both Pharisee and publican, by Christ's conclusion at the end of the parable: "I tell you this man went down to his house justified rather than the other." And [that] it was trusting to their righteousness for acceptance with God that Christ has respect to, is evident by the Pharisee's aim in his prayer in representing his goodness before God, which is evidently to commend himself to God's liking. Secondly, 'tis evident that the trusting in their own righteousness is that trusting that carries pride, or a high conceit of their own excellency

---

9. In 1729 JE began the notebook that he entitled "Signs of Godliness" and continued making entries in it throughout the 1730s and 40s. This reference is to the list of scripture texts demonstrating that "humility, a broken and contrite heart, a being poor in spirit, sensibleness of our own vileness and unworthiness, self-abasement, disclaiming all worthiness and glory, mourning for sin" is a sign of godliness.

in it, in that 'tis said they "trusted in themselves that they were righteous, and despised others."

VIII. Self-sufficiency in religion is fatal to the soul, as is evident by Rev. 3:16–17, "So then because thou art lukewarm, and neither cold nor hot, I will spew thee out of my mouth. Because thou sayst, I am rich, and increased with goods, and have need of nothing; and knowest not that thou art wretched, and miserable, and poor, and blind, and naked." This here mentioned is doubtless the direct contrary of that poverty of spirit that renders blessed.

638. LORD's DAY. There is an harmony between the methods of God's providence in [the] natural and religious worlds in this, as well as many other things. That as when day succeeds the night, and the one comes on and the other gradually ceases, those lesser lights that served to give light in the absence of the sun gradually vanish as the sun approaches; one star vanishes after another as daylight increases, the lesser stars first and the greater ones afterwards; and the same star gradually vanishes, till at length it wholly disappears, and all these lesser lights are extinguished and [the sun] appears in his full glory above the horizon: so when the day of the gospel dawned, the ceremonies of the old testament and ordinances of the Law of Moses, that were only appointed to give light in the absence of the "Sun of righteousness" [Mal. 4:2] or 'till Christ should appear, and shone only with a borrowed and reflected light like the planets; they were gradually abolished one after another, and the same ordinance gradually ceased, and those ordinances that were principal (one of which was the Jewish sabbath) continued the longest. There were a multitude of these ceremonies, which was a sign of their imperfection, but all together did but imperfectly supply the place of the sun of righteousness. But when the sun of righteousness is come, there is no need of any of them. When the true sacrifice is come, there is no need of any of the legal sacrifices. When Christ is come and introduces the gospel that is the ministration of the spirit, there is no more need of ceremonies in worship; but the time is now come that men must worship God in spirit and in truth. So there is a multitude of stars that shine in the night, but they all together do but very imperfectly supply the absence of the sun; but when the sun rises, they all vanish, and we find no want of them.

639. HEAVEN, whether the saints, when they go to heaven, have any special comfort in there meeting with those that were their godly friends on earth. I think that it is evident that they will, by I Thess. 4:13–14 and fol-

lowing verses: "But I would not have you to be ignorant, brethren, concerning them which are asleep, that ye sorrow not, even as others, which have no hope. For if we believe that Jesus died and rose again, even so them also which sleep in Jesus will God bring with him." Here,

1. It seems to me that what the Apostle mentions here as matter of comfort to mourners, is not only that their departed friends, though dead, shall be happy: they are not so miserable in being dead as persons are ready [to] imagine, because they shall rise again; but that they shall meet them and see them again, seems to be intimated in the manner of expression, God shall bring them. Christians mourn when their near friends are dead because they are departed and gone, they are parted from them; but when they rise, God shall bring them to them again. And this is further confirmed by the following verses, especially the 17th and 18th, "Then we which are alive and remain shall be caught up together with them in the clouds, to meet the Lord in the air: and so shall we ever be with the Lord. Wherefore comfort one another with these words"; where the Apostle may well be understood that they should comfort one another, when mourners, with the consideration that they should be hereafter again with their departed friends, and in a glorious and happy state.

2. I think 'tis evident hereby that there will be something else that will be comfortable in meeting them in a future state, than in seeing other saints. The Apostle doubtless mentions it, as what may be a comfortable consideration to them, that they shall again see and converse with the same persons; implying that they will have a different comfort in seeing them, from what they would in seeing other saints. Otherwise, why did the Apostle mention it for their comfort, that they should see them again, rather than any other saints that they had seen or heard of? The Apostle's speaking thus to the Thessalonians might give them just ground to expect that that special, dear affection that they had to their departed friends, which was crossed by their departure, would be again gratified by meeting them again; for this crossing of that affection was the ground of their mourning. If the Thessalonians knew that to see their friends again in another [world], would be no gratification to their affection that they had to them as their friends, and did no way think or conceive of it as such; then to think of it, would be no more comfort to them or remedy to their mourning, than to think that they should see any other saint that lived and died in another country or a past age: and that because it would be no remedy to the ground and foundation of their mourning, viz. the crossing of their affection to them as their friends. And if it would be no rem-

edy to their mourning to think of it, it never would have been mentioned to them by the Apostle as a ground of comfort, or a reason why they need not mourn. That was what they mourned for, viz. that they should not have their affection towards them gratified by seeing of them, conversing [with] them, etc. That was what the heathen here spoken of, that have no hope, mourned excessively for, that they should never more have that affection gratified. The Apostle here would inform them that they have not this ground to mourn that the heathen had, because they should have this affection gratified again.

Hence it follows, that the special affection that the saints have in this world to other saints that are their friends, will in some respects remain in another world. I don't see why we should not suppose that saints that have dwelt together in this world, and have done and received kindness to each others' souls, have been assistant to each others' true happiness, should not love one another with a love of gratitude for it in another world, and that the joy in meeting these and seeing their happiness is part of that joy that is spoken of, II Cor. 1:14, "As also ye have acknowledged us in part, that we are your rejoicing, even as ye also are ours in the day of the Lord Jesus"; and I Thess. 2:19–20, "For what is our hope, or joy, or crown of rejoicing? Are not even ye in the presence of the Lord Jesus Christ at his coming? For ye are our glory and joy"; or why those that have loved one another with a virtuous love, and from such a love have shown kindness one to another, should not love one another the better for it in another world. God and Christ will reward them and favor them the more for such love, and all the fruits of it, to all eternity; and I don't see why they should not love one another the more for it. Neither do I see how it argues infirmity for a saint in glory to have a special respect to another, because God made use of him as an instrument to bring him into being, and so is the remote occasion of his eternal blessedness; or because he himself was the occasion of bringing the other into being; or that the same agreeableness of tempers that is the foundation of special friendship here, may be so also in another world; or even that a former acquaintance with persons and their virtues, may occasion a particular respect in another world. They may go to heaven with a desire to see them upon that account. The idea that they have of them by their acquaintance here, may be what they carry to heaven with them; and the idea we have of a proper object of our love, may be an occasion of the exercises of love, especially towards that object, and more than towards another of which we have not the idea.

This should move us to lay religion and virtue in the foundation of all our friendships, and to strive that the love we have to our friends be a virtuous love, duly subordinated to divine love. For so far as it is so, it will last forever; death don't put an end to such friendship, nor can it put an end to such friends' enjoyment of each other.

640. LOVE OF ENEMIES. PRAYING AGAINST THEM. See No. 600 and note on Ps. 59.[1] Whenever we find David praying against any particular person, we may undoubtedly conclude that he speaks as a prophet in the name of the Lord, as very often he evidently doth when praying against his enemies, mixing prophecies or predictions of their destruction with prayers for it. And 'tis not unlawful for the people of God, as the case may be, whether they speak as prophets or no, to pray in general that God would appear on their side, and plead and vindicate their cause, and punish those wicked men that are entirely and impenitently and implacably their enemies, in a righteous cause. For this is no more than God has often promised, and we may pray for the fulfillment of this as well as other promises. And the making such a prayer is not inconsistent with the love of particular persons, and earnestly desiring that they might repent and be appeased and be forgiven. For when our entire and resolved enemies are a multitude or some great party or combination of wicked men, we have no reason to expect that they will all repent and be reconciled. Especially is it not unsuitable thus to pray against our enemies, if the cause wherein they are our enemies is the cause of God, so that in being our enemies they are also directly God's enemies; and more especially still, if the enemies are public enemies and are enemies in God's cause too, and we pray against them as interested in the public. For here love to men don't only not hinder our praying for the punishment of our implacable enemies, but it inclines us to it, viz. our love to the public, to the people of God that we are chiefly obliged to love and should love more than wicked men; yea, and love to God too, as 'tis in the cause of God. What Christ says evidently supposes that the people of God may pray for the punishment of their enemies. Luke 18:7, "And shall not God avenge his own elect, that cry unto him day and night," with the foregoing parables. See note on Rev. 18:20.[2]

And these following things are to be noted concerning David's praying against his enemies:

1. JE asserts in the "Blank Bible" note on Ps. 59 that when David prays against his enemies, they are not "personal enemies" but rather enemies of the church of Christ. David speaks "as the head of the church and in the person of Christ."

2. The "Blank Bible" note on Rev. 18:20 maintains, "The saints will rejoice in seeing vengeance executed on their enemies." They especially will rejoice to see justice executed on those who injured them.

1. That, unless speaking in the name of the Lord, he is not to be understood as praying against any particular persons, that God would indeed execute vengeance on such and such men, or that he did not desire that they should repent. When David prays against his enemies, there is no necessity of supposing that he desired the hurt of any particular [persons], no not of the head and leader of them. For in the third Psalm, which the title of the Psalm tells us was penned on the occasion of Absalom's conspiracy, he prays against his enemies in the seventh verse. But yet we cannot suppose that he wished any ill to his son Absalom, much less that he would pray for God's curse upon him (see note on Ps. 59),[3] but only that God would fulfill his promises that he has often made of appearing on the side of his people and against their enemies, and avenge them of their adversaries; which promise may be fulfilled, and yet not this and that particular person be punished. David can be understood only as praying against his enemies continuing his enemies.

2. That the enemies that David prays against, are those that are his entire, avowed and mortal enemies. They sought his life, and nothing but his blood would satisfy, and this when he was wholly innocent and righteous in the cause that they were enemies to him in. So that their being thus his enemies evidently denoted [them] to be all wicked men.

3. His enemies were many. It was a great party and combination of men, and seemed exceedingly hardened and very implacable, so that he could not expect that they would all repent and be appeased; and as I said before, [David] can be understood only to pray, as praying against his enemies continuing his enemies.

4. His cause in his difference with Saul was not only a righteous cause, but it was a cause wherein God himself was immediately interested. It was the peculiar favor that God had shown him that was the foundation of their quarrel with him. He prays against them not merely as his own, but as God's enemies (Ps. 21:8–13).

5. David mostly where he prays against his enemies, he don't do it merely as a private person, but, for the most part, he evidently prays against them as public enemies, enemies to the people of God, as in joint interest with them; and often as the head of the church and people of God that were on his side, and many of which were with him, and engaged in his interest in his difference with Saul. And his enemies that he prays against were avowedly at war with him and them. And when he came to the crown, he was the head of all Israel. He prays against his enemies as a public and not a private person.

3. See above, p. 173, n. 1.

6. There is no need, unless when David curses his enemies in the name of the Lord, of understanding him as praying for the destruction of his enemies for the sake of their hurt; but evidently [he] doth it as necessary for his own deliverance and safety, and the safety of God's people, and of religion itself, and for the vindication of his and their cause, and also of God's own cause. When they were unjustly judged and vilified, condemned and persecuted, he prays that God would, in his providence, show himself to be of their side; and he also prays for it as a testimony of the love and tenderness of God to him, according to his gracious promises to his people. It would be very suitable for the persecuted people of God now in like manner to pray against their persecutors. So also may a king pray for the destruction of his enemies whose destruction he seeks in war.

7. 'Tis questionable whether David ever prayed against his enemies, but as a prophet speaking in the name of the Lord. 'Tis evident by the matter of the Psalms that very frequently it was so.

See Neh. 4:5; see No. 1033.

641. CHRIST'S RIGHTEOUSNESS. See note on Ezek. 14:14.[4]

642. CONVICTION. HUMILIATION. *Scriptures.* The leper that had the plague of leprosy on his head, his mouth was to be covered or stopped, and he was to acknowledge how miserable [and] desperately unclean he was, in order to his cleansing. He was to express a sense of his misery by rending his clothes, and [a] sense of his exceeding uncleanness by crying, "Unclean, unclean." Lev. 13:45, "And the leper in whom the plague is, his clothes shall be rent, and his head bare, and he shall put a covering upon his upper lip, and shall cry, Unclean, unclean." See No. 645.

643. RESURRECTION. See note on I Cor. 15:20.[5]

---

4. The "Blank Bible" note on Ezek. 14:14 states, "This shows that it is no new notion lately first thought of in the world that one may be favored of God for the sake of another's righteousness." The righteousness of Noah, Daniel, and Job was great, but not great enough to compensate for the degeneracy of the land. "But the righteousness of Christ is sufficient; 'tis so excellent and worthy in God's account that 'tis sufficient to procure favor for the vilest of sinners. Herein Christ is a more excellent and sufficient mediator than Noah, Daniel or Job, or the most holy and eminent of mere men."

5. Under the law, JE observes in this "Blank Bible" note on I Cor. 15:20, the Jews offered grain offerings of the first fruits of harvest, one sheaf representing the whole harvest. "Now with reference here to [what] the Apostle calls the resurrection of Christ, the 'first fruits,' it having as it were hallowed the dead bodies of the saints, and consecrated them to a new life, he rose not only as first in order, but his resurrection was a representation and figure of our's; [it] showed not only that it might be, but that it should be."

644. RESURRECTION, the complete reward not till then. Redemption is not complete till the resurrection, not only with respect to the positive good and happiness that is obtained, but also with respect to what they are redeemed and delivered from. So long as the separation between soul and body remains, one of those evils remains that is part of the penalty of the law; one of our enemies remains. The last enemy that shall be destroyed is death. Death and hades, or a state of separation, are two evils that shall be at the last day cast into the lake of fire (Rev. 20:14). To be without the body is in itself an evil, because 'tis a want of that which the soul of man naturally inclines to and desires. And though it causes no uneasiness in the departed spirits of the saints, it is not because they don't want it, but because their certain hope and clear prospect of it, and apprehension how much it will be best for them, and most for their happiness to receive it in the time that God's wisdom determines, satisfies them till that time and is a full remedy against all uneasiness; and they perfectly rest in the hope and prospect and trust in God that they have. There is something that they still want, and their rest and satisfaction is not a rest of enjoyment, but a rest of perfect and glorious trust and hope.

645. CONVICTION. HUMILIATION. See No. 642. *Scriptures.* The outward circumstances of Paul's conversion typify what is spiritual in that work, and particularly the spiritual experiences of Paul himself in that work. For instance, the outward light that shone from heaven typified spiritual light. Paul's seeing Christ with the bodily eyes typifies a spiritual sight of Christ; this struck Paul down to the earth. This typifies the humiliation that accompanies conversion; converting light humbles men to the dust before God. His being struck blind typifies the convert's being brought to be blind in his own sense and apprehension. Paul before his conversion was a Pharisee and of a pharisaical spirit. He was brought up at the feet of Gamaliel and had an high opinion of his own wisdom. But he was now brought to be sensible that he was blind, as he was outwardly struck blind. This Apostle tells us that he that thinks he knows anything, knows nothing yet as he ought to know. As he continued three days blind, so he continued so long without meat or drink; which as it signified his concern and sorrow, so it typified his being in his own sense poor and empty. Before he was self-sufficient; now he has nothing of his own to live upon. Before he thought he was rich, and increased with goods, and had need of nothing; now he is miserable, and wretched, and poor, and blind and naked. Note that this humiliation was caused by a sight of the glory [of God], as Isaiah's and Job's sense of their own vileness and misery was from a sight of

God's glory (Is. 5:6; Job 42, at the beginning). II Sam. 23:4, "And he shall be as the light of the morning, when the sun riseth, even a morning without clouds; as the tender grass springing out of the earth by clear shining after rain."

Scriptures. The woman we have an account of in the 7th chapter of Luke, when she comes to Christ, comes in an humble manner, anointing his feet in a sense of her own great unworthiness, and first washes his feet with tears of repentance, before she kisses and anoints them (see note on Luke 7:38).[6] Blind Bartimaeus, when Christ called him, cast away his garment, rose and came to Jesus (Mark 10:50); which probably typifies that when persons truly come to Christ, they cast away their covering—their excuses and false pleas for themselves, their fig leaves and the filthy rags of their own righteousness—and come naked.

Deut. 32:36–39, together with the connection with the foregoing part of the chapter: "For the Lord shall judge his people, and repent himself for his servants, when he seeth that their power is gone, and there is none shut up, or left. And he shall say, where are their gods, their rock in whom they trusted, which did eat the fat of their sacrifices, and drank the wine of their drink offerings? Let them rise up and help you, and be your protection. See now that I, even I, am he, and there is no God with me: I kill, and I make alive; I wound, and I heal: and there is none can deliver out of mine hand." Thus 'tis God's manner to convince men of the vanity of all their other confidences, to strip them wholly and cause them to stand naked and destitute on every side, and to yield up all other hope and give over all vain endeavors, and to see that he only can help, before he helps them.

'Tis very agreeable to the ordinary methods of God's providence, and his way of dealing with men as we learn it in the Scripture, that God should ordinarily bring men to these two things before he reveals his mercy to them, and acceptance of them into his favor, viz. [1] despair in all other help, and (2) humiliation, or a sense of their own unworthiness. For the former, read *Common Place Book to the Holy Scripture,* Consid. 8, pp. 264–66.[7]

6. The "Blank Bible" note on Luke 7:38 states, "She anoints his feet and not his head, expressing her sense of her own unworthiness and her high and exalting esteem of Christ. . . . In this account is represented the manner of a sinner's closure with Christ . . . persons when they first come to Christ come in an humble manner, and ordinarily have first sensible exercises of contrition and repentance before they sensibly embrace Christ by faith and love, and rejoice in him."

7. John Locke, *A Common Place Book to the Holy Bible: or, The Scripture's Sufficiency Practically Demonstrated* (3rd ed., enl., London, 1725). In the 8th Consideration (pp. 264–66) Locke illustrates by biblical example "That the greater the Afflictions and Distresses of the Righteous have been, the more astonishing have their Deliverances been: and then hath Salvation appeared in their Extremity."

Luke 8:43–44, the woman that had the issue of blood twelve years, had spent all her living upon physicians and saw[8] it to be in vain to seek for healing from them any longer; for she could not be healed of any, and besides, she was brought to see herself utterly helpless. She had spent all her stock that she had to depend upon; she had nothing left. And then she comes to Christ and is healed of him by touching the hem of his garment. She believed him; she trusted in his sufficiency, for she said "if I may but touch the hem of his garment, I shall be made whole" (Matt. 9:21). She long labored to buy a cure. She laid out all she had to purchase it, but in vain. And when she comes to Christ, she comes without money, for she had none; and obtained that for nothing of Christ, that she could not obtain of physicians for all her living.

That renouncing of our own righteousness, which the Apostle speaks of in Philip. 3:7–8, which he calls a counting it but loss for Christ, for the excellency of the knowledge of Christ, and counting it but dung that he might win Christ, is evidently a renouncing of his own righteousness that was not antecedent to conversion. We can't renounce our own righteousness for Christ, till we are sensible of the worthiness of Christ and of his preferableness to our own righteousness. We can't do it to win Christ, till we are sensible of the value and preciousness of Christ. We can't esteem it worthless in comparison of the excellency of the knowledge of Christ Jesus our Lord, till we are sensible of the excellency of that knowledge.

Hos. 2:14–15, "And I will allure her, and bring her into the wilderness, and speak comfortably to her. And I will give her her vineyards from thence, and the valley of Achor, for a door of hope: and she shall sing there, as in the days of her youth, and as in the day when she came up out of the land of Egypt." See notes.[9]

See my notes on the story of Joseph in note on Gen. 41:40 ff.[1] See Jer. 3:21 to the end.

---

8. MS: "see."

9. In this "Blank Bible" note JE says that in Hos. 2:14 God speaks as a "young man does to a maid that he courts: 'But I will first bring her into the wilderness, and there bring her to herself, and make her sensible that she needs me, and that I am worthy to be received for an husband.'" Bringing her into the wilderness is "to humble her and fit her to be spoken to comfortably." JE comments on v. 15 that the valley of Achor is where Israel found out "the troubler" and stoned Achan. "The meaning of it seems to be that their being troubled for sin and convinced of it . . . is the way in which God's people shall come to light and comfort."

1. In this "Blank Bible" note JE interprets Joseph as a type of Christ. "This typifies the Father's investing of Christ, the Mediator, with the government of the church and the world," i.e. Joseph was exalted out of a prison, set over Pharoah's house, made ruler of men, invested with king's power, rewarded for being the means of saving the people, and had the people and land put into his hands.

The rain, which in Scripture is spoken of as representing affliction, fits the earth for the clear shining of the sun; and the morning succeeds a dark night. (So it is in God's dealings with his church; see "Notes on Scripture," nos. 359, 366.)[2] So Christ, whom God has appointed to be the ruler over men, is said [to be] as the light of the morning when the sun riseth, even a morning without clouds; and as the tender grass springing out of the earth by clear shining after rain. So is grace, which is Christ in the heart, as the tender grass springing out of the earth.

646. STRICTNESS OF THE LAW. MISERY OF THE DAMNED. We are told, Rom. 6:23, that "the wages of sin is death," and, Ezek. 18:20, [that] "the soul that sinneth, it shall die," by which is undoubtedly meant eternal destruction. The Scripture has sufficiently explained itself in that matter. When it is said, 'tis its wages, the meaning of it is that it is the recompense it deserves, and the recompense that is appointed or stated. And [that] 'tis not only intended that this is the wages of a wicked life or sinful course, but of one sin, of any one thing that is a sin or a breach of the divine law, is evident by these texts: Gen. 2:17, "In the day that thou eatest thereof, thou shalt surely die"; Jas. 2:10, "He that offends in one point, is guilty of all"; Gal. 3:10, "Cursed is every one that continueth not in all things which are written in the book of the law to do them."

That 'tis meant that particular sins distinctly deserve death, is further evident by the following things in Scripture. Job. 32:22, "For I know not to give flattering titles; in so doing my Maker would soon take me away." So the terrible judgments that were inflicted for that one sin of David, his numbering the people [II Sam. 24]. God offered him either seven years of famine, or to flee three months before their enemies, or three days' pestilence. David chose the least of these; yet there died of Israel 70,000 men, and yet God's mercies appeared to be great, in that the judgment was no worse, as David hoped it would be. And God of his mercy repented him of the evil, and commanded the destroying angel to stay his hand when he stretched out his hand upon Jerusalem to destroy it (II Sam. 24:16). And after all, this sin must be atoned by sacrifice, which intimated that this punishment, as terrible as it was, did not satisfy justice or at all take off the desert of death.

How dreadful was God's anger for Achan's sins of taking the accursed thing [Josh. 7]. God was angry with the whole congregation, so that they could not stand before their enemies; and God tells Joshua, Josh. 7:12,

2. Both of these "Scripture" notes discuss Gen. 19:23–24 (*Works*, *15*, 344, 356–57).

"Therefore the children of Israel could not stand before their enemies, but turned their backs before their enemies, because they were accursed." The whole congregation is spoken of as accursed because of that guilt. And it follows, "Neither will I be with you any more, except ye destroy the accursed thing from amongst you." And how terrible [was] the judgment on Achan and his family, vv. 24–26: "And Joshua, and all Israel with him, took Achan the son of Zerah, and the silver, and the garment, and the wedge of gold, and his sons, and his daughters, and his oxen, and his asses, and his sheep, and his tent, and all that he had: and they brought them unto the valley of Achor. . . . And all Israel stoned him with stones, and burned them with fire, after they had stoned them with stones."

And how dreadful was the wrath of God against the men of Beth-shemesh for looking into the ark; he miraculously slew 50,000 and three-score and ten men (I Sam. 6:19). Uzzah only for his mistake—when he put forth his hand to hold the ark when the oxen shook it, when he meant well—was slain by the immediate and miraculous hand of God (II Sam. 6:6–8).

The prophet for his credulity in too soon believing the lies of the other prophet, was slain by a lion (I Kgs. 13).

When God inflicts temporal death on a man for any sin, it truly signifies that that sin deserves eternal death. For temporal death is spoken of by Christ as being significatively eternal destruction. In Luke 13, speaking of those whose blood Pilate mingled with their sacrifices, and those on whom the tower of Siloam fell, [Christ] says, "Except ye repent, ye shall all likewise perish."

And not only overt acts of deliberate willful rebellion are called sins and reputed breaches of God's law in Scripture, but every evil word or thought or exercise of mind, every expression of a depraved disposition of heart or judgment, in short, everything in man that is wrong or as it should not be, everything that is morally amiss, less or more. Matt. 5:28, "But I say unto you, that whosoever looketh on a woman to lust after her hath committed adultery with her already in his heart." A right eye that offends in this respect exposes [one] to be cast into hell fire, as is evident by the next verse. This, with Jas. 2:10, shows that when it is said "the wages of sin is death," it is not to be taken in a restrained sense, as intending only overt acts of sin: for the apostle James says, "He that offends in one point, is guilty of all." Doubtless, he that has the guilt of the breach of the whole law has the wages of sin due to him; and this text sufficiently determines that he that only looks on a woman to lust after her, is guilty in one point.

And death is expressly threatened only for one rash and undue expression or word, yea, for one wrong exercise of heart. Matt. 5:22, "Whosoever is angry with his brother without a cause shall be in danger of the judgment: and whosoever shall say to his brother, Raca, shall be in danger of the council: and whosoever shall say, Thou fool, shall be in danger of hell fire." The judgment and the council were different tribunals among the Jews that had power to inflict death or capital punishments of different degrees. See Turretin, vol. 1, p. 660.[3]

One idle word exposes to condemnation, as is evident by Matt. 12:36–37, "For every idle word that men shall speak, they shall give account thereof in the day of judgment." These words alone show that an idle word exposes to condemnation: for what are men called to judgment for, or called to account there, but only in order to a decision of that point, viz. they shall be justified or condemned. But the following words confirm it: "For by thy words thou shalt be justified, and by thy words thou shalt be condemned."

Any exercise of an ill spirit towards an enemy, though it be only in the heart, is spoken of as sin. Prov. 24:17–18, "Rejoice not when thine enemy falleth, and let not thine heart be glad when he stumbleth: lest the Lord see it, and it displease him." Here 'tis spoken of as a thing that exposes to God's curse, and is mentioned as a thing provoking to God, and is expressly against commands that are found written in the book of the Law (Lev. 19:17–18; see No. 660) and therefore must be included in that threatening, "Cursed is he that continueth not in all things that are found written in the book of the law to do them" [Gal. 3:10]. Job mentions this as a wicked thing. Job 31:29, "If I rejoiced at the destruction of him that hated me, or lifted up myself when evil found him."

Inordinate desire only is a damnable sin because it is contrary to one of those things contained in that book of the Law, in that command, "Thou shalt not covet": which is not only written in the book of the Law, but is one of the commands immediately given by the voice of God from

---

3. "Christus Matth. 5:22, 23 . . . Verba Christi non sunt ad literam urgenda, quasi ageretur proprie in duobus primis gradibus poenae, *judicii* scilicet, & *concilii*, de judicio humano, in tertio vero *gehennae ignis*, de divino tantum, seu morte aeterna: Quia sic sequeretur iram intus conceptam, nec in actum erumpentem humano judicio esse obnoxiam, & aliquod dari peccatum, quod peccatorem judicio Dei non redderet obnoxium, quod absurdum. Sed figurate sunt intelligenda, ut diversitas gradus poenarum in judicio Dei describatur per analogiam & allusionem ad diversos gradus judiciorum & poenarum capitalium usitatos inter Judeaos; Nam praeter judicium infimum quod erat trium virale, quod judicabat de mulctis, sue poenis pecuniariis, debantur adhuc tres gradus poenarum capitalum inter eos" (Francis Turretin, *Institutio Theologiae Elencticae* [4 vols. Rhenum, 1734], Vol. 1, Bk. IX, "De Peccato in Genere, et Specie," Qu. IV, "De Peccato veniali et Mortali," sect. XVII, p. 660).

Mount Sinai, out of the midst of the devouring fire, which voice shook the earth and was attended with thunder and lightning and earthquake, as intimations of his dreadful wrath against those that did not obey; and was one of those commands engraven on the tables of stone.

There is no particular sin but what deserves death, because there was no sin, however light, even those that were committed through ignorance, [but] were to have sacrifices of slain beasts offered for them. That the beast that was substituted in the room of the sinner must die for the sin, evidently signified that the sinner deserved to die. So God broke forth upon Uzzah and miraculously slew him for putting forth his hand to hold the ark when the oxen shook it, though he had a good meaning in so doing. So God said to Abimelech that had ignorantly taken Sarah, "Behold, thou art but a dead man, for the woman which thou hast taken; for she is a man's wife" (Gen. 20:3), which certainly implies that he deserved death; and in the sixth verse God says to him, "Yea, I know that thou didst this in the integrity of thine heart; for I also withheld thee from sinning against me: therefore suffered I thee not to touch her," implying that if he had touched her he would have sinned against God. And Abimelech says to Abraham in the ninth verse, "What hast thou done to us? and what have I offended thee, that thou hast brought on me and on my kingdom a great sin?" He not only calls it a great sin, but signifies that it would have brought guilt not only on himself, but on his kingdom.

An omission of anything whatsoever [it] belongs to us to do, is a sin against God; and therefore, by what was said before, the wages of it is death. Thus Samuel says to Israel, I Sam. 12:23, "God forbid that I should sin against the Lord in ceasing to pray for you"; and that, although the people had very ill treated God and Samuel in rejecting both and desiring a king.

Yea, only a tendency to any such omission in the inclination or thought is a damnable sin. Deut. 15:9, "Beware that there be not a thought (or, as 'tis in the original, "a word") in thy wicked heart, saying, The seventh year, the year of release, is at hand; and thine eye be evil against thy poor brother, and thou givest him nought; and he cry unto the Lord against thee, and it be sin unto thee." This is one of the precepts written in the book of the Law, and then the words imply that the heart would appear wicked in having any such thought.

An ill disposition or temper or inclination, though it be only negatively ill, is spoken of as damnable; as I Cor. 16:22, "If any man love not the Lord Jesus Christ, let him be anathema maranatha."

Doing a thing indifferent with the exercise of an ill disposition of heart, as Hezekiah's showing the ambassadors his treasure, of which it is said, II Chron. 32:25, "But Hezekiah rendered not again according to the benefit done unto him; for his heart was lifted up: therefore there was wrath upon him, and upon Judah and Jerusalem"; and v. 31, "Howbeit, in the business of the ambassadors of the princes of Babylon, who sent unto him to inquire of the wonder that was done in the land, God left him, to try him, that he might know all that was in his heart." Let these texts be compared with the story as related in II Kgs. 20 and Is. 39, and the message that God sent Isaiah with to Hezekiah, and the awful judgments denounced upon this occasion that we have there an account of.

Not only total omissions of what should be in us in heart or[4] life, but the failure of it in any degree wherein it ought to be, is that by which we fail of continuing in all things that are found written in the book of the Law to do them; for we are there commanded to love and serve God with all our heart, and with all our soul, and all our strength (Deut. 6:5 and 10:12 and 11:13).

Expressions of a depraved understanding and judgment are mortal sins. Thus is only an erroneous, unsuitable and dishonorable thought of God, or divine things, [a mortal sin]. Acts 8:20, 22, "But Peter said unto him, Thy money perish with thee, because thou hast thought that the gift of God may be purchased with money. . . . Repent therefore of this thy wickedness, if perhaps the thought of thine heart may be forgiven thee."

So is the not believing the truth of those things that God has revealed. Thus Moses and Aaron were not suffered to enter into Canaan, because they doubted whether water would come out of the rock upon their smiting it, which signified that such unbelief deserves an exclusion from the heavenly Canaan. Num. 20:12, "And the Lord spake unto Moses and Aaron, Because ye believed me not, to sanctify me in the eyes of the children of Israel, therefore ye shall not bring this congregation into the land which I have given them." And in Deut. 3:23–26, how earnestly he besought God that he might go into Canaan; "But," says he, "the Lord was wroth with me, and would not hear me; and the Lord said unto me, Let it suffice thee; speak no more unto me of this matter." See also Deut. 1:32, and II Kgs. 17:14, and Ps. 78:22, 32 and 106:24, and Luke 1:20, and I John 5:10. And how heinous is the sin of not believing in Jesus represented in the Word of God (see note on John 16:8–9).[5] Yea, only ignorance of di-

---

4. MS: "of."

5. The "Blank Bible" note on John 16:8 is simply a cross-reference to "Notes on Scripture," no. 134, which treats the same text. See *Works, 15*, 87–88.

vine things is sin in the sight of God. Rom. 3:17, "And the way of peace they have not known." The Apostle quotes this from the Old Testament to prove that all men are under sin, as may be seen by the foregoing and following verses. Ps. 95:10–11, "Forty years long was I grieved with that generation, and said, It is a people that do err in their heart, they have not known my ways: Unto whom I swear in my wrath that they should not enter into my rest." Their being a people that erred in their heart, and that did not know God's ways, excited his wrath and provoked [him] to swear that they should not enter into his rest, which shows that this deserved damnation. Is. 27:11, "It is a people of no understanding: therefore he that made them will not have mercy on them, and he that formed them will show them no favor." II Thess. 1:8, "In flaming fire taking vengeance of them that know not God, and that obey not the gospel of our Lord Jesus Christ."

And God often speaks with high resentment and indignation of the ignorance, stupidity and inconsiderateness of men, from which, as I observed before, we must needs conclude that God by his law forbids it. Ps. 94:7–10, "Yet they say, The Lord shall not see, neither shall the God of Jacob regard it. Understand, ye brutish among the people: and ye fools, when will ye be wise? He that planted the ear, shall he not hear? he that formed the eye, shall he not see? He that chastiseth the heathen, shall not he correct? he that teacheth man knowledge, shall not he know?" I Sam. 2:12, "The sons of Eli were sons of Belial, they knew not the Lord." Ps. 82:5, "They know not, neither will they learn." Is. 1:3, "The ox knows his owner, and the ass his master's crib: but Israel doth not know, my people doth not consider." Jer. 4:22, "For my people is foolish, they have not known me; they are sottish children, and they have none understanding." Jer. 8:7, "Yea, the stork in the heaven knoweth her appointed times; and the turtle and the crane and the swallow observe the time of their coming; but my people know not the judgment of the Lord." Jer. 5:21, "Hear now this, O foolish people, and without understanding." Hos. 4:1, "The Lord hath a controversy with the inhabitants of the land, because there is no truth, nor mercy, nor knowledge of God in the land." John 8:19, "Ye neither know me, nor my Father"; v. 43, "Why do ye not understand my speech? because ye cannot hear my word." Luke 12:56–57, "Ye hypocrites, ye can discern the face of the sky and of the earth; how is it that ye do not discern the signs of this time? Yea, and why even of yourselves judge ye not what is right?" I Cor. 15:34, "Awake to righteousness, and sin not; for some have not the knowledge of God: I speak this to your shame."

Everything in the heart or life of men that is contrary to any rule of the gospel or anything in the whole Word of God, must merit the curse and must be implied when it is said, "Cursed is every one that continues not in all things that are found written in the book of the law to do them" [Gal. 3:11]; and that, though we should understand the book of the Law to intend only the book of the Law of Moses; and that, because everything that is commanded or any way directed to in the whole Scripture is virtually found written in that book of the Law, viz. in that precept of the book of the Law. Deut. 18:15, "The Lord thy God will raise up unto thee a prophet from the midst of thee, of thy brethren, like unto me; unto him shall ye hearken." If we understand Christ by that prophet, then this brings in all the rules of Christ, all the rules of the gospel, into the book of the Law, which doubtless are so extensive and strict as to include all in the Bible. And if we understand it of prophets in general that God should raise up from time to time of that nation, then all inspired persons of that nation are included, and the whole Bible is the word of God in the mouth of those prophets, and Christ was at least one implied, if not principally intended; and then the disobeying the word of God in the mouths of that prophet or those prophets, has not only God's curse denounced against it annexed to the Law of Moses, but in a particular threatening annexed to this prophecy. Deut. 18:18–19, "I will raise them up a prophet from among their brethren, like unto thee, and will put my words in his mouth, and he shall speak unto them all that I shall command him. And it shall come to pass, that whosoever will not hearken unto my words which he shall speak in my name, I will require it of him."

Corol. Hence, how dreadful will be the punishment of those that go to hell that have lived in sin for many years together. How dreadful a punishment do their sins deserve: for what has been said may in some measure help us to conceive how many sins we are guilty [of], and how vast the number of their sins that live for many years in sin, especially under the light of God's Word. Any one sin we see has eternal destruction and ruin as its due wages; and all sins deserve punishment in proportion to their heinousness and aggravations, and yet the least deserves death. (Concerning[6] what is implied in it, see Nos. 418 and 427.) Men deserve punishment proportionable to the degree of their sin computed by both number and heinousness; and we are assured that wicked men shall be punished as much as their sins deserve. Christ teaches us that it will be required of them that they should pay all the debt, and that the uttermost farthing shall be exacted of them. And God hath said that he "will not at

6. MS: "death which implies concerning"

all acquit the wicked" (Nahum 1:3); and that "he will not be slack to him that hateth him, but will repay him to his face" [Deut. 7:10]; that vengeance belongs to him, and he will repay it [Heb. 10:30]; that he "will recompense, even recompense into their bosom" [Is. 65:6]; and many other passages there are to the like purpose. And it must needs be so, for if God did not exact the whole of the debt, then he forgives some of it; and if unbelievers have anything forgiven them, then there is forgiveness out of Christ, and contrary to God's everlasting and unalterable constitution of grace. Hence then, how many thousands and ten thousands of deaths will many of the damned endure at once, and endure always.

That men's sins will be punished according to their heinousness appears by that, Matt. 5:22, "But I say unto you, that whosoever is angry with his brother without a cause shall be in danger of the judgment: and whosoever shall say to his brother, Raca, shall be in danger of the council: but whosoever shall say, Thou fool, shall be in danger of hell fire"; and according to their aggravations, by that, Luke 12:47–48, "That servant, which knew his lord's will, and prepared not himself, neither did according to his will, shall be beaten with many stripes. But he that knew not, and did commit things worthy of stripes, shall be beaten with few stripes"; and other places.

And that men will be punished according to the multitude and repetition of their sins, appears by the following texts: Matt. 12:36–37, "For every idle word that men shall speak, they shall give account thereof in the day of judgment. For by thy words thou shalt be justified, and by thy words thou shalt be condemned." Num. 14:22–23, "And have tempted me now these ten times, surely they shall not see the land which I swear unto their fathers, neither shall any of them that provoked me see it." Hos. 7:2, "They consider not in their hearts that I remember all their wickedness: now their doings have beset them about; they are before my face." Hos. 8:13, "Now will he remember their iniquity, and visit their sins." Ps. 95:10–11, "Forty years long was I grieved with that generation, and said, It is a people that do err in their heart, and they have not known my ways: to whom I swear in my wrath that they should not enter into my rest." Luke 7:41–42, 47, "The one owed him five hundred pence, and the other fifty. And when they had nothing to pay, he frankly forgave them both. Tell me therefore, which will love him most? . . . Her sins, which are many, are forgiven her." Ezek. 7:3, "I will judge thee according to thy ways, and recompense upon thee all thine abominations"; and v. 8. Job. 9:2–3, "How should man be just with God? If he will contend with him, he cannot answer him one of a thousand." Job 14:17, "My transgression is sealed up in a bag, and thou sewest up mine iniquity." Rom 2:5, "After thy hard-ness and impenitent heart, treasurest up wrath against the day of wrath, and revelation of the righteous judgment of God." II Chron. 28:13, "When we have offended against the Lord already, ye intend to add more to our sins and to our trespass: for our trespass is great, and there is fierce wrath against Israel." Lev. 26:18, "If ye will not for all this hearken to me, then I will punish you seven times more for your sins"; v. 21, "And if ye walk contrary to me, and will not hearken unto me; I will bring seven times more plagues upon you according to your sins"; and so in vv. 24, 28. Ps. 5:10, "Cast them out in the multitude of their transgressions." Jer. 3:1–3, "Shall not that land be greatly polluted? Thou hast played the harlot with many lovers; yet return again unto me, saith the Lord. . . . See where thou hast not been lien with. . . . Therefore the showers have been with-holden." Job 10:14, "If I sin, then thou markest me, and wilt not acquit me from mine iniquity." Job 31:3–4, "Is not destruction to the wicked? and a strange punishment to the workers of iniquity? Doth he not see my ways, and count all my steps?" Ps. 50:21, "These things hast thou done, and I kept silence; thou thoughtest I was altogether such an one as thy-self: but I will reprove thee, and set them in order before thine eyes."

647. FREE GRACE. JUSTIFICATION BY FAITH. There is a twofold fitness to a state. I know not how otherwise to give them distinguishing names, than by calling the one a moral, and the other a natural, fitness. A person is morally fit for a state, when by his excellency or odiousness his excel-lency or odiousness[7] commends him to it. 'Tis suitable that he should be put into such a good or ill state out of respect to his excellency, or hatred of his odiousness; or that a becoming love to his excellency, or hatred to his odiousness, renders it desirable to see him in such a state.

A natural fitness for a state is when there is a good natural agreeable-ness, or accord, between the person or his qualifications and the state; or that there is a good capacity for a state; or that he is so qualified for such a state that will be like to be good effects of his being in such a state; or such as will render it of good and not ill consequence for him to be in such a state. We very often in secular affairs speak of persons as fit or unfit for such a state or such circumstances in this sense, when 'tis no moral but some natural fitness we mean.

There is nothing in man regarded as a moral fitness for a state of salva-tion, or a being in Christ. The moral fitness or suitableness to any good or

7. MS: "loveliness."

happiness is alone in Christ; and we are thus fit or worthy only as being in him, or by the imputation of his worthiness, or by the dignity and value that our persons have; and so our works [are fit only] as we are parts of him, our ill deservings being considered as done away in him.

Whatever qualification, therefore, as that by which we are justified or saved, or what renders it meet that we should be looked upon as being in Christ, and should be in a state of salvation, it must be understood of a natural fitness.

Corol. They therefore that hold that sincere obedience is the condition of being in Christ, or[8] such a moral fitness as is above described, they maintain what is contrary to the Scripture doctrine of justification by faith alone; and commonly to speak of sincere obedience as the condition of having an interest in Christ, is perhaps a way of talking that tends to make persons conceive of it as a moral fitness. 'Tis not St. Paul's way of talking, but what he carefully avoids. See Nos. 632, 627.

648. TRUSTING IN OUR OWN RIGHTEOUSNESS. What some call trusting in the ABSOLUTE MERCY OF GOD, i.e. trusting in his merciful nature without any consideration of a mediator to make way for and obtain the exercises of that mercy, is not much different from trusting in our own righteousness. It arises from the same principle, viz. a want of a sense of our guilt and unworthiness, and too high an opinion of our own moral state as related to the favor of God. Thus for instance, when a person in great outward affliction and distress of soul through fear of hell, on a deathbed or any other, cries earnestly to God, hoping to move the pity of God, thinking that their sorrowful case, their tears and moans and piteous cries, are enough to move the bowels and compassions of God, and that [he] will be hard-hearted if he beholds all without pity: it arises from want of a sense of the greatness and majesty of God, and their heinous guilt in so sinning against him, that they ben't sensible that God might be glorious in refusing to pity them, and could not be glorious in showing them mercy without a mediator.

649. CHRISTIAN RELIGION. CHRISTIANS THE TRUE ISRAEL. See No. 597. We are not to look upon all this time of the rejection and dispersion of the Jews since they have been broken off and the Gentiles grafted in, to be so long a suspension of the fulfillment of the promises made to Abraham, Isaac and Jacob concerning their seed, or an intermission of the be-

8. MS: "as."

stowment of promised mercies and blessings to them. Those promises are now in actual accomplishment in the mercy bestowed on the Christian church, as well as before in his mercy bestowed on the Jewish church, and in much more full and glorious accomplishment. God has not cast off the seed of Abraham and Israel now in the gospel times in no wise, but hath brought them nearer to himself, and hath, according to frequent prophecies of gospel times, abundantly increased their blessings and the manifestations of his favor to them. When the greater part of the nation of the Jews were broken off by unbelief, the seed of Israel were no more cast off then than in the time of the captivity of Israel and Judah into Assyria and Babylon. For then, by far the greater part of that nation were forever removed from being God's people, and it was but a remnant that was preserved and returned. So there was in the beginning of the gospel a remnant [of] that nation that God preserved to be his people that embraced the gospel and believed in Christ. There were many thousands in that one city, Jerusalem (Acts 21:20); and without doubt multitudes in other parts of Judea and in Galilee, and multitudes in other parts of the world where the Jews were dispersed, as we have an account. And this remnant might probably be as great in proportion to the whole nation, as the remnant that were continued and owned as God's people after the captivity into Assyria and Babylon. See Rom. 11, at the beginning: "I say then, hath God cast away his people? God forbid. For I also am an Israelite, of the seed of Abraham, of the tribe of Benjamin. God hath not cast away his people which he foreknew. Wot ye not what the Scripture saith of Elias? how he maketh intercession to God against Israel saying, Lord they have killed thy prophets, and digged down thine altars; and I am left alone, and they seek my life. But what saith the answer of God unto him? I have reserved to myself seven thousand men, who have not bowed the knee to the image of Baal. Even so then at this present time also there is a remnant according to the election of grace." The prophets very often speak of those that shall be owned by God as his people as but a remnant, and that this remnant shall be but a small number in proportion to the whole. Is. 6:13, "But in it shall be a tenth, and it shall return, and shall be eaten: as a teil tree, and as an oak, whose substance is in them, when they cast their leaves: so the holy seed shall be the substance thereof." See Is. 24:13. Is. 10:22, "For though thy people Israel be as the sand of the sea, yet a remnant of them shall return." Is. 1:9, "Except the Lord of hosts had left unto us a very small remnant, we should have been as Sodom, and we should have been like unto Gomorrah." Which two last places the Apostle quotes to this purpose, Rom. 9:27–29. The unbelieving Jews are not the children of Abraham any more than the Ishmaelites and Edomites, because they are disinherited. God threatened in the wilderness that he would disinherit the whole congregation of Israel, and make of Moses a great nation. If he had so done, the promises made to the fathers concerning their seed might have been fulfilled, though it had been only in Moses' posterity. The ten tribes, when they were carried away, they were the greater part of them disinherited and removed from being any more a people, or of Israel; so in gospel times the unbelieving Jews are disinherited. And 'tis only the remnant according to the election of grace that are the seed of Abraham and Israel, though that remnant be exceedingly multiplied by sons and daughters from among the Gentiles, agreeable to ancient prophecies. And this remnant of Israel hath been the mother of thousands of millions, agreeably to the blessing given to Rebekah (Gen. 24:60). The Gentiles are their children in the style of the prophets, and therefore the children of Abraham and Israel. As it was of old before Christ came, the people were not Israel because they all came from Israel by natural generation, but the people as a people were derived from him; and so it is now.

It is prophesied in the 65th chapter of Isaiah that there shall be but a small remnant that shall be God's people, vv. 8 and 9, "Thus saith the Lord, as the new wine is found in the cluster, and one saith, destroy it not; for a blessing is in it: so will I do for my servants' sakes that, I may not destroy them all. And I will bring forth a seed out of Jacob, and out of Judah an inheritor of my mountains: and mine elect shall inherit it, and my servants shall dwell there." And in the same chapter it is prophesied that the Jews should be rejected and another people called in their [stead], and that they should leave their name for a curse unto this chosen remnant or his true people, and that he would call his people by another name. See [No.] 658.

650. BEING OF GOD. NECESSARY EXISTENCE. 'Tis from the exceeding imperfect notions that we have of the nature or essence of God, and because we can't think of it but we must think of it far otherwise than it is, that arises the difficulty in our mind of conceiving of God's existing without a cause. 'Tis repugnant to the nature of our souls, and what our faculties utterly refuse to admit, that anything that is capable of being one part of a proper disjunction should exist and be as it is, rather than not exist or exist otherwise without causes. Our notions we have of the divine nature are so imperfect that our imperfect idea admits of a disjunction, for whatsoever is not absolutely perfect doth so. [In] everything that is im-

perfect there is dependence, or contingent existence implied in the nature of it, or we can conceive of its being a part of a disjunction. There is a THUS and an OTHERWISE in the case. As soon as ever we have descended one step below absolute perfection, possibility ceases to be simple; it divides and becomes manifold. Thus for instance, we can't conceive of God without attributing succession to him; but that notion brings along with it contingent existence, and introduces with it a manifold possibility. There is nothing that exists in a successive duration, but it will necessarily follow from thence that it is simply possible that it might exist infinite other ways than it doth; and that it might not exist at all.

It is a contradiction to suppose that being itself should not be. If anyone says, no, there may be nothing, he supposes at the same time nothing has a being; and indeed nothing—when we speak properly or when the word has any meaning, i.e. when we speak of nothing in contradiction [to] some particular being—has truly a being.

651. ONE GOD. UNITY OF THE GODHEAD. It appears that there is but one creator and governor of the world, by considering how the world is created and governed. The world is evidently so created and governed as to answer but one design in all the different parts of it, and in all ages; and therefore we may justly argue that 'tis but one design that orders the world. This appears,

1. By the mutual subserviency of all the various parts of the world. This great body is as much one, and all the members of it mutually dependent and subservient, as in the body of man. One part is so, and acts so, and is in every respect ordered so, as constantly to promote the design that others are made for. All the parts help one another and mutually forward each other's ends. In all the immense variety of things that there are in the world, every one has such a nature and is so ordered in every respect and circumstance, as to comply with the rest of the universe, and to fall in with and subserve to the purposes of the other parts. This argues that 'tis the same design and contrivance, or the same designing contriving being, that makes and orders one part, as doth the other. It appears also,

2. By this, that the same laws of nature obtain throughout the universe. Every part of matter everywhere is governed by exactly the same law, which laws are only the appointment of the governor. This argues, therefore, that they are all governed by one appointment or will.

3. The same laws obtain in all ages without any alteration. There is no alteration seen in any one instance in all those numberless and infinitely various effects that are the result of those laws in different circumstances.

This argues that 'tis not several that have the government by turns, but that 'tis one being that has the management of the same things in all ages of the world, one design and contrivance.

Not only the identity of laws in inanimate beings, but in the same sort of animals—especially in the nature of man, in all men in all ages of the world—shows that all men in all ages are in the hands of the same being.

[4.] Another thing that argues that the world has but one creator and governor is the great analogy there is in the works of creation and providence; the analogy there is in the bodies of all animals, and in all plants, and in the different parts of the inanimate creation; and the analogy there is even between the corporeal and spiritual parts of the creation; and the analogy in the constitution and government of different orders of beings. This argues that the whole is the fruit of but one wisdom and design.

652. CHRISTIAN RELIGION. MYSTERIES IN RELIGION. I once told a boy of about thirteen years of age that a piece of any matter of two inches square[9] was eight times so big as one of but one inch square, or that it might be cut into eight pieces, all of them as big as that of but an inch square. He seemed at first to think me not in earnest, and to suspect that I only went to make a game of him. But when I had taken considerable pains to convince him that I was in earnest, and that I knew what I said to be true, he seemed to be astonished at my positiveness, and cried out of the impossibility and absurdity of it, and would argue how was it possible for two inches to be eight inches; and all that I could say did [not] at all prevail upon him to make him believe it. I suppose it seemed to him as great and evident a contradiction as that twice one makes eight, or any other absurdity whatsoever, that that [which] was but just twice so long, and twice so broad, and twice so thick, but just so big every way, should yet be eight times so big. And when I afterwards showed him the truth of it by cutting out two cubes, one an inch and another two inches square, and let him examine the measures and see that the measures were exact, and that there was no deceit, and took and cut the two-inch cube into eight equal parts, and he counted the parts over and over, and took the parts one by one and compared them with the one inch cube, and spent some time in counting and comparing; he seemed to [be] astonished as though there were some witchcraft in the case and hardly to believe it after all, for he did not yet at all see the reason of it. I believe it was a much more difficult mystery to him than the Trinity ordinarily is to men. And there

9. I.e. cubed.

seemed to him more evidently to be a contradiction in it than ever there did in any mystery of religion to a Socinian or deist.

And why should we not suppose that there may be some things that are true, that may be as much above our understandings and as difficult to them, as this truth was to this boy. Doubtless, there is a vastly greater distance between our understanding and God's, than between this boy's and that of the greatest philosopher or mathematician.

653. WISDOM OF GOD IN THE WORK OF REDEMPTION. CIRCUMSTANCES OF CHRIST'S DEATH. See No. 621. There are two things that render Christ's sufferings wonderful, viz. (1) that he should voluntarily endure *so great sufferings,* [and] (2) that he should endure 'em to make atonement for *so great wickedness,* or for those that were so unworthy. But in order to its being properly said that Christ of his own act and choice endured so great sufferings to atone for those who were so wicked and hateful, two things were necessary, viz. [(1)] that he should be sensible how great those sufferings were to be; this was given in his agony. And (2) that he should be sensible when he offered himself to suffer, or when he suffered, how great and hateful that sin and wickedness of man was that he suffered to atone for, or how unworthy those were that he died for the sake of. And in order to this, it was seen fit that his sufferings should be immediately caused by that wickedness. It was the wickedness or corruption that is in men that Christ suffered to atone. And Christ had enough to impress upon him a sense of the vileness, unreasonableness and hatefulness of man's corruption and wickedness in the time of his suffering, for it was the wickedness of men that contrived and effected his sufferings. It was the wickedness of men that agreed with Judas. It was the wickedness of men that betrayed him, and that apprehended and bound him, and led him away like a malefactor. It was by men's wickedness that he was deserted and denied by his disciples. It was by men's wickedness that he was arraigned, and falsely accused, and unjustly judged. It was by men's wickedness he was reproached, mocked, buffeted and spit upon. It was by men's wickedness that Barabbas was preferred before him, that he was condemned [and] scourged. It was men's wickedness that laid the cross on him to bear, that nailed him to the cross, and put him to so cruel and ignominious a death. This tended to give Christ an extraordinary sense of the greatness and hatefulness of the sin and depravity, at the time of his suffering to atone for men's sin,

1. Because hereby he had, in the time of his suffering, the corruption and wickedness of men set before him, as it is without disguise. It appeared

in its proper colors, in those that had a hand in his sufferings. Here he saw it; here he saw its true unreasonableness, injuriousness, falseness, baseness and ingratitude (more especially in Judas, his sin) in its maliciousness and contempt and devilish nature. Here he saw sin in its true nature, which is the utmost hatred and contempt of God. Here he saw it in its ultimate tendency or aim, which is to kill God. Christ herein saw the sin of men in its greatest aggravations and highest act.

2. This had a tendency to give him a more lively and strong sense of the greatness and hatefulness of the sin and corruption of man, because he then, in those extreme sufferings, felt the ill effects of man's wickedness. It was then directly leveled against him. It exerted itself against him, to work his reproach and torment and death, which tended to impress a stronger sense of men's hateful wickedness upon his human nature. The wonderfulness of Christ's dying love appears: (1) in that he died for those that were so wicked and unworthy in themselves; (2) in that he died for those who were not only so wicked, but whose wickedness consists in being enemies to him, so that [Christ] did not only die for the wicked, but for his own enemies; (3) in that [he] was willing to die for his enemies at the same time that he was subject to the utmost exertions and efforts of their enmity, in the greatest possible contempt and cruelty towards him, and at the same time that he was feeling the utmost effects of it in his own greatest ignominy, torment and death; (4) in that he was willing to atone for their being his enemies in those very sufferings, by that very ignominy, torment and death that was the fruit of it.

The wickedness that caused the sufferings of Christ tended to give Christ a sense of the same sin and wickedness that he suffered for,

1. Because this wickedness was but a sample of that corruption and depravity of mankind. The sin and corruption of all mankind is of the same nature. 'Tis the very same corruption that all are born with. The wickedness that is in one man's heart, is of the same nature and tendency as that in another's. As in water, face answers to face, so the heart of man to man. This, therefore, was but a sample of that sin of the elect that [Christ] suffered to atone for.

2. Christ suffered to atone for that individual actual wickedness that wrought his sufferings, that reproached, mocked and buffeted him, and crucified [him], with respect to some of his crucifiers, that he prayed might be forgiven while they were in the very act of crucifying him, and who were afterwards, in answer to his prayer, converted and forgiven; as we have an account in the second chapter of Acts.

3. Christ had in the time of his sufferings set before him the sin of those

who were already actually entitled to the benefits of his sufferings, which also had a hand in his sufferings: as the disciples' dullness and unaffectedness in the garden in the time of his agony; their basely flying and forsaking him and being afraid and ashamed to own him in the time of his afflictions; Peter's repeated denying him, and at last with oaths and curses, when he should have stood up for him and pleaded his cause, while others were trampling upon him.

654. MYSTERIES OF RELIGION. ABSOLUTE DECREES. ORIGINAL SIN, ETC. I can conceive how it should be agreeable to divine wisdom, and how it should be for excellent ends, so [that] it should be so ordered that there should be some doctrines taught us in God's words that should be very mysterious, and that should have difficulties in them, inexplicable by us, and particularly that there should be some doctrines very difficult to reconcile with the justice of God. For the time is coming when these mysteries will all be unfolded, and the perplexing difficulties that have attended them will all be perfectly vanished away, as the shades of the night before the sun in a serene hemisphere. And when this time comes, that having formerly [been] so mysterious and difficult to us, will be the occasion of a greater and stronger sense of the truth and knowledge of God, now they are unfolded. It will heighten in us, and greatly fix upon our minds, a sense of his truth, in that he now so clearly appears to be true, perfectly true, in those things that have had the greatest appearance of falsehood, and wherein we have been most liable to temptation to question God's truth, and that have been matter of difficulty to the world for so many ages. And the difficulty and perplexity that has attended those doctrines that have been most difficult to reconcile to God's justice and goodness, will serve to give us a stronger and fuller persuasion, and a higher sense of those perfections of God, when we see him to be perfectly just and holy in those things that have occasioned the blasphemies of multitudes against those perfections of God, and that the whole world, and we ourselves, have been so much perplexed about. When these things shall be fully and perfectly cleared up without any remaining darkness, the former darkness and difficulty will add abundantly to the exultation of our hearts, and will exceedingly exalt our praises of those divine attributes. It will cause us with the more life and joy and greater accent to sing, as Rev. 15:3, "Great and marvelous are thy works, Lord God Almighty; just and true are thy ways, thou King of saints"; and 16:7, "Even so, Lord God Almighty, true and righteous are thy judgments." Preceding darkness does wonderfully prepare the mind for a sense of the glory of succeeding light. We should

not be sensible of the glory of the light of the morning, if no night preceded. We should not know how glorious light is, if we had no darkness to compare it with. I have found something of this effect in myself, after I have, by study, arrived at a great measure of satisfaction in some doctrines that have before [been] very difficult to me. It han't only confirmed me in the belief of that doctrine, and raised my thoughts of those attributes of God, that they seemed most difficult to reconcile with; but has confirmed me in a persuasion of the perfections of God in general, and has enlivened my mind with respect to the whole of religion.

The unfolding of these difficult doctrines may wisely be reserved of God for [the] future appointed time of joy and glory to the church. God may have designed the full explication of some of them for the glorious times of the church here on earth, that we are expecting; and there may be that light bestowed with respect to others, as may give great satisfaction concerning them. But I believe that the perfect and full explication of these mysteries is part of the glory of the last and eternal state of the church, to heighten the joy and praises of the wedding day of Christ and his church.

655. HABIT OF GRACE, NEW NATURE, in what sense man is said to have them. See the latter part of my discourse, in answer to that question that was proposed to the Association, What is the work of the Spirit in a sinner's conversion?[1]

656. MISERY OF THE DAMNED. 'Tis not properly said that the damned are made strong to bear misery. Such an expression seems to hold forth as though they were made strong to bear up and keep from sinking under misery; whereas this is utterly wrong. For the damned in this sense can't bear the misery of hell; it is greater than they can bear. Is. 33:14. "Who among us can dwell with the devouring fire? who among us can dwell with everlasting burnings?" Ezek. 22:14, "Can thine heart endure,

---

1. I.e. the Hampshire County Association. The discourse to which JE refers is quite possibly the sermon on II Cor. 3:18 (n.d., [1728]) because it is written in a lecture format and the subject matter of its "latter part" fits the question posed in the entry. The final section of the sermon is divided into three propositions: (I) "'Tis the Spirit of Christ that is the immediate teacher and instructor to give a true sight of Christ." (II) "'Tis the Spirit of Christ that makes like to Jesus Christ." (III) "These things are done by the Spirit of Christ alone." Suggestively, JE at some point—perhaps in preparation for the association meeting—restitched the sermon MS, placing the "latter part" at the front of the booklet. The Hampshire County Association Minutes (MS, Forbes Library, Northampton, Massachusetts) contain no reference to the sermon or to the discussion leading to it.

or can thine hands be strong, in the day that I shall deal with thee?" There is none that in this sense can bear the torments of hell; nor do they in this sense bear them, but sink and are crushed under them. God enlarges their capableness of receiving misery or being made miserable, but he don't make 'em strong to bear misery. A giving a man a greater strength to support himself under what oppresses him, don't make him more capable of misery, but on the contrary, it renders him a subject less susceptive of misery. And a weakening and disheartening the mind renders it the less able to support itself, and therefore, the more liable to the force of what oppresses it; or, which is the same thing, more capable of suffering misery from it. A weakening the mind, or depriving of it of its firmness or fortitude, does in no respect render it capable of a less misery. It don't make it more liable to be destroyed or annihilated. I can think of no reason why misery should be supposed to have any tendency to annihilate the soul. The bodies of the damned will be in one sense made stronger, so as to last, and not be consumed or dissolved with torment; yet they may, in another sense, be made weaker and more tender, as they may be more sensible of torment.

657. FREE WILL. To place human liberty in a contingency of the will, or the will's having nothing to determine it but its being left to happen this way or that without any determining cause, is contrary to all use and custom of language. It is as far from the meaning of the words *freedom* or *liberty*, in the original and common acceptation, as the east is from the west. The original and proper meaning of a man's being free or at liberty, is that he is in such a state, that he may act his pleasure and do what he will; and there never was any other meaning thought of till philosophers and metaphysicians took it in hand to fix a new meaning to the words.

And besides, when liberty is understood not for this, but for that contingency or sovereignty of the will, as some call it, it not only has not its original true meaning, but no meaning at all. The word liberty used in this [way] is without any sense. It is a word without any notion or distinct consistent meaning to answer it; for, for the will to be determined without any determining cause, [this] is what nobody has any notion of, any more than they have of a thing's coming out of nothing, without any cause. And to suppose that the will does firstly determine itself, or determine itself in its first volition or choice, is a contradiction: for it supposes that there [is] a volition or act of the will before the first act, which is the determining cause of the first act.

658. See [Nos.] 597 and 649. CHRISTIANS THE TRUE ISRAEL. Indeed, it must be confessed that in this affair respect is had to natural generation: for the greater and more visible their relation is to the fathers unto whom the promises are fulfilled, the more evidently is God's respect to those fathers testified in the fulfillment of those promises. And if there be a relation to Abraham and the other fathers otherwise, yet if there be also a relation by natural generation, this adds to the relation and renders it more visible. Natural generation is in some measure concerned in the relation that all the seed bear to the fathers. All are directly or indirectly related to the fathers by natural generation. The Gentile Christians are spiritually from Christ and the apostles, and they[2] were related to the fathers by natural generation; so that natural generation is one thing that intervenes between them and the fathers, by which the relation is connected between the extremes. And though a being directly descended from the fathers by natural generation ben't essential to the being the children of Abraham—there are other ways of being related to him far more considerable—yet the more there is of a relation by natural generation, the stronger and more visible in some respects is the relation. And, therefore, though the promises are fulfilled now in the blessings bestowed on the Gentile church, yet 'tis the will of God to fulfill them in such a manner, as still in a further degree to show his respect to the fathers in calling of the nation of the Jews. For when they shall return to the true religion, their relation to Abraham, Isaac and Jacob will be more visible, and the fulfillment of the promises more conspicuous and remarkable. See that prophecy, Ezek. 47:22–23. See Bp. Kidder's *Demonstration*, Pt. 2, p. 85d, e.[3]

659. JUSTIFICATION. GRACE. TESTAMENTS. DISPENSATIONS. Faith's being the condition of justification don't express the sense of that phrase in Scripture of being justified by faith. There is a difference between being justified by a thing, and that thing's being the condition of justification. We are said to be justified by a thing, as that thing has influence in the affair of our justification, so that there should be [in] some way a depen-

---

2. I.e. the apostles.

3. Richard Kidder, *A Demonstration of the Messias. In which the Truth of the Christian Religion is Proved, against all the Enemies thereof; But especially against the Jews* (2nd ed., corr., London, 1726). Following the table of contents of the second edition, a note informs the reader that "in the second Part, between page 96 and 97, are added twelve other pages, beginning thus (85) and ending thus (96)." JE's reference is to the second page number 85, specifically to Kidder's assertion that "they are said to be *Abraham's* seed, who tread in his steps, and observe his discipline." It is taught not only "in the *new Testament*" but also "among the *Hebrews*" that he is "our father, whom we imitate, tho' we were not born of him."

dence of that effect on its influence. So we are said to be justified by faith, as God, upon the account of faith, looks upon it meet that we should be looked upon as having righteousness, in the manner as has been elsewhere explained.[4] But for anything to be the condition of justification, is to be that with which justification shall be, and without which it shall not be. And God may be said chiefly to give us that as the condition of our justification, which is the condition that he most plainly and fully reveals as the sign and evidence of our justification, by which we can receive God's justification in our consciences. The people of God were always justified by the same thing, viz. by faith (though not always in like exercises of it); but this declared condition of justification, or that condition which God most fully reveals, may be different under different dispensations. Thus universal and persevering obedience was the condition chiefly insisted and most fully revealed in the Law of Moses. Deut. 6:25, "And it shall be our righteousness, if we observe to do all these commandments before the Lord our God, as he hath commanded us." So that the saints of old had not that advantage for comfort and assurance as they have now under the gospel of Jesus, wherein 'tis most clearly revealed that every one that believes is already accepted of God to be everlastingly the object of his favor.

660. CONVERSION. 'Tis probable that most of the first Christians that were turned to Christianity from Judaism or heathenism by the preaching of the apostles, were savingly converted when they were turned, and much more commonly than those that are by long reasoning and persuasion turned from false religions now. For we are to consider that [that] effect of turning them to Christianity was not done ordinarily by any natural influence of means, but by an extraordinary effusion of the Spirit of God, and a supernatural influence upon the minds of those that were turned, as is manifest from the extraordinary success [of] the gospel, and the swift progress it had against the greatest opposition and disadvantages. If there had been no other than a natural influence of means used, 'tis probable there would not have been one proselyte, where there was a

4. In No. 315 JE maintains that faith is not properly called "the only condition of salvation, if by a condition we mean that . . . without which it shall not be, and that with which it shall be; for so are many things that accompany and follow faith." Therefore, "when we say he is justified by faith only, we mean that it's only his having faith that renders him approvable . . . in God's esteem." JE continues this line of reasoning in No. 412 and incorporates it into his 1738 discourse *Justification By Faith Alone.* See *Works, 13,* 396, 471–74, and *Discourses on Various Important Subjects,* prop. I, second pt., subpt. 1, "How justification is by faith," pp. 8–11. See also No. 507.

thousand. And commonly when the effect was wrought by so much of the supernatural power of the Spirit, the Spirit did not do his work to the halves. And then besides, it was a much greater thing then to turn Christian from other religions, than it is now; for then Christianity was a new thing. Never anything like it had been heard of before; [it was] exceeding contrary to the prejudices of the Jews, and all notions of the heathen. And it was a religion professed only by a few poor people. All the powers of the world were against it. The case is exceeding different now, when the greatest powers of the earth and the mightiest nations profess it, and have professed it many ages. Christianity came first abroad in the world under vast disadvantages, with the news of a crucified man as the founder and head of it. It therefore made a contemptible appearance in the eyes of carnal men. The crucifixion of Christ was then a new difficulty. There had not been time for solving the difficulty in the eye of the world, and to remove the stumbling block by reason, and to possess the world with an advantageous notion of it. And in many other respects the difficulties were far greater. So that it can't be thought that very many would openly embrace this religion, separating themselves from all the world, without a mighty power of the Spirit of God on their hearts, changing their very natures.

661. CREATION OF THE WORLD, why God effected it by Jesus Christ. See note on Eph. 3:9.[5]

662. END OF THE CREATION. GLORY OF GOD. It may be inquired why God would have the exercises of his perfections and expressions of his glory known and published abroad. *Ans.* It was meet that his attributes and perfections should be expressed. It was the will of God that they should be expressed and should shine forth. But if the expressions of his attributes ben't known, they are not; the very being of the expression depends on the perception of created understandings. And so much the more as the expression is known, so much the more it is.

663. FAITH. JUSTIFICATION. If faith justifies, or gives us a right to divine benefits, only as 'tis the act [of] uniting to Christ as a savior, then it may

5. The "Blank Bible" note on Eph. 3:9 observes that "the creation of all things was with an aim and subordination to that great work of Christ as Mediator, viz. the work of redemption. It was not only God's design in all the works of providence, from the beginning of the world . . . but also in the creation of the world itself . . . Christ was to be the great means of God's glory, and that by which chiefly he was to be so, was the work of redemption which he was to work out."

be inquired why we have so many instances of the old testament saints obtaining these and those benefits and blessings by their believing of God's promises and trusting in God—that are doubtless recorded as instances of the success of faith, and to show us that it is by faith that we come to have the favor [of God] and to obtain his blessing, and [which] are sometimes mentioned in the New Testament as proofs confirming the doctrine of salvation by faith—when yet they had no distinct respect to Christ in those acts of faith that are mentioned. They believed in God, and trusted in him, without any distinct notion of, or respect to, a distinction of persons and offices in the deity. How then can those instances be examples of the success and validity of faith, in the notion of an act by which we are united to Christ as our Savior?

I answer, it was the Lord Jesus Christ, the second person in the Trinity, that was wont to appear and to reveal himself to the people of God of old, and that manifested himself as the husband of the church, and as the author of all that good and salvation to the saints, that they stood in need of. And by those instances of faith before mentioned, they closed with and cleaved to this their God, husband and Savior, in a way agreeable to the dispensation they were under, and [in] the manner in which Christ revealed himself to them, and according to the manifestations Christ made of himself as their Savior and the author of their good and happiness, in those days. Christ manifested himself then to his people more clearly as the author of temporal salvation and benefits, and they cleaved to him by faith in his promises as such, and were united to him as their Savior, as their spiritual husband, that cared for their welfare and obtained such benefits as Christ then revealed himself the author of, and they trusted in him for. It was, notwithstanding, only as faith was that whereby they closed with Christ as a savior or author of their good, that they by faith obtained the promises they had. Their trusting in God as their helper and the author of their good, was their souls' cleaving to him and active uniting to him in that character.

664a. THE GREATNESS OF THE SIN OF UNBELIEF. The sin of unbelief is exceedingly provoking to God, because thereby his only begotten Son is contemned and ill-treated. And how incensing that must be to the wrath [of God] we may judge by considering how soon, and how greatly, God's wrath was wont to be stirred up by an ill treatment of the saints. They who were but Christ's disciples were so dear to God, and God set so high a value upon them, that he that touched [them], touched the apple of God's eye, and his wrath was effectually roused by it. Despising of them was a great crime. Matt. 18:10, "Take heed that ye despise not one of these little ones: for I say unto you, that in heaven their angels do always behold the face of my father which is in heaven."

Especially if any of the saints came from God with a gracious message to men, if they were then treated with indignity, did God highly resent it. Thus, how highly did God resent it when Korah and his company envied Moses, and treated him ill and rejected him; how terribly were they destroyed [Num. 16]. "But if they escaped not who refused him that spake on earth, much more shall not we escape, if we turn away from him that speaketh from heaven" [Heb. 12:25]. But how much dearer to God is his only begotten Son, and how much higher a value doth he set upon him. John 3:18, "Because he hath not believed on the only begotten Son of God."

664b. Wisdom of God in the Work of Redemption. Fall of Angels. Fall of Man. Confirmation of the Angels. Christ's Righteousness or Obedience. Death and Sufferings of Christ. Day of Judgment. Consummation of All Things. Separate Spirits.

§ 1. 'Tis the will of God that eternal happiness should be bestowed on the creature in reward of obedience, that obedience should first be performed before eternal happiness be bestowed. 'Tis fit, therefore, that every creature, before he receives the eternal reward of his obedience, should have some considerable trial of his obedience. For to what end is any obedience at all required in order to a confirmation in happiness, but as the exercise and manifestation of the creature's respect to God and his authority, or, which is the same thing, the exercise and manifestation of a spirit of obedience? But a respect to God's authority and a spirit of obedience don't appear—is not exercised—unless the creature meets with some trial, i.e. some opposition to obedience, something which, if it were not for a spirit of obedience, would tend to influence to disobedience; something that, if the principle of respect to God did not prevent, would, by working upon other principles, influence to the contrary. Respect to God's authority is not shown in doing those things that other principles would influence to, or not at all oppose, if there were no respect to God's authority. The influence, power or causality of respect to God don't appear in a creature's doing [that] which he would do, or would have nothing influence him not to do, if he was destitute of respect to God's authority.

§ 2. Hence, God might justly suffer Satan to tempt man. For it was fit, as has been shown [§ 1], that man should have a considerable trial, that he should meet with opposition to his obedience, and the angels also doubtless had some remarkable trial of their obedience. I have already shown[6] what a trial they probably had by a revelation that God made to them, and command that he gave them, which tried them as it affected their principle of regard to their own honor.

§ 3. And it would have been no way proper that God should give his creatures any law, or any law with promises and threatenings annexed, or to bring any trial, if at the same time God was bound not to permit any creature to break that law, and to suffer him to fail in the trial. And it was fit that some should be suffered to fail in the trial; otherwise, the rest would not have been duly sensible of the possibility of failing in a trial, and so would not be sensible of the trial, nor of the need of care and watchfulness, nor sensible of the goodness of God in their preservation; as well as could not be sensible of the evil they had escaped, and could not be sensible of the dreadfulness of divine displeasure, wherein God's majesty and the sacredness of his authority appears.

§ 4. It is fit that he that is the most excellent of all creatures, that is nearest and that is to be set highest by him in eternal honor and happiness, should be the greatest instance of obedience, upon several accounts: for,

(1) As has been already observed [§ 1], it is the will of God that all his creatures should receive their eternal happiness as a reward of obedience; and therefore, that creature that is advanced highest in eternal honor and happiness must perform the greatest obedience.

(2) It was meet that it should be so, that the other creatures might see him that was the highest creature, the first born of every creature, the head of all creatures, to be a transcendent instance of obedience to God and respect to his authority, both for God's honor and for an example to the rest: that when they see a person of so great dignity, so great an instance of submission to God, and exceeding respect to his majesty and authority, it might make a strong impression on their minds of the majesty, honorableness and infinite dignity of the Divine Being, and the sacredness of his authority.

(3) 'Tis fit that that creature that is nearest and dearest to God should perform the greatest obedience, if we consider his obedience as an honor to the person that performs it. The elect, holy and blessed creatures, they

6. In No. 320 JE states that "the temptation of the angels that occasioned their rebellion was that when God was about to create man, or had first created him, God declared his decree to the angels that one of that human nature should be his Son . . . and that he should be their head and king; that they should be given to him and should worship him and be his servants, attendants and ministers" (*Works, 13*, 401–02). See also, Nos. 515 and 554.

do esteem it their great honor to do the will of God, and so to pay honor to God's authority, and to give the glory of his majesty and dominion. Love makes them all desirous of opportunity [of] expressing and manifesting their love. But he that has performed the greatest and most remarkable obedience, he has given the highest manifestation of love, and therefore hath the highest honor and happiness. Thus we read of the apostles, who though they were but saints in their imperfect state, yet rejoiced when they had opportunity of expressing their love by obedience under great trials. Acts 5:41, "And they departed from the presence of the council, rejoicing that they were counted worthy to suffer shame for his name." They accounted it their honor and happiness.

Corol. Hence, it was meet that this highest creature should have the greatest trial of his obedience, for the greatness of obedience is that which is performed under the greatest trial. For, as has been observed already (§ 1), a respect to God's authority or a spirit of obedience is not exercised and manifested by obedience, but only as he meets with trial or opposition in his obedience. It was fit, therefore, that the highest and most beloved creature should have the greatest trial, that he might manifest the greatest respect to God's authority and majesty. It was meet, therefore, that this first born of the creatures should obey under the trial of great humiliation and suffering. When persons by obeying must suffer, that is the greatest trial of obedience. It was meet, therefore, that he should have that trial, and not only the[7] trial of suffering, but of the greatest suffering.

§ 5. Christ had immensely the greatest trial of obedience that ever was, upon several accounts:

(1) The sufferings that he underwent in obedience to the Father were by far the greatest that ever any elect creature endured. We may doubtless conclude that they were so by the extraordinary effect that the idea of them had upon him when he had them in view and expectation, when it caused his soul to be exceeding sorrowful, even unto death, and occasioned that strong crying and tears and his sweat to be as it were great drops of blood falling down to the ground. We have reason also to conclude the same from many expressions used to signify them in prophecies, and the types used to represent them.

(2) On [the account of] the dignity and honorableness of the person that suffered. The trial is not great in the simple proportion of the greatness of the sufferings; but to this proportion there is to be added the proportion of the greatness and dignity of the sufferer. For it was a greater

----

7. MS: "that the."

thing for a person of so great dignity to be brought so low, than for others in proportion, as he is greater, for the stoop or humiliation is so much the greater. And so it was proportionably a greater trial. For Christ, when he undertook to suffer, and when he actually suffered, knew how great and honorable a person he was. The sufferings of Christ were a trial not only as what affected a principle of love of his own ease and his aversion to pain, but also as an humiliation, or as they affected a principle of regard to his own honor and dignity.

(3) On the account of the happiness which he was originally in the possession of. It was a greater thing for him that was so happy to be willing to suffer so much, than for another that was not so happy. The degree of trial is not to be measured by the degree of distance of that suffering state from an indifferent state, or such a state as men are in when at ease, but by the distance from that state of happiness that he originally is in; or at least from that state of happiness that the human nature would have been [in], in such a participation of the happiness of the eternal Logos, as would have been answerable to its capacity and state, as being the same person with that eternal Logos. The least degree of diminution of that happiness, or falling below it, would have been some degree of trial. For the loss or privation of happiness is equivalent to suffering; and therefore, so much as Christ in suffering descended below that state of happiness, so much the greater was the trial.

(4) On the account of his great love to God and his remembrance of God's love to him. This rendered his sufferings as from God the greater trial. The sufferings of Christ in great part were from God, from his withdrawing from him and hiding his face; yea, the bitterest and heaviest part, as seems evident by his complaining most of this, when he was in the greatest extremity of his bodily sufferings. That God should hide his face from him, and thus treat him as an enemy, was bitter and grievous to him. In proportion as he loved God and delighted in the manifestations of his favor, the loss or deprivation of these manifestations of his love were so much the more bitter. He remembered how he used to be in the enjoyment of his love, as appears by what he said to the Father in his prayer a little before his crucifixion. John 17:5, "And now, O Father, glorify thou me with thine own self with the glory I had with thee before the world was."

(5) Add to these that he was put to death by that sin and corruption of mankind that he died to atone, and so had even in his very suffering that which tended to give him the greatest sense of the vileness and hatefulness of that which he suffered for, for in suffering he saw and felt the ma-

lignity of it. Yea, it was not only the same corruption of man that was so cruel towards him, that he endured that cruelty for; but it was the same actual sin that put him to death that he was commanded to atone for by that suffering, for he died for some of his crucifiers. Add to this the ill treatment of his disciples that had already received saving benefit by his death. They were never so unkind to him, as when he was in the greatest act of his kindness to them, viz. in offering up himself a sacrifice for them. See [Nos.] 265, 516 and 1005.[8]

N.B. These things that have been mentioned, that were trials of Christ's obedience and render his obedience great and wonderful, were also trials of his love to man. For [there are] these two principles in what he undertook and did and suffered, viz. a principle of obedience to God and a principle of love to man.

§ 6. It is an honor that the holy angels have never had, to obey God in and by suffering. Herein the people of Jesus Christ, as well as Christ himself, have an higher honor in some respect than the angels. The obedience of the angels in other respects is greater and more honorable than theirs: for (1) the angels' obedience is perfect, men's exceeding imperfect; [and] (2) the angels, though they han't had the trial of suffering, yet they have obeyed through great trials of another sort. Trials of obedience are chiefly of two sorts, according to the principles that they affect. The one sort are those that affect a principle of love of ease and pleasure, or aversion to pain. The other are those that affect the creature's principle of affectation of its own dignity and honor. The latter of these the angels have had to a great degree. But Christ hath had both sorts to the greatest degree, immensely beyond any mere creature. There may be a great trial of this latter sort without any suffering; and that notwithstanding, [that] to be degraded in dignity or to be deprived of honor simply considered, is suffering. Because,

(1) God may give the angels a command which obedience to would really be no degradation to them, that yet might be of such a nature that nothing but a great and transcendent regard to God, and honor to him, and high exercise of it at that time, would make 'em think it not a degradation. Without this, they would unavoidably look upon [it] as a degra-

---

8. In the MS JE adds "p. 4 of that No. near the bottom." This reference, a later addition, is to the second paragraph under Pt. II of No. 1005, which is entitled "Christ's Suffering the Wrath of God for the Sins of Men; Satisfaction; Wisdom of God in the Work of Redemption." In this entry JE lists the ways that Christ endured God's wrath. The passage in question begins with the statement, "And then, it was an effect of God's wrath that he forsook Christ," and ends with a cross-reference to Nos. 265, 516, and 664b. See Worcester rev. ed., *1*, 606.

dation. And therefore, their obedience to such a command might be a great manifestation of their respect and honor to God's authority. As for instance, supposing the case to be as I have shown it probably was, that God commanded them to attend upon and minister to a race of beings by nature far inferior in nature to them, and that God revealed that one of that race should be their king and head that they should submit to and serve and worship, perhaps without particularly revealing the constitution and circumstances of his person (Nos. 320, 702, corol. 3, and 710), now an high and extraordinary respect to God might cause the angels to think this no degradation: for such an esteem of God might make them think that, inasmuch as God, of his sovereign pleasure, had been pleased so to set his love on this inferior race, and on that person of that inferior race, and to set such a very high value upon him above them, that upon this account alone they ought to look upon him as so much above them, as that such submission in them might be suitable. They might think that God's sovereign distinguishing love and value alone, without anything else, gave a sufficient superiority. But if they had not an high honor of God and love to him, they would not think thus.

(2) If they did think it a degradation, yet their love to God might make it no suffering to be degraded. They might cast off their own honor from respect to God's honor and love to him, and in compliance with his will, with delight; and it might be a pleasure to them so to do.

Obj. The apostles counted it all joy to suffer for the sake of Christ, and yet it was suffering notwithstanding. *Ans. 1.* Love to God don't hinder a thing's being a suffering to the body, or suffering of sense; but the angels have no bodies. *2.* If the apostles suffered nothing by their outward senses, shame and reproach would have been no suffering at all to them, if their love was perfect, and the exercises of it, and the views of the superior good attained by it, full, perpetual and uninterrupted.

§ 7. 'Tis probable that of the angels that fell, some one or a few of the chief, first entertained the design of rebellion. They, being some of the highest of the angels, could not bear that which they looked upon so great a degradation; and they influenced and tempted others. And the elect angels obeyed through this trial of their temptation, besides the trial that they all had by the command's being of a trying nature. See No. 320.

§ 8. If it was as I have already declared that I think probable (Nos. 515, 570, 591), the elect angels were not confirmed till the trial of their obedience, with respect to that revelation and command wherein their great trial consisted, was perfected; not till their patience, if I may so call it, or their steadfastness in enduring trial, had its perfect work; till they had actually seen that person in that inferior nature that was to be their Lord, and whose servants and worshippers they were to be; till they had seen him not only in that inferior nature that God told them of, but seen him in that nature in a state wherein that nature was depressed vastly below what it was when God first made the revelation, and the fallen angels were overthrown by it. They saw him in a state as much lower than that first state of man, as man's nature in his first state was below theirs, or probably much more. They saw him in the human nature—its mean, defaced, broken, infirm, ruined state—in the form of sinful flesh. And not only so, but they saw him[9] not only in this nature in its broken state, but they saw him in much lower and meaner circumstances than the generality of those in that nature, in beggarly circumstances of mean birth, born in a stable, living in a mean family, and afterwards a poor, despised, rejected person. And not only so, but they saw [him] under his last and greatest humiliation, standing as a malefactor, mocked and scourged and spit upon, and at last put to a most ignominious and accursed death, and continuing under the power of death for a time. They had seen his own disciples forsaking him; yea, and God himself deserting him, and in some respects acting towards him as an enemy in the midst of this disgrace, which gave seeming warrant to them to desert him. Now the trial was thorough; now their steadfastness and perseverance had its perfect work, and their obedience was perfect and entire, lacking nothing. They acquitted themselves well through this trial. When they saw him born of a mean virgin in a stable, in the place where cattle were wont to bring forth their young, it did not overthrow them, but they sang joyful upon that occasion. When they saw him subjected to the power of the devil, to be carried about by him, to be tempted by him, which was a great part of his humiliation, that did not overset them; but they then came and ministered unto him. And when they saw [him] in his agony and distress, in the beginning of his last sufferings and greatest humiliation, we read that they ministered unto him. After his last sufferings were finished, and they had seen the utmost of his humiliation after he had been crucified, and he remained still under the power of death, they came to minister to his resurrection, to roll back the stone from the sepulcher, etc.

§ 9. Though the angels were judged and rewarded at Christ's ascension (as has been already observed, No. 515), yet they don't enter upon their full reward till after the day of judgment, as the devils don't on their full punishment, and as the saints don't receive their complete reward on

---

9. MS: "in."

their first being with their ascended Savior and with the angels. All that are with the ascended Jesus God-man are in a confirmed state of holiness and happiness when they first begin to be with this ascended Jesus. It is meet that it should be so: for the ascended Jesus is in a state of reward, and God sees it meet that all that are with him should be so too, and none in a state of probation. The saints, when they first go to be with Christ in glory, are then judged; and their reward is adjudged to them and bestowed upon them in degree, as it was with the angels at Christ's ascension. But yet they shall be judged again and more fully rewarded at the day of judgment, and so it shall be also with the angels. The day of judgment will be an universal judgment of men, angels and devils. All shall be present, and all shall be judged. The saints shall be judged again, not because their state is not already determined, but to make God's righteousness in their justification manifest before the whole universe convened, and for their more public honor; and there will be the same reason for judging the angels again.

That great day will be a doleful day to both wicked men and devils, because it will be the day of their condemnation and entrance on their utmost misery. But it will be a joyful day to both saints and angels, because it will be the day of their open justification, and of Christ's public acknowledgment and approbation of them and manifestation of his great esteem of them and love to them, and the day of the bestowment of their consummate happiness, and their entrance on their last and most perfect and glorious state. It will be the day of the consummation of all things pertaining to all rational creatures, men, angels and devils. It will be the wedding day of the church; then will be the marriage of the Lamb. It will be the great day of the reward of both saints and angels, and indeed of all elect persons, even of Jesus Christ God-man, Mediator, himself. It will be the day of his highest exaltation, or greatest manifestation of his exaltation, which exaltation is the reward of his righteousness. It will be the day when Christ himself will be most openly and publicly and remarkably justified. He is said to be justified when God raised him from the dead. God the Father then gave an open testimony of his approbation of what he had done. But how much more will God's setting of him to be the universal judge of heaven, earth and hell be a testimony of his approbation, and an open justification of him. Then did God put great honor on his Son when he ascended into heaven. But he will put much greater honor on him, when he shall descend from heaven in the glory of his Father, with all the holy angels with him. This will be an higher step of his exaltation, and a greater manifestation of his glory and of the Father's approbation, than ever was before. Christ will be justified on that day, as well as the other elect persons, but in a different manner: others, in being judged by Christ, but Christ himself in being the judge. The saints and angels will have been justified before, but not till then in so open a manner. And so Christ will have been justified and approved as Mediator before, but not till then publicly, before all heaven, earth and hell convened. 'Tis probable that Christ himself will enter upon a state of higher and more glorious blessedness after the end of the world than he enjoys before; and will then first receive his consummate reward. For then he will have done the whole work that the Father [appointed] for his glory; he will have vanquished all his enemies and perfected everything. Then will he deliver up the kingdom to the Father, and then will he receive his reward from the Father. He, in delivering up the kingdom, won't deliver up any part of his honor or happiness. 'Tis true, his mediatorial kingdom was given him by way of reward; but it was as a means to an end that is better than the means, and wherein Christ's honor and happiness doth more consist. Christ will deliver up the kingdom as having attained this end. He will then have put down all his enemies, and will have gathered in and perfected all that the Father hath given him. He will have received that crown that he has [been] warring with his enemies for. That great day will be the day of his triumph, and it will be the day wherein he will receive his crown. Then the success of his labors and sufferings in the work of redemption will be completed. Then he will fully attain the joy that was set before him, in the perfecting his mystical body in every member of it, in the perfect salvation and full glory of all that the Father hath given him. These will be his joy and crown. If the saints are the joy and crown, in the day of Christ, of faithful ministers that have been the means of their salvation, how much more will they in that day be the joy and crown of Christ, the great author of their salvation, and who has purchased them with his own blood.

So many ways will the day of judgment be the day when Christ himself will be justified, and receive his greatest joy, and highest honor and consummate reward. This day will be a day wherein Christ and his saints and angels will rejoice together in a most glorious [manner]; and from henceforth will they rejoice together in their most consummate joy, before the Father, forever. [See] No. 371. See a part of No. 736.[1]

---

1. JE indicates that the part of No. 736 in question occurs on p. 127 of the MS. See below, p. 362.

Corol. It need not seem strange to us that departed souls of the wicked should be in very miserable circumstances, though they are but in prison in order to their punishment; nor that the souls of the godly should be in an happy state, though they have not received their complete reward: as the angels are in an happy state before their last judgment and complete reward, and the devils are very miserable, though but prisoners against the day of judgment.

665. IRRESISTIBLE GRACE. Grace is said to be irresistible only with respect to the resistance of corruption, not with respect to the resistance of the man, or of the will: because to call it irresistible with respect to the man supposes that there may be such a thing as the man's endeavoring and willing to resist it, and that those endeavors or attempts, and his strength in them, is overcome by the power of grace, when the case is otherwise. For the effect that is wrought by grace is on the will itself, to incline and bring it to a compliance. The very first effect of saving grace that touches the will is to abolish its resistance and to incline the will, and not to stir it up first to opposition, and then to overcome that opposition. Though there be opposition from corruption, yet the will never opposes. There was indeed an opposition of the will to God's commands before. This opposition of the will is overcome by divine grace, or rather abolished, for it never subsists after divine grace enters to fight or struggle with it. As soon as ever divine grace enters, the man is willing. Ps. 110, "Thy people shall be willing in the day of thy power." And therefore grace is not properly called irresistible by the man, for there never can be anything as a trial whether the man can resist it or no. There never can be any endeavor, because such an endeavor and saving grace deny the being of each other. An endeavor or willingness in the man to oppose holiness, supposes that there is no holiness; and grace or holiness supposes that the will don't oppose it. So that these two, viz. grace and an opposing will, never can meet together to have any struggle or combat, because one denies the being of the other. And therefore 'tis not proper to say that one is either resistible or not resistible by the other, unless it be proper to say that the two opposite parts of a contradiction may be supposed to meet and fight with each other.

666. SEPARATE STATE. Texts made use of by Dr. Watts in his *Essay to Prove a Separate State:* Ps. 73:24–26; Eccles. 12:7; Is. 57:2; Luke 9:30–31; Acts 7:59; II Cor. 5:1–2; II Cor. 12:2–3, it shows that St. Paul thought that a soul "might exist, think, know and act in paradise in a state of separation"

(see my note on the text);[2] Philip. 1:21; I Thess. 4:14; I Pet. 3:18–20, "spirits in prison"; Jude 7; Rev. 6:9; Heb. 11:14. The Jews generally supposed separate spirits, and Christ did not correct 'em: Matt. 14:26, Luke 24:36 ff., Acts 23:8–9.

More evident proofs: Matt. 10:28, Luke 16:22 ff., Luke 20:37–38, Luke 23:42–43, II Cor. 5:6–8, Philip. 1:23–24, Heb. 12:23, II Pet. 1:13–14.[3]

To which may be added Acts 1:25.

See my note on Heb. 12:1, "Blank Bible."[4]

667. HADES. Acts 7:59, "And they stoned Stephen, calling upon God, and saying, Lord Jesus, receive my spirit." Without [doubt] Stephen meant, "Receive my spirit to thyself, where thou art." He then at that time, or just before, looking up steadfastly to heaven, saw the heavens opened and Jesus standing on the right hand of God. And when he called to him to receive his spirit, his meaning was to receive him up there into that glorious place where he was at the right hand of God.

668. JUSTIFICATION. FREE GRACE. It may perhaps more adequately express the freedom of grace in justifying us by faith only, and not by the works of the law, that justification, or a right to eternal life, is not given in testimony of God's pleasedness with anything that we do, than to say that 'tis not given as a testimony of his respect to the loveliness of anything that we do. For the freedom of gospel grace consists in that, that God don't give us a right to life for anything that we do as a testimony of his pleasedness with it, either for the sake of the loveliness of it in itself, or from the relation it bears to him, as profiting him, or being done from love to him, or from honor to him, or obedience to him, or any respect to him. These

2. The "Blank Bible" note on II Cor. 12:2–3 concerns the privilege of communication with God enjoyed by Moses. JE concludes that "when the Old Testament saints and prophets have been admitted to so great a privilege, 'tis not unreasonable to suppose that New Testament saints and apostles should be admitted to as great, and greater, of the like kind, considering how much more glorious the dispensation is that the latter are ministers of than the other, and how much more honorable the ministers."

3. Isaac Watts, *An Essay toward the proof of a separate state of souls between death and resurrection, and the commencement of the rewards of virtue and vice immediately after death* (London, 1732). The texts in the first paragraph are from Sec. II, "Probable Arguments for the Separate State," pp. 23–37, 66, the direct quotation being located on p. 31. Those in the second paragraph are from Sec. III, "Some firmer or more evident Proofs of a Separate State," pp. 38–52.

4. This "Blank Bible" note states, "When the Apostle speaks of Christians running the race set before 'em, he undoubtedly alludes to the races in the Olympic games. So when he speaks of their being compassed about with a great cloud of witnesses in running this race, he evidently alludes to the vast crowds of spectators that stood about the racers in the Olympic games."

are really diverse considerations under which our righteousness may be viewed, as men are pleased with others' behavior, either because it appears lovely in itself, without any consideration of any concern they have in it, or they may be pleased with it because of its relation to them, because respect is shown to them in it. And so they will be pleased with others' behavior out of love to themselves, oftentimes when otherwise they would see no loveliness in the behavior considered absolutely in itself. So God may be conceived to have respect to what we do upon either of those accounts; but God don't give us a right to life as a testimony of his pleasedness with what we do either of these ways. Indeed, the freedom of grace may be adequately expressed by that, that God don't give us a title to life in testimony of his respect to the loveliness of what we do, if we understand loveliness in the largest sense in which it may be understood, viz. either for the loveliness of the thing in itself, or its loveliness to him from the particular concern he has in it.

669. JUSTIFICATION, whether FAITH and REPENTANCE are two distinct things that in like manner are the CONDITIONS of justification. The condition of justification, or that in us that we are justified by, is but one, and that is faith. There is nothing else that has a like concern in the affair of justification as that hath. Repentance and faith are not two distinct conditions of justification, nor are they distinct things that both together make one condition of justification. But faith comprehends the whole of that by which we are justified, or by which we come to have an interest in Christ; and there is nothing else that has a parallel concern with it in the affair of our salvation.

It may be objected that repentance is often in Scripture mentioned as the condition of pardon, and sometimes is put with faith as though it had a parallel concern in that affair. To this I answer two things:

1. That where repentance is mentioned in Scripture as the condition of pardon, commonly thereby is not intended any particular grace or act properly distinct from faith, that has a special influence in the affair of our pardon or justification, in like manner with faith. But by repentance is intended nothing distinct from active conversion, i.e. conversion actively considered. So it is to be understood when John the Baptist preached that men should repent because the kingdom of heaven was at hand. So it means when Christ says, "Except ye repent, ye shall all likewise perish" [Luke 13:3]. So it is to be understood when Dives in the parable says, "Nay, father Abraham: but if one went to them from the dead, they would repent" (Luke 16:30). So it is to be understood, Acts

17:30, "But now commandeth all men everywhere to repent"; and elsewhere.[5]

Repentance is conversion. So it is evidently to be understood, Matt. 9:13, "I am not come to call the righteous, but sinners to repentance"; and Luke 15:7, 10, there is "joy in heaven over one sinner that repenteth," etc. And Acts 11:18, "Then hath God also to the Gentiles granted repentance unto life": this is said by the Christians of the circumcision at Jerusalem, upon Peter's giving an account of the conversion of Cornelius and his family and their embracing the gospel, though Peter had said nothing expressly about their sorrow for sin. So II Pet. 3:9, "The Lord is not slack concerning his promise, as some men count slackness; but is long-suffering to us-ward, not willing that any should perish, but that all should come to repentance."

Now 'tis true that conversion is the condition of justification and salvation. But if it be so, how absurd is it to say that conversion is one condition of justification, and faith another, as though they were two distributively distinct and parallel conditions? Conversion is the condition of justification, because it is that great change by which we are brought from sin to Christ, and by which we become believers in him; agreeable to Matt. 21:32, "And ye, when ye had seen it, repented not afterwards, that ye might believe him." When we are directed to repent that our sins may be blotted out, 'tis as much as to say, Let your minds and hearts be changed that your sins may be blotted out. But because it is said, Let your minds be changed that you may be justified, and also said, Believe that you may be justified, it don't therefore follow that the mind's being changed is one condition of justification, and believing another. But our minds must be changed that we may believe, that so we may be justified; our mind's being changed is necessary in order to faith. And indeed, active conversion is not really distinct from faith itself, and so repentance is not really distinct from faith.

2. 'Tis the same active conversion or motion of the soul that there is in justifying faith, which active conversion yet, as it respects the term, is

---

5. At this point in the MS, JE crossed out the following sentences: "And though it may be thought that repentance seems to be distinguished from conversion in Acts 3:19, 'Repent, and be converted,' I answer, it is the same conversion but only differently denominated: in the first word from the term 'from which,' and the latter, the term 'to which'; as Acts 26:20, 'Repent and turn to God.' It don't express two distinct things, one 'repenting' and the other 'turning to God.' They both express the same turning, but only with respect to the different terms: the one 'from which,' and the other 'to which'; the one the turning from sin, and the other turning to God."

called repentance.[6] Active conversion is a motion or exercise of the mind that respects two terms, viz. sin and God. Now when conversion is spoken of under the appellation of repentance, the exercise of mind about the term from which or about sin, is especially respected; as Acts 26:19–20, "Whereupon, O King Agrippa, I showed first unto them of Damascus, and at Jerusalem, and throughout all the coasts of Judea, and then to the Gentiles, that they should REPENT and TURN TO GOD." Both these respect the same turning; but only, with respect to the different terms, in the former is expressed the exercise of the mind that there is about sin in this turning, and in the other, the exercise of [the] mind towards God. But then that exercise of the mind about sin that there is in active conversion, that is an evangelical and saving repentance, as that is spoken of in Scripture as the condition of remission, is not distinct from justifying faith itself. That in faith that does directly and immediately respect sin, is called repentance; and is that very principle or operation of the mind itself that is called faith, so far as it is conversant about sin.

That justifying repentance has the nature of faith seems evident by Acts 19:4, "Then said Paul, John verily baptized with the baptism of repentance, saying unto the people, that they should believe on him which should come after him, that is, on Christ Jesus." The latter words, "saying unto the people, that they should believe on him," etc., are evidently exegetical of the former, and explain how he preached repentance for the remission of sins. When it is said he preached repentance for the remission of sins, saying that they should believe on Christ, it can't be supposed but that 'tis intended that his saying they should believe on Christ was as directing them what to do, that they might obtain remission of sins. And also that forementioned place, Matt. 21:32, "And ye when ye had seen it, repented not afterwards, that ye might believe him." And so II Tim. 2:25, "In meekness instructing those that oppose themselves; if God peradventure will give them repentance to the acknowledging of the truth." That acknowledging of the truth which [is] in believing, is here spoken of as what is attained in repentance.

Justifying faith is conversant about two things. It is conversant about sin to be rejected and to be delivered from, and about positive good to be accepted and obtained. That in justifying faith that directly respects sin is as follows, viz. *a sense of our own sinfulness and the hatefulness of it; and an hearty*

6. MS: "~~If 2 it must be allowed that tho by Repentance when spoken of as the Condition of Pardon he means nothing distinct from~~ ⟨Tis the same ⟨⟨active⟩⟩ ~~motion or~~ conversion or motion of the soul with faith but only that there is in Justifying Faith which⟩ active Conversion yet ~~tis Chiefly~~ as it Respects the Term from which ⟨is called Repentance⟩."

acknowledgement of its desert of wrath, looking to the free mercy of God in a redeemer for deliverance from it, and the punishment of it. Here three things may be noted: (1) That this that has been described is all of it of the essence of justifying faith, and is not different from faith itself, so far as conversant about sin. (2) That 'tis all of it of the essence of repentance, and is the very same with that evangelical repentance to which remission is promised in Scripture. (3) That this is indeed the proper and peculiar condition of remission of sins.

(1) It is all of it of the essence of justifying faith, and not different from faith itself, so far as conversant about sin. For 'tis doubtless of the essence of justifying faith to embrace Christ as a savior from sin and its punishment, and all that is implied and contained in that act is implied and contained in the nature of faith itself. But in the act of embracing of Christ as a savior from sin and its punishment, i.e. from our own sins, is implied a sense of our sinfulness and a hatred of our sins, or a rejecting of them with abhorrence, and a sense of our desert of the punishment of it. An embracing Christ as a savior from sin implies the contrary act towards sin, viz. rejecting of sin. If we flee to the light to be delivered from darkness, the same act is contrary towards darkness, viz. a rejecting it. In proportion to the earnestness or appetite with which we embrace Christ as a savior from sin, in the same proportion is the abhorrence with which we reject sin in the same act. Embracing Christ and rejecting sin is the same motion of the soul, as the same motion of body may be fleeing to one thing and fleeing from another. Yea, if we suppose there to be in the nature of faith as conversant about sin no more than the embracing Christ as a savior from the punishment of sin, this act will imply in it the whole of the above-mentioned description of repentance. It implies a sense [of] our own sinfulness. Certainly, in embracing a savior from the punishment of our own sinfulness, there is the exercise of a sense of our sinfulness; we can't embrace him as a savior from the punishment of that which we ben't sensible we are guilty of. There is also in the same act a sense of our desert of the punishment. We can't heartily embrace Christ as a savior from a punishment that we ben't sensible that we have deserved: for if we thought we had not deserved the punishment, we should not think that we had any need of a savior; or at least [we] must think that the God that offers us a savior unjustly makes him needful, and we can't heartily embrace such an offer. And there is implied in embracing Christ as a savior from punishment not only a conviction [of] the conscience of our having deserved the punishment, such as the devils and damned have; but there is an hearty acknowledgment of it, with the submission of the soul, so as

heartily and with the accord of the soul, to own that God might be just and worthy in the punishment. If the heart rises against the act or judgment of God in holding us obliged to the punishment, when he offers us his Son as a savior from the punishment, we can't with the accord and consent of the soul receive him in that character.

There can be no dispute but only about the former part of this description of evangelical repentance, whether it be properly of the essence of justifying faith. But it not only is evident that it is, by what has been already said, but the Scripture from time to time seems to hold it forth, as particularly Matt. 15:27–28, "Truth, Lord: yet the dogs eat of the crumbs that fall from their masters' table. Then Jesus answered and said unto her, O woman, great is thy faith." And also Luke 7:6–9, "Then Jesus went with them. And when he was now not far from the house, the centurion sent friends to him, saying unto him, Lord, trouble not thyself; for I am not worthy that thou shouldest enter under my roof: wherefore neither thought I myself worthy to come unto thee: but say in a word, and my servant shall be healed. For I am a man set under authority . . . When Jesus heard these things, he marveled at him, and turned him about, and said unto the people that followed him, I say unto you, I have not found so great faith, no, not in Israel." And also vv. 37–38, "And, behold, a woman in the city, which was a sinner, when she knew that Jesus sat at meat in the Pharisee's house, brought an alabaster box of ointment, and stood at his feet behind him weeping, and began to wash his feet with tears, and did wipe them with the hairs of her head, and kissed his feet, and anointed them with the ointment," together with v. 50, "He said to the woman, Thy faith hath saved thee; go in peace." And Luke 23:41–43, "And we indeed justly; for we receive the due reward of our deeds: but this man hath done nothing amiss. And he said unto Jesus, Lord, remember me when thou comest into thy kingdom. And Jesus said unto him, Verily I say unto thee, today shalt thou be with me in paradise." See also about the prodigal son in the 15th chapter of Luke.

(2) That the above description is all of it essential[7] to evangelical repentance, and it is indeed the very thing meant by that repentance to which remission is promised in the gospel. As to the former part of it, nobody will doubt but that it belongs to the proper nature of repentance, viz. *a sense of our own sinfulness and the hatefulness of it, and an hearty acknowledgment of its desert of wrath.* But this don't comprehend the whole essence of evangelical repentance; but what follows does also properly

7. MS: "it is essential."

and essentially belong to its nature, viz. *looking to the free mercy of God in a redeemer for deliverance from it, and the punishment of it.* That repentance to which remission is promised not only always has this with it, but it is contained in it, as what is of the proper nature and essence of it. And respect is ever had to this in the nature of repentance, whenever remission is promised. And 'tis especially from respect to this in the nature of repentance that repentance has that promise made to it; if this latter part be missing, it fails of the nature of that evangelical repentance to which remission is promised. If repentance remains in sorrow for sin, and don't reach to a looking to the sovereign mercy of God for pardon, 'tis not that which is the condition of pardon, neither shall pardon be obtained by it. Evangelical repentance is an humiliation for sin before God, but the sinner never comes and humbles himself before God on any other repentance but that which includes an hoping in his mercy for remission. If his sorrow ben't accompanied with that, there will be no coming to God in it, but a flying further from him.

There is some worship of God in justifying repentance, but there[8] is not in any other repentance, but that which has a sense of, and faith in, the divine mercy to forgive sin. Ps. 130:4, "There is forgiveness with thee, that thou mayst be feared." The promise of mercy to a true penitent is in Prov. 28:13 expressed in these terms, "Whoso confesseth and forsaketh his sins, shall have mercy"; but there is faith in God's mercy in that confessing. The Psalmist says in the 32nd Psalm that "while he kept silence, his bones waxed old," but then he acknowledged his sin unto God, his iniquity he did not hide; he said he would confess his transgressions to the Lord. The manner of expression plainly holds forth that then he began to encourage himself in the mercy of God, when before his bones had waxed old, while he kept silence. When sin is aright confessed to God, there is always faith in that act. That confessing of sin that is joined with despair, such as was in Judas, is not the confession to which the promise is made. In Acts 2:38, the direction that is given to those that were pricked in their heart, was to repent and be baptized in the name of Jesus Christ. A being baptized in the name of Christ implies faith in Christ for cleansing from sin. Repentance for remission of sins was typified of old by the priest's confessing the sins of the people over the scapegoat, laying his hands on him (Lev. 16:21); denoting that 'tis that repentance and confession of sin only that is made over the scapegoat—over Christ the great sacrifice and with dependence on him—that obtains remission. The repentance that Peter

---

8. MS: "that there."

directed Simon Magus to for the obtaining pardon, was that which was with looking to God for mercy. "Repent therefore of this thy wickedness, and pray God, if perhaps the thought of thine heart may be forgiven thee" [Acts 8:22]. There is in true repentance a seeking God's face. Hos. 5:15, "I will go and return to my place, till they acknowledge their offense, and seek my face." Such was the repentance of the prodigal son. Luke 15, "I will arise and go to my father, and I will say unto him, Father, I have sinned against heaven, and before thee, and am no more worthy to be called thy son: make me as one of thy hired servants." Such was also the woman's repentance that we have account of, Luke 7:37–38, "And, behold, a woman in the city, which was a sinner, when she knew that Jesus sat at meat in the Pharisee's house, brought an alabaster box of ointment, and stood at his feet behind him weeping, and began to wash his feet with tears, and did wipe them with the hairs of her head, and anointed them with the ointment." This was repentance, such as is the condition of remission of sins, for Christ upon it declares that "her sins, which are many, are forgiven her"; and tells her, "Thy sins are forgiven thee." But there was faith in [it], and it was by virtue of the faith that was in it, that it had this avail; as appears by the 50th verse, "Thy faith hath saved thee; go in peace."

Not that I suppose that the word repentance, as used in Scripture, is a word of precisely the same signification with the word faith. I don't suppose that the words are used as perfectly synonymous in Mark 1:15, where it is said, "Repent ye, and believe the gospel"; and yet don't imagine that they are mentioned as two distinct parallel conditions of justification. But here I desire that it may be observed, that repentance is sometimes taken more generally and abstractedly, and that repentance in its general and abstract nature don't imply so much in it, as repentance for the remission of sins. It contains no more than the former part of the forementioned description, viz. a sense of our own sinfulness, and a turning of the heart from it. But repentance for the remission of sins contains that and something more, viz. a looking to the free mercy of God in a redeemer for deliverance from it, and the punishment of it. In like manner, as the word faith in the general and abstract nature of it don't imply all in it, as that special faith that we call justifying faith in Christ—though it be the abstract nature of faith that is contained in that act, that is the condition of justification, which is that from whence it is called faith—so[9] it is from the abstract and general nature of repentance that is contained in repentance for remission of sins, whence it has its denomination of repentance. Take repen-

---

9. MS: "and so."

tance only in its general abstract nature, and faith only in the abstract and general nature of that, and so they are entirely and fully distinguished one from the other. But take that special faith that is called justifying faith, and that special repentance that is called repentance for the remission of sins, and they contain and imply one another. Justifying faith contains the whole nature of repentance for the remission of sins in it; and repentance for the remission of sins contains the whole nature of justifying faith in it. Repentance, in its abstract nature, is a constituent part of both justifying faith and also of repentance for the remission of sins; and the abstract general nature [of] faith is also a constituent part of each. And justifying faith and repentance for the remission of sins, they are the very same act and motion of the soul, but that motion is denominated repentance only as respecting, and exercised towards, one of the opposite terms; and faith about both. So that justifying faith is something more comprehensive than the repentance for the remission of sins: for evangelical repentance contains only the exercise of faith as it is conversant about sin, or the evil to be delivered from; and the word faith, when it is used, seems commonly to respect that principle or operation of mind, as exercised both about the evil to be delivered from, and the good to be obtained. Evangelical repentance contains the whole nature of faith as to the kind of the act, though not as to the object, or rather terms; because the same kind of act is exercised towards two objects or terms, viz. evil to be delivered from, and good to be obtained. This principle or operation is called faith as exercised towards either of these; but it is called repentance only as exercised with respect to one of them, viz. the evil to be delivered from. So that there are these three ways that repentance may be distinguished from faith:

    1. The general abstract nature of faith and the abstract nature of repentance, which are both contained in justifying faith, and in repentance for the remission of sins, are entirely and fully distinguished one from another, as two distinct parts of an whole are distinguished one from another.

    2. Repentance in its general abstract nature is distinguished from justifying faith as a part is distinguished from a whole, and no otherwise.

    3. Repentance for the remission of sins differs from justifying faith not at all in the principle or nature of the operation, nor as a part from a whole, but only as the same principle and operation may be differently denominated by different terms that it is related to and exercised towards. And they are not distinguished thus, as one being related only to one of the terms, and the other to the other; but as one being related to the one only, and the other to both.

And therefore when it is said, Mark 1:15, "Repent ye, and believe the gospel," there is no need of understanding these as two distinct conditions of salvation, but the words are exegetical one of another. It is to teach us after what manner we must repent, viz. believing the gospel; and after what manner we must believe the gospel, viz. as repenting.

(3) That repentance that has been described is especially the condition of the pardon of sin. Though it be true that faith is that only by which we are justified, yet evangelical repentance is in a peculiar and special manner that by which persons obtain a being justified, or cleared from the guilt of sin. That it is so is evident by the Scripture, as particularly Mark 1:4, "John did baptize in the wilderness, and preach the baptism of repentance for the remission of sins." So Luke 3:3, "And he came into all the country about Jordan, preaching the baptism of repentance for the remission of sins"; and Luke 24:47, "And that repentance and remission of sins should be preached in his name among all nations, beginning at Jerusalem"; and Acts 5:31, "Him hath God exalted with his right hand to be a prince and a savior, for to give repentance unto Israel, and forgiveness of sins"; and Acts 2:38, "Repent, and be baptized every one of you in the name of Jesus Christ for the remission of sins"; and 3:19, "Repent ye therefore, and be converted, that your sins may be blotted out, when the times of refreshing shall come from the presence of the Lord." Lev. 26:40–42, "If they shall confess their iniquity, . . . if then their uncircumcised hearts be humbled, and they accept the punishment of their iniquity: then will I remember my covenant with Jacob, and also my covenant with Isaac, and also my covenant with Abraham." Job 33:27–28, "If any say, I have sinned, and perverted that which was right, and it profited me not; he will deliver his soul from going into the pit, and his life shall see the light." Ps. 32:5, "I acknowledged my sin unto thee, and mine iniquity have I not hid. I said, I will confess my transgressions unto the Lord; and thou forgavest the iniquity of my sin. Prov. 28:13, "He that confesseth and forsaketh his sin shall have mercy." Jer. 3:13, "Only acknowledge thine iniquity, that thou hast transgressed against the Lord thy God." I John 1:9, "If we confess our sins, he is faithful and just to forgive our sins, and cleanse us from all unrighteousness."

And the reason may be plain from what has been said. We need not wonder that that in faith that especially respects sin should be especially the condition of remission of sin; that this motion or operation of the soul, as it rejects and flies from evil and embraces Christ as a savior from it, should especially be the condition of being free from that evil, in like manner as the same principle or motion, as it seeks good and cleaves to Christ as the procurer of that good, should be the condition of obtaining that good. Faith, with respect to good, is accepting, and with respect to evil, it is rejecting; and free grace appears in like manner, in that we may have good for accepting, and may be free from evil for rejecting. Yea, this rejecting evil is an act of acceptance; it is accepting freedom or separation from that evil, and this freedom or separation is the very benefit bestowed in remission. No wonder that that in faith which immediately respects this benefit, or our acceptance of this benefit, should be the especial condition of our having it. 'Tis so with respect to all the benefits that Christ has purchased: the trusting in Christ for eternal life is the especial condition of our having eternal life; the looking to Christ for protection and defense from enemies is the especial condition of protection; those acts of faith that respect supplies of God's Holy Spirit is the especial condition of those supplies. "Seek and ye shall find," says Christ [Matt. 7:7], having respect to seeking by faith, or in the name of Christ as the condition of finding. But the directest way to find a particular blessing is to seek that blessing. As Christ says, "how much more shall God give his Holy Spirit to them that ask him"; and whatsoever ye shall ask the Father in my name ye shall receive [Luke 11:13, John 14:13]. Hence, the inward sense that God is wont to give his people of his mercy, whether in the pardon of their sins or their adoption or right to eternal life, is wont to be much according to [the] manner of the exercises of faith. When there have been special actings of faith with respect to sin, there is wont to follow a special sense of pardon; when [there have been] special[1] acts of faith with respect to a right to glory, they are wont to be attended with a joyful sense of a title to glory, and so of other benefits of Christ's purchase. See No. 712.

670. FREE GRACE. JUSTIFICATION BY FAITH. OBEDIENCE. When it is said, "Forgive, and ye shall be forgiven" [and], "Blessed are the merciful: for they shall obtain mercy" [Luke 6:37, Matt. 7:7],

1. There is no necessity of supposing that 'tis out of respect to the moral fitness there is between one that forgives and a being forgiven, or between one that shows mercy and receiving mercy: for there is a natural fitness and suitableness between these things. 'Tis acknowledged that God has a respect to a natural suitableness between the subject and the gift. In a person's forgiving of injuries, there is a special manifestation of a natural suitableness and concord between his soul and the benefit of forgiveness. So in a person's showing mercy, there is [a] peculiar manifestation of the

---

1. MS: "a special."

agreeableness there is between him and the benefit of receiving mercy. By those things, that accord and consent of the soul that there is in faith to those particular benefits, is especially exercised and manifested. A forgiving disposition is fundamentally implied in a principle of faith. In repentance and faith in Christ for forgiveness, is the foundation of a forgiving spirit and practice; it lies in repentance, or a sense of our own injuries towards God and unworthiness on that account, and closing with Christ for forgiveness. And so a merciful disposition and practice has its foundation in a sense of our misery and unworthiness, and closing with Christ for mercy. So far as forgiveness or showing mercy is an expression of the suiting, according and closing of the soul with these benefits, so far God bestows these benefits from respect to them. And so it may be said of evangelical obedience in general: so far as it is an expression of the soul's according and closing with Christ and his salvation, so far it is an expression and manifestation of a principle of faith, and so far doth God bestow salvation on men out of respect to their obedience. Men are saved only by faith; but yet they are saved by evangelical obedience so far as it is an expression of faith, and as that in faith which especially respects a particular benefit is especially the condition of that benefit, as was shown, No. 669. So is any benefit especially promised to that part of obedience or holy practice that especially expresses and manifests the accord and consent of the soul to that benefit, or (which is the same thing) which especially manifests faith as related to that benefit. Hence, that part of Christian obedience, which consists in forgiveness, is especially a condition of forgiveness; so that part of evangelical obedience, which consists in showing mercy, is especially a condition of receiving mercy.

2. Though God's forgiving us and showing us mercy is not for any worthiness in our forgiving or showing mercy, or any moral fitness therein for those benefits, yet God's denying forgiveness and mercy may properly be for the unworthiness and ill-deserving of our refusing to forgive and to show mercy, or the moral fitness there is between such sin and such a judgment. See No. 672. Add to this, No. 714.[2]

671. FREE GRACE. JUSTIFICATION. OBEDIENCE. REWARDS. See Nos. 627 and 688. 'Tis most agreeable to the Scriptures to suppose not only that certain additions to the happiness and glory of the saints are given as a reward of their inherent holiness and good works, but heaven itself with all

2. No. 672 contains a third point and No. 714 states an objection to the position advocated by JE in this entry. See below, pp. 229 and 344.

its glory and happiness. The same heaven and the same happiness that is purchased by Christ's righteousness is in some respect the reward of the saints' own holiness and obedience. Indeed, there is not so much that is the reward of their holiness as there is of Christ's righteousness, because Christ by his righteousness has purchased their holiness and obedience itself, as well as all that happiness that is consequent on it. But the whole of man's salvation itself, so far as consequent on the saints' holiness, is given as a reward of their holiness and good works. Man's happiness is in great measure the natural consequent of man's holiness; and as there is a natural consequence, so by God's grace and Christ's merit there is a moral consequence, of all the same life and happiness that is the natural consequence of it.

But here it may be objected: How can the same happiness be wholly the reward of Christ's righteousness, and yet the reward of their own holiness too?

I answer, that although eternal life be the reward of both, yet Christ's righteousness and the saint's inherent holiness are far from having a parallel concern in the affair. It is not the reward of both in the same manner, and that on several accounts:

1. The bringing men into a state of salvation and justification, and favor with God and right to eternal life, is the reward of Christ's righteousness alone.

2. The reward of Christ's righteousness includes both the holiness of the saints, and the reward of it; and it includes their justification, which makes way for[3] their good works being rewardable, and also the reward itself. Salvation in the sum of it is only the reward of Christ's righteousness. The sum of salvation includes the saints' conversion, and justification, and holiness, and good works, and also their consequent happiness. Christ has purchased holiness and happiness both, but only he has purchased one as consequent on the other. But if we speak of salvation as the reward of the holiness of the saints, it must be taken in a more restrained sense, viz. for that happiness that is consequent of their holiness.

3. That the holiness and good works of the saints are rewardable, is what is merited and purchased by the righteousness of Christ. His righteousness not only purchased the holiness itself, but also purchased that it should be rewardable. 'Tis from Christ's righteousness that their holiness derives the value that it has in the eyes of God; so that eternal life and blessedness is primarily only the reward of Christ's righteousness, and is

---

3. MS: "for that."

the reward of the holiness of the saints secondarily and derivatively. Men's holiness is so far from having a parallel concern in this affair with Christ's righteousness, that the rewardableness itself of men's holiness is included in the reward of Christ's righteousness. 'Tis part of the reward of his righteousness that the saints' holiness should be rewarded.

But here another objection may be raised, viz. How can the same things be given as a reward of both Christ's righteousness, and man's own inherent holiness.

But if the matter be duly considered, there will appear no inconsistency in it. In order to any benefit's being a reward of any goodness two things are requisite, viz. 1. that the bestowment of the benefit should be from respect to that goodness, and 2. that the bestowment of it should be in testimony of that respect.

[1.] As to the first of these things, 'tis no way impossible that God may bestow blessedness on men out of respect to Christ's righteousness, and men's holiness, in different ways. He may have respect to Christ's righteousness for its own sake, as worthy in itself; and he may have respect to the saint's own holiness for Christ's sake, as being dependently and derivatively worthy, or as deriving value from Christ's merit or righteousness. They being looked on as in Christ and members of him, there is a great value hereby set on their obedience; 'tis valued in some respect as if it were the righteousness of Christ himself. The righteousness of his members is looked on by the Father as in some respect his, so that for his sake heaven is looked upon as no more than a meet reward for it: as the sufferings of believers, by reason of the respect that God has to them as members of Christ, are by him looked upon in some respect as the sufferings of Christ himself. Hence the Apostle, speaking of his sufferings, says, Col. 1:24, "Who now rejoice in my sufferings for you, and fill up that which is behind of the afflictions of Christ in my flesh." To the same purpose is Matt. 25:35–40, "I was an hungered, naked, sick and in prison," etc. And so that in Rev. 11:8, "And their dead bodies shall lie in the street of the great city, which spiritually is called Sodom and Egypt, where also our Lord was crucified."

By the merit and righteousness of Christ, such favor of God towards the believer may be obtained, as that God may hereby be already as it were disposed to make them perfectly and eternally happy. But yet that don't hinder but that God in his wisdom may choose to bestow this perfect and eternal happiness in this way, viz. as a reward of their holiness and obedience. 'Tis not impossible that the blessedness may be bestowed as a reward for that which is done after that favor is already obtained, which (to speak after the manner of men) disposes God to bestow the blessedness. This may in some measure [be] illustrated by this: a father may already have that favor for a child, whereby it may be thoroughly disposed to give the child an inheritance, because it is his child; and yet that don't hinder but that it should be possible that the father may choose to bestow the inheritance on the child in a way of reward, for his dutifulness and behaving becoming a child. Thus believers for the sake of Christ's righteousness are admitted into favor with God, and into great favor as towards his children, which favor that God has towards them as it were influences God to make them exceeding happy, and give them a glorious inheritance; but yet that don't hinder but that he may choose to do it in a way of reward for their childlike obedience. And so great and exceeding a reward is not judged to be more than a meet reward for their dutifulness. And yet that so great a reward is judged meet, don't arise from the excellency of the obedience, but from their standing in so near and dear and honorable a relation to God, as that of children, which is obtained only by the righteousness of Christ. And thus the reward, and the greatness of it, arises properly from the righteousness of Christ, though it be indeed the reward of their obedience: as a father might justly esteem the inheritance no more than a meet reward for the obedience of his child, and yet esteem [it] more than a meet reward for the obedience of a servant. As 'tis in this case of a child with regard to a parent, the inheritance is not given it so merely as a reward, as that the favor that disposes the father to bestow it does properly arise from the mere worth of the obedience simply considered, but from the relation that he that obeys stands in to him, and the favor he has founded on that relation; and yet it may properly be called a reward of the child's obedience. So it is in this case of the believer with regard to his heavenly Father, the favor that disposes him to bestow so great a reward is purchased by Christ, and is founded on that relation of a child which Christ by his righteousness has obtained for him.

2. Another thing needful in order to the blessedness of the saints being properly in reward for their holiness and good works, is that the bestowment of that happiness should be in testimony of his respect to, and complacence in, their holiness and good works, that that respect should be testified in the bestowment. But this respect is thus testified in the bestowment (1) in that the bestowment of the happiness is in some respect suspended on their holiness and good works as a condition, as has been elsewhere shown;[4] (2) in that when the Judge comes to bestow the reward, it will be

4. In No. 627 JE maintains that "God, in rewarding the holiness and good works of believers,

declared to be in respect to their holiness and good works, as Matt. 25:34–35, "Come, ye blessed of my Father, inherit the kingdom prepared for you from the foundation of the world: for I was an hungered, and ye gave me meat: I was thirsty, and ye gave me drink: I was a stranger, and ye took me in." The Judge in pronouncing this sentence shows, first, that that love and good will of God that the bestowment of this glorious kingdom is the fruit [of], don't arise from anything in them, but is absolutely free: because God had this love, and a design of bestowing this reward on them, long before they had a being, in that this kingdom was prepared of God for them from the foundation of the world. And yet, nextly, here is manifested and testified that this kingdom is bestowed on them in reward for their good works, in these words, "For I was an hungered, and ye gave me meat," etc.

3. God's respect to their holiness and good works shall be testified in the particular manner and degree of the reward. Though the happiness of all the saints be in general of the same nature, as also their holiness is in general the same; yet the reward will differ in different saints, as to the particular mode of it, and there will be a peculiar answerableness in it, to the particular holy disposition and practice that they were chiefly remarkable for. And then the degree of their happiness will be according to the degree of their holiness and good works.

That the reward is infinitely more than in proportion to the degree of goodness, is no evidence that it can't be all given as a reward of the goodness of the saints. The reward that sometimes men bestow on their fellow creatures for what they have done or for kindness received, is vastly greater than the kindness received; and yet it don't thence follow that it can't be a reward. Though the householder that we read of in the 20th chapter of Matthew gave the laborers, that had wrought in the vineyard but one hour, much more than their labor was worth, and made them equal with them that had borne the burden and heat of the day; yet it don't follow that what he gave them was not in reward for their hour's work. God has promised that he will give to those that charitably give to others "good measure, pressed down, shaken together, and running over" [Luke 6:38]; but it don't follow that all this is not in reward for their charity. So Christ promised to his disciples, that had forsaken all to follow him, that they should receive an hundredfold in this life [Matt. 19:29]; but it won't hence follow that but an hundredth part of that could be a proper

---

does in some respect give them happiness as a testimony of his respect to the loveliness of their holiness and good works." However, "their good works are not lovely to God in themselves, but they are lovely to him in Christ and beholding them not separately and by themselves, but as in Christ" (see above, p. 155–56).

reward for their forsaking all. The reward the Christian obtains by his good works is compared to the crop that a man has from his seed that he has sown (II Cor. 9:6), but in the crop the seed is abundantly multiplied. Men from peculiar favor and love that they bear to others may reward them exceeding richly and abundantly, and far beyond the proportion of the goodness of what is rewarded; and yet that don't hinder but that it may be given as a reward nevertheless. Thus God has such a peculiar favor to his saints that he rewards them infinitely above the proportion of the goodness of what they do, and that he has such a favor for them is owing [to] the merits of Jesus Christ.

By the following texts it seems plain that the sum of the happiness of the saints, and not only certain additaments, are given in reward for the saints' inherent holiness and their good works. Matt. 19:27–29, "Behold, we have forsaken all, and followed thee; what shall we have therefore? And Jesus said unto them, . . . every one that hath forsaken houses, or brethren, or sisters, or father, or mother, or wife, or children, or lands, for my name's sake, shall receive an hundredfold, and shall inherit everlasting life." Mark 10:30, "He shall receive an hundredfold now in this time . . . and in the world to come eternal life." Col. 3:23–24, "Whatsoever ye do, do it heartily, as to the Lord, and not to men; knowing that of the Lord ye shall receive the reward of the inheritance." Matt. 25:34–35, "Come, ye blessed of my Father . . . for I was an hungered, and ye gave me meat: thirsty, and ye gave me drink: I was a stranger, and ye took me in." Matt. 10:41, "He that receiveth a righteous man in the name of a righteous man shall receive a righteous man's reward." Heb. 10:34–36, "Ye took joyfully the spoiling of your goods, knowing that ye have in heaven *a better and an enduring substance.* Cast not away therefore your confidence, which hath *great recompense of reward.* For ye have need of patience, after ye have *done the will of God,* that ye might receive the *promise*"; and the like expression in many other places. Matt. 25:21, "His lord said unto him, Well done good and faithful servant: thou hast been faithful over a few things, I will make thee ruler over many things: enter thou into the joy of thy Lord." Rom. 2:6–7, 10, "Who will *render* to every man according to his deeds: to them who by patient continuance in well doing seek for glory, honor and immortality, eternal life . . . glory, honor and peace to every man that worketh good." Rev. 22:12, "Behold, I come quickly; and my reward is with me, to give every man according as his work shall be." Matt. 16:27, "For the Son of man shall come in the glory of his Father with his angels; and then shall he REWARD every man according to his works." Rev. 7:14–17, "These are they which came out of great tribulation . . . Therefore are they before the throne of God, and serve him day and night in his temple: and he that sitteth on the throne shall dwell among them. They shall hunger no more, neither thirst any more; neither shall the sun light on them, nor any heat. For the Lamb which is in the midst of the throne shall feed them, and shall lead them unto living fountains of waters: and God shall wipe away all tears from their eyes." Rev. 2:10, "Be thou faithful unto death, and I will give thee a crown of life." Rev. 14:13, "Write, Blessed are the dead that die in the Lord from henceforth: Yea, saith the Spirit, for they rest from their labors, and their works follow them." Here the sum of their blessedness is spoken of as consisting in these two things, viz. in resting from their labors and receiving the reward of their works.

672. FREE GRACE. JUSTIFICATION. OBEDIENCE. REWARDS. This in addition to No. 670.[5]

3. As I have observed in No. 671, the blessedness that God bestows on the saints, and their salvation so far as consequent to their holiness and good works, may be and is in reward for their holiness and good works, though their salvation is wholly the reward of Christ's righteousness; and so receiving mercy is the reward of showing mercy. And God in Christ shows mercy to us out of respect to the goodness of our mercy to our fellow creatures; and so God will exercise forgiving mercy towards us, in reward for our forgiving our fellow creatures. For though a sinner is forgiven and justified once for all at his first closing with Christ, and there is no occasion for forgiveness in that sense any more, yet God exercises forgiving mercy towards his people oftentimes after their conversion: as the forgiveness of a father, after he is become a father, and has adopted an enemy to be a son, is not of the same nature with that which he exercised at first receiving of him as his child. Yet a father may be angry with his child, that yet he is far from casting off from being his child, and may exercise forgiveness often without such a casting off previous to it. This kind of forgiveness God bestows as a reward of our forgiveness; and not only so, but also grants, though not justification itself and that forgiveness there is in it, yet the comfortable sense and manifestation of this forgiveness, and applying of it inwardly by the Spirit to the conscience. And also God's manifesting of it in providence, and God's dispensations towards us, may be and often is in reward for our forgiving one another.

5. In No. 670 JE lists the two preceding points. See above, p. 222.

673. [That] Saving Grace differs not only in degree, but in nature and kind, from Common Grace, or anything that is ever found in natural men, seems evident by the following things:

1. Because conversion is a work that is done at once, and not gradually. If saving grace differed only in degree from what went before, then the making a man a good man would be a gradual work; it would be the increasing the grace that he has, till it comes to such a degree as to be saving—at least it would be frequently so. But that the conversion of the heart is not a work that is thus gradually wrought, but that it is wrought at once, appears by Christ's converting the soul being represented by his calling of it. Rom. 8:28–30, "And we know that all things work together for good to them that love God, to them who are the called according to his purpose. For whom he did foreknow, he also did predestinate to be conformed to the image of his Son, that he might be the first born among many brethren. Moreover, whom he did predestinate, them he also called: and whom he called, them he also justified: and whom he justified, them he also glorified." Acts 2:37–39, "Men and brethren, what shall we do? Then Peter said unto them, Repent, and be baptized every one of you in the name of Jesus Christ for the remission of sins, and ye shall receive the gift of the Holy Ghost. For the promise is unto you, and to your children, and to all that are afar off, even as many as the Lord our God shall call." Heb. 9:15, "That they which are called might receive the promise of the eternal inheritance." I Thess. 5:23–24, "And the very God of peace sanctify you wholly; and I pray God your whole spirit, soul and body be preserved blameless unto the coming of our Lord Jesus Christ. Faithful is he that calleth you, who also will do it." Nothing else can be meant in these places by calling, but what Christ does in a sinner's saving conversion, by which it seems evident that this is done at once and not gradually. Hereby Christ shows his great power. He does but speak the powerful word, and it is done. He does but call, and the heart of the sinner immediately comes, as was represented by his calling his disciples and their immediately following him. So when he called Peter and Andrew, James and John, they were minding other things, and had no thought of following Christ; but at his call immediately followed. Matt. 4:18–22, Peter and Andrew were casting a net into the sea, and Christ says to them as he passed by, "Follow me"; and it is said, they straightway left their nets and followed him. So James and John were in the ship with Zebedee their father, mending their nets; and he called them. And immediately they left the ship and their father, and followed him. So when Matthew was called, Matt. 9:9, "And as Jesus passed forth from thence, he saw a man, named Matthew, sitting at

the receipt of custom: and he saith unto him, Follow me. And he arose, and followed him." The same circumstances are observed by other evangelists, which doubtless is to represent the manner in which Christ effectually calls his disciples in all ages. There is something immediately put into their hearts at that call that is new, that there was nothing of there before, that makes them so immediately act in a manner so altogether new, and so alien from what they were about before.

And that the work of conversion is wrought at once, is further evident by its being compared to a work of creation. When God created the world, he did what he did immediately. He spake and it was done; he commanded and it stood fast; he said, "Let there be light: and there was light." And by its being compared to a raising from the dead. Raising from the dead is not a gradual work, but 'tis done at once. God calls, and the dead come forth immediately. The change in conversion is in the twinkling of an eye, as that, I Cor. 15:51–52, "We shall be changed, in a moment, in the twinkling of an eye, at the last trump: for the trumpet shall sound, and the dead shall be raised incorruptible, and we shall be changed."

And it appears by the manner in which Christ wrought all those works that he wrought when on earth, that were types of his great work of converting sinners. Thus when he healed the leper he "put forth his hand, and touched him, and said, I will; be thou clean. And immediately his leprosy was cleansed" (Matt. 8:3, Mark 1:42, Luke 5:13). And so in opening the eyes of the blind men, Matt. 20:30–34, he "touched their eyes: and immediately their eyes received sight, and they followed him" (and so Mark 10:52, Luke 18:43). So when he healed the sick, particularly Simon's wife's mother, he "took her by the hand, and lifted her up; and immediately the fever left her, and she ministered unto them" [Mark 1:30–31]. So when the woman that had the issue of blood touched the hem of Christ's garment, immediately her issue of blood stanched (Luke 8:44). So the woman that was bowed together with the spirit of infirmity, when Christ "laid his hands on her: immediately she was made straight, and glorified God" (Luke 13:11–13). So the man at the pool of Bethesda, when Christ bid him rise, and take up his bed, and walk, he was immediately made whole (John 5:8–9). After the same manner Christ raised the dead, and cast out devils, and stilled the winds and seas.

2. There appears to be a specific difference between saving grace or virtue from all that was in the heart before, by the things that conversion is represented by in Scripture, particularly by its being represented as a work of creation. When God creates he don't merely establish and perfect the things that were made before, but makes [them] wholly and im-

mediately. The "things that are seen are not made of things that do appear" [Heb. 11:3]. Saving grace in the heart is said to be the new man or new creature, and corruption the old man.[6] If that virtue that is in the heart of a godly man ben't different in its nature and kind, then the man might possibly have had the same seventy years before, and from time to time from the beginning of his life, and has it no otherwise now but only in a greater degree. And how then is it a new creature?

Again it is evident also by its being compared to a resurrection. Natural men are said to be dead; but when they are converted, they are by God's mighty and effectual power raised from the dead. Now there is no medium between being dead and alive. He that is dead has no degree of life. He that has the least degree of life in him is alive. When a man is raised from the dead, life is not only in a greater degree, but 'tis all new. And 'tis further evident by that representation that is made of Christ's converting sinners in[7] John 5:25, "Verily, verily, I say unto you, The hour is coming, and now is, when the dead shall hear the voice of the Son of God: and they that hear shall live." This shows conversion to be an immediate and instantaneous work, like to the change made in Lazarus when Christ called him from the grave: there went life with the call, and Lazarus was immediately alive. It shows that immediately before the call they are dead, and therefore wholly destitute of any life, as is evident by that expression "the dead shall hear the voice"; and immediately after the call they are alive. Yea, there goes life with the voice, as is evident not only because it is said, they shall live; but also because 'tis said, they shall hear his voice. 'Tis evident that the first moment they have any life is the moment when Christ calls. And when Christ calls, or as soon as they are called, they are converted: as is evident from what is said in the first argument, wherein it is shown that to be called and [to be] converted are the same thing.

3. Those that go furthest in religion that are in a natural condition, have no charity, as is plainly implied in the beginning of I Cor. 13, by which we must understand that they have none of that kind of grace, or disposition, or affection, that is so called. So Christ elsewhere reproves the Pharisees, those high pretenders to religion among the Jews, that they had not the love of God in them.

---

6. At this point, JE deleted the following lines: "by which it appears that it is all new at conversion, for conversion is its creation. If there ben't a specific difference, and there was the same before but only not perfected, then God sometimes fails in the work of creation. He begins to create, and his work is never perfect but comes to nothing again."

7. MS: "in the."

4. In conversion stones are raised up to be children unto Abraham. While stones, they are wholly destitute of all those qualities that afterwards render them the living children of Abraham, and not only had them not in so great a degree. Agreeable to this, conversion is represented by the taking away the heart of stone, and giving an heart of flesh [Ezek. 11:19]. The man while unconverted has a heart of stone, which has no degree of that life or sense in it that the heart of the flesh [has]⁸ because it yet remains a stone, than which nothing is further from life and sense.

5. A wicked man has none of that principle of nature that a godly man has, as is evident by I John 3:9, "Whosoever is born of God doth not commit sin; for his seed remaineth in him: and he cannot sin, because he is born of God." The natural import of the metaphor shows that by a seed is meant a principle of nature. It may be small as a grain of mustard seed. A seed is a small thing; it may be buried up and lie hid, as a seed sown in the earth. It may seem to be dead, as seeds for a while do, till quickened by the sun and rain. But any degree of such a principle of nature, or a principle of such a nature, is what is called the seed. It need not be to such a degree, or have such a prevalency, in order to be called a seed. And 'tis further evident that this seed or this inward principle of nature is peculiar to the saints: for he that has that seed cannot sin; and therefore he that sins, or a wicked man, has it not.

6. Natural men, or those that are not savingly converted, have no degree of that principle from whence all gracious actings flow, viz. the Spirit of God, or of Christ; as is evident, because 'tis asserted both ways in Scripture that those that have not the Spirit of Christ are not his (Rom. 8:9), and also that those that have the Spirit of Christ are his. I John 3:24, "Hereby we know that he abideth in us, by the Spirit which he hath given us." And the Spirit of God is called the earnest of the future inheritance (II Cor. 1:22 and 5:5, Eph. 1:14). Yea, that a natural man has nothing of the Spirit in him, no part nor portion of it, is still more evident because having *of the Spirit* is given as a sure sign of being in Christ. I John 4:13, "Hereby know we that we dwell in him, because he hath given us *of his Spirit.*" Hereby 'tis evident that they have none of that holy principle that the godly have; and if they have nothing of the Spirit, they have nothing of those things that are the fruits of the Spirit, such as those mentioned in Gal. 5:22–23, "But the fruit of the Spirit is love, joy, peace, long-suffering, gentleness, goodness, faith, meekness, temperance." These fruits are here mentioned with that very design, that we may know whether we

---

8. JE, Jr., overwrote this word, obliterating the text underneath.

have the Spirit or no. In the 18th verse the Apostle tells the Galatians that if they are led by the Spirit, they are not under the law; and then directly proceeds, first, to mention what are the fruits or works of the flesh, and then, nextly, what are the fruits of the Spirit, that we may judge whether we are led by the Spirit or no.

7. That natural men, or those that are not born again, have nothing of that grace that is in godly men, is evident by John 3:6, where Christ, speaking of regeneration, says, "That which is born of the flesh is flesh; and that which is born of the Spirit is spirit." By flesh is here meant nature, and by spirit is meant grace, as is evident by Gal. 5:16–18, Gal. 6:8, I Cor. 3:1, Rom. 8:7. And that natural men han't the Spirit is evident, because by this text with the context it is most evident that those that have the Spirit, 'tis by regeneration. It is born in them; it comes into them no otherwise than by birth, and that birth is in regeneration, as is most evident by the preceding and following verses. That is Christ's very argument. By this it is that Christ in these words would show Nicodemus the necessity of regeneration, because by the first birth [we] have nothing but nature, and can have nothing else without being born again; by which it is exceeding evident that they that are not born again have nothing else. See No. 683.[9]

In godly men there are two opposite principles: "the flesh lusteth against the spirit, and the spirit against the flesh," as Gal. 5:17. But 'tis not so with natural men. Rebekah, in having Esau and Jacob struggle together in her womb, was a type only of the true church.

674. CONVICTION. HUMILIATION. The king, before he forgives the servant that owed him 10,000 talents, he terrifies and humbles [him] with threatenings, commanding him to be sold, and his wife and children, and all that he had, and payment to be made. By this means he brought the servant to fall down before his lord and then forgave the debt [Matt. 18:23–26].

Jer. 23:29, "Is not my word like a fire, and like an hammer that breaketh the rock in pieces?" As the founder first breaks the ore in pieces with the hard and mighty blows of the hammer and then melts it in the fire, [so] the law, it with hard blows does as it were break the heart in a legal repentance, and then the Holy Spirit (which is called fire) by the gospel (which is called the dispensation of the Spirit) melts the heart in gracious and evangelical repentance. When Christ was casting out devils (which is a type of conversion), we have two instances of the devils' first tearing the

9. This entry is continued in No. 683, which contains four additional points.

possessed as they came out of them, one in Mark 1:26 and the other Mark 9:26; which it is not probable that Christ would have suffered had there not been a mystery in it.

'Tis natural to suppose that persons in the work of conversion should be made conformable to Christ: that as he underwent such humiliation and sufferings, such terrors in a sense of imputed guilt and wrath, and was killed by the law before his resurrection and comfort, so[1] the soul that is to be one of Christ's members should be first distressed and abased and killed by the law and a sense of wrath, before its spiritual resurrection and comfort.

II Cor. 1:8–10, "For we would not, brethren, have you ignorant of our trouble which came to us in Asia, that we were pressed out of measure, above strength, insomuch that we despaired even of life: but we had the sentence of death in ourselves, that we should not trust in ourselves, but in God which raiseth the dead: who delivered us from so great a death, and doth deliver: in whom we trust that he will yet deliver us." Hence we may observe that 'tis God's manner oftentimes, and doubtless in spiritual cases as well as others, to bring persons into such exceeding great difficulty, that they seem to themselves even past hope; when God's end in it is only to convince them not to depend on themselves, but alone on God. See note on Mark 10:50, and on Deut. 34:5.[2] See note on Gen. 3:7–8.[3] See Is. 57:15, taken with the following verses; and also Is. 61, with following verses; and also Ps. 34:18, with the context.

See my note concerning the golden calf, Ex. 32.[4] Job 5:17–18, "Behold, happy is the man whom God correcteth: therefore despise not thou the chastening of the Almighty: for he maketh sore, and bindeth up: he woundeth, and his hands make whole." It shows that 'tis God's manner first to make sore and wound, to make way for his giving true health and

---

1. MS: "so that."

2. Both of these "Blank Bible" notes concern the futility of works-righteousness. Mark 10:50 "probably typifies that when persons do truly come to Christ, they cast away their coverings, their excuses and pleas, their fig leaves and the filthy rags of their own righteousness, and come naked." That Moses' death (Deut. 34:5) prevented him from bringing the people of Israel into the promised land "seems to signify to us that we can never obtain heaven or saving blessings by the law."

3. According to the "Blank Bible" note on Gen. 3:7–8, Adam and Eve's hiding themselves "well represents the manner of sinners' flying from one refuge to another when awakened with apprehensions of God's approaching wrath. The trees of the garden well represent the ordinances and duties of religion that God has appointed in his church to be means of grace, and of our spiritual nourishment; that garden was a type of the church, and the trees of the garden were what yielded outward nourishment for men. Sinners under awakening are wont to fly to those to hide their nakedness from God."

4. This note is a reference to "Notes on Scripture," no. 441, which comments on Ex. 32–34. See *Works*, *15*, 522–24.

soundness. See Is. 28:23 to the end, with my note upon it.[5] John 9:6–7, Jesus "spat on the ground." Christ did at first as it were spit in his face before he opened his eyes; he first defiled him, made him sensibly defiled, before he sent him to the Pool of Siloam to wash. He first blinded [him] — covered his eyes with clay—to make him as it were sensibly, or to appearance, further from seeing before he opened his eyes. See Acts 8:7; Is. 59:16 and 63:5 and 41:27–29, together with 42:1; Jer. 23:29; II Sam. 23:4, with Ps. 72:6. See note on last place.[6]

675. SPIRIT'S OPERATION IN CONVICTION. The proper work of the Spirit of God is to sanctify. This is the work wherein he acts his own nature. But yet the Spirit of God does other things besides this: he also works those works that have a relation to it, and are in order to it, as particularly he indited the Scriptures, and he ingenerated the human nature of Christ; which is a work to which conversion is compared, which is an ingenerating Christ in the heart, as that was an ingenerating Christ in the virgin's womb. So the Holy Ghost works miracles, casting out devils, healing the sick, etc. "If I by the Spirit of God cast out devils" [Matt. 12:28]. So the gifts of healing and miracles are gifts of the Holy Ghost. These works are images of the work of the Spirit of God in sanctifying the soul. So the Spirit of God in the first creation brought things into their order and beauty, and gave them their excellency and perfection. Gen. 1:2, "And the Spirit of God moved upon the face of the waters." So the Spirit of God causes conviction of sin in natural persons, that is in order to sanctification and tends to prepare for it. Yea, there are many common gifts and endowments of mind that seem to be spoken of as being from the Spirit of God, such as extraordinary skill in any affair, a spirit of judgment and discerning, a spirit of extraordinary courage, or spirit of government, etc.

676. ALL THAT A NATURAL MAN DOTH IS SIN. See Shepard's *Sincere Convert*, p. 40.[7] "Let a woman seek to give all the content to her husband that

5. In the "Blank Bible" note on Is. 28:23–29 JE observes, "What is designed here seems to be that God deals with his people as a prudent husbandman with his field and with his grain, for God's people are his husbandry." This is so, first, as God "plows his field, and breaks the hard clods, and makes smooth the roughnesses of it"; and secondly, "in the afflictions he brings upon them, as the husbandman deals with his grain when he threshes it."

6. The "Blank Bible" note on Ps. 72:6 begins: "The soul, before it is refreshed and renewed with the consolations of Christ, is wounded and as it were cut down with the scythe of the law. And in order to our having the benefit of Christ's salvation, we must be cut down; we must be cut down as to our former sinful life. We must die to sin that we may live to Christ."

7. In the 1st edition (1640) of *The Sincere Convert* this passage occurs on p. 60 (see above, No. 520, p. 64, n. 1).

may be, not out of any love to him, but only out of love to another man, he abhors all that she doth."

677. SABBATH. LORD'S DAY. 'Tis evident that the fourth commandment, as well as the rest of the ten, is of perpetual obligation, by Matt. 5:18–19, "For verily I say unto you, Till heaven and earth pass, one jot or one tittle shall in no wise pass from the law, till all be fulfilled." 'Tis implied here that no command of the law shall pass as to its obligation, even in gospel times, or in the Christian church, as is evident by the following verse. "Whosoever therefore shall break one of these least commandments, and shall teach men so, he shall be called the least in the kingdom of heaven: but whosoever shall do and teach them, the same shall be called great in the kingdom of heaven." By the kingdom of heaven here is meant that gospel kingdom that Christ was about to set up, that state of the church that he was about to establish. And by the commandments seem to be meant the ten commandments; for these are what Christ especially treats of in the following part of the chapter, and these were what were then called the commandments by way of specialty, as they are now. Mark 10:19, "Thou knowest the commandments." Matt. 19:17, "If thou wilt enter into life, keep the commandments." But if hereby is meant all the commandments of the Mosaic Law, ceremonial and all, then hereby must be understood that the obligation will remain in force till they be fulfilled. And those laws that were typical of Christ are fulfilled in Christ, and so cease; but the fourth commandment can't be shown to be typical of Christ.

678. BEATIFICAL VISION, whether there be any visible appearance or glory that is the symbol of the divine presence in which God manifests himself in heaven, besides the glorified body of Christ. See of the beatifical vision in my sermon from those words, "But glory, honor, and peace, to every one that worketh good" (Rom. 2:10).[8]

679. GOODNESS OF GOD. LOVE OF GOD. HAPPINESS OF HEAVEN. God stands in no need of creatures, and is not profited by them; neither can his happiness be said to be added to by the creature. But yet God has a real and proper delight in the excellency and happiness of his creatures.

8. For the sermon on Rom. 2:10 (Dec. 17[35]), see Dwight ed., *8*, 227–79. JE devotes a large portion of this sermon to a description of the beatifical vision. He maintains that "the saints in heaven shall see God. They shall not only see that glorious city [of the heavenly Jerusalem], and the saints there, and the holy angels, and the glorified Christ; but they shall see God himself" (p. 264).

He hath a real delight in the excellency and loveliness of the creature, in his own image in the creature, as that is a manifestation, or expression, or shining forth of his own loveliness. God has a real delight in his own loveliness, and he also has a real delight in the shining forth or glorifying of it. As it is a fit and condecent thing that God's glory should shine forth, so God delights in its shining forth. So that God has a real delight in the spiritual loveliness of the saints, which delight is not a delight distinct from what he has in himself, but is to be resolved into the delight he has in himself: for he delights in his image in the creature, as he delights in his own being glorified, or as he delights in it, that his own glory shines forth. And so he hath real proper delight in the happiness of his creatures, which also is not distinct from the delight that he has in himself, for 'tis to be resolved into the delight that he has in his own goodness. For as he delights in his own goodness, so he delights in the exercise of his goodness; and therefore, he delights to make the creature happy, and delights to see him made happy, as he delights in exercising goodness or communicating happiness. This is no proper addition to the happiness of God because 'tis that which he eternally and unalterably had. God, when he beholds his own glory shining forth in his image in the creature, and when he beholds the creature made happy from the exercises of his goodness, because these and all things are from eternity equally present with God this delight in God can't properly be said to be received from the creature, because it consists only in a delight in giving to the creature. Neither will it hence follow that God is dependent on the creature for any of his joy, because 'tis his own act only that this delight is dependent on, and the creature is absolutely dependent on God for that excellency and happiness that God delights in. God can't be said to be the more happy for the creature, because he is infinitely happy in himself; and he is not dependent on the creature for anything, nor does he receive any addition from the creature. But yet in one sense it can be truly said that God has the more delight for the loveliness and happiness of the creature, viz. as God would be less happy if he were less good, or if it were possible for him to be hindered in exercising his own goodness, or to be hindered from glorifying himself. God has no addition to his happiness when he exercises any act of holiness towards his creatures; and yet God has a real delight in the exercises of his own holiness, and would be less happy if he were less holy, or were capable of being hindered from any act of holiness.

Corol. 1. Hence when the saints get to heaven they will [have] this to rejoice them and add to their blessedness, that God hath a real delight and joy in them, in their holiness and happiness.

Corol. 2. Hence God's love to the saints is real and proper love; so that those have been to blame who have represented, much to the prejudice of religion, the love of God to creatures as if it were merely a purpose in God, of acting as the creature does that has love.

Corol. 3. Hence we learn how all God's love may be resolved into his love to himself and delight in himself, as asserted in my Discourse on the Trinity.[9] His love to the creature is only his inclination to glorify himself and communicate him[self], and his delight in himself glorified and in himself communicated. There is his delight in the act, and in the fruit. The act is the exercise of his own perfection, and the fruit is himself expressed and communicated.

680. TRINITY. How OIL, that was the great type of the Holy Ghost, represented LOVE. See Bedford's *Scripture Chronology*, p. 152, col. 1.[1] "And as the olive branch was a sign of peace between God and Noah; so from hence, so universal a custom arose, that an olive branch was a sign of peace between man and man. Virgil saith of Æneas that he brought the bough of a peace-making olive tree in his hand. Polybius saith, that when Hannibal passed the Alps the people brought him such boughs as a sign of peace and subjection. Livy saith, that the ten ambassadors from Lorin, when the consuls were in the senate house, stretched out their hands with the olive branches, according to the custom of the Greeks, and fell before the throne on the ground with a lamentable cry, desiring peace. And Columbus tells us the same of the Americans upon the first discovery of that country, when they had no other way to express their inclinations."

681. ANGELS. HEAVEN. SAINTS. DEGREES OF GLORY. INCARNATION AND DEATH OF CHRIST. WISDOM OF GOD IN THE WORK OF REDEMPTION.

The angels of heaven, though a superior order of beings and of a more exalted nature and faculties by far than men, are yet all ministering spirits sent forth to minister to them that shall be the heirs of salvation, and so in some respect are made inferior to the saints in honor. So likewise the angels of the churches—the ministers of the gospel—that are of an higher order and office than other saints, yet they are by Christ's appointment ministers and servants to others, and are least of all: as Matt.

9. See Fisher, ed., *An Unpublished Essay*, pp. 79–92.
1. Arthur Bedford, *The Scripture Chronology, Demonstrated by Astronomical Calculations, and also by the Year of Jubilee, and the Sabbatical Year among the Jews: or, an Account of Time from the Creation of the World, to the Restoration of Jerusalem; as it may be proved from the writings of the Old and New Testament* . . . (London, 1730), p. 152, col. 1. See *Works, 15*, 19, 21, 42.

20:25–27, "Ye know that the princes of the Gentiles exercise dominion over them, and they that are great exercise authority upon them. But it shall not be so among you: but whosoever will be great among you, let him be your minister; and whosoever will be chief among you, let him be your servant"; Matt. 23:8–12, "But be ye not called Rabbi: for one is your Master, even Christ; and all ye are brethren. And call no man your father upon the earth: for one is your Father, which is in heaven. Neither be ye called masters: for one is your Master, even Christ. But he that is greatest among you shall be your servant. And whosoever shall exalt himself shall be abased; and he that shall humble himself shall be exalted"; and Mark 9:35, "If any man desire to be first, the same shall be last of all and servant of all." 'Tis as 'tis in the body natural: those parts that we account more noble and honorable are as it were ministers to the more inferior, to guard them and serve them; as the Apostle observes, I Cor. 12:23–24, "And those members of the body, which we think to be less honorable, upon these we bestow more abundant honor; and our uncomely parts have more abundant comeliness. For our comely parts have no need: but God hath tempered the body together, having given more abundant honor to that part which lacked." God's ways are all analogous, and his dispensations harmonize one with another. As 'tis between the saints that are of an inferior order of beings, and the angels who are of more exalted nature and degree, and also between those Christians on earth that are of inferior order, and those who are of superior, being ministers of Christ; so without doubt it also is in some respect in heaven between those that are of lower, and those that are of higher degrees of glory. There, those that are most exalted in honor and happiness, though they are above the rest, yet in some respects they are least, being ministers to others and employed by God to minister to their good and happiness. Those forementioned sayings of Christ, in the forequoted texts, Matt. 20:25–27 and Mark 9:35, were spoken on occasion of the disciples manifesting an ambition to be greatest in his kingdom, by which they meant his state of exaltation and glory. And so it is in some sort even with respect to the man Christ Jesus himself, who is the very highest and most exalted of all creatures, and the head of all: he, to prepare him for it, descended lowest of all, was most abased of any, and in some respect became least of all. And therefore, when Christ, in those forementioned places, directs that those that would be greatest among his disciples should be the servant of the rest, and so in some respect least, he enforces it with his own example. Matt. 20:26–28, "Whosoever will be great among you, let him be your minister; and whosoever will be chief among you, let him be your servant: even as the

Son of man came not to be ministered unto, but to minister, and to give his life a ransom for many." And Luke 22:26–27, "He that is greatest among you, let him be as the younger; and he that is chief, as he that doth serve. For whether is greater, he that sitteth at meat, or he that serveth? is not he that sitteth at meat? but I am among you as he that serveth." None in the kingdom of heaven ever descended so low as Christ did, who descended as it were into the depths of hell. He suffered shame and wrath and was made a curse. He went lower in these things than ever any other did; and this he did as a servant not only to God but to men, that he undertook to serve us and minister to us in such dreadful drudgery while we sit at meat in quietness and rest, and partake of those dainties that he serves up to us. Christ took upon him to minister to us in the lowest service, which he represented and typified by that action of washing the disciples' feet, which he did chiefly for that end. Thus Christ is he that seems to be intended, in Matt 11:11, by him "that is least in the kingdom of heaven," who is there said to be greater than John the Baptist.

The design of God in thus ordering things is to teach and show that he is all, and the creature nothing, and that all exaltation and dignity belongs to him; and therefore, those creatures that are most exalted shall in other respects be least and lowest. Thus the glorious angels, they excel in wisdom and strength and are advanced to glorious dignity. They are principalities and powers and are kings of the earth, yet God makes them all ministers to them that are much less than they, of inferior nature and degree; and so the saints that are most exalted in dignity are servants to others. The angelical nature is the highest and most exalted created nature; but yet God is pleased to put greater honor upon an inferior nature, viz. the human, by causing that the head of all, and the king of all creatures, should be in the human nature, and the saints in that nature in Christ to be in many respects exalted above the angels, that the angelical nature mayn't magnify itself against the human. And that creature that is above all, its superiority and dignity is not at all in itself, but in God, viz. union with a divine person. And though it be above all, yet in some respect 'tis inferior: for 'tis not in the highest created nature, but in a nature that is inferior to the angelical. And to prepare it for its exaltation above all, it was first brought lowest of all in suffering and humiliation, and in some respects in office, in those parts of that office that were executed in his state of humiliation. And though the saints are exalted to glorious dignity, even to union and fellowship with God him[self], to be in some respects divine in glory and happiness, and in many respects to be exalted above the angels, yet care is taken that it should not be in themselves, but in a person that is God; and they must be as it were emptied of themselves in order to it.

And though the angels are exalted in themselves, yet they are ministers to them that are not exalted in themselves, but only in communion with a divine person, as of free grace partaking with him. Thus wisely hath God ordered all things for his own glory, that however great and marvelous the exercises of his grace and love and condescension are to the creature, yet he alone may be exalted, that[2] he may be all in all. And though the creature be by God's grace unspeakably and wonderfully advanced and honored of God's grace and love, yet it is in such a way and manner that even in its exaltation it might be humbled, and so as that its nothingness before God, and its absolute dependence on God and subjection to him, might be manifested. And yet this humiliation or abasement that is joined with the creature's exaltation, is so as not to detract from the privilege and happiness of the exaltation. So far as exaltation is suitable for a creature, and is indeed a privilege and happiness to the creature, it is given to the creature and nothing taken from it. That only is removed that should carry any shadow of what belongs only to the Creator, and that might make the distance between the Creator and creature, and its absolute infinite dependence on the Creator, less manifest. That humiliation only is brought with the exaltation that is suitable to that great humility that becomes the creature before the Creator. And this humiliation don't detract anything from the happiness of elect holy creatures but adds to it, for it gratifies that humble disposition that they are of. It is exceeding sweet and delightful to them to be humbled and abased before God, to cast down their crowns at his feet, as the four and twenty elders do in Rev. 4:10, and to abase themselves, and appear nothing, and ascribe all power and riches and wisdom and strength and honor and glory and blessing to him. They will delight more in seeing God exalted than themselves; and they won't look on themselves the less honored because that God appears to be all, even in their exaltation, but the more. And those creatures that are most exalted will delight most in being abased before God, for they will excel in humility as much as in dignity and glory, as has been elsewhere observed. The man Christ Jesus, that is the head of all creatures, is the most humble of all creatures. That in Matt. 18:4, "Whosoever therefore humbleth himself as this little child, the same is greatest in the kingdom of heaven," is true both with respect to the humility that they exercise in this, and in another world. And they that have most humility in this world will

2. MS: "and that."

continue to excel in humility in heaven. And the proposition is recipro-
cal: they that have the greatest humility shall be most exalted, and shall
be greatest in the kingdom of heaven; and they that are greatest in the
kingdom of heaven are most humble.

Corol. 1. What has been said above confirms that some in heaven will be
a kind of ministers in that society—teachers, ministers to their knowledge
and love, and helpers of their joy, as ministers of the gospel are here.

Corol. 2. Hence we may learn the sweet and perfect harmony that will
reign throughout that glorious society, and how far those that are lowest
will be from envying those that are highest, or the highest from despising
the lowest.[3] For the highest shall be made ministers to the happiness of
the lowest, and shall be even below them in humility; and the lowest shall
have the greatest love to the highest for their superior excellency, and the
greater benefit which they shall receive from their ministration: as 'tis the
disposition of the saints to love and honor their faithful ministers here in
this world.

682. FREE GRACE. JUSTIFICATION BY FAITH. It may be an objection
against what has been supposed, viz. that an interest in Christ and a right
to his benefits is not given as a reward or from respect to the moral fitness
of anything in us, what Christ says in Matt. 10:37–39, "He that loveth father or mother more than me is not worthy of me: and he that loveth son
or daughter more than me is not worthy of me. And he that taketh not his
cross, and followeth after me, is not worthy of me. He that findeth his life
shall loose it: and he that loseth his life for my sake shall find it." Worthiness is a moral fitness; and this place seems to intimate that it was from respect to a worthiness or moral fitness that men were admitted even to an
union with Christ, or an interest in him. And therefore, this worthiness
can't be consequent on being in Christ by the imputation of his worthiness, or from any value that is in us, or our actions on God's account, as
beheld in Christ.

To this I answer, that though persons when they are accepted are not
accepted as worthy, yet when they are rejected they are rejected as unworthy. He that don't love Christ above other things, that treats him with
such indignity as to set him below earthly things, shall be treated as unworthy of Christ. His unworthiness of Christ, especially his unworthiness
in that particular, shall be marked against him and imputed to him.
Though he be a professing Christian, and live in the enjoyment of the

3. MS: "highest."

gospel, and has been visibly ingrafted into Christ and admitted as one of his disciples as Judas was, yet he shall be thrust out in wrath as a punishment of his vile treatment of Christ. But the abovementioned words don't imply that if he did [put] Christ above father or mother, etc., that he would be worthy, but it implies that he would not be treated as unworthy. He that believes is not received for the worthiness of faith, but yet the visible Christian is rejected and thrust out for the unworthiness of unbelief. Being accepted is not the reward of believing, but being thrust out from being one of Christ's disciples is properly the punishment of unbelief. John 3:18–19, "He that believeth on him is not condemned: but he that believeth not is condemned already, because he hath not believed in the name of the only begotten Son of God. And this is the condemnation, that light is come into the world, and men loved darkness rather than light, because their deeds were evil." Salvation is promised to faith as a free gift, but damnation is threatened to unbelief as a debt, or punishment due to unbelief. They that believed in the wilderness did not enter into Canaan because of the worthiness of their faith, but God sware in his wrath that they that believed not should not enter in, because of the unworthiness and baseness of their unbelief. The design of this saying of Christ is to make them sensible of the unworthiness of their treatment of Christ that professed him to be their Lord and Savior, and set him below father and mother, etc., and not to persuade of the worthiness of loving him above father and mother. They that don't prize the benefit in any wise in proportion to the greatness of it, that don't treat the gift or possession in any wise suitably to the value of it, shall be rejected as unworthy to have it; and yet it won't follow but that, if they had received it, it would have been a free gift. As if a beggar should be offered a very great and precious gift, but as soon as offered should trample it under his feet, it might be taken from him as unworthy to have it; or if a malefactor should have his pardon offered him and to be freed from execution, and he should only scoff and jeer at it, his pardon might be refused him as unworthy of it, though if he had received it, he would not have had it for his worthiness: for his being a malefactor supposes him unworthy, and its being offered him only on his accepting it supposes that the king looks for no worthiness, nothing in him for which he should bestow pardon as a reward. And this may teach us how to understand Acts 13:46, "It was necessary that the word of God should first be spoken to you: but seeing ye put it from you, and judge yourselves unworthy of everlasting life, lo, we turn to the Gentiles." See No. 687; see also [No.] 705.

683. COMMON GRACE. SPECIAL GRACE. Join this to No. 673.[4]

8. Natural men have nothing of that nature in them that true Christians have; and that appears, because the nature that they have is divine nature, which the saints alone have. 'Tis not only they alone that partake of such degrees of it, but they alone that are partakers of it. To be a partaker of the divine nature is mentioned as peculiar to the saints in II Pet. 1:4. 'Tis evident that it is the true saints that the Apostle is there speaking of. The words in this verse, with the foregoing are thus: "According as his divine power hath given us all things that pertain unto life and godliness, through the knowledge of him that hath called us to glory and virtue: whereby are given unto us exceeding great and precious promises; that by these you might be partakers of the divine nature, having escaped the corruption that is in the world through lust." Divine nature and lust are evidently here spoken of as two opposite principles in men. Those that are in the world, or that are the men of the world, have only the latter principle; but to be partakers of the divine nature is spoken [of] as peculiar to them that are distinguished and separated from the world by the free and sovereign grace of God—giving of them all things that pertain to life and godliness, giving the knowledge of Christ and calling them to glory and virtue, and giving them the exceeding great and precious promises of the gospel—and that have escaped the corruption of the world of wicked men. 'Tis spoken of not only as peculiar to the saints, but as one of the highest privileges of the saints.

9. A natural man has no degree of that relish and sense of spiritual things, or things of the Spirit, of their divine truth and excellency which a godly person has; as is evident by I Cor. 2:14, "The natural man receiveth not the things of the Spirit of God: for they are foolishness unto him: neither can he know them, because they are spiritually discerned." Here a natural man is represented as perfectly destitute of any sense, perception or discerning of those things: for by the words, he neither does, nor can know them, or discern them—so far from that, that they are foolishness unto him. He is a perfect stranger, so that he knows not what the talk of such things means. They are words without a meaning to him; he knows nothing of the matter any more than a blind man of colors. Hence it will follow, that that sense of things of religion that a natural man has, is not only not to the same degree, but nothing of the same nature, with what a godly person has. And besides, if a natural person has that fruit of the Spirit which is of the same kind with what a spiritual person has, then

---

4. This entry was begun in No. 673, which contains points 1–7.

he experiences within himself the things of the Spirit of God: and how then can he be said to be such a stranger to them, and to have no perception or discerning of them? The reason why natural men have no knowledge of spiritual things, is because they have nothing of the Spirit of God dwelling in them. This is evident by the context, for there we are taught that 'tis by the Spirit that these things are taught (vv. 10–12). And godly persons in the text we are upon are called spiritual evidently on this account, because they have the Spirit; and unregenerate men are called natural because they have nothing but nature. Hereby the sixth argument is confirmed, for natural men are in no degree spiritual. They have only nature and no spirit. If they had anything of the Spirit, though not in so great a degree as the godly, yet they would be taught spiritual things, or the things of the Spirit, in proportion. The Spirit that searcheth all things would teach them in some measure. There would not be so great a difference that the one could perceive nothing of them, and that they should be foolishness to them, while to the other they appear divinely and unspeakably wise and excellent, as they are spoken of in the context in vv. 6–9. And as such the Apostle speaks here of discerning them.

The reason why natural men have no knowledge or perception of spiritual things is because they have none of that anointing spoken of, I John 2:27, "But the anointing which ye have received of him abideth in you, and ye need not that any man should teach you: but as the same anointing teacheth you of all things, and is truth, and is no lie, and even as it hath taught you, ye shall abide in him." This anointing is evidently spoken of here as a thing peculiar to true saints. They never had any of that oil poured upon them; and because ungodly men have none of it, therefore they have no discerning of spiritual things. If they had any degree of it, they would discern in some measure. Therefore, none of that sense that natural men [have] of things, is of the same nature with what the godly have. And that natural men are wholly destitute of this knowledge is further evident, because their conversion is represented in Scripture by opening the eyes of the blind. But this would be very improperly so represented if a man might have some light, though not so clear and full, time after time, for scores of years, before his conversion.

10. The grace of God's Spirit is not only a precious oil with which Christ anoints the believer by giving it to him, but the believer anoints Christ with it by exercising of it towards him, which seems to be represented by the precious ointment that Mary poured on Christ's head. Herein it seems to me that Mary is a type of Christ's church, and of every believing soul (see

note on Mark 14:3);[5] and if so, doubtless the thing that she typifies the church in, is in something peculiar to the church. That would not be a type ordered on purpose to represent the church, that shall represent only something that is common to the church and others. Therefore, unbelievers pour none of that sweet and precious ointment on Christ.

11. That unbelievers have no degree of that grace that the saints [have] is evident because they have no communion with Christ. If unbelievers partook of any of that Spirit—those holy inclinations, affections and actings that[6] the godly have from the Spirit of Christ—then they would have communion with Christ. The communion of saints with Christ does certainly partly consist in receiving of his fullness and partaking of his grace, which is spoken [of], John 1:16, "Of his fullness have all we received, and grace for grace." And in partaking of that Spirit which God gives not by measure unto him, partaking of Christ's holiness and grace, his nature, inclinations, tendencies, affections, love, desires, must be a part of communion with him. Yea, a believer's communion with God and Christ does mainly consist in partaking of the Holy Spirit, as is evident by II Cor. 13:14.

But that unbelievers have no communion or fellowship with Christ appears,

(1) Because they ben't united to Christ. They are not in Christ; and those that ben't in Christ, or are not united to him, can have no degree of communion with him: for union with Christ, or a being in Christ, is the foundation of all communion with him. The union of the members with the head is the foundation of their communicating or partaking with the head; and so the union of the branch with the vine is the foundation of all communion it has with the vine, of all partaking of any degree of its sap or life or influence. So the union of the wife to the husband is the foundation of her communion in his goods. But no natural man is united to Christ because all that are in Christ shall be saved. I Cor. 15:22, "As in Adam all die, so in Christ shall all be made alive," i.e. all that are in Christ, for this speaks only of the glorious resurrection and eternal life (see my note on the text).[7] Philip. 3:8–9, "Yea doubtless, and I count all things but

5. Concerning the woman with the alabaster box, JE comments in his "Blank Bible" note on Mark 14:3, "Pouring this precious ointment on Christ seems to be ordered as a type of the church's or believing soul's exercise of the grace of the Holy Spirit towards Christ, which does primarily and summarily consist in love."

6. MS: "of that."

7. In his "Blank Bible" note on I Cor. 15:22, JE asserts that the words of the text relate only to "all that are in Christ. The words impart no more, for the Apostle speaks of no more being made alive in Christ than are in him. The Apostle in these words has respect only to the resurrection of the saints."

loss for the excellency of the knowledge of Christ Jesus my Lord: for whom I have suffered the loss of all things, and do count them but dung, that I may win Christ, and be found *IN HIM*, not having on my own righteousness, which is of the law, but that which is through the faith of Christ, the righteousness which is of God by faith." II Cor. 5:17, "Now if any man be *IN CHRIST*, he is a new creature: old things are past away; behold, all things are become new." I John 2:5, "Hereby know we that we are in him"; 3:24, "And he that keepeth his commandments *dwelleth in him, and he in him. And hereby we know that he abideth in us*, by the Spirit which he hath given us"; and 4:13, "Hereby know we that *we dwell in him, and he in us*,because he hath given us of his Spirit."

(2) The Scripture does more directly teach that 'tis only true saints that have communion with Christ, as particularly this is most evidently spoken of as what belongs to the saints and to them only in I John 1:3, 6–7, "That which we have seen and heard declare we unto you, that ye also may have fellowship with us: and truly our fellowship is with the Father, and with his Son Jesus Christ. . . . If we say that we have fellowship with him, and walk in darkness, we lie, and do not the truth: but if we walk in the light, as he is in the light, we have fellowship on with another, and the blood of Jesus Christ his Son cleanseth us from all sin"; and I Cor. 1:8–9, "Who shall also confirm you unto the end, that ye may be blameless in the day of our Lord Jesus Christ. God is faithful, by whom ye were called unto the fellowship of his Son Jesus Christ our Lord." By this it appears that they that have fellowship with Christ are those that can't fall away, whom God's faithfulness is bound to confirm to the end that they may be blameless in the day of Jesus Christ.

684. JESUS, WHY CALLED MESSIAH, OR CHRIST, OR ANOINTED. See note on Dan. 9:25.[8]

685. RIGHTEOUSNESS OF CHRIST. Deeds of love and respect towards God are more valuable in God's sight, in proportion as the person is in his eyes of greater dignity: for in the deeds that he offers to God, so far as they are deeds of love or respect, he offers himself to God; so far as he loves, he offers his heart to God. But this is a more excellent offering in

---

8. In his "Blank Bible" note on Dan. 9:25, JE maintains that Jesus is called the Messiah, or Christ, or the Anointed: (1) "in his divine nature only, without any consideration of his human nature or his office of Mediator"; (2) "in his human nature . . . as the Spirit is given not by measure to him"; (3) "in his office of Mediator, for God poured forth the Holy Spirit abundantly on him"; and (4) "as he is anointed by the church or by every believing soul."

proportion as the person whose self or whose heart is offered is more worthy.

686. SPIRIT'S WITNESS. See No 375. Sometimes the strong and lively exercises of love to God do give a kind of immediate and intuitive evidence of the soul's relation to God. Divine love is the bond by which the soul of the saint is united to God, and sometimes when this divine love is strong and lively, this bond of union can be seen as it were intuitively. The saint sees that he is united to God, and so is God's, for he sees and feels the union between God and his soul. He sees clearly and certainly that divine love that does evidently, beyond all contradiction or exception, unite his soul to God. He knows there is an union, for he sees it, or feels it, so strong that he can't question it, or doubt of it. I John 4:18, "There is no fear in love; but perfect love casts out fear." How can the saint doubt but that he stands in a childlike relation to God, when he plainly sees a childlike union between God and his soul? He that has such a strong exercise of a divine and holy love to God, he knows at the same time that 'tis not from himself. This that he feels so strong in his own heart brings its own evidence with it that it is from God. It is a childlike union of his heart to God, that God himself gives; and therefore, in seeing and feeling this union, he sees and feels that God has taken his soul, and has united it as a child to him, so that he does as it were see that he is a child of God. This seems to be that in Scripture which is called the Spirit of God bearing witness within our spirits that we are the children of God (Rom. 8:16); or "the Spirit of adoption, whereby we cry, Abba, Father," as in the preceding verse. The Spirit of God gives those motions and exercises of a childlike love to God that naturally inclines the heart to look on God as his Father, and behave towards him as such (see note on Rom. 8:16).[9] God, in giving this, does manifest himself to be our Father, for the soul does as it were feel itself to be God's child. It feels beyond doubting as it were a childlike union to God in the heart.

687. FREE GRACE. JUSTIFICATION. Add this to No. 682. And besides, Christ in this place seems not to have respect to God's treatment of persons in his invisible transacting with them as the searcher of hearts, by the rules he has established for the justification or condemnation of the souls of men in his sight, or to their being invisibly admitted to or debarred

---

9. The "Blank Bible" note on Rom. 8:16 states, "The Spirit of God and our spirit are not spoken of here as two witnesses separate and independent; but 'tis by one that we receive the witness of the other."

from an interest in Christ; but rather to Christ's treatment of them acting as the head of the visible church, after they in the visible covenant have been admitted or received by him as his disciples, when that question comes to be decided, whether they shall be owned and continued as his disciples, or cast out and removed from the station they have been admitted to as such: for Christ evidently has respect to his treatment of those that are visibly his disciples, and that have appeared and professed to be his followers. Christ in thus transacting with visible disciples, as the head of the visible church, in deciding that forementioned question whether they shall be owned before his Father and continued in their station, or cast out, has indeed respect to a moral fitness in them. When they are cast out, it will be as a punishment, as unworthy of their station. When they shall be owned and continued, it shall be as having an evangelical worthiness of it. See No. 689, of the visible church, especially § 10.

688. FREE GRACE. JUSTIFICATION. See Nos. 627, 671. As to that passage in Rev. 3:4, "They shall walk with me in white: for they are worthy," even according to our scheme of grace and justification, it may be said without the least strain upon the words, that God accepts of persons into his favor and to a right to eternal life, as being in his sight worthy of it, not only that he bestows heaven and all those parts of salvation that are consequent on justification, but he bestows the whole of salvation upon them, and even that admission to a right to salvation that is granted in justification, as looking upon them worthy of it; 'tis on the account of that value that God sets upon them, or their preciousness in God's sight. All that are in Christ are precious in God's eyes. They are precious jewels in his account; and their preciousness with him is such as to render them worthy to be thus accepted and admitted to such privileges as they are in justification, though they become so valuable and precious only as being in Christ, and by being members of him. Though they are not worthy in themselves, yet they are worthy in Christ; but yet the value or preciousness is truly and properly the preciousness of them. The preciousness is of the jewel; and 'tis on the account of this their preciousness that they are worthy—are thought worthy—to be admitted to such privileges, though the way they come by that preciousness is by being in such circumstances, viz. by being in Christ, or by standing in such a relation to him. Jewels of great value and preciousness are worthy to be set in the king's crown, and may properly be said to be set there as worthy of it, when it is on the account of the degree of its preciousness that it was thought fit to be set there, by what means soever they come to be of such high value. Thus God's jewels are

set in his crown, as being looked upon by him to be worthy. Zech. 9:16, "They shall be as the stones of a crown." So far as the saints may [be] said to be properly valuable in God's sight, so far may they properly be said to be worthy, though neither their worthiness nor valuableness is in themselves separately. A child of a prince is worthy to be treated with great honor; and therefore, if a mean person should be adopted to be a child of a prince, it would [be] proper to say that it was worthy of such and such honor and respect, or that it ought to have such respect, because it is worthy; and there would be no force upon words to say so, though it be only on the account of its relation to the prince that it is so. That preciousness or high valuableness of believers is a moral valuableness, and yet the righteousness of Christ is the foundation of it. The thing that respect is had to, is not the excellency that is in them separately by themselves, but to the value that God sets upon them on other considerations: as is the natural import of these expressions, Luke 20:35, "But they which shall be *accounted worthy* to obtain that world, and the resurrection of the dead"; and Luke 21:36, "Watch ye therefore, and pray always, that ye may be *accounted worthy* to escape all these things that shall come to pass, and to stand before the Son of man"; and II Thess. 1:5, "Which is a manifest token of the righteous judgment of God, that ye may be *accounted worthy* of the kingdom of God, for which ye also suffer."

689. VISIBLE CHURCH.

§ 1. When persons regularly enter into the visible church, we are not to look on their admission as what is done merely by man. They ben't merely admitted by man, nor are they admitted merely to be treated as some of God's people by man; they are admitted or accepted of God: for the officers of the church, when they admit, are to act in the name of God in admitting. To them are committed the keys of the kingdom of heaven; and when they open the door it is to admit not only into their society, but into God's kingdom, into the kingdom of heaven. So that when they act regularly, God concurs with them in admitting, and what they do is done in heaven.

§ 2. But God acting as the head of the visible church, as he transacts by man, so he is wont to conform to man, and to transact with us in our own way: as we by reason of our want of omniscience, and ability to search the heart, are forced to do one with another. Thus the officers, when they admit any person into the church, they admit them on presumption that they are sincere, upright, and that they will be faithful in that station and approve themselves as God's faithful people. So God conforms to man herein, and don't act as the searcher of hearts, but admits and receives persons to be his people, as it were, on presumption of their sincerity and faithfulness. God's admission of them to be his people and his treating them as such, and as being himself their God, is not absolute and unalterable, as his invisible justification of them is; nor yet is it merely conditional, i.e. his admitting them is not put off as suspended on conditions yet to be fulfilled, but 'tis presumptive. God admits them as his people and for the present treats them as his people, as it were, trusting to it that they are sincere and will be faithful, though as to future blessings it is in fact conditional. It is as when a man marries a woman, he enters into covenant with her and receives her to be his wife, to live with him as such. The promises that he makes, and his transacting with her to receive and treat her as a wife, are not properly conditional; that is, his thus doing is not suspended on her future faithfulness, because he proceeds forthwith to to take her to communion with him in his goods, and to treat her as his wife. Nor yet is it absolute and unalterable, without any manner of conditions, so as to be engaged that, let her carry herself how she will, whether she be true to his bed or not, yet she shall remain in the enjoyment of the privileges of his wife. But it is presumptive. He trusts to it, and presumes so far upon it that she will be faithful to him, that he don't wait to see whether she will or no, but forthwith proceeds to treat her as his wife; though as to what is future, the covenant is in fact conditional, or, his continuing to treat her as a wife is suspended on conditions yet to be fulfilled.

Christ deals with men as he directed his disciples to deal with them. When he sent them forth he directed them to inquire who in it was worthy, i.e. who were reputed virtuous or of good conversation, and that they should go and desire entertainment [of] them. And if they received them into their houses, when they first entered, they should say, Peace be to this house. And if the Son of Peace was there—if they proved as they hoped—their peace should rest upon it; but if otherwise, their peace should return to them again [Matt. 10:11–13]. So those persons that are of good behavior, and in their profession receive and entertain him, he gives his peace to them, as it were hoping that they are and will prove as they appear. But if in the trial it proves otherwise, his peace returns to him again.

§ 3. When persons regularly enter into God's visible church, God proceeds immediately to treat them as his people. He gives them means of grace, not merely as such and such external things, but as means of grace as they are by his blessing made ordinary means of grace. In themselves, they are no means of grace at all, any more than any other things; but there is a blessing of God with them. There is a connection established by that blessing between these external things and his grace, though not absolute and certain, yet in some manner and degree; and as such these means are given to them that regularly enter the visible church. The Word of God and the gospel of Christ is a ministration of the Spirit, and as such God gives it to them; and the ordinances are conveyancers of the Spirit, and as such God gives them to them. And so God appears ready to succeed their worship when they worship him in those duties that he has appointed. He is more ready to hear and answer their prayers; and he not only is more ready to bless means of good to them, but to defend them against means of evil. So God is wont the more to defend them from Satan, and his power and influence. He in primitive times of the church gave them miraculous gifts of the Spirit and still gives them the common gifts of the Spirit. Thus God admits them into his house, or dwelling place, to an enjoyment of the good things and the protection of his house. And as they are now admitted, so God becomes engaged that they shall always abide there and never be turned out, on condition that they prove faithful and overcome in times of trial. Rev. 3:12, "He that overcometh I will make a pillar in the temple of my God, and he shall go no more out." And eternal life is promised on condition of perseverance, in case there be opportunity for that trial.

§ 4. That God as the head of the visible church thus conforms to man, and acts as presuming on man's faithfulness, is evident, Is. 63:7–10, "I will mention the loving-kindnesses of the Lord, and the praises of the Lord, according to all that the Lord hath bestowed on us, and the great goodness towards the house of Israel, which he hath bestowed on them according to his mercies, and according to the multitude of his loving-kindnesses. For he said, Surely they are my people, children that will not lie: so he became their Savior. In all their affliction he was afflicted, and the angel of his presence saved them: in his love and in his pity he redeemed them; and he bare them, and carried them all the days of old. But they rebelled, and vexed his Holy Spirit: therefore he was turned to be their enemy, and he fought against them." And God is represented in the 16th chapter of Ezekiel, and elsewhere, as receiving his visible people and entering into covenant with them in the same manner as an husband does with a wife, bestowing his goods upon her and admitting her to great privileges, though she afterwards played the harlot and so provoked him to cast her off. Hence also, God is often represented as proving his people to see whether they will be faithful to their promises, or no. And this is further evident in that God often represents himself as disappointed by the unfaithfulness of his people. Ps. 78:54–57, "And he brought them to the border of his sanctuary, even to this mountain, which his right hand had purchased. And cast out the heathen . . . Yet they tempted and provoked the most high God, and kept not his testimonies: but turned back, and dealt unfaithfully, like their fathers: they were turned aside like a deceitful bow." God particularly represents himself as disappointed by the unfaithfulness of his visible people, as a man is disappointed by the unfaithfulness of a wife. Hence also, jealousy is so often ascribed to God as the head of the visible church.

And hence, Christ is represented as spewing visible Christians out of his mouth when they prove naught. As a man doth food that he has received into his mouth on presumption that it was good and wholesome, but when it proves otherwise, and he is disappointed and finds it offensive or unwholesome, he spits it out or vomits it up; so Christ is represented as enrolling of visible Christians amongst his people on presumption of their being such indeed, and afterwards, if they prove unfaithful, blotting their names out of the book of life; and as giving visible Christians a part in the book of life and holy city and promises of God, but as taking away from them these privileges if they afterwards prove unfaithful. So Rev. 3:5, "He that overcometh, the same shall be clothed in white raiment; and I will not blot out his name out of the book of life, but I will confess his name before my Father, and before his angels"; and Rev. 22:19, "And if any man shall take away from the words of the book of this prophecy, God shall take away his part out of the book of life, and out of the holy city, and from the things which are written in this book."

§ 5. Christ as head of the visible church deals with professing Christians as he did when on earth with his disciples, who were then his visible church. The visible church has still a head, which is not the Pope, but 'tis the same that it was when Christ was on earth: for though he be not present, yet he may act as head of the visible church, as a king that is absent his administration may be upheld by his laws and commissioners. So Christ administers the affairs of his visible kingdom by his Word, and by his ministers, and his Spirit (see No. 1011).[1] Christ's way of dealing with his visible church when he was on earth is a true example or specimen of his method of dealing with the visible church to the end of the world. He then in receiving and admitting persons into the number of his disciples did not deal as the searcher of hearts, though he then knew the hearts of all men, and knew what was in man, and was indeed the searcher of hearts

1. The previous two sentences are an interlineation that JE probably added at the same time he wrote No. 1011.

then, as well as now. But he received Judas to be a disciple and treated him as such, though he knew he was not a disciple, but that he was a devil. He received him not only to be one of his church, but to be an officer in his church. He made him a minister of the gospel. For Judas was the very man, or the same sort of man, spoken of in Ps. 50:16–18, "But unto the wicked God saith, What hast thou to do to declare my statutes, or that thou shouldst take my covenant into thy mouth? Seeing thou hatest instruction, and castest my words behind thee. When thou sawest a thief, then thou consentedst with him, and hast been partaker with adulterers," for he was a thief, as we are told (John 12:6), and Christ knew it and yet made him a minister. Yea, he made him an officer of the highest kind, viz. an apostle. He sent him forth with the rest of the apostles to preach and to do miracles, and endued him with miraculous gifts of his Spirit, because Christ did not see cause to act in this matter as the searcher of hearts, but governed himself by what was visible. And Judas was not rejected and deprived of his office and privilege, though he was a wicked treacherous man, till he proved so by his behavior; and then he fell from his place and office in the church by his transgression, and then it was said concerning him, "Let his habitation be desolate, and let another take his office" (Acts 1:20). And as Christ behaved himself in the visible church then, so he doth now. He is the searcher of hearts now, and so he was then; but as the head of the visible church, he did not act as such then, no more doth he now.

Thus Christ promised unto Judas the kingdom of heaven and its glorious privileges (Luke 22:28–30, Matt. 19:28–29).

§ 6. When persons therefore do regularly enter into the Christian church, God receives [them] into his family as his children, and Christ receives them as his spouse, and they are as it were then redeemed. Christ gives them the price of his redemption, and they are as it were then justified and adopted on presumption of their being sincere, i.e. Christ for the present accepts them into his house, and treats them as such, as though they were now free from guilt, and had a title to life. Those blessings that were mentioned that he gives them at present are given on that supposition that they are now justified, for they don't belong to those that ben't justified. They are not fit to have them. And promises of future blessings are as it were made to them on a supposition that they are sincere, as the husband's promises are to the wife when he marries her. The present blessings that they have as Christ's people, and inhabitants of his house, are the fruits of Christ's purchase. They would not have had them had it not have been for Christ's redemption. There would have been no room for such a transacting with fallen men. And if they fail of obtaining those promises that Christ has presumptively made over to them, they must not lay it to Christ's unfaithfulness, but to their own, to their own guile and deceit in covenanting, and their own treachery towards him, by proving otherwise than they pretended to him, and as he graciously trusting in them received them. In this manner it is that they that we are speaking of are cleansed from sin; and thus they have the benefits of the body and blood of Christ given them in the Lord's Supper. They have the Holy Ghost given them in baptism, as they have the means of grace given them as such, that are so only through the blessing of the Holy Ghost attending them. They have the gospel given them as a ministration of the Spirit, and have the common gifts of the Spirit, as before mentioned. And they are in their baptism and admission into the church presumptively justified and cleared from guilt through the blood of Christ, separated from the impure world and consecrated to God as his people.

Hence we may be helped to understand the meaning of those texts, II Pet. 2:1, "Denying the Lord that bought them"; and Heb. 10:29, "And hath counted the blood of the covenant, wherewith he was sanctified, an unholy thing."

§ 7. That covenant transaction that there is between God as the husband of the visible church and men, is not the same with that which there is between God as the searcher of hearts and the soul of a believer at its closing with Christ. The covenant in the foundation and drift of it is the same, but the transaction of covenanting is different. The covenant of grace is the foundation of the transaction, and the same blessedness and glory that is promised in the covenant of grace is the ultimate drift of it; but the covenanting is different from God's covenanting with those that before his allseeing[2] eyes perform that condition of the covenant of grace. And that in the following respects:

(1) Eternal benefits are not absolutely bestowed and confirmed on the fundamental condition being already certainly fulfilled, but are[3] only presumptively promised on a supposition or presumption of the fulfillment of that condition; and the actual possessing of eternal benefits is suspended on a condition yet to be fulfilled.

§ 8. (2) The condition on which future benefits are suspended is in effect the same, but in some respects different. The condition of the covenant of grace is the performance or existence of sincere faith and repentance; in the other, it is the proof or evidence of such a faith and

2. MS: "allseeing seeing."
3. MS: "is."

repentance. The condition in this latter case is not so properly their being sincere, as their proving sincere in the trial. This trial is twofold: either in this life, or in the life to come. The trial in this life is perseverance in good works; in the life to come it is standing the test of the judgment. If it should be so that there should be no opportunity for the former trial, then the latter is the condition: for God as the head of the visible church acts as though the day of judgment discovered the reality of things to him, as well as to others. The day is to try and declare every man's work before God and man; and one reason why Christ don't for the present treat men as the searcher of hearts, is because he would not anticipate the work of the future judgment. Judging men is reserved for a day appointed to that end. Though Christ receives 'em now and treats them as children, yet if they appear to be false, guileful and deceitful when the light of that day comes to shine through all their veils, [then will Christ cast them off]. If they appear as they pretend when the fire of that day comes to burn up all coverings and disguises, then will Christ own them and never will cast them off. (See No. 722.)[4] But perseverance in good works is the main condition of this covenant, in case there be opportunity for this trial (I John 2:24–26, Rom. 11:22). If there be, they will be judged by this in the day of judgment, for everyone shall be judged according to his works.

§ 9. (3) The thing promised also, though in effect the same, yet is in some respects different. The thing promised in the invisible justification of a sinner, is the bestowment of eternal benefits. The thing promised in this transaction is the everlasting continuance of a benefit already bestowed, viz. a continuance in the house of God. What is given in the covenant transaction that there is at the admission of a person into the visible church, is either what is present or what is future: what is present is on presumption of a condition already performed, viz. sincere profession, and this is an actual[5] admission of them into God's house; the future good promised, which is on condition yet to be performed, viz. perseverance, and this is continuance in the house of God into which they have been admitted. I John 2:24–26; and John 15:1–11; Rom. 11–22; Rev. 3:12, "Him that overcometh will I make a pillar in the temple of my God, and he shall go no more out"; and v. 5, "He that overcometh, I will not blot out his name out of the book of life."

---

4. With a cue mark JE indicates that the entirety of No. 722 should be inserted at this point in the MS. See below, p. 351.

5. MS: "actually."

§ 10. (4) Another thing wherein this covenant transaction differs from that in the invisible justification of a sinner, is that the benefit promised is connected with the condition of perseverance in good works, with some respect to an evangelical worthiness in the condition. Rev. 3:4, "Thou hast a few names even in Sardis which have not defiled their garments; and they shall walk with me in white, for they are worthy." II Thess. 1:4–5, "So that we ourselves glory in you in the churches of God, for your patience and faith in all your tribulations that ye endure: which is a manifest token of the righteous judgment of God, that ye may be counted worthy of the kingdom of God, for which ye also suffer." And they that have professed faith and obedience, and so have been admitted, and afterwards prove treacherous and false to Christ, they shall be rejected and cast out of the house of God, and from being the spouse of Christ as unworthy of him. Matt. 10:37, "He that loveth father or mother more than me is not worthy of me: and he that loveth son or daughter more than me is not worthy of me." I have elsewhere shown[6] how that eternal life is in the gospel promised to the good works of the saints as a reward of their good works, and how that God[7] in bestowing the reward has respect to the evangelical worthiness of the saints' obedience.

§ 11. The covenant that God and the visible Christian enter into at his admission can't in strictness be called a distinct covenant from that which [is] established between God and a soul in his invisible justification, but yet may be distinguished from it, as well as the former dispensation of the covenant of grace may be called another covenant from that under the new testament, as it is in Scripture. This covenant therefore may for distinction's sake be called the visible covenant, for want of a better name to call it by.

§ 12. There is just so much difference between this covenanting and the invisible covenanting with a believing soul, and no more, as will naturally and necessarily arise from God's acting in the one case as the searcher of hearts, and in the other not, supposing God in both cases to proceed on the same foundation and with the same drift.

§ 13. One thing among others that may show the wisdom of God in such a method of dealing with men, is the tendency it has to men's conviction. It tends to convince men's consciences how it is of themselves if they perish: in that Christ shows himself ready to receive them, and does actually

---

6. In No. 671 JE explains how it is that "heaven itself with all its glory and happiness" is given to the saints "as a reward of their inherent holiness and good works." He begins this discussion in No. 627 and continues it in No. 688.

7. MS: "the Promise had."

receive them on their profession of faith and obedience, trusting to their sincerity and promising never to cast them off if they persevere and don't prove treacherous and unfaithful. If they perish, it will be by as it were casting themselves out of God's house—into which they have been admitted—by their own voluntary unfaithfulness to their promises on which they have been admitted and received of Christ, because Christ promises never to remove them from the station he has admitted them to, unless they depart from him and prove false to him. God in his dealings with men with relation to their eternal state, has a great respect to that, viz. that his justice be made manifest, and especially to the conviction of men's own consciences. For this end a day of judgment is appointed, wherein God, though he needs it not, being omniscient, will yet judge men in a formal manner to make his justice manifest to the world and to men's own consciences. Therefore that day is called the day of the "revelation of the righteous judgment of God" (Rom. 2:5). And hence, God in judging men will make so much of works, though works are not that by which they are primarily entitled to justification, but being visible evidences of that which is so to the world and to their own consciences. Hence, everyone shall be judged according to his works.

§ 14. It may be objected against what has been said that [a] person, when he is admitted into the church, though he may be regularly admitted so far as the church or its officers are concerned, yet may know in his own conscience his own insincerity, and that he lives in a way of wickedness at that time. Must we suppose that God as the head of the visible church acts as being ignorant of this, and admits and receives him as presuming on his sincerity, though it may be he lives at the same time secretly in adultery or some other like wickedness?

Ans. I have spoken hitherto only of those that regularly enter the visible church in order to this. Both what the church does in admitting, and also what he does in coming, should be regular; neither the church must know, nor his own conscience, of his insincerity and treachery at that time. If he knows that he lives in wickedness, he don't do regularly in coming, nor can he think that God accepts him, nor can he expect any blessing with ordinances, but a curse. These don't need those means of conviction of their consciences spoken of, § [13].

§ 15. If persons after they have been admitted fall into sin, that seems to hold forth unfaithfulness, and to have a show of want of sincerity; yet if there be seeming repentance and disposition to amendment, God will accept them still, as it were on hope of their amendment, after the same manner as he directs the church to do. He still receives them on presumption on their sincerity. When the church forgives them and receives them, God receives them (Matt. 16:19).

§ 16. *Corol.* 1. Hence we may see that which seems to be a ground of the institution of infant baptism. For, as when persons enter into the church as acting for themselves, God receives them on presumption of their own faithfulness; so when they are received as children, they are received on presumption of their parents' faithfulness that they do sincerely and with their whole hearts give up their children to him, and will be faithful to bring them up for him.

§ 17. *Corol.* 2. Hence we learn that when persons are regularly excommunicated they ben't merely cast out by men out of their society. For, as when they are regularly admitted, God admits them into his house and the privileges thereof, so when they are regularly excommunicated, they are cast out of God and are treated by him as those that have proved treacherous and unfaithful to him. He is[8] deprived of the protection of God's [house] and so exposed to his enemies, and is deprived of all blessings to which he was admitted; and not only so, but becomes a subject of special tokens of wrath, as God's wrath is greater towards those that have been admitted into his house and have proved false and treacherous than towards those that never were admitted.

§ 18. *Corol.* 3. Hence we have a solution of the main objections against the doctrine of perseverance, as particularly the apostles' frequently speaking of the obtaining future glory and blessedness as what is suspended on the perseverance of Christians. For the apostles evidently speak to them as visible Christians. Their epistles are directed to all the visible Christians in such a city or region or through the world, excepting those that are directed to particular persons; and perseverance, as has been observed, was the main condition of that covenant they were under as such. The apostles treat them in their epistles in the same manner as God treats them in the visible covenant, as 'tis most proper and fit that the ministers of the visible church to treat visible Christians in the same manner as God treats them as head of the visible church. If God, though the searcher of hearts, conforming himself to man and transacting by man, will thus treat Christians, as it were divesting himself of the character of searcher of hearts; much more is it proper that man himself who is not a searcher of hearts, when a minister under that head of the visible church, should thus treat them.

And again, this may help us to understand what is said in Ezekiel about

8. MS: "They are."

the righteous man's falling away from his righteousness [Ezek. 3:20]. By a righteous [man] must there doubtless be understood one that is righteous with a visible righteousness, i.e. as to what is visible either to men or his own conscience, and that is accepted as righteous in the visible covenant. Such are in Scripture often called saints or holy persons, or, which is the same thing in Scripture language, righteous persons. And such are liable to fall away from their righteousness and often do, and as such the condition of their living and not perishing is perseverance.

690. EXTREMITY OF HELL TORMENTS. The torments of the damned, though so very great, will not rise to a greater extremity than their wickedness. The dreadfulness of the wickedness of a fallen creature unrestrained, appears by the greatness of the spite of the devils against both God and man. Their malice against both appears by their extreme and incessant endeavors through so many ages, through so many disappointments and bafflings, to dishonor one and undo the other. The degree of their cruelty towards man appears by his[9] so earnestly desiring and seeking the utmost possible degree of eternal misery and torment for man. No degree of misery, though it be eternal, will satisfy him so, but that he would be glad to have it greater. How great is this cruelty, and how great must all other wickedness be that is in proportion to it!

691. SABBATH. LORD'S DAY.
§ 1. We are taught in Deut. 5:15 that the Jewish sabbath was instituted in commemoration of the deliverance out of Egyptian bondage, which was a great type of the work of redemption by Jesus Christ, the chief type of it in all the Old Testament. Bedford in his *Scripture Chronology*[1] supposes it to be appointed on the day when the children of Israel came up out of the Red Sea, and rested from their march through the same; and there are several things to be considered, which being put together, do make it very evident that it was so. The day when the children of Israel first began their journey from Egypt appears[2] by Num. 33:3, "And they departed from Rameses in the first month, on the 15th day of the first month; on the morrow after the Passover the children of Israel went out with an high hand in sight of all the Egyptians," and Ex. 12:17–18; but Mr. Bedford proves by astronomical calculations that that day fell that

9. I.e. the devil's.
1. Bedford, *Scripture Chronology*, pp. 298–99, 378–79. Much of the entry is a paraphrase of these pages of Bedford's text.
2. MS: "as appears."

year on the first day of the week. And that the day of the children of Israel's departure was Sunday may be argued from the time of the day of Pentecost, which was kept in commemoration of God's descending on Mt. Sinai and giving the Law from thence. And this day of Pentecost was by divine appointment always to be kept on the first day of the week, as is evident by Lev. 23:15–16; and therefore, doubtless the thing that it was to commemorate came to pass on that day of the week. And it was called the feast of weeks because it was appointed to be kept always at the end of seven weeks, or on the 50th day from a certain time whence God appointed them to begin to reckon. And the most rational account why God should appoint the day to be found or determined in this way, is that it was so long a time after the children of Israel came out of Egypt before God gave the Law on Mt. Sinai; and if so, then the day that the children of Israel came out of Egypt was on a Sunday. And then it appears very probable that the giving the Law at Mt. Sinai was 50 days after they departed out of Egypt, from the account we have of the time when the children of Israel came into the wilderness of Sinai; which we are told in Ex. 19:1 was in the third month when the children of Israel were gone forth out of the land—the same day, that is, on the very day when the third month began. But they came out of Egypt on the 15th day of the first month; so that there were 16 days of that month after they came out, including the day when they came out, the months consisting of 30 days; which being added to the 30 days of the second month makes 46 days. But the first day of the third month seems to have been spent in their journey from Rephidim to the desert of Sinai (Ex. 19:1–2), and that makes 47 days. And on the next day, Moses went up to God and brought the message from God, that they should sanctify themselves that day and the next, which makes 49; and that the third day, which was the 50th, He would come down on the mountain, which was done accordingly. And hence, God appointed the children of Israel should count 50 days from the day after the Sabbath that next followed the Passover, or the first Sunday after the Passover, and that the 50th day from thence should be the feast of Pentecost: because that on the first Sunday after the first-born of Egypt were slain, and the Lord past over their first-born, the children of Israel came out of Egypt, and on the 50th day from thence the Law was given at Mt. Sinai. God had probably reference to this first feast of Pentecost when he said, as in Ex. 5:1, "Let my people go, that they may hold a feast unto me in the wilderness"; and so, 10:9. But the children were so long, viz. 50 days traveling, before they held this feast: and if so, the day of their departure was a Sunday.

And it could not be in a much shorter or a much longer time after that, that they past through the Red Sea, than seven days after. For doubtless, on the first day of their march they came to Succoth—the going from Rameses to Succoth seems to be spoken of as what was done on that day, Ex. 12:37, 41–42, 51 and 13:1–4; what is said there seems to be spoken to Moses in Succoth—where they built booths for their conveniency a little while, till the company that was driven out of Egypt in haste could be got together (see Ex. 12:37, together with Num. 33:3–5). The place in all probability was called Succoth from their building booths there to lodge under (see Gen. 33:17) till they could get together, for they were under a necessity of stopping somewhere for that end. And 'tis not likely that less than a day would suffice to this end, for so vast a multitude of both sexes and all ages, with flocks and herds, to get together, who were driven out in haste, without any times to get into a company or body before they came away. And they would hardly build booths to stop less than a day. And then there was need of a little time to communicate to that vast congregation those instructions we have an account of in Ex. 13, and also to give directions for their march, how they should follow the pillar of cloud and fire, etc. And probably it was not much longer than a day that they would stay here so near the Egyptians, that had been so urgent with them to be gone, and were in no good temper towards them, having so lately suffered so bitterly by reason of them. So that here are two days spent, the first and second days of the week. After they had formed themselves into something of a body in Succoth, then the pillar of cloud and fire appeared to be thenceforward their guide; and on the next day, the third day of the week, they went to Etham (Ex. 13:18, 20–22 and Num. 33:6). On the next day, the fourth day of the week, they came to Pihahiroth (Ex. 14:2 and Num. 33:7). And Pharaoh did not entertain a resolution of pursuing them till he had heard that they turned towards Pihahiroth: for upon that, it was told him[3] that they fled, or turned out of their course, towards the wilderness where they had asked to go, as Ex. 14:5–6; and there must at least be that day and another allowed for Pharaoh to hear of it, and to get such great forces ready, as we have an account of, Ex. 14:6–7, and not much more: for doubtless their motions were well observed and Pharaoh, when he heard where they went, was in great haste to pursue them, which carries us through the fifth day of the week. On the next day, which was the seventh day of the week, Pharaoh overtakes them; and that very night the children of Israel passed through the Red Sea, for Moses tells the peo-

3. MS: "them."

ple when the Egyptians came that the Egyptians, whom they had seen that day, they should see no more forever. And it is also evident by the story that follows. On the seventh day in the morning watch, God looks unto the host of the Egyptians through the pillar of cloud and fire, and troubled the host and took off their chariot wheels; and that morning the children of Israel came up out of the sea, and the Egyptians were drowned.

§ 2. Mr. Bedford quotes a passage to the present purpose out of Abp. Ussher. The words he quotes are these, "Factum verò hoc esse mensis primi die vicessimo primo, postremo videlicet azymorum, quo convocatio sancta ex Dei instituto erat habenda, constans Hebraeorum, eaque veritati maximè consentanea, est sententia."[4] Here see Poole's *Synopsis Criticorum* on Ex. 12:16.[5]

§ 3. Another argument that the day when the children of Israel came up out of the Red Sea was on the seventh day after they departed from Rameses, is that the feast of unleavened bread, which was to begin on the very day of their departure, lasted seven days and no longer. For the people being about to depart out of Egypt, they went about to prepare bread for their journey, but were hurried away by the Egyptians, so that they were forced to take their dough before it was leavened, as Ex. 12: 34. And as the feast of unleavened bread was appointed in remembrance of this, so 'tis reasonable to suppose that the feast lasted for so long a time as the necessity of their circumstances at that time obliged them to live upon bread that was unleavened, for want of rest and leisure to do, which in all probability was till the hurry and danger of their flight was over; which was not before they came up out of the Red Sea, when they were first clear of Egypt, being quite out of the country, and were wholly delivered from the Egyptians. They doubtless lived on their unleavened dough that they brought with them till then: for if we consider their circumstances before,

4. Bedford's reference is to James Ussher, *Annales Veteris et Novi Testamenti, A Prima Mundi Origine Deducti*... (London, 1650), 12–13. The quotation appears in Table 28 of Bedford's *Scripture Chronology* (p. 302), which is entitled "Occurrences before and at the Departure out of Egypt." The passage, as translated in an early edition, reads: "Now that this fell out, upon the 21 [st] day of the first month, to wit, the last day of the feast of *sweat bread* (whereon a solemne assembly by Gods appointment was to be held) is the general opinion of the Iewes, and most agreeable to truth" (*The Annals of the World*, trans. E. Tyler [London, 1658], 15).

5. "*Et dies septima*] *Prima* quidem, quod tunc interfecit primogenita Aegyptiorum; & *septima*, quia tum submersit Aegyptios. Inter ista facinora 7 dies intercessisse Hebraei uno ore tradunt. Et convenit hoc cum itinerum ratione. Nam *Succothas* venerunt 15. die, *Ethan* 17. ad fauces *Chirotharum* 18. (ubi jussu Dei substiterunt expectantes adventum Pharaonis;) die 20. occurrit Pharao, & nocte sequente submersus est" (Matthew Poole, *Synopsis Criticorum Aliorumque Sacrae Scripturae Interpretum* [5 vols. London, 1669], vol. 1, pt. 1, col. 366). On Poole's *Synopsis*, see *Works*, *13*, 127, n. 3.

we can't think that they had any leisure to think of going about to make any other preparation till then. And 'tis evident that they had leisure enough then; so that we may hence argue that the seven days in remembrance of which the days of unleavened bread were kept, were not out before that time, and must be ended at that time, unless that day was the day of the sabbath: which if it was, they could not have opportunity to make leavened bread till the next day, because the sabbath is a day of rest. And if it was so, it will be both the sabbath and the last day of unleavened bread, as we suppose.

So that that morning when the children of Israel came up out of the Red Sea must be the morning either of the seventh or the eight day of their departure. It could not be short of the seventh, because then the time of their haste, when they had no opportunity to leaven their bread, would be out in less than seven days: for their haste was ended, and nothing then remained to hinder their leavening their bread, unless it was the day of the sabbath; which if [it] were short of the seventh, it could not be after the eighth, for then the time of their haste would last more than seven days. It must therefore be either the seventh or the eighth; and if it was on the eighth, then God so ordered it that the seventh or sabbath was spent in flying and the eighth in resting, which is not probable. It therefore remains that it must be on that very day, even the seventh after their coming out of Egypt, and on the sabbath day.

§ 4. We can't find out any way wherein all that was accomplished from the children of Israel's departure, before they came up out of the Red Sea, could be accomplished in less than six complete days. Not one day can by any means be spared; and if so, and never a sabbath had passed from their departure till that time, then the day of their coming up out of the Red Sea must be the very seventh day of their departure, and also the day of the sabbath. And 'tis not probable that any sabbath had past from the time of their departure till that time, because they had no convenient opportunity to keep a sabbath till then; there was no day wherein they could have rest till that day. Upon two accounts especially it is unlikely that any sabbath had past before:

(1) That God had brought the children of Israel out of Egypt for that end that they might serve him, that they might be at liberty to worship him, free from molestation from the Egyptians and separate from the pollutions of that land. 'Tis highly probable that when God had brought them, that he would, when the sabbath came, the day designed for his worship and service, give them opportunity to serve him at rest and freedom from molestation from the Egyptians, and without being distracted by

fear of them, and also without the borders of the polluted Egyptian land. But the first day that they had such an opportunity was the day when they came up out of the Red Sea. While they were in Egypt, they had not liberty to serve God; and what they were especially hindered in was keeping the sabbath, the day that God had appointed for rest and for his special service. They were hindered from this by their taskmasters, that would let 'em have no rest from their service to keep a sabbath or to serve God. And therefore, God's end in bringing them out (which we are often told was that they might serve God) was especially to give them opportunity to serve him on the sabbath, the day appointed for his service. And therefore without doubt, God, when he had brought them, would give them liberty to keep his sabbath in perfect freedom from any fear of the Egyptians or molestation from them, in spite of all that they could do to hinder. But this could not be till the day that they came up out of the Red Sea.

§ 5. (2) Another thing that strengthens the probability that God would give the children of Israel opportunity to keep the first sabbath that there was after they came out of Egypt in rest and quiet, is that it was also one of God's ends in bringing them out of Egypt to[6] give them rest. In Egypt they had no rest. They were kept continually at hard labor and made to serve with a cruel service, and their taskmasters would suffer 'em to have no time of rest; but God brought them out of this house of bondage for that end, that they might enjoy rest. Jer. 31:2, "Even Israel, when I went to cause him to rest." Seeing therefore this was God's very design, 'tis highly probable that God would not suffer it still to be so after he had brought them out, that they should still be deprived by the malice of the Egyptians of opportunity to rest on God's day of rest, even the sabbath. Their cruel masters, the Egyptians, would not so much as suffer 'em to rest on the sabbath. But if the Egyptians should through their obstinate opposition to God and malice against his people still prevail to deprive the people of rest on the very day appointed for the rest of the people of God, God would seem to be frustrated by the rebellious obstinate Egyptians that [he] was now set to overcome in this matter.

§ 6. And this argument is abundantly strengthened by this, viz. that the Jewish sabbath was appointed of God for this very end, viz. to commemorate God's giving of them rest from their Egyptian bondservice, as in Deut. 5:14–15. There, 'tis particularly insisted on that the manservant and maidservant should rest on that day from their service; that reason is given there for it, that they were servants in the land of Egypt, and God gave

6. MS: "was to."

them rest from that service, and therefore commanded them to keep the sabbath day. Seeing that God appointed the sabbath day to be kept throughout their generations, in joyful remembrance of God's giving them rest when he brought them out of the land [of] Egypt, would not God give them opportunity to rest in the time of their deliverance, on that day that was from age to age to be kept as a day of rest in remembrance of that deliverance? If God thought the sabbath a proper time for them to keep rest upon throughout their generations, in remembrance and representation of the rest he gave them when he brought them out of Egypt, was it not a proper time for them to enjoy rest on in the time of their deliverance out of Egypt? They were commanded to rest in all their generations on the sabbath day, in conformity to their rest when God brought them out of Egypt. Therefore, doubtless God gave them rest on the sabbath day when he brought them out, to be conformed to and remembered. Seeing God appointed the sabbath to be kept from age to age in joyful remembrance of their rest that God gave them then, would not God then on the sabbath day give them opportunity, in rest and quietness, to solace themselves and rejoice in their deliverance, in the time whereon it was bestowed. But 'tis evident that the day of the children of Israel's coming up out of Egypt was the remarkable time of the beginning of the rest and joy of their deliverance out of Egypt. They had no quiet day before, no day free from Egypt and the troubles of it, and the molestation of the Egyptians, till that day.

§ 7. These things considered conjunctly, viz. that God brought out the children of Israel from their Egyptian bondage for those ends, viz. to give them rest and that they might serve him; and there being a day appointed of God wholly for those very ends, viz. for rest and for his service; and [that] the hardness of their Egyptian masters towards [them] had chiefly appeared in denying liberty for these things so much as on that day: they make the probability strong that God, when he had brought them, did set them free of this difficulty, and did give them rest and opportunity to serve him on the sabbath free of any molestation from their Egyptian masters, however great endeavors those Egyptians used to hinder; and especially, seeing that God ordained that that nation should rest on that day as long as their state continued, in remembrance of this rest.

§ 8. And another argument that renders it probable that the day of the children of Israel's passing through the Red Sea was the seventh day of the feast of unleavened bread, or the seventh day of the children of Israel's departure out of Egypt, is that the first and the seventh days were by God's appointment remarkably distinguished from the other days, as the greatest days of the feast of unleavened bread, in that there was an holy convocation on each of these days (Ex. 12:15–16), which denoted them to be the greatest days of the feast, as appears by Lev. 23:2. And as the Passover and the days of unleavened bread that followed it were appointed in commemoration of what came to pass in those days of the year, at the time of the children of Israel's deliverance out of Egypt, so it is probable that the first and last days of unleavened bread were thus distinguished and appointed to be holy convocations, in respect to remarkable events that those days were distinguished by, when the children of Israel departed. The first day we know was distinguished by that, that it was the day of their departure. But the next remarkable event that we read of was their passing through the Red Sea, which has been shown could not be within less than six days after; and therefore that probably happened on the seventh day of unleavened bread.

§ 9. But the principal argument that the day of the children of Israel's coming up out of the Red Sea was on the same day of the week, is that the Jewish sabbath was appointed in remembrance of that very event, and what was implied in it, as appears by Deut. 5:12–15, being one of the two places where the Ten Commandments are rehearsed. The words are these, "Keep the sabbath day to sanctify it, as the Lord thy God hath commanded thee. Six days thou shalt labor, and do all thy work: but the seventh is the sabbath of the Lord thy God: in it thou shalt not do any work, thou, nor thy son, nor thy daughter, nor thy manservant, nor thy maidservant, nor thine ox, nor thine ass, nor any of thy cattle, nor thy stranger that is within thy gates; that thy manservant and thy maidservant may rest as well as thou. And remember that thou wast a servant in the land of Egypt, and that the Lord thy God brought thee out thence through a mighty hand and by a stretched out arm: therefore the Lord thy God commanded thee to keep the sabbath day." Here it may be noted:

§ 10. (1) That here is no mention of God's creating the heavens and the earth, and resting from that, which was the ground of God's institution of a sabbath at first; but only God's delivering the children of Israel. And this is expressly said to be the ground of the institution God had given to the Jews, distinct from a former appointment: for it is said, "Therefore the Lord thy God commanded thee to keep the sabbath day." And most probably it is thus said because that was the reason that [the] Mosaic sabbath was appointed, or that such a day was appointed for a sabbath.

§ 11. (2) It is evident that God's delivering the children of Israel out of Egypt was not only the ground of the institution of the Mosaic sabbath, but that the resting on that sabbath was appointed in remembrance of the Israelites' resting from the toil and affliction of their Egyptian bondservice. For here it is particularly insisted on and repeated that their manservant and maidservant should rest on that day; the last clause of the command is "that thy manservant and thy maidservant may rest as well as thou." And then the reason by which it is enforced is plainly this, that they themselves were servants in the land of Egypt, and that God brought them out of Egypt [and] caused them to rest from their service, and that in commemoration of that very rest, God commanded them to keep the sabbath day.

§ 12. But the first day wherein the children of Israel were out of the land of Egypt was the day when they passed through the Red Sea. Till that day they were in the land of Egypt, in the land that was under the dominion of Pharaoh their cruel oppressor, for the Red Sea was the boundary of the country on that side; and that was the first day of their rest and deliverance from their affliction, distress and oppression from the Egyptians, and no day before. That was the day of their deliverance from their enemies and old taskmasters, in the destruction of those taskmasters, and was the day of Israel's salvation. Ex. 14:13, "And Moses said unto the people, Fear ye not, stand still, and see the salvation of the Lord, which he will show unto you this day: for the Egyptians whom ye have seen today, ye shall see them again no more forever." This day was a day of sweet rest to the Israelites, and the only day of rest they had had for many years. It was the day when they were wholly set at liberty and had no more to feel or fear from their cruel oppressors; a day wherein they were refreshed; a day of great joy to them, whereon they sang a song of praise and deliverance, the first song that is recorded in the Scripture. It was the happiest and best day that ever that people had seen, a day most worthy to be commemorated. Here add No. 719.[7]

§ 13. Seeing therefore that the rest of the Jewish sabbath was appointed in remembrance of the rest that God gave the Israelites that day, doubtless it was appointed on the day of their rest; as the sabbath that was appointed in commemoration of God's rest from the work of creation, was appointed on the day of his rest. God thought that rest worthy to be thus commemorated; and therefore God did not only set apart a certain day of rest, but he blessed that day and hallowed it. So seeing that God thought that the rest he accomplished for the children of Israel when he brought them up out of the Red Sea worthy to be thus commemorated, doubtless he blessed that very day and hallowed it.

---

7. JE indicates by a cue mark that the whole of No. 719 should be inserted at this point. See below, pp. 349–50.

§ 14. Having thus considered what reason we have to conclude that the Jewish sabbath was appointed on the day of the children of Israel's coming up out of the Red Sea, and in commemoration of that event, and of their redemption out of Egypt then perfected, and the rest they then obtained, I proceed to consider how this confirms the divine appointment of the Christian sabbath, or that the weekly sabbath now ought to be kept in commemoration of the work of redemption by Jesus Christ, and on the day when he rose from the dead, and so finished and rested from that great and hard work. And here,

(1) The redemption of the children of Israel out of Egypt was a little thing in comparison of the great and eternal redemption of Jesus Christ; 'tis nothing and less than nothing in comparison of it. Therefore, if God thought that petty redemption worthy to be so commemorated as to have the sabbath appointed to be kept in remembrance of the finishing of it, and on the day in which Christ, the angel of God's presence who redeemed them, finished it and rested from it, and whereon the children of Israel rested from that temporal bondage: how much more is the great redemption of Christ worthy to be thus commemorated, and to have the weekly sabbath appointed to be kept on the day whereon Christ finished and rested from that, and whereon the church in him were set at liberty from their spiritual bondage and eternal misery.

§ 15. (2) This redemption of the children of Israel out of Egypt was a type of the great and eternal redemption of Jesus Christ. 'Tis the most eminent type of it that we have in all the Old Testament; [it] was ordered in all its circumstances for that end, to be an image of it. Christ, who was the angel of God's presence, who redeemed the children of Israel and carried them all the days of old, managed this whole affair in an absolute subordination to that great redemption that was so much on his heart. And the principal end of the being of such an event seems to be to shadow forth the great and eternal redemption. If therefore Christ, who is Lord of the sabbath, had so much respect to the redemption which was the shadow as to appoint the weekly sabbath to be kept in remembrance of it, and on the day when it was finished and rested from: how much more would he appoint the sabbath to be kept in remembrance of the great antitype, and cause that the time of it should be regulated by that. Is it not agreeable to the Scripture that the shadow should give place to the substance? It was probably more out of respect to the antitype, or for the sake of the typical relation that the redemption out of Egypt had to the spiritual and eternal redemption that was thus honored in the institution of the Mosaic sabbath, than out of respect to the greatness of the event in itself considered.

See how often the children of Israel's passing through the Red Sea is spoken of as a resemblance of what is brought to pass for God's people by the Messiah, "Miscellanies," [No.] 1069.[8]

§ 16. (3) Not only was the redemption out of Egypt, which was finished and which Christ rested from in the coming up of the children of Israel out of the Red Sea, a type of the great spiritual redemption which Christ rested from when he rose from the grave; but that particular event of the children of Israel's coming up out of the Red Sea was a remarkable type of the resurrection of Jesus Christ (see note on I Pet. 3:18–20).[9] To illustrate this matter several things may be considered:

1. That that congregation that came up out of the Red Sea was the mystical body of Christ. The congregation of [the] church of Christ's people is often called his body, by which 'tis evident that there is in it a lively representation of Christ's body. So that when the children of Israel came up out of the Red Sea, that which then rose out of the sea, was what represented the body of Christ, the same which rose from the dead.

§ 17. 2. Not only the real body of Christ on the first day of the week rose from the dead, but the church did as it were rise in him: for he neither died nor rose again as a private person, but as representing the church. So that that day that Christ rose might be looked upon as the day of the church's resurrection from death and from hell: for it was a state of spiritual and eternal death, as well as temporal death, that the church was brought up from by the resurrection of Christ and were begotten again to a living hope. Is. 26:19, "Thy dead men shall live, together with my dead body shall they arise. Awake and sing, ye that dwell in the dust: for thy dew is as the dew of herbs, and the earth shall cast out the dead." And a number of the dead bodies of the saints did actually rise from their graves with Christ (see Hos. 6:2, with note).[1] This resurrection of the spiritual Israel in and with Christ might therefore be well represented by the children of Israel's rising up out of the Red Sea.

§ 18. *3.* Moses, who was the leader of Israel, their great prophet and teacher, and who was king in Jeshurun, and led and conducted that congregation as a shepherd does his flock, and was a great type or image of

8. MS: "Miscell. B. 7. p. 9." No. 1069, entitled "Types of the Messiah," is published in *Works,* *11;* this reference is to pp. 210–14 of that volume.

9. In the "Blank Bible" note on I Pet. 3:18–20 JE observes that "the destruction of God's visible church of old by the flood, and the wonderful preservation of Noah and his family, and their revival of the church afterwards from thence, is a type of the death and resurrection of Christ; as our baptism is."

1. The "Blank Bible" note on Hos. 6:2 consists simply of a cross-reference to Col. 2:12. Both texts refer to the rising up of believers by the Lord.

Christ by God's own testimony (Deut. 18:15, 18), he came up on that day out of the Red Sea and brought up the congregation with him: in like manner as Christ, on the first day of the week, rose from the dead, and brought up his church with him from death and hell, and an exceeding depth of woe and misery; which shows the resemblance to be yet more exact. See Is. 63:11.

§ 19. *4.* Christ himself came up on that day out of the Red Sea, with the children of Israel, in the pillar of cloud and fire, who was [with] them then as their shepherd and captain, to defend them from their enemies and from being overwhelmed with the waters, and to bring them out and destroy their enemies. He that in all this affair acted as their Redeemer came out of the sea with them. Christ did as it were go both before and behind them: before, he led the people by his Spirit in Moses, who was a type of him;[2] and he went behind them in the pillar of cloud and fire to defend them. Thus the Lord went before them, and the God of Israel was their rearward, as Is. 52:12 and 58:8.

§ 20. *5.* When the children of Israel came up out of the Red Sea, they rested from those sufferings that were typical of the humiliation and suffering of Christ. Israel's sufferings in Egypt and Christ's sufferings represented one the other, as is evident because both were represented by the burning bush and also by the smoking furnace in Abraham's vision (see notes on these places).[3] God, in speaking of this deliverance from Egyptian sufferings, calls Israel his son. Hos. 11:1, "When Israel was a child, then I loved him, and called my son out of Egypt." By which it is evident that Israel, in their deliverance from their Egyptian sufferings, did resemble Christ; which is a further argument that they were a type of Christ in their coming up out of the Red Sea, which was their final deliverance from their Egyptian sufferings.

§ 21. *6.* The children of Israel's being in the Red Sea was typical of Christ in his suffering state, and also the miserable and dreadful state and condition that Christ's people are in before they are delivered by his redemption. Misery and wrath and sore affliction are often in Scripture compared to great waters (Job 22:11), to waves and billows, to great deeps, and the like. And their redemption from misery is called their be-

---

2. MS: "them."

3. In the "Blank Bible" note on Ex. 3:1–3 JE states that the burning bush represents (1) "the human nature of Christ, whose name is the branch"; and (2) "the church, the mystical body of Christ," as it was a "tender plant." The "Blank Bible" note on the smoking flax (Gen. 15:17) is a cross-reference to "Notes on Scripture," nos. 75 and 353, which comment upon Matt. 17:21 and Gen. 15:17 respectively. See *Works, 15,* 71–72, 339–40.

ing brought back "from the depths of the sea" (Ps. 68:22). See Zech. 10:11.

§ 22. *7.* Christ's being in his state of humiliation and suffering is particularly represented in Scripture by his being in great waters, as Ps. 69:1–3, 14–15. For that is spoken of Christ, as is evident because many passages in that Psalm are expressly applied to Christ in the New Testament. Compare v. 4 with John 15:25; v. 9 and John 2:17; v. 21 and Matt. 27:34, 48 and Mark 15:23 and John 19:29; v. 22 and Rom. 11:9–10; v. 25 and Acts 1:20.

§ 23. *8.* As Christ's state of humiliation and suffering is in that Psalm represented[4] by his being in great waters, so his deliverance from this state by his resurrection is represented by being delivered out of deep waters (vv. 14–15). There, Christ prays for his deliverance after this manner, "Deliver me out of the mire, and let me not sink: let me be delivered from them that hate me, and out of the deep waters. Let not the waterflood overflow me, neither let the deep swallow me up, and let not the pit shut her mouth upon me." The deliverance Christ has here respect to, is that in his resurrection: for that was the deliverance appointed and promised, and that he expected. And this is further evident in that he, in these verses, prays that the pit may not shut her mouth upon him. By the pit in Scripture is commonly meant the grave. So that what he prays for is that he mayn't continue in the grave. Christ's resurrection is also, in like manner, compared to a being delivered out of great waters in Ps. 42:7–8, 11, and so II Sam. 22:5–6, etc.

§ 24. *9.* The place of the dead, or the region of the dominion of death and destruction, or hell, is represented as being down under the waters, or at the bottom of the sea in Scripture (Job 26:5–6).

§ 25. *10.* The children of Israel's coming up out of the Red Sea was the more lively image of the resurrection of Christ, because in rising out of that sea they escaped the hand of Pharaoh and his host, who was a type of the devil and his host, and therefore is called the Leviathan and "the dragons in the waters" (Ps. 74:13–14). So Christ and his church, in his resurrection, eternally escaped the hand of Satan, and were delivered from all the powers of darkness. The sea from whence, and by which, the Israelites were delivered was the sea in which their enemies were destroyed. So that passion and humiliation of Christ, from which Christ and his church were delivered, and by which they were saved, was that which was the means of the destruction and ruin of Satan.

---

4. MS: "is represented."

§ 26. *11*. What makes this very clear is that Jonah's being brought up out of the sea, was by Christ's own testimony a type of his resurrection from the grave. Matt. 12:40, "For as Jonas was three days and three nights in the whale's belly; so shall the Son of man be three days and three nights in the heart of the earth"; which demonstrates that a coming up out of the sea is a fit type of the resurrection of Christ. That case of Jonah is exceeding parallel to this of the children of Israel. As Jonah in coming up out of the sea escaped the whale that had swallowed him, so the children of Israel escaped Pharaoh, that is in this case called Leviathan, or the whale who had in his expectation swallowed them up, as Ex. 14:3 and 15:9.

§ 27. *12*. This event resembled the resurrection of Christ in the time of its accomplishment, for it was about the breaking of the day. We have an account that in the morning watch the Lord looked unto the host of the Egyptians through the pillar of fire and of the cloud, and troubled all their host, and took off their chariot wheels. And then the children of Israel came up out of the Red Sea; and as soon as ever they were all come up, Moses stretched forth his hand over the sea, and the sea returned to his strength. And that was when the morning first appeared, which was the time when Christ arose from the dead. And by what has been said before (§ 1), it is very probable that the time that the children of Israel had been in the sea and on the Egyptian shore of it, was about as long as the time from Christ's death to his resurrection. On account of the things that have been mentioned, not only God's leading the children of Israel through the Red Sea, but his bringing 'em up out of the Red Sea, is particularly spoken of as a glorious work of God in Is. 63:11.

§ 28. (4) Another way that this confirms that the sabbath now, in the days of the gospel, ought not to be kept on a Saturday, but on the first day of the week [is this]: for this proves that the day of the sabbath among the Jews was a day of rejoicing, and therefore was abolished by Christ's lying in the grave on that day. For the church—the bride and the children of the bridechamber—were then called not to rejoice but to mourn, because the bridegroom was taken from her (Matt. 9:15 and Mark 2:19–20, Luke 5:34–35). But the day following was the day of the bride's rejoicing, when the bridegroom returned to her from the dead and from such extreme sufferings, from the land of darkness and out of the belly of hell; and came to her with salvation, with deliverance from everlasting misery, and eternal life and glory for her in his hand. This was a day wherein the disciples were as it were raised from the dead: for while Christ remained dead, their spirits were sunk as it were into the shades of death, but when he revived, how were their spirits revived. And Peter doubtless spake very feelingly when he said, Christ had begotten them again to a living hope by the resurrection of Christ from the dead (I Pet. 1:3). See what a time of joy this was to the Lamb's wife, in note on Matt. 28:9.[5] See [No.] 748.

§ 29. *Corol.* BEGINNING OF THE SABBATH. Hence, no argument to prove that the sabbath ought to begin in the morning can be drawn from Christ's rising in the morning: for it was at the same time of day that the children of Israel came up out of the Red Sea, in commemoration of which the Jewish sabbath was appointed, and yet their sabbath began in the evening. They were to keep that day wherein this event happened, but were to have no regard to the time of day in the beginning of the sabbath, but the days were to begin and end as they used to do.

692. SABBATH. LORD'S DAY. Mr. Bedford in his *Scripture Chronology* shows it to be exceeding probable that Christ was born and circumcised on the first day of the week (Bk. IV, ch. IV).[6] If he was born on the feast of tabernacles, which there are solid arguments for, then both his birth and circumcision that year happened on the first day of the week.

693. SABBATH. LORD'S DAY. If the sabbath was originally kept on a Sunday, or the day that answers to the Christian sabbath, till it was changed by Moses, as Bedford in his *Scripture Chronology* renders exceeding probable, then it must return again when the Jewish dispensation comes to be abolished.[7] And therefore, the change must begin from the time of Christ's resurrection, and no other time: for it was Christ's resurrection that abolished the Mosaic dispensation, and on that is built the Christian church, or dispensation, as is many ways evident. And seeing that Christ rose on the morning of that day, the day of his resurrection must be the first Christian sabbath, because as soon as ever he was risen the Mosaic dispensation ceased and things returned immediately to their old channel.

See an argument for the Christian sabbath in note on Ex. 19:10–11.[8]

5. JE considers in the "Blank Bible" note on Matt. 28:9 "the various passions" the women must have felt on visiting Jesus' tomb, such as sorrow over the death of Christ and puzzlement over finding the sepulcher empty. But on hearing the angel's message, "now suddenly did this turn them from the deepest sorrow to overflowing joy. . . . How eager were they to impart the joyful news to their fellow disciples that were sharers in sorrow for his death." And then they see Christ "with their own eyes. How did it heighten their joy now, to see their Lord himself."

6. Bedford, *Scripture Chronology*, pp. 399–433, esp. p. 415.

7. Bedford, *Scripture Chronology*, pp. 6–8.

8. In the "Blank Bible" note on Ex. 19:10–11 JE uses Bedford to argue that the "third day" spoken of in the text, "or the day in which God came down on Mt. Sinai, was the first day of the week."

694. BAPTISM BY SPRINKLING. See note on Ps. 68:8–9, in the book of notes, no. 210, corol. 2.[9]

That the pouring of water on the person to be baptized is properly called "baptism," in the Scripture use of the phrase, and is also a more lively representation of the thing signified by baptism than dipping or plunging, are both evident by the words of John the Baptist, who said to the Pharisees and Sadducees, "I indeed baptize you with water: but he that cometh after me shall baptize you with the Holy Ghost, and with fire" [Matt. 3:11]. Here John's baptizing, and the baptizing with the Holy Ghost, are both called baptizing, and the one as the antitype and end of the other. But what is here called baptizing with the Holy Ghost is the pouring out of the Holy Ghost upon them, which was also typified by the pouring [of] oil on the heads of those that were anointed; and it was especially fulfilled on the day of Pentecost, when the Holy Ghost was so remarkably poured out on the Christian church, because that baptizing with water was designed as a shadow of baptizing with the Holy Ghost. Therefore both were conjoined when Christ was baptized. When John baptized him with water, God remarkably poured out the Spirit from heaven upon him. And it seems to me much the most probable, therefore, that John baptized by affusion, and not by dipping or plunging; and that so there was a greater agreement between the type and the antitype that were then conjoined, than there would have been if John had baptized by dipping.

695. PERSEVERANCE. Concerning the reasons why grace to persevere is promised in the covenant of grace.

God, when he had done such great things to redeem men, and had not spared his own Son, had so completely provided for men's redemption in the dignity of the person that he had provided, and in the greatness of the things that he did and suffered to magnify his grace towards poor fallen men: I say, God, when he had thus laid out himself to glorify his mercy and grace in the redemption of poor fallen men, did not see meet that those that are redeemed by Christ should be redeemed so imperfectly, as still to have the work of perseverance left in their own hands; which they had already been found insufficient for, even in their perfect state, and are now ten times so insufficient for, as before, in their fallen broken state, with their imperfect sanctification, wherein they are ten times so liable to fall away and not to persevere, as before, if the care of the matter be be-

9. This reference to the "Notes on Scripture" is found in *Works*, *15*, 139–40.

trusted with them. The poor creature, though redeemed by Christ so as to have the Holy Spirit of God and spiritual life again restored in a degree, yet is left a very poor piteous creature notwithstanding: because all is suspended on his perseverance, as it was at first, and the care of that affair is left with him, as it was then, and he is ten times so likely to fall away, as he was then, if we consider only what he has in him[self] to preserve him from it. The poor creature sees his own insufficiency to stand from what has happened in time past; his own instability has been his undoing already. And now he is vastly more unstable than before; and now, though he be redeemed to spiritual life, yet he has no remedy provided against that which has once proved his ruin, and is so much more likely to do so again. The more considerate and wise he is, the more will he be sensible of his own insufficiency, and how little his own strength is to be depended on, and how much he needs God's help in this matter; but yet he has nothing to trust to but his own strength. He wants some person that is to be depended on, to fly to for help here; but there is none provided.

God in his providence made void the first covenant to make way for a better covenant; one that was better for man. It was the will of God that it should first appear by the event wherein the first was deficient, or wanting of what man needed, which was manifest in the fall. Therein it appeared that the great thing wherein the first covenant was deficient, was that the fulfillment of the righteousness of the covenant, and man's perseverance, was betrusted with man himself, with nothing better to secure it than his own strength. And therefore, God introduces a better covenant that should be an everlasting covenant, a new and living way, wherein that which was wanting in the first covenant would be supplied, and a remedy should be provided against that which under the first covenant proved man's undoing, viz. man's own weakness and instability, by a mediator's being given, who is the same yesterday, today and forever, who cannot fail, who would undertake for them, who should take the care of them, that is able to save to the uttermost all that come unto God through him, and who ever lives to make intercession for them. God did not see it fit that man should be trusted to stand in his own strength a second time. God at first entered into such a covenant with man wherein he was left to stand in his own strength, for that end, that the event might show the weakness and instability of man and his dependence on God. But when the event has once proved this, there is no need of entering into another covenant of the same tenor to manifest it.

'Tis not fit in a covenant that is distinguished from the first covenant as a covenant of grace, wherein all is of mere free and sovereign grace, that the reward of life should be suspended on man's perseverance as dependent on the strength and steadfastness of his own will. 'Tis a covenant of works and not a covenant of grace that suspends eternal life on what is the fruit of a man's own strength. Eternal life was to have been of works in these two respects, viz. as it was to have been for man's own righteousness, and as it was suspended on the fruit of his own strength. For though our first parent depended on the grace of God—the influences of his Spirit in their hearts—yet that grace was given him already, and dwelt in him constantly and without interruption, in such a degree as to hold him above any lust or sinful habit or principle. And eternal life was not merely suspended on that grace that was given him and dwelt in him, but on his improvement of that grace, his persevering by his own strength with that grace which he already had: for, in order to his perseverance, there was nothing further promised beyond his own strength; no extraordinary occasional assistance was promised. It was not promised but that man should be left to himself as he was (though God did not oblige himself not to afford extraordinary assistance on occasion, as doubtless he did to the angels that stood). But the new covenant is of grace in a manner distinguishing from the old in both these respects, that the reward of life is suspended neither on his own strength or worthiness. It provides something above either. But if eternal life under the new covenant was suspended on man's own perseverance, or his perseveringly using diligent endeavors to stand, without the promise of anything further to ascertain it than his own strength, it would herein be further from being worthy to be called a covenant of grace than the first covenant, because now man's strength is exceedingly less than it was then, and he is under far less advantages to persevere. Perseverance is much more difficult; and if he should obtain eternal life by perseverance in his own strength now, eternal life would, with respect to that, be much more of himself than it would have been by the first covenant, because perseverance would now be a much greater thing than under those circumstances. And he has [now] but an exceeding small part of that grace dwelling in him to assist him than he had then; and that which he has don't dwell in him in the exercises of it by such a constant law as grace did then, but is put into exercise by the spirit of grace in a far more arbitrary and sovereign way.

And again Christ came into the world to do what mere man failed of. He came as a better surety, and that in him those defects might be supplied that proved to be in our first surety, and that we might have a remedy for that mischief that came by those defects. But the defect of our first surety was that he did not persevere; he wanted steadfastness. And therefore, God sent us in the next place one that could not fail, that should surely persevere. But this is no supply of that defect to us, if the reward of life be still suspended on our perseverance, which has nothing greater to secure it still than the strength of mere man. And the perseverance of our second surety is no remedy against the like mischief, which came by failure of our first surety; but, on the contrary, we are exposed by far more to the mischief than before. The perseverance on which life was suspended, depended then indeed on the strength of mere man; but now it is suspended on the strength of fallen man.

In that our first surety did not persevere, we fell in and with him; and so[1] doubtless if he had stood, we should have stood with him. And therefore, when God in mercy has given us a better surety to supply the defects of the first surety, a surety that might stand and[2] persevere, and one that has actually persevered through the greatest imaginable trials, doubt[less] we shall stand and persevere in him after all this. Eternal life won't be suspended on our perseverance by our own poor, feeble, broken strength.

Our first surety, if he had stood, would have been brought to eat of the tree of life as a seal of a confirmed state of life in persevering and everlasting holiness and happiness; and he would have eat of this tree of life as a seal of persevering confirmed life, not only for himself, but as our head. As when he eat of the tree of knowledge of good and evil, he tasted as our head, and so brought death on himself and all his posterity: so if he had persevered, and had eat of the tree of life,[3] he would have tasted of that as our head, and therein confirmed holiness and life would have been sealed to him and all his posterity. But Christ the second Adam acts the same part for us that the first Adam was to have done, and failed in. He has fulfilled the law, and has been admitted to the seals of confirmed and everlasting life. God, as a testimony and seal of his acceptance of what he had done as the condition of life, raised him from the dead and exalted him with his own right hand, received him up into glory and gave all things into his hands. And thus the second Adam has persevered not only for himself, but for us; and has been sealed to confirmed, persevering and eternal life as our head. So that all those that are his, and that are his spiritual posterity,[4] are sealed in him to persevering life. Here it will be in vain to object and say that persons' persevering in faith and holiness is the condition of their being admitted to the state of Christ's posterity, or to a right

1. MS: "~~so~~ ⟨as⟩."
2. MS: "but."
3. MS: "knowledge of good and evil."
4. MS: "prosperity."

in him; and that none are admitted as such till they have first persevered. For this is as much as to say that Christ has no church here in this world, that there are none on this side the grave that are admitted as his children or people, because they han't yet actually persevered to the end of life, which is the condition of their being admitted as his children and people; which is contrary to the whole Scripture.

Christ being the second Adam, and having finished the work of Adam for us, he don't only redeem or bring us back to be in the probationary state of Adam while he had yet his work to finish, having his eternal life uncertain because suspended on his uncertain perseverance. That is very inconsistent with Christ's being a second Adam and having undertaken and finished the work of Adam for us: for if Christ, succeeding in Adam's room, has done and gone through the work that Adam was to have done and did—this as our representative or surety—he han't only thereby set us that are in him, and represented by him, in Adam's probationary uncertain state, having the finishing or persevering in the work on which eternal life was suspended yet before him and uncertain, or the state that Adam was in on this side[5] [of] a state of confirmed life. But if Christ has finished the work of Adam for us, as representing us and acting in our stead, then doubtless he has not only gone through himself, but has carried us who are in him and are represented by him, through the work of Adam, or through Adam's working probationary state, unto that confirmed state that Adam should have arrived at if he had gone through his own work.

To suppose that a right to life is suspended on our own perseverance that is uncertain, and has nothing more sure and steadfast to secure it than our own good wills and resolutions (which way soever we suppose it to [be] dependent on the strength of our resolution and will: either without assistance, or in the improvement of assistance, or in seeking assistance) is exceeding dissonant to the nature and design of the gospel scheme. For if it were so, it would unavoidably have one of these two effects: either (1) exceedingly to deprive the believer of the comfort, hope and joy of salvation. But this is very contrary to God's intention in the scheme of man's salvation, which is to lay a foundation for man's abundant consolation every way, and to make the ground of our peace and joy in all respects strong and sure. Or else (2) he must depend much on himself, and the ground of his joy and hope must in a great measure be his own strength, and the steadfastness of his own heart, the unchangeable-

5. I.e. the state prior to the fall.

ness of his own resolutions, etc., which would be very dissonant from the gospel scheme.[6]

That the saints shall surely persevere will necessarily follow from that, that they have already performed the obedience which is the righteousness by which they have justification to life, or it is already performed for them and imputed to them: for that supposes that it is the same thing in the sight of God as if they had performed it. Now when once the creature has actually performed and finished the righteousness of the law, he is immediately sealed and confirmed to eternal life. There is nothing to keep him off from the tree of life, to seal him to it, any longer; but as soon as ever a believer has Christ's righteousness imputed to him, he has virtually finished the righteousness of the law. To this add No. 711.

696. EXCELLENCY OF CHRIST. See sermon on Cant. 1:3, and also on Rev. 5:5.[7]

697. UNITY OF THE GODHEAD. The unity of the Godhead will necessarily follow from God's being infinite: for to be infinite is to be all, and it would be a contradiction to suppose two ALLS, because if there be two or more, one alone is not all, but the sum of them put together are all. Infinity and omneity, if I may so speak, must go together, because if any being falls short of omneity, then it is not infinite therein; it is limity therein; there is something that it don't extend to, or that it don't comprehend. If there be something more, then there is something beyond; and wherein this being don't reach and include that which is beyond, therein it is limited. Its bounds stop short of this that is not comprehended. An infinite being, therefore, must be an all-comprehending being. He must comprehend in himself all being. That there should be another being underived and independent, and so no way comprehended, will argue him not to be infinite, because then there is something more. There is more entity. There is some entity beside what is in this being; and therefore, his entity can't be infinite. These two beings put together are more than one, for they taken together are a sum total. And one taken alone is but a part

6. At this point in the MS, JE began an entry and then deleted it with a large X mark. It reads: "696. How RENEWED ACTS OF FAITH and PERSEVERANCE IN FAITH DO influence [us] in our salvation. The first act of faith is that which first obtains a title to salvation; and therefore though salvation be promised to after acts of faith and to perseverance in faith, yet they don't give a right to salvation in the same manner as the first act doth."

7. For the sermon on Cant. 1:3 see above, No. 625, p. 154, n. 7. This 1733 sermon is an earlier exploration of the theme JE develops in the sermon on Rev. 5:5–6 (Aug. 1736), which was published in 1738 as *The Excellency of Christ*. See Worcester rev. ed., *4*, 179–201.

of that sum total, and therefore is finite, for whatsoever is a part is finite. God—as he is infinite, and the being whence all are derived, and from whom every thing is given—does comprehend the entity of all his creatures; and their entity is not to be added to his, as not comprehended in it, for they are but communications from him. Communications of being ben't additions of being. The reflections of the sun's light don't add at all to the sum total of the light. 'Tis true, mathematicians conceive of greater than infinite in some respects, and of several infinites being added one to another; but 'tis because they are in some respect finite: as a thing conceived infinitely long may not be infinitely thick, and so its thickness may be added to; or if it be conceived infinitely long one way, yet it may be conceived having bounds, or an end, another. But God is in no respect limited, and therefore can in no respect be added to.

698. THE SUFFERINGS OF CHRIST from the beginning of his life to the end of it. See sermon on Is. 53:3.[8]

699. END OF THE CREATION. GLORY OF GOD. God don't seek his own glory for any happiness he receives by it, as men are gratified in having their excellencies gazed at, admired and extolled by others. But God seeks the display of his own glory as a thing in itself excellent. The display of the divine glory is that which is most excellent. 'Tis good that glory should be displayed. The excellency of God's nature appears in that, that he loves and seeks whatever is in itself excellent. One way that the excellency of God's nature appears is in loving himself, or loving his own excellency and infinite perfection; and as he loves his own perfection, so he loves the effulgence or shining forth of that perfection, or loves his own excellency in the expression and fruit of it. 'Tis an excellent thing that that which is excellent should be expressed in proper act and fruit. Thus, 'tis an excellent thing that infinite justice should shine forth, and be expressed in infinitely just and righteous acts, and that infinite goodness should be expressed in infinitely good and gracious deeds.

700. PREDESTINATION. REPROBATION. SUPRALAPSARIANS. SUBLAPSARIANS. See No. 704. God, in the decree of election, is justly to be consid-

---

8. JE preached on Is. 53:3 several times during his ministerial career. The topic of the entry indicates that he is referring to a lengthy sermon delivered in Aug. 1736, which has as its doctrine "Our Lord Jesus Christ when he dwelt here on earth was one that was very much used to affliction" and which considers in great detail the humiliations and sufferings that Jesus underwent during his lifetime.

ered as decreeing the creature's eternal happiness antecedent to any foresight of good works, in a sense wherein he does not, in reprobation, decree the creature's eternal misery antecedent to any foresight of sin: because the being of sin is supposed in the first things in order in the decree of reprobation, which is that God will glorify his vindictive justice; but the very notion of revenging justice simply considered supposes a fault to be revenged. But faith and good works is not supposed in the first things in order in the decree of election. The first things in order in this decree are that God will communicate his happiness and glorify his grace (for these two seem to be coordinate). But in neither of these is faith and good works supposed: for when God decrees, and seeks to communicate his own happiness in the creature's happiness, the notion of this simply considered supposes or implies nothing of faith or good works. Nor does the notion of grace in *itself* suppose any such thing. It don't necessarily follow from the very nature of grace, or God's communicativeness of his own happiness, that there must be faith and good works. This is only a certain way of the arbitrary appointment of God's wisdom, wherein he will bring men to partake of his grace. But yet God is far from having decreed damnation from a foresight of evil[9] works in the sense of the Arminians: as if God in this decree did properly depend on the creature's sinful act, as an event the coming to pass of which primarily depends on the creature's determination; so that the creature's determination in this decree is properly to be looked upon as antecedent to God's determination, and [that] on which his determination is consequent and dependent.

701. HAPPINESS OF HEAVEN INCREASING. 'Tis certain that the inhabitants of heaven do increase in their knowledge. "The angels know more than they did before Christ's incarnation; for they are said to know *by the church*, i.e. by the dealings of God with the church, *the manifold wisdom of God;* and to *desire to look into* the account the gospel gives of the *sufferings of Christ, and the glory that should follow.*" Ridgley's *Body of Divinity*, vol. 1, pp. 61–62.[1]

702. WORK OF CREATION. PROVIDENCE. REDEMPTION. God's providence taken summarily, or in general, is an operation and work of his, su-

---

9. MS: "good."

1. Thomas Ridgley, *A Body of Divinity: Wherein the Doctrines of the Christian Religion are Explained and defended. Being the Substance of several Lectures on the Assembly's Larger Catechism* (2 vols. London, 1731–33). This passage occurs in vol. 1, Quest. VII, which is entitled "What is God?" (pp. 61–62).

perior to the work of creation: for providence may in some respect be called the end of the work of creation, as the use and improvement any artificer makes of an engine, or the work he intends with it, is superior to his making the engine. God created the world to glorify himself; but it was principally that he might glorify him[self] in his disposal of the world, or in the use he intended to make of it, in his providence. And God's providential disposals of the material part of the world are all subordinate to his providence towards the spiritual and intelligent part of it.

And that work of God's providence to which all other works of providence, both in the material and immaterial part of the creation, are subservient, is the work of redemption. All other works of providence may be looked upon as *appendages* to this great work, or *things* which God does to subserve that grand design. The work of redemption may be looked upon as the great end and drift of all God's works and dispensations from the beginning, and even the end of the work of creation itself; yea, the whole creation. It was the end of the creation of heaven: the preparing that blessed and glorious habitation was with an eye to this. It was the end of the creation of the angels: it was with an eye to the Son of God, and their subserviency to him in the government God intended him as God-man Mediator, and the service and ministration they were to be improved in, in his mediatorial kingdom. They were created that they might be ministering spirits sent forth to minister in the service of that kingdom. And the creation of the visible world [was] in order to it. And therefore,

1. Hence, all things in the formation and constitution and disposal of it, in heaven above and in the earth, and the inhabitants of it among all the brute animals, and especially in the state and circumstances of the world of mankind, shadow forth the things that appertain to this work and do point to them many ways.

2. It may be further argued that the creation of the visible world was in order to the work of redemption, that not only the things made do shadow forth things that appertain to this work, but the work of creation itself seems to be so done that it should shadow forth the work of redemption in the manner of doing of it. Thus everything was first a chaos and things were brought out of a state of utter darkness and confusion and (as it were) ruin. And the first thing that appeared, by which the world began to come out of this state, was light; which seems well to shadow forth and represent three things, viz.

(1) That the recovery of the world from confusion and ruin is by Christ, who is the wisdom of God and the brightness of his glory and the light of

the world; and that the first thing that was done in order to the recovery of the ruined world, was the giving of Jesus Christ to be the light of the world to put an end to its darkness and confusion.

(2) As the light was the first thing come out of darkness and confusion (for it is said, II Cor. 4:6, God caused "the light to shine out of darkness"), so Christ was in a sense the first that rose out of the dismal darkness, ruin and death that was occasioned by sin (Acts 26:23; Col. 1:18; I Cor. 15:20, 23; Rev. 1:5).

(3) Spiritual light is the first thing in the new creation, or in the recovery of the redeemed out of sin and misery. The first thing that God doth is to cause the light to shine into the dark heart; and this work of God is expressly compared to that of his causing light to shine out of the chaos (II Cor. 4:6). And the manner of God's doing this is well represented by the manner of his doing that, viz. by speaking the powerful word, his saying "Let there be light" [Gen. 1:3].

And after the light all things were brought to beauty, and perfection and excellent order out of this dark chaos; but yet gradually, one thing after another, till the seventh day, the day of holy rest, when all things appeared very good, in their complete beauty and perfection, and all remainders of chaos were perfectly done away. Gen. 1:31, "And God saw every thing that he had made, and, behold it was very good"; which well represents two things, viz.

1. How that the work of grace that is begun in the soul is gradually carried on, till it is brought to its perfection without any remains of sin or misery in the heavenly rest and eternal sabbath, to which that sabbath of the seventh day is expressly compared. Heb. 4:4, "For he spake in a certain place of the seventh day on this wise, And God did rest on the seventh day from all his works"; v. 9, "There remaineth therefore a rest to the people of God," together with the rest of the context.

2. How that the work of redemption is gradually carried on in the world, till the church shall be brought to the most perfect and glorious and happy state on earth, to a state of rest; which will probably be after the expiration of the first six thousand years of the world, which answer to the six days of the creation, putting a thousand years for a day.

Again, the state that the earth was brought into out of the chaos seems well to represent the state that the church, or the soul of a believer, is brought into by the new creation while here in the present earthly state, in two respects. For the sin and misery that the soul is involved in before redemption seems in the first creation to be represented by two things, viz. (1) darkness, and (2) chaos, which is called the waters. Neither of

these was wholly and perfectly abolished, but only their power and dominion was broke. Darkness was no longer suffered to possess the whole
world; but God set bounds to the darkness and divided the light from the
darkness. So the waters were no longer suffered to fill heaven and earth
as the chaos did before. But (1) there was a firmament made to divide the
waters from the waters, a space free from water; and (2) the waters were
not suffered to overwhelm and cover all, and bear dominion over all, as
they did before. But God confined the waters to certain bounds and limits. He said, "Let the waters be gathered together into one place, and let
the dry land appear" [Gen. 1:9]. God set "bars and doors" to restrain the
waters (Job 38:10), and "set a bound that they may not pass over" (Ps.
104:9; Jer. 5:22), "and said, Hitherto shalt thou come, and no further: and
here shall thy proud waves be stayed" [Job 38:11]. So in the present state
of the church in this world, the darkness, sin and misery is not totally abolished, but only the reigning power of it. They are kept under, confined to
certain bounds, by God's power and brace. God's limiting and restraining the waters of the sea is expressly compared to his ruling and curbing
the corruptions of man, and conquering his enemies (Ps. 65:7 and Ps.
89:9). By the waters being removed from off the land the earth had opportunity to bring forth grass and plants and fruit in abundance. So 'tis
by the breaking the reigning power of sin in the soul that it can be fruit-
ful in graces and good works.

Waters is very often put in Scripture to represent misery and calamity[2]
(see No. 691, §§ 20–23). Thus the remainders of waters in the creation
represent the remainders of sin and misery in the present state of the
church. But in the future triumphant state of the church there shall be
no remains of these; and therefore, in the description of that 'tis said,
"There was no more sea" (Rev 21:1).

And the creation of man in particular seems to have been in such a manner, as it was that it might shadow the manner of his greater creation, viz.
his new creation. It was like it in this respect, that there was as it were a
consultation of the persons of the Trinity about it, as there was about his
redemption. And then he was formed out of the dust of the earth from a
vile original, which represents the mean, low and vile state that man is
brought out of by redemption. He had life given him by God's breathing
into him the breath of life, whereby man became a living soul; which represents the manner in which man has spiritual life given him in the new

---

2. MS: "⟨the waters the the sin & misery⟩ misery & calamity is very often put in SS. to represent
misery & calamity." In the list of Scripture types appended to "Images of Divine Things" JE states,
"Waters represent misery, Job 22:11." *Works*, *11*, 131.

creation, viz. by the communication of the Spirit of God infusing it into him to be in him a vital principle.

Adam in his creation, or in the state wherein he was created, was a remarkable type of Christ. Rom. 5:14, "After the similitude of Adam's transgression, who was the figure of him that was to come." He was so in various respects. He was the first man that was formed of the dust of the earth; so Christ was the first begotten from the dead, or first raised out of the grave or dust. So he was the first that was raised out [of] those mean and low circumstances, from weakness, from disgrace and misery that were the fruits of man's sin. He was the first made of all mankind; so Christ was the first born of every creature. As he was he out of whom the woman was taken, even from near his heart, bone of his bone, and flesh of his flesh, by his deep sleep; so Christ was he out of whom the church is, as it were, taken, from his transcendent love and by the deep sleep of his death. As Adam was the natural father of all mankind; so is Christ the spiritual father of all in the new creation. Adam was made the federal head of all his seed; so Christ is the federal head of all his seed. That blessedness that Adam would have obtained if he had stood for himself and his posterity was but a type of the blessedness that Christ obtained for himself and his seed by his obedience; and therefore, that tree of life he should have eat of as a seal of that blessedness, was but a type of that blessedness that the church is brought to eat of by Christ's obedience (Rev. 2:7). "Adam was the son of God" (Luke 3:38). As Christ was formed immediately out of the womb of a virgin, by the Spirit of God, without the seed of man; so Adam was immediately formed out of the bowels of his mother earth, which is in Scripture made use [of] to represent the formation of the body in the womb (Ps. 139:15); and it was from the womb of the earth while yet as it were a virgin, while in its pure and undefiled state. And this was by the Spirit, as the formation of Christ in the womb of the virgin, for it was that which breathed into him the breath of life. Adam, though made of the mean vile dust of the earth, yet was made in the image of God; as is particularly observed, Gen. 1:27, "God created man *in his own image, in the image of God* created he him." By which four things are typified: (1) Christ, the antitype of Adam, his being the brightness of God's glory, and the express image of his person. (2) The man Christ Jesus being made in union with the divine nature, so as to be in the divine person. He was made in that person that was the essential image of God; and so had in a sense the Godhead communicated to him. (3) Christ's having the image of God as God-man; as such, representing the person of God the Father as his vicegerent in governing and judging the world. (4) The transcendent advancement of men in their union with God, whereby they partake of the beauty, life, honor and joy of the eternal Son of God; and so are made as gods by communion of his Spirit, whereby they are made partakers of the divine nature.

Though made from so vile an original, yet he was crowned with glory and honor, and was set over the works of God's hand, made to have dominion over all brute creatures. That this was a type of the glorious and exalted state that man is brought into—particularly Jesus Christ the head of man, and they in him as their head—is evident because what is spoken of the one in the eighth Psalm, is applied to the other by the Apostle in the second chapter of Hebrews. The Psalmist says, Ps. 8:4, "What is man, that thou art mindful of him? and the son of man, that thou visitest him?" Of how mean original is man, that is made of the dust; and how mean is he in himself, that when he is made, he should be set in such dignity? See note on Ps. 8.[3]

And the place that man was introduced into when he was created out of this vile original, viz. into paradise, a garden of sweet delight and pleasure, was a type of heaven, that place of glory that persons are brought into by redemption; as is evident in that heaven is called paradise, or a garden of pleasure, and as such is particularly compared to this garden. Rev. 2:7, "Of the tree of life, which is in the midst of the paradise of God," where is a most evident allusion to the tree of life in the midst of the garden of Eden. Man was not made in this garden, but was made in some more mean place, and then brought and put into the garden (Gen. 2:7–8); as man in the new creation is first brought into being and spiritual life in this earthly country, in this barren wilderness, and then is brought to heaven. And 'tis here also that the saints are raised from the dead, from the *dust of the earth*, and then ascend up into heaven at the last day. And this introduction of Adam, the first head and father of mankind, into paradise, after he was made in the image of [God] and the son of God, and formed of the dust of the earth, represents the ascension of the second man, and spiritual head and father of men, into the heavenly paradise, after the man Christ Jesus was made in the image of God, or state of sonship in this world, and after his body was raised from the grave or dust of the earth.

When God created man, he created them male and female and united them in marriage. Then it was even before the fall that God said, "A man shall leave his father and his mother, and shall cleave to his wife: and they

---

3. There is no note in the "Blank Bible" on this text. It is possibly a reference to "Notes on Scripture," no. 95a. See *Works, 15*, 77.

shall be one flesh"; which we are expressly told is a mystery or type representing the relation that there is between Christ and his church (Eph. 5:32). And the manner of Eve's creation was a remarkable type of the work of redemption. Adam was first made on the later part of the sixth day, but was as it were imperfectly made, because without a companion. And when he had seen his want, probably on the night that followed that day, when he was in a deep sleep, Eve was made of his rib. And when he rose from his deep sleep in the morning, and the sun arose, and all things were renewed, he received his beauteous spouse that had been formed of him. She was brought and presented to him in perfect beauty and purity: which represents being of Christ by his death and his obtaining the church by his death, his dying to present it to himself, a glorious church, without spot or wrinkle or any such thing, his rising from the dead to receive the church that he had purchased. This was on the sabbath day, the day of this resurrection of Adam, and the first complete day of his life, and the first day of his complete life; his life the day before being incomplete because without his companion. So Christ's resurrection, when he rose from that death whereby he had purchased the church, was on the sabbath, the first day of the week, the first day of Christ's immortal life, and the day when he first received what he had purchased by his death, viz. the church actually redeemed, who is the fullness or completeness of him who filleth all in all. See note on Gen. 2:3.[4]

The six days of the old creation typify probably the first six thousand years of the church; and the seventh, which was the sabbath, the glorious millennium, and also that eternal state of the church's consummate rest and glory at the end of the world, of which the glory of the millennium is a type.

3. This seems to have been one reason why God made the world by Jesus Christ, viz. that the creation of the world was a work that was subordinate to the work of redemption. But the work of redemption was properly the work of the Son. It belongs to him to do the whole of it. God hath entirely left it with him; and therefore, whatever is needful to be done in order to it, to prepare the way for it, to introduce it and to complete it, it belongs to him to do. And that this was one reason why God created the world by Jesus Christ seems plainly to be intimated by the Apostle, Eph.

4. In the "Blank Bible" note on Gen. 2:3, JE uses Bedford to argue that Adam must have numbered his sabbath from the first day of his life. Adam arose out of the deep sleep God caused so as to create Eve from his rib on the sabbath day, and she was presented to him on that day, just as Christ was presented to the church, his spouse, on the day he arose from the dead, which was also the sabbath.

3:9–11, "And to make all men see what is the fellowship of the mystery, which from the beginning of the world hath been hid in God, who created all things by Jesus Christ: to the intent that now unto the principalities and powers in heavenly places might be known by the church the manifold wisdom of God, according to the eternal purpose which he hath purposed in Christ Jesus our Lord."

See the argument from these words more fully cleared in notes on the words, "By Christ all things were created, that are in heaven, and that are in earth, visible and invisible, whether they be thrones, or dominions, or principalities, or powers" [Col. 1:16].[5] And therefore were all things made "by him," by the Father's appointment, because they are made "for him": for God has appointed him as God-man and Mediator to be "heir of all things"; and that he should be head over all things to the church; and that all things should be gathered together in him (Col. 1:16–18, with Heb. 1, at the beginning).

4. That the works of creation and the laws of nature, and that course of nature that God established in creation, is subordinate to the work of redemption, is confirmed by this, that the laws and course of nature have often been interrupted to subserve to the designs of the great work of redemption, and never for any other purpose. The laws of nature have often been set aside that they might give place to the designs of redemption, but have never yielded to anything else. The course of nature has been very often stopped and made to stand by, as yielding to this, because God would make the lesser give place to the greater and would make the means to be subject to the end. Thus God divided the sea and made it stand like a wall on each hand for the children of Israel, the redeemed of the Lord, to pass through. This showed that the sea and the dry land were by the creator and upholder of all things subordinated to redemption, and to the good and happiness of the redeemed. So the mighty works which God wrought in Egypt, wherein God made the vermin, the clouds, the River Nilus, the dust of the earth, the thunder and hail, the light and the darkness, to serve his people; and that in a way beyond their natures. He caused them to lay aside their nature, and to act beside its laws, in order to it. And in the wilderness God caused the mountains to skip like rams, and the little hills like lambs, and made the waters of the River Jordan to stand on a

---

5. The "Blank Bible" note on Col. 1:16 consists of a cross-reference to "Miscellanies" No. 838. In this entry JE explains that angels "are called thrones, dominions, principalities, and powers" because they "are appointed to different kinds of work" and "their ministry more especially respects some certain limited parts of the universality of things, which God has in some respect committed to their care."

heap for them. And especially is there a remarkable intimation of this in God's causing the sun and moon to stand still in Joshua's time, for the redemption of his people. This was a great intimation in providence that even the sun and moon were created for Christ's redeemed people, and that the very course of nature was by the God of nature subordinated to them. God showed at that time that the whole frame of the universe was by him put in subjection to Christ's redeemed church; and therefore, the whole frame was as it were arrested and stopped—or at least in the principal wheels of its motion—and the course of their nature to stand by and yield to them, and lay aside what belonged to them by nature, to serve them: as the head of a family employs his servants for the good of his children, and sends them hither or thither, and bids them stay or go as their needs require. But yet there is that which does more abundantly manifest it than this, viz.

5. The Creator of heaven and earth himself coming into this world— his (as it were) leaving heaven, quitting that glorious habitation and coming down from it, and dwelling in this lower world, and even descending into the lower parts of the earth to accomplish the work of redemption— is a great intimation that both the upper and the lower world, heaven, earth and hell, have their being in subordination to the work of redemption and from love to the redeemed. Surely the God of heaven would never himself quit heaven that those that were to be redeemed might have it, if he had not made heaven for them. He that made this lower world would surely never have so abased himself to use this lower world for their good, in such a manner as to make it an habitation for himself, had he not made it from love to them. The God of nature became himself subject in many respects to the laws of nature, in order to redemption and that he might obtain the designed good for the redeemed, in receiving nourishment in the womb of a woman, and being brought forth thence (though not there conceived) in a natural way, his living by meat and drink, sleep, etc. And which is much more, he was subject to pain and death by virtue of the laws of nature. The God of nature never so put himself out of the way in any wise to use nature to accomplish anything else as the work of redemption, or to obtain any other end, as the happiness of his elect, by redemption. And therefore, we may conclude that it was made and established chiefly for this end. So much did he put himself out of the way that he became subject to it himself, that it might be subject to the good of the redeemed. He became subject to nature as he assumed the nature of a creature and lived on earth a natural life. And he yielded his own nature to be destroyed for the good of those that were to be redeemed. 'Tis

an argument that the author of nature subjected nature to their good, that he clothed himself with this created nature for them, and as vested with this created nature subjected himself to their good, gave himself for their good. And yet when he was thus clothed with created nature and so subject to its laws, yet at the same time he appeared as the Lord of nature, and he improved his dominion over it by subjecting of it to the good of his people continually in such a course of miracles, making of it give place to their good.

6. 'Tis evident that all God's works, both of creation and providence, are subordinate to the work of redemption. [It] is manifest by the 136th Psalm, throughout, in which is plainly set forth that all are from mercy to his people, not only for the good of his creatures, but from mercy; which implies their being for their good in way of redemption, or as delivered from misery. The main subject of the psalm is the eternity and perpetuity of God's mercy to his church, or his mercy's being forever (in the literal translation [it] is "his mercy is in eternity"), i.e. his mercy to his church is from everlasting to everlasting, the same, unchangeable. With this the psalm begins, in the four first verses, before the mention of any particular work of mercy; and with this the psalm ends, in the last verse, after the enumeration of many works of mercy. But in the psalm are many great works of God enumerated as works of mercy, and which do show this property of divine mercy to his church, viz. that 'tis eternal and perpetual. Many of God's works are enumerated from the beginning of the world to that time wherein the Psalmist lived, to show that God's mercy is from everlasting to everlasting unchangeable. And first he mentions many great works of God that he had wrought before ever the church had a being, as particularly the creation of heaven, and the earth and waters, making the luminaries of heaven, particularly the sun, moon and stars, to show that his mercy to his people was from eternity. This argues it to be from eternity two ways, viz. (1) as it was before God's people had being, and (2) because it was in the very creation or giving being to the world. If the giving being to the world be from mercy to God's church, then that mercy itself must be before God gives being to the world, and therefore from eternity. Being "before the foundation of the world" is a phrase that signifies a thing's being from eternity. Eph. 1:4, "According as he hath chosen us in him before the foundation of the world"; and so II Tim. 1:9. As Christ says, Prov. 8:22–23, "The Lord possessed me in the beginning of his way, before his works of old. I was set up from everlasting, from the beginning or ever the earth was," etc.; vv. 27–31, "When he prepared the heavens, I was there: when he set a compass on the face of

the depth: when he established the clouds above: when he strengthened the fountains of the deep: when he gave to the sea his decree, that the waters should not pass his commandment: when he appointed the foundations of the earth: then I was by him, as one brought up with him: and was daily his delight, rejoicing always before him; *rejoicing in the habitable part of his earth; and my delights were with the sons of men.*" This is true in this sense, that it was from that delight he had in the sons of men that he was with the Father in this work, and acted from the Father in making these things. And the Psalmist in this psalm argues from the earliness of the manifestations of mercy in God's works, as the argument is in Jer. 31:3, "The Lord hath appeared of old unto me, Yea, I have loved thee with an everlasting love."

Nextly, the Psalmist proceeds to enumerate the great works of God towards the church, and especially after it was gathered, and formed, and settled by Moses; wherein is shown the constancy and unchangeableness of that mercy. He first mentions the great works God did for 'em in Egypt; and then his dividing the Red Sea; and then his leading the people through the wilderness; and then his destroying the great kings, and mighty princes, and giants of the land God intended to give them for a possession; and then his giving them their land and settling them in their land; and then his delivering them from their enemies from time to time after they were settled in the land. Hence, the constancy of God's mercy to his church is argued by such a successive course of wondrous works of mercy, through so many and great changes and so many provocations; agreeable to what God said to Moses when he appeared to him to send him to deliver Israel out of Egypt, that his name was JEHOVAH and I AM THAT I AM [Ex. 3:14], which was especially to signify the eternity and immutability of his mercy to his church, that it was the same now that it was when God made the promises to Abraham, and always would be the same. And that God's mercy to his church was perpetual, and would be to eternity, seems to be argued by the Psalmist from the experience the church had had of it hitherto, that it had remained and appeared in God's works the same from the beginning of the world to this time. God's mercy had never failed, yet one generation had passed away and another had come. The earth had been often emptied of its inhabitants, and yet God's mercy to his church lasted; the exercises of that held on in the great works which God wrought. As it was of old, so it was [in] the Psalmist's days: in his time God had in a wonderful manner delivered and redeemed his people from their enemies, as vv. 23–24. Hence, the Psalmist declares his faith that it never will fail, but as it had been *from* eternity and had hitherto been exercised from the beginning of the world, so it would still, to the end of the world and to eternity. Here see II Chron. 16:9.

7. Another argument that redemption is the work to which all things are subordinate, is that the Redeemer as[6] Redeemer is made head over all things. 'Tis [an] argument that that work of God whereby the good of the redeemed is wrought out is the supreme work of God, because their Redeemer, as united to their nature, or as God-man and Mediator, is made supreme, or set at the head of all things, and has all things put under his feet. He, as their Redeemer, is set over all God's works, over all God's works of creation and over all his works of providence. And 'tis out of respect to the good of the church that he is so, as we are expressly taught, Eph. 1:22, "And hath made him to be head over all things to the church." And 'tis in order to their eternal life, John 17:2, "And thou hast given him power over all flesh, that he might give eternal life to as many as thou hast given him." 'Tis an evidence that all things are for the sake of the happiness of the saints, which they have by redemption, that all things are put under the Redeemer of the saints. As all things are made for the redeemed, so they are all made for Christ as their Mediator. Col. 1:16–18, "All things were created by him, and for him: and he is before all things, and by him all things consist: and he is the head of the body, the church." It is mentioned in Mark 2:27–28 as the reason why the Son of man is made Lord of the sabbath, that "the sabbath was made for man"; and if so, there is doubtless the same reason that the Son of man is made Lord of all things, viz. that all things were made for man, i.e. for those men that are Christ's to be redeemed by him. Because the works of providence are all for the saints, therefore it is that the ministers of providence, the angels, are all put in subjection to their head and Redeemer: it is that they may be all ministering spirits sent forth to minister to them that shall be the heirs of salvation, as we are taught Heb. 1:6 and 14.

8. 'Tis a further evidence that all things are subordinate to the redemption and happiness of the saints, that not [only] is their Redeemer set over all things, but they are set over all things and shall reign over all things in and with him. They shall reign over all things as sitting with Christ in his throne (Rev. 2:26–27). Yea,

9. We are expressly informed in Scripture that all things are theirs who are the redeemed of Christ; as I Cor. 3:21–22, "All things are yours; whether Paul, or Apollos, or Cephas, or the world, or life, or death, or things present, or things to come; all are yours." The angels are expressly

6. MS: "And as."

called their angels, and therefore doubtless were made for them. 'Tis nowhere said that they are the angels, as the angels are said to be theirs. And so the Apostle says of himself that he possesses all things (II Cor. 6:10). Now all things are theirs no otherwise than as they are for their good.

10. 'Tis an evidence that the work of redemption and the making happy sinful men in Christ, is that for which all things are done and to which all things are ultimately directed, that the consummation of all things is committed into the hands of Christ as Redeemer and subjected to the redeemed themselves in him. If we would know what is the end of all things, we must look to the end of all things and see how they conclude. If we look there, we shall see that the concluding or winding up of things (if I may so speak), wherein the final issue and event of things is to be brought about, is committed into the hands of Christ as the head and Redeemer of the church, and they have communion with him in it. 'Tis left with him to finish things off, to bring 'em to their last issue. 'Tis left with him therefore to judge the world, and put an end to the present state of things, and fix all things in their eternal state. This is a plain intimation that the happiness of him whose Redeemer he is, is the end of all things; especially considering that they shall bear a part with him in it as having communion with him, for they shall judge the world and even angels with him (I Cor. 6:2–3). Because all things are subordinate to the work of redemption, therefore both the beginning and the end of the world is by the Redeemer; and he is appointed of the Father to be both the Creator and the Judge of the world, and is, as he says in the Revelation, the Alpha and the Omega.

11. This is further evident by considering what it is that will be brought to pass, introduced and established by this final consummation of all things: and that is the perfection of the redemption of the church and the everlasting kingdom of the redeemed. The last kingdom which God will set up in the world will be a kingdom wherein the saints shall reign, which will be begun in an anticipation of it in the last state of things in this world, before it's destruction by the conflagration. In Rev. 5:10 we have the saints singing to Christ, "Thou hast made us to our God kings and priests: and we shall reign on earth." And this dominion of the saints will be the last kingdom after all the great kingdoms and monarchies of the earth are destroyed, and utterly brought to an end. And the perfection of this kingdom will be after Christ has put down all principality and power. [In] Dan. 7, after giving an account of other great monarchies succeeding one another and the kingdom of Antichrist as the last of them, 'tis said, "But the

judgment shall sit, and they shall take away his dominion, to consume and to destroy it unto the end. And the kingdom and dominion, and the greatness of the kingdom under the whole heaven, shall be given to the people of the saints of the Most High, whose kingdom is an everlasting kingdom, and all dominions shall serve and obey him" (vv. 26–27). In Rev. 20 there is an account of the glorious kingdom of the saints before the end of the world represented by that, that the souls of the saints lived and reigned with Christ a thousand years. But in the 22nd and last chapter is an account of their dominion in the last and consummate state of things, as in vv. 3–5, "And there shall be no more curse: but the throne of God and of the Lamb shall be in it; and his servants shall serve him: and they shall see his face; and his name shall be in their foreheads. And there shall be no night there; and they need no candle, neither light of the sun; for the Lord God giveth them light: *and they shall reign forever and ever.*" We may well conclude that this last and everlasting kingdom is the end of all foregoing kingdoms and monarchies, and all the changes and revolutions and all that comes to pass from the beginning to the end, they all doubtless tended to this consummate state of things.

12. 'Tis represented in Scripture as though the whole creation were laboring and travailing to bring forth this perfect redemption of the elect. Rom. 8:19, "For the earnest expectation of the creature waiteth for the manifestation of the sons of God"; and v. 22, "For we know that the whole creation groaneth and travaileth in pain together until now," with the context. All the creatures in all their motions, operations and changes are seeking this end, viz. the perfect redemption of the elect, and never will be at rest till that glorious and eternal reign of the saints is established. And therefore 'tis said there in that context, vv. 28–30, "And we know that all things shall work together for good to them that love God, to them who are the called according to his purpose." And [in] the verses following it tells what good of theirs all things conspire to seek, viz. that they should be called and conformed to the image of Christ, and that they should be justified, and that they should be glorified.

So that the work of God is but one, so far as the works of God are made known to us, for I would say nothing of possible unrevealed works with which we have nothing to do. 'Tis not many works that are separate and not dependent, or subordinate. 'Tis but one work. 'Tis all one scheme, one contrivance; and that is the scheme, contrivance and work of glorifying himself and his Son Jesus Christ, and gathering and uniting his creatures to himself, and making them happy in himself through Christ Godman by means of that glorious redemption that he has wrought out. And when this design was revealed by [his] coming into the world and accomplishing this great work, it was an opening to the view of angels and saints God's great design in all that he had been doing from the first foundation of the world; which had been till then all along in a great degree a mystery to them, and that seems to be plainly the Apostle's meaning, Eph. 3:9–11, "And to make all men [see] what is the fellowship of the mystery, which from the beginning of the world hath been hid in God, who created all things by Jesus Christ: to the intent that now unto the principalities and powers in heavenly places might be known by the church the manifold wisdom [of God], according to the eternal purpose which he purposed in Christ Jesus our Lord" (see Rom. 16:25–26 and Col. 1:26). The sum of the wisdom of God in all his works appears in bringing to pass this great event; and thus the manifold wisdom of God appeared by it to the angels, who desire to look into these things, in that by this his wise and great design now was made manifest in all his manifold works that they had seen, and till now never understood the meaning of. And that "eternal purpose which God purposed in Christ Jesus our Lord," mentioned here in v. 11, is a comprehension of all God's eternal decrees and purposes. All of [this] was comprehended in that eternal transaction that there was between the Father and the Son, even the covenant of redemption, in the revealing God's purpose of gathering together in one all things in heaven and earth in Christ. By accomplishing it in the fullness of time, the whole mystery of all God's eternal will and sovereign purposes is made manifest; as in Eph. 1:9–10, "Having made known unto us the mystery of his will, according to his good pleasure which he hath purposed in himself: that in the dispensation of the fullness of times he might gather together in one all things in Christ, both which are in heaven, and which are on earth; even in him." Everything that God has purposed he has purposed in Christ the Redeemer. All his purposes are included in the work of redemption and all that [he] has done or will do in fulfillment of those purposes, is done in and by Christ. He created the world by Christ; all things visible and invisible were created by him and for him. He governed the church of old by Christ. He governs heaven and earth by Christ. The consummation of all things will be by Christ. The world will be brought to an end by him; and the last issue of all things in creation and providence will be brought forth by Christ the Redeemer; and the ultimate end of all things in all their motions, changes and revolutions from the beginning, will be accomplished by Christ God-man, Mediator. All God's enemies will be conquered by him. All God's elect will be gathered together to God by him. All rational creatures, angels [and] men, will be judged by him. Reprobate men and angels will be punished by being made his footstool, and dashed in pieces with his rod of iron; and elect men and angels will have the reward and crown from his hands, and will be eternally happy in God through him. The end of the creation of God was to provide a spouse for his Son Jesus Christ that might enjoy him and on whom he might pour forth his love. And the end of all things in providence are to make way for the exceeding expressions of Christ's love to his spouse and for her exceeding close and intimate union with, and high and glorious enjoyment of, him and to bring this to pass. And therefore the last thing and the issue of all things is the marriage of the Lamb. And the wedding day is the last day, the day of judgment, or rather that will be the beginning of it. The wedding feast is eternal; and the love and joys, the songs, entertainments and glories of the wedding never will be ended. It will be an everlasting wedding day.

Corol. 1. Hence [it] is a great confirmation that God's communicating happiness to the creature stands in the place of a supreme end, because we see that that work, even the making the creature happy by redemption, is the end of all God's other works. See Nos. 461, 445.

Corol. 2. Hence we may undoubtedly conclude that the redeemed of Jesus Christ will be advanced to greater honor and happiness, and a more intimate union and communion with God, than the glorious angels, seeing all God's works are in subordination to the work of the redemption of mankind, or making them happy by redemption, which is the same thing. And even the angels themselves were created in order to this; and so their very beings are in order to the happiness of the redeemed. Without doubt their happiness and glory will be superior to that of the angels. The world was created that Christ might obtain a spouse (see note on Eph. 1:22–23, "Notes on Scripture," no. 235).[7] In this way has God been pleased to make it manifest that the happiness and glory of every blessed creature, is purely owing to his sovereign eternal electing love. And therefore, [he] hath not chosen the highest rank of beings to make them the chief objects of his love; but he has chosen those that are much inferior unto them. However God has created various ranks of intelligent beings, yet 'tis but one species that is peculiarly the beloved race; and we are told who they are, Prov. 8:31, "Rejoicing in the habitable parts of his earth; and my delights were with the sons of *men*." Infinite wisdom did not choose those[8] creatures that were in their first creation set in heaven in such an exceeding exaltation;

---

7. See *Works*, *15*, 185–87.
8. MS: "chose to this those."

but these were above all others the elect species or race chosen to have his love most gloriously manifested to them, and to enjoy most of it, and to be brought to the most intimate union with him; should be fetched up from a lower and meaner world, from a weak and feeble state, and not only so, but should be brought up from an universally ruined state, from exceeding depths of sin and misery, hereby gloriously manifesting his sovereignty.

He wisely chose those to the highest happiness in whom appears[9] an absolute and most universal and exceeding dependence on him, on his power and wisdom, and sovereign and infinite goodness, and free love: for happiness might be most conspicuous and in most ways, that they who are most obliged for the greatness of the gift might be most obliged also to gratitude and praise and humble and thankful admiration for the manner of giving, that those who are most honored and exalted might have the most abundant occasion to cast themselves down low in humility.

'Tis an evidence of this, that there has been far the greatest manifestation of the love of God to this race, such as was in sending his only begotten Son into the world to die for them. God never gave any manifestation of his love to the angels in any wise comparable to this. Seeing therefore that the love of God has been most manifested to them, it will doubtless be most enjoyed by them. The manifestation is in order to enjoyment. Those that God is pleased to show most love to, we may well suppose he has set his love most upon. God communicates his love to enjoyment by manifestation. None can enjoy [but] only as God manifests; the enjoyment therefore will be proportionable to the manifestation. The angels admire and desire to look into the manifestations of God's love to men.

And it was a great evidence that the human and not the angelical nature was the nature that God intended to bring nearest to himself, that he took one of this nature into a personal union with himself to be the head and king of the angels; therein as it were assuming all the elect that were in that nature, who are all united to him as members to the head. Heb. 2:16, "For verily he took not on him the nature of angels; but he took on him the seed of Abraham." Elect men have an higher honor than the angels, for concerning them Christ has said the angels are their angels, though they are but little children; but concerning the angels hath he said at any time that the saints are their saints? (See No. 103.) Hence the

9. MS: "in ⟨appears⟩ whom."

church of saints is not only called God's son, as the angels are, but is called God's first born. See note on Ex. 4:22.[1]

If any object against this that it seems not suitable thus to advance an inferior nature above one that is so much superior, a full and sufficient answer to all objections[2] is that, 'tis certain that it has pleased God to advance this very same nature to a vast and immense superiority above the angels in the person of Christ, making the man Christ Jesus Lord of all the angels, in communion with the Logos. So that we see all that in this instance is done that is objected against. If it ben't thought by God improper to so advance this nature in Christ, why should we suppose that God looks on it improper to set this nature higher than they, in those that are Christ's—that are his spouses and his members—the saints in Christ, in this honor of being nearer to God than the angels? As Christ with respect to the angels and every creature is God's firstborn, so the saints are the church of the firstborn, as they are said to be, when mentioned with the company of angels in Heb. 12:22–23. The members of Christ will have communion with Christ in his dominion, for they shall sit with him in his throne. And as Christ is Lord of the angels, so the saints shall in some sort reign over angels in heaven. This dominion will extend to all things that shall be theirs. Whatsoever they shall inherit as joint heirs with Christ, they shall in some respect reign over as kings with Christ. But the angels are some of those things that are theirs, that they inherit as heirs with Christ: for the angels are their angels, and they "shall judge the angels" (I Cor. 6:3); which we have no reason to confine to the fallen angels, when both the elect angels and the fallen angels will doubtless be judged at the day of judgment. But this dominion will be exercised in no wise separately by themselves, only in and through Christ their head, as partaking with him, and as reigning in and by him, and as being honored by the angels in him.

Corol. 3. This greatly strengthens the probability that God's design of accomplishing this work should be early, in some degree, revealed in heaven to the angels, even soon after they were created. Seeing that this was the end of the creation of all things, and seeing that the angels were early created that they might be the spectators of God's work in creating the world—especially of the creation of this lower world that was created

---

1. The "Blank Bible" note on Ex. 4:22 states, "This is especially agreeable to the spiritual Israel, and is spoken of as they were visibly God's saints; and as the spiritual Israel was contained in this nation, and as they were a type of the spiritual Israel." The church will be dealt with "as a first born" that "was to have a double portion." This note includes an integral cross-reference to "Miscellanies" No. 702.

2. MS: "subjections."

or brought into form after they were created, and they beheld it and praised God for it (Job 38:4–7)—and seeing that this world that they beheld the formation of was created to be the seat of this great work, 'tis highly probable that God would give them some notice of his great design in creating this world. And seeing that the angels themselves were created to be the ministers of providence, 'tis probable that God would give them some notice of that work of providence that was the grand design and drift of all God's works of providence; and especially, seeing that the angels had their beings, and station in heaven, and exalted powers given them to that end, that they might be ministers to the Redeemer in that great affair. 'Tis very probable that when God created or was about to create the human nature, the nature that God had determined so to exalt, and to create Adam, one of the elect and beloved race that was to be the spouse and body of Christ, and who in particular is called God's son, and was so eminent a type of Christ, as has been shown,[3] that God then declared the decree to the thrones, dominions, principalities and powers: which God declares to the earthly principalities, dominions and powers in the second Psalm, viz. that this nature that he this day had begotten out of the earthly chaos, should be exalted to the honor of sonship to himself, that one in this nature should be his Son, and as such should be set up as his king on his holy hill of Zion, that he should be king of heaven, and that the uttermost parts of the earth should be given him for his possession, i.e. that he should be king of both heaven and earth, and that those principalities and powers should be required to be subject to him and humbly to worship [him] (vv. 10–12, "Be wise now therefore, O ye kings: be instructed, ye judges of the earth. Serve the Lord with fear, and rejoice with trembling. Kiss the Son, lest he be angry, and ye perish from the way, when his wrath is kindled but a little. Blessed are all they that put their trust in him"); and as 'tis there represented that the kings and princes of the earth, on the notice of this design of God, or when they apprehended such a thing was like to be, took it in disdain and could not bear to submit to this person that God had *anointed* to be king over them, and therefore entered into a conspiracy to oppose and resist this design, and deliver themselves from such subjection (vv. 2–3, "The kings of the earth set themselves, and the rulers take counsel together, against the Lord and against his Anointed, saying, Let us break their bands asunder, and cast away their cords from us"): so that there was such a conspiracy amongst the thrones and principalities

---

3. In the MS JE indicates that he has demonstrated this point on "p. 41." See above, para. 14 of the entry, starting at "Adam in his creation . . . " (pp. 287–88).

in heaven when this decree was declared there, as 'tis there declared that
God in spite of those earthly rulers did set his Son on his holy hill of Zion
according to his decree, and made Christ to rule over these his enemies
with a rod of iron that scorned to submit to his golden scepter, so that he
dashed them in pieces as a potter's vessel, and took the heathen and uttermost parts of the earth that were before under their dominion and gave
'em to his Son for his possession. So hath God done with respect to those
rebelling spiritual dominions and powers. This man whom they despised
and would not submit [to], yet they are subjected to against their wills. He
has power given him over them, and takes the heathen world and uttermost parts of the earth, that they long reigned as gods of gods, out of their
possession into his own; and at last will be their Judge and will rule 'em
with a rod of iron and dash them in pieces as a potter's vessel.

'Tis not unlikely that God in this psalm, in speaking of kings and rulers
of the earth, has an eye both to earthly and also heavenly principalities,
who are often compared one to the other in Scripture, and sometimes are
spoken of under one, as Rev. 21:24 (see my Notes on the Revelation, no.
59).[4] They are both called the sons of God (Ps. 82:6 and Job. 38:7), and
both are called gods, and both seem to be spoken of under one: "Worship
him all ye gods (Ps. 97:7, compared with Heb. 1:6.); which place is parallel with what we have in this second Psalm, "Be wise now therefore, O ye
kings: be instructed, ye judges of the earth. Serve the Lord with fear, and
rejoice with trembling. *Kiss the Son*" [vv. 10–12].

Again, we may argue from the sin of proud ministers who in their office are compared to the angels, as Rev. 2–3. The sin of such ministers the
Apostle signifies to be the same with that of the devil, I Tim. 3:6, "Not a
novice, lest being lifted up with pride he fall into the condemnation of the
devil." The sin and condemnation of such ministers is this, that whereas
they are set to [be] the ministers and servants of a despised and crucified
Christ, and that for his sake they should be the servants of his people that
are committed to their [care], and not carry it as lords over God's heritage (II Cor. 4:5, I Pet. 5:1), and that they should not lift themselves up
above Christ's people of their flock, or exercise dominion over them or
authority upon them, but that they should be least of all and servants of
all (Matt. 20:25–27 and 23:11); they are appointed to serve the members
of Christ and minister unto them, though not set in such place of dignity
as they are, much as the angels are all made ministering spirits to minister to Christ God-man, and sent forth to minister to his saints that are so

---

4. "Notes on the Apocalypse," no. 59 is a comment on Rev. 21–22 (*Works*, 5, 149–158).

much inferior to them: but they being lifted up with pride by the honor they are set in, are not content with this; and being set higher [in] dignity than the rest, scorn to be their servants and ministers, and least of all, as God has appointed, but affect to be lords over God's heritage. And so instead of being ministers for their good, they make merchandise of them, and use them only to aggrandize themselves, and become ravening wolves that devour the flock (Matt. 7:15 and Acts 20:29); as the devil—not content to be a ministering spirit to the beloved race of mankind—has set up himself to be god over men, and is become a roaring lion to devour them. False teachers that thus make merchandise of the flock, instead of being servants for their good, are in their condemnation and punishment compared [to] the angels that fell. "But there were false prophets also among the people, even as there shall be false teachers among you ... And through covetousness shall they with feigned words make merchandise of you: whose judgment now of a long time lingereth not, and their damnation slumbereth not. For if God spared not the angels that sinned, but cast them down to hell, and delivered them into chains of darkness to be reserved unto judgment . . ." (II Pet. 2, at the beginning).

And we may argue particularly from the Romish hierarchy, or *Antichrist*, that [is the] first born of the devil and is his greatest image. As *Christ* is the image of God, so is *Antichrist* the image of the devil (as is evident by comparing these following places in the Revelation: 12:3, 9 and 13:1, 12, 14–15); so that they seem to be often spoken of and signified in Scripture under one. Both are represented by the same types. Thus Pharaoh was a type of the devil, and therefore is called Leviathan and the dragon in the waters. "Thou didst divide the sea by thy strength: thou breakest the heads of the dragons in the waters. Thou breakest the heads of Leviathan in pieces, and gavest him to be meat to the people inhabiting the wilderness" (Ps. 74:13–14). Is. 51:9, "Art thou not it that hath cut Rahab and wounded the dragon?" So Pharaoh is called "the great dragon that lieth in the midst of his rivers" (Ezek. 29:3). So also he was a type of Antichrist: for Egypt in the oppression that the church of Israel suffered there under Pharaoh and his taskmasters, was a type of the church of Rome; as we are directly taught, Rev. 11:8, "And their dead bodies shall lie in the street of the great city, that is spiritually called Sodom and *Egypt*." And therefore the king of Egypt, the oppressor of God's people, is the type of the king of this spiritual Egypt, the persecutor of the Christian church. So also the king of Babylon was a type both of the devil and also Antichrist. He was a type of Antichrist: for the church of Rome is the spiritual Babylon, and therefore is more commonly called in the Revelation by the name of Babylon than anything else. And he was also a type of the devil, as is evident by Is. 14:12–14, for there he is called "Lucifer, a son of the morning," or [the] morning star that fell from heaven. And the devil and Antichrist are both in that place represented under one, as is evident by comparing of it with II Thess. 2:3–4. The ministers of the true church of Christ are the angels of the churches; but the clergy of the false church[5] of Antichrist are devils. But we know the sin of this man of sin is that—whereas he was appointed to be an angel of the church that he should be a minister of a crucified Savior, one that was poor, despised and afflicted, and to be a minister and servant of the people of Christ—he being exceedingly lifted up with pride and affectation of his own dignity and exaltation, scorns the meanness and poverty of Christ, and to be subject to Christ therein, and disdains to be a servant of the people of Christ; and therefore sets up a rebellion against God, seeks to jostle him out of his throne and get into his throne himself (II Thess. 2), and so has set up himself for god of this world, and god over men, and is become a roaring lion to devour the flock, and is drunk with the blood of the saints.

Again, we may argue from various types of the devil that we have in Scripture, as particularly Pharaoh was a type of the devil, as we have shown. His sin that was the occasion of all his other sins that we have an account of, was his proud contempt of the children of Israel and fear lest they should get above him. "And he said unto his people, Behold, the people of the children of Israel is more and mightier than we" [Ex. 1:9]. And at last it was a spirit of envy in Pharaoh against the people of God that occasioned his ruin. He could not bear it, that they were gone forth with an high hand having obtained the victory and gotten as it were above him. And so he pursued after them to bring them under again, and then was drowned in the Red Sea, a type of hell, or the eternal gulf of misery and lake that burns with fire and brimstone. God had made Moses the leader and head of Israel, and therein was a remarkable type of Christ. And God had made him to be, instead of Christ, in the contest with Pharaoh: "See, I have made thee a god to Pharaoh" (Ex. 7:1). He in this contest represented Christ contending with the devil. Pharaoh could not bear that Moses, one of that race that he looked upon so servile and abject, should get above him and obtain victory over him; and therefore, when he went out pursued after him to reduce him, and so was cast from his throne and height of dignity into the bottom of the sea.

We may also argue from the sin and condemnation of the king of Baby-

---

5. MS: "the church of ⟨anti⟩ the false church."

lon, mentioned in Is. 14:12–15, "How art thou fallen from heaven, O Lucifer, son of the morning! How art thou cut down to the ground, which didst weaken the nations! For thou hast said in thine heart, I will ascend into heaven, I will exalt my throne above the stars of God: I will sit also upon the mount of the congregation, in the sides of the north: I will ascend above the height of the clouds; I will be like the Most High. Yet thou shalt be brought down to hell, to the sides of the pit." Here the king of Babylon in his sin and fall is most evidently compared to the devil: for he is called Lucifer, and is represented to be as the devil was before his fall, a morning star (Job. 38:7); his punishment, being cast down from heaven and from exceeding glory there to hell to the lowest disgrace and misery; and the sin mentioned for which he was thus cast down, was that he, being lifted up with pride, was not content to be below but affected to be above the stars of God, i. e. the saints (as is evident by many scriptures), and aspired after the very throne of God himself.

This also appears in Haman, another remarkable type of both the devil and Antichrist. (Concerning his being a type of Antichrist, see my notes on the book of Esther).[6] He seems to be in many things a lively type of the devil: for he was at first a great prince in Ahasuerus' court, was set in exceeding dignity by him but was exceeding proud of his dignity, and was the bitter enemy of the people of God and sought their destruction. He fell suddenly from this height to the lowest disgrace and the most terrible destruction. But the occasion of his fall was that, being exceedingly lifted up, he could not bear that Mordecai, a type of Christ, should appear as one that would not pay honor to him as superior; hence was his enmity against him and all his seed, whence he so exceedingly sought their destruction. But Mordecai, the type of Christ and head of the people of the Jews, the people of God, and their brother, being one of them, was one that King Ahasuerus delighted to honor, as God delighted to honor Jesus Christ God-man. Ahasuerus clothed him with his own royal apparel and set him on the horse that the king was wont to ride upon, and set the crown royal upon his head; as God the Father hath exalted Christ God-man, and hath put his own honor upon him, and hath set his own crown on him, and hath made him King over his kingdom, that all men should honor the Son even as they honor the Father. And Haman himself was appointed to attend on Mordecai in this honor and dignity as his minister and servant, which Haman could not bear. Haman fell into the pit that he had digged, was himself

---

6. The "Blank Bible" note on the book of Esther is simply a cross-reference to "Notes on Scripture," no. 46 (*Works, 15*, 60–63).

hanged on the gallows that he had prepared for Mordecai; and though he intended the destruction of Mordecai and the Queen and all their seed, yet they on the other hand procured his destruction and his friends'. Even as the devil is fallen into the pit that he hath digged, Christ and his church and people that he envied, and would not honor or minister to, whose destruction he sought, are made the means of his destruction, the same destruction that he thought to procure to them. The house of Haman was given to Queen Esther, and Mordecai is put in Haman's place, as Christ and his church shall take the heathen world out of the hands of Satan, and the kingdom of Christ shall be erected on the ruins of Satan's kingdom.

Another remarkable type of the devil is Goliath, who exceedingly lifted up himself in pride in his own strength and monstrous bulk, and disdained the thought of being a servant to Israel (I Sam. 17:9–10); and particularly despised David (the greatest personal type of Christ) in his design of subjecting him to himself, because he appeared in a nature so much inferior to him. But his contempt of David, and defying the armies of Israel, proved his ruin.

This well accounts for that exceeding enmity that Satan manifests against Christ and the race of mankind, in that it was for their sakes that he was cast down from heaven to hell. That was the sin for which he was condemned and cast down, viz. that when God revealed the great love he had to this race, and his design of exceeding honor and happiness to them and to one in their nature, especially that should be his Son, and that the angels should minister to this race, and should be subject to this elect one of the race, and worship him and serve him as their Lord, they envied them this honor, and could not bear to yield it to them, and for this was cast into eternal [misery]. Hence, they have an exceeding inveterate spite against mankind, and against Christ in particular, and do their utmost to prevent that honor and happiness that God has revealed as designed for them, and to prevent their own being subjected to 'em and brought under 'em; which they are aware God is set to bring to pass since their fall, that they may not get their wills in that regard. They look upon the honor and happiness of mankind in all degrees of it as so many steps towards the fulfillment of this, viz. their being set above them and over them. Their pride therefore stirs them up to labor with indefatigable industry and their utmost craft—instead of being subject to them, and to one of them as their King and their God, as God has declared—themselves to rule over them, and reign over them as god, to make himself[7] god of this world:

7. I.e. Satan.

hence, such endeavors to reign over 'em as their god in this world, and such endeavors to carry 'em captives to hell and tyrannize over 'em there; hence, such indefatigable endeavors to get the victory over Christ when he was in the world. Hence, he would fain persuade him to fall down and worship him. Hence, he so indefatigably labored to bring him into the greatest contempt and disgrace, and to be put to the most ignominious death, and the death of a slave in particular; which was most gratifying to him who was cast out of heaven for refusing to be minister and servant to him, and [to] seek humbly to worship him. How pleasing may we well think it was to the devil to see Christ mocked and spit upon and crucified, instead of himself humbly serving and worshipping him, as God had said. See Nos. 320, 438, 664, §§ 6–9.

Corol. 4. Hence also 'tis the more probable that the sin and fall of the reprobate angels should be with reference to this work, but that the confirmation and reward of the elect angels should also have a near concern with this work, since that the work of redemption by Jesus Christ God-man is that work to which all the other works of God are subordinate, and that which all intelligent beings and even the angels were created with an eye to. God hath so ordered it that all the great concerns and events of the universe should be some way concerning of this work, and bearing some respect to it, and as it were some way interwoven with it, that the occasion of the fall of some of the angels should be something about this, and the confirmation and reward of others should be for something relating to this: for seeing this work is their end, 'tis probable that the undoing of those that fell was their opposition to this their end, and that what proves the eternal happiness of the rest is their falling in with their end, and cheerfully submitting to God in it. And as both the occasion of [the fall of] some, and the ground of the reward of others, was something about this work; so God's end in permitting the fall of some, and his preserving others, was this work. The fall of the devils was wisely permitted and ordered to give occasion for a redemption from that evil they should introduce, and that the Redeemer might be glorified in their ruin. And the preservation of the others was that they might minister to the Redeemer in the work; might be to his glory in their submission to him and attendance on him, and might receive their reward at his hands for their submission to him in this work; and that they might employ their glorious wisdom in contemplating the wonders of the work, and praising the Father and the Son for it, and declaring of it to others. See No. 515.

Corol. 5. Hence we may learn a reason why the fall of man was so soon permitted: because the world being made for the work of redemption,

God did not see meet that it should stand long without occasion for that work.

Corol. 6. Hence 'tis no wonder that Christ has been so variously and manifoldly revealed, and that God hath so abundantly spoken of him; that he was so soon revealed and promised to man after he fell, and has been so much spoken to and in the church in all ages from the beginning of the world; and that Christ and his redemption are so much spoken of in the Word of God from the beginning of the Bible to the end of it; so much insisted on [in] the prophecies, promises and song of the Scripture; and that so many things were appointed of God to typify things pertaining to this, and so much done for so many ages in order to it, so many things recorded in history that are typical of it; and that so much is made of this work by Christ and his apostles in the New Testament.

Corol. 7. Hence it is that in this work, though in no other, God doth distinctly manifest himself in each of the persons of the Godhead, in their mutual relations one to another, and in that economy there is established amongst them, and in their distinct persons appearing in the eternal agreement and covenant these divine persons entered into about this work, and in the several offices and parts which each one bears in it, and how they are therein concerned one with another. 'Tis meet that this should be in the greatest and supreme work of God to which all other works are subordinate.

Corol. 8. Hence no wonder that faith in Christ, or the heart's closing with Christ as Redeemer, should be insisted on in the Word of God as so great a duty, so necessary and important, and that it should be made the great condition of salvation. And no wonder that unbelief, or the heart's disallowing and rejecting Christ and his redemption, should be reckoned as so great a sin; and that self-righteousness, or ascribing our salvation to our own works and not Christ's redemption, should be set forth to be so fatal to the soul.

Corol. 9. Hence 'tis no wonder that that design and purpose of the sabbath, that consists in commemorating God's rest from the old creation, should give place to the commemoration of God's finishing this so much greater work of the creation, which the old was but a shadow of, and was done wholly in subserviency to. No wonder that when the Prophet is making comparison between these two creations—the former and the latter—he says, "the former shall not be remembered, nor come into mind" (Is. 65:17).

Corol. 10. Hence how greatly are those ministers to blame who in a great measure neglect Christ in their preaching, who insist on morality only, and that in such a manner as to find but little occasion to mention the name of Christ, the Redeemer, and his glorious work of redemption.

Corol. 11. Hence we may well infer that the glory and happiness that the saints will be brought to by redemption, will immensely exceed the happiness that man was possessed of before the fall, or that he could have expected if he had stood; for this happiness of man by redemption is the great end of all things, the end of the work of creation, the end of all God's dispensations towards man before the fall, and what those things were but types of, as has been shown.[8] Both that happiness that man had before he fell, and that which he had to expect if he did not fall, were but types and shadows of this happiness; so that this happiness exceeds that, as antitypes are wont to exceed types. That garden was but a type of the heavenly paradise; that tree of life, but a type of the true tree of life, and therefore answerably hereto; the blessedness that would have followed the eating of that tree if man had stood, but a type of the blessedness that comes by the eating of the fruit of the true tree of life. Adam, in being the head of that covenant, was but a type of Christ, the second Adam, as has been plainly shown. And therefore, the happiness he by his obedience would have brought his posterity to, is but a type of [the happiness] the second Adam, the Lord from heaven, will bring his children to. As the second Adam is a more worthy and more glorious person than the first, and his obedience immensely more excellent than the perfect obedience of the first Adam would have been; so will the blessedness he procures for his spiritual posterity by his obedience be more glorious than that which the first Adam would have obtained for his posterity.

703. SIN AGAINST THE HOLY GHOST. See No. 475. In order to [commit] the sin against the Holy Ghost, persons must appear in avowed malicious opposition and contumacy against[9] the Holy Ghost in his work and office, and as communicated to men, and acting in them, either in his ordinary or extraordinary influences and operations. This is what is sometimes

---

8. In the MS JE indicates that he demonstrated this point on "p. 40 &c—." See above, pp. 284 ff.

9. At this point in the MS, JE deleted the following lines: "or as acting in the Godhead, or against those things in God that may be resolved into the divine Spirit, as particularly the holiness of God which is not indeed different from the Holy Ghost, for every man that hates God hates him for his holiness. And so if he hates the Father, or hates the Son, he hates him for the Holy Ghost which proceeds from them; and so every man that blasphemes the Father or the Son, and so expresses his malice against them, he blasphemes them for that which is the Holy Ghost in them, or proceeding from them. But Christ has told us that if men blaspheme the Father or the Son they shall be forgiven, but that which they reproach must be."

meant by the Holy Ghost in Scripture. Acts 19:2, "He said unto them, Have ye received the Holy Ghost since ye believed? And they said unto him, We have not so much as heard whether there be an Holy Ghost." It must be against conviction, reproaching the Holy Ghost in his gracious merciful communications to and operations in men, whether those communications and operations are ordinary or extraordinary. 'Tis reproaching the Holy Ghost as the Spirit of grace. Heb. 10:29, He "hath done despite to the Spirit of grace." The word in the original signifies treating with petulant, proud and insolent reproach (see Mastricht, p. 363, col. 1).[1] Reproaching the Holy Ghost in his extraordinary and miraculous gifts and operations was this blasphemy against the Holy Ghost. So did they to a great degree who themselves had those extraordinary gifts, that yet totally apostatized from Christianity and turned persecutors, spoken of, Heb. 6:4–6, "For 'tis impossible for those who were once enlightened, and have tasted of the heavenly gift, and were made partakers of *the Holy Ghost*, and have tasted the good word of God, and the powers of the world to come, if they shall fall away, to renew them again to repentance; *seeing they crucify to themselves the Son of God afresh, and put him to an open shame.*" Reproaching the Spirit of God as thus communicated to men, and operating in them, is blasphemy against the Holy Ghost, whatever man it be in. If it be as being communicated to the man Christ Jesus, there is no reason why it should not be looked upon as a sin of the same nature and kind; as if in any other man to reproach the Holy Ghost in that man that was the elder brother and the head of all the rest, is as much this sin as to reproach him in any of the other brethren. Hence, the Jews reproaching the Holy Ghost in Christ, and calling him Beelzebub, was blasphemy against the Holy Ghost. If they had reproached anything else in Christ, as reproaching him for being the carpenter's son, [it] would not have been this sin, for blasphemy against the Son shall be forgiven.

With respect to the ground of the unpardonableness of this sin, this is not properly the greatness or heinousness of it, or because it brings such a degree of guilt, but God's arbitrary constitution. The exceeding aggravations of this sin, its being the most aggravated sort of sin, may be one reason why God in wisdom has seen meet so to constitute that it never

---

1. "Sic sonat in generaliore vocis significatu: hic autem, magis grave & horrible vilipendium Sp. S. idque malitiosum, adversus cognitionem, id quod alibi Heb. x. 29. Apostolus exprimit per υβριζοντες, quod proprié notat petulantiam & proclivitatem in reprehendendo & contemnendo." Peter van Mastricht, *Theoretico-practica theologia* (see above, No. 609, p. 145, n. 1). In the 1st ed. of the *Theoretico-practico theologia* there are two sets of pp. 325–424; JE's reference is to the second p. 363 [i.e. p. 463], col. 1.

should be pardoned, to be a warning to men to take heed how they go great lengths in sin, and for other wise ends. But the mere heinousness of it or degree of guilt, without regard to these wise ends and good consequences of such a constitution, is not the thing that renders it unpardonable. For if so, then it would follow that the same degree of guilt, wherever it was and however contracted, was always unpardonable; whereas we have no ground to conclude that none are ever pardoned that have contracted as great a degree of guilt as is contracted by an act of this sin: for though we should suppose this sin vastly more heinous than 'tis possible for any other sin to be, yet it can't be supposed impossible for a man, by multiplying other sins, to contract as great guilt as a man contracts by one act of blasphemy against the Holy Ghost. 'Tis possible that a man should fill up great part of his life with acts of blasphemy against the Father and the Son, together with all manner of other most heinous sins, whereby his guilt might doubtless far exceed the guilt of one act of sin against the Holy Ghost, but yet this would not be unpardonable: for Christ has expressly taught us that all manner of sins and blasphemies, wherewith soever they shall blaspheme, shall be forgiven unto men, but the blasphemy against the Holy Ghost. And I don't know that we have any certain ground to conclude that 'tis not possible for any other particular sin to be as heinous as an act of this sin, or that blasphemy against the Father and against the Son can't be so circumstanced and aggravated as to bring equal guilt with it. To suppose that 'tis the degree of guilt that properly rendered this sin unpardonable, is to suppose that God's mercy is not equally sufficient to pardon some sins, as others; or that Christ's blood was not as sufficient to satisfy for the greatest sins as the smallest.

'Tis therefore a grand mistake that persons under trouble, that are tempted to think that they have committed the unpardonable sin, ordinarily argue upon. For this is the principle they most commonly go upon, viz. that some sin is unpardonable, and beyond the reach of pardoning mercy, because of the heinousness of it. And they think some sin of theirs that their minds are fixed [upon], is bad enough to be unpardonable. They therefore conclude it to be the unpardonable sin, without looking into the Word of God to compare it with the description given of that particular sin called blasphemy against the Holy Ghost. See No. 706.

Join this with No. 475, the third particular.[2] Blaspheming against the Holy Ghost possibly may be done without words, but it can't be done

2. See *Works*, *13*, 519.

merely with the heart, or in the thoughts; for whether blaspheming necessarily implies speaking words or no, yet thus much it implies, viz. that
the malice and contempt that there is in the heart be some way professed
and avowed. There is, besides malice, that horrid presumption and contumacy, as in a willful manner openly to appear in it, and profess and
declare it, and stand in it. If it ben't done by words, it must be done by
actions that carry a plain, open, owning and declaring, contemptuous
malice. I can think of but three ways of appearing in avowed contempt
and reproach against the Holy Ghost, viz. either first, by reproaches in
words; or secondly, by appearing in open and declared war against it,
which is done by persecution; or thirdly, by apostasy and open renouncing Christianity, with the Spirit that confirms it. For persecution against
the Spirit of God in the saints—openly and manifestly for that—against
light, seems to be this sin, as well as reproaching the Holy Spirit. Hence
Christ prays that the Father would forgive those that crucified him, because they knew not what they did [Luke 23:34]; signifying that otherwise
there would be no forgiveness (see note on the place).[3] So the Apostle, in
what he is declaring how he persecuted the saints, says he "obtained
mercy, because he did it ignorantly and in unbelief" (I Tim. 1:13); intimating that if he had done it knowingly there would have been no mercy
for him. And indeed, persecuting may well be called a blaspheming that
which is persecuted. 'Tis declaring and avowing malice and contempt as
openly and with as much presumption and boldness as if done in words.
And indeed 'tis difficult to conceive how a man can appear in open war
against the Holy Spirit in the saints by persecution, without also professing and declaring their malice in words; and probably never is, especially
when the persecutors ben't heathen, but professors of religion, and them
that have been enlightened. Thus the Apostle, when he is speaking of
what he did, which if he had done against light he should not have obtained mercy, joins blaspheming and persecuting together. I Tim. 1:13,
"Who was before a blasphemer, and a persecutor and injurious: but I obtained mercy, because I did it ignorantly in unbelief" (see note on the
place).[4]

3. The "Blank Bible" note on Luke 23:34 states, "If they had known what they did, their sin
would have been the unpardonable sin, for their malice and persecution against Christ was principally for that Spirit that he spake and acted by."

4. In the "Blank Bible" note on I Tim. 1:13, JE maintains that Paul, when he persecuted the
church, doubtless committed blasphemies against the Holy Ghost, but "he did it ignorantly and
in unbelief. If he had done it against light and had knowledge, it would have been the unpardonable sin."

Blaspheming and persecuting were joined together in those Pharisees that charged Christ with casting out devils by Beelzebub. They were joined together in those that crucified Christ, who could never have been forgiven if they had done it against light. They knew he had wrought miracles; but they crucified him under that notion, that what he did was by the help of Beelzebub, and by the power of Satan. And their malice against him was for his holy doctrine and practice, which galled them, and which they therefore reproached as being from hell and by the influence of the devil; for the Pharisees had infused that notion into the people that he acted and was assisted by the devil. Blasphemy and persecution are joined together in Antichrist, that greatest of all persecutors. We read of the seven headed beast that on his heads were written the name of blasphemy (Rev. 13:1 and 17:3). And in ch. 13, [the] fifth, sixth and seventh verses of that chapter, 'tis said of him, "And there was given unto him a mouth speaking great things and blasphemies . . . And he opened his mouth in blasphemy against God, to blaspheme his name, and his tabernacle, and them that dwell in heaven. And it was given unto him to make war with the saints." And Dan. 7:25, "And he shall speak great words against the Most High, and shall wear out the saints of the Most High." Persecution and blasphemy are joined together, as what went together, in Jas. 2:6–7. "Do not rich men oppress you, and draw you before the judgment seats? Do not they blaspheme that worthy name by which ye are called?" They were joined together in the Jews at Corinth. Acts 18:6, "They opposed themselves and blasphemed"; v. 12, "The Jews made insurrection against Paul, and brought him to the judgment seat." The Psalmist speaks of them as joined together in the persecutors and enemies of the church: "They said in their hearts, Let us destroy them together: they have burnt up all the synagogues of God in the land" (Ps. 74:8). V. 10, "O God, how long shall the adversary reproach? shall the enemy blaspheme thy name forever?" (See also vv. 18–19 and vv. 21–23.) They were joined together in Rabshakah when he came up against Jerusalem: "This day is a day of trouble, and rebuke, and blasphemy" (II Kgs. 19:3).

And moreover, it seems to be common among those that are professors of the worship of the true God, that are bitter persecutors of the saints for their holiness, but what are guilty of blasphemy this way, viz. in laying that holiness which they persecute them for to the devil. So the papists were wont to put on those that they burnt for the Protestant religion a cap painted with devils.

And as persecution is commonly attended with blasphemy in words, so 'tis probable that those that reproach the Holy Ghost so as to be guilty of this unpardonable sin, are generally, if not universally, persecutors. Those that Christ speaks of were so; and those that the Apostle speaks of in the sixth and the tenth chapters of Hebrews seem plainly to have been so. Heb. 6:6, "They crucify the Son of God afresh," i.e. in his members. And in the tenth chapter, vv. 25–39, he evidently has respect to some that were persecutors, by what follows in the chapter. 'Tis certain they can't be guilty of that sin without a great degree of a persecuting spirit, and a great manifestation of it. That malice that there [is] in it, is of that nature.

Another way of open blaspheming the Holy Ghost indeed possibly may be by apostasy, and open renouncing Christianity, with the spirit that confirms it and is the soul of it. So renouncing can't be done without reproaching, and indeed a declared open renouncing Christianity and its Spirit can scarcely be itself distinguished from reproaching in words, for this renunciation is declared by words. (Of this see more in note on Heb. 6:4–6, no. 227, and also note on Heb. 10:25–29, no. 230.)[5]

There seems to be no hint in Scripture of any other ways of expressing contempt and malice against the Holy Ghost, so as to be the unpardonable blasphemy, but these three. And this last is commonly and perhaps always attended with the other two. The Pharisees that Christ charges with the sin against the Holy Ghost were therein guilty of something that was of the nature of apostasy; as appears by what Christ in the same place says, "When the unclean spirit is gone out of a man, he walketh through dry places, seeking rest; and finding none, he saith, I will return unto my house whence I came out" (Luke 11:24).

704. DECREES. PREDESTINATION. SUPRALAPSARIANS. SUBLAPSARIANS. See No. 700. What divines intend by prior and posterior in the affair of God's decrees, is not that one is before another in the order of time, for all are from eternity, but that we must conceive the view or consideration of one decree to be before another, inasmuch as God decrees one thing out of respect to another decree that he has made; so that one decree must be conceived of as in some sort to be the ground of another, or that God decrees one because of another, or that he would not have decreed one had he not decreed that other.

Now there are two ways in which divine decrees may be said to be in this sense prior one to another:

1. When one thing decreed is the end of another. This must in some respect be conceived of as prior to that other. The good to be obtained is in

---

5. See *Works*, *15*, 176–77, 179–81.

some respect prior in the consideration of him who decrees and disposes to the means of obtaining it. And,

2. When one thing decreed is the ground on which the disposer goes in seeking such an end by another thing decreed, as being the foundation of the capableness or fitness that there is in that other thing decreed to obtain such an end. Thus the sinfulness of the reprobate is the ground on which God goes in determining to glorify his justice in the punishment of his sinfulness, because that his sinfulness is the foundation of the possibility of obtaining that end by such means. His having sin is the foundation of both the fitness and [the] possibility of justice being glorified in the punishment of his sin; and therefore, the consideration of the being of sin in the subject must in some respect be prior in the mind of the disposer to the determination to glorify his justice in the punishment of sin: for the disposer must first consider the capableness and aptness of such means for such an end before he determines them to such an end. Thus God must be conceived of as first considering Adonibezek's cruelty in cutting off the thumbs and great toes of threescore kings, as that which was to be before he decreed to glorify his justice in punishing that cruelty by the cutting off of his thumbs and great toes: for God in this last decree has respect to the fitness and aptness of his thumbs and great toes being cut off, to glorify his justice [Judg. 1:6–7]. But this aptness depends on the nature of that sin that was punished; and therefore, the disposer in fixing on those means for this end must be conceived of as having that sin in view. Not only must God be conceived of as having some end in consideration, before he determines the means in order to that end; but also must he be conceived of as having a consideration of the capableness or aptness of the means to obtain the end, before he fixes on the means. Both these, in different respects, may be said to be prior to the means decreed to such end in the mind of the disposer. Both in different respects are the ground or reason of the appointment of the means. The end is the ground or reason of the appointment of the means, and also the capacity and fitness of the means to the end is the ground or reason of their appointment to such an end. So both the sin of the reprobate, and also the glory of divine justice, may properly be said to be before the decree of damning the reprobate. The decree of damnation may properly be said, in different respects, to be because of both these; and that God would not have decreed the damnation of the sinner, had [it] not been for [the] respect he had both to the one and the other. Both may properly be considered as the ground of the decree of damnation. The view of the[6] sin-

---

6. MS: "their."

fulness of the reprobate must be in some respect prior in the decree, to God's decree to glorify his justice in punishing their sinfulness, because sinfulness is necessarily supposed *or already put* in the decree of punishing sinfulness. And the decree of damnation being posterior to the consideration of the sin of men in this latter respect, clears God of any injustice in such a decree.

That which stands in the place of the ultimate end in the decree, i.e. that is a mere end and not a means to anything further or higher, viz. the shining forth of God's glory, and the communication of his goodness, must indeed be considered as prior in the consideration of the supreme disposer to everything, excepting the mere possibility of it; but this must in some respect be conceived as prior to that, because possibility is necessarily supposed in this decree. But if we descend lower than the highest end, if we come down to other events decreed that ben't mere ends but means to obtain that end, then[7] we must necessarily bring in more things as in some respect prior, in the same manner as mere possibility is in this highest decree; because that more things must necessarily be supposed, or considered as put in the decree, in order to those things decreed reaching the end for which they are decreed. More things must be supposed in order to a possibility of these things taking place as subordinate to their end; and therefore, they stand in the same place, in these lower decrees, as absolute possibility does in the decree of the highest end. The vindictive justice of God is not to be considered as a mere or ultimate end, but as a means to an end. Indeed, God's glorifying his justice, or rather his glorifying his holiness and greatness, has the place of a mere and ultimate end. But his glorifying his justice in punishing sin (or in exercising vindictive justice, which is the same) or by any other particular means, is not to be considered as a mere end, but a certain way or means of obtaining an end. Vindictive justice is not to be considered as a certain distinct attribute to be glorified, but as a certain way and means for the glorifying an attribute. Every distinct way of God's glorifying or exercising an attribute might as well be called a distinct attribute, as this. 'Tis but giving a distinct name to it; and so we might multiply attributes without end. The considering the glorifying [of] vindictive justice as a mere end, has led to great misrepresentations and undue and unhappy expressions about the decree of reprobation. Hence, the glorifying of God's vindictive justice on such particular persons has been considered as altogether prior in the decree to their sinfulness; yea, [to] their very beings. Whereby it being

7. MS: "and then."

only a means to an end, those things that are necessarily presupposed in order to the fitness and possibility of this means obtaining the end, must be conceived of as prior to it.

Hence God's decree of the eternal damnation of the reprobate, is not to be conceived of as prior to the fall, yea, and to the very being of the person; as the decree of the eternal glory of the elect is. For God's glorifying his love and communicating his goodness stands in the place of a mere or ultimate end, and therefore is prior in the mind of the eternal disposer to the very being of the subject, and to everything but mere possibility. The goodness of God gives the being as well as the happiness of the creature, and don't presuppose it.

Indeed, the glorifying God's mercy, as it presupposes the subject to be miserable, and the glorifying his grace, as it supposes the subject to be sinful, unworthy and ill-deserving, are not to be conceived of as ultimate ends, but only certain ways or means for the glorifying the exceeding abundance and overflowing fullness of God's goodness and love. And therefore, those decrees ben't to be considered as prior to the decree of the being and permission of the fall of the subject, and the decree of election, as it implies. A decree of glorifying God's mercy and grace considers man as being created and fallen, because the very notion of such a decree supposes a great sin and misery.

Hence, we may learn how much in the decree of predestination are to be considered as prior to the creation and fall of man, and how much as posterior, viz. that God's decree to glorify his love and communicate his goodness, and to glorify his greatness and holiness, is to be considered as prior to the creation and fall of man. And because the glory of God's love, and the communication of his goodness, necessarily implies the happiness of the creature, and gives both their being and happiness, hence the designing to communicate and glorify his goodness and love eternally to a certain number, is to be considered as prior in both those mentioned respects—to their being and fall—for such a design in the notion of it presupposes neither. But nothing in the decree of reprobation is to be looked upon as antecedent in one of those respects to man's being and fall, but only that general decree that God will glorify his justice, or rather his holiness and greatness, which supposes neither their being nor sinfulness. But whatsoever there is in this decree of evil to particular subjects, is to be considered as consequent on the decree of their creation, and permission of their fall. And indeed, although all that is in the decree of election, all that respects good to the subjects ben't posterior to the being and fall of man; yet both the decrees of election and rejection or reprobation, as so styled, must be considered as consequent on the decrees concerning the creation and fall, for both these decrees have respect to the distinction or discrimination that is afterwards actually made amongst men in pursuance of these decrees. Hence effectual calling, being the proper execution of election, is sometimes in Scripture called election; and the rejection of men in time is called reprobation. And therefore, these decrees of election and reprobation must be looked upon as beginning there where the actual distinction begins, because distinction is implied in the notion of these decrees. And therefore, whatsoever is prior to this actual distinction—the foresight of it, or decree concerning it, or that state that was common, or wherein they were undistinguished, the foresight of it, or decree concerning it—must be considered in some respect as prior to the decree concerning the distinction: because all that is before, is supposed or looked on as already put in the decree, for that is the decree, viz. to make such a distinction between those that before were in such a common state. And this is agreeable to the Scriptural representations of these decrees. John 15:19, "Ye are not of the world, but I have chosen you out of the world, therefore the world hateth you." See also Ezek. 16:1–8.

The decrees of God must be conceived of in the same order, and as antecedent to and consequent on one another, in the same manner as God's acts in execution of those decrees. If this won't hold with regard to those things that are the effects of those acts, yet certainly it will hold with respect to the acts themselves. They depend on one another, and are grounded on one another, in the same manner as the decrees that those are the execution of, and in no other. For, on the one hand, the decrees of God are no other than his eternal doing what is done, acted or executed by him in time; and, on the other hand, God's acts themselves in executing, can be conceived of no otherwise than as decrees for a present effect. They are acts of God's will. God brings things to pass only by acts of his will. He speaks, and it is done. His will says, Let it be; and it is. And this act of his will that now is, cannot be looked upon as really different from that act of will that was in him before, and from eternity, in decreeing that this thing should be at this time. It differs only relatively. There is no new act of the will in God, but only the same acts of God's will that [were] before, because the time was not come [that] respected future time, and so were called decrees. But now the time being come, [they] respect present time, and so ben't called by us decrees, but acts executing decree. But 'tis evidently the same act in God; and therefore, these acts in executing must certainly be conceived of in the same order, with the same dependence, as the decrees themselves.

It may be in some measure illustrated by this. The decree of God, or the will of God decreeing events, may be represented by a straight line of infinite length that runs through all past eternity and terminates in the event. The last point in the line is the act of God's will in bringing the event to pass, and don't at all differ from all the other points throughout the infinite length of the line, in no other respect but this, that this last point is next to the event. This line may be represented as in motion, but yet always kept parallel to itself. The hither end of the line by its motion describes events in the order in which they come to pass, or at least represents God's acts in bringing the events to pass in their order and mutual dependence, antecedence and consequence, by the motion of all the other points of the line. Before the event, or end of the line, in the whole infinite length of it, is represented the decrees in their order; which because the line in all its motions is kept parallel to itself, is exactly the same with the order of the motions of the last point: for the motion of every point of the whole line is in all respects just like the motion of that last point, wherein the line terminates in the event; and the different parts of the motion of every point are in every respect precisely in the same order. And that maxim, that that which is first in intention is last in execution, don't in the least concern this matter, for by last in execution is meant only last in order of time, without any respect to the priority or posteriority that we are speaking of. And it don't [at] all hinder but that in God's acts in executing his decrees one act is the ground or reason of another act, in the same manner precisely as the decree that related to it was the ground or reason of the other decree. The absolute independence of God no more argues against some of God's decrees being grounded on decrees of some other things that should first come to pass, than it does against some of God's acts in time being grounded on some other of his acts that went before. 'Tis just in God's acts in executing, as has been said already of his decreeing. In one respect, the end that is afterwards to be accomplished is the ground of God's acting; in another respect, something that is already accomplished is the ground of his acting, as 'tis the ground of the fitness or capableness of that act to obtain that end. There is nothing but the ultimate end of all things, viz. God's glory and the communication of his goodness, that is prior to God's first act in creating the world[8] in one respect, and mere possibility in another. But with respect to after acts, other ends are prior in one respect, and other preceding acts are prior in another, just as I have shown it to be with respect to God's decrees.

8. MS: "all ~~Gods~~ ⟨first act in creating the world⟩ ~~actions and executions~~."

Now this being established, it may help more clearly to illustrate and fully to evidence what we have insisted on concerning the order of the decrees; and that God's decrees of some things that are to [be] accomplished first in order of time, are also prior in the order so as to be the proper ground and reason of other decrees. For let us see how it is in God's acts in executing his decrees: will any deny that God's act in rewarding for righteousness is grounded on a foregoing act of his in giving righteousness, and that he rewards righteousness in such a person *because* he hath given righteousness to such a person, and that because this latter act necessarily supposes the former act foregoing? So in like manner, God's decree in determining to reward righteousness is grounded on [an] antecedent decree to give righteousness, because the former decree necessarily supposes the latter decree, and implies it in the very notion of it. So who will deny but that God's act in punishing sin is grounded on what God antecedently hath done in permitting sin or suffering it to be, because the former necessarily supposes the latter;[9] and therefore that the actual permission of sin is prior in the order of nature to the punishment of it? So whatever foregoing act of God is in any respect a ground and reason of another succeeding act, so far is both the act and the decree of the act prior to both that other act and decree.

It may be objected to this, that if so, the decree of bestowing salvation on an elect soul is founded on the decree of bestowing faith on him: for God actually bestows salvation in some respect because he has bestowed faith, and this would be [to] make the decree of election succedaneous to the decree of giving [faith], as well as that of reprobation consequent on the decree of permitting sin. To this I answer, that both God's act, and also his decree of bestowing salvation on such a fallen creature, is in some respects grounded on God's act and decree of giving faith; but in no wise as the decree and act of eternal punishing is [grounded] on sin, because punishment necessarily presupposes sin, so that it could not [be] without it. But the decreeing and giving the happiness of the elect is not so founded on faith; the case is very different. For with respect to eternal punishment, it may be said that God would not, yea, could not, have decreed or executed it had he not decreed and permitted sin. But it can't be said either that God could not or would not have decreed or bestowed the eternal happiness of the elect unless he had decreed and given faith. Indeed, the salvation of an elect soul is in this respect grounded on the decree of giving faith, viz. as God's decree of bestowing happiness on the

9. MS: "former."

elect in this particular way, viz. as a fallen creature, and by the righteousness of Christ made his own by being heartily received and closed with, is grounded on the decree of bestowing faith in Christ, because it presupposes as the act that answers to this decree does. But the decree of bestowing happiness in general, which we conceive of as antecedent to this act, presupposes no such thing. Nor does just so much without any more in execution presuppose faith; or indeed the righteousness of, or any act or suffering of, a mediator; nor indeed the fall of man. And the decree of God's communicating his goodness to such a subject don't so much as presuppose the being of the subject, because it gives being; but there is no decree of evil to such a subject [that] can be conceived of as antecedent to a decree of punishment. The first decree of evil or suffering implies that in it, for there is no evil decreed for any other end but the glory of God's justice; and therefore, the decree of the permission of sin is prior to all other things in the decree of reprobation.

Due distinctions seem not to have been observed in asserting that all the decrees of God are unconditional, which has occasioned difficulty in controversies about the decrees. There are no conditional decrees in this sense, viz. that decrees should depend on things, or conditions of them, that in this decree that depends on them as conditions, must be considered as themselves yet undecreed. But yet decrees may in some sort be conditions of decrees, so as that it may be said that God would not have decreed some things had he not decreed others.

705. FREE GRACE. JUSTIFICATION. Join this to No. 682. Though giving an interest in Christ is evermore an act of mere sovereignty, yet denying an interest in Christ may be a judicial act. Though admitting to union with Christ and communion in Christ's benefits be only an act of free and sovereign grace, and no judicial proceeding; yet excluding at the day of judgment those professors of Christianity that have had the offers of a Savior, and have had a time of probation under the gospel, and a trial whether they would accept of a Savior or no, is always a judicial proceeding, and is a just punishment for their unworthy treatment of Christ. And indeed a being denied an interest in Christ is evermore in some respect a judicial proceeding, even in the heathen, for the miserable state that they are in is God's just judgment upon them; and so it is that they are continued in it without a Savior. And even that the devils in hell have no Savior, is in just wrath for their sin. Though God of his free and distinguishing grace don't inflict that just punishment of leaving them finally in their misery without a Savior, yet that don't argue that when God does inflict it, 'tis as be-

ing a just deserved punishment. Yea, it argues that it is so; for if it were [not] a due punishment on those that suffer it, it would not be free grace to be delivered from it.

706. SIN AGAINST THE HOLY GHOST, WHY UNPARDONABLE. See No. 703[1] and No. 475. Though 'tis possible that the highest and most aggravated acts of some other kinds of sin may be more heinous than the lowest acts of this sin, yet this sin seems evidently to be the most heinous *kind* of sin in the world. And 'tis a sort of sin that not only by its degree, but by its particular nature, is above others, inviting and calling for such a judgment and punishment as final dereliction and remediless irrecoverable hardening. There is no other sin to whose nature and properties such a punishment is in every respect so consonant and adapted. There is no sin that does to such a degree and [in] so many ways as it were seek and embrace and challenge God to inflict such a judgment and to oppose[2] and reject a remedy. And however, the heinousness of the sin, and its so much deserving this judgment, ben't the thing that in itself renders this sin unpardonable, but arbitrary constitution; yet that the wisdom of God has respect to these things in this sin in constituting it unpardonable, is evident by the reasons the Apostle gives why God has been pleased so to constitute. Heb. 6, "'Tis impossible to renew them again to repentance; seeing they crucify to themselves the Son of God afresh, and put him to an open shame, for the earth which drinketh in the rain that cometh oft upon it, and bringeth forth herbs meet for them by whom it is dressed, receiveth blessing from God: but that which beareth thorns and briars is rejected, and is nigh unto cursing, whose end is to be burned." Heb. 10:26, "If we sin willfully after we have received the knowledge of the truth, there remaineth no more sacrifice for sin." Vv. 28–29, "He that despised Moses' law died without mercy under two or three witnesses: of how much sorer punishment, suppose ye, shall he be thought worthy, who hath trodden under foot the Son of God, and hath counted the blood of the covenant an unholy thing, and hath done despite unto the Spirit of grace?" But that it is thus with the sin against the Holy Ghost, as has been said, may appear by the following things:

This sin is a sin of the most heinous kind in that it is not a sin of omission but commission.

'Tis a sin of the most heinous kind with regard to the object against

1. JE's cross-reference is to "p. 52," on which appears the penultimate paragraph of entry No. 703. See above, p. 314.
2. MS: "& that & oppose."

whom it is committed. 'Tis a sin committed primarily and most directly against God. I Sam. 2:25, "If one man sin against another, the judge shall judge him: but if a man sin against the Lord, who shall entreat for him?" 'Tis a sin against that great command of the Law: "Thou shalt love the Lord thy God with all thy heart, and all thy soul, and all thy mind, and all thy strength" [Mark 12:30]. 'Tis a sin against the first table of the Law, and against the first and chief precept of that table.

'Tis of the most heinous kind, that 'tis not merely sin in the principle, or a lust that has its being in the heart as a principle of sin there, but 'tis actual sin. In it the principle is brought forth into act and exercise.

'Tis of the most heinous kind, as 'tis not only the sin or corruption of the heart in act or exercise, and that against God; but 'tis the highest kind of the exercise of corruption. The nature of all the corruption of the heart is expressed by that, that 'tis enmity against God.

This enmity is exercised in a various opposition: as in neglecting God, flying from God, disliking and disrelishing the things of God, disregarding the commands of God, being ungrateful towards God, unaffected at the displays of his perfections, etc. But in this sin is enmity against God in the highest sort of exercise of all, both in esteem and affection, viz. direct contemptuous malice or malicious contempt. 'Tis the highest and most direct opposition to the foundation and sum of all duty, and the source and comprehension of all holiness, viz. love to God.

'Tis the most heinous sort of sin, not only as 'tis actual sin, corruption, in exercise, and in the most heinous sort of exercise, but 'tis actual sin in its most perfect production. 'Tis not a lust in the first stirrings and motions of it in the heart, which [is] the lowest sort of sin with respect to the manner and degree of production. Nor is it those motions or stirrings only tolerated and allowed, so far as not presently to be forbidden and expelled; which are the workings of lust in order to conception, and are [the] next degree of production. Nor is it only the act or exercise fully consented to, and allowed, by the explicit deliberate determination of the will, whereby lust has [been] fully conceived. Nor is only the outward act fully resolved upon, whereby what was conceived is fully ripened for the birth, but what is conceived is actually brought forth. This malice against God is vented in outward and open acts. This contemptuous malice against God is expressed in malicious outward acts; and not only so, but 'tis expressed in the highest fullness and perfectness of expression, not only in doing those acts, and speaking those words, that do indeed proceed from such malice, but to do it with such horrid audacious presumption and contumacy, as to be professed and avowed and open in it:

to show and declare this malicious contempt, and that either in blasphemous speeches, or such a behavior as carries a plain, open, owning and declaring this contemptuous malice, so as that it may justly be called blasphemy.

So that 'tis the highest kind of actual sin against God, or against the first table of the Law. There are various kinds of actual sins of this sort. There is profaneness, heresy, idolatry, sacrilege, atheism, blasphemy; but the most heinous of all is blasphemy.

'Tis a sin of the highest kind, as 'tis committed against the greatest and most glorious objective light. 'Tis a sin not only against the light of nature, but against the glorious light of the gospel.

'Tis also of the most heinous kind, not only as 'tis against outward light, but against inward light, against the light of men's own consciences; and 'tis a sin not only against doubts and misgivings of conscience, but against the plain dictates and clear light of conscience.

'Tis a sin of the highest kind, as 'tis in opposition to the greatest means that ever God uses with natural man. 'Tis not only against the means God uses with all mankind in the manifestations he makes of himself in the works of creation and providence, and in his providential dealings with them, preserving them, bestowing good things on them, and correcting them for sin; and also against the much greater external means given and appointed by revelation—his word and ordinances, and the outward warnings, counsels, calls and invitations wherewith God is striving with men, and Christ knocking at the door of their hearts—but [it is also] in opposition to the inward strivings of God's Spirit, whereby Christ comes as it were down from heaven, and stands and knocks at their door. And 'tis against those motions and strivings of the Spirit of God, which is [a] circumstance of sin that does exceedingly provoke God, and tends above all others to harden the heart. And this sin is not only against the inward strivings of God's Spirit, but against those strivings that are of the highest kind that are ever given to natural men, as Heb. 6; so great as to give conviction of the truth, and what is called the knowledge of the truth, viz. the truth of the things of revealed religion.

'Tis a sin of the most inexcusable sort because 'tis the most willful. 'Tis not willful merely as there is an approbation of the will to what is evil in it, as there is in sins of ignorance; nor [is] it willful as the will is gained by being driven against light by fear, or drawn by carnal appetite or the like. But 'tis so willful that 'tis done, ἑκουσίως, *sponte*. They commit it of their own accord for opposition's sake—committed from mere malice and contumacy.

'Tis a sin of the most heinous kind, as 'tis committed against the greatest mercies that ever are bestowed on any natural man. The outward means of grace are much greater mercies than any outward mercies; but the greatest of all are the inward motions and strivings of God's Spirit. Those that commit this sin do it against these; and not only [these], but the highest of this sort, the highest kind of inward motions that ever natural men have.

'Tis a sin attended with those circumstances of the sinner which do above all others render him capable of offering an high injury to God, in that they are such as are, or have been, professors of religion, that have visibly received God, and been visibly received by him. Besides the mercy there is in this to them, this capacitates them to do a greater injury than others these two ways, viz. (1) as hereby they have voluntarily laid themselves under the highest obligation by that holy covenant which they have owned, and bound themselves to God by; and (2) as they by such a visible relation to God and concern with him are capable of casting a greater reproach on God, and putting Christ to a greater shame, than others. And they improve this capacity they are under, in actually committing the greatest injury that their circumstances make them capable of, viz. actually openly renouncing this God that they profess in an apostasy, or something that is equivalent, and in blaspheming him in words or persecuting of him. He that has been owned, between whom and them there has been a visible union, is openly turned out of doors with open malice and avowed contempt. And it seems that this sin most commonly happens in those that are highly exalted in the visible church of God, and that sustain the place of teachers and pastors there; as it did in the Pharisees, and those mentioned in the sixth [chapter] of Hebrews, who had the extraordinary gifts of the Spirit in order to teach and profit others in the church.

Upon this and other accounts, it is the most heinous sort of sin, as it brings the greatest dishonor to God and Christ, and as the greatest scandal ariseth from it. It is that sin which above all others "puts Christ to an open shame" (Heb. 6:6).

He that commits this sin is guilty of reproaching all the persons of the Trinity in their work and office, for the Holy Spirit is the last of them and he by whom both the others act. He acts in the name of both the others, and by him is consummated all that each of them do. He that reproaches the Father in his economical concern reproaches him alone in that respect, for he acts only in his own name. He that reproaches the Son reproaches both the Father and the Son, for he acts not only in his own name but the name of the Father. But he that blasphemes the Holy Ghost in his work and office reproaches and renounces and declares war with them all, in all their distinct concerns and offices; and that not only because the Spirit acts in the name of the other two, but because he is the great and ultimate end of the acting of the other two in the affair of redemption, and all their concern in it. Thus he both tramples under foot the Son of God, and also "does despite to the Spirit of grace," as in Heb. 10:29. He tramples on all the causes [and] means of his own deliverance. He reproaches the Father who elects to that end that men might have the Holy Spirit, and who gives the Son to purchase the Spirit, and accepts the sacrifice of the Son for the Spirit, and sends the Spirit to bring home the sinner to Christ that he may be justified through him, to impute that righteousness to him that is indeed in some respect the Spirit in the Son, the expressions of his influence and actings in him; and he justifies them that so they may have a right to the Spirit. He tramples on the blood of Christ by which he should be cleansed from the guilt of sin. He counts that "an unholy thing" (Heb. 10:29); for 'tis through the Spirit that he offered up that blood, and whence it has its excellency and cleansing virtue, and 'tis by the Spirit that he applies his blood. He tramples on his righteousness, which, as has been said, is in some sort his Spirit, and is applied by his Spirit. He tramples on that Spirit himself by whom he should be brought to repentance and faith and salvation. Thus the whole Trinity is reproached, and so all remedy is maliciously and contumaciously opposed, and openly trampled: for we have no help but in God, no salvation [but] by the persons of the Trinity in their offices. And the last remedy in a particular manner is thus trampled on, viz. the Holy Ghost in his office, so that there is no remedy left according to the order of acting among the persons of the Trinity. It belongs to the Father in the economy of the persons to sustain the dignity of the deity as a lawgiver and judge; and therefore, he is the person whose majesty is to be vindicated, and his law satisfied for sin committed. The Son has the place of a mediator who satisfies for our sins. The Holy Ghost has the office of a sanctifier, who puts the last hand to the work of our salvation by bringing of us to Christ, and by Christ to the Father; so that he that has violated the laws of the Father may have a remedy in the satisfaction of the Son. He that injures the person of the Son, and casts contempt on his satisfaction, there remains hope for him in the grace of the Spirit, which may open his eyes and change his heart, to cast off his enmity against the Son, and bring him to repent of it, and heartily to close with that satisfaction that was before rejected. The Spirit of God does in a sense make intercession for us by working in the heart humble penitent faith in Christ. The Spirit in the heart does as it were look to Christ and come to him for help for the poor sinner. But he that does avowedly reject and trample on[3] the Spirit and declare war against him, there remains nothing else whence any hope can arise to him. There remains never another divine person to appear for his help. The operation of the Spirit is last in the affair of salvation, after which there is no remedy of divine grace to be expected. See Turretin, vol. 1, p. 718, § 16.[4]

And he that commits the sin against the Holy Ghost don't only avowedly resist and reproach the Holy Spirit—the person that is the next and immediate author of repentance, and faith, and saving conversion—but with this exceeding aggravation, that he does it at that very time when the Spirit is mercifully striving with him to bring him [in], and that with his highest and greatest influences that are ever bestowed on natural men, by those operations that are the highest step next to those saving benefits.

Moreover, he that commits this sin don't only reproach each person in the Trinity, but he is guilty of a far greater injury, both to the divine being, and also to each particular person, than if he blasphemed either of the other persons.

1. This is the highest injury to the divine being. The divine nature and essence is more heinously opposed than it would be by reproaching God or the deity undistinguishedly, or than it would be by reproaching either of the two first persons; because in the sin against the Holy Ghost that person is maligned and vilified that is the very excellency of the deity or divine being. The hatred and malice is directed against the very beauty and loveliness of the Godhead, so that the hateful and deformed nature of sin appears in this above all sins. The sin is against the very holiness of God itself, in the most direct manner possible; and not only so, but 'tis most directly against that person who is the very goodness, and love, and grace of

---

3. MS: "on against."

4. "Hoc vero clarius adhuc patet ex diversitate operationum, quae singulis Personis competunt in oeconomia salutis. Nam ut Pater majestatem Numinis laesi refert, & Legum sancitarum custos est & vindex. Filius locum habet Mediatoris & Vadis, qui pro peccatis nostris satisfecit. Et Spiritus Sanctus vices sustinet Sancificatoris, qui ultimam manum operi salutis admovet, nos ad Christum, & per Christum ad Patrem adducendo; Ita qui Patris leges violavit, remedium habere potest in satisfactione Filii; Qui Filii personam, & satisfactionis ejus dignitatem per incredulitatem & ignorantiam laesit, illi spes aliqua superest in gratia Spiritus, qui potest ejus ignorantiam sanare, & incredulitatem corrigere; Sed qui Spiritum Sanctum contumelia afficit, ejusque operationem rejicit, nihil ei superest amplius unde spes aliqua oriatur, quia nulla datur alia Persona divina, quae illi succurrere possit, & Spiritus operatio ultima est in negotio salutis, post quam nullum uterius potest expectari gratiae remedium." Turretin, *Institutio Theologiae Elencticae* (see above, No. 646, p. 181, n. 3), Vol. 1, Bk. IX, "De Peccato in Genere et Specie," Qu. XIV, "In quo consistat ratio formalis peccati in Spirtum S. Et cur sit irremissibile?", sec. XVI, p. 718.

the divine nature. They herein vent malice against divine love itself. They reproach and trample on divine mercy and grace itself; so that both the unholy, and also the ungrateful, nature of sin is expressed and manifested in this sin above all other kinds of sin. And,

2. He that commits the sin against the Holy Ghost is guilty of a far greater injury to each of the other persons than if he reproached them directly; for as has been already observed, in reproaching him in his office, he reproaches them in theirs, for his is subordinate to theirs. He acts in their name and as representing each of them. His work is as their messenger to finish and complete their work; so that, on this account, he reproaches each of the other two as much as if he reproached them singly and directly.

But then he injures them much more than if he reproached them singly and directly, for two reasons.

(1) He reproaches the other two in that which is supreme and ultimate in their work. He reproaches what is ultimate in their work in two respects, viz.

1. As he reproaches that which is the supreme and ultimate aim and end of the work of the other two. Thus the ultimate aim of the Father in electing and sending the Son, etc. is the Spirit. So the thing ultimately sought and aimed at by the Son in satisfying and purchasing was the Spirit. What the Father and the Son make their end in their concern in this affair, they do from two grounds, viz. from the view and consideration of the excellency of the thing aimed at, and the graciousness of it; or otherwise, its goodness or excellency in itself, and its tendency to the happiness of the creature. But the Holy Spirit is ultimate in the operations of the other persons in both these respects. He is sought by them in their concern in the work of redemption as the thing ultimately excellent and ultimately gracious to man, or the ultimate benefit to him. And reproaching of the Holy Ghost is a peculiarly aggravated and heinous opposition of the other persons on each account.

2. He that reproaches the Holy Ghost in his office, reproaches what is ultimate in the work of the other two: as their sending the Holy Ghost in their name, or rather coming by him to apply and actually to accomplish redemption, is the last part of their work, that part of it that completes all, and that crowns all the rest, and immediately attains the end of all in the sinner's actual deliverance and happiness.

(2) He not only reproaches that which [is] ultimate in their work, but he reproaches that which is the very excellency and grace of their work itself. The grace and love of the Father in electing and in sending his Son,

and accepting his sacrifice, consists in the Holy Spirit. The holiness, grace and love of the Son in all that he did, and suffered, and now does, consists in the Holy Spirit.

(3) He that reproaches the Holy Ghost reproaches each person of the Trinity in their whole work. He that reproaches the other persons directly don't reproach them in the whole work. He that reproaches Christ singly in his office, he reproaches him in his satisfying for sin, and interceding for sinners, and other parts of his office performed by him in his own person separately; but he don't reproach him as coming, in and by his Spirit, to make application of this redemption. But he that reproaches the Spirit of God reproaches him in this, and in those other parts of his work too. So he that reproaches the Spirit don't only reproach the Father's election and mission of the Son, but also as coming by his Spirit to bestow salvation and life.

Hence we may learn that this sin is the greatest violation of that great command of gospel revelation—that we should believe on the Son of God—or the highest degree of that great sin of unbelief, or rejection of Christ; which seems to [be] intimated in the Apostle's calling it a trodding under foot the Son of God, and counting the blood of the covenant an unholy thing, and putting Christ to an open shame [Heb. 10:29, 6:6].

He that commits the sin against the Holy Ghost don't only reject and trample on all means of repentance and the favor of God, and spiritual and eternal life and all gospel benefits, but also on the benefits themselves, for the Holy Ghost is the sum of all those benefits. He tramples on the love of the Father, [and] he tramples on the grace of the Son, for these are the Holy Ghost, and the enjoyment of 'em consists in the communion of the Holy Ghost. He maliciously, and contumaciously, and with avowed contempt, rejects and reproaches his own holiness and happiness, love to God, and joy in God; for this is the Spirit of God. He tramples on his own good, both of perfection and happiness, for 'tis that divine person in the communication of which consists both our holiness and joy.

Sins against the persons of the Trinity are great and heinous in the reverse order of their subsisting and acting in the work of redemption. The Son is second in order; but sins against him in his office are much more highly resented by God than sins directly against the Father, for he is the brightness of his Father's glory, and does most remarkably appear as such in the affair of redemption. That peculiar and wonderful glory of God that appears in this work, shines forth in the face of Jesus Christ; and therein Christ acts in the name of the Father. Hence, the heinousness of the sin of unbelief; and hence, sins against the gospel are greater than sins against the Law. The Holy Ghost is last in order of subsisting and acting, but sins against him are greatest of all.

Persecution is one thing wherein this sin commonly, if not always, appears; and therein, it is not only the greatest sin against the first table of the Law, but also against the second. Persecution is a kind of sin above all others, a violation of that second great command of the Law, which is like the first, viz. thou shalt love thy neighbor as thyself. And thus, there is no kind of sin so contrary to that great Christian virtue of charity, and that on several accounts: it consists in malice, and that against those of our neighbors that are most excellent, and that we have most reason to love, viz. the saints; and especially for that which is their loveliness, and is the highest loveliness that our neighbor can have, viz. his holiness and the image of God in him: none so contrary to the foundation and source of this virtue, viz. love to God. And that persecution in which the sin against the Holy Ghost is committed, is the most aggravated sort of persecution.

707. SIN AGAINST THE HOLY GHOST, with respect to the degree of light persons must have. Add this to No. 475.[5] And it don't seem to be sufficient that persons should only be in doubt whether it ben't indeed something divine or no, or that they should have some wavering sort of opinion that it is so; but there must be something that is of the nature of conviction, that may be called a receiving the knowledge of the truth, as Heb. 10:26, so that what they do, they may be said not to do "ignorantly and in unbelief" (I Tim. 1:13), and so that they may be said to know what they do (Luke 23:34).

This light, by being so spoken of, seems to be the highest sort of light that natural men ever attain to, or are capable of, in a natural state, and it is probable is not attained without great inward convictions of the Spirit of God. Those that the Apostle has respect to in the sixth [chapter] of Hebrews evidently had such great enlightenings and convictions of the Spirit. 'Tis evident that they had such a conviction of the truth of things of religion, for without it they could not work miracles or exercise miraculous gifts; which is evident by I Cor. 13:2, "And though I have all faith, so that I could remove mountains, and have no charity, I am nothing." Or at least it is not probable that persons can have this sort of conviction without either great influence of the Spirit of God immediately on their minds, or having extraordinary effects of the power and influence of the Spirit of God immediately set before their eyes, either in miracles, or in

5. JE's cue mark indicates that this entry is to be added to § 2 of No. 475. See *Works*, *13*, 519.

exceeding wonderful works of God, in the pouring out of his Spirit in convincing and converting sinners. And probably both do commonly go together, when this sin is committed. The Pharisees that blasphemed Christ's Spirit, and called it Beelzebub, probably had both. We have reason to think that that nation were subject to very great, and even the greatest, strivings of Christ's Spirit before they were cast off, and particularly their teachers; for we are taught that Christ exceedingly strove with that people before they were rejected, as being loathe to cast them off. He said he was sent to the lost sheep of the house of Israel, and therefore confined his ministry very much to them, preaching and working great miracles, and innumerable miracles, among them; and his miracles were wrought chiefly for them. Hence when the woman of Canaan desired a miracle of him, he told her it was not meet to take the children's bread to cast it to dogs; and he directed his disciples, when he sent them forth, not to go to the Gentiles, but to go to the lost sheep of the house of Israel. And Christ, when the time of his crucifixion drew nigh, spoke as one that had been striving and using all manner of means to gain them, and with tears laments their obstinacy and utter incorrigibleness. "How often," says he, "would I have gathered thy children together, as an hen gathereth her chickens under her wings, and ye would not!" [Matt. 23:37]. From the analogy to these things, we may well suppose that the inward strivings of Christ's Spirit, and knocks at the doors of their hearts, were very great. He who used the greatest outward means with them (for Abraham's and the father's sakes, and because they had long been God's chosen people), before he rejected them doubtless also used the greatest inward strivings, and especially with their teachers and rulers; for a people ben't rejected and destroyed as a people, but for the perverseness and obstinacy of these. And then we have an account that the Pharisees were under great convictions a little before under John's preaching, which wrought without doubt by convincing them of the things which John taught, of which the main thing was that another should come after him whose shoes' latchet [he was not worthy to stoop down and unloose (Mark 1:7)], and that this person was the Christ: for he came as the harbinger of Christ. And the Pharisees understood him to testify of this very person, as appears by Matt. 21:25, what they said there when Christ asked them whence the baptism of John was. And 'tis not to be thought that the Spirit of Christ finally left striving with them, till Christ himself left striving with them; but as Christ used greater means with them after John before he gave them up, so that the Spirit also used greater strivings and convictions, and that they ran parallel with the means Christ used in other respects: in that as Christ used utmost means in other respects before he gave them up, so he did in this respect also, viz. the utmost inward means, and that the highest inward convictions were given that are ever given to natural men. Hence, Stephen charges this sort of men among the Jews with resisting the Holy Ghost, with a thorough and persevering obstinacy. Acts 7:51, "Ye stiff-necked and uncircumcised in heart and ears, ye do always resist the Holy Ghost." And no more likely reason can be given why those that nailed Christ to his cross were not convinced, though Christ had so lately wrought that great miracle of raising Lazarus from the dead, and that the Pharisees were convinced, but that the one had received convincing influences of the Spirit of God, and the other had not. That apostasy is always an ingredient in this sin, see note on Luke 11:24–26.[6]

708. CHRISTIAN RELIGION. Though some may be ready to object against the Christian religion that there seem to be innumerable difficulties and inconsistences attending it, which would appear to be insolvable but only as a multitude of heads have been employed for many ages to find out solutions for 'em, innumerable attempts have been made, and multitudes have been rejected one after another as insufficient, for the sake of others that have been thought less liable to objection, till at length such solutions have been found out for many of them as are in some measure plausible: but there is nothing—no history, nor scheme of doctrine, nor set of principles whatever, however inconsistent, absurd and confused—but what might be made to seem consistent at this rate; no difficulties nor inconsistences, but what something plausible might be found out to color it over and hide it, by so much search and study, by a combination of such multitudes through so many ages.

To this I answer, that as there have been a long time to answer objections, so there have been many ages to strengthen them. As there have been many ages to solve difficulties, so there have been as many to find out difficulties and inconsistences. Falsehood in things that are in like manner complicated, as all that is contained in the whole compass of the scheme of the Christian religion, must needs be attended with numberless things that may discover it, more and more of which will appear by time. And besides, there has been all this time to make difficulties more plain, and bring out inconsistences more to the light, and by thorough

6. In the "Blank Bible" note on Luke 11:24–26, JE observes that "apostasy" is "one great ingredient or constituent of the unpardonable sin." For example, the Pharisees had an awakening as a result of John the Baptist's preaching, but then "their religion greatly degenerated."

and exact consideration to make them more manifest and apparent, by setting all things forth more exactly and minutely as they be. Time is a thing that wonderfully brings truth to light, and wears off by degrees false colorings and disguises. If the truth be of that side that would have most advantage by time, appearing inconsistences, being founded on truth, would grow plainer and plainer, and difficulties more and more evident. It would discover more circumstances to strengthen and confirm them, and pretenses of solution would appear more and more evidently absurd and ridiculous. When there are contending parties that contend by argument and search and inquiry, time greatly helps that party that have truth of their side, and weakens the contrary side. It gradually wears away their sandy foundation, and rots away the building that is not made of substantial materials. The Christian religion has evermore in all ages had its enemies, and that among those that were learned men. Yea, 'tis observable that there have commonly been some of the most subtile of men to scan the Christian scheme, and to discover the objections that lie against it, and have done it with a good will to overthrow it. Thus it was in Judea in the infancy of the church, the scribes and Pharisees and the wise men among the Jews employed all their wisdom against it. Thus in the first ages of the church not many wise, not many mighty, not many noble, were called; but Christianity had the wisdom, learning and subtilty of the world to oppose it. So of latter ages: how many learned and subtile men have done their utmost against Christianity, so that the length of time that there has been for persons to strengthen their own side in this controversy, that is brought as an objection against Christianity, is much more of an argument for it, than an objection against it.

709. INCARNATION. MYSTICAL UNION. See No. 624. A further evidence that the union of the man Christ Jesus to the divine Logos in the same person so as to be the same Son of God, is by communicating the Spirit of God, is the answer Christ gives the Jews when they charge him with blasphemy—in that he, being a man, made himself God—in the tenth chapter of John, v. 36, "Say ye of him, that the Father hath sanctified, and sent into the world, Thou blasphemest; because I said, I am the Son of God?" The Jews objection was that he, *being a man*, made himself one with God [v. 33]. Christ here answers directly to their objection, and shows how *he, a man*, is the Son of God, or how his manhood is united to the deity, and this is by his being sanctified; by which it is evident that it must be by his having the Holy Spirit given to him. The Holy Spirit is the Sanctifier, for the Spirit is the very divine holiness. Hence typical sanctifications, or set-

tings apart to offices, were by those things that represented giving the Spirit of God, as anointing with oil, etc. Christ is sanctified by being anointed; hence he is called Christ, or the anointed. He was sanctified when he was anointed with the oil of gladness. When Christ entered on his public ministry, and solemnly renewedly sanctified and set apart it to his work, it was by giving the Spirit. The Spirit descended like a dove upon him. Christ vindicates his saying that he is the Son of God, though he is a man, in that he was sanctified *and sent into the world.* By sending into the world, Christ doubtless means his incarnation; and herein he shows that he is the Son of God by the manner of his incarnation as it was first brought to pass, which was by the Holy Ghost. He was conceived by the Holy Ghost. He received his first being in this world by the Spirit of holiness. And thus the Father sanctified him when he sent him into the world, and sanctified him in sending him into the world; incarnated him by sanctification. By sending the Spirit, assuming his flesh into being and into the person of the divine Logos, at the same time and by the same act, the Father sent him into the world, or incarnated him by an act of sanctification; for the incarnation was assuming flesh, or human nature, into the person of the Son, or giving communion of the divine personality to human nature, in giving that human nature being. And this was done by giving the Holy Spirit in such a manner and measure to that human nature in making it; and this was sanctifying that human nature. By this sanctifying was given communion in divine personality to human nature. But the giving such communion in the personality of the eternal Son to human [nature], was the very same as sending Christ into the world; there is no other sending the Son into the world. And here is the force of Christ's argument: seeing the Father hath sanctified him and sent him into the world, he has given his manhood being, so as to be the Son of God. It was not properly the making the flesh of Christ that was sending Christ into the world, but *making the Word flesh.* It was not merely giving being to the manhood of Christ, but the communicating the divine personality from heaven to earth in giving being to Christ's manhood, that was sending Christ into the world. And this God did by an act of sanctification, or by an imparting of the Spirit of holiness. So that these two expressions together, "sanctified" and "sent into the [world]," do show the nature of Christ's incarnation, so as to show how that which was produced by it was the Son of God, a divine person, and so united to the Father that he and the Father were one, as Christ had said, v. 30.

It was necessary that the same person that acted as the principle of union between the manhood of Christ and the person of the Son, should make the manhood of Christ. For it must be by that person that acted as the principle of union that the human nature must be assumed, for assuming implies the uniting, and making is what belongs to assuming. This assuming may be considered as one act, but having two effects, viz. the being of the manhood, and his union with the person of the Son. Assuming is the making the human nature in the person of the Logos. It was the uniting something out of nothing (i.e. something as yet unmade) to him. Whatever Christ assumes into union to himself must be by that person that acts as the principle of union; and therefore, when something was to be assumed out of nothing into union to himself, the Logos or Word sent forth this constituent, or principle of assumption or unition, to assume it out of nothing to himself. But this implies making and uniting in one act, or making in union. If the making had been by one person and the unition by another, it must have been by two distinct acts because by two distinct agents; and the humanity would not, by him that made it, be made out of nothing into the Son, nor could the person that made it, be properly said to make the Word flesh.

710. HEAVEN. SEPARATE STATE. RESURRECTION. DISPENSATIONS. How the happiness of the resurrection state will exceed the present happiness in heaven. It looks to me probable that the glory of the state of the church after the resurrection will as much exceed the present glory of the spirits of just men made perfect, as the glory of the gospel dispensation exceeds the Mosaic dispensation, or as much as the glory of the state of the church in its first or purest state of it, or rather in its state in the millennium (wherein alone the glory of the gospel dispensation will be fully manifested) exceeds the state of the church under the law, and as much as the state [of] the company of glorified souls exceeds this. Of old under the Mosaic dispensation the church saw things very darkly. They saw as it were by a reflex light, as we see the light of the sun by that of the moon. They saw gospel things in dark types and shadows, and in dark sayings that were as it were riddles or enigmas. The glory of that dispensation was no glory in comparison of the glory of the evangelical dispensation it so much excels. But under the gospel dispensation those dark shadows are ceased; and instead of enigmas or dark sayings the apostles use great plainness of speech (II Cor. 3:12). The night in which we saw by a reflex light only is ceased, and Christ is actually come. We enjoy daylight. John the Baptist was the day star to usher in the day, and when he was born "the dayspring from on high visited us," as Zacharias his father sang, Luke 1:78–79. And when Christ himself came the sun rose, especially when he rose from the

dead, and shed forth his light and heat on the day of Pentecost. And now we see the sun by his own direct light. We see him immediately; the veil is taken away, and we all see with open face (II Cor. 3:18). But still even under the gospel dispensation we see by a reflex light. We see through a looking glass, in comparison of what we shall in the future state (I Cor. 13:12). We understand not by plain speeches and declarations, but as in an enigma or dark saying (as 'tis said in the same place), for the things of heaven can't be expressed as they be in our language. The Apostle, when he went there, said of them that it was not lawful or possible to utter them [II Cor. 12:4]. But when the souls of the saints are separated from their bodies, they shall no longer see heavenly things as in an enigma or dark saying: for they shall go themselves to heaven to dwell there, and shall immediately see and hear those things that it is not possible or lawful to utter plainly, or know immediately in this world. They shall then no longer see Christ by reflection as in a looking glass, because they shall be where Christ himself shall be immediately present, for they that are departed are with Christ. They that are absent from the body are present with the Lord [II Cor. 5:8]. When that which is perfect is come, then we shall no more see by a looking glass, in an enigma, but shall see face to face, as the Apostle shows (I Cor. 13:10, 12). But that which is perfect is come with respect to the separate souls of the saints, as is evident by Heb. 12:23, for they are there called "the spirits of just men made perfect." And therefore, when the soul of the saint leaves the body and goes to heaven, it will be like coming out of the dim light of the night into daylight. The present state is a dark, benighted state, but when the soul enters into heaven it [will be] like[7] the rising of the sun, for they shall then see the Sun of righteousness by his own direct light. Because they shall be with him, they will be spirits made perfect in that respect, that it will be perfect day with them (Prov. 4:18). We can't in the present state see clearly, because we have a veil before us, even the veil of the flesh. The church is Christ mystical. The church in the old testament state was represented by Christ in his fleshly state, such as he was in before his death; for Christ was the head of that church in that state, and was subject to the same ordinances with them, was under the same dispensation with his church, till his death. See notes.[8]

His flesh was as it were a veil that hindered our access to heavenly things

7. MS: "it we like."

8. This is probably a reference to "Notes on Scripture," no. 46. This note, which ends with a cross-reference to "Miscellanies" No. 710, discusses the book of Esther as "a shadow of gospel times and things." See *Works, 15*, 60–63.

or seeing them immediately. When Christ died this veil was rent from the top to the bottom, and the holy of holies, with [the] ark of the testament, were opened to view. And especially will this be fulfilled in the glorious period of this evangelical dispensation, when "the kingdoms of this world become the kingdoms of our Lord, and of his Christ" (Rev. 11:15, 19). But still the church of Christ has a veil before it, to hinder it from seeing immediately things in the holy of holies; and this veil is their flesh, which is mystically the flesh of Christ. Christ in his members is still in his fleshly state; but when the saints die this veil is rent from the top to the bottom, and a glorious prospect will be opened through this veil. The day is a time of glory in comparison of the night, because of the sun that is then seen, which is the glory of the visible universe and by his light fills the world with glory. So the gospel state of the church is spoken of as a state of glory in comparison of its old testament state. I Pet. 1:11, "Searching what, or what manner of time the Spirit of Christ which was in them did signify, when it testified beforehand the sufferings of Christ, and the glory that should follow." II Cor. 3:10, "For even that which was made glorious had no glory in this respect, by reason of the glory that excelleth." And this state was prophesied of of old as a state of glory, but the state of holy separate souls is a state of glory in comparison of the present state. Ps. 73:24, 26, "Thou shalt guide me with thy counsel, and afterwards receive me to glory. . . . My flesh and my heart faileth: but God is the strength of my heart, and my portion forever." So 'tis said of Moses and Elias, who were in the state that the saints are in now in heaven, that at Christ's transfiguration they appeared in glory (Luke 9:30–31).

But yet the glorified souls of saints in their present state in heaven, though they can't be said properly to see as in an enigma, yet 'tis but darkly in comparison of what they will see after the resurrection. Therefore, though we are said now to see with open face in comparison of what they did under the old testament, and though separate souls in heaven see face to face in comparison of what we do now, yet the sight that the saints shall have at the resurrection is spoken of as if it were the first sight, wherein they should see him as he is. I John 3:2, "Beloved, now are we the sons of God, and it doth not yet appear what we shall be: but we know that, when he shall appear, we shall be like him; for we shall see him as he is." The glory of Christ is what will as it were then first appear to all the church, to all that shall then lift up their heads out of their graves to behold it, as well as to those that will then be alive. 'Tis called the blessed hope and glorious appearing of the great God and Savior Jesus Christ, with respect to both those companies of which the church consists. The Apostle speaks of it as what would be a "glorious *appearing*" to them, to the Christians that were then living (Tit. 2:13); which implies something that will be seen anew, as though he had been till then unseen. That appearing of Christ will be like the appearing of the sun when it rises, to all, both those that shall then be saved alive, and those that will then rise. It will be to them both as the morning succeeding the dim light of the night. Ps. 49:14, "The upright shall have dominion over them in the morning." Though in the state the saints are now in in heaven there is no proper darkness because there is no evil, yet the light they have is dim, like the light of the night, in comparison of the glorious light that shall appear on that morning. The happiness that separate souls have now in heaven is like the quiet rest that a person has in his bed before a wedding day, or some other joyful and glorious day, in comparison of the light and joy after the resurrection. Is. 57:1–2, "The righteous perisheth, and no man layeth it to heart: and merciful men are taken away, none considering that the righteous are taken away from the evil to come. He shall enter into peace: they shall rest in their beds, each one walking in his uprightness." I Thess. 4:14–15, "Them which sleep in Jesus will God bring with him. For this we say unto you by the word of the Lord, that we which are alive and remain unto the coming of the Lord shall not prevent them which are asleep." The morning of the natural day, when the sun rises and persons awake out of sleep, and the face of the whole world seems to be renewed by the light of the sun, seems to be a type of the resurrection, when the saints shall awake out of sweet repose to glory.

The saints now in heaven see God, or the divine nature, by a reflex light, comparatively with the manner in which they will see it after the resurrection; seeing now through the glass of the glorified human nature of Christ, and in the glass of his works, especially relating to redemption, as was observed, No. 702.

Of old, under the old testament, the church of Christ was as a child (Gal. 4:1). So still under the gospel dispensation the church on earth is as a child, in comparison of what the church of glorified souls in heaven is when what is perfect is come. I Cor. 13:10–11, "But when that which is perfect is come, then that which is in part shall be done away. When I was a child, I spake as a child, I understood as a child, I thought as a child: but when I became a man, I put away childish things." But yet the church remains a child, and don't come to the stature of a man till the resurrection. Eph. 4:10–13, "He that descended is the same also that ascended far above all heavens, that he might fill all things. And he gave some, apostles; and some, prophets; and some, evangelists; and some, pastors and teachers; for the perfecting of the saints, for the work of the ministry, for the edifying the body of

Christ: till we all come in the unity of the faith, and of the knowledge of the Son of God, unto a perfect man, unto the measure of the stature of the fullness of Christ." But this won't be till that time comes when the work of these officers ceases, which won't be till the end of the world; and there be no further use of them (Matt. 28:20). It won't be till the time comes when he that is ascended shall descend again. It won't be till the church has all its members, and all the members delivered from all remaining corruption, and all are brought to their consummate glory.

Of old, the church was in a preparatory state, as a woman preparing for the marriage to Christ. The coming of Christ, and destroying the Jewish state and church, and setting up this gospel dispensation is compared to the coming of the bridegroom and his marriage with the church; the gospel day to the wedding day, and the provision of God's house under the gospel to the wedding feast, and gospel ministers to servants sent out to invite persons to the wedding (Matt. 22, at the beginning; and Is. 61:10.) And especially is the most glorious time of the Christian church on earth, when the glories of the gospel dispensation be most fully manifested, called the marriage of the Lamb. Rev. 19:7, "Let us be glad and rejoice, and give honor to him: for the marriage of the Lamb is come, and his wife hath made herself ready," etc. But yet the translation of the soul from the earthly to the heavenly state at death is represented as its marriage to Christ, and therefore Christ's coming by death is called the coming of the bridegroom. In the beginning of the 25th [chapter] of Matthew, one thing that Christ has there respect to is his coming by death; because in the application Christ makes of it in the 13th verse, Christ speaks of the coming of the bridegroom as what would be sudden and unexpected, and as it were at midnight, to them that then were his hearers, and what they therefore should continually watch and wait for, that they might not be found slumbering and sleeping as the foolish virgins were. "Watch therefore; for ye know neither the day nor the hour wherein the Son of man cometh." But this matter[9] is not in this manner applicable to those that were then living, with respect to Christ's last coming at the end of the world, but with regard to his coming by death. But yet the glorification of the church after the last judgment is represented as the proper marriage of the Lamb. Rev. 21:2, "And I John saw the holy city, new Jerusalem, coming down from God out of heaven, prepared as a bride adorned for her husband"; and v. 9, "Come hither, I will show thee the bride, the Lamb's wife." See Luke 14:14–24, compared with Matt. 22 at the beginning. See No. 744, corol. 5.

9. MS: "manner."

711. PERSEVERANCE. Add this to No. 695. 'Tis evident that the saints shall persevere because they are already justified. Adam would not have been justified till he had fulfilled and done his work. If he had stood, he would not have [been] tried or judged in order to his justification till then, and then his justification would have been a confirmation. It would have been an approving of him as having done his work, and as standing entitled to his reward. A servant that is sent out about a piece of work is not justified by his master till he has done [his work]; and then the master views his work and, seeing it to be done according to his order, he then approves or justifies him as having done his work, and being now entitled to the promised reward. And his title to his reward is no longer suspended on any remaining [work]. So Christ having done our work for us, we are justified as soon as ever we believe in him, as being through what he has accomplished and finished, now already actually entitled to the reward of life. And justification carries in it not only remission of sins and a being adjudged to life, or accepted as entitled by righteousness to the reward of life, as is evident because believers are justified by communion with Christ in his justification, which he received when he was raised from the dead. But that justification of Christ that he was then the subject [of] did most certainly imply both these, viz. his being now judged free of that guilt that he had taken upon [himself], and also his having now fulfilled all righteousness, his having perfectly obeyed the Father and done enough to entitle him to the reward of life as our head and surety; and therefore, he then had eternal life given him as our head. That life that [had] begun when he was raised from the dead was eternal life. Christ was then justified in the same sense as Adam would have been justified if he had finished his course of perfect obedience; and therefore, [it] implies in it confirmation in a title to life, as that would have done. And therefore, all those that are risen with Christ and have him for their surety, and so are justified in his justification, are certainly in like manner confirmed.

And again, that a believer's justification implies not only deliverance from the wrath of God, but a title to glory, is evident by Rom. 5:1–2, where the Apostle mentions both these as joint benefits implied in justification. "Therefore being justified by faith, we *have peace with God* through our Lord Jesus Christ: by whom also we have access into this grace wherein we stand, and *rejoice in hope of the glory of God.*" So remission of sins, and inheritance among them that are sanctified, are mentioned together as what are jointly obtained by faith in Christ. Acts 26:18, "That they may receive forgiveness of sins, and inheritance among them that are sanctified through faith that is in me." Both these are without any doubt implied in that passing from death to life, which Christ speaks of as the fruit of faith, and which he opposes to condemnation. John 5:24, "Verily, I say unto you, He that heareth my word, and believeth on him that sent me, hath everlasting life, and shall not come into condemnation; but is passed from death to life."

712. JUSTIFICATION. FAITH. MORAL AND NATURAL SUITABLENESS. God's bestowing Christ and his benefits on a soul in consequence of faith, out of regard only to the natural suitableness that there is between such a qualification of a soul, and such an union with Christ and interest in Christ, makes the case very widely different from what would be if he bestowed these things from regard to any moral suitableness: for in the former case, 'tis only from God's love of order and hatred of confusion that [he] bestows these things on the account of faith; in the latter, God doth it out of love to the grace of faith itself. God will neither impute Christ's righteousness to us, nor adjudge his benefits to us, *unless we be in him;* nor will he look upon us as being in him without an actual unition to him, because he is a wise being and delights in order and not confusion. And his making such a constitution is a testimony of his love of order; whereas, if it were out of regard to any moral fitness, it would be a testimony of his love to the act. The one supposes this divine constitution to [be] a manifestation of his regard to the beauty of the act of faith; the other only supposes it to be a manifestation of his regard to the beauty of that order there [is] in uniting those things that have a natural agreement and congruity, the one with the other.

A moral suitableness or unsuitableness includes a natural, but a natural don't include a moral. While the moral unsuitableness stood in the way, it could[1] in no respect be suitable that men should be accepted; it could not be naturally suitable. But when the moral unsuitableness is removed, it may be naturally suitable.

Goodness or loveliness is not prior in the order of nature to justification, or is not to be considered as prior in the order and method of God's proceeding in this affair. There is indeed something in man that is really and spiritually good, that is prior in the order of nature to justification, viz. faith. But there is nothing that is accepted as goodness till after justification. Though a respect to the natural suitableness between such a qualification and such a state be prior in the order of nature to justification, yet the acceptance even of faith, as any goodness or loveliness in the

1. MS: "there could ~~be no natur.~~"

believer in the order of nature, follows justification. The goodness is justly looked upon as nothing till the man is justified; and therefore, the man is respected in justification as ungodly and altogether hateful in himself (Rom. 4:5). The goodness of faith is not accepted as any goodness or loveliness of the man but in consequence of justification, and therefore is none in God's account. 'Tis not accepted as his loveliness, nor is it meet that it should be, out of Christ. If it could be so that a sinner could have faith or some other grace in his heart and yet remain separate from Christ, it should continue still to be so that he is not looked upon by God as being in Christ, or having any relation to him. It would not be meet that that true grace should be accepted as any goodness or loveliness of the man in God's sight, if it should be accepted as the loveliness of the person; that would be to accept the person as in some degree lovely to God. But 'tis not meet that this should be. Neither can it be, separate from Christ; because the person out of Christ is under the guilt of sin, which has infinite unworthiness, and which that goodness has no worthiness to balance, as long as the man remains under guilt in the sight of God, which guilt is an infinite hatefulness in his eyes. His goodness can't be beheld by God but as taken with this hatefulness or as put in the scales with it, and the excess of the weight in one scale above another must be looked on as the quality of the man, these contraries being beheld and taken together. One takes from another, as one number is subtracted from another; and the man is looked upon in God's sight according to the remainder. And the unworthiness being infinite, and the goodness that subtracts from it being small, the unworthiness and hatefulness that remains must be still infinite. The man is still infinitely unworthy and hateful in God's sight, as he was before, without diminution: because his goodness bears no proportion to his unworthiness, and therefore, when taken with it—or when they are put into the scales together, as they are in God's estimation of the person—is nothing. For [when] a contrary is taken with its contrary, it must be[2] taken according to the proportion it bears to its contrary; and if that proportion be nothing, then being so taken, it must pass for nothing. And besides this, the goodness that is in that faith not only bears no proportion to the guilt of the person, but neither does it bear any proportion to the unworthiness even of that defective polluted act of faith. The odiousness of the act so infinitely exceeds the excellency, that the excellency of that very act is, in the sight of him that judges according to the law and mere justice, nothing. See the next.

2. MS: "to."

713. INFINITE EVIL OF SIN. WORTHLESSNESS OF OUR HOLINESS. FREE GRACE. JUSTIFICATION. That the evil and demerit of sin is infinitely great, is most demonstrably evident because what the evil or iniquity of sin consists in is a violation of an obligation, doing contrary to what we are obliged to do; and therefore, by how much the greater the obligation is that is violated, so much the greater is the iniquity of the violation.[3] But certainly our obligation to fear, or love, or honor any being is great in proportion to the greatness and excellency of the being, or their worthiness to be loved and honored. We are under greater obligation to love a more lovely being, than a less lovely; and if a being be infinitely excellent and lovely, our obligations to love him are therein infinitely great.

Some have argued exceeding strangely against the infinite evil of sin from its being committed against an infinite object. Because if so, then it might as well be argued that there is also an infinite value or worthiness in holiness and love to God, because that also has an infinite object; whereas, the argument from parity of reason will carry it in the reverse. The sin of the creature against God is ill-deserving in proportion to the distance there is between God and the creature; the greatness of the object, and the meanness of the subject, aggravates it. But 'tis the reverse with respect to the worthiness of the respect of the creature to God. 'Tis worthless (and not worthy) in proportion to the meanness of the subject. So much the greater the distance between God and the creature, so much the less is the creature's respect worthy of God's notice or regard. The unworthiness of sin, or opposition to God, rises and is great in proportion to the dignity of the object, and meanness of the subject. But on the contrary, the worth or value of respect rises in proportion to the value of the subject; and that for this plain reason, viz. that the evil of disrespect is in proportion to the obligation that lies upon the subject to the object, which obligation is most evidently increased by the excellency of the object. But on the contrary, the worthiness of respect is in proportion to the obligation that lies on the object (or rather the reason he has) to regard the subject, which certainly is in proportion to the subject's value or excellency. Sin or disrespect is evil or heinous in proportion to the degree of what it takes from the object, viz. the obligation it is under to it; which certainly is great in proportion to the object's excellency and worthiness of respect. Respect, on the contrary, is valuable in proportion to the value of what is given to the object in that respect: which certainly, other things being equal, is great in proportion to the subject's value or worthiness of regard,

3. MS: "obligation."

because the subject, so far as he gives his respect, gives himself to the object; and therefore, his gift is of greater value in proportion to the value of himself.

Corol. Hence the love and honor and obedience of Christ towards God has infinite value, viz. from the infinite excellency and dignity of the person in whom these qualifications were inherent. And the reason why we needed a person of infinite dignity to obey for us, was because of our infinite meanness who had disobeyed, whereby our disobedience was infinitely aggravated. We needed one, the worthiness of whose obedience might be answerable to the unworthiness of our disobedience, and therefore needed one who was as great and worthy as we were unworthy.

Another objection that perhaps may be thought hardly worth mentioning, is that to suppose that sin is an evil infinitely heinous, is to make all sins equally heinous: for how can any sin be more than infinitely heinous? But all that can be argued hence, is that no sin can be greater with respect to that aggravation, viz. the worthiness of the object against whom it is committed. One sin can't be more aggravated than another in that respect, because in this respect the aggravation of every sin is infinite. But that don't hinder but that some sins may be more aggravated and heinous than others in other respects. As if we suppose a cylinder infinitely long, it can't be greater in that respect, viz. with respect to the length of it; yet it may be doubled and trebled, yea, and made a thousandfold more, by the increase of other dimensions. A punishment may be infinitely dreadful, or infinitely exceed all finite punishments in dreadfullness, by reason of the infinite duration of it; and therefore, it can't be more dreadful with respect to that aggravation of it, viz. its length or continuance, but yet may be vastly more dreadful on other accounts.[4]

714. FREE GRACE. JUSTIFICATION BY FAITH ONLY. Let this be in addition to No. 670. It may be objected that if it be allowed that God promises mercy to the merciful, and forgiveness to the forgiving, and love to the loving (Prov. 8:17), and walking with Christ in white to those that keep

---

4. At this point in the MS there is a fragment of an entry No. 714, which JE deleted with a vertical line. It reads as follows:

"714. RIGHTEOUSNESS OF CHRIST, HIS ACTIVE OBEDIENCE. The satisfaction of Christ by bearing the punishment due to sin, and his active obedience to fulfill the law for us and to be imputed to us, can't be separated. To separate them, and to suppose that Christ only suffered our punishment for us to satisfy for our sins, but never fulfilled the obedience of the law for us, but it was left to us to work out our obedience for ourselves to be acepted, instead of the perfect obedience of the law, seems to be unreasonable."

their garments pure (Rev. 3:4), only out of respect to the natural fitness there is in these graces and qualifications to those blessings; yet this will be to make love, and mercy, and meekness, and all graces, the condition of justification and salvation in the same manner as faith: for faith is the condition by virtue of a natural fitness, and so are those other graces conditions of the same the same way.

To which I answer, that they are not conditions of salvation the same way as faith is, for the following reasons:

1. Their fitness or suitableness to salvation is not so direct as that which is in faith. 'Tis true there is a natural agreeableness or suitableness between all graces and a state of salvation, but faith in its very nature and essence consists in nothing else but a direct according, suiting or closing of the soul with the Savior and his salvation, especially that which may be called fundamental actual salvation, viz. justification by Christ. Though there be an agreeableness between other particular graces and salvation,[5] yet suiting and closing with salvation is not their immediate business, and that wherein the proper nature and essence of them consists, as 'tis in faith.

2. As the suitableness of other graces is more indirect, so 'tis more partial. 'Tis more partial on several accounts: (1) They are especially suited only to some particular part of salvation. Thus mercifulness is especially suited to obtaining mercy, and forgiveness to being forgiven, etc., but faith is the direct according and symphonizing of the soul to the whole of salvation, and especially to that which fundamentally comprehends all actual salvation, viz. justification. (2) The suitableness is more partial in other graces, because in them 'tis especially only as it were some part of the soul that is adapted to such spiritual and heavenly benefits, some one faculty, affection or principle of the soul; but faith in the nature of it is the closing of the whole soul. (3) 'Tis more partial because 'tis only some particular kind of suitableness, as between mercifulness and obtaining mercy there is a suitableness of likeness of the qualification to the benefit. But in faith there is not only an harmony of similitude, but that of actual union, which is a more direct harmonizing than merely there being a similitude. And then it is to be considered,

3. That the suitableness of other graces is comprehended in the suitableness of faith, as the natural suitableness that there is in a forgiving spirit to the blessing of being forgiven, is comprehended in the soul's humbly, and in a sense of its own vileness, coming to Christ as a savior from

5. MS: "salvation and especially."

sin. And other graces have a natural fitness to the salvation of Jesus Christ no otherwise than as every grace has faith in it. There is faith in all evangelical virtues; and virtues become evangelical, and can justly be so denominated, no otherwise than as they partake of the nature of faith, and as they flow from faith in Christ and a closing with the gospel, and as such a principle is expressed in them. As 'tis with obedience, it justifies because it has faith in it. Acts of evangelical obedience are exercises and expressions of the heart's closing with Christ, and admitting and yielding to the glorious gospel that reveals him as a savior. So it is with other graces, as love and meekness, etc., they influence in the affair of justification no otherwise than as expressions of the heart's unition with Christ and his salvation. The distinction we make of graces, as if they were entirely distinct things not implying and containing one another, is not according to truth, and many ways confounds in our inquiries and disquisitions about things of this nature.

715. CHRISTIAN RELIGION. CHRIST'S RESURRECTION. Christ hanging so long on the cross, as he did, with wounds open in his hands and feet, and in extreme pain and torture, that must set it[6] into the most violent motion and ferment, and so more apt to issue freely forth at his wounds. His body must needs be exhausted of almost all its blood. But a body so drained of blood, till it is so weak and spent as to be breathless and motionless, and seem to all to be quite dead, and that, though it was narrowly observed to see whether it was dead, and seemed to be quite dead for a considerable time together, some time before they took him down from the cross, and afterwards while they were handling of it, taking it down from the cross, embalming it and wrapping it [in] grave clothes, and laying it in the sepulcher; I say, a body reduced to such a state by the loss of almost all its blood is in most unlikely circumstances to revive, for the vehicle of life, viz. the blood, is gone. When bodies revive after they seem to be dead, 'tis by a new excitation of the circulation of the fluids of the body; but when these fluids are gone, this can't be.

716. IMMORTALITY OF THE SOUL. FUTURE STATE. Dr. Tillotson shows in his 3rd volume of sermons, sermons 120–123,[7] first, what arguments

6. I.e. his blood.

7. JE's reference is to John Tillotson, *The Works of the Most Reverend Dr. John Tillotson, Lord Archbishop of Canterbury* (3 vols. 4th ed., London, 1728). Sermons 120–123, which are collectively titled "Of the Immortality of the Soul, as discover'd by Nature, and by Revelation," appear in vol. 3, pp. 105–34.

natural reason furnishes us with that there is a future state, and how this was a received principle among all nations, both in former and also in latter ages of the world, and how it was looked upon as exceeding probable by the wisest of the philosophers, who yet seemed to long for a greater certainty and to have it plainly revealed, whether it was so or no. And after [having] shown what expectation the Jews had from the light of nature, together with the more obscure revelations made to them of it, he then proceeds to [show] how fully this matter is brought to light by the gospel that seemed somewhat obscure before; in that, first, the gospel makes a most clear and express revelation of it, absolutely and plainly and abundantly discovers the thing; and secondly, that it is not only revealed and declared, but that state is described with its very particular circumstances; and, says the Doctor, third, "The gospel gives us yet farther assurance of these things by such an Argument as is most like to be most convincing and satisfactory to common capacities; and that is by a lively instance of the thing to be proved, in *raising Christ from the dead*, Acts 17:30–31.

"'Tis true indeed, under the Old Testament there were two instances somewhat of this nature; Enoch and Elias were immediately translated, and taken up [alive] into heaven; but these two instances do in many respects fall short of the other. For after Christ was raised from the dead, he conversed forty days with his disciples, and satisfied them that he was risen; after which he was in their sight visibly taken up into heaven: and as an evidence that he was possessed of his glorious kingdom, he sent down, according to his promise, his Holy Spirit in miraculous gifts, to assure them by those testimonies of his royalty, that he was in heaven, and to qualify them by those miraculous powers to convince the world of the truth of their doctrine.

"Now what argument more proper to convince them of another life after this, than to see a man raised from the dead, and restored to a new life? What fitter to satisfy a man concerning heaven, and the happy state of those there, than to see one visibly taken up into heaven? And what more fit to assure us, that the promises of the gospel are real, and shall be made good to us, than to see him who made these promises to us, raise himself from the dead, and go up into heaven, and from thence [to] dispense miraculous gifts abroad in the world, as evidences of the power and authority which he is invested withal? All the philosophical arguments that a man can bring for the soul's immortality, and another life, will have no force upon vulgar apprehensions, in comparison of these sensible demonstrations, which give an experiment of the thing, and furnish us with an instance of something of the same kind, and of equal difficulty with that which is propounded to our belief."[8] See No. 584.

717. FIRST COVENANT. THE FALL. Why only Adam's first transgression is imputed to us. Ridgley's *Body of Divinity*, vol. 1, p. 331.[9] "This appears from hence, that Adam, as soon as he sinned, lost the honor and prerogative, that was conferred upon him of being the federal head of his posterity, though he was their natural head, or common father; for the covenant being broken, all the evils, that we were liable to, arising from thence, were devolved upon us, and none of the blessings, contained therein, could be conveyed to us that way, since it was impossible for him, after his fall, to perform sinless obedience, which was the condition of the life promised therein. This doth not arise so much from the nature of the covenant, as from the change that there was in man, with whom it was made," whereby he became unfit any longer to be a federal head. "The law, or covenant, would have given life, if man could have yielded perfect obedience; but since the fall rendered that impossible, though the obli-gation thereof, as a law, distinct from a covenant, and the curse, arising from the sanction thereof, remains still in force against fallen man; yet, as a covenant, in which life was promised" on condition of obedience, "it was from that time, abrogated" because that matter of man's obedience was already decided, obedience was what man had already failed of. "And therefore the Apostle speaks of it, as weak through the flesh, that is, by reason of Adam's transgression, and consequently he ceased, from that time, to be the federal head, or means of conveying life to his posterity; therefore those sins he committed afterwards, were no more imputed to them, to enhance their condemnation, than his repentance or good works, were imputed for their justification." [The] sentence of condemnation was already immediately passed upon Adam, and on his posterity with him, when he had broken the covenant, agreeable to the threatening contained in the covenant. The covenant was immediately acted upon. And he that gave the covenant proceeded to judgment, and so the whole affair of trying of mankind upon that covenant with Adam was determined. Judgment is the final issue of

8. Tillotson's *Works*, 3, 132–33. In sermons 120–122 Tillotson shows "what arguments natural reason doth furnish us with, for the immortality of our souls" (3, 126). In sermon 123, as JE indicates, he discusses, first, what assurance heathen philosophers and Jews had of immortality, second, "what further evidence and assurance the Gospel gives us of it, than the world had before" (3, 128). JE summarizes the first two points under this second head and quotes directly from the third.

9. Ridgley, *A Body of Divinity* (see above, No. 701, p. 283, n. 1). This passage occurs in vol. 1, Quest. XXII, which is entitled "Did all mankind fall in that first transgression?" (p. 331).

God's transacting with man in a covenant established. When God has already acted upon it, 'tis absurd to suppose that God still treats with man upon that covenant. Though the law or covenant of works stood in force, still yet the covenant with Adam was acted upon and done with. And so with the covenant of works, [it would] have been done with too, as much as it will be after the day of judgment, were it not that there is still a possibility and a trial for obtaining by that covenant under a new head, even under Christ. The voice of that covenant still is directed to us, viz. that if we sin in ourselves, or in our surety, we shall die. But if we obey in ourselves, or in our surety, without sin we shall live. And though it be impossible for us to obtain life by obeying ourselves, as obedience is the price of life, yet there is still encouragement for our obedience, as obedience may be otherwise a means or occasion of life to us, and that no less than before, in those that live under the gospel. So that the sins of such don't only expose 'em to punishment, but to a punishment no less aggravated than if we could obtain life by obedience as its price, and on other accounts much more aggravated. See this matter much more clearly set forth, in answer to the inquiry, in the beginning of my third sermon from Gen. 3:11.[1]

God, not only after Adam had violated the covenant, presently acted upon it and proceeded to judgment; but he before, in the making of the covenant, declared that he would do so. "In the day that thou eatest thereof," said God, "thou shalt surely die" [Gen. 2:17]. So that the very establishment, or covenant itself, as God revealed and stated it, implied that the first, overt, explicit violation should be the abolishing of the covenant as to future proceedings, because that was in the establishment, that on the first violation God would immediately proceed to judgment.

718. CONVICTION. WORK OF THE LAW. Why the enmity of the heart is stirred up against [it] in persons under the work of the law. See "Notes on Scripture," no. 244.[2]

719. LORD'S DAY. Add this to No. 691, at the end of § 12.[3] And besides, the Scripture does expressly call this day the day of their coming up out

1. This four-unit sermon on Gen. 3:11 (Feb. 1739) takes as its doctrine, "The act of our first father in eating the forbidden fruit was a very heinous act." In the third sermon JE answers the inquiry, "Why only that first act of sin in our father Adam, his eating the forbidden fruit, is imputed to his posterity, and not the other sins that he committed afterwards." The reason, JE argues, is that "the time of Adam's trial as the covenant head of his posterity was over as soon as that act was completed."

2. This note considers Rom. 6:14 (*Works, 15,* 198–99).

3. See above, p. 269.

of the land of Egypt. Hos. 2:15, "And she shall sing there, as in the days of her youth, and as in the day when she came up out of the land of Egypt"; referring plainly [to] that triumphant song that Moses and the children of Israel sang when they came up out of the Red Sea.

720. FIRST COVENANT. FALL. "Now that there was a covenant between God and our first parents, tending to this purpose, that if they continued in obedience, that they should never die, but be always blessed and happy, as well as in case of disobedience, be subject to death, and all other calamities, is plain from the preface, which ushers in the prohibition given to Adam concerning his not eating of the tree of knowledge, with this express donation or grant; that 'of every tree of the garden' (not excepting the tree of life) 'he might freely eat.' For whether the tree of life was a sacramental sign, or a natural means of immortality, 'tis evident from the words of God himself, that whoever made use of it, was put in a capacity of living *forever*. Nay, the very commination itself imports all this: for how insignificant would have been the threatening of death to a man's eating of the forbidden fruit, if he should have died, whether he had eaten of it or not?" See *Complete Body of Divinity*, p. 278.[4]

721. HAPPINESS OF HEAVEN AFTER THE RESURRECTION, their external blessedness and delight. See Nos. 95, 182, [and] especially 263. As the saints after the resurrection will have an external part, or an outward man, distinct from their souls, so it necessarily follows that they shall have external perception or sense. And doubtless then all their sense, and all the perception that they have, will be delighted and filled with happiness. Every perceptive faculty shall be an inlet of delight. Particularly then, doubtless they will have the sense of seeing, which is the noblest of all external senses; and then without doubt, the most noble sense will receive most pleasure and delight. The sensory will be immensely more perfect than now it is. And the external light of the heavenly world will be a perfectly different kind of light from the light of the sun, or any light in this world, exciting a sensation or idea in the beholders perfectly different— of which we can no more conceive than we can conceive of a color we never saw, or than a blind man can conceive of light and colors—a sort of light immensely more pleasant and glorious, in comparison of which the

---

4. Thomas Stackhouse, *A Complete Body of Divinity, Consisting in 5 parts . . . The whole extracted from the best ancient and modern writers* (London, 1729), Pt. III, ch. 1, "The most memorable Transactions, from the Creation to the Flood," p. 278.

sun is a shade, and his light but darkness. And this world full of the light of the sun is a world under the darkness of night, but that a world of light, affording inexpressible pleasure and delight to the beholders immensely exceeding all sensitive delights in this world.

That the light of heaven, which will be the light of the brightness of Christ's glo[rified] body, shall be a perfectly different sort of light from that of this world, seems evident from Rev. 21:11. And that it will be so, and will also be ravishingly sweet to the eye, is evident from the circumstances of Christ's transfiguration (see note on II Pet. 1:11 to the end; "Scripture," no. 265);[5] and also from the circumstances of Moses's vision of God in the mount (see note on Ex. 33:18 to the end; "Scripture," no. 266).[6]

But yet this pleasure from external perception will in a sense have God for its object. It will be in a sight of Christ's external glory. And it will be so ordered in its degree and circumstances, as to be wholly and absolutely subservient to a spiritual sight of that divine spiritual glory, of which this will be a semblance and external representation; and subservient to the superior spiritual delights of the saints, as the body will in all respects be a spiritual body, and subservient to the happiness of the spirit. And there will be no tendency to, or danger of, an inordinacy or predominance. This visible glory will be subservient to a sense of mind of spiritual glory, as the music of God's praises is to holy sense and pleasure, and more immediately so, because this that will be seen by the bodily eye will be God's glory, but that music will not be so immediately God's harmony.

722. VISIBLE CHURCH. Add this to No. 689, § 8. They at the day of judgment shall be found not to have been faithful, that have not persevered. They shall be rejected and cast out of Christ's church and out of God's house. Such branches shall be cut off from the vine. Their names shall be blotted out of the book of life. Their talents shall be taken away and given to others. But herein shall only be taken from [them] that which they seemed to have, agreeably to Christ's threatening (Luke 8:18), or that which he visibly had: for he never any otherwise was in the church of Christ or house of God, or [was] a branch in the true vine, or [had] his name in the book of life.

723. WISDOM OF GOD IN THE WORK OF REDEMPTION. CALLING OF THE GENTILES. It was fit that when Christ came into the world on such an

---

5. JE adds "pp. 3–4 and 7–8 of that note." See *Works, 15,* 213–17.
6. See *Works, 15,* 219–20.

errand as to save sinners—those that were in themselves aliens and strangers, children of wrath and without God in the world—that his church that should be gathered to him on his coming should be chiefly made up of those that were visibly such, of those that were not Jews but sinners, of the gentiles that were visibly enemies of God and under darkness, aliens from the commonwealth of Israel, and visible slaves and worshippers of the devil: hereby the design and efficacy of Christ's redemption is made the more conspicuous.

724. PREPARATORY WORK. A being terrified with fears of wrath and seeing the dismal consequences of sin has in itself no tendency to wean the heart from sin: for true weanedness from sin don't consist in being afraid of the mischief that will follow from sin, but in hating sin itself, and don't arise from a sight of the dreadful consequences of sin, but from a sight of the odiousness of sin in its own nature. But yet one may be a good preparation for the other, and is commonly so made use of by God. For a man to meet with many worldly losses and disappointments has in itself no tendency to true weanedness from the world, because true weanedness from the world don't consist in being beat off from the world by the affliction of it, but a being drawn off by the sight of something better.

725. VANITY OF THE WORLD. After the fall, the place of paradise was altered. It was changed from earth to heaven, and God ordered it so that nothing paradisaical should be any more here. And though sometimes there be great appearances of it, and men are ready to flatter themselves that they shall obtain it, yet it is found that paradise is not here, and there is nothing but the shadow of it. Those things that look most paradisaical will have some sting to spoil them.

726. PERSEVERANCE. 'Tis one act of faith to commit the soul to Christ's keeping, in this sense, viz. to keep it from falling. The believing soul is convinced of its own weakness and helplessness, its inability to resist its enemies, its insufficiency to keep itself, and so commits itself to Christ that he would be its keeper. The Apostle speaks of his committing his soul by faith to Christ under great sufferings and trials of his perseverance. II Tim. 1:12, "For which cause also I suffer these things: nevertheless I am not ashamed; for I know whom I have believed, and am persuaded that he is able to keep that which I have committed to him against that day." And we are commanded to commit our way and our works unto the Lord (Ps.

37:5, Prov. 16:3).[7] Faith depends on Christ for all good that we need, and especially good of this kind, that is of such absolute necessity in order to the salvation of our souls. The sum of the good that faith looks for is the Holy Spirit—for spiritual and eternal life, perfect holiness in heaven [and] persevering holiness here—for the just shall life by faith.

727. EXALTATION OF CHRIST, how the divine nature is concerned in that exaltation. The divine nature is concerned in it in two respects: (1) Although the glory of that was not really added to, yet his glory received an additional manifestation. The glory of the divine person was veiled in the meanness and sufferings of the human nature, but now it shone forth gloriously in the exaltation of the human nature. (2) Though Christ's humanity was the more immediate and proper subject of the exaltation, yet the divinity was the especial ground of it. When God[8] was about to exalt Christ, he looked upon [him] not merely as man but as a divine person, for it was on this account that he looked upon it meet that he should be so exalted. In one sense, it was as he was man only that he was capable of being exalted, viz. because it was as such only that he was capable of being higher than he was before. But in another sense, it was as he was God only that he was capable of such an exaltation, for it was only by reason of his being God that he was capable of being made so high.

728. SUFFERINGS OF CHRIST. The divinity supported the humanity of Christ under his sufferings not as it kept his human nature from being annihilated or crushed in that respect, but as it kept him from sinking, and his courage from utterly failing, so as that he should have no command of himself; communicating such a degree of holiness to him, as to keep him from impatience and discontent, and that his love might be so great as to make him voluntary in it, in the midst of it. Probably these sufferings would have overcome the holiness of any mere creature, and that no creature has such love either to God or men as to hold such a trial.

729. PERSEVERANCE, in what sense necessary to salvation. See [No.] 1188. Though perseverance is acknowledged by Calvinian divines to be necessary to salvation, yet it seems to me that the manner in which it is necessary has not been sufficiently set forth. 'Tis owned to be necessary

7. At this point JE deleted the following lines: "Whatsoever is the matter of prayer is the matter of faith. And the prayer of faith can never fail, for it is said, 'Ask and you shall recieve'; which is spoken especially with respect to the needed influences of the Spirit of God."

8. MS: "when as God."

as a *sine qua non;* and also is expressed by that, that though it is not that by which we first come to have a title to eternal life, yet it is necessary in order to the actual possession of it, as the way to it; that it is impossible that we should come to it without perseverance, as 'tis impossible for a man to go to a city or town without traveling throughout the road that leads to it. But we are really saved by perseverance, so that salvation has a dependence on perseverance, as that which influences in the affair, so as to render it congruous that we should be saved. Faith is the great condition of salvation; 'tis that BY which we are justified and saved, as 'tis what renders it congruous that we should be looked upon as having a title to salvation. But this faith on which salvation thus depends, and the perseverance that belongs to it, is one thing in it that is really a fundamental ground of the congruity that such a qualification gives to salvation. Faith is that which renders it congruous that we should be accepted to a title to salvation. And it is so on the account of certain properties in, or certain things that belong to, it; and this is one of them, viz. its perseverance. Without this it would not be fit that a sinner should be accepted to salvation. Perseverance indeed comes into consideration even in the justification of a sinner, as one thing on which the fitness of acceptance to life depends. For though a sinner is justified on his first act of faith, yet even then, in that act of justification, God has respect to perseverance, as being virtually in that first act; and 'tis looked upon as if it were a property of the faith, by which the sinner is then justified. God has respect to continuance in faith, and the sinner is justified by that, as though it already were, because by divine establishment it shall follow; and so it is accepted as if it were a property contained in the faith that is then seen. Without this, it would not be congruous that the sinner should be justified at his first believing; but it would be needful that the act of justification should be suspended, till the sinner had persevered in faith. For a like reason that it is necessary that there should be one act of faith in order to its being congruous that a person should be saved, it is also necessary that there should be perseverance in faith.

Faith gives a title to salvation as it gives an union to Christ, or is in its nature an actual unition of the soul to Christ. But there is the same reason why 'tis necessary that the union between Christ and the soul should remain in order to salvation, as that it should once be, or that it should [be] begun: for it is begun to that end that it might remain, and if it could be begun without remaining, the beginning would be in vain. The soul is saved no otherwise than *in union* with Christ, and so is fitly looked upon [as] his. 'Tis saved *in him;* and in order to that, 'tis necessary that the soul should now be in him, even when salvation is actually bestowed, and not only that it should once have been in him. In order to its being now saved, it must now be one of Christ's; and in order to being fitly or congruously looked on as now one of Christ's, it is necessary that it should now be united, and not only that it should be remembered that he once was united. And there is the same reason why believing, or the quality wherein the unition consists, should remain in order to the union's remaining, as why the unition should once be in order to the union's once being.

The first act of faith gives a title to salvation, because it does, virtually at least, trust in God and Christ for perseverance among other benefits, and gives a title to this benefit with others, and so virtually contains perseverance; otherwise, it would not be congruous that the sinner should be justified on the first act of faith. And therefore God, in justifying a sinner, even in the first act of faith, has respect to the congruity between justification and perseverance of faith. So that perseverance is necessary to salvation not only as a *sine qua non*, or as the way to possession, but 'tis necessary even to the congruity of justification; and that not the less because a sinner is justified on his first act of believing, or because that perseverance is promised when once there has been one act of faith: for God in justifying a sinner, or at least all that in justification that respects a future reward, has respect to his own promise, and to the fitness of a qualification beheld as yet only in his own promise.

That perseverance is thus necessary to salvation not only as a *sine qua non*, but by reason of such an influence and dependence, seems manifest from Scripture, as particularly, Heb. 10:38–39, "Now the just shall live by faith: but if any man draw, back my soul shall have no pleasure in him. But we are not of them who draw back unto perdition; but of them that believe to the saving of the soul." Rom. 11:20, "Well; because of unbelief they were broken off, but thou standest by faith. Be not high-minded, but fear." John 15:7, "If ye abide in me, and my words abide in you, ye shall ask what ye will, and it shall be done unto you." Heb. 3:14, "For we are made partakers of Christ, if we hold the beginning of our confidence firm unto the end." Heb. 6:12, "Be ye followers of them who through faith and patience inherit the promises."

So that not only the first act of faith, but after-acts of faith, and perseverance in faith, do justify the sinner; and that, although salvation is in itself sure and certain after the first act. For the way wherein the first act of faith justifies, is not by making the futurition of salvation certain in itself, for that is as certain in itself by the divine decree, before the first act of faith, as afterwards. But 'tis only [in] these two things that any act of ours can connect salvation with the subject: (1) as it may give a congruity; and (2) as it gives such a divine manifestation of the futurition of salvation to us, that we can lay hold of and depend on as relying on the divine truth and faithfulness that we shall have salvation. Salvation is in some sense the sinner's right before he believes; it was given him in Christ before the world was. But before a sinner believes, he is not actually possessed of that which gives the congruity, nor has he anything from God that he can lay hold of, so as either to challenge it, or on good grounds hope for it. He can't be said to have any right, for he has no congruity; and as to the promise made to Christ, he has no hold of that, because that is not revealed to him. If God had declared and promised to the angels that such a man should be saved, that would not give him any right of his own, or any challenge. A promise is a manifestation of a person's design of doing some good to another, to that end, to enable him, and that he may depend on it, and rest in it. The certainty in him arises from the manifestation; and the obligation in justice to him arises from the manifestation's being made to him, to that tendency and end that he might depend on it. And therefore, after-acts of faith may be said to give a sinner a title to salvation, as well as the first: for, from what has been said, it appears that the congruity arises from them, as well as the first, they in like manner containing the nature of unition to Christ as Mediator. And they may have as great and greater hand in the manifestation of the futurition of salvation to us, for our dependence, as the first act; for our knowledge of this may be mainly from after-acts, and from a course of acts. This is all that is peculiar to the first act: that so far as the act is plain, it gives us evidence from God for our dependence, both for continued acts of faith, and also the salvation that is connected with them. So that so far as this act is plain to us, we can challenge both these as our right. The Scripture speaks of after-acts of faith in both Abraham and Noah, as giving a title to the righteousness which is the matter of justification. See Rom. 4:3, Heb. 11:7.

From this latter part of the foregoing number we may draw two corollaries.

Corol. 1. Hence we may learn that the saints under the old testament had not so much given them, whence they might hope for and challenge salvation, from their first conversion, because the promises of perseverance were much more obscure, and an assurance of perseverance was rather spoken of as a benefit that should be enjoyed in gospel times, than one that was enjoyed by the church already (Jer. 31:31–33 and 32:37–40; Ezek. 11:19–20 and 36:25–27). Seeing 'tis only by the manifestation to us for our dependence that God properly lies under obligation to us, hence a title to life from the first act of faith was more imperfectly made over to the saints under the old testament than now. This is one way in which that dispensation was more legal, and savored more of a covenant of works, in which the reward was suspended on an uncertain perseverance. And by this we may the better understand the meaning of these places in the prophets.

Corol. 2. Hence also we may learn how good works and a course of obedience influence in the affair of justification, or in what sense we are by them entitled to eternal life, viz. as by them, in the latter way mentioned, we have divine manifestations of the futurition of life, which we may lay hold on and depend upon; but not in the former, viz. as giving a congruity to an interest in them.

730. MISERY OF HELL. Instead of the damneds' being comforted in each others' company, 'tis probable that they will be as coals or brands in a fire, that heat and burn one another.

731. LORD'S DAY. Ex. 12:42, "It is a night to be much observed to the Lord for bringing them out from the land of Egypt: this is that night of the Lord to be observed of all the children of Israel in their generations." From this text I would observe several things: (1) That a work of redemption, deliverance or salvation is a sort of work especially worthy and fit to be commemorated, by observing and keeping sacred the time in which it was wrought, or keeping it as holy time, or as the Lord's time, from generation to generation, because it is said, it is to be "observed *to the Lord.*" And again, "this is that *night of the Lord,*" or which is the same thing, the *Lord's night,* and "to be observed of all the children of Israel *in their* generations." (2) That a work of redemption is the more worthy to be thus observed, by keeping holy the time of it, by how much the greater that redemption is; because 'tis evident that this night is here spoken [of], as what is thus to be much observed, upon this account, viz. that the redemption was so great. And therefore, (3) a work of deliverance, or redemption of God's church, or Israel, that is infinitely greater than this, and also that this redemption out of Egypt was wrought on purpose to be an image and type of, is a work that it is a very fit and condecent thing that the church in all ages should commemorate after this manner.

732. COMMON ILLUMINATION. The nature of the work of the Spirit may be learnt from the nature of his work in legal conviction. 'Tis the same common enlightening assistance of both, but only one is of evil, and the

other of good. Those legal convictions that natural men have are from the common illuminations of the Spirit of God concerning evil. Those pleasant religious affections and apprehensions that natural men sometimes have are from the common illuminations of the Spirit of God concerning good. The assistance given is of a like sort in both, but only the object is different. One respects good and the other evil, both which natural men are equally capable of apprehending without any supernatural principle. The mind [of] man, without a supernatural principle, is capable of two things with respect to conviction of evil:

1. The judgment is capable of being convinced of evil. Men's natural reason is capable of discerning force in those arguments that prove it. Though sin greatly clouds the judgment concerning these things, a natural man's reason, by common assistance of it against the clouding, prejudicing and stupefying nature of sin, is capable of seeing the force of many arguments that prove God's anger and future punishment, and the greatness of these things. And so a natural man is capable of being convinced how much there is in him contrary to God's law, and to how great a degree it is contrary, and what connection there is between these faults and God's anger and future punishment.

2. Besides a conviction of truth respecting evil in the judgment, a natural man as such is capable of a sense of heart of this evil, i.e. he is capable of a deeply impressed, and lively and affecting idea and sense of these things, which is something more than a mere conviction in the judgment concerning their truth. The mind of a natural man is capable of a sense of the heart of natural [evil], or of those things that are terrible to nature.

And therefore, what the Spirit of God does in legal conviction, or, which is the same thing, common illuminations of evil, is to assist those principles, viz. the natural reason or judgment, against the prejudicing blinding tendency of sin, and to assist the sense of the heart against the stupefying nature of sin.

And it is the same kind of influence or assistance that is given in common convictions and immuminations of good, whereby the souls of natural men are affected with thoughts of God's love and pity and kindness to them or others, of benefits offered or bestowed on them, of being beloved of God, of being delivered from calamity, of having honor put upon them of God, and the like. For the mind of man, without any supernatural principle, is in like manner capable of two things, viz. (1) of a conviction of the judgment by reasons that evince the truth of the things of religion, that respect natural good; and (2) of a sense of heart of natural good. And so God assists these principles in common illumination.

And 'tis to be noted that a conviction of evil abundantly makes way for such a conviction of good. A conviction of sin and guilt makes way for a conviction of the greatness of mercy held forth. A conviction of [the] danger of misery prepares for a more sensible affecting idea of God's pity, appearing either in comfortable words of Scripture, or in the great works of God in redemption, or in his particular providence towards the person affected.

Such a conviction and illumination of the mind, or such an assistance of the soul to a sense of the good or evil things of religion, is the proper work of the Spirit of God: for the Spirit of God is indeed the author of our capacity of discerning, or having a sense of heart, of natural good or evil, for this really differs not from the faculty of man's will. And it was especially the work of the Spirit of God in creation, wherein the three persons of the Trinity were conjunct, to infuse this principle, this part of the natural image of God: for herein man is made in the image of God, who has understanding and will, which will is the same with the Holy Ghost; and therefore, the assisting this principle in its actings and in giving a sense of good and evil, is proper to the Holy Ghost.

733. WHY THE MEDIATOR [IS] THE SECOND PERSON IN THE TRINITY. WISDOM OF GOD IN THE WORK OF REDEMPTION. The Mediator ought to be the middle person of the Trinity because, in[9] being the mediator between the saints and God, he is intermediate between the Spirit and the Father, or between the third person and the first; for 'tis the Spirit of God in the saints that is that by which they are saints. The Spirit is the sum of all that which they have from the Father through the Son, all that the Father doth through the Mediator, to and for the saints, terminates in the Spirit. And on the other hand, all that by which they come to the Father through the Mediator is the Spirit, and all that they do or transact through the Son, towards God, is by the Spirit. 'Tis the Spirit in them that puts forth acts of faith in God through a mediator. 'Tis the Spirit that prays and that gives praises, etc. See No. 737.

734. PREPARATORY WORK is from the Spirit of God. It is a work that properly belongs to this person of the Trinity, though there be no holiness in it, and so nothing of the nature of the Holy Spirit communicated to the soul, or exerted in the soul in it. As the embryo of Christ in the womb of the Virgin Mary, though it had no spirit or soul, and so no proper

9. MS: "for in."

holiness of nature, and nothing of the nature of the Holy Spirit in it, yet was from the Spirit of God; for it was a work wrought in the womb of the Virgin that was preparatory, or in order, to an holy effect or production in her, for that was an holy thing that was born of her.

735. HUMILIATION. 'Tis true that natural men are capable of being convinced of the justice of God in their own damnation, because they will be convinced of it at the day of judgment; and so they are capable of being convinced of the certain truth of the same great things of religion, that natural men will be convinced of at that day. But yet it don't follow that it ordinarily is so, till saving conversion. The conviction of both will be given at the day of judgment the same way, viz. (1) by strengthening the faculty of understanding, and clear setting forth the reasons and arguments that evince the justice of God in the damnation of sinners, and other great truths of religion; and (2) by the sight of the greatness and majesty of God, which will convince of the infinite greatness of the guilt of sin that is committed against God, and so its proportion to the eternal punishment, and also will convince and assure of other truths that had before been taught concerning God, as his infinite power, his wisdom, his justice, his truth, his holiness, his immutability. For a sight of the greatness of God, with arguments deduced from it, will make 'em know these things, and many others, though it won't make 'em see the beauty and loveliness of these things in God. So that a natural man is capable, while such, to see the truth and certainty of these things, as well as of the justice of God in his own eternal damnation; but it don't follow that such do ordinarily see them in this world, before conversion. No more can we argue that it is ordinary for them to see God's justice in their own damnation before conversion.

736. CONSUMMATION OF ALL THINGS. CHRIST'S DELIVERING UP THE KINGDOM TO THE FATHER. [See] Nos. 609, 664, § 9, 742. After this is done, Christ shall still continue to reign. "Luke 1:33, 'He shall reign over the house of Jacob for ever; and of his kingdom there shall be no end.' . . . Are the gifts of God to his saints without repentance [Rom. 11:29]; and are they not so to his Son? It was long since declared, that 'of the increase of Christ's government and peace there should be no end' (Is. 9:7); and, with respect to his sitting at God's right hand, that his dominion is an 'everlasting dominion,' which shall not pass away; and his kingdom, that which shall not be destroyed (Dan. 7:14); that he shall reign over his people in Mt. Zion, from henceforth, even forever (Mic. 4:7), and that his throne is forever and ever (Heb. 1:8). . . . Christ prayed that his people might be

with him, to behold his mediatorial glory [John 17:24]; and shall this glory cease as soon as they all come to see it? What good then would this prayer do[1] them? How short-lived a happiness would it be to some of them, who should only have a short glimpse of it, after the resurrection, and then behold it no more forever, whilst others have been in the views of it ever since Christ's ascension?"

That prayer of Christ in the 24th verse of the 17th chapter of John never shall be fully answered till the day of judgment. Till then, it shall not be answered at all with respect to many that God hath given him; and it will not be so fully answered with respect to any before, as it will then. The church never will be with Christ to behold his glory in that eminent and glorious manner before, as she will then, when the marriage of the Lamb is come. The bride is never with the bridegroom in that full acquaintance and intimate communion before, as she is after marriage. And marriage is not only for this acquaintance and communion on the wedding day, but in order to it ever after. Therefore we may conclude that the glory and exaltation that the Father gives Christ, will not be diminished after the day of judgment.

Christ in this prayer seems to have a principal respect to his people's being with him after his second coming. It is probable by John 14:3, "And if I go and prepare a place for you, I will come again, and receive you unto myself; that where I am, there ye may be also"; for we may well suppose that he has respect to the same in his prayer with his disciples—when he speaks of their being with him where he is—as in his discourse with them, at the same time and on the same occasion, and wherein he uses almost the same words. By the glory that God had given Christ, he meant the glory that God was about to exalt him to at his ascension into heaven, and sitting at God's right hand, wherein he should be invested with kingly glory; as appears by the beginning of his prayer, where he prays for that glory and exaltation and dominion over all flesh that was approaching, and that God had promised him, and that was to be given him in reward for his going through the work of our redemption, as may be evident by comparing the 1st, 2nd and 4th verses [of John 17]. "Will Christ the chief shepherd hereafter give to his under-shepherds 'a crown of glory that fadeth not away' [I Pet. 5:4], and shall his own wither? Shall he who is chief, have less honor than they who are so much inferior to him? Shall the subjects wear a crown when the King has none?" The reward shall not cease when the work is done, but "the reward is rather to begin than end,

1. MS: "to do."

when that which is procured it is accomplished." And therefore, Christ's crown and kingdom, that he has in reward for his doing the work of redemption, shall not cease at the day of judgment, for not till then will he have perfected all that belongs to this work.

And therefore, we may argue that Christ's glory will then be greatly increased, rather than diminished (see No. 664, § 9). It will be with the head as with the members in this respect. As the saints that are now in heaven—Enoch, Elias and others—han't their full glory, their consummate reward, but it is to be given at the day of judgment; so will it be with the head. When the Son of God, as a son over his own house, hath faithfully finished and completed his vicegerency, and comes and delivers it up to the Father as a betrustment that had been committed to him of the Father, as having faithfully and fully discharged the trust reposed in him, then will the Father accept of him as having been faithful, and then will he reward [him]. When he lays down his work of vicegerency and delivers up his betrustment into the hands of the Father, then shall the Father give the reward into his hands. Then will Christ come to the Father and say, "I have glorified thee on the earth: I have finished the work which thou givest me to do," in an yet higher sense than he did, when he finished the work of his life on the earth, in the 17th chapter of John, v. 4. And then will he make use of this as a plea for his reward and glory, as he did then, saying, "and now, O Father, glorify me with thine own self" (v. 5). And then will he say, "I have manifested thy name to the men which thou gavest me out of the world: thine they were, and thou gavest them me; and they have kept thy word," in a more full sense than he did then (v. 6); for then will this be true of all that the Father has given him out of the world. "The members of Christ shall reign in life forever, and that as sitting together with Christ in heavenly places, and as being made partakers of Christ's exaltation; and shall not their head, who procured them this dignity," and in communion with whom they have it? "How can the saints reign with Christ forever if he himself don't reign forever? . . . The Scriptures . . . tell us that Christ is a 'priest forever, after the power of an endless life' [Heb. 7:16], and that he sat down forever on the right hand of God."

Christ will to all eternity continue the medium of communication between God and the saints. "That God, who gathers all the things in heaven together in Christ, will doubtless continue him, as an everlasting bond of union, and medium of communion, betwixt himself and the glorified saints. If the elect angels were chosen and confirmed forever in Christ, as their head, as the scripture seems to intimate [Eph. 1:10], what reason can there be that those redeemed from among men, should not forever abide in him? The whole family in heaven, and on earth, good angels, and redeemed men, are named of Christ: he is their head, the head of all principalities and powers; the angels worship him, and are part of the general assembly gathered together in Christ; in him all the members of this family are united, and in him they forever abide; he therefore is forever their Lord and head. Christ is the eternal head of the whole family; God hath placed one head over angels and men. Thus there is a strict union and conjunction, all having one heavenly necessary bond of union, as one of the ancient writers has expressed it.[2] . . . Christ's sitting at God's right hand, and being 'head over all things to the church' [Eph. 1:20, 22], are joined together in Scripture; and certainly there is a very close connection betwixt them. It is said of the heavenly Jerusalem, that 'the Lamb is the light thereof' [Rev. 21:23]; this may respect that unction from Christ, the holy one, the emanations of light from the Holy Spirit, derived from Christ, the eternal head of the glorified church; and if so, then Christ forever sits at the Father's right hand, not only as King and priest, but also as prophet; from whom, by his Spirit, light is continually communicated to that blessed assembly." Hurrion, *Of the Knowledge of Christ Glorified*, pp. 196–98.[3] See note on I Cor. 15:24, and the things there quoted.[4]

737. MEDIATOR, WHY THE SECOND PERSON IN THE TRINITY. See No. 733. This was necessary that so the Mediator might be a person beloved of God. The third person may be said to be beloved of God, but not so

2. Hurrion cites "Chrysostom in loc." See the next footnote.

3. John Hurrion, *The Knowledge of Christ Glorified, opened and applied in twelve sermons on Christ's resurrection, ascension, sitting at God's right hand, intercession and judging the world* (London, 1729), from which JE quotes intermittently throughout No. 736. The discourse was later reprinted in *The Whole Works of John Hurrion* (3 vols. London, 1823), 2, 128–32.

4. The "Blank Bible" note on I Cor. 15:24 includes cross-references to "Miscellanies" Nos. 86 and 609 (*Works, 13*, 250–51, and above, pp. 143–45); to van Mastricht's *Theoretico-Practica Theologia*, p. 1096b (see above, No. 609, p. 145, n. 1); and to a "Blank Bible" note on I Cor. 15:28, which itself includes cross-references to "Notes on Scripture," no. 158 (*Works, 15*, 95–96) and to Christoph Matthew Pfaff's *Institutiones theologiae dogmaticae et moralis* (Tübingen, 1720), p. 439. By his reference to "the things there quoted," JE probably intends to cite not only van Mastricht but also Pfaff, who makes the following comment on I Cor. 15:24 on p. 439 of the *Institutiones:* "Illa traditio non est actus depositionis sed propositionis: non deponet regnum, quod usque ad consummationem seculi gratiose gubernavit Christus, in ist a consummatione, sed proponet Deo Patri ad lustrationem quasi & gloriam. Sicut belli dux destructis omnibus hostibus, Regi, qui per ipsum hucusque bellum gesserat, victoriosum ac triumph abundant exerciutium, servatos cives populos liberos, praesentat & exhibit, ut judicet ac juidicio suo comprobet praeclare & ad Regis gloriam gesta, non tamen depunit potestatem, quam in exercitum habiuit, ita multo magis Christus tamquam filius consummato seculo & summotis hostibus universis sistet exercitum suum ecclesisticum coram DEO Patre."

properly, because he is the infinite love of God itself. He is the delight that
the Father and the Son have in each other. A person may be said to love
the delight he has in a person that he loves, but not so properly as he loves
that person, because this would make love to that love, and delight in that
delight, and again delight in the delight that he has in that delight, and
so on in infinitum. It was above all things necessary in a mediator between
God and his enemies that were justly the objects of his wrath, that he
should be a person beloved of God. The success of everything in his mediation depends upon that.

738. UNION OF THE DIVINE AND HUMAN NATURE OF CHRIST IN ONE
PERSON. The divine Logos is so united to the humanity of Christ that it
spake and acted by it, and made use of it as its organ, as is evident by the
history of Christ's life, and as it is evident he will do at the day of judgment. And this he does not occasionally once in a while, as he may in the
prophets, but constantly, not by an occasional communication, but a constant and everlasting union. Now 'tis manifest that the Logos, in thus acting by the humanity of Christ, did not merely make use of his body as its
organ, but his soul, not only the members of his body, but the faculties of
his soul; which can be no otherwise than by such a communication with
his understanding as we call identity of consciousness. If the divine Logos
speaks in and by the man Christ Jesus, so that the man Christ Jesus in his
speaking should say, I say thus or thus, and his human understanding is
made use of by the Logos, and it be the speech of his human understanding, it must be by such a communication between the Logos and the
human nature as to communicate consciousness.

739. LOVE TO GOD. PREDOMINANCY OF GRACE. See [No.] 567. Though
it be by many things most evident that there is but little grace in the hearts
of the godly in their present infant state, to what there is of corruption,
yet 'tis also very evident by the Scripture that grace is the principle that
reigns and predominates in the heart of a godly man, in such a manner
as that it is the spirit that he is of, and so that it denominates the man so.
Goodness or godliness prevails in him, so that he is called a good man, a
godly righteous man, a saint or holy man. Humility predominates; therefore, all good men are called humble men. Meekness predominates, so
that all good men are denominated the meek. Mercifulness prevails, so
that all good men are called merciful men. So godly persons are represented as such as love God, and not the world; for 'tis said, "if any man love
the world, the love of the Father is not in him" [I John 1:15]. A true dis-

ciple of Christ is represented as one that loves Christ above father and mother, and wife and children, houses and lands, yea, than his own life, that loves him above all and therefore sells all for him. Now how can these things consist with his having so little grace and so much corruption, his having so little divine love and so much love to the world? And why can't it be so that a man may [have] some true love to God, and yet that love be so little and the love of the world so much, that he may be said to love the world a great deal better than God?

I answer, 'tis from the nature of the object loved, rather [than] from the degree of the principle in the lover. The object beloved is of supreme excellency, of a loveliness immensely above all, worthy to be chosen and pursued and cleaved to and delighted [in] far above all. And he that truly loves [God], loves him as seeing this superlative excellency, seeing of it as superlative, and as being convinced that [it] is far above all. Though a man has but a faint discovery of the glory of God, yet if he has any true discovery of him, so far as he is discovered, he sees this. He is sensible that [it] is worthy to be loved far above all. The Spirit of God is a Spirit of truth; and if he makes any true discovery of God, it must be a discovery of him as lovely above all. If such an excellency is not discovered, there is no divine excellency discovered, for divine excellency is superlative supreme excellency.

Now that wherein a godly man may be said to love God above all seems to be built [on], and seems all to be no more than, [what] immediately follows. He that has God's supreme excellency thus discovered to him, has a sense of heart of his being lovely above all, for spiritual knowledge and conviction consists in the sense of heart. And having such a sort of conviction and sense of heart, it follows that he doth in his heart esteem God above all, so that the love of God reigns in his practical judgment and esteem. And it will also follow that God predominates in the stated established choice and election of his heart: for he that [has] a conviction and sense of heart of anything, as above all things eligible, must elect that above all; and therefore godly men are often in Scripture represented as choosing God for their portion, as choosing the pearl of great price above all. And from this it will follow that God and holiness predominates in his established purpose and resolution; he cleaves to the Lord with purpose of heart, and so in the sense of the Scripture, with his whole heart.

Though there may be but little of the principle of love, yet the principle that there is, being built on such a conviction, will be of that nature, viz. to prize God above all. There may be an endless variety of degrees of the principle, but the nature of the object is unalterable; and therefore, if there be a true discovery of the object, whether in a greater or lesser degree, yet if it be true or agreeable to the nature of the object discovered, the nature of that principle that is the effect of the discovery will answer the nature of the object, and so it will evermore be the nature of it to prize God above all, though there may be but little of such a principle.

And so may it be said of the man's love to and choice of holiness, and of particular graces, such as meekness, mercifulness, etc. He sees the excellency of these things above all other qualifications; hence they predominate in the judgment and choice.

And then another way whereby grace predominates in the soul of a saint is by virtue of the covenant of grace, and the promises of God, on which Christian grace relies, and which engage God's strength and assistance to be on its side, and to help it against its enemy, when otherwise it would be overpowered. Where God infuses grace, he will give it a predominance by his upholding of it, and time after time giving it the victory, when it seemed for a time to be overborn and ready to be swallowed. This is not owing to our strength, but to the strength of God, who won't forsake the work of his hands, and will carry on his work where he has begun it, and always causeth us to triumph in Christ Jesus, who is the author, and has undertaken to be the finisher, of our faith.

740. MILLENNIUM. That there are remaining glorious times of the church, see note on Matt. 28:18–19.[5]

741. HAPPINESS OF HEAVEN. There is scarce anything that can be conceived or expressed about the degree of the happiness of the saints in heaven, the degree of intimacy of union and communion with Christ, and fullness of enjoyment of God, but what the consideration of the nature and circumstances of our redemption by Christ do allow us, and encourage us, to hope for. This redemption leaves nothing to hinder our highest exaltation, and the utmost intimacy and fullness of enjoyment of God. Our being such guilty creatures need be no hindrance, because the blood of Christ has perfectly removed that; and by his obedience he hath procured the contrary for us, in the highest perfection and glory. The meanness of our natures need be no hindrance, for Christ is in our natures. There is an infinite distance between the human nature and the divine.

5. According to the "Blank Bible" note on Matt. 28:18–19, the text shows that "it was Christ's aim to assert his right over mankind that he had acquired by the labors he went through . . . and therefore inasmuch as this has never been accomplished, we may suppose that there is a day remaining in which it will be accomplished."

The divine nature has that infinite majesty and greatness, whereby 'tis impossible that we should immediately approach to that, and converse with that intimacy as we might do one that is in our own nature. Job wished for a near approach to God, but his complaint was that his mean nature did not allow of so near an approach to God as he desired. God's majesty was too great for him (Job 9:32–35). But now we han't this to keep us from the utmost nearness of access, and intimacy of communion, with Christ; for to remove this obstacle wholly out of the way, Christ has come down and taken upon him our nature. He is, as Elihu tells Job he was, according to his wish: he is a man as we are, he also is formed out of the clay [Job 33:6]. This the church anciently wished for, before it came to pass, to that end, that she might have greater opportunity of near access and intimacy of communion. Cant. 8:1, "O that thou wert my brother, that sucked the breasts of my mother! when I should find thee without, I would kiss thee; yea, I should not be despised." Christ, descending so low in uniting himself to our nature, tends to invite and encourage us to ascend to the most intimate converse with him, and encourages us that we shall be accepted and not despised therein. For we have this to consider of, that let us be never so bold in this kind of ascending, for Christ to allow us and accept us in it won't be a greater humbling himself than to take upon him our nature. Christ was made flesh, and dwelt among us in a nature infinitely below his original nature, for this end, that we might have as it were the full possession and enjoyment of him.

Again it shows how much God designed to communicate himself to men, that he so communicated himself to the first and chief of elect men, the elder brother and the head and representative of the rest, even so that this man should be the same person with one of the persons of the Trinity. It seems by this to have been God's design to admit man as it were to the inmost fellowship with the deity. There was [as] it were an eternal society or family in the Godhead in the Trinity of persons. It seems to be God's design to admit the church into the divine family as his son's wife, so that which Satan made use [of] as a temptation to our first parents, "*Ye shall be as gods,*" shall be fulfilled contrary to his design [Gen. 3:5]. The saints' enjoyment of Christ shall be like the Son's intimate enjoyment of the Father. John 17:21–24, "That they may be all one; as thou, Father, art in me, and I in thee, that they also may be one in us: that the world may believe that thou hast sent me. And the glory which thou gavest me have I given them; that they may be one, even as we are one: I in them, and thou in me, that they may be made perfect in one; that the world may know that thou hast sent me, and hast loved them, even as thou hast loved me. Father, I will that they also, whom thou hast given me, be with me where I am; that they may behold my glory, which thou hast given me: for thou lovedst me before the foundation of the world." V. 26, "That the love wherewith thou hast loved me may be in them, and I in them." The Son's intimate enjoyment of the Father is expressed by that, that he is in the bosom of the Father; so we read that one of Christ's disciples leaned on his bosom (John 13:23).

These things imply not only that the saints shall have such an intimate enjoyment of the Son, but that they, through the Son, shall have a most intimate enjoyment of the Father. Which may be argued from this, that the way that God hath contrived to bring 'em to their happiness, is to unite them to the Son as members: which doubtless is that they may partake with the head that they are so united to in his good; and so "our fellowship is with the Father, and with his Son Jesus Christ" (I John 1:3).

We have all reason to conclude that no degree of intimacy will be too much for the manhood of Christ, seeing that the divine Logos has been pleased to assume him into his very person; and therefore, we may conclude that no degree of intimacy will be too great for others to be admitted to, of whom Christ is the head or chief, according to their capacity: for this is in some sort an example of God's love to manhood, that he hath so advanced manhood. He hath done this to the head of manhood to show forth what honor and happiness God designs for manhood, for the end of God's assuming this particular manhood, was the honor and happiness of the rest; surely therefore, we may well argue the greatness of the happiness of the rest from it. The assumption of that particular manhood of Christ was but as a means of the honor and advancement of the rest; and we may well argue the end from the means, and the excellency of the one from the excellency of the other.

Christ took on him our nature, that he might become our brother and our companion. The saints are called Christ's brethren (Heb. 2), and his fellows—"hast anointed him with the oil of gladness above thy fellows" (Heb. 1:9, Ps. 45:8). The Hebrew word properly signifies a companion, חֲבֵרִים; [it] comes from a root that properly signifies to "consociate" or "be joined with." This teaches both the saints' intimate converse with and enjoyment of Christ, and their fellowship with him, or being joined with him in partaking with him in his glory and happiness.

But nothing so much confirms these things as the death and sufferings of Christ. He that hath not witheld his own Son, but hath freely delivered him up for us all in death, how shall he not with him also freely give us all things? If the consideration of the greatness of Christ's condescension in taking on him our nature, invites us to ascend high in our intimacy with him, and encourages us that he will condescend to allow us, and accept us in it, much more does his so condescending and humbling himself, as he did in his last sufferings. No degree of the enjoyment of God that we can suppose, can require grace and condescension that exceeds what was requisite in order to God's giving Christ to die, or will be a greater expression of love. Christ will not descend lower, nor shall we ascend higher, in having Christ for us, and giving himself to us, in such a high degree of enjoyment, than to give himself to us to be our sacrifice, and to be for us in such a degree of suffering. It is certainly as much for God to give his Son to bear his wrath towards [us], as 'tis to admit us to partake of his love towards him. The latter in no respect seems too much to do for a creature, and for a mean worthless creature, than the former. Surely, the majesty of God that did not hinder the one, won't hinder the other, especially considering that one is the end of the other. We may more easily conceive that God would go far in bestowing happiness on an inferior nature, than that he would go far in bringing suffering on an infinitely superiour divine person; for the former is in itself agreeable to his nature, to the attribute of his goodness, but bringing suffering and evil on an innocent and glorious person is in itself in some respect against his nature. If, therefore, God hath done the latter in such a degree for those that are inferior, how shall he not freely do the former? It will not be in any respect a greater gift for Christ thus to give himself in enjoyment, than it was for him to give [himself] in suffering.

The sufferings of Christ for believers also argues the greatness of intimacy with Christ, and fullness of enjoyment of him, that believers shall have, as it shows the fullness of propriety they shall have in him, or right that they have[6] to him. Propriety in any person is just ground of boldness of access and freedom in enjoyment. The beloved disciple John would not have made so free with Jesus Christ as to lean on his bosom had not he looked upon him as his own. Christ did, in effect, give himself to the elect to be theirs from eternity in the same covenant with the Father in which the Father gave them to him to be his. And therefore, Christ ever looked on himself to be theirs, and they his; and Christ looked on himself to be so much theirs that he, as it were, spent himself for them when he was on the earth. He had in the eternal covenant of redemption given his life to them, and so looked upon it theirs, and laid it down for them when their good required it. He looked on his blood theirs and so spilt it for them

6. MS: "he has."

when it was needed for their happiness. He looked on his flesh theirs, and so gave it for their life. John 6:51, "The bread I will give is my flesh." His heart was theirs; he had given [it] to them in the eternal covenant; and therefore, he yielded it up to be broke for them, and to spill out his heart's blood for them, being pierced by the wrath of God for their sins. He looked on his soul to be theirs; and therefore, he poured out his soul unto death, and made his soul an offering for their sins. Thus he from eternity gave himself to them, and looked on them as having so great a propriety in him, as amounted to his thus spending and being spent for them; and as he gave himself to them from eternity, so he is theirs to eternity. The right they have to him is an everlasting right; he is theirs, and will be forever theirs. Now what greater ground can there be for believers to come boldly to Christ, and use the utmost liberty in access to him and enjoyment of him? Will it argue Christ to be theirs in an higher degree for them to be admitted to the most perfectly intimate free and full enjoyment of Christ, than for him so to be as it were perfectly spent for them, and utterly consumed in such extreme suffering and in the furnace of God's wrath?

Christ won't descend lower to admit us to the kisses of his mouth, who are not worthy to kiss his feet, than he did to wash our feet.

Again, if enemies were admitted to be so free with Christ in persecuting and afflicting, if Christ as it were yielded himself wholly into their hands to be mocked and spit upon, and that they might be as bold as they would in deriding and trampling on him, and might execute their utmost malice and cruelty to make way for his friends enjoyment of him, doubtless his friends for whom this was done will be allowed to be as free with him in enjoying of him. He will yield himself as fully up to his friends to enjoy him, as he did to be abused by them, seeing the former was the end of the latter. Christ will surely give himself as much to his saints as he has given himself for them.

He whose arms were expanded to suffer, to be nailed to the cross, will doubtless be opened as wide to embrace those from whom he suffered. He whose side, whose vitals, whose heart, was opened to the spear of his enemies to give access to their malice and cruelty, and to let out his blood, will doubtless be[7] opened to admit the love of his saints. They may freely come, even *ad intima Christi;* whence the blood hath issued for them, the blood hath made way for them.

God and Christ, who have begrutched nothing as too great to be done,

7. MS: "to."

too good to be given, as the means of the saints' enjoyment of happiness, won't begrutch anything in the enjoyment itself.

The awful majesty of God now won't be in the way to hinder perfect freedom and intimacy in the enjoyment of God, any more than if God were our equal, because that majesty has already been fully displayed, vindicated and glorified in Christ's blood. All that the honor of God's awful majesty requires is abundantly answered already by so great sufferings of so great a person. A sense of these wonderful sufferings of Christ for their sins will be ever fixed in their minds, and a sense of their dependance on those sufferings as the means of their obtaining that happiness. Sufficient care is taken in the method of salvation that all that have the benefit of Christ's salvation, and the comforts and joys of it, should have 'em sensibly on that foundation, that with their joys and comforts they should have a sense of their dependence on those sufferings, and their validity, and that comforts should arise on the foundation of such a sense. And as God begins to bestow comforts in this way here, so he will go on in heaven; for the joy and glory of heaven shall be enjoyed as in Christ, as the members of the Lamb slain, and the divine love and glory shall be manifested through him. And the sense they will have of this, together with a continual sight of the punishment of affronting this majesty, in those who were of the same nature and circumstances with themselves, will be sufficient to keep up a due sense of the infinite awful majesty of God, without their being kept at a distance, and though all possible nearness and liberty should be allowed. All the ends of divine majesty are already answered fully and perfectly, so as to prepare the way for the most perfect union and communion, without the least injury to the honor of that majesty.

Though an admission to such a kind of fellowship with God perhaps could not be without God's own suffering, yet when a divine person has been slain, way is made for it, seeing that he has been dead. The veil is rent from the top to the bottom by the death of Christ. The debt is all paid to the awful attributes of God; there is no need of any more. Nothing of awful distance towards the believer can be of any use after this. Now the veil is removed, the way is all open to the boldest and nearest access; and he that was dead and alive again is ours fully and freely to enjoy.

Again, we may further argue from the misery of the damned: as God will have no manner of regard to the welfare of the damned, will have no pity, no merciful care, least they should be too miserable. They will be perfectly lost and thrown away by God as to any manner of care for their good, or defence from any degree of misery. There will be no merciful restraint to God's wrath; so, on the contrary, with respect to the saints, there will be no happiness too much for them. God wont begrutch anything as too good for them. There will be no restraint to his love, no restraint to their enjoyment of himself; nothing will be too full, too inward and intimate for them to be admitted to, but Christ will say to his saints, as in Cant. 5:1, "Eat, O friends; drink, yea, be drunken, O beloved."

This is agreeable to what is revealed of the blessedness of the church in the 21st Psalm, and in the book of Solomon's Song. That song in all parts of it is an abundant revelation of such a nearness, and intimacy of union and communion, and fullness of enjoyment, as we have been speaking of; and particularly such expressions in it as, "Let him kiss me with the kisses of his mouth"; "the king hath brought me into his chambers," i.e. the chambers of a bridegroom; "come let us go forth into the villages, and there will I give thee my love"; "a bundle of myrrh is my well-beloved unto me; he shall lie all night betwixt my breasts"; also, "our bed is green"; "Solomon made a bed of the wood of Lebanon," etc. [Cant. 1:1, 4; 7:11–12; 1:13, 16; 3:9]. And also the 45th Psalm; and innumerable other places of Scripture that compare the union and communion that is between Christ and his church to that which is between a bridegroom and bride.

Corol. 1. HUMILIATION. Hence we may see a reason why HUMILIATION should be required in order to a title to these benefits, and why such abundant care has been exercised in all God's dispensations with fallen man to make provision for man's humiliation, and self-diffidence, and self-emptiness; why 'tis so ordered and contrived that it should not be by our own righteousness, but altogether by the righteousness of another, viz. that there might be the more effectual provision to keep the creature humble, and in the place of a creature, in such exceeding exaltation, and that the honor of God's majesty and exaltation above the creature might in all be maintained; and how needful is it to believe those truths; and how far those DOCTRINES are FUNDAMENTAL or important that tend to this; and how much they militate against the design and drift of God in the contrivance for our redemption that maintain contrary doctrines.

Corol. 2. Hence we may learn that a believer has more [liberty] to be free and bold in access to Christ, than to any other person in heaven or earth. The papists WORSHIP ANGELS and SAINTS as intercessors between Christ and them, because they say it is too much boldness to go to Christ without some[one] to intercede for them. But we have far more to embolden and encourage us to go freely and immediately to Christ, than we can have to any of the angels. The angels are none of them so near to us as Christ is; we han't that propriety in them. Yea, we have a great deal more to encourage and invite us to freedom of access to and communion with

Christ, than with our[8] fellow worms; there is not the thousandth part of that to draw us to freedom and nearness towards them, as there is towards Christ. Yea, though Christ is much above us, yet he is nearer to us than the saints themselves, for our nearness to them is by him; our relation to them is through him.

742. CONSUMMATION OF ALL THINGS. CHRIST'S DELIVERING UP THE KINGDOM TO THE FATHER. That kingdom that Christ shall deliver up to the Father at the end of the world is not properly his mediatorial kingdom but his representative kingdom. Christ God-man rules now as representing the Father's person in his government, and therefore that work is committed to Christ that according to the economy of the Trinity is properly the work of the Father, as particularly the work of a lawgiver and judge. The Father is properly the lawgiver and judge of the world. Christ now is not only the natural representative, or the *natural* perfect image of the Father's person, and effulgence and expression of his glory, but he is his *constituted* representative to be his delegate image or representative in the Father's economical work, viz. the work of governing as lawgiver and judge. But this state of things won't last always. God the Father has committed his work to the Son for a season, for special and glorious reasons; but things are not thus fixed to be thus ultimately and eternally, for that would amount even to an overthrowing the economy of the persons of the Trinity. But doubtless this representative kingdom, when the special ends of it shall be answered, shall be delivered up, and things shall return to their own primæval original order, and every person of the Trinity, in the ultimate and eternal state of things, shall continue each one in the exercise of his own economical place and work.

This representative delegated kingdom of Christ is not just the same with his mediatorial kingdom. Indeed, the kingdom that he has as the Father's vicegerent is given and improved to subserve to the purposes of his mediation between God and the elect; but yet 'tis not the same with his mediatorial kingdom. 'Tis rather something that is superadded to that which is most essential in his mediatorial office and work, to subserve to the purposes of it; and therefore his mediation or mediatorial work will continue after that which is thus superadded ceases. Christ's mediatorial kingdom never will be delivered up to the Father. It would imply a great absurdity to suppose that Christ should deliver up or commit the work of a mediator to the Father, as if the Father himself should thenceforward

8. MS: "a."

take upon him the work of mediating between himself and men. Christ's mediation between the Father and the elect will continue after the end of the world; and he will reign as a middle person between the Father and them to all eternity, though he won't continue to do the same things as Mediator then as he does now, as he now does not do the same things as Mediator that he has done heretofore—and particularly the work which he did when he was here on earth, called the impetration of redemption, which work he finished and rested from when he rose from the dead— but still continues as much the Mediator as he was then, and doing the work of a mediator now as well as then. So after the end of the world, though he won't continue to do the same parts of his mediatorial work after the end of the world as he [now] does, such as delivering the saints from the remains of sin, and interceding for them as sinful creatures, and conquering their enemies (to subserve to which parts of his mediatorial work his kingdom of vicegerency is committed to him), yet he will continue a middle person between the Father and the saints to all eternity, and as the bond of union with the Father, and of derivation from him, and of all manner of communication and intercourse with the Father.

When the end comes, that relation that Christ stands in to his church, as the Father's viceroy over her, shall cease, and shall be swallowed up in the relation of a vital and conjugal head, or head of influence and enjoyment, which is more natural and essential to the main ends and purposes of his union with them. And henceforward, his dominion or kingship over them will be no other than what naturally flows from, or is included in, such an headship. And now God will be all; the church now shall be brought nearer to God the Father, who by his economical office sustains the dignity and appears as the fountain of the Deity. And her enjoyment of him shall be more direct: Christ God-man shall now no longer be instead of the Father to them, but, as I may express it, their head of their enjoyment of God, as it were, the eye to receive the rays of divine glory and love for the whole body, and the ear to hear the sweet expressions of his love, and the mouth to taste the sweetness and feed on the delights of the enjoyment of God—the root of the whole tree planted in God to receive sap and nourishment for every branch.

That it should be thus is much more agreeable with that supreme state of happiness and consummate enjoyment of both the Father and the Son, which the saints shall be admitted to at the end of the world. 'Tis more agreeable to a state of consummate enjoyment of God, for hereby God's communication of himself to them shall be more direct than when it was by a vicegerent. And 'tis more agreeable to their state of consummate enjoyment of the Son of God, God-man; for Christ, while he rules as the representative of the person of the Father, and as his vicegerent as lawgiver and judge, appears with something to represent the awe of his Father's majesty, for the manifestations of the awe of his Father's majesty must ever be maintained, because his economical part is to sustain the dignity and majesty of the Deity. And the way in which the saints will come to an intimate full enjoyment of the Father is not by the Father's majesty, its being as it were softened by his descending to them in a created nature, as 'tis in Christ the Son, but by their ascending to him by their union with Christ's person. And therefore Christ, while he appears as representing the Father's person in governing and judging, must have represented in him the Father's awful majesty, which tends to keep at a distance in some measure, though Christ also appears in the character of an husband to his church; but then will way be made for the most perfect intimacy, when this awe shall as it were be laid aside, and be swallowed up in the gentleness and sweetness of a conjugal head.

The alteration that will be made in Christ's relative circumstances when he shall thus have delivered up the kingdom to the Father will be no diminution of his glory, but a great increase of it: for when the glory of the members is perfected, and brought to its highest pitch, without doubt the glory of the head will not be diminished, but greatly increased. The honor and glory that Christ has now in possessing this delegated kingdom is that which consists in an honorable *work under the Father*, as his great and high officer; but the glory that he will receive in lieu of it, when he shall deliver up the kingdom, is the honor and glory of an high *enjoyment of the Father*, a kind and manner and degree of enjoyment as the Father's only begotten Son, and the brightness of his glory, and express image of his person, which shall be manifest to all in that glory which they shall see him in; which will be more glorious than this kind and manner of work that he is now employed in, as the Father's vicegerent. To be received to an honorable kind of enjoyment of a glorious being is certainly more honorable than to have committed to him an honorable employment by a glorious being. That glorious being's love is more manifested in the former than in the latter.

Christ's enjoyment of the Father, that he shall be admitted to after he has completed his work, will be his reward of his work. Enjoyment of the person that employs is the proper reward of well-discharging the employment. But surely the reward is more excellent and honorable than the work; a state of reward is more glorious than a state of work. Christ shall then be rewarded in a complete, perfect and glorious possession of the end of that kingdom which he now has by the Father's delegation. But the end is more excellent and glorious than the work, as Solomon observes, "Better is the end of a thing than the beginning thereof" [Eccles. 7:8]. He then shall have brought in all that the Father hath given him, all that he died for; and[9] shall possess his church complete in all its members, and all the members made perfect, without spot or wrinkle, or any such thing, all in their consummate beauty, as a bride adorned for her husband, and all in their consummate happiness. And the glory and beauty of the man Christ Jesus, and his happiness in the enjoyment of the Father, shall be increased proportionably; for the increase must be in him first, as the head, and through him derived to his church. He shall now fully obtain, and be possessed of, all that honor and glory in himself that is the end of his administration of his delegated kingdom. Christ will reign till all his enemies are put under his feet; but the glory that he has in that state, wherein he has all his enemies wholly under his feet, is doubtless greater than that wherein his enemies yet remain in power and unsubdued, and wherein he is yet conflicting with them in order to bring them under his feet.

The Roman generals, when they came back to Rome after noted victories in the office in which they were sent forth, as representatives of the Roman power in the field, had their glory chiefly manifested in the triumph in which they entered the city after they had finished their work as Roman officers and representatives. Now the glory that Christ will have when he returns to heaven after the day of judgment, when he shall have subdued all his enemies, and even the last enemy, death, will be the glory of a triumph: he will enter the heavenly city with his redeemed people, and the spoils of all his enemies, in triumph; and the glory of that triumph will be eternal. See Nos. 609, 664, §9, 736.

743. NEW HEAVENS AND NEW EARTH. CONSUMMATION OF ALL THINGS. HEAVEN. See [Nos.] 634 and 745; Discourse on Is. 51:8, Sermon 18.[1] See Revelation, [nos.] 62, 64, and 73a.[2] The place of God's eternal residence, and the place of the everlasting residence and reign of Christ and his church, will be heaven and not this lower world purified and refined. Heaven is everywhere in Scripture represented as the throne of God, and that part of the universe that is God's fixed abode and dwelling place, and

---

9. MS: "as."

1. The last reference, added slightly later, is to the discourse known as "A History of the Work of Redemption." For the 18th sermon, see *Works*, 9, 344–56.

2. This is a reference to "Notes on the Apocalypse" (*Works*, 5, 158, 159, 166–67).

that is everlastingly appropriated to that use. Other places are mentioned in Scripture as being places of God's residence for a time, as Mt. Sinai, and the land of Canaan, the temple, the holy of holies, but yet God is represented as having dwelt in heaven before he dwelt in those places (Gen. 11:5, 19:24; Ex. 3:8; Job 22:12 and 14; Gen. 28:12). And when God is spoken of as dwelling in those places, he is represented as coming down out of heaven: so he is represented as coming on Mt. Sinai (Ex. 19:11, 18, 20; 20:22; Deut. 4:36; Neh. 9:13); so he is represented as coming to the temple (II Chron. 7:3). And so when the cloud of glory first came on the tabernacle, in Ex. 40:34, it doubtless was the same cloud that till then abode on Mt Sinai; but God had first descended from heaven on Mt. Sinai. And while God did dwell in the tabernacle and temple he was represented as still dwelling in heaven, as being still his original proper and everlasting dwelling place, and dwelling in the temple and tabernacle in a far inferior manner. I Kgs. 8:30, "When they shall pray towards this place: then hear thou in heaven thy dwelling place." So vv. 32, 34, 36, 39, 43, 45, 49. Ps. 11:4, "The Lord is in his holy temple, the Lord's throne is in heaven." Deut. 33:26, "There is none like the God of Jeshurun, who rideth on the heavens in thine help, and in his excellency on the sky." Ps. 20:6, "Now know I that the Lord saveth his anointed; he will hear him from his holy heaven." Deut. 26:15; Is. 63:15; Lam. 3:50; I Chron. 21:26; II Chron. 6:21, 23, 27, 30 and 7:14; Neh. 9:27–28; Ps. 14:2 and 53:2. Ps. 33:13–14, "The Lord looketh from heaven; he beholdeth all the sons of men. From the place of his habitation he looketh on all the inhabitants of the earth." Ps. 57:3, 76:8, 80:14. Ps. 102:19, "For he hath looked from the height of his sanctuary; from heaven did the Lord behold the earth." Eccles. 5:2, "God is in heaven, and thou on the earth." II Kgs. 2:1, "Would take up Elijah into heaven"; and so we have an account how he was taken up, v. 11. II Chron. 30:27, Ps. 68:4, 33. Ps. 123:1, "Unto thee lift I up mine eyes, O thou that dwellest in the heavens." Ps 115:2–3, "Wherefore should the heathen say, where is now their God? Our God is in the heavens: he hath done whatsoever he pleased." Lam. 3:41, II Chron. 20:6, Job 31:2, Ps. 113:5, Is. 33:5, Jer. 25:30, Is. 57:15.

The manner in which God dwells in heaven is so much superior to that wherein he dwells on earth, that heaven is said to be God's throne and the earth his footstool. Is. 66:1, "Thus saith the Lord, the heaven is my throne, and the earth is my footstool: where is the house that he build unto me? and where is the place of my rest?"

The holy places on earth where God is represented as dwelling are called his footstool. Lam. 2:1, "And remembered not his footstool in the day of his anger." I Chron. 28:2, "As for me, I had in mine heart to build an house of rest for the ark of the covenant of the Lord, and for the footstool of our God, and had made ready for the building." Ps. 132:7, "We will go into his tabernacles: we will worship at his footstool." God's sanctuary is called the place of his feet. Is. 60:13, "To beautify the place of my sanctuary; and to make the place of my feet glorious." The inferior manner in which God dwelt in the Jewish sanctuary was expressed by that, that God placed his name there. Earthly holy places, which were called God's house or places of his habitation, were so in such a manner, and a manner so inferior to that in which heaven is God's house, that they are represented as only outworks or gates of heaven. Gen. 28:17, "This is none other but the house of God, this is the gate of heaven." Yea, though God is represented as dwelling in these earthly holy places, yet he was so far from dwelling in them as he does in heaven, that when he appeared in them from time to time, he is represented as then coming from heaven to them, as though heaven were his fixed abode, and Mt. Sinai and the tabernacle and temple places into which he would occasionally turn aside and appear. Thus God is said to have descended in a cloud and appeared to Moses, when he passed by him and proclaimed his name, though he had before that from time to time appeared there, as in the Mount of God, and though Moses had at that time been long conversing with God in the mount (Ex. 34:5). And so God descended from time to time on the tabernacle (Num. 11:25 and 12:5). Heaven is always represented as the proper and fixed abode of God, and other dwelling places but as occasional abodes. When the wise man speaks of worshipping God in his house, he at the same time would have those that worship him there be sensible that he is in heaven, and not on the earth. Eccles. 5:1–2, "Keep thy foot when thou goest to the house of God, . . . let not thy heart be hasty to utter any thing before God: for God is in heaven, and thou upon the earth."

So God, when he withdrew from the land of Israel, is spoken of as returning to heaven, which is called his place, as though the land of Israel were not his place. Hos. 5:15, "I will go and return to my place." And God is spoken of as being in heaven in the time of the captivity, as he is in the prophecy of Daniel (Dan. 4:37, Dan. 5:23), and in Daniel's visions (Dan. 4:13, 23, 31).

And heaven is also in the New Testament everywhere represented as the place of God's abode. Christ tells us that 'tis God's throne (Matt. 5:34). This we are taught in the New Testament to look on as God's temple, after all that was legal and ceremonial concerning holy times and holy places ceased. Acts 7:48–49, "Howbeit the most high dwelleth not in temples made with hands; as saith the prophet, Heaven is my throne, and the earth is my footstool: what house will ye build me? saith the Lord: and where is the place of my rest?" This is the true temple and the true holy of holies, as it is represented in the Epistle to the Hebrews. Heaven is the place whence Christ descended, and it is the place whither he ascended. It was the place whence the Holy Ghost descended on Christ, and whence the voice came saying, "This is my beloved Son, in whom I am well pleased" [Matt. 3:17], and is the place whence the Holy Ghost was poured out at Pentecost; and whatever is from God is said to be from heaven (Matt. 16:1, Mark 8:11, Luke 11:16, Matt. 21:25, Luke 9:54, Luke 21:11, John 3:27, John 6:31, Acts 9:3 and 11:5, 9; Rom. 1:18, I Cor. 15:47, I Pet. 1:12, Heb. 12:25, Rev. 3:12, and other places). The angels are spoken of as coming from heaven, from time to time in the New Testament; and visions of God are by heaven's being opened. And prayers and divine worship are commanded under the new testament to be directed to heaven: we are to pray to our Father, which is in heaven, which appellation is very often given to God in the New Testament; so we are to lift up our eyes and hands to heaven in our prayers. And heaven is everywhere in the New Testament spoken as the place of God, and Christ, and the angels, and the place of blessedness, and all good. Whatever is divine is called heavenly, and is always spoken of as the proper country of the saints, the appointed place of all that is holy and happy.

Whenever God comes out of heaven into this world he is represented as bowing the heavens, and rending the heavens, intimating that heaven is so much the proper place of God's abode, that 'tis something very great and extraordinary for him to manifest himself—as he is pleased to do in this world among his people—that heaven, the proper place of his abode, is as it were rent or bowed, and brought down in part to the earth to make way for it (II Sam. 22:10, Ps. 18:9 and 144:5, and Is. 64:1). God is called the God of heaven, Lord of heaven, King of heaven (Dan. 5:23 and 4:37 and 2:44).

Heaven is so much the proper place of God's abode that by a metonymy heaven is put for God himself (II Chron. 32:20); and for this cause Hezekiah the king, and the prophet Isaiah, the son of Amoz, prayed and cried to heaven. Ps. 73:9, "They set their mouth against the heavens." And when anything is spoken of in Scripture as being from heaven, the same is to be understood as to be from God; the prodigal says, "I have sinned against heaven," i.e. against God (Luke 15:21).

Heaven is a part of the universe that,[3] in the first creation and the dis-

---

3. MS: "that God."

position of things that was made in the beginning, was appropriated to God to be that part of the universe that should be his residence, while other parts were destined to other uses. Ps. 115:15–16, "You are blessed of the Lord who hath made heaven and earth. The heaven, even the heavens, are the Lord's: but the earth hath he given to the children of men." God having taken this part of the universe for his dwelling place in the beginning of the creation, he will retain it as long as the creation lasts.

When man was in a state of innocency, before the world was polluted and brought into the present state of confusion, God was in heaven. Heaven was God's dwelling place, for the angels fell from thence. We read that when they fell, God cast 'em down from heaven; and therefore, when this polluted confused state of the world is at an end, and elect men shall be perfectly restored from the fall, to another state of innocency and perfect happiness after the resurrection, heaven will also then be the place of God's abode.

This lower world in its beginning was from God in heaven. He dwelt in heaven when he made it, and brought it out of its chaos into its present form; as is evident, because we are told that when God did this, the morning stars sang together, and all the sons of God, i.e. the angels, shouted for joy. Without doubt, the habitation of the angels was from the beginning that high and holy place where God dwells; and their habitation was heaven in the time of the creation, because those that fell were cast down from thence. But if this lower world in its beginning was from God in heaven, without doubt in its end it will return thither. As he dwelt in heaven before and when he made it, and brought it out of its chaos into its present form, so he will dwell in heaven when and after it is destroyed, and reduced to a chaos again.

Heaven is that throne where God sits in his dominion, not only over some particular [part] of the universe, as the mercy seat in the temple, but 'tis the throne of his universal kingdom. Ps. 103:19, "The Lord hath prepared his throne in the heavens; and his kingdom ruleth over all," i.e. over all his works, or all that he hath made; which appears by v. 22, "Bless the Lord, all his works in all places of his dominion." Because it is the throne in which God rules over the whole universe, therefore 'tis the uppermost part of the universe as above all; as 'tis evident that the heaven where God dwells is far, 'tis said to be far above all heavens. And as 'tis the throne of his universal kingdom, so it is the throne of his everlasting kingdom; as he here reigns by a dominion that is universal with respect to the extent of it, so he does also with respect to the duration of it. The Psalmist in this same place is speaking of things that are the fruits of God's everlasting dominion, especially his everlasting mercy to his people (which mercy will be especially manifested after the day of judgment), as in the words immediately preceding in the two foregoing verses. "But the mercy of the Lord is from everlasting to everlasting upon them that fear him, and his righteousness unto his children's children; to such as keep his covenant, and to those that remember his commandments to do them." The word here used [v. 19] that is translated *"prepared"* also signifies "established," having respect to its firmness and durableness. 'Tis fit that as God's kingdom is an everlasting [kingdom], so the[4] throne of that kingdom should be everlasting, and never should be changed, for that which moves is ready to vanish away. The everlastingness of God's kingdom is signified by the same word in the original that in the place now mentioned is translated *"prepared."* Ps. 93:2, *"Thy throne is established of old: thou art from everlasting,"* together with the context.

If God should change the place of his abode, and his throne, from heaven to some other part of the universe, then that which has hitherto been God's chief throne, and his metropolis, his royal city, must either be destroyed, or put to a so much meaner use, and be deprived of so much of its glory, as would be equivalent to a destruction; which is not a seemly thing for the chief city, palace and throne of the eternal king whose royal throne never shall be destroyed. Ps. 45:6, "Thy throne, O God, is forever and ever."[5]

This heaven that is so often spoken of as the place of God's proper and settled abode is a local heaven, a particular place or part of the universe, and the highest or outermost part of it, because 'tis said to be the heaven of heavens. 'Tis the place where the body of Christ is ascended, which is said to be far above all heavens, and is called the third heaven.

Is it likely that God should change the place of his eternal abode, and remove and come and dwell in another part of the universe? or that he should [not] gather men and bring 'em home to himself, as to their great end and center, whither all things should tend, and in which all should rest?

'Tis fit that an immutable being, and he who has an everlasting and unchangeable dominion, should not move the place of his throne.

---

4. MS: "that the."

5. JE deleted at this point the following paragraph: "The everlastingness of Christ's kingdom is signified in Ps 89:29, 'that his throne shall be as the days of heaven.' Seeing therefore Christ's throne is to be eternal, and the eternity of his throne is here spoken of as commensurate with the duration of heaven, and seeing that heaven is God's throne, we may—putting these things together—infer that heaven as Christ's throne will be forever."

The apostle John, even when he is giving a description of the state of the church after the resurrection, represents the place of God's abode as being then in heaven, for he says he saw the New Jerusalem descending from God out of heaven [Rev. 21:2].[6]

The dwelling place of the saints is said to be "eternal in the heavens" in II Cor. 5:1, "For we know that, if our earthly house of this tabernacle were dissolved, we have a building of God, an house not made with hands, eternal in the heavens."

If any say that this earth will be heaven after the day of judgment, is it not as easy to say that after the resurrection heaven will be the new earth? Is there any more force upon words one way than the other?

The natural images and representations of things seem to represent heaven to be the place of light, happiness and glory, such as the serenity and brightness of the visible heavens, of which I have spoken elsewhere.[7]

'Tis an argument that this globe we now dwell upon is not to be refined to be the place of God's everlasting abode, because 'tis a moveable globe, and must continue moving always if the laws of nature are upheld. It being so small, it can't remain and subsist distinct among the neighboring parts of the universe without motion. But it is not seemly that God's eternal glorious abode, and fixed and everlasting throne, should be a moveable part of the universe.

As heaven will be everlastingly the place of God's chief, highest and most glorious abode, so without doubt it will be the place of Christ's everlasting residence, and therefore, the place whither he will return after the day of judgment. He who has had the honor and glory of dwelling in this glorious abode of God hitherto, won't have his honor diminished after he has completed all his work as God's officer by then dwelling in a place far separated from God's dwelling place. If he returned in triumph to heaven, entering into the royal city after his first victory in his terrible conflict under suffering, much more shall he return thither after his more perfect and complete victory, when all his enemies shall be put under his feet, after the day of judgment. And if Christ after the day of judgment returns to heaven to dwell, doubtless all his saints shall go there with him; he will invite them to come with him, and inherit the kingdom prepared for them before the foundation of the world.

---

6. At this point, JE deleted the following paragraph: "This heaven is the place where Christ is said to have sat down forever, which implies that it is to dwell and reign there forever (Heb. 1:3)."

7. "The purity, beauty, sublimity and glory of the visible heavens," writes JE in "Images of Divine Things," no. 21, "livelily denotes the exaltedness and purity of the blessedness of the heavenly inhabitants." See *Works, 11*, 56. He also describes the "light of heaven" in "Miscellanies" No. 721.

The place of both Christ and his church, their everlasting residence, will be heaven. When Christ comes forth at the day of judgment with the armies of heaven, the saints and angels attending him, it will be as it were [on] an white horse going forth to a glorious victory. And as the Roman generals after their victories returned in triumph to Rome, the metropolis of the empire, delivering up their power to them that sent 'em forth, so will Christ return in triumph to heaven, all his armies following him, and shall there deliver up his delegated authority to the Father. As Christ returned to heaven after his first victory, after the resurrection of his natural body, so he will return thither again after his second victory, after the resurrection of his mystical body. See [No.] 745.

744. CONFIRMATION OF THE ANGELS BY JESUS CHRIST. That Christ in his ascension into heaven gave to the angels the reward of eternal life, or confirmed immutable happiness, may be argued from Eph. 4:10, "He that descended is the same also that ascended up far above all heavens, that he might fill all things"; i.e. all things not only on the face of [the] earth where he dwelt before he descended into the lower parts of the earth, as in the foregoing verse, and all things in the lower parts of the earth whither he descended, but[8] all things in heaven. By *all things*, agreeable to the Apostle's way of using such an expression, is meant *all persons* or intelligent beings, as in Philip. 2:9–10, "Wherefore God hath highly exalted him, and given him a name which is above every name: that at the name of Jesus every knee should bow, of things in heaven, and things in earth, and things under the earth." As there, so here the Apostle is speaking "of things in heaven, and things in earth, and things under the earth," as appears by comparing this with the foregoing verse. And the Apostle there in Philippians mentions these three as therein[9] enumerating all things whatsoever, for certainly whatever things there are, they must be either in heaven, or in the earth, or under the earth; and doubtless by all things there, that are spoken of as being included in these three, is intended the same with all things spoken of here, as included in the same three divisions of the universe. But 'tis evident that by "things" there is meant persons or intelligent creatures; 'tis they who shall bow the knee to him, and whose tongues shall confess to him. And as there God is said highly to have exalted Christ, and to have given him a name above every name, i.e. above the highest angel in heaven, as well as above the highest prince upon

8. MS: "and."
9. MS: "in therein."

earth; so here he is said to have ascended up far above all heavens, or above the highest part of heaven, and therefore above the seat of the highest angel, that he might fill all universally, the highest as well as the lowest, that all might depend on him and receive their fullness from him. By "things in heaven" in that place in Philippians, and so doubtless here, is meant the angels; and by "things in earth" is meant elect men living on earth. By "things under the earth," or in the lower parts of the earth, is meant the souls of departed saints whose bodies are gone under the earth, and especially the saints that were dead and buried before Christ came, or before Christ descended into the lower parts of the earth. Christ died and was buried that he might fill those that were dead and buried. Rom. 14:9, "For to this end Christ both died, and rose, and revived, that he might be Lord both of the dead and of the living." By things or creatures under the earth is meant souls of buried saints, and not devils and damned souls in hell, is manifest from Rev. 5:13, "And every creature which is in heaven, and on the earth, and under the earth, and such as are in the sea, and all that are in them, heard I saying, Blessing, and honor, and glory, and power, be unto him that sitteth upon the throne, and unto the Lamb forever and ever." This would not be said of devils and wicked damned souls, who are far from thus praising and extolling God and Christ with such exultation; instead of that, they are continually blaspheming them.

And again, by "all things" is meant all elect intelligent creatures in the first chapter of this epistle to the Ephesians, 10th verse, "That in the dispensation of the fullness of times he might gather together in one all things in Christ, both which are in heaven, and which are on earth; even in him." And if he means all intelligent elect creatures there, by all things in heaven and earth, doubtless he also does when he speaks of all things in heaven, and on the earth, and the lower parts of the earth, in this 4th chapter of the same epistle where he is treating of the same thing, viz. the glory of Christ's exaltation. So again, Col. 1:20, "And (having made peace through the blood of his cross) by him to reconcile all things to himself; by him, I say, whether they be things in earth, or things in heaven." In these two places last mentioned are mentioned only things in heaven and things in earth, those which in those other places are called things under the earth being here ranked among things [in] heaven, because their souls are in heaven, though their bodies are in the lower parts of the earth.

Christ is said to have descended and ascended that he might *fill* all things, not only in earth, and under the earth, but in the highest heaven. Now by his filling all things or all elect creatures, according to the Apostle's common use of such an expression, must be understood filling them with life and the enjoyment of their proper good, giving them blessedness and perfecting their blessedness, making them complete in a happy state, as in the third chapter of this epistle, 19th verse, "And to know the love of Christ, which passeth knowledge, that ye might be filled with all the fullness of God." Col. 2:10, "Ye are *complete* in him." Rom. 11:12, "Now if the fall of them be the riches of the Gentiles; how much more their fullness?" So that when we are put in mind that Christ, who dwelt once on the earth, descended into the lower parts of the earth and then ascended far above all heavens, that he might fill all things, the meaning is that Christ came down from heaven and dwelt among us on the earth; the Word was made flesh and dwelt amongst us, full of grace and truth, that we might partake of his fullness and might be made happy by him and in him; agreeable to John 1:14, 16, "And the Word was made flesh, and dwelt among us (and we beheld his glory, the glory as of the only begotten of the Father), *full* of grace and truth. And of his *fullness* have all we received, and grace for grace." And then Christ descended into the lower parts of the earth in a state of death, that he might bless those that were in a state of death; agreeable to Rom. 14:9, "For to this end Christ both died, and rose, and revived, that he might be Lord both of the dead and of the living." So we read that when he died the graves of many saints were opened, and that many bodies of saints that slept arose and came out of their graves after his resurrection, and went into the holy city and appeared unto many. And then Christ ascended into heaven and filled them, bestowing eternal life and blessedness upon them, that the angels in heaven might all receive the reward of confirmed and eternal glory from him and in him.

That Christ at his ascension into heaven thus *filled* the angels of heaven is also plainly taught in the last verse of the first chapter of this epistle, "Which is his body, the fullness of him that *filleth all in all*." The Apostle here has a special respect to his filling the angels, and particularly their being subjected to him, to receive their fullness from him as their head and as their Lord at his ascension, for he in these foregoing verses is speaking of Christ's being made the Lord and head of the angels at his ascension. "Which he wrought in Christ, when he raised him from the dead, and set him at his own right hand in the heavenly places, far above all principality, and power, and might, and dominion, and every name that is named, not only in this world, but that which is to come: and hath put all things under his feet, and given him to be head over all things to the church" [Eph. 1:20–22]. By "all things" is here meant, as in the verse we are upon especially, all intelligent creatures, men and angels, as in that verse in the fourth chapter that we are upon. God has given him to be head over the angels to the church, agreeably to Heb. 1:14, "Are they not all ministering spirits, sent forth to minister to them that shall be the heirs of salvation?" The same "all things" that Christ is here said to be made head over, he is said in the next verse to fill [Eph. 1:23]. By this it appears that the angels at Christ's ascension received their fullness, i.e. their whole reward, all their confirmed life and eternal blessedness, from Christ as their judge, because they received it from him as their Lord or head of government, for they are said to be put under his feet; and also that they received it in him as the fountain of communication. He did not only adjudge it to them, but he gives it to them; and they possess it as united to him in a constant dependence on him, and have that more full enjoyment of God than they before had, as beholding God's glory in his face and as enjoying God in him, for he is here spoken of not only as their Lord but their head, as a natural head to a body, as appears by comparing the two last verses together.

This [is] confirmed again by the tenth verse, "That in the dispensation of the fullness of times he might gather together in one all things in Christ, both which are in heaven, and which are on earth; even in him." The Apostle adds *even in him* at the end of the verse because it might seem wonderful that not only things on earth, but even things in heaven or the angels, should be gathered together in him, who was one that existed in the human nature. By gathering together in one is meant making happy together in one head, or uniting all in one fountain of life and happiness, as appears by John 17:20–23.

The same thing is taught again in Col. 2:9–10, "For in him dwelleth all the fullness of the Godhead bodily. And ye are *complete* in him, which is the head of all principality and power." What is rendered *complete in him* in the original, [is] properly signified *filled up* or *filled full in him*. He is he in whom all the fullness of the Godhead dwells, and in whom the creature receives that fullness; and he is the head of communication whence ye receive fullness, or in whom ye are filled full, who is the same person who is also the head in whom the angels receive their fullness, as it is added, who "is the head of all principality and power."

This is very agreeable to what the Apostle says, vv. 18–19 of the first chapter of Colossians, "And he is the head of the body, the church: who is the beginning, the first-born from the dead; that in all things he might have the preeminence. For it pleased the Father that in him all fullness should dwell." By this it appears that it was the design of God so to exalt and glorify his Son that all his intelligent creatures should in everything be after him, inferior to him, subject to him, and dependent on him, and should have all their fullness, all their supplies from him and in him; especially if we compare this verse with the context, and with many other places in the New Testament.

That the angels have their fullness, and their eternal good and happiness, not only from the hands of Christ, but also in him as the head and fountain of it, and as enjoying God in him, and that they have their confirmation in and by him, is confirmed in Christ's being called angels' food. The Psalmist, speaking of manna, says, Ps. 78:25, "Man did eat angels' food," which can be understood no otherwise than that which manna was the type of, was angels' food; but this Christ tells us is himself in John 6:31–32. There Christ tells us that that bread from heaven spoken [of] in this very place in the 78th Psalm, is him; for the Jews [are] quoting the beginning of this passage, that is, the verse immediately preceding in the psalm [v. 24], "Our fathers did eat manna in the wilderness; as it is written, He gave them bread from heaven to eat" (John 6:31). But then we have Christ's answer in the two next verses, "Moses gave you not *that* bread from heaven" (i.e. *that* bread from heaven spoken of in that place that you cite); "but my Father giveth you the true bread from heaven. For the bread of God is he which cometh down and giveth life unto the world" [vv. 32–33]. Christ is called the tree of life that grows in the midst of the paradise of God [Rev. 2:7]; but we know that the use of the tree of life in paradise was that they that eat of that fruit might have confirmed life, and never die, but live forever. And the same is signified by Christ's being called in the sixth chapter of John "the bread of life," viz. that he that eats of this bread should have confirmed life, and not die, but live forever; as Christ himself there teaches, vv. 48–51, "I am the bread of life. Your fathers did eat manna in the wilderness, and are dead. This is the bread which cometh down from heaven, that a man may eat thereof, and not die. I am the living bread which came down from heaven: if any one" (for so the original signifies) "eat of this bread, he shall live forever." But we are taught from the forementioned place that 'tis the angels' bread of life, as well as ours; and therefore, 'tis that bread by which they have eternal life, or which they eat of and live forever, and is a tree of life to them, as well as to us, a tree the fruit whereof they eat and live forever, as well as we.

Corol. 1. Here we may take occasion to observe the sweet harmony that there is between God's dispensations, and particularly the analogy and agreement there is between his dealings with the angels and his dealings with mankind: that though one is innocent and the other guilty, the one having eternal life by a covenant of grace, the other by a covenant of works, yet both have eternal life by his Son Jesus Christ God-man; and both, though different ways, by the humiliation and sufferings of Christ, the one as the price of life, the other as the greatest and last trial of their steadfast and persevering obedience. Both have eternal life, though different ways, by their adherence and voluntary submission and self-dedication to Christ crucified. And he is made the Lord and king of both, and head of communication, influence and enjoyment to both, and a head of confirmation to both, for as the angels have confirmed life in and by Christ, so have the saints; all that are united in this head have in him a security of PERSEVERANCE. Thus Christ is the tree of life that grows in the paradise of God to all that belong to that paradise, and to all that ever eat of the fruit of that tree. As Adam, if he had persevered through his trial would have eat of the fruit of the tree of life, and after that would have had confirmation and been secure of perseverance, so are all that taste of the fruit of this tree, this branch that grows out of the stem of Jesse, this tender plant and root out of a dry ground, this branch of the Lord and fruit of the earth, this bush that God dwells in, this low tree which God exalts. Seeing the saints and angels are forever to be one society dwelling together as one company to all eternity, it was fit that they should be thus united in one common head, and that their greatest interests and those things that concern their everlasting happiness should be so linked together, and that they should have such communion or common concern in the same great events in which God chiefly manifests himself to them, and by which they come to the possession of the eternal reward.

Corol. 2. Here also we may observe that God's work from the beginning of the universe to the end, and in all parts of the universe, appears to be but one. 'Tis all one design carried on, one affair managed in all God's dispensations, towards all intelligent beings, viz. the glorifying and communicating himself in and through his Son Jesus Christ as God-man and by the work of redemption of fallen man. Those that [were] of the angels that fell are destroyed for their opposition to God in this affair, and are overthrown and condemned and destroyed by the Redeemer. Those of [them] that stood are confirmed for their submission and adherence to God in this great affair. So the work of God is one, if we view it in all its parts: what was done in heaven, and what was done on earth and in hell, in the beginning and since that, through all ages, and what will be done at the end of the world.

Corol. 3. From this we may see that the angels are interested in Jesus Christ God-man, as well as elect men, and that the INCARNATION of Christ was not only for our sakes (though chiefly for ours), but also for the sake of the angels. For God having from eternity from his infinite goodness designed to communicate himself to creatures, the way in which he designed to communicate himself to elect beloved creatures, all of them, was to unite himself to a created nature, and to become one of the creatures, and to gather together in one all elect creatures in that creature that he assumed into a personal union with himself, and to manifest to them and maintain intercourse with them through him. All creatures have this benefit by Christ's incarnation, that God thereby is as it were come down to them from his infinite height above them, and is become a fellow creature, and all elect creatures hereby have opportunity for a more free and intimate converse with God, and full enjoyment of him than otherwise could be; and though Christ is not the Mediator of the angels in the same sense that he is of men, yet he is a middle person between God and them, through whom is all their intercourse with God and derivations from him.

Corol. 4. That the person that is the head of all elect creatures, in whom all are gathered together in one, by whom they all have their eternal fullness and glory, and who is the common fountain of all their good and the common medium through [whom] God communicates himself to all, is so much nearer to men than to the angels, confirms it [that] the SAINTS ARE HIGHER IN GLORY THAN THE ANGELS.

Corol. 5. This confirms it, that the church or blessed assembly in HEAVEN is in a like PROGRESSIVE STATE with the church on earth: for at the same time that the church in this world was advanced to a state of new light and glory by the dawning of the gospel day, the angels in heaven were advanced to a new state of glory and happiness, and not only so, but the souls of the SAINTS that died UNDER THE OLD TESTAMENT were ADVANCED much HIGHER IN GLORY at CHRIST'S RESURRECTION and ASCENSION. For the text in Eph. 4:10 teaches that at that time of the manifestation of Christ God-man in this universe, each of these three were advanced to a state of new blessedness, viz. the church on earth, and departed souls of saints whose bodies were in the lower parts of the earth, and also the angels in heaven. He came and dwelt upon earth amongst us, and we beheld his glory and received of his fullness. When he rose from the dead he begat the church again to a living hope, as it were raised the church from the dead with him, and the church here was advanced to so much higher glory that her former glory was no glory in this respect, by reason of the glory that excelleth; and then descended into the lower parts of the earth, and filled those that were there, advanced the souls of departed saints in glory in becoming Lord of the dead; and a token of it, and one instance of it then, was his granting a resurrection to many of them whereby the future glory of the resurrection was in a great measure anticipated. Doubtless those saints that rose with Christ ascended triumphing with him into heaven into new glory and blessedness. These things confirm that the assembly in heaven has all along been in a like progressive state with the church on earth, and is in a preparatory state, and that things there from the beginning of the world hitherto have been working towards a great end and glorious issue, and consummation at the end of the world, as 'tis here.

The church of angels and saints there at first was in a state of infancy to what it is now, as it was with the church on earth, and have been brought forward to greater fullness and perfection by great events of providence, as it has been with the church here; and things there will arrive at a consummation at the same time, and in the same great event at the end of the world, that they will here. The church in heaven was greatly advanced in happiness at Christ's exaltation, whence commenced the gospel day to the church in this world; and so again the church in heaven will receive another still much higher advancement in glory at the time of the fall of Antichrist, as appears by several passages in the book of Revelation; as abundantly appears by Rev. 18:20, 19:1–9 and 20:4. And both that part of the church that is on earth, and that which is in heaven, shall at the same time receive their highest advancement in glory, together with consummation of Christ's exaltation at the day of judgment. See No. 777, corol. 3.

745. NEW HEAVENS AND NEW EARTH. See [No.] 743. 'Tis manifest that the world of the blessed, that is, the new world, or the new heavens and earth, or the next world that is to succeed this as the habitation of the church, is heaven, the same world that is now the habitation of the angels; for heaven, or the world of the angels, is called the world that is to come. Eph. 1:20–22, "Which he wrought in Christ, when he raised him from the dead, and set him at his own right hand in the heavenly places, far above all principality, and power, and might, and dominion, and every name that is named, not only in this [world], but that which is to come, and hath put all things under his feet." Heaven, the habitation of principalities and powers, is that which is here called the world to come, as being the world that was to succeed this as the habitation of the church. It can't be understood in any other sense, or only that Christ was to be at the head of things in the new world when it did [come]; but it speaks of what is already done, and was done at Christ's ascension, a past effect of God's mighty power, *according to the working of the exceeding greatness of his power, which [he] wrought in Christ Jesus when he raised him from the dead, and set him at his own right hand in the heavenly places.*

746. HADES. That the place of the departed souls of saints is heaven, appears by Col. 1:19–20, "For it pleased the Father that in him should all fullness dwell; and (having made peace by the blood of his cross) by him to reconcile all things unto himself; by him, I say, whether they be things on earth or things in heaven." By things in heaven must be meant chiefly the departed souls of saints in heaven. For there can be nothing else in heaven that can have been at any time the subjects of reconciliation to God, or at least such a reconciliation as the Apostle here explains himself to intend, viz. a making peace through the blood of his cross. There can be no others in heaven that Christ died to make atonement for, or to reconcile and make peace for, by the blood of his cross, but these. Departed saints, that the papists worship, are in heaven (see Rev. 13:6). Prophets and apostles are in heaven (Rev. 18:20).

747. SELF-RIGHTEOUSNESS. PRIDE. Self-righteousness is a certain kind of sin of the heart that is especially contrary to Christ and the gospel, displeasing to God and fatal to the soul. Now it may be worthy of an inquiry what lust, or which of the cardinal principles of corruption mentioned, No. [1032],[1] it is that is exercised in self-righteousness, that belongs to the nature of this hateful disposition, and wherein its sinfulness does most essentially consist: and this is *PRIDE*, or an inordinate affecting our own comparative dignity, or an inordinate disposition to self-exaltation, as is evident by Luke 18:9, "And he spake this parable unto certain which trusted in themselves that they were righteous, and despised others"; together with v. 14, "I tell you, this man went down to his house justified rather than the other: for every one that exalteth himself shall be abased; and he that humbleth himself shall be exalted." Self-righteousness is a self-glorying; and therefore, persons are said not to be justified by their own righteousness, but by faith, that boasting might be excluded, and that no flesh should glory in God's presence. Self-righteousness is the same with a spirit of pride, as it tends to a particular kind or sort of exercise: a self-righteous principle or disposition is the same as a disposition to exercise pride with regard to our own supposed righteousness, or moral dignity.

1. The phrase "or which of the cardinal principles of corruption mentioned, No. . . ." is an interlineation, which JE evidently made before he had assigned a number to the entry in question. No. 1032, entitled "Humiliation and Mortification to the World. Corruption of Nature," states, "The corruption of nature, as to all that is positive in it, does primarily consist in these two things: *self-exaltation* and *worldlimindedness.* There are no other idols but self and the world." Similarly, in *Charity and Its Fruits* JE states that the "two cardinal vices or fountains of sin and wickedness in the heart" are the "two lusts of pride and covetousness" (*Works, 8,* 272).

Now pride consists mainly and most essentially in the disposition or heart, and not in the understanding, as all lusts do. Pride don't most essentially consist in a too high conceit of one's self, but in a disposition inordinately to affect our own comparative dignity. Hence, the wrong thought that children have of themselves, of their own understanding and strength and self-sufficiency, is on this account far more innocent than the inordinate conceit grown persons have of themselves, because it arises more from mere ignorance, and so less from a proud disposition. A wrong conceit of one's own dignity is a proud haughty conceit no farther and no otherwise than as it proceeds [from] a self-exalting disposition.[2]

748. LORD'S DAY. See [No.] 691, § 28. That the Jewish sabbath was a day of rejoicing is further evident from Ps. 92 that, we are told, is a psalm or song for the sabbath day; which it is evident is a joyful song, or a psalm to express joy and gladness, as v. 4, "For thou, Lord, hast made me glad through thy work: I will triumph in the works of thine hands."

And besides, the festivals or holy days of the Jews were all joyful[3] days, excepting the Day of Atonement. Ps. 42:4, "For I had gone with the multitude, I went with them to the house of God, with the voice of joy and praise, with a multitude that kept holyday."

749. BEING OF GOD. THE FIRST CAUSE AN INTELLIGENT VOLUNTARY AGENT. Nothing can be more plain than [that] the make and constitution of the world, in all parts of it, is with respect to final causes, or with an aim at these and those ends to be obtained; and therefore, it seems to be plain that the world must have a cause, and that this cause is an intelligent and voluntary, or designing agent.

1. It shows that the world must have an efficient cause: for how can anything but an efficient cause have respect to an end in an effect? If the world be disposed and ordered for an end, then there must have been some being that has disposed and ordered it for that end. Its being ordered for a future end must be from something that has some regard to futurity, or to what as yet is not, for the end is what is not as yet obtained when the dis-

2. JE drew a line down the entire length of this entry, through the text of the entry about one-half inch to the right of its left-hand margin. Ink comparisons suggest that JE probably drew this use line when he composed No. 950. In this entry JE developed at greater length a definition of pride essentially identical to that given in No. 747, although in the latter entry he emphasizes the relation between pride and humility, not pride and self-righteousness. The comparative nature of pride is also reflected in JE's discussion of spiritual pride in *Religious Affections* (*Works, 2,* 320–40). See also his discussions of envy and humility in *Charity and Its Fruits* (*Works, 8,* 218–51).

3. MS: "holy."

posal first is, but is a consequence of the disposal. It can't be without any cause, or from nothing, for in nothing there can in no respect be any regard or relation to a future thing. It can't be from the thing itself that is disposed, for the relation to futurity is by the supposition the thing that governs the disposal; and therefore, the relation or regard to futurity can't be consequent on the disposed, or be from the thing itself disposed. As for instance, the clock's disposal to tell the hours of the day can't be from the clock disposed, because a respect to the notification of the hours of the day is supposed to govern the disposal of the clock. The world's therefore being so disposed that respect is had to final causes, or to future good, must be from something prior to the world, for any other supposition carries in it a contradiction. To suppose it is from the world itself carries a contradiction; and to suppose that it is from nothing is a contradiction, for it supposes that nothing carries in it some regard, or respect, or relation to future good to be obtained, so as to govern in the disposal of things in order to that good.

2. It shows that the efficient cause of the world must be an intelligent voluntary agent. For in the first place, by things being disposed to an end, something that is future, and that as yet has no actual being, has influence and governs in the effect that is produced; for the good that is the final cause as yet is future. But this future thing, that has no actual existence yet, has a present existence some way or other, otherwise it could have no present influence in any effect at all. For that which in no respect whatsoever *is* can in no respect whatsoever have influence in an effect, for it is a contradiction to suppose that that which absolutely and in all respects is not, or is nothing, should have influence or causality, or that mere nothing can do something. But there is no other way that that which has no actual existence can have existence but only by having existence in the understanding, or in some idea. For instance, there is no way that things that are first to begin to be the next year, can be now—before they begin to be—but by their being foreseen. Therefore, if any cause be now seen acting with evident respect to something that is first to begin to be the next year, so as that its effects shall be disposed in order to it, and the production of that future thing governs in the ordering and disposal of the effect, it argues that that cause is intelligent, and that he foresees that future thing, or that it exists already in his idea, just as much as if he foretold it. To foretell an event to come is to hold forth those things that are signs conformed to the future event, and by their conformity manifestly show that that future event is present with the efficient of those signs, and that there is an aim or respect of the efficient to the event in directing and or-

dering and designing those things wherein the sign consists in conformity to the event signified, and for an end, viz. to signify or give notice of that future event. There is nothing in foretelling events, however particularly or exactly, that manifests intelligence and design any other ways than these two, viz. (1) conforming things present, viz. sounds or marks, to things future; and (2) doing this with a certain design, viz. giving notice. But there is the very same evidence of an intelligent and voluntary agent in ordering and disposing *things* in conformity to future events, as *words*, as much in conforming *other things*, as *sounds* or *marks*.

Things are so disposed to future ends, so perfectly ordered to bring about such and such necessary and good ends, that there [is] as it were an exact and perfect conformity, or rather correspondence, between the means and the end, as there is between a stamp and the picture that is designed to be stamped with it, or as there is in the types in the press and the impression intended by it, or as there is between the letters and their combinations on paper and the words that are intended should be spoken by him that shall read them. We may as well, and as reasonably, suppose that words, yea, a great multitude of them, may be in exact and precise conformity in innumerable particulars to something future, without understanding, as that a great multitude of things shall be in as exact and particular conformity to future events, without understanding. There are two things in foretelling future events that argues intelligence, viz. conformity to something future, and design or aim at an end; and there is the same in directing or ordering things for future good, or for final causes.

If a cause may conform and direct effects to final causes without understanding, as if it had exceeding great understanding, then there is nothing that we expect of intelligent beings but what we may expect from such an unintelligent cause: for there is nothing whatsoever that we look upon as a sign or mark of intelligence in any being, but it is in thus directing and ordering things for final causes. For we can see no signs of intelligence in any but these three, viz. (1) that he acts and produces effects; and (2) that in acting or producing effects, he shows that things not present in their actual existence are yet some way present with him as in idea, by a conformity of his acts to things distant or future, as it is in one that conceives of things distant and future; and (3) that he acts with design, or [by] aiming at that which is future. But he that evidently acts for final causes does all these things.

If a cause without understanding can do all these things, then we may expect that he will do all the acts that intelligent beings do in as great perfection as they, viz. determine between good and bad, reward, punish, instruct, counsel, comfort, give answers, and converse. For all that in any or all of these things argues intelligence, is a conformity of acts to things absent, or future, as if present in idea, and acting with design or ends; and though the designs or ends in such a way of acting is exceeding various and manifold, yet the multiplicity and variety of ends argues intelligence no otherwise than as it the more plainly manifests that there is indeed a presence of things absent, as in idea, and that there is indeed an ordering of effects for final causes, as in design. But this is not the thing now in question. But the question is whether or no, if that be granted that future things are manifestly so present as if in idea, and things are indeed so ordered for final causes, it argues intelligence; not but that there is [as] great an evidence of real intelligence and design in God's works of creation and providence, by multiplicity and variety of good ends evidently aimed at, as there can be in conversing as intelligent beings do.

In an efficient cause's disposing things for a final cause, it appears that things not actually in being are present with it, but present with it so as to determine it in acting; just as intelligent beings are determined by choice, and by a wise choice, rejecting the bad and choosing the good, and choosing the good with admirable distinction, choosing the best in millions of cases out of an infinite variety that are equally possible, and equally before this cause. It argues perception in the cause that thus selects the best out of infinite numbers in all cases, though the cases are as it were infinite [in] number, because 'tis good that governs the determination of this cause; but things are neither good nor bad but only with relation to perception.

There is no other way that a being can exist before its actual proper existence, but only existing in some representation. For if the thing itself is not, nor anything that represents it, then surely it is not at all, or in any wise; but there is no representation present with an efficient to make that aim at the thing represented, as that for which he effects, but an idea, no other representation, but a perceived representation. The representation of the future thing aimed at by the first cause is no otherwise present with that first cause, before actual existence, than all other possible being not actually existing; but only this is selected by the first cause, out of all other possible things, for its goodness, which argues that the first cause perceives the goodness, for goodness has no existence but with relation to perception.

Why should there be a backwardness in us to conceive of this first cause of things as a properly intelligent and voluntary agent; or why should we look upon it as a strange thing that it should be so? Is it because 'tis a strange thing that there should be any intelligent and voluntary beings at all? If it be so, it argues against the first cause's being such a being, no otherwise than it argues against there being any such being at all; and if it ben't forcible against the existence of any such being, then it is not against the first cause's being such a being. But we know that there are intelligent and voluntary beings, and that more certainly than we know the existence of any other kind of being, because we know it by our own immediate consciousness. And we that are intelligent and voluntary beings are the effects of this first cause; 'tis it that has made and made us intelligent beings. And why is it more strange that the cause should be intelligent, than the effect? Why should it appear strange that the intelligent creatures that it has made, are more in his image, than any other effects that it hath made? We see they are in its image in all other things far more than any unperceiving beings. They are so in the manner of their acting. The first cause acts from him[self], so these act more from themselves than any other beings. The first cause acts for final causes, so do these his creatures and these only. The first cause is chief of all beings. Those intelligent beings that he has made are chief among creatures, and so in his image in that respect; and are next to the first cause, and 'tis more likely that those effects of the first cause that are nearest to it should be most like it. Those intelligent creatures are evidently set over the rest; the rest are put more in subjection to them than to any other, and more in their power. In this respect they bear the image of the first [cause] who has all things under it, and in its power.

We have all reason to think that this first cause of all things, that is the cause of all perception and intelligence in the world, is not only not an unintelligent, unknowing, and insensible being, but that he is infinitely the most intelligent and sensible being of all; that he is more perceiving than any; that his perception is so much more sensible and lively and perfect; that created minds are in comparison of him like dead, senseless, unperceiving substances; and that he infinitely more exceeds them in the sensibility and life and height (if I may so speak) of his perception than the sun exceeds the planets, in the intensive degree of his brightness, as well as the bulk or extent of his shining disk. And as he is more sensible, so he is as I may express it more voluntary than created minds. He acts more of himself, infinitely more purely active, and in no respect passive, as all created minds are in a great measure passive in their acts of will. And the acts of will are more voluntary. Though there be no proper passions as in created minds, yet voluntariness is exercised to an infinitely greater height. The divine love, which is the sum of all the exercises of the divine will, is infinitely stronger, more lively and intense, as not only the light of the sun, but his heat, is immensely greater than that of the planets whose light and heat is derived from him.

Corol. 1. WORSHIP OF GOD. Hence how rational is it to suppose, contrary to the principles of the deists, that God ought to be worshipped by prayer, confession, praise and thanksgiving, and those duties in which we speak to God, and have to do with [him] as a properly intelligent being, or one that perceives and knows what we say to him; that we ought to show respect to him by voluntary acts, as expressions of our thoughts and volitions and motions of our hearts, purposely expressed before him and directed to him, as all intelligent creatures do to all other intelligent beings with whom they are concerned, or have intercourse. Never to go to God, or to purpose to exhibit our thoughts to him, or to direct any expression of any motion of our hearts to him, as we naturally do to all properly intelligent beings with whom we are concerned, certainly is not to treat him as a properly intelligent voluntary being.

Corol. 2. Hence also it appears most rational to suppose that God should make some REVELATION of himself to his intelligent creatures by his Word; and seeing he is properly an intelligent voluntary being, that he should maintain intercourse with them by voluntarily expressing and signifying his mind to them, as intelligent voluntary agents do one to another, and as they only can do. And as 'tis hence rational to suppose that it should be required of us that we should speak to God, so 'tis as rational to suppose that he should speak to us.

Corol. 3. This also renders it most credible that God should maintain a moral government over mankind by revelation, giving laws, promising rewards and threatening punishments, and appointing a judgment; managing the affairs of his kingdom by revelations made, or his word spoken, from time to time; making constitutions; appointing means of reconciliation for those that have offended; counseling, directing, encouraging, ordering and altering dispensations, or forms of administration of government, according to the different states of things, and diverse exigencies of his kingdom, in different ages of mankind; with wonderful contrivance disposing the affairs of his kingdom; and with a manifestation of a sovereign will contriving and bringing to pass things unthought of, and beyond all human contrivance; and foretelling many future things of importance: for herein he does but act as an intelligent voluntary head of infinite wisdom and sovereign will, over a society of intelligent voluntary creatures.

Seeing that God is certainly an intelligent and voluntary being, it is rational to suppose that in his government of the world there should not only be a series of events that he brings to pass in a constant uninterrupted series, by certain fixed unvaried laws, such as the laws of nature; but that he should manifest himself in his dealings with his intelligent and voluntary creatures in a series of more arbitrary acts and dispensations, not confined to certain unalterable rules and laws in all circumstances, but acts done more in the manner of intelligent voluntary creatures, and more directly showing the will and arbitrament of the governor, as it is in God's dispensations towards his church from the beginning of the world, both in the extraordinary dispensations of his providence in miracles, and the arbitrary influences of his Spirit on their hearts, in the course of his ordinary dispensations in his church and kingdom.

750. PERSEVERANCE. Grace is that which God implants in the heart against great opposition of enemies, great opposition from the corruption of the heart, and from Satan and the world. These all are great in their efforts against the implantation of it, and labor as it were to the utmost to keep it out. Seeing therefore that God manifests his all-conquering power in giving grace a place in the heart in spite of those enemies, he will doubtless maintain it there, against their continued efforts to root it out. He that has so gloriously conquered them in bringing in grace, won't at last suffer himself to be conquered, by their expelling that which he has so brought in by his mighty power. He that gloriously subdued those enemies under his feet by bringing this image of his into the soul, won't suffer this image of his finally to be trampled under their feet. God alone could introduce it. It was what he undertook, and it was wholly his work, and doubtless he will maintain it. He will not forsake the work of his own hands. Where he has begun a good work, he will carry it on to the day of Christ [Philip. 1:6]. Grace shall endure all things, and shall remain under all things, as the expression πάντα ὑπομένει literally signifies in I Cor. 13:7.

751. LORD'S DAY. Though every day ought to be dedicated to God's service, "yet this doth not hinder but that some days should be dedicated in another manner, and to other parts of his service, than it is possible for us to dedicate every day" (so Abp. Sharp).[4] When we argue that 'tis but reasonable to suppose that certain appointed days should be wholly dedicated

4. John Sharp, *Works of the Most Reverend John Sharp, Late Lord Archbishop of York* (7 vols. London, 1729; 5th ed., 1754),6, "Of the Change of the Sabbath: The Great Advantages of Strictly Observing the Lord's Day; and the Manner of Observing it," on Ex. 20:8. The quote appears on p. 239.

to God's service, what the anti-sabbatarians reply, viz. that we ought to dedicate all our time to God; we ought to serve him in ploughing the field and in merchandising, etc., don't at all weaken the force of the argument. For though we allow this, yet it don't at all hinder but that 'tis necessary that some time should be spent in other parts of God's service, viz. the exercises of his more immediate worship; and that the time that is spent in these should be set apart or separated from that which is immediately spent in those others; and that it is absolutely necessary that one should be attended free from the entanglements of the other, and not mixed with them.

A seventh part of time being appointed to be kept holy to God from the beginning of the world, seems to prove that a seventh part of time should be kept holy to God throughout all ages. Thus Christ himself argues that men should not put away their wives now in these days of the gospel, because from the beginning it was not so, "but he that made them in the beginning made them male and female, saying, For this cause shall a man leave his father and his mother, and cleave unto his wife: and they twain shall be one flesh. What therefore God hath joined together, let not man put asunder" [Matt. 19:4–6]. So we may with equal reason argue concerning sanctifying the seventh part of time, that from the beginning it was so, that God that made the days in the beginning made the seventh holy, resting on the seventh day, and making it a sabbath, and blessed[5] and hallowed. Therefore what God hath hallowed, let not men profane.

And if we suppose a prolepsis in these words of Moses [Gen. 2:2–3], and that they are only the occasional remark of the historian as giving a reason of what came to pass afterwards, yet it shows that the command of resting a seventh part of time is founded on that which did not at all concern the Jews more than other nations, but is of universal and equal concernment to all mankind, and what was many ages before the being of their dispensation and church; which argues that the command itself is not confined to their nation or dispensation but respects all nations and all dispensations. For 'tis but reasonable to suppose that the obligation of the command should be of equal extent with its foundation, and that as the duty has its foundation in that which came to pass in the beginning so it is to remain to the end of the world.

If we take this passage in Moses' history of the creation as proleptical, or an occasional remark, yet it seems[6] to show the great and extraordinary weight that Moses laid on that command, and the regard that God had to

5. MS: "blessing."
6. MS: "shews."

it. Thus to finish the first part of all writings in the history of the greatest thing that he wrote the history of; thus as soon as he had finished it, to turn aside from it to make this remark, and as the only improvement he expressly makes of it, when he has filled his reader with admiration of this glorious work of God, he straightway leads him off from it, by it to observe the ground of that great duty of sanctifying the seventh part of time which God had commanded Israel in the wilderness: this strongly argues that this is something more than a ceremonial.

But there seems to be no reason to suppose that this is a proleptical occasional observation, for the manner of expression seems plainly to denote it to be a part of the history. Gen. 2:2–3, "And on the seventh day God ended his work which he had made; and he rested on the seventh day from all his work which he had made. And God blessed the seventh day, and sanctified it." It seems manifestly to [be] a continuation of the story. There is the same conjunction and prefix before the two verbs, rested and blessed: "*and he rested*"; "*and he blessed.*" And both seem to have reference to the same thing; his resting was some way or other with respect to his creatures, angels or men, either a peculiar manifestation God on that day made of his rest and well-pleasedness in his works to Adam and Eve, or to the angels, for that end that he might set mankind an example: for God with respect to himself only rested no more, and rejoiced no more, on that day than on any day following. But God's giving a manifestation of his rest for an example to mankind is as much to our present purpose as his then hallowing and blessing the seventh day.

The Apostle argues from things that came to pass in the beginning of the creation, as things that should have universal influence in the regulation of the state and behavior of mankind in all ages—as from the woman's being taken out of man, and the woman's being first in the transgression. I don't see why we may not as well suppose that the state and practice of mankind in all ages should be governed and regulated from God's resting on the seventh day.

We have no reason to suppose that any one of the Ten Commands are abolished, for the whole of the Decalogue seems to be confirmed in the New Testament. Christ says he came not to destroy the law but to fulfill [Matt. 5:17]. Christ in that sermon where he says he came to fulfill the law, much blames the Pharisees for making void that law of God in the Decalogue by their perverse glosses, and elsewhere for making void one of them, viz. that of honoring our father and mother, by a precept contrary to it. Therefore, when Christ, in the midst of his reprehensions of them, professes to do the contrary of what they did, by saying that he came not to destroy the law but to fulfill, we may conclude that he makes void no one of them. One way in which Christ fulfills them is in vindicating them from the false glosses of the Pharisees, and explaining them in their full meaning, wherein they by their false interpretations of them, and by their human precepts, had curtailed them. Another way is by obeying them. Another way is by satisfying them. Another way is by bringing the substance, by which the shadows of the ceremonial law are fulfilled, in the same manner as a prophecy is fulfilled by the accomplishment.

'Tis this that in the New Testament is especially called the law, as appears, Rom. 13:8–10, where this law is spoken of as that which must yet be fulfilled or obeyed by us. So Gal. 5:14 and Jas. 2:8–11. I Cor. 7:19, "Circumcision is nothing, and uncircumcision is nothing, but the keeping the commandments of God." The Ten Commandments are in the New Testament especially called *the commandments;* so Christ says to the young man, "If thou wilt enter into life, keep the commandments" [Matt. 19:17]. So Rom. 13:9. See also Matt. 15:3 and 6; Matt. 22:36 and 38; and Mark 12:30 and 7:9; Luke 23:56; Rom. 7:7–8, 10, 12–13; Eph. 6:2, which last place shows that the Ten Commands are yet in force. See also I [Tim.] 1:5.

752. CHRISTIAN RELIGION. If there be a revelation that God makes to the world, 'tis most reasonable to suppose, and natural to expect, that he should therein make known not only what manner of being he is, but also that he should lead mankind to an understanding of his works of creation and providence; that he should give 'em some account how the world came into being, and also some account of his works of providence, that mankind may understand something of God's scope and design in continuing the world in being for so many ages, and [of] that series of events, great changes and revolutions, and many strange things that are brought to pass in it, in the successive ages in it; and that men may know something of God's scheme of providence, and so much of his scope and design, as to be able to see something of the wisdom and other perfections of God in the course of things; and that may be of some direction to them how to regulate themselves so as to concur with, and not to contradict, the holy and wise scheme of the governor of the world.

These things the Christian revelation opens to us in such a manner as might be expected. This only gives any tolerable account of the work of creation. And this reveals to us the scheme of providence, and what is God's particular main design in the whole series of providences, a design worthy of himself; what great work, that is his main work, the main design of providence, to which all events and revolutions of providence are subordinate; what is the thing that God is doing; what contrivance he is accomplishing; what God has done in order to it from the beginning of the world in the several ages of it. And we are shown how these events all point to the main great work of power, wisdom and grace that is the hinge of all. We have a particular account how this greatest work of all has actually been wrought in the fulness of time, as to those great acts that are the main ground of it, how this was foretold in the several ages of the world; and we have these prophecies still extant in this revelation. And we have a history of the series of events down from the creation of the world to that time that were preparatory to it; and then after that of the great events and works of God's providence that were immediately consequent on it, to establish the first fruits of it in the world, with a prophecy of the main events yet to be accomplished in pursuance of the same great scheme, and a description of the end of the world, an account of the winding up of things, and after what manner the scheme of God shall be finished, and his great design and great work consummated, and all things brought to their last end, and settled in their ultimate state to remain throughout eternity.

These things are such as are exceeding agreeable to a most natural and rational supposition, in case God makes a revelation to mankind. But if the Scriptures are not a revelation of God, then mankind, the principal creature God has made in this world, the only intelligent creature to whom he has subjected this lower part of the creation, are left wholly and entirely in the dark both about God's works of creation and providence, and have nothing to guide [them], whereby to judge what God's scheme is in all the great changes they see come to pass in the world from one age to another, or what he aims at or intends to accomplish. Everything lies in darkness and confusion before 'em, without any possibility of their determining anything as to direct 'em what to think of God's works which they behold, or what affections they should exercise towards the supreme governor on occasion of them, or how they shall in the course of their practice conform themselves to his scope, or admire and adore him, submit to him, serve him and praise him as the supreme Lord of the world and orderer of all things, or act towards the governor of the world as becomes a rational and intelligent subject of his kingdom.

753. CONVICTION, why it is necessary that a man should be convinced of his guilt in order to salvation. See sermon on Matt. 9:2, first direction under first use.[7]

---

7. The MS of the sermon on Matt. 9:2 is not extant.

754. SPIRITUAL KNOWLEDGE. 'Tis rational to suppose, that seeing God with such great care has so abundantly provided for the giving most convincing, assuring, satisfying and manifold evidence of his faithfulness in the covenant of grace, and as David says, made a covenant "ordered in all things, and sure" [II Sam. 23:5], that at the same time he would not fail of ordering the matter so that there should not be wanting as great and clear evidence that this is his covenant and that these promises, or which is the same thing, that the Christian religion, is true and that the Scriptures are his Word. Otherwise, those great assurances God has given of his faithfulness in his covenant are in vain, for the evidence that it is his covenant is properly the foundation on which all the force and effect of those other assurances stand. We may therefore undoubtedly suppose that there is some sort of evidence that God has given of this covenant's, and these promises', being his beyond moral evidence; that there is some ground of assurance of it held forth, which if we are not blind to them, tend to give an higher assurance of it than any arguing from history, human tradition, etc.; and that which is good ground of the highest and most perfect kind of assurance that mankind have in any case whatsoever.

It is also upon other accounts reasonable to suppose that God would give the greatest evidence of those things that are greatest, and the truth of which is of greatest importance to us; and that we therefore, if we are wise and act rationally, shall have far the greatest desire of having full, undoubting and perfect assurance of.

755. PERSEVERANCE. The Spirit of God was given at first, but was lost; but God gives it a second time, never to [be] utterly lost. The Spirit is now given in another manner than he was then. Then indeed he was communicated and dwelt in their hearts, but this communication was made without conveying at the same [time] any proper right or sure title to it. But when God communicates it a second time, as he does to a true convert, he withal gives it to him to be his own. He finally makes it over to him in a sure covenant. He is their purchased and promised possession. If our first parents had had a right to the Holy Spirit made over to them at first, he never would have departed from them.

Man in his first state had no benefit at all properly made over to him: for God makes over benefits only by covenant, but then the condition of the covenant had not been fulfilled. But now man at his first conversion is justified and adopted. He is received as a child and an heir, as a joint heir with Christ. His fellowship is with the Father and with his Son Jesus Christ. God is theirs, and Christ is theirs, and the Holy Ghost is theirs, and all things are theirs. The Holy Spirit, who is the sum of all good, is their inheritance; and that little of it that they have in this life, is the earnest of their future inheritance, till the redemption of the purchased possession. Heaven is theirs; their conversation is there [Philip. 3:20]. They are citizens of that city, and of the household of God. Christians are represented as being come already to heaven, to Mount Zion, the city of the living God, to an innumerable company of angels, etc. Heaven is the proper country of the church. They are raised up together with Christ, and made to sit together with him in heavenly places. Eph. 1:3, "They are blessed with all spiritual blessings in heavenly places." The whole tenor of the gospel shows that Christians have actually a full and final right made over to them, to spiritual and heavenly blessings.

756. MILLENNIUM, whether or no the miraculous gifts of the Spirit of God will be restored then. See sermon on I Cor. 13:8, first inference.[8] See also note on vv. 8–12, "Scripture," no. 305.[9]

757. JUSTIFICATION BY FAITH ALONE. The law which is God's original constitution and that is prior to the covenant of grace, won't allow of persons being in any respect accepted for their virtue, or any of their virtues, or any offering being accepted of God at their hands before they are in Christ, because the law sentences all such persons to be utterly rejected of God and treated with total abhorrence; for by the sentence of the law they are cursed, and to be treated of God as accursed persons, as appears by Gal. 3:10. But certainly for God to accept their offerings, and to accept them and to give testimonies of his delight in them for them, especially to that degree as to bestow such an exceeding and infinite reward upon them, as a saving interest in his Son, is not to treat them as accursed and an execration.

It was implied in any person's being accursed that he was wholly abhorred of God, as appears by Deut. 21:22–23, "And if a man have committed a sin worthy of death, and he be put to death, and thou hang him on a tree: his body shall not remain all night on the tree, but thou shalt in any wise bury him that day; for he that is hanged is accursed of God; that thy land be not defiled, which the Lord thy God giveth thee for an inheritance." So abominable was an accursed person to God that God looked

8. This is the 14th sermon in the series known as *Charity and Its Fruits*. For the first inference, see *Works, 8*, 361–63.

9. "Notes on Scripture," no. 305, is in *Works, 15*, 277–79. JE probably added this reference shortly after writing the entry.

on the very land as defiled on which they long remained. God did not see meet that that which was a curse and execration should remain in open sight, for [it was] an abomination and offense to the pure eyes of that God that dwelt in that holy land. They were therefore to remove such abominable things out of God's sight, that God might dwell and walk in the land and not withdraw from it. And such a curse, rendering us in like manner abominable in the eyes of God, are we naturally under, because Christ bore such a curse in our stead, as appears fully by the testimony of the Apostle in Gal. 3:10–14. Therefore, by a prior constitution we are condemned to be wholly an abomination. The abomination, and the accursed thing, are spoken of as the same; and the children of Israel, God's people, were commanded utterly to detest and utterly to abhor the accursed thing, and not to receive or take it to themselves, or bring it into their houses. Deut. 7:26, "Neither shalt thou bring an abomination into thine house, least thou be a cursed thing like it: but thou shalt utterly detest it, and thou shalt utterly abhor it; for it is a cursed thing." Doubtless therefore, the infinitely pure and holy God of this people himself will utterly abhor and utterly detest that which is accursed, and will not receive it, or accept anything in it or from it, and will in no wise manifest any delight in anything of it that is offered to him. He will not receive it into his house, much less bestow infinite blessings out of his house in reward for it. If God accepts something of their acts, offerings or virtues, he accepts something of themselves, for in offering their respect to God they can offer nothing diverse from themselves. And if God accepts it, he accepts themselves, and so receives the accursed thing before the curse is removed by Christ, because, by the supposition, before justification or pardon.

The cities that were accursed, everything in them was accursed and abominable, even their silver and gold and most precious things. To be accursed of God, and to be accepted of God, are utterly inconsistent; and the one can't be, till the other ceases to be. They can[not] subsist at the same time with respect to the same person.

758. DISPENSATIONS. TESTAMENTS. JUSTIFICATION BY FAITH ALONE. Whether or no we are not obliged to obey the precepts of the moral law by virtue of that prescription by which they are enacted in the law of Moses, as some that oppose justification by faith think we are not: see these texts, Acts 23:5, Eph. 6:2–3 and Jas. 2:8.

759. WISDOM OF GOD IN THE WORK OF REDEMPTION. Mercy and justice do gloriously and wondrously illustrate one another in the work of re-

demption. The immutability of justice makes the greatness of mercy to appear, in that, when justice was inexorable, mercy was so great towards the sinner that it rather gave God's only begotten Son to suffer than that the sinner should not be saved. The greatness of mercy shows the immutability of justice, in that, when mercy towards man was so great that it insisted that the sinner should be saved, God's justice was so unalterable that it would execute the full punishment of sin on the Son of God himself, rather than that sin should not have its just punishment.

760. CHRISTIAN RELIGION. THE HOLY SCRIPTURE. As providence is a far greater work than the work of creation, and its end, so the history of Scripture is much more taken up in works of providence, than in the work of creation. Things that appear minute in comparison of the work of creation are much insisted on in Scripture, for they become great by their relation to Christ and his redemption, of which creation was but a shadow. And the history of Scripture, which gives an account of the works of providence, are all taken up in the history of Christ and his church; for all God's works of providence are to be reduced to his providence towards Christ and his church.

761. FREE WILL. MAN'S IMPOTENCE. If men are wholly unable to believe of themselves, or unless God works faith in them, yet that is no argument that they are not chargeable with the blame of their own unbelief: for though man can't believe in Christ of himself, yet that is no argument that he can't reject him of himself. 'Tis no argument that because one of two opposites is of God, that therefore the other is so too; but the contrary. If sweet water proceed from a certain fountain, that is no argument that bitter water is from the same fountain; but on the contrary, an argument that it is from some other source (Jas. 3:11). Sinners, in laying the blame of their rejection of Christ to God from that, that all faith must be of God, and not of themselves, argue in this manner: God is the fountain of all light and, therefore, he must be the fountain of all darkness too; he is the author of all good and, therefore, the blame of all evil must be laid to him: whereas it would certainly be more natural and rational to argue contrariwise. If the sun be the fountain of light, then certainly darkness don't come from the sun, but that must proceed from some other cause. If all faith and receiving Christ be from God, and that be true in John 6:44, "No man can come to me, except the Father that hath sent me draw him," then 'tis natural to suppose that unbelief is not of God, but of ourselves. 'Tis no argument that man can't hate Christ of himself, because God is the bestower of all love to Christ.

762. WISDOM OF GOD IN THE WORK OF REDEMPTION. The sin of crucifying Christ seems to have been designed of God to be a representative of
the sin of mankind in general. The sin of mankind was that which slew
Christ, for he bore[1] our sins; it was our sin that stood against him. This was
the enemy that was so cruel to him, that nailed him to the cross, that
pierced his side, and let out his heart's blood. We who have sinned, that
he came into the world to redeem, are the crucifiers of Christ; therefore,
the sin of mankind in general is fitly represented by the sin of the immediate crucifiers of Christ. As the sin of mankind crucified Christ by procuring his crucifixion, so the sin of the Jews immediately executed his crucifixion, and so fitly represents the other. Their sin is a fit representative of
the sin of mankind in general, as therein the nature, tendency, and malignity of the sin of man does most eminently appear. The act of Christ's
crucifiers shows what is the nature of the sin of man, for those that put
him to death had no other corruption naturally in their hearts than is in
all of us. It was that very same corruption that we have, that crucified
Christ, for no other corruption exerted itself in that wicked act of theirs.
There never was opportunity but once for it to appear in fact, what the
corruption of man would do to God or a divine person if it had him within
its reach: for a divine person never was put within the reach of the malignity of man's sin, but only when the Son of God became man and dwelt
here on earth. Then he was liable to the malignant power of sin; and at
last he was delivered up into their hands a prisoner, to execute their will
upon him. And therefore sin, as it exerted itself then against this divine
person, appeared in such an act as fitly represents all the sin of man. In
that instance, it appeared that sin aimed at nothing short of the life of
God, that in its nature it was a murderer of God, and implied a mortal enmity against him; yea, that it not merely seeks the life of God, but to bring
all evil upon him, all ignominy, torment, and misery. For the Jews exerted
themselves to the utmost, to bring ignominy and torment and misery on
Christ to the utmost of their power. They were insatiable in it; they seemed
as if they never could be satisfied with mocking of him, and venting their
cruelty towards him. And that that sin might be the fitter to represent the
sin of mankind in general, there were both Jews and Gentiles concerned
in it, and persons of all ranks of both, great men and mean men, the rulers
of the Jews, and the common people, and Pilate the Gentile governor, and
the soldiers. There was Herod, that was originally of Gentile ancestors, being Idumeans; but by profession a Jew. There were persons both of the sa-

1. MS: "bear."

cred and civil order, and one of Christ's disciples, viz. Judas, and his true disciples in some sort concurring, all forsaking him at that time, and one of them denying him with oaths and curses. Christ, in dying for the sinful children of men, dies for those that are his crucifiers and murderers. As he died for some that actually and immediately put him to death, as he called for mercy for them when he was suffering, so his voice in that prayer showed what was the voice of his blood, that spoke better things than the blood of Abel. For Abel's blood cried for vengeance on him that shed it, but Christ's blood cries for the forgiveness of them that shed it, saying, "Father, forgive them; for they know not what they do" [Luke 23:34]. His dying for those that immediately crucified him, and interceding for their forgiveness, was to represent his dying for all the elect Jews and Gentiles, and his forgiving their enmity against him.

Corol. 1. WONDERFUL LOVE OF CHRIST. This shows the greatness and constancy of the love of Christ to his elect people. It appears in the circumstances of his last sufferings, that when his passion approached, and he had an extraordinary and near view of [it] in the time of his agony, and was sensible how great his approaching sufferings were, and then knew how that those sufferings should be brought on by the malignity of that sin that he was going to die to make atonement for, and when he was actually under his extreme sufferings, when he had more to give him a view of the hatefulness, and malignity, and baseness of that sin that he was going to suffer for the atonement of, out of love to the sinners; he then actually feeling the torments and cruelties, and suffering the reproach and contumely that was the fruit of the malignity and venom of that sin, yet his love did not fail. All this baseness did not overcome his love; but he was willing to yield himself a sacrifice, and endure such extreme sufferings out of love to those who were so cruel towards [him], and to expiate that very iniquity that appeared in that cruelty. When he saw the hatefulness and baseness of all the sin that he died for, in this representative iniquity that was now before his eyes, and that he now suffered from, it did not overcome his love.

Corol. 2. GOD DECREES MEN'S SIN. Hence that sin being foreordained of God in his decree, and ordered in his providence—as we have abundant evidence from the nature of the thing, from the great ends that God had to accomplish by means of this wicked act of crucifying Christ, it being as it were the cause of all the decrees, the greatest of all decreed events, and that on which all other decreed events depend on as their main foundation, being the main thing in that greatest work of God, the work of redemption, that [which] is the end of all other works—and it being so much prophesied of and so plainly spoken [of] as being done according to the determinate counsel and foreknowledge of God: I say, seeing we have such evidence of this sin being foreordained in God's decrees, and ordered in providence, and this being as it were the head sin and representative of the sin of men in general; hence is a clear argument that all the sins of men are foreordained, and ordered by a wise providence.

763. ABSOLUTE DECREES. SINCERITY OF GOD'S INVITATIONS. 'Tis objected against the absolute decrees of God respecting the future actions of men, and especially the unbelief of sinners and their rejection of the gospel, that this don't consist with the sincerity of God's calls and invitations to such sinners as he has willed in his eternal secret decree never should accept of those invitations. To which I answer: that there is that in God—respecting that acceptance and compliance of sinners, which God knows will never be, and which he has decreed never to cause to be—which though it ben't just the same with our desiring and wishing for that which never will come to pass, yet there is nothing wanting but what would imply imperfection in such a case. There is all that in God, that is good and perfect and excellent in our desires and wishes for the conversion and salvation of wicked men; as for instance, there is a love to holiness absolutely considered, or an agreeableness of holiness to his nature and will, or in other words, to his natural inclination. So the happiness of the creature absolutely considered, is a thing that he loves. Those things are infinitely more agreeable to his nature than to ours. There is all in God that belongs to our desire of the holiness and happiness of unconverted men and reprobates, excepting what implies imperfection; all that is consistent with infinite knowledge, wisdom and power, self-sufficience, infinite happiness, and immutability. And therefore, there is no reason that his absolute prescience, yea, or his wise determination and ordering what is future, should hinder his expressing this disposition of his nature, in like manner as we are wont to express such a disposition in us, viz. by calls, and invitations, and the like.

The disagreeableness of the wickedness and misery of the creature, absolutely considered, to the nature of God, is all that is good in good and holy men's lamenting the past misery and wickedness of men. Their lamenting these is good no farther than it proceeds from the disagreeableness of these things to their holy and good nature. So this is also all that is good in wishing for the future holiness and happiness of men. And there is nothing wanting in God, in order to his having such desires and such lamentings, but imperfection; and nothing is in the way of his having them, but infinite perfection. And therefore it properly, naturally, and necessarily came to pass that when God, in the *manner* of *existence*, came down from his infinite perfection, and accommodated himself to our nature and manner by being made man, as he was in the person of Jesus Christ, he really desires the conversion and salvation of reprobates, and laments their obstinacy and misery; as when he beheld the city Jerusalem and wept over it, saying, "O Jerusalem, Jerusalem, thou that killest the prophets, and stonest them which are sent unto thee, how often would I have gathered thy children together, even as a hen gathereth her chickens under her wings, and ye would not" [Matt. 23:37]. So in like manner, when he comes down from his infinite perfection, though not in the manner of being, but in the manner of manifestation, and accommodates himself to our nature and manner, in the manner of expression, 'tis equally natural and proper that he should express himself as though he desired the conversion and salvation of reprobates, and lamented their obstinacy and misery.

764a. CHRIST'S SATISFACTION. It was needful that he that was a mediator between two parties, that are distant and alienated one from the other, to be the middle person to unite them together, should himself be united to both; otherwise he could not, by coming between them, be a bond of union between them. And if he be a mediator between God and guilty men, it was necessary that he should unite himself to them, or assume them as it were to himself. But if he unites himself to guilty creatures, he of necessity brings their guilt on himself; if he unites himself to them that are in debt, he brings their debt on himself. He can't properly unite himself to a rebel against God, and one that is obnoxious to God's wrath, and is condemned to condign punishment, to be a mediator, to bring God to be at peace with him, without voluntarily taking his suffering on himself; because otherwise his undertaking for such an one, and uniting himself to such an one, will appear like a countenancing his offense and rebellion. But if at the same time that he unites himself to him, he takes it upon himself to bear his penalty, it quite takes off all such appearance. He shows that though he loves the rebel that has affronted the divine majesty, yet he at the same time has the greatest possible abhorrence of the injury to God's majesty, and dishonor to his name, in that he regards the honor of God's majesty so much as to be willing [to endure] so extreme [suffering], that the divine majesty and glory may not be injured, but fully maintained.

764b. INCARNATION OF CHRIST. UNION OF THE TWO NATURES IN CHRIST. What Christ says in the 3rd [chapter] of John, vv. 33–34, confirms that the Holy Spirit is the bond of union by which the human nature of Christ is united to the divine, so as to be one person. "He that hath received his testimony hath set to his seal that God is true. For he whom God hath sent speaketh the words of God: for God giveth not the Spirit by measure unto him." Which words may be thus paraphrased: he that hath received my testimony as true, and sets to his seal that I speak true, he therein sets to his seal that God speaks true, for in my speaking of it God speaks it. There is such an union between this human nature that immediately speaks with God's [words], that the words in being my words are God's words; which union is the consequence of God's communicating his Spirit without measure to my human nature, so as to render it the same person with him that is God. Something more is doubtless intended than that he was an inspired person, and spake the Word of God as the prophets did. When Christ says that he that receives his testimony sets to his seal that God is true, because his words were God's words, he doubtless has respect to something that is peculiar to himself, something that is his own prerogative; and therefore, the reason that he gives for it is something peculiar to him, viz. God's giving the Spirit not by measure unto him. When he says that he that hears his words hears God's words, and he that owns him to be true owns God to be true, 'tis most natural to understand him in a sense analogous to what he says elsewhere: "My Father worketh hitherto, and I work"; and "he that hath seen me hath seen the Father" [John 5:17, 14:9].

765. MYSTERIES IN RELIGION. If one seeks for anything in the dark, by so low a faculty of discerning as the sense of feeling, or by the sense of seeing with a dim light, sometimes we cannot find it, though it be there. It seems to [be] impossible that it should be there; but yet when a clear light comes to shine into the place, and we discern by a better faculty, viz. of sight, or the same faculty in a clearer manner, the thing appears very plain to us. So doubtless many truths will hereafter appear plain, when we come to look on them by the bright light of heaven, that now are involved in mystery and darkness.

766. INCARNATION OF THE SON OF GOD. UNION OF THE DIVINE AND HUMAN NATURE OF CHRIST. The bond of this union is the Holy Spirit. 'Tis manifest that the divine speeches that Christ uttered, and the divine works that Christ wrought, were by the Spirit of God. The divine words

that he uttered, with which he taught the world divine things, and revealed God and the things of God to mankind, were[2] by the Spirit of God; as is evident by John 3:34, "For he whom God hath sent speaketh the words of God: for God giveth not the Spirit by measure unto him." And the divine works that Christ wrought, wherein he manifested divine power, were by the Spirit of God; as is evident by what Christ says on occasion of the Pharisees blaspheming him, as though he cast out devils by Beelzebub (Matt. 12). That both Christ's outward and inward divine teachings, and also both his outward and inward divine works of power and grace, were wrought by the Spirit of God, is manifest by Luke 4:18–19. "The Spirit of the Lord God is upon me, because the Lord has anointed me to preach the gospel to the poor; he hath sent me to heal the brokenhearted, to preach deliverance to the captives, and recovering of sight to the blind, to set at liberty them that are bruised, to preach the acceptable year of the Lord." It will therefore follow that the union of Christ's human nature with the divine is by the Spirit of God. For those divine works that he wrought were his own works; they were not wrought by the Spirit, as the apostles and prophets wrought miracles by the power and in the name of another, but as wrought in his own name and by his own power. Though he was directed by the Spirit of God when and how to work those works, and was moved by the Spirit to work them, yet he wrought them as of his own wisdom and his own will; as he says, "I will; be thou clean" [Matt. 8:3]. Now this can't be, that he should [be] directed by the Spirit to work, and his will moved by the Spirit of God, and yet they be done as of his own will any otherwise than as the Spirit of God directed the human understanding, and moved the human will, as a bond of union between the understanding and the will of the divine Logos, and the understanding and will of the human nature of Christ. For those works of the divine power were his own no otherwise than as they were the works of the divine Logos, united to the human nature, or to the human understanding and will. But if that human understanding and will was directed and moved by the Holy Ghost, and yet it might be said to be done as of his own wisdom and will, the Holy Ghost must in this act as a means of conveyance of the understanding and will of the divine Logos, to the understanding and will of the human nature, or of the union of these understandings and wills. And so, though it was of the motion of the Spirit of God, yet it was of himself, because these motions of the Spirit themselves were of himself, i.e. of his divine person, the person of the Logos,

2. MS: "was."

conveying and uniting the divine understanding and will, and so of the divine nature with the human.

Christ taught the things of God as of his own knowledge, as being in the bosom of the Father, as he that had seen the Father and knew the Father. He revealed the Father as one that knew him of himself, without a revelation. And yet the knowledge of divine things that the human nature had was by the Spirit of God, by his inspiration or revelation: for he taught and did the business of the great prophet of God by the Spirit. But these things can't consist together any other way, than that the Spirit of God is the bond of union between the knowledge of the divine nature of Christ and the human, so that the knowledge of the divine Logos was his knowledge. But that which so unites the human nature of Christ with the divine, that the knowledge of the one is the knowledge of the other, is doubtless the same thing that unites them so together, that the person of the one is the person of the other. That by which the knowledge and the power of the eternal Logos came to dwell in Jesus the son of Mary, is that by which the eternal Logos himself dwelt in Jesus the Son of Mary. The union of the eternal Logos with the man Christ Jesus was doubtless by some communication or other, by that means some way peculiarly communicating with that divine Logos in what was his, or by having something dwelling in [him] that was divine, that belonged to the Logos. If there is no more communication between this individual human nature and the eternal Son of God than others, there is no more real union. But all that was divine in the man Christ Jesus is from the Spirit of God—divine power, and divine knowledge, and divine will, and divine acts—and therefore, it must be that the divine Logos dwelt in him by the Spirit, or which is the same thing, was united to him by the Spirit. When the man Christ Jesus said, "I will; be thou clean," or speaking in the name and person of the eternal Son of God, *spake* by the Holy Ghost, then it will follow that it was by the Holy Ghost that the man Christ Jesus *was* in the name and in the person of the eternal Son of God. But he spake this by the Holy Ghost, for it was at the direction, motion, and influence of the Spirit of God on Christ's will that he wrought miracles.

Corol. This shows how much the man Christ Jesus must needs be the most holy of all creatures. For the creature is more or less holy according as it has more or less of the Holy Spirit dwelling in it; but Christ has so much of the Spirit, and hath it in so high and excellent a manner, as to render him the same person with him whose Spirit it is. This shows how much fuller his heart is of love for holiness, and [how] the Spirit of God consists in love. And his acts show the same: never any gave such manifestations of love in their acts as he did. The love of his heart is as much above the love of any other creature as his acts of love were greater. This shows how excellent and sufficient Christ's righteousness must needs be.

767. INCARNATION OF CHRIST, AND HIS PERFECT HOLINESS. Though Christ was conceived in the womb, and of the substance of a mother that was one of the corrupt race of mankind, and born of her, yet being conceived by the power of the Holy Ghost, which is the omnipotent holiness of God itself, that which was conceived and formed must needs be a perfectly holy thing; as Luke 1:35, "The Holy Ghost shall come upon thee, and the power of the Highest shall overshadow thee: therefore also that holy thing which shall be born of thee shall be called the Son of God." Here it seems to be supposed, that seeing this thing is formed by the Holy Ghost, it must needs be an holy thing. Seeing it was the immediate work of infinite, omnipotent, holiness itself, the thing wrought must needs be perfectly holy, without any unholiness. Though wrought in the midst of pollution and brought out of it, yet this agent being infinitely powerful, its influence must needs infinitely prevail over any ill influence, that the nature of the mother might be supposed to have. It is the proper work of this infinite, divine, holy energy to bring good out of evil, light out of darkness, life out of death, holiness out of impurity.

768. ABRAHAM IS THE FATHER OF BELIEVERS. Christ is our father in other virtues, but only those that [he] himself as our Savior is the object of, and that are proper for us as sinners, these Christ could not set us an example of. And therefore, another one that is naturally a sinful man as we are, is appointed to be our father. Abraham is the father of believers, as Jabal was the father of such as dwell in tents, and as Jubal was the father of such as handle the harp and the organ (Gen. 4:20–21); that is, he was set as the great example and pattern for them to follow. And he [was the one] that the church of believers, that was afterwards, came from; he [the one] that by his faith laid the foundation of the church of believers: for the promises, that in him all the families of the earth should be blessed, were by faith; as well as because the church of believers either were of, or are[3] come by means of, his natural posterity.

769. CHRIST is often spoken of in Scripture as being by way of eminency THE ELECT or chosen of God. Is. 42:1, "Behold my servant, whom I up-

---

3. MS: "were of ore."

hold; mine elect, in whom my soul delighteth." Luke 23:35, "If he be the Christ, the chosen of God." I Pet. 2:4, "A living stone, chosen of God, and precious." Ps. 89:3, "I have made a covenant with my chosen"; v. 19, "I have exalted one chosen out of the people." Hence those persons in the Old Testament that were the most remarkable types of Christ, were the subjects of a very remarkable election of God, by which they were designed to some peculiar honor of the prophetical, priestly or kingly office. So Moses was called God's chosen in that wherein he was eminently a type of Christ, viz. as a prophet, and ruler, and mediator for his people. Ps. 106:23, "Had not Moses his chosen stood before him in the breach." So Aaron was constituted high priest by a remarkable election of God, as in Num. 16:5 and 17:5; Deut. 21:5. So David the king was the subject of a remarkable election. Ps. 78:67–72, "Moreover he refused the tabernacle of Joseph, and chose not the tribe of Ephraim: but chose the tribe of Judah, the Mt. Zion which he loved. And he built his sanctuary like high palaces, like the earth which he hath established forever. He chose David also his servant, and took him from the sheepfolds: from following the ewes great with young he brought him to feed Jacob his people, and Israel his inheritance." I Sam. 16:7–10, "The Lord hath not chosen this. [. . .] Neither hath the Lord chosen this. . . . The Lord hath not chosen these."

Christ is the chosen of God both as to his divine and human nature. As to his divine nature he was chosen of God, though not to any addition to his essential glory or real happiness which is infinite, yet to [his] great declarative glory. As he is man, he is chosen of God to the highest degree of real glory and happiness of all creatures. As to both, he is chosen of God to the office and glory of the Mediator between God and man, and the head of all the elect creation. His election as it respects his divine nature was for his worthiness, and excellency, and infinite amiableness in the sight of God; and perfect fitness for that which God chose him to his worthiness, was the ground of his election. But his election as it respects his human nature was free and sovereign, not being for any worthiness, but his election was the foundation of his worthiness. His election as he is God is a manifestation of God's infinite wisdom. The wisdom of any being is discovered by the wise choice he makes. So the infinite wisdom of God is manifest in the wisdom of his choice, when he chose his eternal Son— one so fit upon all accounts for the office of a Mediator—when he only was fit, and when he was perfectly and infinitely fit; and yet his fitness was so difficultly to be discerned that none but one of infinite wisdom could discover it. See sermon on Eph. 3:10, the first particular insisted on under the doctrine; and also sermon on Heb. 2:3, beginning with the second page of the seventh leaf.[4]

His election as he was man was a manifestation of God's sovereignty and grace. God had determined to exalt one of the creatures so high that he should be one person with God, and should have communion with God, and glory in all respects answerable, and so should be the head of all other elect creatures, that they might be united to God and glorified in him. And his sovereignty appears in the election of the man Jesus various ways. It appears in choosing the species of creatures of which he should be, viz. the race of mankind, and not the angels, the superior species. God's sovereignty also appears in choosing this creature of the seed of fallen creatures, that were become enemies and rebels, abominable, miserable creatures. It appears in choosing that he should be of such a branch of mankind, in selecting the posterity of David, a mean person originally and the youngest of the family. And as he was the seed of the woman, so his sovereignty appears in his being the seed of such women as he was: as of Leah, the uncomely wife of Jacob, whom her husband had not chosen; and of Tamar, a Canaanitess and a harlot; and Rahab, a harlot; and Ruth, a Moabitess; and of Bathsheba, one that had committed adultery; and the immediate seed of Mary, a mean person. And his sovereignty appears in the choice of that individual female seed of mankind. As all the future seed of Adam were in some respect in his loins, so all the future posterity of the woman were in the womb or ovary of Eve. There are the first principles, the stamina, of every human body, long before it becomes the body of the human being. There is a seed of the woman to be afterwards impregnated in the immediate mother, if not in the first mother of mankind. And what number of these ova or seeds should be impregnated, is determined of God beforehand, and so every individual human being that should have existence from thence. God's sovereignty appears in choosing this individual seed of the woman to advance to such glory and blessedness. 'Tis this free, sovereign and gracious election that is the prime ground of any distinction among those seeds of the woman considered antecedent to this. They are all in like circumstances: they are all alike seeds of the woman, all have the same nature, are all alike liable to begin their proper human existence the same way, are all alike liable to the guilt and pollution, and so to the misery and damnation, that comes

4. In the first particular under the doctrine of the sermon on Eph. 3:10 (March 1733) JE addresses the proposition "that there is great wisdom manifested in contriving the way of salvation by Christ." Published in Worcester rev. ed., *4*, 133–68; see esp. p. 135. The MS of the sermon on Heb. 2:3 is not extant.

by the fall. That Christ was conceived by the power of the Holy Ghost was a fruit of his election. For that seed of the woman—those stamina and first principles of his human being that were in the womb of the virgin, that was one of those seeds that had future humanity and that [had] individual humanity annexed to it by God's decree—was as liable to be impregnated by man as any other seed of the woman whatsoever. So that it was owing to this election of God that the man Jesus was not one of the corrupt race of mankind. So that freedom from sin and damnation is owing to the free, sovereign, electing love of God in him, as well as in the rest of elect men. All holiness, all obedience, and good works, and perseverance in him, was owing to the electing love of God, as well as in his elect members. And so his freedom from eternal damnation was owing to the free electing love of God another way, viz. as it was owing to God's electing love to him and his members; but to him in the first place, that he did not fail in that great and difficult work that he undertook, that he did not fail under his extreme sufferings, and so eternally continue under them. For if he had failed, [if] his courage, resolution and love had been conquered by his sufferings, he never could have been delivered from them: for then he would have failed in his obedience to God and, his love to God failing and being overcome by sufferings, those sufferings would have failed of the nature of an acceptable sacrifice to God, and the infinite value of his sufferings would have failed, and so must be made up in infinite duration to atone for his own deficiency. But God having chosen Christ, he could not fail in this work, and so was delivered from his sufferings, from the eternity of them, by the electing love of God. Justification and glorification were fruits of God's foreknowledge and predestination, in him as well as in his elect members.

So that the man Christ Jesus has the eternal electing love of God to him to contemplate and admire, and to delight and rejoice his heart, as all his elect members have. He has it before him eternally to praise God for his free and sovereign election of him, and to ascribe the praise of his freedom from eternal damnation (which he with his elect members beholds, and has had a taste of far beyond all the rest, and so has more to excite joy and praise for his deliverance from it), and the praise [of] the glory he possesses to that election, as others have. This election is not for Christ's works or worthiness, for all his works and worthiness are the fruits of it. God had power over this seed of the woman to make it either a vessel to honor or dishonor, as he had over the rest.

Christ is by way of eminency called THE ELECT of God: for though other elect men are by election distinguished from the greater part of mankind, yet they in their election have that which is common to thousands and millions, and though the elect angels are distinguished by election from the angels that fell, yet they are chosen among myriads of others; but this man by his election is vastly distinguished from all other creatures in heaven or earth. And Christ in his election is the head of election, and the pattern of all other election. He is the head of all elect creatures, and both angels and men are chosen in him in some sense, i.e. chosen to be in him. All elect men are said to be chosen in Christ in Eph. 1:4. Election contains two things, viz. foreknowledge and predestination, which are distinguished in the eighth chapter of Romans. The one is choosing persons to be God's, which is a foreowning them; and the other a destining them to be conformed to the image of his Son, both in his holiness and blessedness. The elect are chosen in him with respect to these two, in senses somewhat diverse. With respect to foreknowledge or foreowning, we are chosen in him as God chose us to be actually his, in this way, viz. by being in Christ, or being members of his Son. This is the way that God determined we should actually become his. God chose Christ and gave them to him, and so looking on them as his, owned them for his own. But by predestination, which is consequent on this foreknowledge, we are elected in Christ, as we are elected in his election. For God having in foreknowledge given us to Christ, he thenceforward beheld us as members or parts of him; and so ordaining the head to glory, he therein ordained the members to glory. Or, in destining Christ to eternal life, he destined all parts of Christ to it also, so that we are appointed to eternal life in Christ, being in Christ his members from eternity. In his being appointed to life, we are appointed. So Christ's election is the foundation of ours, as much as his justification and glorification are the foundation of ours. By election in Scripture is sometimes meant this latter part, viz. destination to conformity to Christ in life and glory; as II Thess. 2:13, "God from the beginning hath chosen you to salvation." And it seems to be spoken of in this sense chiefly in Eph. 1:3–5, "Who hath blessed us with all spiritual blessings in heavenly places in Christ: according as he hath chosen us in him before the foundation of the world, that we should be holy and without blame before him in love: having predestinated us to the adoption of children by Jesus Christ to himself, according to the good pleasure of his will." See [No.] 1245.

770. MYSTERIES. How are we ready to trust to the determinations of a man that is universally reputed a man of great genius, of vast penetration and insight into things! If he [be] positive in anything that appears to us

very mysterious, and is quite contrary to what we thought ourselves clear and certain in before, how are we ready in such a case to suspect ourselves, especially if it be a matter wherein he has been very much versed, has had much more occasion to look into it than we, and has been under greater advantages to know the truth. How much more still, if one should be positive in it as a thing that he had clearly and undoubtedly seen to be true, if he were still of ten times greater genius and more penetrating insight into things, than any that ever have appeared. And in matters of fact, if some person that we had long known, that was a person of great judgment and discretion, justice, integrity and fidelity, and had always been universally so reputed by others, should declare to us that he had seen and known to be true that [that] appeared to us very strange and mysterious, and what we can't see how it is possible that it should be, how in such a case should we be ready almost to suspect our own faculties, and to give credit to such a testimony in that which, if he had not positively asserted it and persisted in it, we should have looked upon as perfectly incredible and absurd to suppose.

771. CONVICTION. HUMILIATION. Its being needful that a person that is saved should be sensibly saved, and so first sensible of his misery, don't prove that persons universally are first in great terror before they are converted. For whether any are converted in proper infancy or no, yet doubtless some are converted in early childhood when, if they have great terror, yet the sense of it in a course of nature will in a great measure wear off, so that so far as the sensibleness of their salvation depends on that terrible sense of their own misery that they had before they were converted, their salvation will cease to be sensible when they are grown up. They will not be more sensibly delivered by reason of that, than if they were converted when adult with far less terror.

772. MEDIATION OF CHRIST. The business of a mediator is as a middle person between two parties, at a distance and at variance, to make peace between them. Christ is Mediator between God and man to make peace between them, by reconciling God to man [and man] to God. He alone is fit to be the Mediator. He only of the persons of the Trinity is fit, being the middle person between the Father and the Holy Ghost, and so only is fit to be a mediator between the Father and sinners, in order to their holiness and happiness. For in so being, he is a middle person between the Father and the Holy Ghost in them, in that he is the means or middle person by which holiness and happiness is purchased for them of the Father,

or which is the same thing, by which the Holy Ghost is purchased for them: for the conferring of holiness and happiness consists in conferring the Holy Ghost. The purchaser and the price are intermediate between the person of whom the purchase is made, and the thing purchased of him. So he acts intermediately as between the Father and the Holy Ghost not only as he is the person by whom the Holy Ghost is purchased of the Father, but also by whom it is conferred on sinners from the Father. Thus the Mediator acts as a middle person between the Father and the Holy Ghost in transacting with sinful men from the Father. So also is he, in transacting for them and from them with the Father when their desires, their prayers and praises, their love, their trust and their obedience, is offered to God through Christ as Mediator, and these are presented to the Father through his hands: for that love and those prayers, etc., are from the actings of the Holy Spirit in them.

Christ God-man is a fit person for a mediator between God and man not only as he is a middle person between the Father and the Holy Ghost, but also between God and man. But as he is a middle person between God and men themselves, he is nearly allied to both; he is the Son of God and the Son of man. He is both God and man. He is God's Son and our brother. And as he has the nature of both, so he has the circumstances of both: the glory, majesty and happiness of the one, and the infirmity, meanness, disgrace, guilt and misery of the other. As it was requisite in order to his being Mediator between God and man that he should be the subject of our calamities, that he might know, on the one hand, how to pity us who suffer or are exposed to those calamities; so on the other hand, it was requisite that he should be possessed of the glory and majesty of God, that he might know how to value that glory and majesty, and to be careful and tender of them, and effectually engaged to see to it that they are well secured, and gloriously magnified. And he undertakes for each with the other. He undertakes for man with God. He becomes surety for him; he undertakes that the law shall be answered, God's majesty vindicated and glorified with respect to man. Yea, he so undertakes for sinners that he assumes them to himself; he puts himself before the Father in the sinner's stead, that whatever justice has to demand of the sinner, it may demand it of him. He takes the sinner's debt, becomes bound for him, so that justice no longer looks to the sinner for a discharge of the debt, but to Christ. And so he also undertakes for the Father with men, in order to their being reconciled to God, and resting in him as their sure and everlasting portion, that God will preserve them and keep them, that none shall pluck them out of his hands, away from this portion and inheritance, that so they may rest in him without having all rest in him destroyed through continual fear of a dissolution of their union with him, through their great weakness and continual sins. Christ therefore undertakes with men to be their advocate and intercessor, and therein engages them the continuance of God's favor. See the next, No. 773.

Christ, being Mediator between God and man, appears in the stead of each to the other, and is the representative of each before the other. He appears in God's stead to us in his prophetical and kingly office. He pleads and manages the cause of each with the other. He manages the cause of God with us as prophet, and he manages our cause with God as priest. He acts for both as king. As prophet he is God's representative to us; as priest he is our representative to God. As king he reigns as God's representative, but as our head, and for our benefit. He is head of the church, and head over all things to the church. He reigns as God's vicegerent and delegate, and our Mediator and spiritual husband. He reigns in some sort in the name of both.

He, as Mediator between both, brings to each what is said by the other. He brings the Word of God to man as prophet in his instructions and counsels; and he carries our words to God in our prayers, confessions and praises, as priest in his intercession.

By his death he has reconciled each to [the] other. By his blood he has taken away that on our part which was the partition wall and the cause of God's enmity towards us, viz. our sin. And by the same he has taken away that which was the partition wall on God's part, that was the occasion of our enmity to him, viz. the law of the commandments, the law or covenant of works which condemned us, and so rendered God the object of our slavish fear and hatred.

Christ, by dying, has offered to God the strongest inducement to him to receive man into his favor, as it was the most glorious act of righteousness; and he has also by the same offered to man the strongest inducement to man to love God, as it was the most glorious manifestation of his amiable holiness, and winning grace, and mercy. Christ, being Mediator between God and man, goes from one to the other. He in the first place came down from God to man and dwells in this world, and then ascends to God again and to obtain salvation. And at the last day he will come down from God hither again. He will appear the second time, having obtained salvation, actually to bestow it; and then will ascend to God again with his people, bringing them to God, to an everlasting enjoyment of him. His first coming was from God; and his last return is to God, for God is the Alpha and Omega in this affair.

Christ brings God and man to each other, and actually unites them together. This he does by various steps and degrees, which terminate in the highest step, in that consummation of actual union, which he will accomplish at the end of the world. First, he came into this world and brought God or divinity down with him to us; and then he ascended to God and carried up humanity or man with him to God. And from heaven he sent down the Holy Spirit, whereby he gives God to man, and hereby he draws them to give up themselves to God. He brings God to dwell with their souls on earth in their conversion, and he brings their souls to dwell with God in heaven at their death. The time will come when he will come down again from heaven in person, and will bring God with him and to man a second time, and will a second time ascend to carry up man with him. God, at his first descent, he brought divinity down to us under a veil; at his second coming he will bring divinity with him without a veil, appearing in its glory. At his first ascension after his own resurrection, he carried up our nature with him to God. At his second ascension after the general resurrection, he will carry up our persons with him. At death he brings the souls of the saints to God in heaven, whereby a part of the church is gloriously united to God. At the end of the world he will bring them in both body and soul to heaven, and will bring all the church together to their highest and consummate union with God. And this will be the last step that he will take in the office of a Mediator to unite God [and man], having presented all his church together in body and soul to the Father, without spot or wrinkle, or any such thing, perfectly delivered, and perfectly restored, and perfectly glorified; saying, "Here am I, and the children which thou hast given me." Having finished the work which the Father gave him to do, then cometh the end when he will deliver up the kingdom to the Father.

Christ is an advocate for each with the other. He is an advocate for us with the Father in intercession in heaven; and he is an advocate for the Father with us by his Spirit, that is therefore called the Advocate.

773. PERSEVERANCE. CHRIST'S MEDIATION. The doctrine of perseverance is manifest from the nature of the mediation of Christ, spoken of in the proceeding number. For Christ, being a mediator between God and man, to reconcile God to man and man to God, and as he is a middle person between both, and as he has the nature of both, so he undertakes for each, and in some respect becomes surety for each with the other. He undertakes and becomes a surety for man to God. He engages for him that the law that was given him shall be answered, and that justice with respect

to him shall be satisfied, and the honor of God's majesty vindicated. So he undertakes and engages for the Father with men, in order to their being reconciled to God, and induced to come to him, to love him, and trust confidently in him, and rest quietly in him. He undertakes for the Father's acceptance and favor. John 14:21, "He that loveth me shall be loved of my Father." He undertakes that the Father shall hear and answer their prayers. He becomes as it were surety to see their prayers answered. John 14:13, "Whatsoever ye shall ask the Father in my name, that will I do, that the Father may be glorified in the Son." He undertakes that they shall have all needed supplies of grace from the Father; and he engages for the continuance of God's presence with them, and the continuance of his favor, and of the supplies of grace necessary to uphold and preserve them, and keep them from finally perishing. John 14:16, "And I will pray the Father, and he shall give you another Comforter, that he may abide with you forever"; and v. 23, "If a man love me, he will keep my words: and my Father will love him, and we will come to him, and make our abode with him." Christ don't only declare that God will give us needed grace, but he himself undertakes to see it done. He promises that he will bestow it from the Father. John 15:26, "But the Comforter whom I will send you from the Father." It was necessary that someone should thus undertake for God with men, for the continuance of his pardoning and sanctifying grace, in order to the sinner's being fully reconciled to God, and brought fully and quietly to rest in him as his God. Otherwise the sinner, conscious of his own weakness and sinfulness, could have no quiet rest in God for fear of the union's being broken between God and him, and for fear of incurring God's displeasure and wrath, and so having God an enemy forever; which man in himself in his fallen state is a thousand times as liable to, as he was under the first covenant. He is in a capacity to undertake for us and be surety for us with the Father because he puts himself in our stead; and he also is [in] a capacity to undertake for the Father and be surety for him with us, because the Father hath put him in his stead. He puts himself in our stead as priest, and answers for us, and does and suffers in that office what we should have done and suffered. And God puts him in his stead as king. He is appointed to the government of the world as God's vicegerent, and so in that office answers for God to us; [he] does that and orders and bestows that which we need from God. He undertakes for us in things that are expected of us as subjects, because he puts himself into our subjection. He appears in the form of a servant for us. So he undertakes for the Father in that which is desired and hoped for of him as king, for the Father hath put him into his kingdom and dominion, and has committed all authority and power unto him. He is in a capacity to undertake for the Father with us, because he can say as in John 16:15, "All things that the Father hath are mine."

774. PERSEVERANCE. The first covenant failed of bringing man to the glory of God through man's instability, whereby he failed of perseverance. Man's changeableness was the thing wherein it was weak; it was weak through the flesh. But God had made a second covenant in mercy to fallen man, that in the way of this covenant he might be brought to the glory of God, which he failed of under the other. But 'tis God's manner in things that [he] appoints and constitutes, when one thing fails of its proper end, and he appoints another to succeed in the room of it, to introduce that the second time in which the weakness and defects of the former are supplied, and which never shall fail, but shall surely reach its end; and so shall remain as that which needs no other to succeed it. So God removed the first dispensation by Moses. Heb. 8:7–13, "For if the first covenant had been faultless, then should no place have been sought for the second. For finding fault with them, he saith, Behold, the days come, saith the Lord, that I will make a new covenant with the house of Israel and with the house of Judah: not according to the covenant that I made with their fathers . . . because they continued not in my covenant, and I regarded them not, saith the Lord. For this is the covenant that I will make with the house of Israel after those days, saith the Lord; I will put my laws into their mind, and write them in their hearts: and I will be to them a God, and they shall be to me a people: and they shall not teach every man his neighbor, and every man his brother, saying, Know the Lord: for all shall know me, from the least to the greatest. For I will be merciful to their unrighteousnesses, and their sins and their iniquities will I remember no more. In that he saith, A new covenant, he hath made the first old. Now that which decayeth and waxeth old is ready to vanish away."

So the priesthood of the order of Aaron ceases because of the weakness and insufficiency of it to answer the ends of priesthood, which are to reconcile God to man. Therefore God introduces another priesthood after the order of Melchizedek, that is sufficient, and can't fail, and remains forever. Heb. 7:11–12, "If therefore perfection were by the Levitical priesthood (for under it the people received the law), what further need was there that another priest should arise after the order of Melchizedek, and not called after the order of Aaron? For the priesthood being changed, there is made of necessity a change also of the law"; vv. 15–19, "After the similitude of Melchizedek there ariseth another priest, who is made, not after the law of a carnal commandment, but after the power of an endless life. For he testifieth, Thou art a priest forever after the order of Melchizedek. For there is verily a disannulling of the commandment going before for the weakness and unprofitableness thereof. For the law made nothing perfect, but the bringing in of a better hope did." What the law failed of, being weak through the flesh, Christ performed. Rom. 8:3–4, "For what the law could not do, in that it was weak through the flesh, God sending his own Son in the likeness of sinful flesh, and for sin, condemned sin in the flesh: that the righteousness of the law might be fulfilled in us, that walk not after the flesh. but after the Spirit." So the old heavens and earth are destroyed because of their defects, and a new heavens and earth introduced, that are to remain forever. Heb. 12:26–28, "But now hath he promised, Yet once more I shake not the earth only, but also heaven. And this word, Yet once more, signifieth the removing of those things that are shaken, as of those things that are made, that those things which cannot be shaken may remain. Wherefore we receiving a kingdom which cannot be moved, let us have grace, whereby we may serve God acceptably with reverence and godly fear." So Moses the first leader of Israel failed of bringing them into Canaan; but Joshua the second leader did not fail. The kingdom of Saul, the first anointed of the Lord, did not continue, but the kingdom of the second anointed remains forever. The first sanctuary that was built in Israel was a movable tabernacle, and therefore ready to vanish away, or be removed finally; and God forsook the tabernacle of Shiloh. But the second sanctuary was a firm building, an immovable temple, which was typically an everlasting sanctuary, and that which God never would forsake (II Sam. 7:10–11). So the first covenant that God made with Adam failed because it was weak through the flesh, or through the weakness of human nature to whose strength and stability the keeping was betrusted. Therefore God introduces another, better covenant, committed not to his strength, but to the strength of one that was mighty and stable; and therefore is a sure and everlasting covenant. God betrusted the affair of man's happiness on a weak foundation at first, to show men that that foundation was weak and not to be trusted to, that he might trust in God alone. The first was only to make way for the second. God lit up divine light in man's soul at the first, but it remained on such a foundation that Satan found means to extinguish it; and therefore when God lights it up a second time, it is that it never may be extinguished.

775. HAPPINESS OF SEPARATE SAINTS. The proper time of Christ's reward is not till after the end of the world, for he will not have finished the

work of Mediator till then; but yet he has glorious rewards in heaven before. The proper time of the angels' reward is not till the end of the world. And their work of attending on and ministering to Christ in his humbled, militant state, both in himself, and members or body mystical, is not finished till then; but yet they are confirmed before, and have an exceeding reward before. The proper time of the saints' reward is not in this world, nor is their work, their hard labors, trials and sufferings, finished till death; but yet they are confirmed as soon as they believe, and have an earnest of their future inheritance, the first fruits of the Spirit, now. And so though the proper time of judgment and reward of all elect creatures, is not till the end of the world, yet the saints have glorious rewards in heaven immediately after death.

776. SAINTS IN HEAVEN know what comes to pass in the CHURCH ON EARTH. MILLENNIUM. The glory of Christ—the chief of elect men and head of the whole—that he has in reward for his labors and sufferings here in this world, consists in great measure in the glorious flourishing of the church and success of the gospel after he is gone to heaven. Is. 49:4–6, "Then I said, I have labored in vain, and spent my strength for nought, and in vain: yet surely my judgment is with the Lord, and my work" (in the margin "reward") "with my God. And now, saith the Lord that formed me from the womb to be his servant, Though Israel be not gathered, yet shall I be glorious in the eyes of the Lord, and my God shall be my strength. And he said, It is a light thing that thou shouldest be my servant to raise up the tribes of Jacob, and to restore the preserved of Israel: I will also give thee for a light to the Gentiles, that thou mayst be my salvation to the end of the earth." So Is. 53:10–12, "When thou shalt make his soul an offering for sin, he shall see his seed, he shall prolong his days, and the pleasure of the Lord shall prosper in his hand. He shall see of the travail of his soul, and be satisfied: by his knowledge shall my righteous servant justify many; for he shall bear their iniquities. Therefore will I divide him a portion with the great, and he shall divide the spoil with the strong; because he hath poured out his soul unto death: and he was numbered with the transgressors; and he bare the sins of many, and made intercession for the transgressors." And there are multitudes of passages of Scripture that show the same thing.

So doubtless much of the reward of others of the company—the members of the body as well as the head, that have prayed and labored for the advancement of Christ's kingdom, and have suffered for it, and therein been made partakers with their head in his labors and sufferings, have filled up what is lacking in the sufferings of Christ for the same end—will be in seeing that glory accomplished after their death. As they partook in desires, and prayers, and labors, and sufferings for this, with their head and elder brother in this world, so they shall partake with him in the reward, that consists in the attainment of the scope and end of those desires, prayers, labors and sufferings of them both. Christ is our forerunner in the reward he receives. He is the first fruits and the pattern of the saints not only in deeds and sufferings, but in his reward and glory. See next [No. 777], corols. 2 and 3. See No. 778.

777. HAPPINESS OF HEAVEN IS PROGRESSIVE, and has various periods in which it has a new and glorious advancement, and consists very much in BEHOLDING the manifestations that God makes of himself in the WORK OF REDEMPTION. There can be no view or knowledge that one spiritual being can have of another, but it must be either immediate and intuitive, or mediate, or [by] some manifestations or signs. An immediate and intuitive view of any mind, if it be consequent and dependent on the prior existence of what is viewed in that mind, is the very same with consciousness: for to have an immediate view of a mind is to have an immediate view of the thoughts, volitions, exercises, and motions of that mind, for there is nothing else in any mind to be beheld. But to have an immediate view of the ideas and exercises of any mind consequent on their existence, is the same as to have an immediate perception, sense, or feeling of them as they pass or exist in that mind. For there is no difference between immediate seeing ideas, and immediate having them; neither is there any difference between a created mind's immediate view of the sense or feelings of a mind, either of pleasure or pain, and feeling the same. Therefore a spiritual, created being can't have an immediate view of another mind without some union of personality. If two spirits were so made of God that the one evermore necessarily saw all that passed in the other's mind fully, and perceived it as in that mind, so that all the ideas and all the sense of things that was in one was fully viewed by the other, or a full idea of all was necessarily constantly excited in the one consequent on its being in the other, and beheld as in the other, those two would to all intents and purposes be the same individual person. And if it were not so constantly, but only for a season, there would be for a season an union of personality; and if these seasons were determined by the will of one of them, viz. of him whose ideas were consequent on those of the other, when he pleased to turn the attention of his mind to [the] other, still the effect is the same: there is for a season an union of personality. If the ideas and

sense that pass in one, though immediately perceived, yet are not fully perceived, but only in some degree, still this don't hinder the effects being the same, viz. an union of personality in some degree.

Therefore, there is no creature can thus have an immediate sight of God, but only Jesus Christ, who is in the bosom of God: for no creature can have such an immediate view of another created spirit, for if they could they could search the heart and try the reins. But to see and SEARCH THE HEART is often spoken of as GOD'S PREROGATIVE, and as one thing God's divinity and infinite exaltation above all creatures appears. And God, who is called the "invisible God" (Col. 1:15), and the "King eternal, immortal, invisible" (I Tim. 1:17), and "he that is invisible" (Heb. 11:27); and of whom it is said, I John 4:12, "No man" (in the original "no one") "hath seen God at any time"; and, I Tim. 6:16, "Who only hath immortality, dwelling in the light which no man can approach unto; whom no man" (or "no one") "hath seen, or can see": I say, this being is doubtless as invisible as created spirits; and 'tis not to be thought, that he that gives no mere creature to an immediate sight or knowledge of any created spirit, but reserves it to himself and his Son as their great prerogative, properly belonging to them as God, would admit 'em to an immediate sight or knowledge of himself, whom to know is an infinitely higher prerogative of the only-begotten Son of God, who is in the bosom of the Father. Jesus Christ is admitted to know God immediately; but the knowledge of all other creatures in heaven and earth is by means, or by manifestations or signs held forth. And Jesus Christ, who alone sees immediately, [is] the grand medium of the knowledge of all others; they know no otherwise than by the exhibitions held forth in and by him, as the Scripture is express. Matt. 11:27, "No man" (in the Greek,[5] "no one") "knoweth the Son, but the Father; neither knoweth any one the Father, save the Son, and he to whomsoever the Son will reveal him"; and John 1:18, "No one hath seen God at any time; the only begotten Son, which is in the bosom of the Father, he hath declared him." John 6:46, "Not that any one hath seen the Father, save he which [is] of God, he hath seen the Father."

But the other kind of view, or knowledge, that one spiritual being may have of another, is mediate, or by manifestations or signs held forth. And there are but four[6] sorts of signs by which anything that is in another spiritual being can be manifested, or made known: either (1) images or resemblances; (2) words and declarations, or voluntary significations, ei-

5. MS: "Hebrew."
6. MS: "three."

ther inward or outward, equivalent to speaking; and (3) effects, by which what is in the mind may be argued as cause is argued from the effect; or (4) a priori, by arguing from the causes, or from something that must be conceived of after the manner of a cause, or something prior on which the thing argued in the manner of arguing is consequent and dependent. There are no other ways than these four in which we can have any view or knowledge of a created mind. 'Tis in these ways only that we see and know one another's souls or minds: either by that image and resemblance there is in the body, and its air and motions of the sense and affections, and motions of the mind; or by words or voluntary significations we make to each other, of what we are conscious of[7] in our own minds, by voice, writing, or other signs; or from the effects we see of each other's thoughts, choice, sense, and exercises of mind in our actions and works; and as we may argue something about each other a priori. So these are the only ways in which any creature can see or know God. We see him either in images, either something that is intended on purpose for a representation of him—such as the visible symbols of his presence of old to the prophets and others, and such is the man Christ Jesus—or anything that being from him has some resemblance of him, as the sun has some shadow of his glory, the clouds and mountains of his majesty, and the green fields and pleasant flowers of his grace and mercy; such also is the soul of man that is made in the image of God, and especially souls endowed with holiness; such are the angels; and such above all is the soul of Jesus Christ. Or we see him in his Word, or voluntary signification of what is invisible in him, either internally speaking by impulses made on the mind, as in inspiration, or externally by voices, or by his written Word. Or else we behold him in the effects of what is in him, in his works of creation and providence; and the manifestations that are made of God by his Word, are chiefly as showing us the manifestations that there are of him in his works. Or lastly, we argue the things of God a priori from the necessity of his existence and perfections. And there are no other ways but these four that the saints can see God. They see him in his image; which especially is his Son Jesus Christ, who is said to be the "image of the invisible God" (Col. 1:15), chiefly for that reason, because he is that visible image, by which God who in himself is invisible, is pleased to manifest himself to[8] the creature. "He that seeth the Son seeth the Father" [John 14:9]. And they see and know God in heaven by his Word or speech, for there the saints are with God,

7. MS: "to."
8. MS: "by to."

and converse with God, and God converses with them by voluntary manifestations and significations of his mind, either by external signs or by
impulses of his Spirit; and this also is by Christ. They converse with God
by conversing with Christ, who speaketh the words of God (see John
3:33–34, with note).[9] And "no one hath seen God at any time; but the
only begotten Son, who is in the bosom of the Father, he hath declared
him"; and "no one knows the Father, but the Son, and he to whom the
Son will reveal him." 'Tis God's pleasure that Christ should be the light,
the Sun of heaven, by which God should be seen and known there, for it
pleases the Father that in him all fullness should dwell. And again they
see and know God in heaven in his works, which are the effects of the glorious perfections there are in him; and this also is in Christ, for all the
works of God are wrought in him by whom all things are made, in heaven
and earth, whether they be thrones, or dominions, or principalities, or
powers; and by him all things consist. And especially do they see his glory
as it is manifested in the work of redemption, which the angels desire to
look into, and by which the manifold wisdom of God is made known to
the angels. So far as they see God and know him in his works (which is the
principal way in which God manifests himself, and to which the manifestation of himself in his Word is subordinate: the manifestations God
makes of himself in his works are the principal manifestations of his perfections, and the declarations and teaching of his Word are to lead to
those; by God's declaring and teaching that he is infinitely powerful or
wise, the creature believes that he is powerful and wise as he teaches, but
in seeing his mighty and wise works, the effects of his power and wisdom,
the creature not only hears and believes, but sees his power and wisdom:
and so of his other perfections) they see and know [him] as he manifests
himself in the work of redemption, which [is] the greatest and most glorious of all God's works, the work of works to which all God's works are
reduced. And [this] is the end, and as it were the sum of all God's works,
to the purposes and ends of which work heaven and all its angels were created; and which is a work that the redeemed saints in heaven are concerned [with] far above all other works of God, in which the glory of the
divine perfections, and especially the glory of his love, appears as much
more brightly than in any other work, as the light of the sun is above that
of the stars, and of which work all their glory and blessedness in heaven
is a fruit and a part. And this work by way of eminency is THE WORK of Je-

9. The "Blank Bible" note on John 3:33–34 is simply a cross-reference to "Miscellanies" No.
764[b].

sus Christ, the image of the invisible [God], by whom alone God is seen and known by the saints.

Corol. 1. Hence that BEATIFICAL VISION that the saints have of God in heaven, is in beholding the manifestations that he makes of himself in the work of redemption: for that arguing of the being and perfections of God that may be a priori, don't seem to be called seeing God in Scripture, but only that which is by [the] manifestations God makes of himself in his Son. All other ways of knowing God are by seeing him in Christ the Redeemer, the image of the invisible God, and in his works, or the effects of his perfections in his redemption, and the fruits of it (which effects are the principal manifestation or shining forth of his perfections); and in conversing with them by Christ, which conversation is chiefly about those things done and manifested in this work—if we may judge by the subject of God's conversation with his church—by his work[1] in this world. And so we may infer that [the] business and employment of the saints, so far as it consists in contemplation, praise, and conversation, is mainly in contemplating the wonders of this work, in praising God for the displays of his glory and love therein, and in conversing about things appertaining to it.

Corol. 2. This greatly confirms that the SAINTS IN HEAVEN see what comes to pass in the CHURCH ON EARTH. For seeing their happiness in so great part consists in beholding the work of redemption, and their business so much in contemplating of it, hence 'tis most reasonable to suppose that they see this work as it is carried on in the world in the various steps of it; that they saw those things that were preparatory to it, from age to age, before Christ came; and that they saw Christ's birth, and the acts of his life, and his death and resurrection, by which this redemption was procured; and afterwards saw the success of it in the church of God, that was founded on Christ's blood, and saw the overthrow of Satan's heathenish kingdom; and so have seen the various steps of the progress of redemption, and the erection of Christ's kingdom, and will behold the future remaining great events by which the success of Christ's redemption is to be obtained in the world. See Nos. 776 and 778.

Corol. 3. Seeing that the happiness of heaven is in Christ the Redeemer, and their vision and enjoyment of God is through him and his redemption, this renders it more probable that the happiness of heaven is PROGRESSIVE, having[2] several PERIODS of new accession of glory and blessedness to their state, answering to the several periods of the accomplishment

---

1. MS: "word."
2. MS: "have."

and advancement of this work; and that the same periods that are happy and blessed periods to the church on earth, are so also to the church in heaven: as particularly, that the church in heaven had a new accession of glory when the church on earth was redeemed out of Egypt, and settled in Canaan, in such a series of glorious and wonderful works of God; and that again they had another happy period of glorious advancement in the time of the establishment of the throne of David, and the great prosperity of God's church on earth under David and Solomon; and again had another happy period of new accession of glory at the redemption of the church on earth out of Babylon; and that the light, and love, and glory of the church in heaven was as much advanced from the period of Christ's first coming, especially from his ascension into heaven, as of the church on earth; and again had a new period of advancement in Constantine's time, and at the Reformation; and again, far above all that has been hitherto, in the fall of Antichrist, and the beginning of the millennium; and that last period of all, whence will begin[3] the consummate glory both of the church in heaven and that on earth, when they shall be united in one, will be at the end of the world.

This seems to appear by the promises made to the fathers of those several periods on earth, and their so wishing for the accomplishment of them, and rejoicing in the foresight of them. So Abraham rejoiced and rested in hope of the coming of the children of Israel out of Egypt; and God fulfilled those promises to Abraham in the character of the God of Abraham and Isaac and Jacob, as not the God of the dead, but of the living. So Abraham rejoiced to see Christ's day; that is, he rejoiced in hopes of the coming of the glorious day of the gospel: and therefore, when he sees it, has doubtless answerable happiness and satisfaction in the accomplishment (John 8:56). So David exceedingly rejoiced in the foresight of gospel times that should come; and doubtless therefore, when he saw them his satisfaction was answerable. Therefore it was promised to Daniel that he should have a lot and portion in the future glorious times of the church, when they should be accomplished (Dan. 12:13). This is one sense wherein the saints of old—the church in heaven—are not made perfect without the accomplishment of the glorious periods of the church's prosperity on earth: that the church in heaven and the church on earth are so united, that the glory of the one is not advanced and perfected without the perfecting of the glory of the other. As is meet in those that are one body, 'tis meet that all the members should rejoice together,

3. MS: "beginning."

and be honored and glorified together. Heb. 11:39–40, "And all these, having obtained a good report through faith, received not the promise: that they without us should not be made perfect." By this also we may happily understand Heb. 11:13, "These all died in faith, not having received the promises, but having seen them afar off" (viz. at the distance of their times from the days of the gospel), "and were persuaded of them, and embraced them." This shows how that Christ's promise to his disciples—that when he should sit on the throne of his glory, they should sit on twelve thrones, judging the twelve tribes of Israel, in the glorious accomplishment of it in this world, which is principally after their death, especially in the millennium—will be their real glory and happiness. And this explains how in the millennium "the SOULS of them that were beheaded for the witness of Jesus, and for the word of God, and which had not worshipped the beast, neither his image, neither had received his mark upon their foreheads, or in their hands; live and reign with Christ a thousand years" (Rev. 20:4). And 'tis observable, and very much confirming and evidencing what I have here supposed that, in the book of Revelation, all along the periods of new advancement of glory to the church on earth, seem to [be] so, no less to the church in heaven. Hence the saints in heaven rejoice and praise Christ in the thoughts of that they shall "reign on earth" (Rev. 5:10). Hence the departed souls of the martyrs are represented as being so deeply concerned for the flourishing of the church on earth; Rev. 6:9–11, "I saw under the altar the souls of them that had been slain for the word of God, and for the testimony which they held: and they cried with a loud voice, saying, How long, Lord, holy and true, dost thou not judge and avenge our blood on them that dwell on the earth? And white robes were given to every one of them; and it was said to them, that they should rest yet for a little season, till their fellow servants also and their brethren that should be killed as they were, should be fulfilled." Hence the church in heaven is represented as so rejoicing in the victory of the church over Antichrist (Rev. 7:9–12); and hence those great rejoicings in heaven at the overthrow of Satan's kingdom, and the beginning of the glorious times of the church, in Rev. 11:15–17 and ch. 19. And their rejoicing is represented as not only being on the account of the prosperity of the church on earth with whom they sympathize, but as that wherein they are immediately concerned; Rev. 19:6–7, "And I heard as it were the voice of a great multitude, and as the voice of many waters, and as the voice of might thunderings, saying, Alleluia: for the Lord God omnipotent reigneth. Let us be glad and rejoice in him, for the marriage of the Lamb is come, and his wife hath made herself ready." In the 18th chapter, 20th [verse], heaven and the holy apostles and prophets are called upon to rejoice on this occasion, as what they are immediately concerned in: "Rejoice over her, thou heaven, and ye holy apostles and prophets: for God hath avenged you on her." The success and victory of the church on earth over her enemies is represented as the success and victory of the saints and angels in heaven. See Rev. 19:11 to the end, with 11:3. See No. 744 (corol. 5).

778. SAINTS IN HEAVEN see what comes to pass in the CHURCH on earth. For 'tis evident by many places that they see the sufferings and torments of the damned in hell, and are they so much less concerned in the happiness of that part of the same family that they are of, the members of the same body on earth, than they are in the state of the damned? Be they less nearly related to the saints on earth than to the devils and wicked souls in hell? See Nos. 776 and 777 (corols. 2, 3).

779. THE NECESSITY OF SATISFACTION for sin, the reasonableness of that Christian doctrine.

1. Justice requires that sin be punished, because sin deserves punishment. What the merit of sin calls for, justice calls for, for 'tis only the same thing in different words: for the notion of a desert of punishment, is the very same as a just connection with punishment. None will deny but that there is such a thing in some cases as the desert or merit of a crime, its calling for or requiring punishment; and to say that the desert of a crime does require punishment, is the same thing as to say the reason why it requires it, is because it deserves it. So that the meetness or suitableness of the connection between the crime and punishment consists in the desert; and therefore wherever desert is, there is that meetness or suitableness.

None will deny but that some crimes are so horrid and so deserving of punishment, that 'tis requisite that they should not go unpunished without something very considerable in some wise to make up for the crime, either some answerable repentance or some other compensation, that in some measure at least balances the desert of punishment, and so as it were takes it off, or as it were disannuls it. Otherwise, the desert of punishment remaining, all will allow that 'tis fit, and becoming, and to be desired that the crime should be severely punished. And why is it so, but only from the merit of the crime, or because the crime so much deserves such a punishment? It justly excites so great abhorrence and indignation, that 'tis requisite that there should be a punishment answerable to this abhorrence and indignation, that is fitly excited by it. But by this all is granted that needs to be granted, to show that desert of punishment carries in it a requisiteness of the punishment deserved: for if greater crimes do very much require punishment because of their great demerit, lesser crimes will also require punishment, but only in a lesser degree, proportionably to their demerit; because the ground of the requisiteness of the punishment of great crimes is their demerit. 'Tis requisite that they should be punished on no other account but because they deserve it.

And besides, if it be allowed that it is requisite that great crimes should be punished with punishment in some measure answerable to the heinousness of the crime, with[4] something to balance them, some answerable repentance or other satisfaction, because of their great demerit, and the great abhorrence and indignation they justly excite: it will follow, that 'tis requisite that God should punish all sin with infinite punishment; because all sin, as it is against God, is infinitely heinous, and has infinite demerit, is justly infinitely hateful to him, and so stirs up infinite abhorrence and indignation in him. Therefore, by what was before granted, 'tis requisite that God should punish it, unless there be something in some measure to balance this desert, either some answerable repentance and sorrow for it, or other compensation. But there can be no repentance of it, or sorrow for it, in any measure answerable, or proportionable, to the heinousness of the demerit of the crime, because that is infinite; and there can be no infinite sorrow for sin in finite creatures. Yea, there can be none but what is infinitely short of it, none that bears any proportion to it, or but what is as nothing in comparison of it; and therefore, can weigh nothing when put in the scales with it, and so does nothing at all towards compensating it, or diminishing the desert or requisiteness of punishment, any more than if there were no repentance. And if any ask why God could not pardon the injury on repentance, without other satisfaction, without any wrong to justice; I also ask the same person, why he could not also pardon the injury without repentance? For the same reason, could he not pardon with repentance, without satisfaction: for all the repentance man is capable of, is no repentance at all, or is as little as none in comparison to the greatness of the injury, for it bears no proportion to it; and it would be as dishonorable and unfit for God to pardon the injury without repentance at all, as merely on the account of a repentance, that bears no more proportion to the injury, than none at all. And therefore, we are not forgiven on repentance because it in any wise compensates, or takes off, or diminishes the desert or requisiteness of punishment, but because of

4. MS: "without."

the respect that evangelical repentance has to compensation already made.

If sin therefore deserves punishment, that is the same thing as to say that 'tis meet and proper that it should be punished. If the case be so, that sin deserves punishment from men, in those cases it is meet and proper that it should receive punishment from men. A fault can't be properly said to deserve punishment from any but those to whom it belongs to inflict punishment, when it is deserved. In those cases, therefore, wherein it belongs to men to inflict punishment, in those cases, is it meet and proper for them to inflict the punishment that is deserved of them.

Again, if sin's desert of punishment be the proper ground of the fitness of its connection with punishment, or rather be that wherein fitness of connection consists, it will then follow not only that 'tis fit that sin that deserves punishment should be punished, but also that it should be punished as it deserves.

'Tis meet that [a] person's state should be agreeable to the quality of their dispositions and voluntary actions. Suffering is a thing that is answerable and suitable to the quality of sinful dispositions and actions. 'Tis suitable that they that will evil and do evil, should receive evil in proportion to the evil that he does or wills; 'tis but justice that it should be so. And when sin is punished, it receives but its own, or that which suitably is connected with it; but it is a contradiction to say that it is suitably and meetly connected, or that it is suitable and meet that it should be connected, and yet suitable and meet that it should not be connected.

All sin may be resolved into hatred of God and our neighbor, as all our duty may be resolved into love to God and our neighbor. And 'tis but meet that this spirit of enmity should receive in its own kind, that it should receive enmity again. Sin is of such a nature that it wishes ill, and aims at ill, to God and men, but to God especially. It strikes at God; it would, if it could, procure his misery and death. It is but suitable that with what measure it meets, it should be measured to it again. 'Tis but suitable that men should reap what they sow, and that the reward of every man's hands should be given him. This is what the consciences of all men do naturally declare. There is nothing that men know sooner, after they come to the exercise of their reason, than that when they have done wickedness, they deserve punishment. The consciences not only of Christians, and those that have been educated in the principles of divine revelation, but also the consciences of the heathen, inform them of this. And therefore, unless conscience has been stupefied by frequent violations, when men have done wickedness there remains a sense of guilt upon their minds, a sense of an obligation to punishment. 'Tis natural to expect that which conscience or reason tells 'em it is suitable should come; and therefore, they are afraid, and are jealous, and ready to flee when no man pursues.

Seeing therefore 'tis requisite that sin should be punished, as punishment is deserved and just, therefore the justice of God obliges him to punish sin: for it belongs to God as the supreme Rector of the universality of things, to maintain order and decorum in his kingdom, and to see to it that decency and right takes place at all times, and in all cases. That perfection of his nature whereby he is disposed to this, is his justice; and therefore, his justice naturally disposes him to punish sin as it deserves.

2. The holiness of God, which is the infinite opposition of his nature to sin, naturally and necessarily disposes him to punish sin. Indeed, his justice is part of his holiness; but when we spoke of God's justice inclining of him to punish sin, we had respect only to that exercise of his holiness whereby he loved that holy and beautiful order that consisted in the connection of one thing with another according to their[5] nature, and so between sin and punishment, and his opposition to that which would be so unsuitable as a disconnection of these things. But now I speak of the holiness of God as appearing, not directly and immediately in his hatred of an unsuitable, hateful disconnection between sin itself, and that which is proper for it, but in his hatred of sin, or the opposition of his nature to the odious nature of sin.

If God's nature be infinitely opposite to sin, then doubtless he has a disposition answerable to oppose it in his acts and works. If he by his nature be an enemy to sin with an infinite enmity, then he is doubtless disposed to act as an enemy to it, or to do the part of an enemy to it; and if he [be] disposed naturally to do the part of an enemy against sin, or, which is the same thing, against the faultiness or blameworthiness of moral agents, then it will follow that he is naturally disposed to act as an enemy to those that are the persons faulty and blameworthy, or are chargeable with the guilt of it, as though they were the persons faulty. Indignation is the proper exercise of hatred of anything as a fault, or thing blamable; and there could be no such thing, either in the Creator or creature, as hatred of a fault, without indignation, unless it be conceived or hoped that the fault is suffered for, and so the indignation be, as it were, satisfied. Whoever finds a hatred to a fault, and at the same [time] imputes the fault to him that committed it, he therein feels an indignation against him for it:

5. MS: "the."

so that God, by his necessary infinite hatred of sin, is necessarily disposed to punish it with a punishment answerable to his hatred.

'Tis not becoming of the sovereign of the world, a being of infinite glory, purity, and beauty, to suffer such a thing as sin, an infinitely uncomely disorder, an infinitely detestable pollution, to appear in the world subject to his government without his making any opposition to it, or giving some public manifestations and tokens of his infinite abhorrence of it. If he should so do, it would be countenancing of it, which God cannot do: for "he is of purer eyes than to behold evil, and cannot look on iniquity" (Hab. 1:13). 'Tis natural in such a case to expect tokens of the utmost opposition. If we could behold the infinite fountain of purity and holiness, and could see what an infinitely pure flame it was, and with what a pure brightness it shone, so that the heavens appeared impure when compared with it, and then should behold some infinitely odious and detestable filthiness brought and set in its presence, would it not be natural to expect some ineffably vehement opposition [to be] made, and would not the want of it be indecent and shocking?

If it be to God's glory that he is in his nature infinitely holy and opposite to sin, then it is to his glory to be infinitely displeased with sin; and if it be to God's glory to be infinitely displeased with sin, then it must be to God's glory to exercise and manifest that displeasure, and act according to it. But the proper exercise and testimony of displeasure against sin, in the supreme being and absolute governor of the world, is taking vengeance. Men may show their hatred of sin by lamenting it, and mourning for it, and taking great pains and undergoing great difficulties to prevent or remove it, or by approving God's vengeance for it. Taking vengeance is not the proper way of fellow subject's [showing] hatred of sin; but it is in the supreme Lord and Judge of the world, to whom vengeance belongs, because he has the ordering and government of all things. And therefore, a suffering sin to go unpunished would in him be a conniving at it. Taking vengeance is as much the proper manifestation of God's displeasure at sin, as a mighty work is the proper manifestation of his power, or as a wise work is the proper manifestation of his wisdom. There may be other testimonies of God's displeasedness with and abhorrence of sin, without testifying his displeasure in condign punishment; he might declare that he has such a displeasure and abhorrence. So there might be other testimonies of God's power and wisdom, besides a powerful and wise effect; he might have declared himself to be infinitely wise and powerful. But yet there would [have] been wanting the proper manifestations of God's power and wisdom, if God had only declared himself to be possessed of those attributes. The creature might have believed him to be all-wise and almighty, but by seeing his mighty and wise works, they see his power and wisdom. So if there had been only a declaration of God's abhorrence and displeasure against sin, the creature might have believed it, but could not have seen it, unless he should also take vengeance for it.

3. The honor of the greatness, excellency, and majesty of God's being requires that sin be punished with an infinite punishment. Hitherto I have spoken of the requisiteness of God's punishing sin, on the account of the demerit and hatefulness of it absolutely considered, and not directly as God is interested in the affair. But now if we consider sin as leveled against God, not only compensative justice to the sinner, but justice to himself, requires that God should punish sin with infinite punishment. Sin casts contempt on the greatness and majesty of God. The language of it is that he is a despicable being, not worthy to be honored or feared, not so great that his displeasure is worthy to be dreaded; and that his threatenings of wrath are despicable things. Now the proper vindication or defense of God's majesty in such a case, is for God to contradict this language of sin in his providence towards sin that speaks this language, or to contradict the language of sin in the event and fruit of sin. Sin, says God, is a despicable being, and not worthy that he, the sinner, should fear him, and so affronts him without fear. The proper vindication of God's majesty from this, is for God to show by the event that he is worthy that the sinner should have regarded him and feared him, by his appearing in the fearful, dreadful event to the person guilty, that he is an infinitely fearful and terrible being. The language of sin [is] that God's displeasure is not worthy that the sinner should regard it. The proper vindication of God from this language is to show, by the experience of the event, the infinite dreadfulness of that slighted displeasure. In such a case the majesty of God requires this vindication. It can't be properly vindicated without it; neither can God be just to himself without this vindication, unless there could be such a thing as a repentance, humiliation, and sorrow for this, proportionable to the greatness of the majesty despised. When the majesty of God has such contempt cast upon it, and is trodden down in the dust by vile sinners, 'tis not fit that this infinite and glorious majesty should be left under this contempt, but that it should be vindicated wholly from it; that it should be raised perfectly from the dust wherein it is trodden by something opposite to the contempt that is equivalent to it, or of weight sufficient to balance it, either an equivalent punishment, or an equivalent sorrow and repentance, so that sin must be punished with an infinite punishment.

Sin casts contempt on the infinite glory and excellency of God. The language of it is that God is not an excellent being, but an odious one, and therefore that 'tis no heinous thing to hate him. Now 'tis fit that on this occasion omniscience should declare and manifest that it judges otherwise, and that it should show that it esteems God infinitely excellent, and therefore that it looks on it as an infinitely heinous thing to cast such a reflection on God, by infinite tokens of resentment of such a reflection and such hatred.

God is to be considered in this affair not merely as the governor of the world of creatures, to order things between one creature and another, but as the supreme regulator or Rector of the universality of things, the orderer of things relating to the whole compass of existence, including himself, to maintain the rights of the whole, and decorum through the whole, and to maintain his own rights, and the due honor of his own perfections, as well as to keep justice among creatures. 'Tis fit that there should be one that has this office, and the office properly belongs to the supreme being. And if he should fail of doing justice to him[self] in a needed vindication of his own majesty and glory, it would be an immensely greater failure of his rectoral justice than if he should deprive the creatures, that are beings of infinitely less consequence, of their rights.

4. There is a necessity of sin's being punished with condign punishment, from the law of God that threatens such punishment. All but Epicureans will own that all creatures that are moral agents are subjects of God's moral government, and that therefore he has given a law to his creatures. But if God has given a law to his creatures, that law must have sanctions, i.e. it must be enforced with threatenings of punishment; otherwise, it fails of having the nature of a law, and is only of the nature of counsel or advice, or rather of the nature of a request. For one being to express his inclination or will to another, concerning anything that he would receive from him, any love or respect, without any threatening annexed, but leaving it with the person applied to whether he will afford it or no, whether he will grant it or no, supposing that his refusal will be with impunity, is properly of the nature of a request. It don't amount to counsel or advice, because when we give counsel to others it is for their interest; but when we express our desire or will of something we would receive from them, with impunity to them whether they grant it or no, this is more properly requesting than counseling. Be sure, it falls far short of the nature of law-giving, for such an expression of one's will as this, is an expression of will without any expression of authority. It holds forth no authority for us merely to manifest our wills or inclinations to another; nor

indeed does it exhibit any authority over a person applied to, to promise him rewards. So persons may do, and often do, for doing those things that they have no power to oblige them to. So may persons do to their equals. So may a king do to others that are not his subjects. This is rather bargaining with others, than giving them laws. That expression of will only is a law that is exhibited in such a manner as to express the lawgiver's power over the person to whom it is manifested, expressing his power of disposal of him according as he complies or refuses, that which shows power over him so as to oblige him to comply, or to make it to be to his cost, that he refuses.

And for the same reason that it is necessary the divine law should have a threatening of condign punishment annexed, it is also necessary that the threatening should be fulfilled, for the threatening wholly relates to the execution. If it had no connection with execution, it would be wholly void, and would be as no threatening; and so far as there is not a connection with execution, whether that be in a greater or lesser degree, so far, and in such a degree, is it void, and so far [it] approaches to the nature of no threatening, as much as if that degree of unconnection was expressed in the threatening. As for instance, if sin fails of threatened punishment half the time, this makes void the threatening in one half of it, and brings it down to be no more, than if the threatening had expressed only so much, that sin should be punished half the times that it is committed. But if it be needful that all sin in every act should be forbidden by law, i.e. with a prohibition and threatening of condign punishment annexed, and so that the threatening of sin with condign punishment should be universal, then 'tis necessary that it should be universally executed. A threatening of an omniscient and true being can be supposed to signify no more punishment than is intended to be executed, and is not necessarily to be understood of any more. A threatening, if it signifies anything, is a signification of some connection between the crime and punishment; but the threatening of an omniscient being, can't be understood to signify more connection with punishment than there is.

If it be needful that there should be a divine law, 'tis needful that that law should be maintained in the nature, life, authority, and strength that is proper to it as a law. The authority, life, and strength of every law consists in its sanction, by which the deed is connected with the compensation; and therefore, depends on the strength and firmness of that connection. In proportion as that connection is weak, in such proportion does the law lose its strength, and fails of the proper nature and power of a law, and degenerates towards the nature of request, and expression of will or desire to receive love or respect, without being enforced with authority.

Dispensing with the law in the lawgiver, so as not to fulfill it or execute it, in its nature don't differ from an abrogation of it; unless the law itself contains in it such a clause, that it shall or may be dispensed with, and not fulfilled in certain cases, or when the lawgiver pleases. But this would be a contradiction: for if the law contained such a clause, then not to fulfill it would be according to the law, and a fulfillment of the law; and therefore, there would be no dispensing with the law in it, because 'tis doing what the law itself directs to. The law may contain clauses of exception, wherein particular cases may be excepted from general rules, but it can't make provision for a dispensation; and therefore, for the lawgiver to dispense with [it], is indeed to abrogate it. Though it may not be an abrogating of it wholly, yet 'tis in some measure changing it. To dispense with the law in not fulfilling it on him that breaks it, is making the rule give place to the sinner. But certainly 'tis an indecent thing, that sin which provokes the execution should procure the abrogation of the law. (The necessity of fulfilling the law in the sense that has been spoken of, appears from Matt. 5:18; the words will allow of no other tolerable sense.)

'Tis necessary that the law of God should be maintained and executed, and not dispensed with or abrogated for the sake of the sinner, on the following:

(1) The nature and being of the law requires it: for, as has been already shown, by such dispensation it loses the life and authority of a law, as it respects the subject. But it don't only fail of being a law in this respect, but it fails of being a rule to the supreme Judge. The law is the great rule of righteousness and decorum, that the supreme and universal Rector has established and published, for the regulation of things in the commonwealth of the universality of intelligent beings and moral agents, in all that relates to them as concerned one with another; a rule by which things are not only to be regulated between one subject and another, but between the King and [his] subjects, that it may be a rule of judgment to the one, as well as a rule of duty to the other. 'Tis but reasonable to suppose, that such a rule should be established and published for the benefit of all that belong to this universal commonwealth, to be a rule to direct both their actions towards each other and their expectations from each other, that they may have a fixed and known rule by which they are to act and to be dealt with, to be both active and passive as members of this commonwealth. The subject is most nearly concerned, not only in the measure of

its own actions, but also in the consequences of them, or the method of his Judge's determinations concerning him.

None that own the being of a divine law with threatenings annexed, can deny that there actually is such a rule as this, that relates both to the manner of the creature's acting, and also the Judge's acting towards him as subject to that law: for none will deny but that the precepts relate to the manner of the subject's acting, and that the threatenings relate to the manner of the Judge's proceeding with the subject, in consequence of his obedience or disobedience.

'Tis needful that this great rule of regulation of things in this universal commonwealth, should be fixed and settled, and not vague and uncertain. So far as it fails of this, it ceases to be of a nature of a rule, for 'tis essential to the nature of a rule, that it be something fixed. But if it be needful that it be something fixed, then it is needful that the author, and he by whom it subsists, should maintain and fulfill it, and not depart from it, because that is in a measure to disannul it. If he doth so, therein the rule becomes unfixed; it so far ceases to be a rule to the Judge.

(2) That the law should be made to give place to the sinner, is contrary to the direct design of the law. For the law was made that the subject should be regulated by it, and give place to it, and not to be regulated by the subject, and to give place to him, especially a wicked, vile, rebellious subject. 'Tis made that [it] might prevent sin, and cause that not to be, and not that sin should disannul that, and cause it not to be; and therefore, it would be very indecent for the supreme Rector to cause this great rule to give place to the rebellion of the sinner.

(3) 'Tis in no wise fit, that this great rule should be abrogated, and give place to the opposition and violation of the rebellious subject, on account of the perfection of the law, and as it is an expression of the perfection of the Lawgiver. The holiness and rectitude and goodness of this great rule, that the supreme Lawgiver has established for the regulation of the commonwealth of moral agents, and its universal fitness and wisdom and absolute perfection, render a partial abrogation for the sake of them that dislike it, and won't submit to it, needless and unseemly. If the great rule should be set aside for the sake of the rebel, it would carry too much of the face of an acknowledgment in the Lawgiver, of want of wisdom and foresight, or of some defect in point of holiness or righteousness in his law. He that breaks the law finds fault with it, and casts that reflection on it, that 'tis not a good law; and if God should in part abrogate the law upon this, it would have too much of a face of a conceding to the sinner's objection against the law. But God will magnify his law, and make it honor-

able, and give no occasion for any such reflection upon it, nor leave the law under such a reflection.

If this great rule of righteousness be so excellent and good a law, 'tis not only unfit that it should give place to rebellion, as this would be a dishonor to the excellency of the law and Lawgiver, but also a wrong to the public good, which the supreme Rector of the world has the care of and is the guardian of. If the rule be perfect, perfectly right and just and holy, and with infinite wisdom adapted to the good of the whole, then the public good require that it be strongly established. The more firmly 'tis settled, and the more strongly it is guarded and defended, the better, and the more is it for the public benefit; and everything by which it is weakened, is a damage and loss to the commonwealth of being. But I have already shown how every departure from it unfixes it, and causes it to fail of the nature of a settled rule, and in a degree disannuls it.

(4) The sacredness of the authority and majesty of the Lawgiver requires that he should maintain and fulfill his law, when it is violated by a rebellious subject. I have before spoken of the majesty and greatness of his being, how that is concerned in it; I now would consider the sacredness of his authority, as he stands related to the creatures as their Lawgiver. The majesty of a ruler consists very much in that which appears in him, that tends to strike the subject with reverence and awe, and dread of contempt of him, or rebellion against him; and 'tis fit that this awe and dread should be in proportion to the greatness and dignity of the ruler, and the degree of authority that he is vested with. But this awe and dread is not by an apprehension of the terribleness of the consequences of that contempt and rebellion, and the degree of the danger of those terrible consequences, or the degree of connection of that rebellion with those consequences. Therefore, if it be meet that this awe, or this apprehension, should be in proportion to the greatness and dignity of the ruler, then 'tis fit that the consequences of contempt of the supreme ruler of the world, should be infinitely terrible, and the danger that it brings of it, or connection that it has with it, strong and certain; and consequently, that the threatenings that enforce his laws, should be sure and inviolable. 'Tis fit that the authority of a ruler should be sacred proportionably to the greatness of that authority, i.e. in proportion to the greatness of the ruler, and his worthiness of honor and obedience, the height of his exaltation above us, and the absoluteness of his dominion over us, and the strength of his right to our submission and obedience. But the sacredness of the authority of a sovereign consists in the strength of the enforcement of it, and guard that is about it, i.e. in the terrible consequences of the viola-

tion to him that is guilty, and the degree of danger of those consequences. For authority of a ruler don't consist in the power or influence he has on another by attractives, but coercives. The fence that is about the authority of a prince, that guards it as sacred, is the connection there is between the violations of it and the terrible consequences, or, in other words, in the strength or sureness of the threatening. And therefore, if this connection be partly broken, the fence is partly broken; in proportion as the threatenings are weak, the guard is weak. But certainly it is fit that the authority of the supreme and infinitely great and absolute Lord of heaven and earth should be infinitely sacred, and should be kept so with an infinitely strong guard, and a fence without any breach in it. And it is not becoming the sacredness of the majesty and authority of the great παν-τοκράτωρ that that perfectly holy, just, and infinitely wise and good law that he has established, as the great rule for the regulation of all things in the universal commonwealth of beings, should be set aside to give place to the infinitely unreasonable and vile opposition that sinners make to it, and their horrid and daring rebellion against it.

(5) The truth of the Lawgiver makes it necessary that the threatenings of the law should be fulfilled in every punctilio. The threatening of the law is absolute: "Thou shalt surely die" [Gen. 2:17]. 'Tis true, the obligation don't lie in the claim of the person threatened, as 'tis in promises; for 'tis not to be supposed that the person threatened will claim the punishment threatened. And indeed, if we look upon things strictly, those seem to reckon the [wrong] way that suppose the necessity of the futurity of the execution to arise from an obligation on God in executing, properly consequent on his threatening. For the necessity of the connection of the execution with the threatening seems to arise the directly other way, viz. from the obligation that was on the omniscient God in threatening, consequent on the futurity of the execution; though strictly speaking, he is not properly obliged to execute because he has threatened, yet he was obliged not absolutely to threaten, if he at the same time knew that he should not and would not execute, because this would not have been consistent with his truth. So that from the truth of God there is an inviolable connection between absolute threatenings and execution, not so properly from an obligation on God to conform the execution to the past absolute threatenings, as on his obligation to conform his absolute threatenings to the future execution. This God was absolutely obliged to do, as he would speak the truth. For if God absolutely threatened contrary to what he knew would come to pass, then he absolutely threatened contrary to what he knew to be truth; and how any can speak contrary to what they

know to be truth, in declaring, promising, or threatening, or any other way consistent with perfect and inviolable truth, I can't conceive.

Threatenings are significations of something; and if they are made consistent with truth, or are true significations, they are significations of truth, or significations of that which is true. If absolute threatenings are significations of anything, they are significations of the futurity of the thing threatened; but if the futurity of the thing threatened is not true, then how can the threatenings be true significations? And if God in them speaks contrary to what he knows, and contrary to what he intends, how he can speak true, is to me inconceivable. It is with absolute threatenings, as 'tis with predictions: when God has foretold something that shall come to pass hereafter, that don't concern our interest, and so is of the nature neither of a promise nor threatening, there is a necessary connection between the prediction and the fulfillment; but not by virtue of any claim that we have to make, and so not properly by virtue of any obligation to fulfill, consequent on the prediction, but by virtue of an obligation on an omniscient being in predicting, consequent on what he knew he would fulfill, an obligation to conform the prediction to the future event. And it is as much against the veracity of God absolutely to threaten what he knows he will not accomplish, as to[6] predict what he knows he will not accomplish: for to do either would be to declare that that will be, which he at the same time knows will not be, and that he intends to do, that which he does not intend to do. Absolute threatenings are a sort of predictions. God in them foretells or declares what shall come to pass. They don't differ from mere predictions in their nature, of the declaration or foretelling, but only in that, that the thing declared or foretold is an evil to come upon us. And a mere prediction is a thing indifferent, and is[7] the end of foretelling. In a threatening, the end of foretelling is to deter us from sinning; and predictions of things indifferent are for some other end. Absolute threatenings are God's declarations of something future, and the truth of God does as much oblige him to keep to truth in declarations of what is future, as of what is past or present. For things past, present, and future are all alike before God, all alike in his view; and when God declares to others what he sees himself, he is equally obliged to truth, whether the thing declared be past, present, or to come. And indeed, there is no need of the distinction between present truth, and future, in this case. For if any of God's absolute threatenings are not to be fulfilled,

6. MS: "not to."
7. MS: "in."

those threatenings are declarations, or revelations, contrary not only to future truth, for such a threatening is a revelation of the futurition of a punishment. That futurition is now present with God when he threatens—present in his mind, his knowledge—and if he signifies that a thing is future, which he knows not to be future, then the signification he gives is contrary to present truth, even contrary to what God now knows is future. Again, an absolute threatening is a signification of the present intention of him that threatens; and therefore, if he threatens what he don't intend to fulfill, then he signifies an intention to be, which is not, and so the threatening is contrary to present truth. God's absolute threatenings are a revelation to his subjects of the appointed measures of their Judge's proceeding, with respect to their breaches of his law; and if they don't reveal what is indeed the intended method of the Judge's proceeding, then it is not a true revelation.

There is a necessity of the fulfillment of God's absolute promises both ways, viz. both by an obligation on God to foretell or fore-declare the future benefit according to what he foresaw would be, and intended should be; and also by an obligation on him to fulfill his promise consequent on his predicting, and by virtue of the claim of the person to whom the promise was made. And there is also an obligation on God to fulfill his absolute threatenings consequent on his threatening, indirectly, by virtue of many ill and undesirable consequences of the event's being, beside the certain dependence or certain expectations raised by God's threatening, in the persons threatened, and others that are spectators: which consequences God may be obliged not to be a cause of. But threatenings don't properly bring an obligation on God that is consequent on them as threatenings, as it is with promises.

As to those threatenings that ben't positive or absolute, they ben't necessarily followed with the punishment mentioned in them, because a possibility of escaping the punishment is either expressed or understood in the threatening; but the divine truth makes it necessary that there should be a certain connection between them, and as much as is signified by them. If certain suffering be not signified by them, then there is no necessary connection between them and certain suffering. If it be only signified in them, that there is great danger of the suffering according to God's ordinary method of dealing with men; and that therefore they, as they would act rationally, have great reason to fear it, seeing that God don't see cause to reveal what he will do to them: if this be all that is really contained and understood in the threatening, then this is all that the threatening is connected with. Or if the proper meaning of the threatening be that such suffering shall come unless they repent, and this be all that can fairly be understood, then the truth of God makes no more necessary. But God's truth makes a necessary connection between every threatening and every promise, and all that is properly signified in that threatening or promise.

NECESSITY OF EXECUTION OF ABSOLUTE THREATENINGS. See in what precedes under this fifth particular.[8] Also here add No. 798.[9]

As to any OBJECTION that may be made against the force of the foregoing arguments, from the practice of all, and even the wisest of human legislatures: their dispensing with their own laws, and forbearing to execute them, and pardoning offenders without anyone's being substituted to suffer in their stead; the case is vastly different in the supreme Lawgiver, and subordinate lawgivers, and in the supreme Judge, and subordinate judges. The case is vastly different in them that give rules only to a certain small part of the commonwealth of moral agents, and with relation only to some few of their concerns, and for a little [while], by lawgivers that are weak and fallible and very imperfect, in the exercise of a limited, subordinate, and infinitely inferior authority; from what it is in him who is the great, infinitely wise, omniscient, holy, and absolutely perfect Rector of all, to whom it belongs to establish a rule for the regulation of the whole universality of beings, throughout all eternity, in all that concerns them, in the exercise of an infinitely strong right of supreme, absolute dominion and sovereignty. The laws of men may be dispensed with, who can't foresee all cases that may happen; and if they could, han't both the laws and the state of the subject perfectly at their own disposal, so that it should be possible for them universally and perfectly to suit one to the other. And moreover, there is a superior law that all are subject to, and a superior tribunal to which all are obnoxious, to which inferior tribunals, when the exigence of affairs or anything extraordinary in the case requires it, may refer offenders, dispensing with inferior, subordinate laws. But there is no wise and good law, but that care should be taken, that it ordinarily be put in execution; and the nearer any law approaches to the supreme in perfection and in extent of jurisdiction, the more care should be taken of its execution. The wisdom of nations teaches this. And besides, persons' re-

---

8. In the MS JE adds: "in this and the two foregoing pages," referring to subsection (5) of section 4 of the current entry, immediately above, which begins in the MS two pages prior to this statement, where he argues that absolute threatenings necessarily must be executed.

9. JE's cue marks indicate that he intended to add at this point the whole of No. 798; see below, p. 498.

pentance may be proportionable and answerable at least in some measure to offenses against men. And as to public truth, that is to be upheld in execution of the threatenings of human laws; there ought to be great care to uphold it, according to the true intent and meaning of those threatenings. If all that is meant by them, and all that by the very nature of the public constitution (that is the foundation on which all their laws stand) is to be understood by those threatenings, is that this punishment shall be inflicted, but only when the exigence of [the] public requires otherwise, or when the pleasure of the prince is otherwise, then the public truth obliges to no more.

780. JUSTIFICATION, that the ACCEPTANCE of the saints' WORKS is consequent on the acceptance of their persons. Now, under the covenant of grace, God accepts their persons[1] and then accepts their deeds or offerings. So it was with Abel, in that acceptance which the Apostle, in Heb. 11:4, says he had by faith; as appears by Gen. 4:4, "The Lord had respect unto Abel and to his offering." So God accepted the offerings and prayers which Job offered up for his three friends, because of the acceptance which his person had found with him. Job 42:8, "Therefore take unto you now seven bullocks and seven rams, and go to my servant Job, and offer up for yourselves a burnt offering; and my servant Job shall pray for you: for him will I accept." When the prophet Isaiah is speaking of the calling of the Gentiles, God's accepting their offerings is spoken of as consequent on his accepting them. Is. 56:3, "Neither let the son of the stranger, that hath joined himself to the Lord, speak, saying, the Lord hath utterly separated me from his people"; together with vv. 6–7, "Also the sons of the stranger, that join themselves to the Lord, to serve him, and to love the name of the Lord, to be his servants, every one that keepeth the sabbath from polluting it, and taketh hold of my covenant; even them will I bring to my holy mountain, and make them joyful in my house of prayer: their burnt offerings and their sacrifices shall be accepted upon mine altar." So Is. 60:5–7, "The forces of the Gentiles shall come unto thee. The multitude of camels shall cover thee, the dromedaries of Midian and Ephah; all they from Sheba shall come: they shall bring gold and incense; and they shall show forth the praises of the Lord. All the flocks of Kedar shall be gathered together unto thee, the rams of Nebaioth shall minister unto thee: they shall come up with acceptance on mine altar." So when the Jews' return to God is spoken of, 'tis represented as though God would accept

1. MS: "deeds."

them first, and then their offerings shall be loved and sought of God, and delighted in of him, in consequence of his accepting them. Ezek. 20:40–41, "For in mine holy mountain, in the mountain of the height of Israel, saith the Lord God, there shall all the house of Israel, all of them in the land, serve me: there will I accept them, and there will I require your offerings, and the firstfruits of your oblations, with all your holy things. I will accept you with your sweet savor." That God's having pleasure in men's persons is the ground of his accepting an offering at their hands, is evident by Mal. 1:10, "I have no pleasure in you, saith the Lord of hosts, nor will I accept an offering at your hands."

781. CHRIST'S MEDIATION. The WISDOM of God in the WORK OF REDEMPTION. How God gathers together in one all things in Christ. Christ God-man is not only Mediator between God and sinful men, but he acts as a middle person between all other persons, and all intelligent beings, that all things may be gathered together in one in him, agreeable to Eph. 1:10. He is the middle person between the other two divine persons, and acts as such in the affair of our redemption, as has been shown, No. 772. Though he ben't properly a mediator between God and angels, yet he acts in many respects as a middle person between them; so that all that eternal life, glory, and blessedness that they are possessed of, is by his mediety. And he is a kind of mediator between one man and another, to make peace between them; as he reconciles God and man together, by his blood, and by his Word, and by his Spirit, so by the same he reconciles one man to another. He reconciles one man to another by his blood, by taking away all just cause one can have to hate another—for what is indeed hateful in them, and for which they deserve to be hated of both God and man—by suffering for it fully as much as it deserves; so that what the hatred of both God and man desires, is here fully accomplished in a punishment fully proportionable to the hatefulness of the crime. Were it not that the sins of men are already fully punished in the sufferings of Christ, all, both angels and men, might justly hate all sinners for their sins. For appearing as they are in themselves, they are indeed infinitely hateful, and could appear no otherwise to any than as they are in themselves, had not another been substituted for them; and therefore, they must necessarily appear hateful to all that saw things as they be. It is impossible for any to hate a crime as a crime or fault, without desiring that it should be punished. For he that hates sin is thereby an enemy to it, and therefore necessarily is inimical or inclined to act against it, that it may suffer or to see it suffer; and if we impute men's sins to them, i.e. if we look on the hatefulness of their sins as their hate-

fulness, we necessarily hate them, and are inclined that the sufferings that we desire for their sins, should be their sufferings. But now Christ has suffered for the sins of the world, we ought to hate no man, because there is room to hope that Christ has suffered and satisfied for his sins; and therefore, we should endeavor to bring him to Christ. A right consideration of Christ's sufferings for the sins of others is enough to satisfy all just indignation against them for their sins. When once the saints and angels come to know certainly that Christ has not satisfied for any man's sin, they will hate them, and will rejoice in their infernal and eternal sufferings, which they will see to be no more than in proportion to the hatefulness of their sins. So that Christ by his sufferings has in a sense made propitiations for men's sins not only with God, but with their fellow creatures; and so by his obedience, he recommends them not only to the favor of God, but of one another. For Christ's righteousness is exceeding amiable to all men and angels that see it aright, and Christ himself is amiable to them on that account; and it renders all that they look upon to be in him amiable in their eyes, to consider 'em as members of so amiable an head, as we naturally love the children of those that we have a very dear love to.

Christ by his death also has laid a foundation for peace and love among enemies, in that therein he has done two things; first, in setting the most marvelous, affecting example of love to enemies, an example in an instance wherein we are most nearly concerned, for we ourselves are those enemies that he has manifested such love to. And second, he has done the greatest thing to engage us to love him, and so to follow his example, for the examples of such as we have a strong love to have a most powerful influence upon us. And again, as Christ unites mankind with the Father, by being the bond of union between them, as the third person in whom both are united (for the Father and he from eternity are one); and therefore, by making sinful men one with himself, as he does by three things, viz. by substituting himself in their stead from eternity, and by taking on their nature, and bringing them home to an union of hearts, and vital union: I say, by thus bringing them to himself he unites them to the Father. So also he unites mankind one to another by being a middle being in which all are united: for he brings and unites 'em all to himself as in their head; and thereby, without more ado, they become nearly related and closely united one to another, for they become members of the same body. And again as Christ reconciles man to the Father by his Word, preaching the word of reconciliation, and powerfully drawing and uniting their hearts to God by his Spirit, so he also unites them one to another. He by his Word and Spirit, as it were, does the part of an intercessor between them.

Christ was a mediator between the Jews and Gentiles to reconcile them together, breaking down the middle wall of partition; and he also unites men and angels. He unites angels to men by the following things: by taking away their guilt by his blood, and suffering for that which otherwise would necessarily have rendered them hateful to the angels; and by taking away sin itself by sanctification; and by rendering those that are so much inferior to them in their natures, honorable in their eyes, and worthy that they should be ministering spirits going forth to minister to them; by his taking their nature upon him, and by dying for them, and uniting them to be members of himself; and by setting them such a wonderful example, manifesting God's and his own eternal transcendent love to them by the great things he did and suffered for them; and by being an intermediate person as a bond and head of union, being a common head to each, in which both are united; and by confirming their hearts by his Spirit against all pride, which was the thing that caused such an alienation between the angels that fell and man, so that they could not endure to be ministering spirits to him, which was the occasion of their fall.

782. IDEAS. SENSE OF THE HEART. SPIRITUAL KNOWLEDGE or CONVICTION. FAITH.[2] Great part of our thoughts, and the discourse of our minds concerning [things], is without the actual ideas of those things of which we discourse and reason; but the mind makes use of signs instead of the ideas themselves. A little attentive reflection may be enough to convince any one of this. Let any man for his own satisfaction take any book, and read down one page of it as fast as he ordinarily is wont to read with understanding. He finishes perhaps the whole page in about a minute of time, wherein, it may be, were many such terms as "God," "man," "angel,"

---

2. JE deleted the first introductory paragraph that he composed for this entry. In the MS the last two sentences of this paragraph are separated from the foregoing by a horizontal line and deleted with an X. The first part of the paragraph is deleted with a single vertical line. The deleted text states: "FAITH. SPIRITUAL CONVICTION of the truth of divine things. If by a sense of the excellency of divine things we intend, we mean only a spiritual sense or taste of that moral excellency, beauty or sweetness that is in divine things, which is properly called their spiritual excellency and beauty, because the source and sum of this beauty and sweetness is God's spirit of holiness, love and grace; I say, if we intend this only by a sense of the excellency of divine things, this is not the only ideal apprehension of the things of religion that contributes to a saving conviction of the truth of the gospel: though there can be no saving conviction without it, and this be principal in every saving conviction, and all other possible sense of things of religion will work no degree of saving conviction without it. The sense of heart that persons may have of things of religion is twofold. [1] There is a sense of the natural good and evil that relates to those things consisting in happiness or misery, and (2) a sense of their spiritual good or evil that relates to 'em consisting in beauty or deformity."

"people," "misery," "happiness," "salvation," "destruction," "consideration," "perplexity," "sanctification," and many more such like. And then
let him consider whether he has had the actual ideas of all those things,
and things signified by every other word in the whole page, in this short
space of time. As particularly, let him consider whether or no, when in the
course of his reading he came upon the word God, in such a line which
his mind dwelt not a moment upon, whether or no he had an actual idea
of God, i.e. whether he had an actual idea that moment, of those things
that are principally essential in an idea of God: as whether he had an actual idea of supremacy, of supreme power, of supreme government, of
supreme knowledge, of will, etc. I apprehend that diligent attention will
convince him that he has no actual idea of one of these things, when he
understandingly reads, or hears, or speaks the Word of God. I will instance
but in one thing that seems most fundamental of all in the idea of God,
viz. understanding or knowledge. He will find that in such cases he had
no actual idea at all of this: for if he had an actual idea of understanding
or knowledge, then he had an actual idea of ideas, or ideas of perception
or consciousness, of judging or perceiving connections and relations between different ideas, and so had an actual idea of various ideas and relations between them. So when he read the word "man,"[3] let him inquire
whether he had any actual idea of that which was signified by this word.
In order to this he must have an actual idea of man. I don't mean only a
confused idea of an outward appearance, like that of man, for if that was
all, that was not an idea of man properly, but only a sign made use of instead of an idea; but he must have an actual idea of those things wherein
manhood most essentially consists: as an idea of reason, which contains
many other actual ideas—as an actual idea of consciousness, an actual
idea of a disposal of ideas in the mind, an actual idea of a consequent perception of relations and connections between them, etc.; and so he must
have an actual idea of will, which contains an actual idea of pleasure or
pain, agreeableness or disagreeableness, and a consequent command, or
imperate act of the soul, etc. So when he read the word "perplexity," let
him consider whether he had an actual idea of that actual thing signified
by that word, which contains many actual ideas: as an actual idea of
thought, and an actual idea of intenseness of thought, and also earnestness of desire, then an actual idea of disappointment or crossness to
desire, which contains many other actual ideas, and an actual idea of man-
ifoldness of troubles and crosses, etc. So when he read the word "sancti-

3. MS: "~~man~~ ⟨people⟩."

fication," the actual idea of which contains a great many actual ideas, viz. an actual idea of what is implied in the faculties of an intelligent voluntary being, and then an actual idea of holiness, which contains a great number of other actual ideas. But I need not insist on more instances; I should think that these might be enough to convince anyone that there is very often no actual idea of those things when we are said to think of them, and that the thought is not employed about things themselves immediately, or immediately exercised in the idea itself, but only some sign that the mind habitually substitutes in the room of the idea.

Our thoughts are oftentimes ten times swifter than our reading or speech. Men oftentimes think that in a few minutes, which it would take 'em a long time to speak; and if there be no room to suppose that all the ideas signified by the words of a discourse can be actually excited in the mind in reading or speaking, much less can it be in such swift discourse of thought.

We thus in the discourse of our minds generally make use of signs instead of ideas, especially with respect to two kinds of subjects of our thoughts, viz.

1. With respect to general things, or kinds and sorts; such are kinds of substances, and such also are what Mr. Locke calls mixed modes.[4] When we in the course of our thoughts, in reading, or hearing, or speaking, or meditation, think of any sort of substances, or distinct beings—as particularly of men—instead of going about with attention of mind actually to excite the ideas of those things that belong to the nature of man, that are essential to it, and that distinguish it from other creatures, and so having actually such an abstract idea, as Mr. Locke speaks of; we have only an idea of something in our minds, either a name, or some external sensible idea, that we use as a sign to represent that idea. So, when in the discourse of our minds, there passes a thought of that sort of creatures called lions, or that sort of natural bodies called metal, or that called trees. So in mixed modes, such as confusion, decency, harmony, and the like.

2. 'Tis commonly so in our discourses of those things that we can know only by reflection, which are of a spiritual nature, or things that consist in the ideas, acts, and exercises of minds. It has been shown elsewhere,[5] that

4. JE used the 7th ed. (London, 1716) of John Locke's *An Essay Concerning Human Understanding.* Locke develops the concept of "mixed modes" in Bk. II, ch. 22, pp. 235–42.

5. In No. 238 JE argues that "ideas of reflection . . . are not properly representations, but are indeed repetitions of those very things, either more fully or more faintly; they therefore are not properly ideas. Thus 'tis impossible to have an idea of [a] thought or of an idea but it will [be] that same idea repeated." See *Works, 13,* 353–54.

there is no actual idea of those things, but what consists in the actual existence of the same things, or like things, in our own minds: as for instance, to excite the idea of an idea, we must renew that very idea in our minds; we must have the same idea. To have an actual idea of a thought is to have that thought that we have an idea of then in our minds. To have an actual idea of any pleasure or delight, there must be excited a degree of that delight. So to have an actual idea of any trouble, or kind of pain, there must be excited a degree of that pain or trouble, and to have an idea of any affection of the mind there must be then present a degree of that affection. This alone is sufficient to show that, in great part, our[6] discourses and reasonings on things, are without the actual ideas of those things of which we discourse and reason: for most of our discourses and reasonings are about things that belong to minds, or things that we know by reflection, or at least do involve some relation to them in some respect or other; but how far are we when we speak, or read, or hear, or think of those beings that have minds, or intelligent beings, or of their faculties and powers, or their dispositions, principles, and acts, and those mixed modes that involve relations to those things, from actually having present in our minds those mental things, those thoughts and those mental acts, that those spiritual things do consist in, or are related to. Very commonly we discourse about them in our minds, and argue and reason concerning them, without any idea at all of the things themselves in any degree, but only make use of the signs instead of the ideas. As for instance, how often do we think and speak of the pleasure and delight, or pain and trouble, that such have or have had in such and such things, or things that do in some respect involve pleasure or pain in their idea, without the presence of any degree of that pleasure or that trouble, or any real idea of those troublesome or pleasing sensations.

Those signs that we are wont to make use of in our thoughts for representatives of things, and to substitute in the room of the actual ideas themselves, are either the ideas of the names by which we are wont to call them, or the ideas of some external sensible thing that some way belongs to the thing, some sensible image or resemblance, or some sensible part, or some sensible effect, or sensible concomitant, or a few sensible circumstances. We have the ideas of some of these excited, which we substitute in the room of those things that are most essential, and use 'em as signs as we do words, and have respect to 'em no further in our discourse.

Hence we don't stand at all on the clearness and distinctness of that ex-

6. MS: "of our."

ternal idea that we thus make use of, but commonly 'tis very dim and transient, and exceeding confused and indistinct. As when in a course of meditations we think of man, angels, nations, conversion, and conviction, if we have anything further in our thoughts to represent those things than only the words, we commonly have only some very confused passing notion of something external, which[7] we don't at all insist on the clearness and distinctness of, nor do we find any need of it, because we make use of that external idea no otherwise than as a sign of the idea, or something to stand in its stead. And the notion need not be distinct in order to that, because we[8] may habitually understand the use of it as a sign without it; whereas it would be of great consequence that it should be clear and distinct if we regarded it as an actual idea and proper representation of the thing itself.

The signs that those that have the use of speech do principally make use of in their thoughts are words or names, which are indeed very frequently accompanied with some slight confused glance of some sensible idea that belongs to the thing named, but the name is the principal sign the mind makes use of. Others that are deaf and dumb do probably make use of the ideas of those signs, which they have been accustomed to signify the thing by; or (if we may judge by what we find in things that we have no names for, as there are many such) they make use of some sensible effect, part, concomitant, or circumstance as the sign.

'Tis something external or sensible that we are wont to make use [of] for signs of the ideas of the things themselves, for they are much more ready at hand, and more easily excited, than ideas of spiritual or mental things; which for the most part can't be without attentive reflection, and very often the force of the mind is not sufficient to excite them at all, because we are not able to excite in our minds those acts, exercises, or passions of the mind that we think of.

We are under a necessity of thus putting signs in our minds, instead of the actual ideas of the things signified, on several accounts. Partly by reason of the difficulty of exciting the actual ideas of things, especially in things that are not external and sensible, which are a kind of things that we are mainly concerned with; and also because, if we must have the actual ideas of everything that came in our way in the course of our thoughts, this would render our thoughts so slow as to render our powers of thinking in a great measure useless, as may be seen in the instance men-

7. MS: "some way which."
8. MS: "if we."

tioned of a man reading down a page. Now [if] we use signs instead of the actual ideas themselves, we can sufficiently understand what is contained in that page in a minute of time, and can express the same thoughts to another in as little time by our voices, and can think ten times as swiftly as we can read or speak; but if in order to an understanding of what was contained in that page we must have an actual idea of everything signified by every word in that page, it would take us up many hours to go through with it. For taking in all the ideas that are either directly signified, or involved in relations that are signified by them, it would take us up a considerable time before we could be said to understand one word; but if our understandings were so slow, it would frustrate all use of reading or writing, all use of speech, yea, and all improvement of a faculty of thinking too; and if all our thoughts must have proceeded after this slow manner from our infancy, we must have remained infants all the days of our lives, and seventy years would have been sufficient to have proceeded but a few steps in knowledge.

This way of thinking by signs, unless as it is abused to an indulgence of a slothful, inattentive disposition, very well serves us to many of the common purposes of thinking. For in many respects, we, without the actual presence of the idea, know how to use the sign as if it were the idea itself, having learned by frequent experience, and our minds on the presence of the sign being habitually led to the relations and connections with other things. The presence of the sign in the mind does by custom as naturally and spontaneously suggest many relations of the thing signified to others as the hearing of such a certain sound, or seeing such letters, does by custom and habit spontaneously excite such a thought. But if we are at a loss concerning a connection or consequence, or have a new inference to draw, or would see the force of some new argument, then commonly we are put to the trouble of exciting the actual idea, and making it as lively and clear as we can; and in this consists very much of that which we call attention of the mind in thinking, and the force or strength of a mind consists very much in an ability to excite actual ideas, so as to have them lively and clear, and in its comprehension, whereby it is able to excite several at once to that degree as to see their connection and relations.

Here, by the way, we may observe the exceeding imperfection of the HUMAN UNDERSTANDING, and one thing wherein it appears immensely BELOW GOD'S UNDERSTANDING, in that he understands himself, and all other things, by the actual and immediate presence of an idea of the things understood. All his understanding is not only by actual ideas of things, without ever being put to it to make use of signs instead of ideas, either through an inability or difficulty of exciting those ideas, or to avoid a slow progress of thought that would arise by so manifold and exact an attention; but he has the actual ideas of things perfectly in his mind, without the least defect of any part, and with perfect clearness, and without the imperfection of that fleetingness or transitoriness that attends our ideas, and without any troublesome exertion of the mind to hold the idea there, and without the trouble we are at to have in view a number at once, that we may see the relations. But he has the ideas of all things at once in his mind, and all in the highest possible perfection of clearness, and all permanently and invariably there, without any transitoriness or fading in any part. Our understandings are not only subject to the imperfection that consists in those things which necessitate us to make use of such signs as we have been speaking [of], but this is a source of innumerable errors that we are subject to; though, as was said before, such a use of signs serves us well to many purposes, yet the want of the actual ideas, and making use only of the signs instead of them, causes mankind to run into a multitude of errors the falsity of which would be manifest to them if the ideas themselves were present.

From what has been said, we see that there are two ways of thinking and understanding, especially of spiritual or mental things, that we receive a notion of by reflection or consciousness; viz. (1) that wherein we don't directly view the things themselves by the actual presence of their ideas, or (which is the same thing in mental matters) sensation of their resemblances, but apprehend them only indirectly in their signs, which is a kind of a mental reading, wherein we don't look on the things themselves, but only on those signs of them that are before our eyes. This is a *mere cogitation* without any proper apprehension of the things thought of. (2) There is that which is more properly called *apprehension*, wherein the mind has a direct *ideal view* or *contemplation* of the thing thought of.

This ideal apprehension or view of mental things is either (1) of things that pertain merely to the faculty of understanding, or what is figuratively called the head, including all the modes of mere discerning, judging, or speculation; or (2) of things that appertain to the other faculty of the will, or what is figuratively called the heart, whereby things are pleasing or displeasing, including all agreeableness and disagreeableness, all beauty and deformity, all pleasure and pain, and all those sensations, exercises, and passions of the mind that arise from either of these. An ideal apprehension or view of things of this latter sort, is what is vulgarly called a having

A SENSE. 'Tis commonly said when a person has an ideal view of any thing of this nature, that he has a sense of it in his mind, and 'tis very properly so expressed. For, by what has been said already, persons can't have actual ideas of mental things without having those very things in the mind, and seeing all of this latter sort of mental things, that belong to the faculty of will or the heart, do in great part at least consist in a sensation of agreeableness or disagreeableness, or a sense or feeling of the heart of pleasedness or displeasedness; therefore it will follow that everyone that has an ideal view of those things has therein some measure of that inward feeling or sense.

Hence arises another great distinction of the kinds of understanding of mental things, or those things that appertain or relate to spiritual beings, which is somewhat diverse from the former, viz. of speculative and sensible, or (1) that understanding which consists in mere SPECULATION or the understanding of the head, or (2) that which consists in the SENSE OF THE HEART. The former includes all that understanding that is without any proper ideal apprehension or view, or all understanding of mental things of either faculty that is only by signs, and also all ideal views of things that are merely intellectual, or appertain only to the faculty of understanding, i.e. all that understanding of things that don't consist in or imply some motion of the will, or in other words (to speak figuratively) some feeling of the heart, is mere speculative knowledge, whether it be an ideal apprehension of them, or no. But all that understanding of things that does consist in or involve such a sense or feeling, is not merely speculative but sensible knowledge; so is all ideal apprehension of beauty and deformity, or loveliness and hatefulness, and all ideas of delight or comfort, and pleasure of body or mind, and pain, trouble, or misery, and all ideal apprehensions of desires and longings, esteem, acquiescence, hope, fear, contempt, choosing, refusing, accepting, rejecting, loving, hating, anger, and the idea of all the affections of the mind, and all their motions and exercises, and all ideal views of dignity or excellency of any kind, and also all ideas of terrible greatness or awful majesty, meanness or contemptibleness, value and importance.

All knowledge of this sort, as it is of things that concern the heart, or the will and affections, so it all relates to the good or evil that the sensible knowledge of things of this nature involves; and nothing is called a sensible knowledge upon any other account, but on the account of the sense, or kind of inward tasting or feeling, of sweetness or pleasure, bitterness or pains, that is implied in it, or arises from it. Yet 'tis not only the mere ideal apprehension of that good or evil that [is] included in what is called a[9] being sensible, but also the ideal apprehensions of other things that appertain to the thing known, on which the goodness or evil that attends them depends. As, for instance, some men are said to have a sense of the dreadfulness of God's displeasure. This apprehension of God's displeasure is called having a sense, and is to be looked upon as a part of sensible knowledge, because of that evil or pain in the object of God's displeasure that is connected with that displeasure, [which is] an idea of what God is supposed to feel in his own heart in having that displeasure. But yet in a sense of the terribleness of God's displeasure, there is implied an ideal apprehension of more things than merely of that pain, or misery, or sense of God's heart, there is implied an ideal apprehension of the being of God, or of some intellectual existence, and an ideal apprehension of his greatness and of the greatness of his power.

An ideal apprehension or view of these things is in vulgar speech called an having a sense of them; and in proportion to the intensive degree of this ideal apprehension, or the clearness and liveliness of the idea of them, so persons are said to have a greater or lesser sense of them, and according to the easiness or difficulty of persons receiving such a sense of things, especially things that it much concerns them to be sensible of, are they called either sensible or stupid.

This distribution of the human knowledge into SPECULATIVE and SENSIBLE, though it seems to pertain [to] only one particular kind of the objects of our knowledge, viz. those things that appertain or relate to the will and affections, yet indeed may be extended to all the knowledge we have of all objects whatsoever. For there is no kind of thing that we know, but what may be considered as in some respect or other concerning the wills or hearts of spiritual beings; and indeed we are concerned to know nothing on any other account, so that perhaps this distinction of the kinds of our knowledge into speculative and sensible, if duly weighed, will be found the most important of all. The distribution is with respect to those properties of our knowledge that immediately relate to [the] end of all our knowledge, and that in the objects of our knowledge, on the account of which alone, they are worthy to be known, viz. their relation to our wills, and affections, and interest, as good or evil, important or otherwise, and the respect they bear to our happiness or misery.

The will in all its determinations whatsoever is governed by its thoughts and apprehensions of things, with regard to those properties of the ob-

9. MS: "of."

jects of its thoughts, wherein the degree of the sense of the heart has a main influence.

There is a twofold division or distribution [that] may be made of the kinds of sensible knowledge of things that men have. The

First respects the ways we come by it. (1) There is that which is purely natural, either such as men's minds come to be impressed with by the objects that are about them, by the laws of nature: as when they behold anything that is beautiful or deformed, by a beauty and deformity that men by nature are sensible of, then they have a sensible knowledge of their beauty or deformity. As when the ear hears a variety of sounds harmoniously proportioned, the soul has a sensible knowledge of the excellency of the sound. When it tastes any good or ill savor or odor, it has a sensible knowledge of the excellency or hatefulness of that savor or odor. So it may have a sensible knowledge of many things by memory and reflection. So a man may have a sensible apprehension of pleasure or sorrow that others are the subjects of, indirectly by reflection, either by exciting from the memory something that he has felt heretofore, which he supposes is like it, or by placing himself in others' circumstances, or by placing things about himself in his imagination, and from ideas so put together in his mind, exciting something of a like pleasure or pain transiently in himself; or if these ideas come so together into the mind by the senses, or by the relation of others, such a sensation will spontaneously arise in the mind in like manner. Men may have a sense of their own happiness or misery conceived as future. So men may by mere nature come to have a sense of the importance or terribleness or desirableness of many things. (2) That sense of things which we don't receive without some immediate influence of the Spirit, of impressing a sense of things that do concern our greatest interest on our minds. 'Tis found very often a very difficult thing to excite a sense of temporal things in the mind, requiring great attention and close application of thought; and many times it is not in our power, and in many instances wherein we have a sense of temporal things that is purely natural, it depends not merely on the force of our thoughts, but the circumstances we are in, or some special accidental situation and concurrence of things in the course of our thoughts and meditations, or some particular incident in providence that excites a sense of things, or gives an ideal view of them in a way inexplicable. But the exciting a sense of things pertaining to our eternal interest, is a thing that we are so far from, and so unable to attain of ourselves, by reason of the alienation of the inclinations and natural dispositions of the soul from those things as they are, and the sinking of our intellectual powers, and the great subjection of the soul in its fallen state to the external senses, that a due sense of those things is never attained without immediate divine assistance.

'Tis in this that the ORDINARY WORK OF THE SPIRIT OF GOD in the hearts of men CONSISTS, viz. in giving a sense of spiritual and eternal things, or things that appertain to the business of religion and our eternal interest. The extraordinary influence of the Spirit of God in inspiration, imparts speculative knowledge to the soul. But the ordinary influence of God's Spirit communicates only a sensible knowledge of those things, that the mind had a speculative knowledge of before; and an imagination that some have of speculative knowledge received from the Spirit of God, in those that have no real inspiration, is that wherein ENTHUSIASM consists.

Secondly. The other distribution that may be made of the kinds of sensible knowledge is according to the different nature of the objects of it, into a sense of things with respect to the natural good or evil that is in them, or that they relate to, or a sense of them with respect to spiritual good or evil. By spiritual good I mean all true moral good, all real moral beauty and excellency, and all those acts of the will, or that sense of the heart, that relates to it, and the idea of which involves it, as all sense of it, all relish and desires of it, and delight in it, happiness consisting in it, etc. By natural good and evil I mean all that good or evil which is agreeable or disagreeable to human nature as such, without regard to the moral disposition: as all natural beauty and deformity, such as a visible sensible proportion or disproportion in figures, sounds, and beauty of colors; any good or evil that is the object of the external senses, and all that good or evil which arises from gratifying or crossing any of the natural appetites; all that good and evil which consists in gratifying or crossing a principle of self-love, consisting in others' esteem of us and love to us, or their hatred and contempt; and that desirableness or undesirableness of moral dispositions and actions, so far as arising from hence, and all that importance, worth, or terribleness arising from a relation to this natural good or evil.

Persons are capable of some sensible knowledge of things of religion of the former sort, viz. with respect to the natural good or evil that attends them, of themselves, with the same improvement of their natural powers that they have a[1] sensible knowledge of temporal [things], because this good and evil consists in an agreeableness or disagreeableness to human nature as such, and therefore no principles are required in men, beyond those that are contained in human nature, to discern them. But yet by rea-

1. MS: "this."

son of the natural stupidity of the soul, with respect to things so diverse from all the objects of sense, and so opposite to the natural disposition of the heart, 'tis found by experience that men never will obtain any very considerable sense of them, without the influence of the Spirit of God assisting the faculties of human nature, and impressing a lively sense of them. But as to the other, viz. a sense of divine things with respect to spiritual good and evil, because these don't consist in any agreeableness or disagreeableness to human nature as such, or the mere human faculties or principles, therefore man, merely[2] with the exercise of these faculties and his own natural strength, can do nothing towards getting such a sense of divine things; but it must be wholly and entirely a work of the Spirit of God, not merely as assisting and co-working with natural principles, but infusing something above nature.

By the things that have been said, we may see the difference between the influences of the Spirit of God on the minds of natural men in AWAKENINGS, COMMON CONVICTIONS, and ILLUMINATIONS, and his spiritual influences on the hearts of the saints at and after their conversion. (1) Natural men, while they are senseless and unawakened, have very little sensible knowledge of the things of religion, even with respect to the natural good and evil that is in them, and attends them, and indeed have very little of an ideal apprehension of any sort of divine and eternal things, by reason of their being left to the stupefying influence of sin, and the objects of sense. But when they are awakened and convinced, the Spirit of God, by assisting their natural powers, gives 'em an ideal apprehension of the things of religion with respect to what is natural in them, i.e. of that which is speculative in them, and that which pertains to a sensibleness of their natural good and evil, or all but only that which involves a sense of their spiritual excellency. The Spirit of God assists to an ideal view of God's natural perfections, wherein consists his greatness, and gives a view of this as manifested in his works that he has done, and in the words that he has spoken, and so gives a sensible apprehension of the heinousness of sin and his wrath against it, and the guilt of it, and the terribleness of the sufferings denounced against it. And so they have a sense of the importance of things of religion in general, and herein consists what we commonly call conviction. And in a sense of the natural good that attends the things of religion, viz. the favor of so great a being, his mercy as it relates to our natural good or deliverance from natural evil, the glory of heaven with respect to the natural good that is to be enjoyed there, and the like, consists

2. MS: "only merely."

those affecting, joyful, common illuminations that natural men sometimes have. In thus assisting men's faculties to an ideal apprehension of the natural things of religion, together with what assistance God may give men's natural reason and judgment, to see the force of natural arguments, consists the whole of the common work of the Spirit of God on men; and it consists only in assisting natural principles without infusing anything supernatural. (2) The special work of the Spirit of God, or that which is peculiar to the saints, consists in giving the sensible knowledge of the things of religion, with respect to their spiritual good or evil: which indeed does all originally consist in a sense of the spiritual excellency, beauty, or sweetness of divine things, which is not by assisting natural principles, but by infusing something supernatural.

The ideal apprehension and sensible knowledge of the things of religion will give that conviction of their truth or reality which can no otherwise be obtained, and is the principal source of that CONVICTION of the TRUTH of the things of religion, that is given by the immediate influence of the Spirit of God on men's hearts. (1) An ideal apprehension and sensible knowledge of the things of religion, with respect to what is natural in them, such as natural men have that are under awakenings, will give some degree of conviction of the truth of divine things, further than a mere notion of them in their signs, or only a speculative apprehension of them, because by this means men are enabled to see, in many instances, the agreement of the declarations and threatenings of the Word of God with the nature of things, that without an ideal and sensible knowledge of them they could not have: as, for instance, they that from the tokens of God's greatness, his power and awful majesty, in his works and in his words, have an idea or sense of that greatness and power and awful majesty, and so see the agreement between such works and such words, and such power and majesty; and therefore[3] have a conviction of that truth that otherwise they could not have, viz. that it is a very great being that made those things, and spake those things. And so from a sense they may hence have of the dreadfulness of the wrath of such a being, they have a conviction of the truth of what the Scripture teaches about the dreadfulness of God's wrath, and of the punishment of hell; and from the sense they hereby have of the heinousness or dreadfulness of sin against such a God, and the natural agreement between affronts of such a majesty, and the suffering of extreme misery, it appears much more credible to them, that there is indeed an extreme misery to be suffered for sin. And so a

3. MS: "therefore hence."

sense of the natural good that there is in the things of religion, such as is given in common illuminations, makes what the Scriptures declare of the blessedness of heaven, etc. more credible.

(2) An ideal and sensible apprehension of the spiritual excellency of divine things, is [the] proper source of all SPIRITUAL CONVICTION of the truth of divine things, or that belief of their truth, that there is in SAVING FAITH. There can be no saving conviction without it; and it is the great thing that mainly distinguishes saving belief or conviction from all other, or the thing wherein its distinguishing essence does properly lie, that it has a sense of the divine or spiritual excellency of the things of religion, as that which it arises from.

Saving conviction of divine truth does most essentially arise from the spiritual sense of the excellency of divine things. Yet this sense of spiritual excellency is not the only kind of ideal apprehension, or sense of divine things, that is concerned in such a conviction, but it also partly depends on a sensible knowledge of what is natural in religion, as this may be needful to prepare the mind for a sense of its spiritual excellency, and as such a sense of its spiritual excellency may depend upon it. For as the spiritual excellency of the things of religion itself does depend on and presuppose those things that are natural in religion—they being as it were the substratum of this spiritual excellency—so a sense, or ideal apprehension, of the one, depends in some measure on the ideal apprehension of the other. Thus a sense of the excellency of God's mercy in forgiving sin, depends on a sense of the great guilt of sin, the great punishment it deserves. A sense of the beauty and wonderfulness of divine grace, does in great measure depend on a sense of the greatness and majesty of that being whose grace it is, and so indeed a sense of the glory of God's holiness and all his moral perfections. A sense of the excellency of Christ's salvation, depends on a sense of the misery and great guilt of those that are the subjects of this salvation. And so, though a saving conviction of the truth of things of religion does most directly and immediately depend on a sense of their spiritual excellency, yet it also in some measure, and more indirectly and remotely, depends on an ideal apprehension of what is natural in religion, and is a common conviction.

Common conviction, or an ideal and sensible apprehension of what is natural in the things of religion, contributes to a saving conviction of the truth of the gospel, especially this way. Men, by being made sensible of the great guilt of sin, or the connection or natural agreeableness there is between that and a dreadful punishment, and how that the greatness and majesty of God seem to require and demand such a punishment, they are brought to see the great need of a satisfaction, or something to intervene to make it honorable to that majesty to show 'em favor. And being for a while blind to the suitableness of Christ's satisfaction in order to this, and then afterwards having a sense given them of Christ's divine excellency, and so of the glorious dignity of his person, and what he did and suffered for sinners; hereby their eyes are, as it were, opened to see the perfect fitness there is in this to satisfy for sin, or to render their being received into favor consistent with the honor of God's offended majesty. The sight of this excellent congruity does very powerfully convince of the truth of the gospel, or that this way of satisfying for the sins, which now they see to be so congruous, is certainly a real way, not a mere figment, but a divine contrivance, and that there is indeed acceptance to be had with God in this; and so the soul savingly believes in Christ. The sight of this congruity convinces the more strongly, when at last it is seen, because, though the person was often told of it before, yet could see nothing of it; which convinces that it was beyond the invention of men to discover it. For by experience they found themselves all their lifetime wholly blind to it, but now they see the perfect suitableness there is; which convinces 'em of the divine wisdom, that is beyond the wisdom of man, that contrived it.

The truth that the soul is most immediately convinced of in this case, by a sense of the divine excellency of Christ, with a preparatory sense of the need of satisfaction for sin, is not that the gospel is the Word of [God]; but this is the truth the mind firstly and more directly falls under a conviction of, viz. that the way of salvation that the gospel reveals, is a proper, suitable, and sufficient way, perfectly agreeable to reason and the nature of things, and that which tends to answer the ends proposed. And the mind being convinced of this truth, which is the great subject of the gospel, it then naturally and immediately infers from this fitness, and sufficiency of this salvation, which the mind has experienced to be so much [beyond] the power of human reason of itself to discern, that it is certainly a contrivance of a superhuman, excellent wisdom, holiness, and justice, and therefore God's contrivance.

783. JUSTIFICATION. CHRIST'S RIGHTEOUSNESS. See "Notes on Scripture," no. 318.[4]

784. ASCENSION OF CHRIST. See "Notes on Scripture," no. 319.[5]

---

4. See Works, 15, 294–96.
5. See Works, 15, 297–302.

785. The DEATH threatened in the COVENANT OF WORKS. When God said to Adam, "in the day that thou eatest thereof thou shalt surely die" [Gen. 2:17], was [implied] not only, or principally, temporal death, or a becoming mortal, or annihilation; but it was the utter, final, and sensible ruin, or destruction of his whole man, which the following things tend to confirm.

1. The expression that God used, "dying thou shalt die," naturally implied thus much; signifying not only the certainty of death as the wages of sin, but that he should be the subject of all manner of death. The punishment threatened when God said thus, was what Adam never had had any experience of, and never had seen any instance of; and therefore was not liable to be deceived as to the import of the expression, from being prepossessed with any other notion of death, or having been wont to use the words in another [sense]; and had nothing else to form his notion of it by, but only conceiving in his own mind of his utter, sensible, and dreadful destruction with respect to all that good that he now enjoyed. Though he knew nothing what death or any evil was by experience, yet by the idea he was capable of forming of the abolition of his present good, he could excite an idea of misery, or that which was very dreadful, and especially if he withal conceived of this as being from God's displeasure and wrath. And from the emphasis and force of the redoubled expression, he would naturally think that God meant a very dreadful destruction, and that it would be executed from a terrible degree of divine displeasure, hatred, and wrath. The manner of the threatening was sufficient to impress a sense of this on his mind, as it appears to have been actually impressed by the fear that he manifested after he had sinned. So that the punishment Adam naturally expected from this threatening, was a being utterly and finally destroyed in his whole man, and with a destruction that was the opposite of all good that he now possessed, and to have it inflicted in its greatest extremity, or in the most terrible manner, and sensibly to lie under this destruction, and therein to suffer the dreadful hatred and wrath of God, and so to suffer misery in death answerable to that hatred.

2. When God threatened thus, Adam would naturally conceive of that death as a state of sensible ruin and horrible misery. For we still find by experience that we naturally conceive of death as a sensible destruction, or a state of dismal darkness and horrible [ruin], and as Job expressed it, "a land of darkness, as darkness itself" [Job 10:22], and without any order, where the light is as darkness; and that the misery is answerable to those dismal appearances that death is attended [with], a ghastly aspect, confinement to the dark and silent grave, rotting and moldering there, a

being eaten of worms, etc. All mankind, throughout all ages and nations, have a horrible sense of this, beyond a mere state of nonexistence. We find when we are children, we naturally conceive of it as a sensibly most dismal state, which notion we can never conquer when we grow up and grow old, and no consideration or learning will thoroughly root it out; but we still naturally conceive of death after this manner, when thinking of our own death, and when mourning for the death of our dear friends. Those dismal appearances in temporal death that strongly impress the mind with an idea of sensible amazing darkness, destruction, and horror, are an indication that death in itself is something more than mere ceasing of temporal life, or ceasing to be, and that it is indeed a state of such real misery, as these are the appearances of; and so doubtless Adam conceived of it, and would naturally conceive of a great deal more misery in it, than we do. For when we think of it, we conceive of it as a sensible destruction with regard to all that good that we now enjoy in our fallen state, and the suffering the contrary of that good; but he would naturally conceive of it as a sensible destruction with regard to all that good which he enjoyed, and enduring the contrary of that good. But the good that he enjoyed was much greater than we enjoy, and more manifold: for besides the great outward happiness that he enjoyed, he enjoyed also great spiritual happiness in the image and favor of God; and besides, he had that which tended to make him conceive of all this as the fruit of the great wrath of God, and his suffering that wrath in a state of death, from his peremptory and awful manner of threatening.

3. 'Tis evident by many passages of the Old Testament that God's people, from the beginning, did conceive of a state of death [as] a state of sensible, dismal darkness and misery, though they seemed to have conceived of the righteous[6] as redeemed from that misery. So in that forementioned place in Job. See also Ps. 88:4–12. They conceived of the souls of the dead as descending lower than the grave, even into a pit of darkness, in the inner or lower parts of the earth. See Job 26:5–6, with note,[7] compared with Ps. 88:6; and Job 33:22. This place they called hell, Prov. 9:18, Job 28:22, Ps. 55:23, Prov. 15:11, Job 11:8, Deut. 32:22, Ps 9:17, Ps. 139:8, Is. 14:9, 15, Amos 9:2, Jonah 2:2, Ezek. 32:18. And that they looked on a state of

6. MS: "righteousness."

7. In the "Blank Bible" note on Job 26:5–6 JE speculates on the meaning of the Hebrew word "Rephaim" or "dead things." It "seems to [be] a word by which they signified the inhabitants of the infernal world, which indeed only are dead . . . They had this notion of old that down in the lower parts of the earth was the place of those Rephaim; to this abode they supposedly descended . . . when they died."

death as a state of sensible misery, is further evident by Ezek. 32:27, Job 20:11.

Seeing therefore the word "death" was so understood by God's people of old, and amongst the Israelites in particular, we may well suppose that Moses, who was an Israelite when giving an account of God's threatening to Adam in the language of the Israelites, might think it sufficient to express it thus; though we should suppose that the thing that was really threatened to Adam, was a sensible, total, perfect, and final, most dreadful destruction of his whole man in enduring the terrible wrath of God, seeing such an expression naturally imparted thus much in that language, and as it was then used. For we are not necessarily to suppose, that God spake to Adam in that very language, and in those very words, that Moses gives the account in; 'tis sufficient that the thing that he expresses was, some way or other, plainly made known to Adam.

4. 'Tis manifest that the word death, as used in Scripture, is of much larger signification than as commonly used now, so that any destruction, or any very dreadful calamity, bringing any considerable destruction of any kind with it, is called death in Scripture. So Pharaoh says of the plague of locusts, Ex. 10:17, "Intreat the Lord, that he may take away from me this death only." So that when God, with such repetition and emphasis, threatens "Dying thou shalt die," it is natural to understand it, that God would inflict all manner of misery and destruction, even to universal and final destruction.

5. The death that God at first threatened for sin, is doubtless the same—that perishing or destruction, that is so often spoken of throughout the Old Testament—as what the wicked shall suffer, but the righteous shall be delivered from, in places too many to be mentioned. But this is not temporal death, for the righteous are not delivered from that.

6. The misery that is the punishment that wicked men shall suffer, and that the righteous shall be delivered from, is in the Scripture, and even the Old Testament, not only called perishing, or being destroyed, but 'tis in innumerable places called death. We find death or dying threatened to wicked men all over the Old Testament, as that which the righteous shall escape; and the reward of life is promised to them. Now by this cannot be meant temporal death, for this the righteous do [no] more escape than the wicked. It can't be meant only an untimely death, for there is particularly observed in the Old Testament, that the wicked do grow old in sin, and are in great prosperity while they do live. It can't be meant some more dreadful kind of temporal death, for 'tis particularly observed in the Old Testament, that wicked men sometimes die quietly, having no bonds

in their death. And in the general 'tis observed, that as to all visible things, all things come alike to all; and that there is one event to the righteous, and to the wicked, so that there is no knowing either love or hatred, by all that is before us.

7. That death that we are saved from, by him who is in Scripture called the second Adam, is doubtless the same that came by the sin of the first. It is most manifestly so by Rom. 5 at the latter end, and I Cor. 15:21–22 and 45.

8. Not only the ruin or destruction of the body, that is in temporal death, is called death; but that ruin of the soul, that is entirely different from the death of the body, is expressly and often called death in Scripture. And we are moreover taught that 'tis a death that Christ, or the second Adam, came to save us from, John 5:25, Eph. 2:1, 5, Col. 2:13, Matt. 8:22.

9. The death that was at first threatened for sin, was doubtless the same with what is in Scripture metonymically called "damnation" or "condemnation," when speaking of the punishment of sinners. For the word damnation or condemnation as used in Scripture, in this case signifies as much a condemnation to death, or such a condemnation as men were brought under for capital crimes; and indeed the Scripture is plain in this, that the condemnation the Scripture means in this case, is a condemnation to death, and to that death that came by Adam's sin, by Rom. 5, 16th and 18th verses, with the context. But this damnation or condemnation is not to temporal death, because we are abundantly taught in the Scripture, that 'tis what believers shall not come into, as there, and Rom. 8:1, 34; I Cor. 11:31–32, 34; II Cor. 3:9; Jas. 3:1, and 5:12; John 3:17; Matt. 12:37; John 3:18. That by the condemnation which sinners are exposed to, is meant the same with condemnation to suffer that death that God has threatened for sin, is particularly manifest by John 5:24. "Verily, verily, I say unto you, He that heareth my word, and believeth on him that sent me, hath everlasting life, and shall not come into condemnation; but is passed from death to life." And that this death is not temporal death, is exceeding manifest by the 29th verse of that context: "And shall come forth; they that have done good, to the resurrection of life; and they that have done evil, to the resurrection of damnation," or condemnation, for the word in the original is the same as v. 24. Now nothing can be more manifest, than that by the condemnation that the wicked shall rise to, is not a condemnation to temporal death, for that is what the verse speaks of their coming out of; now how absurd is it to suppose, that Christ means that they shall rise and come out of a state of bodily death, that they may

be condemned to a state of bodily death. And 'tis also evident in this same verse, that the condemnation they shall rise to, is a condemnation to that death that is the threatened punishment of sin, because 'tis opposed to resurrection of life. And 'tis further manifest that this death is not natural death, by the same antithesis or opposition to that life that the godly shall rise to, for that life is not natural life. For 'tis evident the life they rise to, is a life wherein they are distinguished from the wicked, but they are not distinguished by rising to natural life, for both shall rise to natural life, consisting in the life of the body, and the union of soul and body. And further,

10. We are expressly taught that the punishment which wicked [men] shall be condemned to after the resurrection, which is the proper and full punishment of sin (for the proper time of both rewards and punishments is after the resurrection, and what is before is only by anticipation; and the misery of the wicked before, is therefore reckoned as a state of imprisonment in order to judgment, condemnation, and execution): I say, we are expressly taught both that this punishment of sin that the wicked shall then be condemned to is not a state of natural death or annihilation, but a state of continual torment, and also that this state of torment is death, yea, moreover, that death that was principally threatened to Adam for his sin in Rev. 20:10, "And the devil that deceived them was cast into the lake of fire and brimstone, where the beast and the false prophet are, and shall be tormented day and night forever and ever"; with v. 14, "And death and hell were cast into the lake of fire. This is the second death"; and 21:8, "But the fearful, and unbelieving, and abominable, and murderers, and whoremongers, and sorcerers, and idolaters, and all liars, shall have their part in the lake which burneth with fire and brimstone: which is the second death," alluding to the double expression in the threatening to Adam, "Dying thou shalt die." See note on Rev. 20:14, and compare those places with 14:10–11, and Matt. 25:41.[8]

11. Without doubt, that death that was threatened to man at first, in case he sinned, was that same death, if any such there be, that the Scripture declares to be the proper and the threatened punishment of sin, or

---

8. The "places" to which JE refers in the "Blank Bible" note on Rev. 20:14 are Rev. 20:14 and 8:13; this note also includes cross-references to "Notes on Scripture," no. 77 (*Works, 15,* 72) and to the second of the sermons in his series on Gen. 3:11 (see above, No. 717, p. 349, n. 1), pp. 8–10. These pages contain a discussion of God's injunction to Adam not to eat the forbidden fruit. "The command," JE states, "was enforced with a very terrible threatening, denounced in a most awful preemptory manner." The sentence, "Dying thou shalt die," expresses at once the "certainty" and the "extremity of it." JE also suggests that this sentence also "may intimate more death than one," i.e. temporal death of the body and eternal death of the soul.

the wages of sin, by which we can understand nothing else, but the proper and appointed recompense of sin; but this wages is called death. Rom. 6:23, "The wages of sin is death; but the gift of God is eternal life through Jesus Christ our Lord." Now in order to know what the proper and appointed wages of sin is, we must look and see what is the wages appointed and given, when judgment comes to be passed by the proper judge, and in the proper time of judgment. When he comes thus to reckon with the servants, he will doubtless assign every one his proper wages; when he comes to call all to an account, he will doubtless give every one their proper and appointed recompense. But we have seen what this is under the preceding particular. And we may also judge by the death that Christ suffered, who not only suffered the dissolution of the frame of his body, but extreme agonies in his soul, which made him say, "My soul is exceeding sorrowful, even unto death" [Matt. 26:38]. 'Tis also manifest that this death that is the wages of sin, is not the death of the body: for doubtless this is the same death that Christ has respect to when he says, that he that believes on him shall not die, but shall live forever (John 6:49–51, 58).

786. How that PERFECT OBEDIENCE is the CONDITION of the first covenant, is implied in the words of that covenant, as God expressed it to Adam, Gen. 2:17, "Thou shalt not eat thereof: for on the day that thou eatest thereof thou shalt surely die." See note on the verse.[9]

787. FUTURE STATE. IMMORTALITY OF THE SOUL. Our existence in ANOTHER WORLD after this. It don't appear reasonable to me to suppose that there never shall be any communication between the different parts of the universe. The universe is evidently one. It has one architect and is one frame. The parts have evidently relation and connection one with another, and there is a mutual dependence and subserviency. And that the parts should be thus u nited, and yet in this sense eternally remain separate, that one part should have no communication with another, by the knowledge and intelligence and activity that there is in the different parts, which is *instar totius* as it were, the soul and sum of those several parts, and which lies in the intelligent inhabitants of the several parts; I say, that the several parts of the universe so sweetly having respect one to another, har-

9. In the "Blank Bible" note on Gen. 2:17, JE asserts that the "words signify that perfect obedience was the condition of God's covenant that was made with Adam, as they signify that for one act of disobedience he should die." The note also includes a cross-reference to "Notes on Scripture," nos. 77, 320, and 325 (*Works, 15*, 72, 302, 310); and to the second in his series of sermons on Gen. 3:11, pp. 8–11 (see above, No. 785, p. 471, n. 8 and No. 717, p. 349, n. 1).

monizing one with another, and orderly united and connected together, should in this respect remain totally and eternally separate, don't appear to me reasonable. But they will remain totally separate, without communication, unless there be such a thing as a transition or translation of the inhabitants from one part of the universe to another.

788. IMPUTATION of ADAM's SIN. How the whole of the style or language used in the three first chapters of Genesis proves that in those words, "In the day that thou eatest thereof thou shalt surely die," God had respect not only to Adam but his posterity. See my third sermon from Gen. 3:11, the first use.[1] And also [proved] from the nature of all covenant transactions in Scripture.

789. IMMORTALITY OF THE SOUL. FUTURE STATE. "The theory of the perpetual progress of the soul to its perfection, without a possibility of ever arriving at it, is to every candid and virtuous mind, the most convincing proof and demonstration of its immortality. 'For how can it enter into the thoughts of a man, that the soul, which is capable of such immense perfections, and of receiving new improvements to all eternity, shall fall away into nothing almost as soon it was created? Are such abilities made for no purpose? A brute arrives at a point of perfection that he can never pass: in a few years he has all the endowments he is capable of; and were [he] to live ten thousand more, would be the same thing he is at present. Were a human soul thus at a stand in her accomplishments, were her faculties to be full blown, and incapable of further enlargements, I could imagine it might fall away insensibly, and drop at once into a state of annihilation. But can we believe a thinking being, that is in a perpetual progress of improvements, and traveling on from perfection to perfection, after having just looked abroad into the works of its Creator, and made a few discoveries of his infinite goodness, wisdom, and power, must perish at her first setting out, and in the very beginning of her inquiries?

"'A man considered in his present state indeed, does not seem so much born to enjoy life, as to deliver it down to others. This is not surprising to consider in animals, which are formed for our use, and can finish their

1. For the third sermon in the series on Gen. 3:11, see above, No. 717, p. 349, n. 1 (see also No. 785, p. 471, n. 8 and No. 786, p. 472, n. 9). In the first use JE maintains that Adam's "sin is imputed to all the posterity of Adam by ordinary generation." This is "manifest from the Scripture both of the Old and New Testaments," and it is also demonstrated by "experience." "We see that the sin of Adam is imputed to his posterity, because we every day see 'em punished for it."

business in a short life. The silkworm, after having spun her task, lays her eggs and dies. But a man can never have taken in his full measure of knowledge, has not time to subdue his passions, establish his soul in virtue, and come up to the perfection of his nature, before he is hurried off the stage. Would an infinitely wise Being make such glorious beings for so mean a purpose? Can he delight in the production of such abortive intelligences, such short-lived reasonable beings? Would he give us talents that are not to be exerted? Capacities that are never to be gratified? How can we find that wisdom, which shines through all his works, in the formation of man, without looking on this world as only a nursery for the next, and believing that the several generations of reasonable creatures, which rise up and disappear in such quick successions, are only to receive their first rudiments of their existence here, and afterwards to be transplanted into a more friendly climate, where they may spread and flourish to all eternity?'" *Republic of Letters*, vol. 6, pp. 284–86.[2]

790. SIGNS OF GODLINESS. *Ques.* What are the best signs of godliness—those by which persons may try themselves with the greatest safety and certainty; and therefore, those that ministers ought chiefly to insist upon with their hearers?

Ans. This matter is most properly determined by the Word of God, the searcher of hearts, the being to whom it belongs to appoint the terms of salvation and acceptance with himself, and the being who is finally to [be] our Judge.

The holy Scriptures have not left this matter in the dark or doubtful, but have plainly answered this question, and han't only told us what are good evidences of a good estate, but have also very plainly [pointed] out to us those that are chiefly to be looked at, and most safely to be depended on. Concerning good works as the proper evidences of godliness, see various parts of Dr. Manton's Exposition on James.[3]

And by what the Scriptures have taught us in this matter, we must determine that good fruits, or good works and keeping Christ's commandments, are the evidences by which we are chiefly and most safely and surely

2. *The Present State of the Republick of Letters, For October 1730*, Vol. VI (London, 1730), pp. 284–86. This passage occurs in Article XXVIII, "A Discourse Concerning the Nature and Faculties of the Mind: In which are contained some general hints for the Understanding and Will, and the comparative Value and Excellence of each. Done up on new principles, and in a new Method." It includes a quotation from a person identified on p. 282 only as "a learned and ingenious author."

3. Thomas Manton, *A Practical Commentary: an exposition with notes on the epistle of James* (London, 1651).

790. Signs of Godliness.

The beginning of entry No. 790, "Signs of Godliness," in "Miscellanies," Book 3. Courtesy Beinecke Rare Book and Manuscript Library, Yale University.

to be determined, not only concerning the godliness of others, but also concerning our own godliness. Christ, when giving his dying counsel to his disciples, and when[4] giving them directions for their own comfort— John 14:15–16, "If ye love me, keep my commandments. And I will pray the Father, and he will give you another Comforter, that he may abide with you forever"; and v. 21, "He that hath my commandments, and keepeth [them], he it is that loveth me: and he that loveth me shall be loved of my Father, and I will love him, and will manifest myself to him"—such is the emphasis and manner of expression that it plainly carries this in it, that this is the great thing, and the [thing] mainly to be looked at; as also does Christ's so much insisting on it, and so often repeating it in this his last discourse with his disciples. As again, v. 23, "If any man love me, he will keep my words: and my Father will love him, and we will come to him, and make our abode with him." V. 24, "He that loveth me not keepeth not my sayings." And again, 15:10, "If ye keep my commandments, ye shall abide in my love"; and v. 14, "Ye are my friends, if ye do whatsoever I command you." And so the beloved disciple from him in like manner insists on the same, as that by which we are chiefly to try ourselves and not others only. I John 2:3–6, "Hereby do we know that we know him, if we keep his commandments. He that saith, I know him, and keepeth not his commandments, is a liar, and the truth is not in him. But whoso keepeth his word, in him verily is the love of God *perfected* (this is "the *perfect* love that casts out fear," I John 4:18; that is the same with the "Spirit of adoption, bearing witness with our spirits, that we are the children of God," Rom. 8:[15–16]): hereby know we that we are in him. He that saith he abideth in him ought also to walk, even as he walked." I John 5:3, "For this is the love of God, that we keep his commandments: and his commandments are not grievous." Where have [we] anything else in such a manner insisted on in Scripture as a sign of a good estate? So Matt. 7:16–20, "Ye shall know them by their fruits. Do men gather grapes of thorns, or figs of thistles? Even so every good tree bringeth forth good fruit; but a corrupt tree bringeth forth evil fruit. Every tree that bringeth not forth good fruit is hewn down, and cast into the fire. Whereby by their fruits shall ye know them." Here good fruits seem to be especially given as a sign by which we should know others; but Christ, by what he says next [vv. 21–27], lets us know that he would also be understood of ourselves, as well as others: that we are to judge ourselves also mainly by our fruits. "Not every one that saith unto me, Lord, Lord, shall enter into the kingdom of heaven; but he that doth

4. MS: "is."

the will of my Father which is in heaven. Many will say unto me in that day, Lord, Lord, Have we not prophesied in thy name? and in thy name have cast out devils? and in thy name done many wonderful works? And then will I profess unto them, I never knew you: depart from me, ye that work iniquity. Therefore whosoever heareth these sayings of mine, and doth them, I will liken him unto a wise man, that built his house upon a rock: and the rain descended, and the floods came, and the winds blew, and beat upon that house; and it fell not: for it was founded upon a rock. And every one that heareth these sayings of mine, and doth them not, shall be likened unto a foolish man, which built his house upon the sand: And the rain descended, and the floods came, and the wind blew, and beat upon the house; and it fell: and great was the fall of it." The testimony of our own consciences, with respect to doing good works and living a holy life, is spoken [of] as that certain sign which especially tends to give good assurance of godliness. I John 3:18–22, "My little children, let us not love in word and in tongue, but in deed and in truth. And hereby we know that we are of the truth, and shall assure our hearts before him. For if our heart condemn us, God is greater than our heart, and knoweth all things. Beloved, if our heart condemn us not, then have we confidence towards God. And whatsoever we ask, we receive of him, because we keep his commandments, and do those things that are pleasing in his sight."

The apostle Paul (Heb. 6) mentions good works and righteous fruits in the Christian Hebrews both as that evidence that gave him hope concerning them, that they had something more than the highest common illuminations and gifts of hypocrites mentioned in the beginning of the chapter, and also as that evidence which tended to give them the highest assurance of hope concerning themselves. Vv. 9–11, "But, beloved, we are persuaded better things of you, and things that accompany salvation, though we thus speak. For God is not unrighteous to forget your work and labor of love, which ye have showed toward his name, in that ye have ministered to the saints, and do minister. And we desire that every one of you do show the same diligence to the full assurance of hope unto the end." And Gal. 6:4, "Let every man prove his own work, so shall he have rejoicing in himself alone, and not in another." And works are spoken of by the apostle James as the best sign of a man's good estate to his own conscience, as well as to his neighbor, as is manifest by his saying that "Abraham was justified by works (i.e. approved of God as in a good estate), when he offered up his son Isaac on the altar" [Jas. 3:4]; referring to that in which God said to Abraham on that occasion, "Now I know that thou fearest God, because thou hast not withheld from me thy son, thine only son

Isaac" [Gen. 22:12]: which was a testimony of God to Abraham himself of his good estate. The Psalmist says then shall I not be ashamed when I have respect to all thy commandments [Ps. 119:80], i.e. then shall I be bold, and assured, and steadfast in my hope. But that keeping God's commandments is insisted upon throughout the Old Testament as the main evidence of godliness, is manifest beyond all dispute, so as [not] to need enumeration of places.[5]

That by which principally Christ tries men in this, and by which he will judge them hereafter, is doubtless the main evidence by which we are to judge of ourselves. But 'tis principally by men's keeping God's commandments, and bringing forth the fruits of righteousness, that he both tries them here, and judges them hereafter. 'Tis by this chiefly that he judges them here. Thus God tempted or tried Abraham when he commanded him to offer up his only son. It was the way that Christ took to try men's sincerity, viz. to try their obedience. Thus Christ tried the rich young man (Matt. 19:16–21). He made a show of respect to Christ, and a willingness to do anything he should direct him to, but Christ bid him "go and sell all that he had, and give to the poor, and thou shalt have treasure in heaven: and come and follow me." So Christ tried another that we read of (Matt. 8:19–20). He made a great profession of respect to Christ in words; says he, "Lord, I will follow thee whithersoever thou goest." He thought he experienced in his heart such a love to Christ that he could follow him whithersoever he went, but Christ tries how he would do in practice, by telling him that "the foxes had holes, and the birds of the air had nests; but the Son of man had not where to lay his head"; and his practice consequent hereupon showed what he was. Hence difficulties and sufferings laid in the way of our keeping God's commands, do by way of eminency in Scripture, both in the Old Testament and New, obtain the name of temptations or trials, because by these especially men's sincerity is tried.

Again, 'tis principally by men's works, practice, or fruits that they are to be judged at the last day. This is declared in places too many to be mentioned; and 'tis not only in general, but in that most particular description of the day of judgment that is in the whole Bible, which we have in the 25th chapter of Matthew. 'Tis described how both good and bad will be judged by their works; but those signs by which we are to be judged at the last day are doubtless the best evidences both to our own consciences

---

5. Both in this entry and in the "Signs of Godliness" notebook the texts JE lists indicating that obedience is the principal sign of grace are primarily drawn from the New Testament.

and to others. For the end of the day of judgment is to *manifest* the righteous judgment of God, and so the state of men, both to men's own consciences and to the world, and who can suppose that the infinitely wise Judge of the world, when he is about such a work, would not make use of the best *manifestations* to that end. Thus the Scriptures make it very plain and manifest, that good works and fruits and keeping Christ's commands are the best evidences of sincerity of heart, and a good estate of soul. But then several things are here to be observed.

1. The Scripture don't speak only of obedience in one or two particulars, or a partial obedience, but is to be understood of that kind of obedience which is universal. See the evidences of this in the catalogue of Scriptures that speak of evidences of godliness.[6]

2. The Scripture has especially, and above all, respect to keeping Christ's commands, and doing good works, and bringing forth good fruit perseveringly, through trials—or in cases wherein Christ and other things that are dear to the flesh stand in competition—so that in continuing in holy practice we deny ourselves and sell other things for Christ. This also is manifest from the Scriptures cited in the forementioned catalogue.[7] The expression of keeping Christ's commandments imports thus much, and has reference to the opposition that is made to our retaining them, or endeavors to take them away from us, or us from them. Then are we found faithful to *keep* that which is committed to our trust, when others oppose us in it, and try to get the depositum from us, or to tempt us to let it go. Ps. 18:17, "He delivered me from my strong enemy, and from them which hated me: for they were too strong for me"; together with v. 21, "For I have kept the ways of the Lord, and have not wickedly departed from my God."

3. We cannot reasonably suppose that when the Scripture in this case speaks of good works, good fruit, and keeping Christ's commandments, that it has respect merely to what is external, or the motion or action of the body, without including anything else, any aim or intention in the agent, or any act of the understanding or will, in the case: for consider the actions of men so, and they are no more good works, or acts of obedience, than the regular motions of a machine. But doubtless the obedience and

---

6. In the "Signs of Goliness" notebook JE lists numerous texts indicating that obedience must be universal to be a genuine sign of grace.

7. "What can be the proper evidence of a person's loving God above all," JE asserts in the "Signs of Godliness" notebook, "but his actually preferring him indeed when it comes to a trial?" The paragraph in which this statement is made also contains a cross-reference to "Miscellanies," No. 790.

fruit that is spoken of is the obedience and fruit of the man, and therefore not only the obedience of the body, but the obedience of the soul, as
consisting in acts and practice of the soul. Doubtless the Scripture speaks
of these acts or works as ours; but they are ours no further than they are
from the inward actings of our minds, and exercises of our inclinations
and wills. Indeed, by these expressions I don't suppose that the Scripture
intends to include all inward piety, both principle and exercise, both spirit
and practice, because then on these things being given as signs of godliness, the same thing would be given as a sign of itself. But only the exercise and inward practice of the soul is meant. The holy exercise is given as
the sign of the holy principle and good estate, and the manner of exercise, viz. it being that manner of exercise of soul and exertion of inward
holiness that there is in the soul in a truly obediential act: which is something more than the mere being of the principle or merely that principle's being in exercise. 'Tis that exertion of the soul, and of the disposition of the soul, issuing and terminating in imperate acts of the will, the
act that is in what we call practice, or an act of obedience: this I call the
practice of the soul, being something more than the mere immanent exercise of grace. The act of the soul, and the exercise of grace that is exerted in the performance of a good work, is the good work itself so far as
the soul is concerned in it, or so far as it is the soul's good work; and thus
the Scripture gives such a kind of exercise, or exercition, or practice of
the soul, and grace in the soul, as the surest sign of the sincerity of grace,
and the reality of the principle, and so of the goodness of the state. And
this is the obedience and the good fruit that God mainly looks at, as he
looks at the soul more than the body, as much as the soul in the constitution of the human nature is the superior part. As he looks at the obedience and practice of the man, he looks at the practice of the soul chiefly,
as the soul chiefly is the man and *instar totius* in God's sight: for God seeth
not as man seeth, for he looketh on the heart. True godliness consists not
in an heart to intend to keep God's commandments, but in an heart to do
it, Deut. 5:27–29. See sermon on this text.[8]

   So that in this keeping Christ's commands, not only is the exercise of
the faculties of the soul included, but also the end for which a man acts:
for not only should we not look on the motions of a statue, doing justice
by clockwork, as an act of obedience to Christ in that statue, but neither

8. The reference to the sermon on Deut. 5:27–29 (Nov. 1743) is a later addition. The doctrine of the sermon is almost identical to the sentence preceding this reference: "Godliness consists not in an heart to purpose to do the will of God, but in an heart to do it."

would anybody call the voluntary actions of a man, externally and materially agreeable to a command of Christ, an act of obedience to Christ, if he never had heard of Christ, or any of his commands, or never thought of them at that time.

If the acts of obedience and good fruits spoken of be looked upon not as mere motions of the body but as acts of the soul, the whole exercise of the spirit of the mind must be taken in, with the end acted for, and the respect the soul then has to God, his will and authority; otherwise, 'tis no act of denial of ourselves, or obedience to God, or service done to him, but to something else. See papers of minutes, no. 9, p. 16.[9] See also "Miscellanies," No. 1031.[1]

But at the same time it must also be observed that the external act is not excluded in that obedience that is in Scripture so much insisted on as a sign of godliness, but the internal exertion of the mind, and the external act as connected with [it] are both included and intended. And though in this great evidence of godliness what is inward is of greatest importance, yet hereby are effectually cut off all pretensions that any man can have to evidences of godliness that externally lives wickedly: because the great evidence lies in the inward exercise, or practice of the soul, that accompanies and issues in imperate acts of the will. But 'tis known that the imperate acts of the will are not one way and the actions of the bodily organs another: for the unalterable law of nature is that they should be united, or that one should follow another, as long as soul and body are united, and the organs are not so destroyed as [not] to remain capable of those motions that the soul commands. Thus it would be ridiculous for a man to plead that the imperate act of his will was to go to the public worship, while his feet carried him to a tavern or public stew, or that the imperate act of his soul was to give such a sum that he had in his hand to a poor beggar, while his hand at the same instant retained it.

The words, "fruits," "works," "keeping or breaking commandments,"

---

9. Given the close relation between the content of No. 790 and *Religious Affections*, this is probably a reference to the ninth in a series of small notebooks that JE constructed while preparing to write that treatise. Only the seventh of these notebooks is now extant, but JE must have compiled at least nine, because on the first page of the notebook entitled "no. 7" is a reference, "see no. 9, p. 2." This reference is very similar to JE's direction, "see papers of minutes, no. 9, p. 16."

1. JE's cue marks indicate that he intended the entirety of No. 1031 to be inserted at this point. That entry, entitled "Signs of Godliness. Faith. Obedience," is a paraphrase of a sentence from Phillip Doddridge's sermon, "The Scripture Doctrine of Salvation by Grace through Faith," stating, "The determinations of the will are indeed our very actions so far as they are properly ours" (*Practical Discourses on Regeneration* [2nd ed., Philadelphia, 1794], p. 284). JE quoted this entry in *Religious Affections* (*Works*, 2, 423).

are used in Scripture sometimes in a more restrained and sometimes in a larger sense. Sometimes for outward acts: so they are to be understood when they are given as signs by which we are to judge of others, and it may be in some other cases; and sometimes not only for outward, but also inward acts. By works sometimes is meant all acts that are liable to a reward or punishment, as is evident by Job 34:11, "The work of a man will he render unto him"; and Rev. 14:13, "Their works do follow them"; and a multitude of parallel places. But inward exercises are liable to a reward or punishment. We find promises and threatenings often made to good or evil thoughts and exercises of the heart; and works are to be understood in this extensive sense where the Apostle speaks of works, works of the Law and works of righteousness, in the affair of justification. And so Prov. 20:11, "Even a child is known by his doings, whether his work be pure, and whether it be right"; here external deeds are spoken [of] as a sign of the quality of something internal, that is called work. And Col. 1:21, "Enemies in your mind by wicked works." Heb. 6:1, there repentance of sin is called "repentance from dead works." John 6:28–29, "What [shall we do, that we might work the works of God? Jesus answered and said unto them, this is the work of God, that ye believe on him whom he hath sent]." Both the terms, works and fruits, are used in this extensive sense in Gal. 5, beginning at the 19th v., "Now the works of the flesh are manifest, which are these; adultery, fornication, uncleanness, lasciviousness, idolatry, witchcraft, hatred, emulations, wrath, strife, seditions, heresies, envyings. But the fruit of the Spirit is love, joy, peace, long-suffering, gentleness, goodness, faith, meekness, temperance: against such there is no law. And they that are Christ's have crucified the flesh with the affections and lusts."

Though all exercises whatsoever, of either grace or corruption, are what we either keep or break God's commandments by, and though they are all sometimes called works and fruits, yet where good works and fruits and keeping God's commands are insisted on as the great evidences of godliness in the places forementioned, those exercises of grace and exertions of soul whence good external practice in speech or behavior immediately result, seem chiefly to be aimed at.

However, 'tis beyond dispute that inward exercises of grace are included. Thus the good fruits that Christ mentions as the sure signs of the tree, and the doing the things that Christ says, so much insisted on in the conclusion of Christ's sermon on the mount as the great sign of being on a sure foundation, implies many inward exercises: for doubtless Christ, by doing the things that he says, has a special respect to those things that he had been saying in that sermon, the commands he had then been giving.

But many of those sayings of his respect acts of the mind, as in those that follow. "Blessed are the poor in spirit." "Blessed are they that mourn." "Blessed are the meek." "Blessed are they which do hunger and thirst after righteousness." "Blessed are the merciful." "Blessed are the pure in heart." "Whosoever is angry with his brother without a cause shall be in danger of judgment." "But I say unto you, whosoever looketh on a woman to lust after her hath committed adultery with her already in his heart." "Love your enemies, bless them that curse you, do good to them that hate you, and pray for them which despitefully use you, and persecute you." "No man can serve two masters: for either he will hate the one, and love the other; or else he will hold to the one, and despise the other." "Take no thought for your life, what ye shall eat, or what ye shall drink; nor yet for your body, what ye shall put on. Is not the life more than meat, and the body more than raiment?" "Seek first the kingdom of God, and his righteousness; and all these things shall be added unto you." "Judge not, that ye be not judged" [Matt. 5:3–8, 22, 28, 44; 6:24–25, 33; 7:1].

And when Christ, in his dying discourses to his disciples, so much insists on keeping his commandments as a sign of sincerity, 'tis manifest that he has a special respect to a command that mainly respects the exercise of the heart, viz. loving one another; which he once and again in that same discourse calls his commandment, as John 13:34–35, "A new commandment I give unto you, that ye love one another; as I have loved you, that you also love one another. By this shall all men know that ye are my disciples, if ye have love one to another." Here he mentions it as that by which others should know that they were his disciples; but in what follows—the places that have been already cited—he also insists on it as a sign by which they should know themselves, in insisting on keeping his commandments as the great sign. As also does the penman of this book in his first epistle, ch. 2, [vv.] 3–6, "Hereby do we know that we know him, if we keep his commandments. He that saith, I know him, and keepeth not his commandments, is a liar, and the truth is not in him. But whoso keepeth his word, in him verily is the love of God perfected: hereby know that we are in him. He that saith he abideth in him ought himself also so to walk, even as he walked"; together with what follows in v. 7, "Brethren, I write no new commandment unto you, but an old commandment which ye had from the beginning. The old commandment is the word which ye have heard from the beginning," there insisting on love to the brethren. And again, 3:23, there speaking of keeping Christ's commands as a sure sign, he adds, "And this is his commandment, that we should believe on the name of his Son Jesus Christ, and love one another, as he gave us commandment";

both which are acts of the mind. And both these the Apostle seemed to take from that dying discourse of Christ that he rehearses in his Gospel, as you may see by comparing John 13:34–35 with 14:10–15, 21–25. See II John 5–6, "That we love one another. And this is love, that we walk after his commandments. This is the commandment, that ye have heard from the beginning, that ye should walk in it."

And when we are told in Scripture that men shall at the last day all be judged according to their works, and all shall receive according to the things done in the body, whether good or bad, it is not to be understood only of outward acts; for if so, why is God so often spoken of as he that searches the heart and the reins, at the same time that he is spoken of as judge of the world, and as he that render to every man according to his works? Rev. 2:23, "And all the churches shall know that I am he which searcheth the reins and the hearts: and I will give unto every one of you according to your works." Ps. 7:8–9, "The Lord shall judge the people: judge me, O Lord, according to my righteousness, and according to mine integrity that is in me. Oh let the wickedness of the wicked come to an end; but do thou establish the just: for the righteous God trieth the hearts and the reins." Jer. 11:20, "But, O Lord of hosts, that judgest righteously, that triest the reins and the heart." Jer. 17:9–10, "The heart is deceitful above all things, and desperately wicked: who can know it? I the Lord search the heart, I try the reins, even to give every man according to his ways, and according to the fruit of his doings." Prov. 17:3, "The fining pot for silver, and the furnace for gold: but the Lord trieth the hearts." Prov. 21:2, "Every way of a man is right in his own eyes: but the Lord pondereth the hearts." Prov. 16:2, "All the ways of a man are clean in his own eyes; but the Lord weigheth the spirits." I Cor. 4:5, "Therefore judge nothing before the time, until the Lord come, who will both bring to light the hidden things of darkness, and make manifest the counsels of the hearts: and then shall every man have praise of God."

So that 'tis this keeping Christ's commandments that is spoken of in Scripture as the best sign of godliness, viz. not only in outward practice, but also in the practice of the soul, in the sense that has been explained. It is such a keeping God's commands that Hezekiah pleads in his sickness; Is. 38:3, "Remember now, O Lord, I beseech thee, how I have walked before thee in truth and with a perfect heart."

There can be no sufficient objection against universally keeping Christ's commands in this sense as being the best sign of godliness, especially when the commandments are thus kept through such trials as providence lays in our way.

1. It can be no objection against it that 'tis reasonable to suppose that those things must be the best evidences of a good estate wherein godliness does most essentially consist, and are themselves the very condition of a good estate by God's revealed constitution. For, take good works or holy practice in this sense, and godliness does most essentially consist in it, so far as it consists in act, or in anything visible or sensible: for the essence of godliness, so far [as] that lies in anything sensible or perceivable, doubtless lies in the inward exercises of grace or holiness; but good works in the sense that has been explained are grace itself, they are proper exercises of grace. Such practical exertions of faith and love are exercises of faith and love, and they are the highest and most essential sort of the exercises of these graces. For what is called the imperate act of the will in which these exercises issue and terminate, is indeed nothing else but the preponderating of the inclination or disposition of the soul in its exercise in the present trial, which is to be decided by the following motion of the body, by the law of the union of soul and body, which law is fixed and upheld by the omniscient God himself. And especially does godliness most essentially consist in such practical exercises of grace, in cases wherein Christ and other things are especially set in competition.

That loving Christ and believing in him, hoping and trusting in him, that are chiefly insisted on as notes of a good [estate] and evidences of acceptance with God and true happiness, are chiefly these effective exercises and acts of faith and love and hope under trials. Jas. 1:12, "Blessed is he that endureth temptation: for when he is tried, he shall receive the crown of life, which the Lord hath promised to them that love him." I John 5:3, "For this is the love of God, that we keep his commandments: and his commandments are not grievous." II John 6, "And this is love, that we walk after his commandments." So [when] the trusting in God, and believing in him, exercising confidence and hope in him, are chiefly prescribed, it is chiefly with respect to such trials.

So when FAITH is insisted on as the great CONDITION OF SALVATION, practical exertions[2] and effective expressions of faith, appearing when faith is thus tried, are mainly pointed at. It was by faith appearing thus that Abraham was justified, which the apostle James takes notice of [Jas. 3:21]. They did not perform the condition of salvation who believed for a while and in a time of temptation fell away, but they do who believe with that faith that overcomes the world. They are entitled to the promises that are made to those that overcome in the 2nd and 3rd chapters of Revelation.

2. MS: "expressions and practical exertions."

Rom. 10:9, "If thou shalt confess with thy mouth the Lord Jesus, and shalt believe in thine heart that God hath raised him from the dead, thou shalt be saved." I Thess. 2:13–14, "Which effectually worketh also in you that believe. For ye, brethren, became followers of the churches of God which in Judea are in Christ Jesus: for ye also suffered like things of your own countrymen." Heb. 10:39, "Ye are not of them that draw back unto perdition; but of [them] that believe to the saving of the soul," with the context. And to this purpose are the many examples of faith mentioned in the 11th chapter of Hebrews. (Here insert No. 800.)[3] Thus that faith that is called a work, and is one thing implied in those forementioned expressions in Scripture of good works and keeping Christ's commandments, is the great condition of salvation. John 6:28–29, "Then said they unto him, What shall we do, that we may work the works of God? Jesus answered and said unto them, This is the work of God, that ye believe on him whom he hath sent." So in this manner faith is mentioned as the condition of receiving an answer to our prayers. I John 3:22–23, "And whatsoever we ask, we receive of him, because we keep his commandments, and do those things that are pleasing in his sight. And this is his commandment, that we should believe on the name of his Son Jesus Christ, and love one another, as he gave us commandment." See No. 996.

And thus what Hezekiah pleaded on his sick bed (Is. 38:3) was not only a sign of his title to the fruits of God's favor, but was the condition of a title to them.

2. WITNESS OF THE SPIRIT. It can be no sufficient objection against good fruits and keeping Christ's commandments being the best sign of grace, that the Scripture speaks of a certain kind of evidence of a good estate, that is represented as the immediate testimony of the Spirit of God himself to our souls that we are the children of God, and the seal of the Spirit, and the earnest of the Spirit in our hearts, which is the experience of the exercise of the Spirit of adoption, or Spirit of love, which seems to be the same with that love which the beloved disciple speaks of that casts out fear, and that white stone and new name written that Christ gives which no man knows but he that receives it. Such an evidence as this, one would think by the things that are said, must needs be the highest and most certain and assuring kind of evidence that any person can receive. And it must be allowed to be so. But yet, I say, this don't argue but that keeping Christ's commands in the sense that has been spoken of through trials is the high-

---

3. JE's cue marks indicate that he intended the insertion to include only the first paragraph of No. 800. See p. 500.

est evidence. This witness of the Spirit, or a Spirit of adoption, must be the experience of the exercise of such a spirit, or a spirit of love, which is a childlike spirit, in opposition to a spirit of fear, which is the spirit of bondage. But it has been already observed that the keeping Christ's commands that has been spoken of consists mainly in the exercise of grace in the heart; and that kind of exercise of love, or the spirit of adoption that there is in such practical exertions and effective exercises of love, are the highest and most essential and distinguishing kind of exercises of love: and therefore in them this testimony and seal and earnest of the Spirit of love is given in its clearest and fullest manner. And the Apostle, when he speaks of the testimony of the Spirit of God in Rom. 8:15–16, in that very place he principally and most immediately has respect to such effective exercises of love as those whereby Christians deny themselves in times of trial; as appears by his manner of introducing what is there said, which is to be seen in vv. 12–13, "Therefore, brethren, we are debtors, not to the flesh, to live after the flesh. For if we live after the flesh, ye shall die: but if ye through the Spirit do mortify the deeds of the flesh, ye shall live"; and also by what immediately follows in vv. 17–18, "And if children, then heirs; heirs of God, and joint heirs with Christ; if so be that we suffer with him, that we may also be glorified together. For I reckon that the sufferings of this present time are not worthy to be compared with the glory which shall be revealed in us." That exercise of love, or the filial spirit that the Apostle here speaks of as the highest ground of hope, is the same with that exercise of the love of God that Christians experience in bearing tribulation for his sake; whence arises that hope that makes not ashamed, that he had before spoken of, ch. 5, at the beginning; and the same with that white stone and new name which is obtained by overcoming, spoken of in Revelation; and that seal of the Spirit that the Apostle speaks of as what he had in going through extreme suffering (see II Cor. 1:8–9, together with 21–22); and that earnest of the Spirit that he had under afflictions and persecutions, which he speaks of, II Cor. 5:5, together with the preceding part of the chapter and the latter part of the foregoing. So that keeping Christ's commands is the highest evidence of a good estate, and yet the witness of the Spirit of adoption or love is the highest evidence: for they are both the same. Therefore the apostle John, where speaking of keeping Christ's commands as the great evidence of our good estate, does in the same place speak of our partaking of the Spirit of God as a spirit of love, as the great evidence of a good estate (I John, 3rd chapter, at the latter end). V. 19, "And hereby we know that we are of the truth, and shall assure our hearts before him"; v. 22, "And whatsoever we ask, we receive of him, because we keep his commandments"; [vv.] 23–24, "And this is his commandment, that we should believe on the name of his Son Jesus Christ, and love one another, as he gave us commandment. And he that keepeth his commandments dwelleth in him, and he in him. And hereby we know that he abideth in us, by the Spirit that he hath given us." The same he insists on again in the next chapter, 12th and 13th verses, "If we love one another, God dwelleth in us, and his love is perfected in us. Hereby we know that we dwell in him, and he in us, because he hath given us of his Spirit"; and this is the same evidence with that spoken in the 18th verse there following in the same chapter, which we have observed is the same with the sure testimony of the Spirit of adoption spoken of in the 8th of Romans. "There is no fear in love; but perfect love casteth out fear: because fear hath torment. He that feareth is not made perfect in love." And this again is the same with that evidence, consisting in keeping God's commandments, spoken of in the 3rd verse of the chapter next following, in a continuation of the same discourse. "This is the love of God, that we keep his commandments: and his commandments are not grievous."

Here add No. 800.[4]

791. CHRIST'S EXAMPLE. THE EXCELLENCY OF CHRIST. RIGHTEOUSNESS OF CHRIST. The time of Christ's last suffering, beginning with the night wherein he was betrayed, till he expired on the cross, was in almost all respects more [excellent] than all the rest of his life. He suffered more in that time than he did in all the rest of his life. His satisfaction for sin was mainly by what passed in that time, and his purchase of heaven was chiefly in that time: for that obedience and righteousness by which we are justified was more by what he did in that time than by all that he did before; as much as his propitiation for sin was more by what he suffered in that time than by all that he suffered before. And so the excellency of Christ mainly appears in what he did then; and the example that he has set us in the amiable virtues he expressed, lies as much in what appeared in him in the time of his last sufferings, as his propitiation and righteousness. Therefore, when we look for the example that Christ hath set us, and the distinguishing amiableness and excellency of the virtue which appeared in him, though we may find much of it in other parts of his life, yet we are chiefly to look here where was the main trial of his. Strict and eminent virtue always appears brightest in the fire. Pure gold shows its purity chiefly in the furnace.

---

4. JE adds, "the paragraph thus marked," followed by a cue mark, which indicates that JE intended the insertion to include the second and third paragraphs of No. 800. See pp. 500–01.

To be sensible of the greatness of the trial of those virtues in Christ that were exercised under his sufferings, two things must be considered: (1) the infinite height and dignity of his person and state, and (2) the degree of suffering and humiliation that he was subject to. Both these are to be considered jointly, for 'tis a greater thing for one that in himself is very great and honorable to stoop low, and to be the subject of great abasement, than for a meaner person; 'tis a greater trial of reverence, obedience, submission, humility, meekness, and patience, and every virtue that is exercised in humiliation. The dignity of the nature of the angels and the honorableness of their state was their temptation, and was a trial of their obedience and subjection and humility, when the subjection that was required of them implied no abasement, nothing but what properly and originally belonged to beings of their rank. How much more was it a trial of the virtue of Christ, when it was to be exercised in those things that were infinitely below his degree, and what originally belonged to his person.

Christ expressed great reverence towards God in his last sufferings, as in the manner of his praying to the Father in the garden, when he kneeled down and prayed (Luke 22:41); yea, he fell prostrate on the ground (Matt. 26:39, Mark 14:35). His infinite dignity, which the human nature knew was a great trial of his reverence, and especially under God's terrible dealings with him at that time, when he felt the rod of God upon him for our sins, in those stripes by which we are healed, when his Father thus chastened him, he thus gave him reverence. He also at this time manifested perfect submission to the will of God, though he was a person so honorable that in his original nature he was equal with God, and in his original circumstances he was subject to the will of none, and knew that he was the sovereign Lord of heaven and earth, and was to reign as such as God-man, and though the will of God was so terrible to his human nature. In his last sufferings he manifested the most wonderful humility. Though the man Christ Jesus knew that he was the most excellent and honorable of all men, yea, of all creatures, yet was he the most humble; no man nor angel ever equaled him in humility. He was least of all in this respect, and therefore he mentions and recommends his example in making himself least of all in his last sufferings. Mark 10:44–45, "And whosoever of you will be the chiefest, shall be servant of all. For even the Son of man came not to be ministered unto, but to minister, and to give his life a ransom for many." The man Christ Jesus would have been under the greatest temptation to pride, if it had been possible that anything could have been a temptation to him. The temptation of the angels that fell was the dignity of their natures and the honorableness of their circumstances, but Christ knew himself to be infinitely more honorable than they. The human nature of Christ was so honored as to be in the same person with the eternal Son of God, that was equal with God, yet was he not at all lifted up with pride; nor was the man Christ Jesus at all lifted up with pride with all those wonderful and divine works that he wrought, not as the prophets wrought miracles in the name of another, but in his own name, and as of his own will, as the God of nature and the sovereign of the world. And he knew that God had appointed him as God-man to be king over angels, and over the heavens of heavens, and over the universe, and to be the judge of all; as appears by what he says Matt. 11:27, "All things are delivered unto me of my Father: and no man knoweth the Son, but the Father; neither knoweth any man the Father, save the Son, and he to whomsoever the Son will reveal him." Though he knew that he was the heir of his Father's kingdom, for these things had been promised him by the Father in covenant, yet such was his humility that he did not disdain to be abased and depressed into lower and viler circumstances by far, than ever any other elect creature was. The proper trial and evidence of humility is stooping or complying with those acts or circumstances when called to it, that are very low and imply great abasement; but none ever stooped so low as Christ, if we consider either the infinite height he stooped from, or the great depth to which he descended. Such was the humility of the man Christ Jesus, though he knew the immense height of dignity and honor in which he stood, and that he was worthy of ten-thousand times more honor than the highest prince on earth or angel in heaven, yet he did not think it too much when called to it to be bound as a malefactor, to be after such a manner the mock stock and spitting stock of the vilest of men and his most haughty, unreasonable, malignant and cruel enemies, to be crowned with thorns and a mock robe, to be scourged and crucified like an abject slave, and detestable cursed vagabond, and miscreant and enemy of God and man, and one not fit to live upon earth; and that not for himself [but] for such cursed malignant wretches as those his crucifiers, and for some of those very crucifiers.

In his last sufferings were also the highest manifestations and fruits of his love to God, for his offering up himself under those sufferings was an act of love and obedience to God, and regard to his glory. God was the being to whom he offered up that sacrifice, and the gift was a gift of love to God. This sacrifice was offered in a twofold flame, viz. the flame God's wrath, and yet (wonderful mystery) the flame of his own love to God. The wrath was God's wrath for our sins. The ardency of one of those flames was as great as the other, unless we may look on the flame of love in some respects as exceeding and conquering the other. Christ's love in making him willing to offer himself up in the fire of God's wrath, and carrying him through the torments of that flame, even till it was extinguished, did as it were conquer and quench it. Never was there such a gift of love and labor of love as this. It as more exceeds all the expressions of love in any man or angel, than the treasures of the most wealthy prince exceed the stores of the meanest peasant.

In this also was the greatest exercise of the virtue of love to man. The flame of love in which Christ offered up the sacrifice of himself was twofold, viz. love to God and love to man; and both these flames did as it were overcome the flame of wrath. There have been very remarkable manifestations of love to men in some of the saints, as in the Apostle Paul, and the Apostle John, and others; but the love to man that Christ showed when on earth as much exceeded the love of all other men, as the ocean exceeds a small stream.

So Christ's meekness here has its highest exercise. Christ's meekness was his humble calmness of spirit under the provocations that he met with. The degree of meekness appears in two things, viz. the degree of quietness and humble calmness, and in the degree of provocation under which this quietness is maintained. None ever met with so great provocations as Christ did. The degree of provocation lies in two things: (1) in the degree of the opposition by which the provocation is given, and (2) in wthe degree of the unreasonableness of that opposition, or in the degree of the obligation to the contrary. Now if we consider both these things, no man ever met with such provocation as he did—if we consider the degree in which he was hated, and the degree in which he suffered from that hatred, and the degree of contempt that was offered, and also consider how causeless and unreasonable those abuses were, and how deserving he was of the contrary, of love and honor and good treatment at their hands. But his composure and quietness of spirit was perfect under all these provocations. And how wonderful was his spirit of forgiveness under them, which is something more than mere meekness. The virtue of the most glorious angel in heaven would have carried him but little way towards such forgiveness, exercised under such trials, and in such a manner. And so his patience, which is somewhat diverse from his meekness, has the most glorious manifestation under these sufferings.

And also his contempt of the glory of the world has its highest manifestation under these sufferings, when he rather chose this meanness, reproach and suffering, than to wear a temporal crown and to be invested with the glories of the highest earthly princes.

Wherever anything in particular in Christ's example is recommended to our imitation in the Scripture, regard is manifestly chiefly had to what was expressed in his last sufferings. So Matt. 20:26–28, "But it shall not be so among you: but whosoever will be great among you, let him be your minister; and whosoever will be chief among you, let him be your servant: Even as the Son of man came not to be ministered unto, but to minister, and to give his life a ransom for many." So after that act of his washing the disciples' feet, which was symbolical of his great humiliation in becoming servant of all, and least of all, in his last sufferings to cleanse his people from their[5] sins he recommends his example. John 13:15, "For I have given you an example, that ye should do as I have done unto you"; and I Pet. 2:21–24, "For even hereunto were ye called: because Christ also suffered for us, leaving us an example, that we should follow his steps . . . who, when he was reviled, reviled not again . . . who his own self bare our sins in his own body on the tree." Matt. 16:24–25, "Then said Jesus unto his disciples, If any man will come after me, let him deny himself, and take up his cross, and follow me. For whosoever will save his life shall lose it: and whosoever will lose his life for my sake shall find it." I Pet. 3:17–18, "For it is better, if the will of God be so, that ye suffer for well doing, than for evil doing. For Christ also hath once suffered for sins, the just for the unjust, that he might bring us to God." I John 4:19, "We love him, because he first loved us"; with v. 10, "Herein is love, not that we loved him, but that he loved us, and sent his Son into the world to be the propitiation for our sins." John 15:12–13, "This is my commandment, that ye love one another, as I have loved you. Greater love hath no man than this, that a man lay down his life for his friends"; and 13:31–34, "Now is the Son of man glorified, and God is glorified in him. If God be glorified in him, God shall also glorify him in himself, and shall straitway glorify him. Little children, yet a little while am I with you. And as I said unto the Jews, Whither I go, ye cannot come; so now I say unto you. A new commandment I give unto you, That ye love one another; as I have loved you, that ye also love one another." And Eph. 5:2, "And walk in love, as Christ also hath loved us, and hath given himself for us an offering and a sacrifice to God for a sweet smelling savor." Eph. 5:25–27, "Husbands, love your wives, even as Christ also loved the church, and gave himself for it; that he might sanctify and cleanse it with the washing of water by the word, that he might present it

5. MS: "his."

to himself a glorious church, not having spot, or wrinkle, or any such thing; but that it should be holy and without blemish." I John 3:16, "Hereby perceive we the love of God, because he laid down his life for us; and we ought to lay down our lives for the brethren." Philip. 2:5–8, "Let this mind be in you, which was also in Christ Jesus: who, being in the form of God . . . humbled himself, and became obedient unto death, even the death of the cross." I Cor. 10, last [verse] and 11:1, "Even as I please all men in all things, not seeking mine own profit, but the profit of many, to their edification. Be ye followers of me, even as I also am of Christ." Rom. 15:2–3, "Let every one of us please his neighbor for his good to edification. For even Christ pleased not himself; but, as it is written, The reproaches of them that reproached thee fell on me." Philip. 3:10, "Being made conformable to his death." Rom. 8:17, "If so be that we suffer with him, that we may also be glorified together"; to the same purpose, II Tim. 2:11–12.

If we consider the perfection of the virtue that Christ exercised, his virtue did more exceed that of the most eminent saints than the purest gold exceeds the leanest and foulest ore. If we consider the latter of those two great trials of virtue that were first mentioned, under which this perfect virtue was exercised, viz. the degree of suffering and humiliation, so Christ's virtue exceeds that of all other perfectly innocent creatures, and even the brightest angel, as the sun in his glory exceeds the stars. And if we consider the dignity of his person, and the value that arose to his virtue directly from thence, as the excellent qualities of gold are more valuable when joined with greater weight and dimensions, than when with smaller, or with respect to the value that arose to his virtue from hence, as this dignity and honorableness of his person was a trial of his virtue (it being the former of those two forementioned kinds of trial), the dignity of his person both these ways gives such value to the virtue he exercised under his sufferings, that it doth truly, infinitely exceed the virtue of all men and angels.

It pleased God that trials of both men and angels should meet in Christ, i.e. that he should be tried with those temptations which were the trial of their obedience, by which men and the angels that fell were overthrown. He was subject to a trial like that which was the temptation of man, and peculiar to him, viz. the importunate desires and inclinations of animal nature. These he was tempted by in the wilderness, when [he] was hungry after his forty days' fast in the wilderness, and the devil tempted him to take an unlawful course to gratify that appetite. But above all was he subject to an exceeding great trial from the inclinations of his animal nature, and of the whole human nature, which so exceedingly dreaded and shrunk at those torments that it was to undergo, and solicited to be delivered from the bitterness of that cup that was given into Christ's hands to drink, with immensely greater importunity than ever the human nature solicited to taste the sweetness of the forbidden fruit, and which bitterness was represented to Christ in a far more lively manner than the sweetness of the forbidden fruit was set forth to our first parents by Satan, or their own imaginations. So also was Christ's virtue tried with that kind of trial that was the temptation of the angels, which was the knowledge of their dignity, for Christ was in immensely higher dignity than they. But Christ overcame in both these kinds of trial, that in all things he might have the preeminence, and that he might be honorable in the eyes of men and angels, over both which God had appointed him to be the head. Yea, not only was Christ subject to all those kinds of trials that creatures have had while innocent, but also a kind of trials that no other innocent person but he ever was subject to, and the greatest kind that guilty creatures are ever subject to, viz. suffering, and far more extreme sufferings than ever fallen creature that was in a state of trial was subject to; and he conquered in this trial and triumphed over all these temptations, so glorious in all respects was his virtue and obedience.

All the virtue that Christ exercised in the human nature in any respect belongs to that righteousness which is imputed to believers for their justification, even his wonderful dying love to man is so, as it was the most glorious exercise of the virtue of charity to man, and the greatest instance of the fulfillment of the second great commandment of the law, viz. thou shalt love thy neighbor as thy self; and as he was called of God, and his duty required him to exercise such love to man. And by such an act as the offering up himself a sacrifice to God, his so loving and so expressing his love was as much a part of his obedience to the law of God, as he was subject to it, as our love to our neighbors is part of our obedience to the law of God, as we are subject to it. So that believers are saved by the dying love of Christ in several respects. They are saved by it as this was the internal moving cause of his offering himself a sacrifice to God; and they are also saved by it as it is part of that righteousness that is imputed to them.

From things being thus as has been observed, it comes to pass that whenever the saints behold the beauty and amiable excellency of Christ as appearing in his virtues, and have their souls ravished with it, they may behold it in its brightest effulgence, and by far its most full and glorious manifestation, shining forth in a wonderful act of love to them, exercised in his last sufferings, wherein he died for them. They may have the pleasure to see all his ravishing excellency in that which is the height, and, as it were, the sum of its exhibited and expressed glory, appearing in and by the exercise of dying love to them; which certainly will tend to endear that excellency, and make that greatest effulgence of it the more ravishing in their eyes. They see the transcendent greatness of his love shining forth in the same act that they see the transcendent greatness of his loveliness shining forth, and his loveliness to shine in his love; so that 'tis most lovely love. Their seeing his loveliness tends to make them desire his love, but the sight of his loveliness brings satisfaction to this desire with it, because the appearance of his loveliness as they behold it, mainly consists in the marvelous exercise of his love to them. It being thus, his excellency both endears his love, and his love endears his excellency; and the very beholding his excellency, as thus manifested, is an enjoying of it as their own. And while the saints have the pleasure of these views, they may also have the additional pleasure of considering that this lovely virtue is imputed to them. 'Tis the lovely robe, and robe of love, with which they are covered. Christ gives it to them, and puts it upon them, and by the beauty of this robe recommends 'em to the favor and delight of God the Father, as well as of all heaven besides.

792. JUSTIFICATION. When the Scripture says we are not justified by works, 'tis meant, as good works, or as our virtue; because 'tis evident the expression is used as signifying the same as our own righteousness.

793. JUSTIFICATION. REWARDS. Believers may be heirs of eternal life prior to their good works. They may have a right by Christ's righteousness received by faith that may be prior to any regard to anything in them as a good work, or any virtue or lovely qualification in them; and yet [it] may be the pleasure of God to bestow heaven upon them in that way, viz. in reward for their good works, as lovely to God in Christ. And this contains no more absurdity or inconsistency than Christ himself, his being the heir of the kingdom of the world as a Son prior to his good works, and its being yet the pleasure of God that he should have the possession of the kingdom given him in reward for his labors. He was the Son of God, and so the heir of the world, and that was the reason that God appointed him to those labors, that he might obtain the possession of it in that way. So believers being heirs as children (which they are by the righteousness of Christ), is the reason that God appoints them to obtain heaven in a way of good works, which God hath before ordained that they should walk in them.

794. CHRIST'S RIGHTEOUSNESS. JUSTIFICATION. See [Nos.] 399 and 381. Every command that Christ, when he was in his state of humiliation, obeyed may be reduced to one law, and that is that which the Apostle calls the law of works, to which indeed all laws of God properly so called may be reduced (Rom. 3:27). But the commands that Christ obeyed may be distributed into three particular laws, viz. the law that he was subject to merely as man, which was (1) the moral law; and the law that he was subject to as a Jew, which includes (2) the ceremonial law, and all the positive precepts that were peculiar to that nation. (3) The mediatorial law, which contained those commands of God that he was subject to purely as he was mediator, to which belong all those commands that the Father gave him to work such miracles, and teach such doctrines, and so to labor in the works of his public ministry, and to yield himself to such sufferings: for as he often tells us, he did all those things agreeable to the Father's direction, and in obedience to his Father's commandments.

The righteousness of Christ, by which he merited heaven for himself and all that believe on him, consists principally in his obedience to the last of these laws. For in the fulfilling of this law consisted his chief work and business in the world, and this part of his obedience was attended with the greatest difficulties and trials of all, and so this obedience was most meritorious; and therefore, the history of the evangelists is chiefly taken up in giving an account of the acts of his obedience to this mediatorial law. As the obedience of the first Adam, wherein his righteousness would have mainly consisted if he had stood, would not have been in his obedience to the moral law that he was subject to merely as man, or as one possessed of the human nature, but in his obedience to that special law that he was subject to as a moral head and surety; so the righteousness of the second Adam consists mainly in his obedience to the special law that he was subject to, in his office of mediator and surety.

795. CONDITION OF SALVATION. HOLY LIFE. PERSEVERANCE. Some things may yet remain that are properly the conditions of salvation, on which salvation may be so suspended, that it may well excite to the utmost caution lest we should come short of eternal life, and should perish for want of them, after it is already become impossible that we should fail of salvation. For the condition of the man Christ Jesus, his obtaining eternal life, was his doing the work which God had given him to do, his performing perfect persevering obedience, and his therein conquering Satan, and the world, and all opposition, and enduring all sufferings that he met with. And therefore Christ used the utmost diligence to do this work, and

used the utmost caution lest he should fail of it, and prayed with strong crying and tears, and wrestled with God in a bloody sweat, that he might not fail, but might have God's help to go through, so that he might not fail; and yet it was impossible that he should fail of eternal life. And the whole reward that had been promised him, the joy that was set before him, it was not only certain to him, but [he] had a proper title to it as God's heir, by reason of his relation to God the Father, as being his only begotten Son. And it was impossible that he should fail in his work to which he was appointed; God had promised him sufficient and effectual grace and help to persevere, and already had made known his election. Ps. 110:7, "He shall drink of the brook in the way: therefore shall he lift up the head." Is. 42:1, "Behold my servant, whom I uphold; mine elect, in whom my soul delighteth; I have put my spirit upon him: he shall bring forth judgment to the Gentiles"; v. 4, "He shall not fail nor be discouraged"; and v. 6, "I the Lord have called thee in righteousness; I will hold thine hand, and will keep thee." And Is. 41:8, "But thou, Israel, my servant, Jacob whom I have chosen, the seed of Abraham my friend"; v. 10, "Fear thou not; for I am with thee: be not dismayed; for I am thy God: I will strengthen thee; yea, I will help thee; yea, I will uphold thee with the right hand of my righteousness." So it was in effect promised in the revelations that were made to Mary and Joseph, Zechariah, etc.; and so to Himself in answer to His prayers, by a voice from heaven, "I have both glorified it, and will glorify it again" [John 12:28]; and so probably by Moses and Elias in the mount, and by the voice from heaven there; and by the angel strengthening Him in answer to His prayer in His agony. It appears by this that all was certain beforehand, by God's actually saving great numbers beforehand, on the ground of his future perseverance in his work.

796. CHURCH IN HEAVEN IN A PROGRESSIVE PREPARATORY STATE. 'Tis a wrong idea some seem to have of the heavenly world, as if it so differed from the visible world with respect to its constancy, that the state of things were, as it were, immovable and immutable; whereas there is no reason to suppose but that 'tis a world wherein are many and great changes or, as it were, revolutions. It has heretofore been a world of probation, and where multitudes have sinned and fallen and passed under the greatest imaginable change; and though now we have reason to think that it is subject to no evil changes, yet 'tis subject to great changes and revolutions of the contrary nature. How great a change will it pass under at the day of judgment, when all the saints shall be there with their glorified bodies; and there is no reason to think that before that it passes under no great

changes. 'Tis God only that is unchangeable. The whole universe, consisting in upper and lower worlds, is in a changing state, especially before the consummation of all things at the day of judgment.

797. That there is No Good Work Before Conversion, and actual union with Christ, is manifest from that, Rom. 7:4, "Wherefore, my brethren, ye also are become dead to the law by the body of Christ; that ye should be married unto another, even to him who is raised from the dead, that we should bring forth fruit unto God." Hence we may argue that there is no lawful child brought forth before that marriage. Seeming virtues and good works before, are not so indeed; they are a spurious brood, being bastards and not children. Essential difference between common and saving grace.

798. The Necessity of Christ's Satisfaction. Add this to [No.] 779.[6] If the threatening of death be not executed, the devil's horrid suggestion and our first parents' vile suspicion, will be verified and fulfilled; viz. that God said otherwise than what he knew when he threatened, "Thou shalt surely die." See further, No. 915.

799. Perseverance. Concerning the objection from Ezekiel. God's saying in Ezek 18:24, "if the righteous shall fall from his righteousness, and commit iniquity, all his righteousness shall not be remembered; but in his iniquity that he hath done, shall he die," and the like, don't at all prove that 'tis supposed to be possible that a truly righteous man should fall from his righteousness; any more than God's saying, Lev. 18:4–5, "Ye shall do my judgments, and keep mine ordinances, to walk therein: I am the Lord your God. Ye shall therefore keep my statutes, and my judgments: which if a man do, he shall live in them"; and in Ezek. 20:11, "And I gave them my statutes, and showed them my judgments, which if a man do, he shall even live in them"; and the same, vv. 13 and 21; and to the same purpose, ch. 18, v. 22, the next verse but one before that whence the objection is taken, "In his righteousness that he hath done he shall live." These two assertions are again joined together in Ezek. 33:18–19. I say, what is said in the forementioned place no more proves it to be possible for a truly righteous man to fall from righteousness, so as to die in his iniquity, than these places prove that 'tis possible for a man to do those

6. MS: "last page of that number, at this mark." JE's cue marks indicate that he intended this entry to be inserted immediately prior to the last full paragraph of No. 779. See above, p. 448.

things required in God's statutes and judgments, so as to live in them, or to perform righteousness, so that in the righteousness that he hath done, he shall live. But these last mentioned places do not prove that it is possible for a man to do righteousness, and the things required in God's statutes, so as to live in them, by the express sentence of the Apostle, when speaking of those very passages of the Old Testament, Rom. 10:5 and Gal. 3:12. The truth concerning both these assertions of the Old Testament seems to be that they are proposed to us as signifying and containing diverse verities, and for a diverse use in application to ourselves.

1. For wise ends they are proposed to us, as supposing something that is (though not in itself yet) in the present state of things impossible; to declare the certain connection of the impossible thing supposed with something else. So that all that is taught is the certain connection between the antecedent and the consequent; but it is not taught that the antecedent shall ever be, or that it ever can be. So the Scripture in saying, "He that doth these things shall live by them," don't design to teach us that in the present state of things it is possible for us to do these things in a legal sense (in which sense the words are certainly proposed, as the Apostle teaches), but only teaches the certain connection there is between doing these things and living in them, for wise ends; particularly to lead us by such a legal proposal to see our utter inability to obtain life by our own doings, so the law is our schoolmaster to bring us to Christ.

Especially was it proper that those things should both be proposed, the one to be earnestly sought, though impossible to be obtained; and the other to be carefully avoided, though impossible to be fallen into under the old testament, when the impossibility of either the one or the other [was] not so clearly and fully revealed, as now under the gospel. So also the Scripture in saying "if the righteous shall fall away from his righteousness, he shall die" don't teach us that in the present state of things since the fall, 'tis possible for a truly righteous man to fall from his righteousness; but only teaches us the certain connection between the antecedent and the consequent, for wise ends, and particularly that those that think themselves righteous may beware of falling from righteousness. For 'tis not unreasonable to suppose that God should put us on bewaring of those things that are already impossible, any more than that he should direct us to seek and pray for those things, that are promised and certain.

2. In another way both these things are proposed more evangelically, as having respect to that doing those things, and that falling from righteousness, that are possible, viz. doing those things in an evangelical and believing obedience, which in strictness is not a proper doing them; and

a falling from a visible and external, material righteousness or godliness, which is not in strictness a proper godliness. Concerning the former of these—concerning [the] doing those things—'tis certain both senses are to be taken in: the legal one, as is evident by the Apostle, and the evangelical, possible one must also be understood, as is plain from the context of those places of the Old Testament; and that we should so understand the latter is equally free of difficulty and objection.

800. SIGNS OF GODLINESS. Insert this, No. 790.[7] 'Tis the essence and life of faith that is doubtless principally intended by faith when spoken of as the condition of salvation, and is the most essential condition of salvation. But the apostle James teaches us that works is the life of faith; which signifies its working nature, and especially its working nature in act, in such exercise as it is in in producing good works (for this exercise, as was observed before, is the work itself so far as anything is the immediate work of the soul). 'Tis not only principles, but especially acts, that are the condition of salvation, for acts are the end of principles, and principles are in vain without 'em.

Add this at the end of No. 790.[8] And when the Apostle speaks of that perfect love that casts out fear, 'tis most agreeable to the style of Scripture to understand love that is perfect in this sense, viz. love that is so thorough and effectual as to appear in a readiness to devote ourselves to God, and his service, under all opposition and difficulties; a love that carries in it a conquest of the world, a renunciation of ourselves for God's sake, our own ease, our own appetites, etc.; and an heart to sell all for God. I John 2:3–6, "Whoso keepeth his commandments, in him verily is the love of God perfected." So love is made perfect by works, in the same sense in which the Apostle James says, Jas. 2:22, "By works was faith made perfect." This is the perfect love that casts out fear, that perfect spirit of adoption that casts out a spirit of bondage, as Sarah and Isaac cast out the bondwoman and her son. An inward feeling and consciousness of such victorious triumphant love as this, in the acts of its victory, does above all things tend to assure the heart of a good estate, and of a childlike relation to God. Such an inward sense and experience as this, is that which above all things

7. In the MS JE adds: "sixth page of that number." His cue marks indicate that he intended this paragraph to be inserted in the middle of the third to last paragraph of No. 790. See above, p. 486.

8. JE's cue marks indicate that he intended the following two paragraphs to consititute the final two paragraphs of No. 790. See above, p. 488.

naturally, and[9] as it were necessarily, disposes the soul to look on God, and go to God, as its Father, or to cry, "Abba, Father." Unless we are conscious within ourselves of this love conquering the flesh and the world, and of this conquest of love, our way will not be open; we shall not feel that entire boldness and confidence in approaching God as a Father.

This removes the objection against inward experience, as the witness of the Spirit, being the best evidence of a good estate, viz. that some men wicked in life would pretend that though they[1] han't evidence of holiness of life, yet they have that which is more certain, viz. the inward witness of the Spirit, the feeling of soul-assuring inward experience: because everyone can see the ridiculousness of a man's pretending that he feels such an all-conquering love, disposing him to sell all for God, and to adhere to him, and be devoted to his service through all temptation, yea, and experiences the actual conquest of this love in its trial; and yet at the same time lives in sin against God, and really yields to the flesh and the world as conquerors in the trial. Everybody has sense enough to see that this is just the same contradiction as to say that he lives holily, and strictly adheres to God in his practice under temptations, at the same [time] that he lives wickedly, and don't cleave to God, but forsakes him for the world.

801. DEACONS, their office. See sermon on Rom. 12:4–8, and Acts 6:1–3, and on Gen. 4:3–4, and on these words, "I will have mercy and not sacrifice" [Hos. 6:6].[2]

802. PROGRESS OF REDEMPTION. Add this to Discourse on Is. 51:8, sermon 18, at the end of the second particular, under the fourth general observation.[3] In these three great successive dispensations of providence, that are compared in Scripture to Christ's coming to judgment,

9. MS: "as."

1. MS: "that tho' that they."

2. On the MS JE notes that he delivered the sermon on Rom. 12:4–8 "on the occasion of the ordination of the deacons," which occurred on Aug. 9, 1739. The previous June he preached the sermon on Acts 6:1–3 that has the doctrine "that the main business of a deacon by Christ's appointments is to take care of the distribution of the church's charity, for the outward supply of those in need." The later addition of the reference to the sermon on Gen. 4:3–5 (Nov. 1743) is to a Thanksgiving sermon that also addresses the issue of charity; its doctrine states, "It has been a thing established in the church of Christ from the very beginning that his people should publicly offer up a part of their worldly subsistence to God as a part of the stated public service of his visible church." The MS of the sermon on Hos. 6:6 is not extant.

3. The 18th sermon of the series known as *A History of the Work of Redemption* contains a cross-reference that reads "See 'Miscell.' No. 802." For the location of the insertion, see *Works, 9*, 353, n. 3.

those things were done spiritually that in Christ's last coming will be done externally. In each of them Christ comes down from heaven spiritually, by his Holy Spirit and in the wonderful works of his providence, but[4] at the day of judgment he will come externally. In these preceding dispensations, Christ comes with multitudes of angels in a spiritual sense attending on him, and acting as his servants, ministers, and instruments of bringing to pass the glorious effects that attend him in each of those preceding dispensations, as Christ in them comes with a great number of gospel ministers, angels of the churches, fervent in spirit, serving him as instruments to bring to pass the effects of his coming. As at Christ's coming to judgment God "sends forth his angels with the great sound of the trumpet," or with some mighty sound made by them called the sound of the trumpet, thereby to "gather together the elect from the four winds, from one [end] of heaven to the other": so this is done mystically in those preceding dispensations in sounding the gospel trumpet, especially in that which ended in the destruction of Jerusalem (Matt. 24:31), and that which brings the fall of Antichrist and the destruction of Satan's visible kingdom on earth, when it is said "the great trumpet shall be blown" (Is. 27:13), which was typified by the trumpet of the Jubilee in Israel.

At the last judgment, at the sound of the trumpet, the dead are raised and the living changed. Both these things are represented by that spiritual change that is made in men at the sound of the gospel trumpet in those preceding dispensations. The change made in men's souls at the call of the gospel is "in a moment, or twinkling of an eye," as that will be [I Cor. 15:52]. It is a change of the soul from an earthly, carnal, dull, sluggish [state] to a spiritual, heavenly, active, vigorous state, in the image of Christ and likeness to him, as that will of the bodies of the saints; and 'tis a resurrection of their souls from death to life, as at the last trumpet the bodies of the saints will rise. As at the last judgment the elect shall literally be gathered together to Christ, from one end of heaven to the other, by the angels, which is compared to gathering in Christ's harvest (Matt. 13:30, and vv. 39–41), so in the preceding dispensation Christ's ministers do gather together the elect from one end of heaven to another, in a spiritual sense, as in Matt. 24:31; which kind of gathering is often in Scripture compared to Christ's harvest, and particularly that gathering in of the elect that will be at the time of the fall of Antichrist (Rev. 14:15–16). At the last judgment, when the trumpet has sounded, all the elect being risen

4. MS: "in."

and changed, shall mount up as with wings, shall leave this earth to go heavenwards, to meet Christ never to return to this earth anymore; so at the sounding of the gospel, souls being converted are weaned from the world, and caused as it were to soar aloft towards heaven, where Christ is never anymore to return to this world, but to be ever with the Lord. At the last judgment, the elect shall be seen flocking together in the air, in the region of the clouds, coming multitudes after multitudes, one mighty flock after another, appearing like a great cloud flowing together, to that place where Christ has fixed his throne, coming from all countries; so it is in a spiritual sense, at those preceding dispensations. Is. 60:8, "Who are these that fly as a cloud, and as doves to their windows?" This, [which] is spoken of these glorious times of the church spiritually, will be literally fulfilled at the day of judgment. Those remarkable seasons of the church are more like the day of judgment in that respect, than any other times that such multitudes are, as it were, raised from the dead, and brought home to Christ in so little a time: that the work is carried on so swiftly; that the earth does, as it were, "bring forth in one day" as it will at the day of judgment (Is. 66:8). In the beginning of those glorious days of the church, not only are multitudes of sinners converted, and so dead souls raised, but also saints are wonderfully renewed and altered, as at the day of judgment the dead shall be raised and the living changed. At the day of judgment Christ comes to the destruction of the wicked and to the salvation of the elect. So it is in those mystical comings of Christ; they issue in the great happiness of the elect, especially that at the fall of Antichrist—very much an image of their heavenly happiness—and in amazing destruction of the wicked (of which, see sermons on Is. 51:8 concerning those dispensations).[5] The last trumpet sounds to call reprobates to condemnation; so in those preceding dispensations, that preaching of the gospel that issues in the life and salvation of the elect, issues in the condemnation of reprobates. At the day of judgment reprobates will in a sense be raised to life, but it will be worse than no resurrection: for, indeed, it will be a resurrection to a more terrible death. So in those former dispensations, though many reprobates will have a kind of a conversion, multitudes of 'em are enlightened and converted from heathenism, Judaism, and popery, Mahometanism, and a state of visible spiritual death, to be visible Christians; yet it not being a real holy change, shall only issue in their far more dreadful death. The world at the day of judgment shall come to an end in an external sense, as it does in those preceding dispensations in a spiritual

5. See *Works, 9,* sermons 26–29, pp. 455–514.

sense. *See sermons.*[6] The everlasting kingdom of Christ is in each of these dispensations set up. See sermon 18.[7]

803. PROGRESS OF REDEMPTION. CHRIST'S COMING TO JUDGMENT. See [No.] 835. Join this to what is said concerning the state of things requiring Christ's coming to judgment at the time that he will come, in Discourse from Is. 51:8, sermon 28, the 3rd particular concerning the last apostasy.[8]

The wickedness of the world will be such at that [time], as immensely more to require Christ's immediate appearance in flaming fire, to take vengeance on his enemies, than ever before, by reason of the great light that the wicked world will then have sinned against, and their great apostasy. If the whole habitable world were full of people, as England is now, and all had as great light, and immensely greater than England has, but most of the world had apostatized from Christianity notwithstanding this great light, and had turned infidels as the deists in England have, and scoffed at Christianity as many of them do, and not only so, but persecuted the church, and were on a design of extirpating it from the earth, how much should we think that the state of things required that the world should be immediately destroyed by fire from heaven!

The world before the flood was in a state of great temporal prosperity; the earth was exceeding fertile, the air wholesome, men's lives very long. But they abused their prosperity by giving themselves up to their lusts. So Sodom, and the cities of the plain, also enjoyed exceeding great prosperity; their land was fertile as the garden of God, and it was well watered everywhere, and they also abused their prosperity. So also it will be a great time of outward prosperity, in the future glorious times of the church. "The plowman shall overtake the reaper, and the treader of grapes him that soweth seed; and the mountains shall drop sweet wine" (Amos 9:13). The earth shall then yield her increase. And it shall be a time of great health and prolongation of men's lives—Is. 33:24, "And the inhabitant shall not say, I am sick"—probably by a great improvement of the art of physic, and the discovery of new sovereign remedies for diseases, which have hitherto not been discovered, the discovery and use of which God has reserved for that time. And this prosperity they shall abuse as they did in the old world and in Sodom, as Luke 17:26–30.

6. Undoubtedly another reference to *A History of the Work of Redemption.* See *Works, 9.*

7. See *Works, 9,* 344–356.

8. This reference, a slightly later addition, is to the 28th sermon of *A History of the Work of Redemption,* which contains a cross-reference that reads "See 'Miscell.' No. 803." For the location of the insertion, see *Works, 9,* 491, n. 4.

Considering the great health, and long lives, and prosperity of the world for so long a time before, 'tis probable there may be an hundred times so many people then in the world, as are in it now, and most of these will be very presumptiously and contemptuously wicked, and all against such great light and mercies. How much, therefore, will the state of the world require Christ's immediate appearance, in the most visible signal manner of all, to vindicate his own cause.

God don't see meet to destroy all nations with flaming fire, till all nations have had the gospel preached to them. But when they have had it preached to them for so long a time together, in the fullest manner, and after all have apostatized and rejected the gospel, as growing sick and weary of it, then will the end come. By this means it will be so ordered, that when the inhabitants of the world see Christ coming to judgment, they will all know what it means, having[9] been instructed concerning Christ's coming. They will have had much warning of [it] beforehand; and especially a little before, the church will warn 'em of the approach of it from the word of God, as Noah warned the old world of the approach of the flood, and as Lot warned the inhabitants of Sodom of the approach of their destruction. And then they will actually have despised this person that they will see coming to judgment, and will have despised the warnings of his coming to judgment, being those scoffers that will say, "Where is the promise of his coming?" [II Pet. 3:4]. And therefore, this sight of Christ coming in the clouds of heaven will terribly smite their consciences. 'Tis the will of God not only that the world should far more universally have the gospel preached to 'em before its last and most dreadful destruction comes upon it, but also that it should be preached in a vastly fuller and clearer manner than ever yet it has been, with immensely greater light; and then, when the world have rejected the gospel, will it be ripe for its last destruction. The cluster of the vine of the earth will be fully ripe [Rev. 14:18]. See Discourse on Is. 51:8, sermon 28, 3rd particular concerning the last apostasy.[1]

804. SAINTS IN HEAVEN, in their present state of SEPARATION from the body, are acquainted with the STATE OF THE CHURCH ON EARTH. 'Tis manifest that the saints in heaven, holy martyrs and others, do behold and rejoice in the prosperity of Christ's church on earth, and do rejoice in the nations of the world, and the heathen, being brought under Christ, and

9. MS: "have."

1. This cross-reference, which repeats almost verbatim the instruction at the beginning of the entry, is a slightly later addition to the MS.

have a great share in this prosperity by that kind of union and communion that the Scripture reveals that they have with Christ. Christ beholds this prosperity of his church, for 'tis the prosperity of his kingdom. 'Tis all his glory, his victory; he is infinitely more concerned in it than any of the angels that minister in it, or any of the saints that are then on earth. 'Tis the joy that was set before him, for which he endured the cross. 'Tis given him as the reward of what he did and suffered in the work of redemption. But the saints in heaven are his disciples, his members, that are with him to behold the glory that God gives him to see, the reward that God bestows upon him; and not only so, but to partake in it, that his joy may be fulfilled in themselves. For that righteousness and those sufferings by which Christ purchased this reward is imputed to them; and therefore, they partake with the head in the reward itself, as at the last day they shall partake with him in that part of the joy that was set before [him], consisting in his judging the world, for they shall judge the world with him. So they do as much partake with him in those preceding glorious events, by which Christ's kingdom is set up in the world, and that are compared in Scripture to his last judgment of the world, and that are part of the joy set before him, as the glory of the last judgment is; and therefore, their reigning with Christ in those times of the church's prosperity, is promised to them in like manner, as their judging the world with him at the last day is promised to him. So it is said in the 20th chapter of Revelation, that they shall "reign with Christ a thousand years" [v. 4]. As they shall at the last day sit with Christ in his throne of judgment, judging the nations, so it is promised also that they shall sit with Christ in his throne of government, when he reigns over the nations. So in the second and third chapters of Revelation, Christ promises that they shall sit with him in his throne, and that he will give them power over the nations, that they shall rule over them with a rod of iron, etc., as he himself received of his Father [3:21, 2:26–27]. And the saints themselves greatly rejoice in that, and praise Christ for it, in the fourth chapter of Revelation, that they shall reign on earth. And so [is] it represented all along in the course of that prophecy in the Revelation, that the saints in heaven seem to be as nearly and immediately concerned in those glorious revolutions, as the saints on earth.

And how meet and suitable is it, and agreeable to the gospel scheme, that, as Christ's mediatorial glory, and that reward that he has for his own sufferings and righteousness, is progressive and is bestowed and advanced in various successive steps and degrees, is given first in a degree in his resurrection, and then in a far more glorious degree in his ascension, and then still in a yet far more glorious degree in that first great dispensation that is in Scripture called Christ's coming in his kingdom; which was in the days of the apostles beginning with the pouring out of the Holy Ghost at Pentecost, and ending with the destruction of Antichrist, and is advanced much higher still at the second great dispensation of providence that is called his coming in his kingdom, viz. that in the days of Constantine the Great, and much higher still at the third dispensation so called, viz. that at the destruction of Antichrist, and at last vastly higher still, at the day of judgment: I say, how reasonable is it to suppose that the glory of the church in heaven, that part of the mystical body of Christ that is with him, reigning with him, and who are partaking of his reward, and whose glory and happiness is all a reward of the same righteousness, should be advanced by like steps and degrees, at the same time, and in the same dispensations of providence. See, concerning Ezekiel's wheels, "Scripture" no. 391, corol.[2]

805. MISERY OF DEVILS AND SEPARATE SOULS IS PROGRESSIVE, as well as the happiness of the separate souls of saints, and is advanced at the same time and by like degrees. As each extraordinary advancement of the prosperity of God's church on earth is attended with proportionable terrible judgments on the enemies of God and his church in this world, so those judgments on those that are of Satan's kingdom on earth have been attended with dreadful judgments on Satan and those that are of his kingdom in hell, in like manner as the prosperity of Christ's church and kingdom on earth have been attended with an advancement of glory to Christ, and those that are of his church and kingdom in heaven, even the saints and angels there. Thus when God redeemed his people out of Egypt, and executed judgments on the church's enemies on earth, at the same time he executed judgments on the gods of Egypt, who were the devils of hell. Ex. 12:12, "For I will pass through the land of Egypt this night, and I will smite all the firstborn in the land of Egypt, both man and beast; and against all the gods of Egypt will I execute judgment: I am the Lord." So Num. 33:4. So when God overthrew Pharaoh and his host in the Red Sea, God is said to have broken the heads of the dragons in the waters, to have broken the heads of leviathan in pieces [Ps. 74:13–14], not only that Pharaoh, a type of the dragon, was destroyed, but also that terrible judgments were then executed on the devil himself. So on the destruction of Babylon, and the deliverance of the church from the Babylonish captiv-

---

2. "Notes on Scripture" no. 391 discusses Ezek. 1; its corollary includes a cross-reference to "Miscellanies" No. 804 (*Works, 15*, 385–86).

ity, God executed judgments on the idols and gods of Babylon (Is. 21:9, 46:1–2, Jer. 50:2). Jer. 51:44, "And I will punish Bel in Babylon, and I will bring forth out of his mouth that which he hath swallowed up." So on the birth of Christ the devil's misery is increased. Hence the oracle at Delphos, when inquired of why it ceased to give answers, answered that an Hebrew boy that was king of the gods had commanded [it] to be gone thence to hell. See Millar's *History of the Propagation of the Gospel*.[3] And so in those glorious revolutions that are mentioned in the book of Revelation, 'tis all along represented as though judgments were then executed on the devil. Hence no wonder that he so dreads and opposes the accomplishment of those glorious revolutions.

And not only is the misery of the devils in hell greatly increased at those times, but also the misery of damned souls, especially those that had been, when on earth, the greatest enemies and opposers of the church, and the chief instruments of the devil. At the destruction of particular kingdoms of the devil, those wicked souls will especially have their torment increased that have been before the chief instruments of the devil, and opposers of the church in that kingdom; as at the destruction of the heathen Roman Empire in the days of Constantine the Great, we may suppose that the misery of the souls of persecuting emperors, and other persecutors that had been dead before, was greatly increased; as those SAINTS will especially have their HAPPINESS INCREASED at that time, that were the greatest defenders of Christ's cause against that opposition, and were the greatest sufferers in it; as it will also be at the destruction of Antichrist "the souls of those that were beheaded for the witness of Jesus, and for the word of God, and which had not worshipped the beast, nor his image, neither had received his mark in their foreheads, nor in their hands, lived and reigned with Christ a thousand years" (Rev. 20:4).

So at the fall of Antichrist the [misery of the] separate souls of persecuting popes, and other popish persecutors, shall especially be increased;

3. Robert Millar, *A History of the Propagation of Christianity, and the Overthrow of Paganism. Wherein the Christian Religion is Confirmed. The rise and progress of heathenish idolatry is considered. The overthrow of paganism, and the spreading of Christianity in the several ages of the church is explained. The present state of heathenism is inquired into; and methods for their conversion proposed* (2 vols. Edinburgh, 1723). Millar notes that during the "first Ages of the Christian Church . . . The Heathen Oracles were struck dumb; the famous Oracle at *Delphos*, which both *Greeks* and *Romans* consulted at or before our Saviour's Incarnation, Had lost its Reputation, and Began to cease to give any Answers." His authority for this fact is Suidas, to whom he attributes the verse: "A Hebrew Boy who reigns in Heavens high, / To leave these Altars, hath Commanded me, / And pack to Hell, to silence and Wo; / Then therefore silent from our Altars go" (ch. III, pp. 473–74). JE used this comment about the silencing of the oracles in *A History of the Work of Redemption* (*Works*, 9, 392).

which is one thing meant by the beast's being then "cast into the lake that burns with fire and brimstone" [Rev. 20:10]. And on this account the times of those great dispensations of providence are the more fitly compared to the day of judgment, when devils and wicked souls shall have their misery so greatly increased, and the saints their reward so increased.

806. NEW HEAVENS AND NEW EARTH. It was proper and natural, considering the nature and end of Christ's redemption, to represent that new state of things that the saints shall enjoy by Christ's redemption as a new heaven and a new earth: for Christ came to restore all things, and that in him there might be a remedy for every calamity that came by the fall. One calamity that was the consequence of the fall was the dissolution of the body. There is in Christ a remedy for this calamity; the body is through him restored, and comfort is administered to the saints against the apprehensions of it, by the promises of the resurrection. Another calamity that comes by the fall is the dissolution of heaven and earth, our dwelling place. The remedy that is promised in Christ is a new heaven and a new earth, a new and much better habitation and state of things, instead of it; and this is the comfort we have by Christ against this sorrow. This restoration is equivalent to a resurrection of heaven and earth, and is more than a mere restoration: for it shall be a far more glorious state of things, not only than is immediately before the dissolution or conflagration, but more glorious than the state of the world was before the fall, as the resurrection of the bodies of the saints is more than a mere restitution. For the body shall [not] only return to life, but to a much more glorious state than it was in before its dissolution, yea, a much more glorious state than the body of man was in before the fall; for it shall not be conformed to the body of the first Adam, which was a natural body, but to the body of Christ, which is a spiritual body (see I Cor. 15:44–49). Hence this new state of things is called a new heaven and a new earth. Christ came to restore all things with respect to the elect that, whatever there is of the ruinous effects of the fall through the whole universe, all might be fully and perfectly healed in Christ; that old things might pass away and all things become new; that man himself might be a new *creature*, both in his soul by conversion and sanctification, and in his body by the resurrection, and the world as to him might become a new *creation;* and so not only himself created anew in Christ Jesus, but everything created anew as to him fully and perfectly. Rev. 21:5, "Behold, I make all things new." Hence the end of the world, when this shall be perfected, is called the "times of refreshing" and the "times of restitution of all things" (Acts 3:19–21).

Christ came to restore all things only with respect to the elect. The bodies of the wicked will not be restored from the calamity and ruin it fell under by the fall. And so the world, as to the wicked, which are far the greater number, will not be restored; but with respect to the elect, it will be restored, for they shall receive a new heaven and a new earth, instead of it. If this individual world belonged to the elect as much as their bodies, then would it be requisite that this individual world should be restored, as well as their bodies. But this is not the world that properly belongs to them. This is not their native world. 'Tis not the land of the church. They are not of the world. They ben't the men of this world, but heaven is their country. The world as to them is to be restored: for they are to be delivered from all the evil of it, all the calamity that came by the evil state and course of it, and are to be more than restored to all the comfort and benefit they had by its first perfect state. Everything in the whole universe is to be new as to them, and to be as well, and better, than if there never had been any sin.

807. WORK OF REDEMPTION THE GREATEST OF GOD'S WORKS. God, who doth all things in amiable harmony, hath been pleased to put so much greater honor and dignity on the new creation than he did the old, that, whereas the old heavens and earth were finished in about six days, he spends on the new all the time from Christ's resurrection to the end of the world; which we may well suppose to be at least 3,000 years, besides 4,000 years before spent in making preparation for it. See Discourse on Is. 51:8, first inference at the close of sermon 29.[4]

808. JUSTIFICATION by faith alone. PERSEVERANCE OF FAITH, how the condition of justification. That the perseverance of faith is necessary to a congruity to salvation. For it is implied in several places of Scripture, that if true believers should fail of a persevering in faith they would[5] therein fail of a title to salvation, or a state of salvation, and would be in a lost state. John 18:8–9, "Jesus answered, I have told you that I am he: if therefore ye seek me, let these go their way: that the saying might be fulfilled, which he spake, Of them which thou gavest me have I lost none"; i.e. Christ took care that they might go away, that they might not be in the way of such temptation as would be in danger of overthrowing them, so that they should not persevere. And it is implied that if they were overthrown, and

4. This inference states, "Hence we may learn how great a work the Work of Redemption is"; see *Works*, 9, 510–14.
5. MS: "were."

should not persevere, Christ would have lost them; the saving relation that they stood in to Christ would have been dissolved. The same seems fully implied in Christ's prayer in the 17th chapter of John. Thus he makes use not only of their having received God's word, and believed that God had sent him, but their having kept his word, as a good plea for their title to that favor and acceptance of the Father, which he asks of the Father for them, as vv. 6–10. The same is implied in the 11th verse, "Holy Father, keep through thine own name those whom thou hast given me, that they may be one, as we are." This implies that their being one, or their standing in a saving relation to him, and [in] union with his mystical body, depends on the perseverance of their faith, even that union on which a title to all spiritual and saving benefits depends; which is more fully spoken of in the 21st and following verses. This perseverance of believers seems to be the benefit that is the principal subject of this whole prayer. And in Luke 22:31 'tis implied that if Peter's faith had failed Satan would have had him. Luke 22:31–32, "And the Lord said, Simon, Simon, Satan hath desired to have you, that he may sift you as wheat: but I have prayed for thee, that thy faith fail not." I Pet. 1:5, "Who are kept by the power of God through faith unto salvation"; where it seems implied that if they were not kept through faith, or if their faith did not persevere, they would never come to salvation.

So believers being overthrown in their faith, or their [not] knowing Christ's voice and following him, is called a being plucked out of Christ's hand; and it is implied that the consequence would be their perishing. And it also seems to be implied [that] their possession to eternal life by Christ's gift depends on their perseverance. John 10:27–28, "My sheep hear my voice, and I know them, and they follow me: and I give unto them eternal life; and they shall never perish, neither shall any pluck them out of my hand." And in the 15th chapter of John, believers persevering in faith in Christ, or their abiding in him, is spoken of as necessary to the continuance of the saving union and relation that is between Christ and believers, and Christ's abiding in them; as vv. 4–5, "Abide in me and I in you. As the branch cannot bear fruit of itself, except it abide in the vine; no more can ye, except ye abide in me. I am the vine, ye are the branches. He that abideth in me, and I in him, the same bringeth forth much fruit." And in the sixth verse it is spoken of as the necessary consequence of their not abiding in Christ, if that were possible, that the union should be utterly broken between Christ and them, and that damnation should be the consequence. "If a man abide not in me, he is cast forth as a branch, and is withered; and men gather them, and cast them into the fire, and they are burned." And in the seventh verse this perseverance of faith is spoken of as the necessary means of the success of faith, as expressed in prayer, which is faith's voice, necessary to obtain those good things that faith and prayer seek. "If ye abide in me, and my words abide in you, ye shall ask what ye will, and it shall be done unto you." And in the ninth and tenth verses it is implied that Christ's acceptance of us, and favor to us as his, depends on our perseverance. "As the Father hath loved me, so have I loved you: continue ye in my love. If ye keep my commandments, ye shall abide in my love; even as I have kept my Father's commandments, and abide in his love." So the same perseverance is spoken of as necessary to our continuing in the favor and grace of God. "Now when the congregation was broken up, many of the Jews and religious proselytes followed Paul and Barnabas: who, speaking to them, persuaded them to continue in the grace of God" [Acts 13:43]. And so it is spoken [of] as necessary to continuing in the goodness of God, and a being cut off is spoken of as the certain consequence of the contrary. Rom 11:22, "Behold therefore the goodness and severity of God: on them which fell, severity; but towards thee, goodness, if thou continue in his goodness: otherwise thou also shalt be but off." That expression of standing fast IN THE LORD (I Thess. 3:8 and Philip. 4:1) implies that perseverance is necessary to a continuing in Christ, or in a saving relation to him; and more plainly still in I John 2:24, "Let that therefore abide in you, which ye have heard from the beginning. If that which ye have heard from the beginning shall remain in you, ye also shall continue in the Son, and in the Father." See I Cor. 15:2, and II Tim. 4:7–8, and Heb. 12:28. See Jer. 3:19.

809. HEAVEN is not the promise of the FIRST COVENANT WITH ADAM, but is only the promise of the covenant of grace, and the inheritance which is alone by the purchase of Christ. For no more is promised in the covenant made with Adam than is some way implied in what God said to Adam, as we have an account of the covenant in the Word of God; but all that is implied is that man's life should be perpetuated, and the happy circumstances of it on eating the fruit of the tree of life. There is not a word tending to lead Adam to a thought of another unseen world. And if God did not by anything he said lead him to expect it, then it is certain that he did not promise it and make it over to him by covenant. If there had been any such promise in that covenant on condition of Adam's perfect obedience, it must have been to the end that Adam might have it before him as an enforcement of the commandment God had given, and to encourage him to perform the condition of the covenant. Promises and threat-

enings are enforcements of laws to which they are annexed, and engagements to a performance of the condition of covenants they belong to; but if Adam had nothing said to him tending to lead him to an expectation of heaven on his perfect obedience, it is impossible that the performance of this condition should be enforced by it.

Adam, our first head, was a native of this world; he was of the earth, earthly. And if he had stood he would have obtained eternal happiness here in his own country for himself [and] all his earthly posterity. But Christ, our second head, is one that properly belongs to heaven; he is the Lord from heaven, and the happiness he obtains by his obedience for himself and his spiritual posterity is eternal blessedness in his country, even heaven. The Apostle, speaking of our being conformed to Christ in glory at the resurrection, and of our natural body and spiritual body, says, I Cor. 15:44–45, "It is sown a natural body; it is raised a spiritual body. There is a natural body, and there is a spiritual body. And so it is written, The first Adam was made a living soul; the last Adam was made a quickening spirit." The Apostle is here speaking of what the first Adam was made in his state of innocency, and goes on in the 47th [to] 49th verses, "The first man is of the earth, earthy: the second man is the Lord from heaven. As is the earthy, such are they also that are earthy: and as is the heavenly, such are they also that are heavenly. And as we have born the image of the earthy, we shall also bear the image of the heavenly." Thus the Apostle shows in this place how the posterities of the two Adams shall be conformed to the state of their respective heads. And what he is speaking of here is not our conformity to the first Adam in the state whereinto he fell, though he had spoken of that before, but our conformity to him in that state wherein he was made. And therefore, if he had never fallen, we should have been conformed to him in these respects. We should have dwelt in natural earthy bodies, though in the most perfect state of such bodies, and without sin. So we should, by a parity of reason, have been conformed to him in the place of his habitation. The first Adam was earthy and of the earth in respect to the place of the habitation of his person, in the world he was of and belonged to, as well as in the habitation of his soul, or the body that [he] dwelt in; and in both we should have been conformed to him. And so in both Christ's posterity are conformed to him. He is from heaven and is heavenly in both these respects. He dwells in an heavenly body, and heaven is his proper country and dwelling place; and in both these respects his posterity shall be conformed to him. They shall have spiritual heavenly bodies, and shall dwell in heaven; and they would have had neither of these had it not been for the redemption of Jesus

Christ. New bodies and the new world are both of them [to] be by the redemption of Jesus Christ (see No. 806). The new sort of bodies which the
saints will have, viz. their spiritual and heavenly bodies, whereby they are
fitted to dwell in heaven, which they will have by the resurrection or that
change that passed on the bodies of the living, this change of the body
shall be only by the second Adam in distinction from the first, as the Apostle is very express and full, I Cor. 15:22, and vv. 44–52. But if Adam and
his posterity would have been translated to heaven for his perfect obedience, then doubtless their natural bodies must have passed under this
change, and made spiritual and heavenly: for as the Apostle says, v. 50,
"Flesh and blood shall not inherit the kingdom of God"; and then this
would have been by the first Adam, which is quite contrary to the doctrine
of the Apostle. And the new world, or the new heavens and new earth, is
as much by the redemption of Jesus Christ as the new body (see No. 806).
But this—so far as a place of habitation is meant—is heaven. This world
don't pass away but by a dissolution occasioned by the fall. And therefore,
mankind would not have ascended and left this world, for if they had so
done, this world would have passed away without a fall. One reason why
heaven is bestowed is because this world is ruined by the fall, and is to be
destroyed; therefore, Christ will come and take away his elect to another
world, a better world than this is, or ever was.

'Tis said, John 3:13, "No man hath ascended up to heaven, but he that
came down from heaven, even the Son of man which is in heaven"—
where Christ's coming down from heaven, and his properly belonging to
that country, seems to be spoken of as the proper ground of man's ascending up to heaven. And therefore, if one of mankind, even the head
of elect mankind, had not belonged to heaven and come from thence, no
man would ever have ascended up to heaven. None ever ascended to
Christ but Christ himself and his members. None ever ascended to heaven
but mystical Christ, and there is no way of any others' ascending to heaven
but by being members of him. We are made to sit together (i.e. with Christ
Jesus) in heavenly places, in Christ; and it is the only way that men come
to sit in heavenly places, even by being in Christ, and having communion
with him.

'Tis only the promise of the covenant of grace to sit down with Christ
in his throne, as he is set down with his Father in his throne. This benefit
is obtained only by Christ's purchase: for Christ obtained it for himself,
to sit in that throne, by his purchase that he made, by that victory that he
obtained (Rev. 3:21). And therefore 'tis only by the purchase of Christ that
men go, or ever would have gone, to heaven, which is Christ's throne.

The only way that ever has been contrived for the gathering together angels and men into one society, and one place of habitation, is by Christ. Eph. 1:10, "That in the dispensation of the fullness of times he might gather together in one all things in Christ, both which are in heaven, and which are on earth; even in him."

Corol. 1. Hence we may learn how vastly HIGHER and more glorious the happiness is that is purchased for the elect by Christ, than that which Adam would have obtained if he had stood. We have now shown how it is so with respect to the place of habitation: instead of the glory of an earthly paradise, there is purchased the glory of the heaven of heavens; instead of the earth that is the habitation of men, they shall have heaven, the palace and throne of the most high God; and without doubt the difference will be proportionable in other respects. The happiness that is by Christ is as much above what would have been by Adam, as heaven is high above the earth. We should have had the happiness of men by Adam, but by Jesus Christ, who is a divine person, we are brought to partake in a sort of the very happiness of God himself: for our fellowship is with the Father and with his Son Jesus Christ, in heaven the place of the residence of God's glory. Little did the devil think of any such thing as this being the consequence of man's fall when he said, "Ye shall be as gods" [Gen. 3:5].

Corol. 2. This shows how SATAN WILL BE DEFEATED. For not only will his temptation prove an occasion of man's being advanced so much higher in glory, and of verifying that "ye shall be as gods", which was intended by him as a mere illusion; but it proves an occasion of man's being advanced to that very world of glory from which he fell. Satan, by what he does for the destruction and misery of man, is an occasion, instead of their being eternally ruined, of their being advanced from the comparatively low state of happiness they were in then, to fill up the place in heaven that he was cast out from. He is cast down from his high seat of glory in heaven, and men, that he envied and destroyed, are taken in his room; and what he does against [them] to destroy them is made an occasion of bringing it about.

Corol. 3. Hence we may see one reason why it is fit why the new covenant should so differ from the old: that FAITH that believes, and looks to, and receives things invisible and of another world, should be the great CONDITION of the COVENANT OF GRACE.

Corol. 4. Hence we may see a reason why all things in the evangelical constitution should be so spiritual, and not savoring of the things of this world; why Christ did not appear in earthly glory; why his kingdom is not of this world, nor is to be managed by worldly means; why mortification is so much required in Christians; and why the state of the church for the most part is a state of such suffering.

Corol. 5. That heaven is not the promise of the first covenant but is the peculiar promise of the covenant of grace, and that the NEW HEAVENS AND NEW EARTH, so far as a place of habitation is meant by 'em, are heaven and not this lower world, are doctrines that strengthen and establish one another. I have shown how the heavenly world being the new heaven and new earth, is an argument that heaven is only by the redemption [of Christ]; and from this truth, viz. that heaven is only by the purchase of Christ, as it is established by other arguments, we may strongly argue that the place of the eternal abode of the church of Christ shall not be this lower world refined, but the highest heavens, the country that Christ has purchased for them, the land of the promise of the covenant of grace; wherein lies one great difference between the covenant of grace and the first covenant made with Adam.

810. SCRIPTURES of the Old Testament, why constituted of such parts; and particularly, why such a book as the book of JOB is inserted. Add this at the end of No. 359.[6] Seeing the church of God in this world is in a militant state, and 'tis so appointed of God that his people should through much tribulation enter into the kingdom of heaven, and especially seeing that it was appointed of God that the church of Christ should for so long a time be for the most part in a state of great trouble, in an afflicted and travailing state, even from the resurrection of Christ till the fall of Antichrist, and great part of this time under those troubles that are very extreme, how much does the wisdom of God appear in giving his church such a book as the book of Job, written on occasion of the great and sore affliction of a particular eminent saint. God's people in no circumstances do more stand in need of revelation from God than when in dark times, or in times of great affliction and distress; then especially do the saints need some revelation from God to instruct them that when chastened they may be taught out of God's law. The saints, in such circumstances especially, are ready to be confounded in their minds, as appears in Job and the Psalmist. They then stand in extraordinary need of a revelation from God to comfort and strengthen [them]. Christ, himself the head of the church, when in his agony especially stood in need of a revelation from God; and therefore then there was sent an angel from heaven strengthening him. 'Tis therefore a great instance of the fatherly mercy

6. For the location of the addition, see *Works*, *13*, 433.

and tenderness of God towards his church that he has given one book of divine revelation on purpose to instruct them and direct them, strengthen and comfort them, under such circumstances. This book is exceedingly fitted for these ends. The circumstances of Job are very agreeable to the afflicted circumstances of the church. They were from the envy and malignity of the devil, as the afflictions of the church are. He was deprived of all his substance, all the comfortable possessions of this life, and was called to part with all his nearest and dearest friends, as Christians are called to forsake houses and lands, wife and children. Job had none to stand by him. All that formerly used to be friendly to him now forsook him. Their love was turned into hatred, and their honor into contempt, as it is with the little flock of Christ in times of persecution, and as it very often is with particular saints that will steadfastly adhere to Christ, and follow the Lamb whethersoever he goes. The wife of his bosom forsook [him]; as he says, his "breath was strange unto his wife" [19:17]. So Christ tells us it should be with his people; a man's enemies should be those of his own house. His wife proved a tempter to him; she tempted him no longer to hold his integrity, but "to curse God and die" [2:9]. Thus it very commonly is with God's people in time of persecution; wives and other dear friends will hang about them to persuade them to forsake the cause of God, and they must violently break off from them if they would hold fast their integrity. Job was accused of the devil before God, as being an hypocrite; so the devil is the accuser of the brethren, and accuses them before God day and night in the time of the church's afflicted state. The devil exercised Job with sore and grievous torments of body; so he does the church in times of her persecution. Job was the object of great derision; so are God's people. Job was looked upon as an hypocrite and enemy of God; so it is with God's people in time of persecution. He was so esteemed and treated by those that used to be his friends and brethren, as Christ was ill treated by his own familiar friends. So God's saints, in their suffering state, are treated by those that used to be God's people, and so their friends. Thus the apostles and primitive Christians were treated by the Jews, that formerly had been God's people. So afterwards the saints are treated by the church of Rome, that formerly used to be of the church of God. Job's friends make use of that as a great argument, that God was not his friend, that he did not protect and deliver him, but saw such terrible calamities come upon him without relieving him. So did the Jews make use of the same argument against Christ, and so have the persecutors of the church all along pleaded against the people of God. The infirmity of human nature, with its sinful

corruption, under sore affliction is livelily represented in Job. And yet
there is also livelily represented in him the integrity and perseverance of
true saints through their greatest trials, by God's help. Job was under all
[trials] very dear to God. God had not forsaken him, nor had he taken
his faithfulness away from him, though he seemed for a while so to hide
his face from him, and set him as his mark; so is it with God's afflicted
church. And God at last delivered Job out of trouble, as he also will his
church. His deliverance was preceded by God's sending Elihu as his messenger, and as God's forerunner, to preach to him and his three friends,
and to reprove them, and teach them the mind and will of God. So the
deliverance of the Christian church will be preceded by God's raising up
a number of eminent ministers that shall more plainly and fervently and
effectually preach the gospel than it had been before, and reprove his
own church, and show her her errors, and also shall convince gainsayers,
and shall thoroughly detect the errors of the false church; as Elihu did
of Job's three friends, who though they were godly men, yet were in this
matter false friends. (See how [the] everlasting gospel is preached just
before the fall of Antichrist, Rev. 14:6–8.) Elihu was God's forerunner;
so before the end of the church's suffering state shall there be those
raised up that shall come in the spirit and power of Elias, going before
the Lord to prepare his way. Before Job was delivered, God appeared
greatly to humble [him], and make him sensible of his infinite greatness
and sovereignty, and his own nothingness, blindness, and unworthiness.
So before God delivers his church from her suffering state, he will appear by the pouring [out] of a remarkable spirit of conviction and, it may
be, also in terrible providences, as God appeared to Job in a whirlwind,
abundantly to convince his professing people of their meanness, empti-
ness, blindness, and sinfulness, and his sovereignty and greatness; which
the church now exceedingly needs, her greatest error being her being
so insensible of these things, and her[7] entertaining so may conceits to
the contrary of these things.

Job lost his children under his sufferings. So the church in her persecuted state loses her children by the storm of persecution; they are put to
death. Especially in the times of Antichrist has the church been bereaved
of her children, and brought to be very solitary, being reduced to very
strait limits. Job lost his servants. The Chaldeans, the people that were subject to Babylon, fell upon them and slew them with the edge of the sword.
So the church is bereaved of her ministers. Christ mystical loses his ser-

7. MS: "are."

vants; they are slain with the sword of the spiritual Chaldeans, and under the persecutions of the spiritual Babylon.

God in the end brought Job to a state of glorious prosperity. The hearts of all were wonderfully turned to him, and all liberally contributed of their substance to comfort and enrich and adorn him with silver and gold and jewels (Job 42:11). So shall God at the close of the church's suffering state wonderfully turn the hearts of men to her, who shall in like manner abundantly contribute of their wealth to enrich and adorn her; as appears by many passages in Isaiah. God gave Job much more than he had before his affliction; so Christ has promised that they that forsake fathers, and mothers, and houses, and lands, etc., shall have in this life an hundred-fold (see note on the place [Matt. 19:29]).[8] And so shall it be in the glorious times of the church. This prosperity continued to Job a long time; so shall the future prosperity of the church be long continued.

Because this instance of Job is so wonderfully accommodated to the circumstances of the Christian church in its afflicted state, and adapted for her instruction and comfort, therefore the Apostle recommends this instance to the consideration of the church in this afflicted state for these ends. Jas. 5:11, "Behold, we count them happy which endure. Ye have heard of the patience of Job, and have seen the end of the Lord; that the Lord is very pitiful, and of tender mercy."

'Tis probable the time that this book was first given to the church of Israel was either the time of their affliction in Egypt, which was a type of the suffering state of the Christian [church] under Rome, or the time of their travail in the wilderness, a type of the same afflicted state of the church, wherein she is represented as the woman in the wilderness; and that Moses either wrote the book in Midian, or brought it thence with him, written by another, to his own people in Egypt, or else it was brought to him in the wilderness by Jethro, or written by Moses there. And so the time of its being first given to the church of Israel agrees with that which I have supposed to be the special design of the book. See further, [No.] 878.

Another end of inserting this book into the canon of the Old Testament might be that the church of God might thereby have some view of the ancient theology that the church and people of God had before the giving of the Law at Mt. Sinai.

8. The "Blank Bible" note on Matt. 19:29 states, "How this argues that the saints in heaven share in the glory of the glorious things done for the church on earth, see 'Miscellanies' No. 811." For JE's discussion of this text, see the next entry, pp. 520–22.

811. SEPARATE SOULS OF SAINTS IN HEAVEN, acquainted with what is done on earth. Rev. 12:10, "And I heard a loud voice saying in heaven, Now is come salvation, and strength, and the kingdom of our God, and the power of his Christ: for the accuser of *OUR BRETHREN* is cast down, that accused them before God day and night." By this it appears that when there is mention made in this book (as there very often is) of the praises of the inhabitants in heaven, and great rejoicings among them on occasion of the glorious works of God towards his church on earth, that thereby is really intended the church in heaven, the assembly of saints and angels, as distinguished from the church on earth. For here the distinction is made: those that are here represented as rejoicing in heaven, praise God for the deliverance of the saints on earth, which they call their brethren. But it would hardly be thus represented time after time in this book, as though there were such great rejoicings and praises in heaven when glorious things were accomplished for the church on earth, if the church in heaven were not indeed sharers in the joy.

Again, the same may be argued from what God says in the book of Job of the hosts of heaven singing and shouting for joy when they saw the formation of this lower world [Job 38:6–7]. If they beheld the work of God in the old creation, and it was an occasion of great joy with them, much more may we suppose that they behold the work of God in the new creation, and greatly rejoice on occasion of the glorious progress of that work; which is so much more glorious, and wherein they are so much more concerned and employed as ministering spirits, and which is a work so much more nearly concerning the end of their creation, for they were made to be ministering spirits in this affair. And if they behold these works, we may argue that so do the saints in heaven also that are of the same worshipping, praising, and rejoicing society with them, and are those that are received into that society to fill up the gap that was made by the fall of some of them, and who are much more nearly concerned in this work of redemption than the angels, as being some of the subjects of it, and are more nearly related by far to the church on earth, being more properly of the same family and members of the same body.

Again, the same may be argued from Matt. 19:28–29. In the 28th [verse] 'tis promised to the disciples that hereafter "when the Son of man should sit on the throne of his glory, they should sit on twelve thrones, judging the twelve tribes of Israel"; which seems especially to relate to the glorious times of the church on earth after the fall of Antichrist, concerning which time the apostle John, one of those to whom Christ spake this, says in the 20th [chapter] of Revelation, that he "saw thrones, and them that sat upon them, and judgment was given unto them: and that they reigned with Christ a thousand years." Then shall the apostles, as it were, sit on twelve thrones, judging and reigning over God's church or spiritual Israel, in that glorious success that their doctrine shall then have to subdue the world, and govern the hearts of men. But what benefit will this be [to] them if they never see it, and never rejoice in it, as here 'tis promised to them as a reward, in such terms that tended to lead them to expect that it should be something that they should *ENJOY*, so doubtless it will be. And in the 29th verse 'tis said, "And every one that hath forsaken houses, or brethren, or sisters, or father, or mother, or wife, or children, or lands, for my name's sake, shall receive an hundred-fold, and shall inherit everlasting life." In [one of the] other Evangelists 'tis said that they "shall receive an hundred-fold in this time, and in the world to come everlasting life" [Mark 10:30]. Their receiving an hundred-fold of houses and lands, etc., has its accomplishment especially in the glorious times of the church on earth, when the meek shall inherit the earth, and shall reign on earth. 'Tis said in one [of the] Evangelists [Mark 10:30], "shall receive an hundred-fold with persecutions," i.e. they shall obtain the possession of this hundred-fold in a way of first suffering persecution. This argues that the saints in heaven shall enjoy the glory of those times, and shall properly have the possession of this hundred-fold of houses and lands, etc., and shall enjoy the inheritance of the earth.

So 'tis promised to Daniel [12:13] that he shall "stand in his lot" in the happy days of God's church, which seems to imply that he shall share in the glory of them.

So the promises made to Abraham, Isaac, and Jacob, and David of the glorious things God would bring to pass on earth in their posterity, doubtless implies that they should see the fulfillment of the promises, and should enjoy the glory and blessedness thereof. God would not make so much of promises that they were never properly to enjoy, or be the better of, any other way than in a thought of what would be long after they were dead, and which they should never see and enjoy. God is not the God of the dead but of the living; and when he fulfills promises that he has made he don't fulfill 'em to them that are dead, and wholly insensible of the fulfillment, and have no share in it, but to those that are alive to enjoy them, and know that they are accomplished. Therefore 'tis said in the 20th [chapter] of Revelation, of saints that had lived in former ages, that "they *LIVED* and reigned with Christ a thousand years." When God says to Moses, "I am the God of Abraham, and of Isaac, and of Jacob," whence Christ argues that he is "not the God of the dead but of the living" [Matt. 22:32], 'tis especially with respect to promises that God had made to them, glorious things to be accomplished to their seed on earth. Therefore, Christ's argument proves that they were alive to enjoy the fulfillment of these promises. See "Scripture," no. 381.[9]

812. JUSTIFICATION is not only PARDON of sin; and indeed it don't in strictness consist at all in pardon of sin, but in an act or sentence approving of him as innocent and positively righteous, and so having a right to freedom from punishment, and to the reward of positive righteousness. Pardon, as the word is used in other cases, signifies a forgiving one freely, though he is not innocent, or has no right to be looked on as such. There is nothing of his own he has to offer that is equivalent to innocence, but he justly stands guilty; but notwithstanding his guilt, he is freed from punishment. But the pardon we have by Christ is a freeing persons from the punishment of sin, as an act of justice, and because they are looked upon and accepted as having that which is equivalent to innocence, viz. satisfaction. 'Tis called pardon because, though in itself it be an act of justice, and strictly speaking the person pardoned has no sin or guilt to be pardoned, yet considered with those preceding free and sovereign acts of God that are its foundation, viz. the free gift of Christ, and the free establishment of the covenant of grace, the free giving us repentance and faith in Christ for remission, I say, considered with these things, 'tis a most free and wonderfully gracious act, and may well be called pardon.

What is done for a sinner on his repentance respecting sin consists in two things, viz. in accepting him as innocent, or as having that which is equivalent to innocence, and in establishing a freedom from punishment consequent upon it. But in strictness that in his justification which respects sin consists only in the former, viz. in accepting him as innocent or negatively just; and pardon most properly consists in the latter, viz. freeing him from punishment, which is consequent on the other: for freeing from punishment is consequent on satisfaction, or acquired innocence, for it depends on it as its foundation. Justification consists in imputing righteousness. To pardon sin is to cease to be angry for sin. But imputing righteousness and ceasing to be angry for sin are two things; one is the foundation of the other. God ceases to be angry with the sinner for his sin because righteousness is imputed to him.

Mere pardon can in no propriety be called justification. If one that is called before a judge, and is tried—whether he be guilty of such a crime,

9. This entry in "Notes on Scripture" discusses Matt. 22:31–32 (*Works*, *15*, 365–66).

and so whether he be bound to the punishment of it—be acquitted in judgment as being found innocent, and so under no obligation to punishment, then he may properly be said to be justified. But if he be found guilty, and is condemned, but afterward, as a justly condemned malefactor, is freely pardoned, whoever calls that justifying of him?

Corol. Hence we may see how that persons cannot be justified without a righteousness consistent with God's truth, for it would be a false sentence. It would be to give sentence concerning a person, that he is approvable as just, that is not just, and cannot be approved as such in a true judgment. To suppose a sinner pardoned without a righteousness implies no contradiction, but to justify without a righteousness is self-contradictory.

813. CHRIST, why the JUDGE of the WORLD. Christ is a fit person to judge between God and man, being a middle person between both the divine and human nature, and having manifested infinite regard both to the honor of God's majesty and justice, and to the welfare of mankind.

814. PROGRESS OF REDEMPTION. DELUGE. It was wisely determined of God that the effect of the fall should be seen in a very conspicuous and visible and universal manner, both with respect to temporal and spiritual death, before Christ came into the world to work out redemption: with respect to spiritual death, in the apostasy of the world to visible wickedness, casting off the true God and worshipping of idols, and into that gross heathenism wherein the things that appertain to spiritual death, such as man's ignorance and blindness, unreasonableness, and brutality, and slavery to the devil, etc., are remarkably conspicuous; and with respect to temporal death, in the destruction of the universal deluge, wherein the effect of the fall, in the temporal destruction of the fallen world, as the fruit of sin, and as inflicted by God's wrath was most remarkably conspicuous, much more than in the death of mankind, as it happens in the ordinary course of nature. The hand of God and his wrath were more visible in it; and the awfulness of the tendency of the fall with respect to temporal destruction was much more manifest many ways. Though all men are subject to death as it comes in the ordinary course of nature, yet the world of mankind is not so properly destroyed by death in this way; though all men die one after another, yet the world of mankind yet lives. Men do, as it were, live in their families; and death in this way, though it be universal, yet is so gradual that it is not set before us in one view, as the destruction of the world of mankind, but little is seen at a time: death not

gaining the conquest, and triumphing in universal awful devastation, as in the other case, but the world still rejoices in life; and natural generation, as it were, maintaining its ground against death, yea, gaining ground of it by giving more life than death takes away, and so gradually increasing the number of living men on earth. And especially before the flood was it thus, when men's lives were so long and mankind increased and multiplied so fast. God was pleased by the flood to give one example of the mischief of the fall, the ill effects of sin in the ruin that it has exposed all mankind to, by the temporal destruction of the world at once; and a very remarkable image of their awful eternal destruction, before he accomplished the salvation of the world by Christ, and in a sense before the work of redemption of the world by Christ was begun, as it was begun after the flood in the CALLING OF ABRAHAM. This, in some sense, may be looked upon as the beginning of the work of redemption. It was the planting of the tree, whence that branch of the righteousness should sprout forth. It was the planting of that tree, the church of God, or rather mystical Christ, including both the head and the members, the stock and all the branches, the great branch of righteousness, and all the lesser branches and twigs that were to grow out of it. It was the first planting of that tree that was to grow till its top should reach unto heaven, and its roots and its branches and fruit were to fill the whole earth.

God saw meet greatly to diminish the temporal prosperity of the world by the flood, by destroying almost all its inhabitants, and by greatly diminishing the days of the lives of the residue, and more fully bringing the curse on the ground by diminishing its fertility, and the pleasantness and wholesomeness of its fruits, and destroying the ancient purity and healthiness of the air and water, and all the aliment of human bodies, before he thus began the salvation of the world by Christ.

God gave Adam before he fell a grant of the earth founded on the covenant of works, but when he fell he lost the inheritance of the earth by this grant. And God was pleased once to take the earth away from mankind by the deluge, to let 'em see the dire effects of the fall in this forfeiture before he[1] gave 'em a new grant of the earth founded on the covenant of grace, and the redemption of Jesus Christ.

The destruction of the world by the flood was in the fullness of time, for it was needful that before God gave such an example of the destructive tendency of the fall the world should be full of people, that the terribleness of the effect might be greater, and [the] awful tendency of men's

1. MS: "have."

sin the more visible. But yet it was wisely ordered that this destruction should not be at a very great distance from the fall, not so great but that the world had a fresh remembrance of it, and of God's awful threatening denounced on the world thereupon; so that some that were alive till the flood came, or till just before it, might have had it from Adam at first hand. And it was also wisely ordered so early that that preparation for the redemption of Christ that was to be begun afterwards might not be too long delayed.

ABRAHAM was CALLED in the fullness of time. The destruction of the world by sin having been exemplified in the eyes of angels and men, and it being now apparent that though the wicked world was destroyed, and only one family preserved, which was God's visible church; I say, it being notwithstanding now become apparent, that the world notwithstanding still is in a ruined condition, is a wicked world and stands in absolute need of a Redeemer—the world that was now only of the posterity of that righteous person that was saved from the flood being now generally become visibly wicked, apostatizing from the worship of the true God to the worship of idols—now God begins the great preparation for the redemption of the world by Jesus Christ by the calling of Abraham, that person of whose seed the Redeemer was to be, that in his seed the church might be upheld, and that the way might be prepared for the coming of Christ, by God's dispensation towards them for a succession of ages.

815. The world is vastly more extensively peopled now than it was before Christ. Then, very great part, and perhaps the greater part, of the inhabitants of the world were within the limits of the Roman Empire, or on its borders; but now what is confined within those limits is but a little part of the world. And 'tis very probable that the devil, who had for so many ages reigned as god of this world, and had miserably enslaved the nations of it, did after Christ's ascension, when he saw how wonderfully the gospel prevailed, lead away many people into the more remote corners of the earth. And this may account for the people of the northern cold regions of the earth where the climate seems to be almost intolerable, which perhaps can scarcely be accounted for otherwise. And particularly 'tis probable that it is hence that AMERICA was first peopled, some of the Americans giving this account when the Europeans first came hither, that their god had led them hither.

But SATAN in the end will be DEFEATED in this: for he only has prepared the way for the more extensive and glorious kingdom of Jesus Christ, which shall be at that time, when the whole earth shall be given to him for his possession; and prepared the way for a new triumph of Christ over him, and one that is far greater, and obtained by a far more extensive victory, than [that] which Christ obtained over him in the days of Constantine the Great.

816. The following reasons seem to render it probable that FEW ARE CONVERTED IN INFANCY.

1. Those that are converted in infancy never know by experience what their state is by nature. They may believe it to be totally corrupt, and that by nature no goodness [is] in them, and that they are altogether slaves to sin and Satan, and that they are the children of wrath, and without any favor of God. They may believe it from what they are taught in the Word, and they may in a sense know it by experience, i.e. they may rationally argue it from what they find themselves to be now. At some seasons when the Spirit of God is withdrawn, they may see enough to convince 'em that they are totally corrupt, and utterly ruined, as they are in themselves; but they can't know by immediate experience what their state by nature is. And if any of those that are converted in infancy should be called to be ministers, they would be under great disadvantage in dealing with those that are in a natural condition, and in teaching others the difference between a converted and an unconverted state, for they would not know by experience.

2. Such persons as are converted in infancy are never sensibly delivered from their natural, blind, wicked, miserable condition, and never would be the subjects of any sensible redemption from this state, in that which is most properly their redemption from it, viz. their conversion. Though they might be sensible of redemption from remains of corrupt nature, and slavery to sin, and from such sorrowful circumstances wherein they suffer much of the darkness and misery of a natural condition in renewed conversions, we know how very much God seems to insist on it that his mercy and salvation should be sensible, and therefore is wont so to order the circumstances of it as to make it most sensible and visible. He hath concluded all in unbelief (i.e. in visible unbelief) that he might have mercy upon all.

How far God may go out of his usual way in this respect in extraordinary times, and particularly in those glorious times of the church that are approaching (as he doubtless will then go out of his usual way with respect to there being but few saved), I can't tell.

817. DEGREES OF GLORY will not be precisely in proportion to the degrees of grace in this [world], without any respect to anything else; but by

the Scriptures it seems as though, in proportioning the degrees of glory, these four things would chiefly come in consideration.

1. The degrees of grace and holiness here; not only the degree of the principle, but of the exercises and fruits. God will reward a principle of grace, as well as punish a principle of corruption, or a corrupt nature; and God will also reward all the exercises and fruits of grace, for all these are good works. But no one good work shall go without its reward, though it be only in the heart. When grace is exercised only in the heart, the saints do well; as God said to David, "Thou didst well that it was in thine heart" [I Kgs. 8:18]. But especially shall grace be rewarded when exercised in voluntary and overt acts. As sin is perfected in such acts—agreeable to the Apostle, "When lust hath conceived, [it] bringeth forth sin: and sin, when it is finished, bringeth forth death" [Jas. 1:15]—so it is in grace. And God in both rewards and punishments has not only respect to the corruption or grace itself, but to the expression and manifestation.

2. Another thing by which the degree [of] glory is proportioned is the degree of good that is done by the exercise and fruits of grace: the degree of glory to the name of God, and the degree of good done to men, especially to the household of faith. That the degree of both punishments and rewards will be in some measure proportioned [to] the good or hurt done, is manifest by innumerable passages of Scripture. How terrible are those sins of the wicked especially threatened, by which they offend Christ's little ones, or hurt the church of God; and what rewards are promised to those that [do] good to the bodies of men, that give to the poor. 'Tis said that such do lend to the Lord, and that that which they give, he will pay 'em again; he will pay 'em "good measure, pressed down, shaken together, and running over" [Luke 6:38]. How much is this way of doing good spoken of as a way of laying up treasure in heaven, and "laying up in store a good foundation against the time which is to come" (I Tim. 6:17–19). And especially giving to the poor saints, or members of Christ: Christ says that what is done to them he shall look upon as done to himself, and that he that gives to a disciple in the name of a disciple shall in no case lose his reward [Matt. 25:40, 10:42]. And doing [good] to the souls of men shall yet be more highly rewarded. 'Tis said that they that "turn many to righteousness shall shine as the stars forever and ever" [Dan. 12:3]; so the Apostle speaks of those that were converted by his ministry as his "joy and crown" of rejoicing in the day of the Lord Jesus [Philip. 4:1]. These words of Christ are remarkable in John 4:35–36, "The fields are already white unto the harvest; and he that reapeth receiveth wages."

3. Future degrees of glory will be in proportion to [a] person's self-denial and suffering in the exercises and fruits of grace: for when grace is exercised and manifested in this manner, it is especially to the glory of God, for hereby the creature makes a sacrifice of himself and all things to the Creator. And this kind of exercises of grace are especially evidential of the truth and reality and strength of grace; and besides, God has regard in the reward not only to the goodness there is in this kind of exercises of grace, but to what the creature has lost in them to make it up to him. Hence David said when Shimei cursed him, "It may be the Lord will reward me for his cursing this day" [II Sam. 16:12]. And hence such declarations and promises in Scripture as these: Matt. 5:11–12, "Blessed are ye, when men shall revile you, and persecute you, and shall say all manner of evil against you falsely, for my sake. Rejoice, and be exceeding glad: for great is your reward in heaven." II Tim. 2:11–12, "It is a faithful saying: for if we be dead with him, we shall also live with him: if we suffer, we shall also reign with him." I Pet. 4:13, "But rejoice, inasmuch as ye are partakers of Christ's sufferings; that, when his glory shall be revealed, ye may be glad also with exceeding joy"; and many other places. And what great rewards are especially promised to suffering Christians in the Revelations.

4. Eminency in humility: for not only will the degree of grace, that consists most essentially in the degree of love, be regarded in the reward, but the particular manner of the exercise of grace. One way of the exercise of love may be such as is more especially becoming and beautiful in a creature, and such a creature as man, and may be that which more especially exalts God; and God may especially be concerned to reward this by exalting and glorifying the subject of such exercises. And besides, as in suffering so in humility, the saint does as it were lose [himself]; he denies himself; he casts away himself; he renounces his own glory for God. Now God, in the reward, is concerned to make up this loss. Hence we are so often told that God looks to him, and will dwell with him, that is of a humble and contrite spirit, and that he that humbles himself shall be exalted. And hence Christ, when inquired of who should be the greatest in the kingdom of God, makes answer, Matt. 18:4, that he that "humbles himself as this little child, the same is greatest in the kingdom of God."

818. Grace, How a Principle in the Heart. Rightly to understand the nature of the habit of grace, it must be observed that the Spirit of God in the heart of a saint acts both as a natural vital principle, and also as a voluntary agent manifesting care of that heart that it is in, lest it should be overcome by temptations, and lest it should fall away. The heart some-

times seems to be going on in a way to ruin for some time, and comes just to the edge of it, does but just escape going over the brink once and again; and sometimes seems as if it was gone and would not revive again, but yet the indwelling Spirit takes care of the heart, and wonderfully, and with great care and wisdom, conducts, preserves it, and restores it. The exercises and operations of this Spirit are after the manner of a natural principle in many respects; but yet there is that in it that shows it [to] be something supernatural, not only in such a sense as to be a principle besides all the principles of human nature as such, but also so as to be above all nature, above all laws of any nature, and all natural principles whatsoever. It acts both after the manner of a natural principle or seed, and yet after the manner of a voluntary agent, yea, and a most sovereign agent, and yet of a wise, careful, and faithful agent; and so every way as a divine agent, or as God acting in the soul. That indwelling vital Spirit acts so as to punish miscarriages, and reward diligence, and to answer prayer. The continuance of its actings are in many respects like the continuance of the exercises of a nature; the exercises of that wherein nature consists will be continual because nature can't be destroyed. But in other respects the continuance of its actings is after such a manner as to show plainly that 'tis owing to a covenant faithfulness. And more especially does the indwelling Spirit appear in its manner of acting as a voluntary agent—more than a natural necessary principle—in times of the greatest exigence, and in it highest acts and fruits, as in those extraordinary exercises of grace that are often given under great trials, terrible persecutions, and the like.

Corol. Hence we may observe that GRACE is a SUPERNATURAL thing in these three respects. (1) 'Tis from the supernatural and immediate operation of the Spirit. 'Tis given at first by an efficiency that is not such an efficiency as is confined to the laws of nature, but 'tis immediate and arbitrary. (2) The effect itself is supernatural.[2] The principle and exercises are something diverse in nature and kind from, and above all that belongs to, or proceeds from, human nature as such. See sermons on the parable of the ten virgins.[3] (3) They are supernatural so as not only to be above all the principles and exercises of human nature as such, but so as to be

2. MS: "supernature."

3. Beginning in Nov. 1737, JE preached a nineteen-unit sermon series on Matt. 25:1–12, the parable of the wise and foolish virgins. In the 12th unit JE maintains that true Christians differ from false insofar as they have "a spiritual and abiding principle in their hearts, that may be said to be a new nature in the soul, consisting in the Christian spirit that they are of." This spiritual principle is "not from nature but is wrought in the heart wholly by the Spirit of that which is supernatural, or above nature." And it "dwells in the hearts of the saints . . . as an inward, ardent, powerful principle of operation" and action.

above all nature whatsoever. That is, its exercises are after the manner not of a mere natural [principle], or a principle that in its exercises is subject to laws of nature, but above all stated fixed laws; and so is a divine thing that acts[4] in divine manner, as God himself is a being above all nature, a voluntary, sovereign, arbitrary agent, not subject to laws of nature in his acting, but above all those laws, being the arbitrary author of all those laws.

819. How Evangelical Obedience influences in the Affair of Justification. It seems to be a mistaken notion that many have of God's looking at the heart, as though all that God looked at, or had respect to in his dispensations towards men, with respect to their state towards him, or relating to their own welfare, was only the inward principle or habit, and the immanent acts of the principle; whereas, it is plain by the tenor of the whole Bible, that God has respect not only to principles and immanent acts, but also to overt and transitory acts, and especially to them. And though he looks at the heart, and not at what is merely outward—for so 'tis no more than the act of a machine—but yet he looks chiefly at the heart as exercised in those acts, in punishing and rewarding, in accepting and rejecting, or granting or denying any favor or privilege, or appointing men in any respect to any state; and in all his dealings with men in his moral government of them. So it is in God's punishing men. The transitory and overt acts of sin are especially forbidden in Scripture, and 'tis they that are especially threatened. And we find everywhere that they are[5] those that do especially excite God's wrath and bring on his vengeance: for 'tis in them that lust, or the corruption of the heart, is brought forth and is perfected, as the Apostle observes [Jas. 1:15]. So it is in rewards. We find the transitive exercises and good fruits of grace are they that rewards are especially promised to throughout the Bible; and that 'tis they that have especially been rewarded from time to time according to the account of the Scripture.

And it is these kinds of acts that have especially been regarded in the covenants that God has made with mankind. Thus it was in the first covenant. It was actually abstaining from the tree of knowledge that was the main thing in the express condition; and it was Adam's eating in the overt act that was chiefly that[6] by which the covenant was broken, and the curse brought upon him, though there were many inward corrupt acts

4. MS: "it acts."
5. MS: "&."
6. MS: "the."

tending to it before. And so it is in the covenant of grace. 'Tis a coming to Christ, cleaving to him, and expressing a choice of him and trust in him, in act and practice, that is the thing chiefly looked at in the condition of this covenant. 'Tis true the covenant of grace vastly differs from the first covenant in that, that the moral quality, the goodness or badness of the thing, that was the condition, was the thing that was looked at in the first; but 'tis only the natural quality of the thing that is the condition [that] is looked [at] in the second covenant. But yet this affords not the least reason why the overt or transitive act should be more looked at in the one case than in the other: for both the moral and natural *qualities* of those things in us, that are the conditions of both these covenants, are more or less in the inward principle and exercises, or the transitive and overt acts, according as the *being* of those things lies more or less in them. The being of obedience lay[7] more in the overt practical act of obedience to the law of the first covenant, and so the moral goodness of the obedience lay more in them. So the being of a closing with and adhering to Christ lies more in the transitive practical acts of a principle of unition and adherence; and therefore, the natural quality of it that is looked at in the covenant of grace lies more in it. For not only does the manifestation and outward appearance of a closing with Christ lie more in the practical exercises of such a spirit; but also the very being of it lies more in such exercises, and therefore is chiefly looked at in the covenant of grace.

820. JUSTIFICATION. REPENTANCE for the remission of sins is a particular kind of exercise of justifying FAITH. Add this to the definition given of repentance for the remission of sins in the Discourse on Justification.[8] Though this condition of the remission of sins don't take the denomination of repentance equally from all this, but especially from some part of it; yet it don't follow but that all is of the essence of it. For justifying faith itself don't take its denomination of faith from all that is of the essence of it: for love is of the essence of faith, yea, is the very life and soul of it, and the most essential thing in it. See note on Jas. 2, last verse.[9]

7. MS: "law."

8. In Nov. 1734 JE preached a lecture on Rom. 4:5, the doctrine of which states, "We are justified only by faith in Christ, and not by any manner of goodness of our own." In 1738 he revised this sermon and published it, along with four other sermons, in *Discourses on Various Important Subjects*. In the revised text of *Justification By Faith Alone* (pp. 103–14), JE defines repentance for the remission of sins at the outset of a discussion of the relation between repentance and faith.

9. There is no note in either the "Blank Bible" or the "Notes on Scripture" on the "last verse" (v. 26) of Jas. 2. The last verse of Jas. 2 on which JE comments in the "Blank Bible" is v. 18, which, like v. 26, addresses the relation between faith and works. In this note JE states that the words of

821. SELF-LOVE. COMMON GRACE. SAVING GRACE. There are two affections that are natural to men that do especially seem to imitate virtue. [1.] The one is gratitude, or a disposition to love others that love them. 'Tis as easy to account for such an affection's arising from self-love as anger and revenge, whereby men are disposed to hate those that hate them. Matt. 5:46, "For if ye love them that love you, what reward have ye; do not even the publicans the same?"

2. 'Tis very plain by experience that pity is an affection natural to men. But this don't argue that men naturally have any true or proper love to others that don't arise from self-love: for men may pity those that they have no love to, provided they don't hate them; or if they do hate them, they may pity them, if they see that their misery goes beyond their hatred. Pity is a painful sensation in us, arising from the sight or sense of misery in others, that is disproportionable to our disposition towards them. Whenever there is a disproportion between our disposition towards others and the state we see them in, it has a tendency to excite uneasiness in us. Let that disposition be what it will, when we see those happy that we don't love, or when their happiness exceeds our love, or when their misery is less than our hatred, that excites our envy. And on the other hand, when we see those miserable that we don't hate, or when their misery exceeds our hatred, or when their happiness is less than our love, it excites our pity. This natural pity may excite in men hatred of many acts of sin. We have a remarkable instance in David when he don't seem to have been much in the exercise of grace. II Sam. 12:5–6, "And David's anger was greatly kindled against the man; and he said to Nathan, As the Lord liveth, the man that hath done this thing shall surely die: and he shall restore the lamb fourfold, because he did this thing, and because he had no pity."

And self-love may have influence to cause men to love virtue many more ways than one would be ready to imagine. The ways of the working of a man's heart are so mysterious that in many instances it may be difficult to give an account how such and such things should arise from self-love.

That natural men should love just, generous, meek and benevolent persons, and persons possessed of such like virtues, with a love of appetition and complacence, though they have never received any benefit by those virtues in them, and possibly have no expectation that ever they shall, is no more unaccountable than that they should love that sweet fruit and

---

the text refer to Is. 32:17: "the former part of the verse declares what is the genuine exercise or work of righteousness, viz. peaceableness or peacemaking; the latter part expresses the effect, consequence and reward of righteousness to those who have it, in this its genuine nature, and who exercise it, in this its genuine work."

pleasant food the sweetness of which they are sensible of, or have an idea of, though they as yet receive no benefit of it, and don't know that ever they shall: yet they love it because they conceive of it as in itself tending to their pleasure, if there were opportunity and due application; so they conceive of those mentioned virtues as in like manner, in their own nature, tending to their good. Self-love makes them love the quality in general in one case, as in the other.

A natural [man] may love others, but 'tis some way or other as appendages and appurtenances to himself. But a spiritual man loves others as of God, or in God, or some way related to him.[1]

822. DEGREES OF GLORY. PERFECTION OF HAPPINESS. What I mean by the largeness of capacity for happiness don't consist only in the strength and extent of the faculties, but in the actual views which God gives, whereby the appetite of the soul is excited and extended, and the enjoying faculty (if I may so speak) is, as it were, opened and prepared to receive such a degree, and such a manner, of delight and satisfaction. And their capacity will also partly depend on their particular station and circumstances God sets 'em in in heaven, the degree and place they stand in in the heavenly society. For not only the knowledge they have will excite their desires, but also the consideration of the place they stand in in the body, and so the consideration of what is suitable for them in their place.

Wherein the degree of capacity depends on the degree of knowledge, it depends on three things: (1) the extent and strength of the faculty; (2) the degree of notional knowledge. But it won't depend only on these two: for the angels do doubtless far excel the saints in both, in the extent and strength of their faculties, and also in the degree of notional knowledge. But it will depend (3) on the degree and manner of those spiritual views that God lets into their minds, and the particular manifestations that he is pleased to make of himself, enlarging the appetite, and opening the heart, and extending the vessel, viz. the enjoying faculty opening the mouth wide to receive the more.

Everyone shall have his cravings filled, i.e. in such a sense as to leave no uneasiness of craving, but not so as to leave no desire of increasing: for doubtless when they study and contemplate [it will be] with a desire of gaining knowledge, and the satisfaction that arises from it; so we are told the angels desire to look into these things. But they shall have no uneasy

1. In the MS this entry has a use line along the entirety of its left margin. JE incorporated the substance of it into *The Nature of True Virtue*, chs. IV and VI (see *Works, 8*, 575–88, 600–608).

desires. Their desires shall be no more than a suitable preparation for delight in their satisfaction. Now the views we have cause uneasy desires. We find obstructions and opposition in the way of our obtaining those things that our spiritual views excite an appetite after, and great failing of such a satisfaction as we stand in great need of for the present, and many and great frustrations in our desires. Hence we read of groanings that cannot be uttered; and the Psalmist says "My soul breaketh for the longing it hath" [119:20].

823. PERSEVERANCE. It shows the infallible perseverance of true Christians, that the spiritual life that they have is as partaking with Christ in his resurrection life, or the life that he has received as risen from the dead; and not as partaking of that life that he lived before his death. For they live by Christ living in them (Gal. 2:20); this is by the life that he has received since his resurrection, and by communicating to them that fullness that he received when he rose from the dead. When he rose he received the promise of the Father, the Spirit of life without measure, and [he] sheds it forth on believers. The oil poured on the risen head goes down the skirts of the garments [Ps. 133:2]. And thus Christ lives in believers by his Spirit's dwelling in them. Believers in their conversion are said to be risen with Christ. Col. 2:12–13, "Ye are risen with him through the faith of the operation of God, who hath raised him from the dead. And you, being dead in your sins and the uncircumcision of your flesh, hath he quickened together with him"; and 3:1, "If ye then be risen with Christ, seek those things which are above, where Christ sitteth on the right hand of God"; and Eph. 2:5–6, "Even when we were dead in sins, hath quickened us together with Christ, and hath raised us up together." Rom. 5:10, "For if, when we were enemies, we were reconciled to God by the death of his Son, much more, being reconciled, we shall be saved by his life." Philip. 3:10, "That I may know him and the power of his resurrection." Rom. 6:4–5, "Therefore we are buried by him by baptism unto death: that like as Christ was raised up from the dead by the glory of the Father, even so we also should walk in newness [of life]"; and so on throughout that chapter.

This spiritual resurrection and life is procured and purchased for Christ's members by Christ's suffering obedience, in the same manner as his own resurrection and life is purchased by it; and they receive life as united to him, as members of a rising Savior, and as being married in their conversion to him, as in the beginning of the seventh chapter of Romans, which [is] a continuation of that forecited discourse in the sixth chapter. That justification that believers have at their conversion is as partaking of the justification that Christ had in his resurrection; and so all the benefits that believers [have], their comfort and hope and joy here, and their eternal life hereafter, is as partaking with a risen Savior. We are begotten again to a living hope by the resurrection of Christ from the dead to an inheritance incorruptible. See Eph. 1:18–20, "The eyes of your understanding being enlightened; that ye may know what is the hope of his calling, and what the riches of the glory of his inheritance in the saints; and what is the exceeding greatness of his power to us-ward who believe, according to the working of his mighty power, which he wrought in Christ Jesus, when he raised him from the dead, and set him at his own right hand in heavenly places."

Hence it follows that the saints shall surely persevere in their spiritual life and their justified state. The Apostle hence argues in the sixth [chapter] of Romans that believers are finally freed from sin, and shall live forever with Christ, and that sin shall no more have dominion over them: v. 9, "Knowing that Christ being raised from the dead dieth no more; death hath no more dominion over him"; compared with vv. 5–7, 10, 14. Christ's resurrection life is an immortal unfailing life. Rev. 1:18, "I am he that liveth, and was dead; and, behold, I am alive for evermore." Hence the benefits that believers receive being converted and risen with Christ are sure and unfailing mercies. Acts 13:34, "And as concerning that he raised him up from the dead, now no more to return to corruption, he said on this wise, I will give you the sure mercies of David." This is the living bread, and hence he that eateth thereof shall not die, but shall live forever (John 6:50–51). The saints can't die, for their "life is hid with Christ in God," who is risen and ascended, and is with God in glory in immortal life (Col. 3:3–4).

824. SAINTS HIGHER IN GLORY THAN THE ANGELS. 'Tis not in all respects that the saints will be higher in glory than the angels: for the angels will be superior in greatness, in strength and wisdom, and so in that honor that belongs to 'em on that [account]; but they will not be superior in beauty and amiableness, and in being most beloved of God, and most nearly united to him, and having the fullest and sweetest enjoyment of him. It hath pleased God in his infinite wisdom that the superior greatness, and the highest beauty and blessedness, in the most intimate union with him, and enjoyment of his love, should not go together: that creature greatness mayn't lift up itself, that it may appear that good don't depend on creature greatness, that creature greatness is nothingness before God, and that all good is of God.

The nobles and barons, and great ministers of a prince's court may in strength and wisdom be superior to the queen or the king's children, and so in some respects may have peculiar honor put upon them in that honorable business, and those great employments they have answerable to their great abilities, and that special sort of respect that is due such abilities; but yet the queen and the king's children are indeed, all things considered, most exalted.

In that the saints will be superior in goodness and happiness, they will have the most excellent superiority. Goodness is more excellent than creature greatness; 'tis more divine. God communicates himself more immediately in it. And therefore God is pleased to make goodness the end of greatness: for he would make that in the creature, which is properly belonging to the nature of the creature, subordinate to that which is of God, or a communication of the divine nature in the creature. And accordingly has he disposed things between the two kinds of intelligent creatures that he has made. He has made the good creature the end of the great creature. He has made saints the end of the angels, rather than the angels the end of the saints. He has subordinated that kind of creatures wherein is most creature greatness, to another sort of creatures that have not so much greatness, but are appointed to more goodness, i.e. more divine beauty and joy in the communications of the Spirit of God.

Obj. The angels are called thrones, dominions, principalities, and powers, and how does this consist with their being inferior to the saints?

Ans. This can't be understood as though they had principality and dominion over the saints, for being princes over the saints, and their being their angels and ministering spirits to them, hardly consist together. But they may be called thrones and dominions, etc., in two respects: (1) with respect to their dominion in the earth, or this lower visible world; or (2) with respect to the various degrees and orders of angels, whereby some are princes over others, as 'tis among evil angels. Or if they are princes with respect to the saints, it must be only in some particular respects, only wherein they are superior, the saints remaining still in the general superior.

825. COVENANT OF GRACE AND REDEMPTION. See Nos. 617, 919, 1091. There are two covenants that are made that are by no means to be confounded one with another.

1. The covenant of God the Father with the Son, and with all the elect in him, whereby things are said to be given in Christ before the world began, and to be promised before the world began. This is what properly

succeeds, as 'tis revealed in the world in the room of God's covenant with Adam, and stands in direct opposition to it. For as God made the first covenant with Adam for himself and all his posterity, so God makes this covenant with Christ, as second Adam, for himself and all his posterity.

2. There is another covenant that is the marriage covenant between Christ and the soul, the covenant of union, or whereby the soul becomes united to Christ. This covenant before marriage is only an offer or invitation. "Behold, I stand at the door, and knock: if any man hear my voice, and open the door, I will come in to him, and will sup with him, and he with me" [Rev. 3:20]. In marriage, or in the soul's conversion, it becomes a proper covenant. This is what is called the covenant of grace, in distinction from the covenant of redemption.

826. INDEFINITE PROMISES, as they are called, seem to be no other than promises of the public covenant, or the promises made to a professing covenant people. God has promised to his visible church a blessing on his ordinances; and with respect to the public society, the visible church to whom the promises are made, they are absolute promises. But not being limited to particular persons, to them they are no more than encouragements; such promises as these children are interested in by baptism. God has promised to bestow salvation in his church, and in the way of his appointed worship. "In all places where I record my name, there will I come unto thee, and will bless thee" [Ex. 20:24]. When God sets his tabernacle amongst a people, he has annexed a promise of his blessing.

827. MILLENNIUM, concerning Christ's HUMAN presence on earth then. It is a greater privilege to the church on earth to have Christ, her head and Redeemer, in heaven at the right hand of God, than for him to be in this lower world: for Christ in heaven is in his glorious throne. For him to come down to this earth to dwell here, would be a second humiliation, a descending from an higher glory to a lower. Christ's exaltation and ascension to heaven is spoken of as cause of exceeding joy to his church. It was an instating him in his throne in his people's name. 'Tis a glorious privilege to the church to have their Mediator in heaven, in the holy of holies, at the right hand of God; it tends to strengthen their faith, and greatly to encourage and comfort them. No saint that considers things aright will desire that he should leave heaven. Christ signified to his disciples that, if they saw things aright, they would rejoice when he said he was going away. Christ's reigning on earth by his Spirit is more glorious and happy for his church than his human presence would be, as

Christ intimates when he says, "Except I go away, the Comforter will not come" [John 16:7]. Christ's ascension is spoken of as the most glorious cause of rejoicing in those psalms that are penned on occasion of the ascension of the ark into Mt. Zion.[2]

828. RULE OF FAITH. SCRIPTURE. HISTORY. FATHERS. The way that history is to be made use of for our instruction and guidance in matters of faith is twofold: 'tis either in interpreting the Scriptures, or confirming the things that are taught in the Scripture.

1. There is no doubt but that what is to be learned of the ancient customs and state of things at the time when the Scriptures were written, as this is to be learned from other authors, may be made use of in interpreting the Scripture; as well as the ancient use of that language in which the Scriptures are written, as it is to be learned from other authors, is to be made use of in interpreting the words and phrases that are found in the original of the Scriptures: for the customary use of words and phrases is one instance of ancient customs, and what is found in other authors may be as much relied upon with respect to other customs, as the customary use of words and phrases. And the knowledge of ancient customs and the state of things is needful to [be] known in order to an interpretation of the Scripture, the same way as the knowledge of the custom of speech. For, from knowing what was the custom of speaking from other authors, we argue that the penmen of Scripture speak in the same manner: for 'tis a known and manifest thing that custom governs the use of speech and language, and so also it is a known and manifest thing that the state of affairs, in every age and country, governs the use of speech in many respects.

Indeed, so hath God wisely ordered that the Scripture, in both these respects, is more sufficient for itself by far than any other book. Both the use and force of its own phrases is more fully to be learned from the Scriptures themselves, and also the customs and state of things on which the interpretation mainly depends. The manifest design of God in the Scripture, is to speak so plainly as that the interpretation should be more independent than that of any other book which is ever to be remembered, and should always be of great weight with us in our interpretation of the

---

2. In "Notes on Scripture" no. 319, which discusses Ps. 68, JE argues that the "bringing up the ark of God out of the house of Obed-edom the Gittite, into the city of David on the top of Mt. Zion, on which occasion this psalm was penned, was the most remarkable type of the ascension of Christ that we have in the Old Testament." According to this note, the "other songs penned on this occasion" are "Ps. 47, and that which is given us in the I Chronicles, 16th chapter" (*Works*, *15*, 297–302).

Scripture; and so we should chiefly interpret Scripture by Scripture.

2. Another way that we may make use of history, etc., in affairs of this nature, is to help our weakness and unbelief, and to confirm the truths taught us in the Scripture. History and other ancient writings may, as well, be made use of to confirm anything in the Scripture, according to the force of reason that is in them; as reason may be made use of for this purpose from experience, from our present observation of what passes in our own hearts, or what we observe among our neighbors, or what is to be seen or heard of in the present state of God's church, or the world of mankind, or the present dispensations of God's providence.

Whatever affords a just argument to reason, whether history or anything else, may and ought to be made use [of] fully, according to the proportion of weight, or force of real argument, there is in it. The only question there can be is concerning the proportion of weight of argument between the Scripture and other things; and the danger is of not laying weight enough on what we find in the Scripture, not laying such weight on it as God expects we should, on that which he has given to us on purpose, that it might be a sufficient, perfect, and infallible rule.

829. JUSTIFICATION. MERIT. MORAL FITNESS. The Arminians suppose their scheme of justification don't imply that we are justified by our own merit. They utterly disclaim the doctrine of our own merit. But though they disclaim the *word*, yet they fully maintain the thing signified by that word. Whoever maintains that men are justified by their own virtue, or goodness considered as his goodness, therein does, to all intents and purposes, maintain that they are justified by their own merit or worthiness. If our virtue and obedience is, according to the strict truth of things, all things considered, to be looked upon as some moral goodness of our person, or we are to be looked upon as in some degree morally good upon the account of it, there is no dispute but that there is merit or worthiness. Worthiness is of the essence of moral goodness, and universally and necessarily attends it, as much as guilt or blame attends sin or moral evil. As all moral evil is blameworthy, and worthy of abhorrence and the fruits of abhorrence, so all moral goodness is praiseworthy, worthy of acceptance, approbation, and of the fruits of acceptance and approbation; and therefore, that scheme that supposes that a man's virtue and good works are accepted as some moral goodness of him, and that he is accordingly justified on the account of it, that scheme supposes a man is justified by his merits. And though it is true their scheme may be inconsistent with itself, and some parts of their scheme may contradict this, to suppose that a man

is looked upon as in any degree morally good, is to suppose him in some degree worthy, and that, though we suppose him to have more sin than goodness: for still, if he is to be looked upon according to truth as in some degree good, he is worthy of a reward, or an abatement of punishment, which is equivalent to a reward.

Indeed, there is a sort of merit or worthiness that this scheme of justification don't necessarily suppose, and that is that sort that is peculiar to Christ as a divine person, whose worthiness differed from that of all others, in that what he offered to God was what originally was not due by a debt of subjection; but it implies fully the highest possible kind of merit or worthiness of a creature, though not the highest degree of that kind.

830. FREE WILL. According to the present prevailing notion of liberty, it consists in a state of indifference that the soul was in antecedent to the act of choice: so that if, when the two opposites are proposed—set before the will in order to its determination or choice—the soul is not found hitherto in a state of indifference, and don't so remain till it has determined itself by its own act of choice, the proposal did not find the soul in a state of liberty, neither is the choice that is made upon it a free choice; and that anything done can be no further blameworthy than it is the fruit of a choice made by the will in this sense, left to itself and to its own sovereignty, without any weight lying upon it antecedent to its own determination and act of choice, to put it out of its balance, to bias and sway it one way, and in any measure by its power to govern its determination, because they suppose that a free will must be determined only by its self, and that nothing but its own sovereign command of itself can have any hand in its determination. But in case of such an antecedent, biasing power affecting the will to turn it one way, the will is, in some measure at least, determined by something out of itself; so that, according to this notion of liberty, if there be any original corruption, any evil inclination of nature, that, so far as it prevails, excuses any evil act of choice, because so far the corruption of nature took from the liberty of the will. And hence it will follow that, if a man be naturally a very ill-natured man, and from that ill nature does often treat his neighbors maliciously, and with great indignity, his neighbors ought to excuse and not to be angry with him, so far as what he does is from ill nature. And so, if he be naturally of a very proud, haughty spirit, 'tis unreasonable in his neighbors to resent his haughty, contemptuous carriage towards them, so far as it arises from a proud natural temper. And so, on the other hand, if any person be naturally of an excellent spirit, a disposition strongly inclining him to virtue and the most

amiable actions, so far does it take from the commendableness and praise-worthiness of his actions. And so, none of the holy excellent actions or voluntary sufferings of Jesus Christ are worthy of any reward or commendation, because he was naturally perfectly holy. He had a nature so strongly inclining him to holiness that it certainly and indeclinably determined him to holy actions. And so of the holy actions of the angels; and above all, of the holy and righteous and excellent acts of God himself, for he by nature is infinitely holy. He is so far from exercising liberty in any of his holiness or virtue, according to this notion of liberty, that he is infinitely far from it: for his will, antecedently to the act, is infinitely out of the balance; his inclination one way is so strong, and makes it so necessary that he should choose on the holy side, that 'tis infinitely impossible that his will should be determined the other way.

And so 'tis equally against this notion of liberty if there was, previous to the act of choice, a preponderancy in those visible circumstances of the two opposite proposed objects of choice, so that, antecedent to its act of choice, there was more manifested or apparent to the soul on one side, that naturally tended to bias and sway the choice on that side, than on the other. When the will proceeds in its act of choice according to such a bias, it is not a free choice, because it was not determined only by itself, but partly at least by something without itself, viz. that apparent preponderance of circumstances that put the will out of its balance, so that it was not under equal advantages to choose either in the mere exercise of its own sovereignty. A preponderance in visible circumstances that naturally tend to sway the disposition on one side is equivalent to a preponderance of the natural disposition on one side; and indeed it is the same thing, for 'tis supposed that in such circumstances nature preponderates that way. To say that there is a preponderance of such circumstances as naturally tend to turn the disposition that way is the same thing as to say that the disposition in the view of such circumstances naturally tends that way; as for instance, when the circumstances of a case proposed to the will for its choice are such that most of the visible pleasure and advantage, which we naturally incline to, is on one side. This is equivalent to a preponderating of nature towards one side, and can't be distinguished from it, because it is supposed that the natural inclination preponderates towards the greatest apparent advantage. Hence, it is scarcely worth the while to offer any arguments to persuade men to choose that which is good and refuse that which is evil. 'Tis not worth the while to set before men the wisdom of ways of virtue and piety, and the folly of ways of vice, by showing the great advantages and benefits of the former, and the mischievous tendency of the latter; no, nor the deformity of the one, and the beauty and amiableness of the other (for men naturally incline to what appears beautiful to them and abhor deformity). This notion of liberty seems to frustrate all such endeavors to persuade men to virtue: for though these things may induce 'em to what is materially virtuous, yet at the same time they take away the form of virtue, because they put the soul out of its equilibrium wherein its liberty consists, and occasion something else to determine the will besides its own sovereignty. And the more powerful the arguments are, the more likely are they to be in vain in this respect: for the more is the inclination put out of its balance, and the greater hand has something external in determining the will, and so the more effectually is the form of virtue destroyed. And so, likewise, when men are led into the practice of virtue or vice by powerful example, the form of virtue and vice are wanting, because men naturally incline to follow example.

But how absurd are these things.

Corol. 1. From the absurdity of this notion of liberty we may infer that it is false, and that the liberty of men don't at all consist in, or depend upon, such an equilibrium, but is entirely of another nature; and that whether the will or inclination be more or less out of its equilibrium before the act of choice, it don't at all concern the liberty of that act of choice.

Corol. 2. And from hence it follows that necessity, if by necessity is meant only certain connection of nature between one thing and another, is not a thing opposite to liberty, or at all inconsistent with it, though compulsion or force be inconsistent with it. For, as has been just shown, it is not in any measure inconsistent with liberty that the soul be out of an equilibrium, or that its nature preponderates before the act of choice, let it preponderate more or less. But no one will deny that the preponderance may be, and often is, such as to imply a necessity or certain connection with an act of choice agreeable to it.

Corol. 3. From what has been said also it appears that 'tis not against human liberty for the will to be determined by something out of itself, as when it is determined by such a preponderating of circumstances.

Corol. 4. Hence, it is not at all inconsistent with human liberty for man's will to be determined by the ordering of divine providence: as when providence orders that the prevailing natural inclination, or that preponderating visible circumstances, should be on one side; yea, though providence should so order it as that a particular determination of the will should in nature be certainly connected with such a disposal of providence, and so that neither the commendableness nor blameworthiness of the acts of the will is hereby infringed.

Corol. 5. Hence, it is not at all against human liberty for God absolutely to decree that such a determination of the will shall come to pass, or to decree to order circumstances so that such a determination of the will shall certainly follow.[3]

831. JUSTIFICATION BY FAITH, i.e. by reason of the NATURAL FITNESS there [is] between faith in Christ, and a being looked upon as united to Christ. It has been objected by some against what is here advanced that this scheme of things seems to suppose that a believer's being justified has its foundation in nature, and not in God's pleasure, in that it supposes that if a person believes in Christ there is a natural fitness in it that he should have an interest in Christ, prior to any constitution of God; which seems to suppose that 'tis so far from being owing to God's arbitrary constitution that he makes faith the condition of an interest in Christ, that he could not fitly or suitably have done otherwise.

To this objection I answer,

1. This don't suppose that it is depending on God's sovereign will and mere pleasure whether or no he would give mankind a Savior to be their head and surety, and to suffer all their punishment as their head and substitute, and to fulfill the law, and perform all the obedience required by the law in order to a title to eternal life. This gift of Christ to do and suffer such things for us, in such a manner, and for such purposes, I suppose to be altogether the fruit of God's sovereign good pleasure.

2. This don't suppose that it is not a thing that depends on God's mere good pleasure when a Savior is thus given, and has thus been substituted for us, and as our substitute has thus perfectly obeyed and satisfied, whether or no this Savior shall be offered to all, or whether it shall be limited, and whom in particular it shall be made to; so that the offer of salvation, or opportunity for salvation by Christ, on any terms at all, as to every individual person, or whether it shall be offered wholly to all, or to some in part only, depends wholly on God's arbitrary pleasure.

3. These things being already thus fixed by a divine constitution, to fix the particular way in which persons should become interested[4] in this Savior still depends on God's arbitrary constitution in the sense in which we

---

3. In the MS this entry has a use line along the entirety of its left margin. In it JE lays out an argument that he develops at length in *Freedom of the Will.* Note also the resemblance between the first line of this entry and the full title of the treatise: *A Careful and Strict Enquiry into the Modern Prevailing Notions of that Freedom of the Will. . . .* See *The Works of Jonathan Edwards, 1, Freedom of the Will,* ed. Paul Ramsey (New Haven, Yale Univ. Press, 1957), v, 195–212, and *passim.*

4. MS: "interest."

commonly use such an expression, i.e. God still remains absolutely at liberty from any such thing as we call obligation, or any indebtedness to men to fix one way and not another; but God may fix the way in which an interest in the Savior shall be determined as his own will and wisdom shall direct, free from any tie in justice, (for 'tis moral fitness only, and not natural, that ever more brings what we call obligation). But yet I don't suppose that anyone will say that, since God has of his mere good pleasure given his Son to be the Savior of sinners, and substituted him for them, and he as their substitute has perfectly answered the law both in its threatenings and precepts, and this Savior is revealed to be for all to seek an interest in without limitation; I say, I do not suppose that after this anyone will say, everything relating to the way in which persons should become interested in this Savior, and what he has done and suffered, is still in such a sense wholly depending on God's arbitrary constitution that no one way is in itself more fit than another, and more agreeable to things as thus already constituted, so that there can be no more suitableness in appointing one than another. (Will anyone say so?) Particularly it would not in itself be suitable after this, that the way of being interested in Christ should be by their own virtue or righteousness, because this contains an inconsistency with the giving a Savior to perform all righteousness for us, as will be hereafter shown.[5] And so I suppose that[6] would be in itself unsuitable, that some wholly indifferent thing, that has neither any moral goodness in it, nor any relation to Christ the Mediator, or to God that has given him, or [to] any of his benefits, should be the great thing by which persons should become interested in Christ.

4. I would ask of anyone that makes the foregoing objection whether or no—things relating to our redemption being as they are in the forementioned respects, abating any consideration of any further constitution, and only considering the nature of things in themselves—one, that by the sincere act of his own heart unites and closes with Christ as his Head and Savior, and the way of salvation by his satisfaction and righteousness, and so as a rational voluntary agent is one with Christ by his own act, is not on that account much more *fitly* and *suitably* to be looked upon as [Christ's], and belonging to him, and legally one with him, than

---

5. JE does not, in the remainder of the entry, return to the question of the suitableness of gaining an interest in Christ through one's "own virtue or righteousness." He does, however, consider whether "no one way is in itself more fit than another." In both this entry and No. 877, which is referenced at the end of the entry, JE maintains that faith is a particularly suitable means of justification, "because the very nature of it is to apprehend Christ."

6. MS: "there."

others in whom there never has been any such active union with Christ. And,

5. I would further ask whether or no, if the case be so indeed—and all must needs acknowledge it—that there is a great *suitableness*, and it is a thing more wise, that those that, as creatures capable of act and choice, should be required, actively and in heart, to unite to Christ as their head, in order to a being accepted of God as one with Christ; and that this is more fit than those others, that don't close with him, should be looked upon as one with him, prior to any divine constitution about this matter; and we now see that God has actually constituted that he will accept such and such only as one with Christ, and that BY or on the ACCOUNT of this active union: where is the absurdity of our supposing that he doth thus accept such, rather than others, as one with Christ, because of that wisdom, suitableness, and fitness there is in so doing, and that the wisdom of God appears therein?[7] When reason shows us that [the] things that God does have a suitableness in their own nature, is it absurd for us to suppose that God does it because it is suitable and wise?[8] When reason shows us that they, and they only, that believe in Christ are suitably qualified to be looked upon as in him, and God declares that he will accept of them, and them only, as suitably qualified, and that he does it *by* or on the *account* of that qualification, is it unreasonable for us to suppose that he does it because they are suitably qualified, or is it not indeed fully implied?

6. I would ask such an objector whether or no, if it be not allowed that believers are accepted as one with Christ *by faith* in this sense, viz. that it is from respect to something in faith, whereby it does in its *own nature* especially qualify a person or (which is the same thing) render him fit to be looked upon as one with Christ; it be possible to find out any sense wherein it may be said to be *by faith* that we are accepted as being in Christ, but that the same may, in the same sense, be equally said of any other grace?

---

7. JE revised this rather convoluted sentence at some point subsequent to composition. The MS originally read: "I would further ask whether or no, if the case be so indeed—and all must needs acknowledge it—that there is a great *suitableness* that those that, as creatures capable of act and choice, actively and in heart unite to Christ as their head, should be accepted of God as one with Christ, rather than others that don't close with him prior to any divine constitution about this matter; and we now see that God has actually constituted that he will accept such and such only as one with Christ, and that BY or on the ACCOUNT of this active union: where is the absurdity of our supposing that he doth thus accept such, rather than others, as one with Christ because of that suitableness and fitness there, and that the wisdom of God appears therein?"

8. JE added the words "and wise" when he revised the previous sentence.

The objection is against persons' being accepted in Christ by faith, on the account of any relation that faith in Christ has to a being in Christ, in the nature of things, and so it is insisted that faith has no relation to a being in Christ, only by positive constitution; and if it be so, wherein has faith any relation to this benefit different from that which [is] common to every other grace? For the relation that is by constitution can be nothing more than a constituted connection between the grace and the benefit, so that the benefit shall not be without the grace, nor the grace without the benefit, without any regard to any real fitness or qualification, or any relation in nature whatsoever. But what grace is [there] that is not, in this sense, fully as much connected with this benefit as faith?

7. Some that have made this objection seem to suppose it a new notion, that it should be supposed that God justifies so *by faith* as that he has in that act respect to any relation that faith has to an interest in Christ in its own nature; when, indeed, it is far from being a new thing. For all that suppose that men are justified by faith, or are accepted as being in Christ by faith, because faith is *the instrument* by which Christ is received, do suppose that men are accepted in Christ by faith because of the relation that [it] stands in to Christ and his righteousness, in its own nature, viz. because the very nature of it is to apprehend Christ, or that is in its own nature related to the benefit, as the hand that receives is to the gift received. See No. 877.

832. PREFACE TO RATIONAL ACCOUNT. To mention some things that may justly make us suspect that the present fashionable divinity is wrong.

1. Whether or no it be likely that an age, that is distinguished from all other ages of the Christian church for deadness in the practice of religion and for practical licentiousness, and so of the absence of the Spirit of God and prevalence of the spirit of the devil, should be distinguished from all latter ages in purity of doctrine, and in being conducted by the providence and Spirit of God into the knowledge of the truth as it is in Jesus, and enjoying glorious light, being delivered from the errors of former generations. If we look into past ages, was ever anything seen parallel with this? When the world had new light breaking forth after heathenism, it was accompanied with a glorious reformation of manners. So, when new light broke forth at the Reformation. And has it always been so in ages past, that the most corrupt times with respect to practice have most abounded with error. And how strange would it be in its own nature if it should be; and how diverse from what God declares he will do, who will not lead the wicked into his truth. But "the secret of the Lord is with them

that fear him, and he will show them his covenant" [Ps. 25:14]. And "the meek are those that he will guide in judgment, and teach in his way" [Ps. 25:9]; and those that do his commandments shall know what doctrines are of God [John 7:17]. And besides, the Scripture teaches that 'tis God's manner to bless his truth, and to cause that the pure doctrines of the gospel should be accompanied with the power of his Spirit, and with a powerful effect on the hearts and lives of men.

Since this fashionable divinity has been growing and getting ground, han't vice and deadness and a decay of vital Christianity kept pace with it? The dissenters have of late for some time been refining on their principles. They see, as they imagine, the errors and impertinence of the tenets of their fathers; but han't unsuccessfulness in their ministry kept pace with their refinings?

2. Has there ever been any instance, in any age, of any great reformation of manners wrought in any society whatever, by proceeding on the foot of those principles that are now so fashionable? Incontestable and plentiful instances can be produced of this effect of other principles.

GENERAL INDEX

INDEX OF BIBLICAL PASSAGES

565

NEW TESTAMENT